# INTRODUCTION TO INTERNATIONAL POLITICAL ECONOMY

FOURTH EDITION

# INTRODUCTION TO INTERNATIONAL POLITICAL ECONOMY

**DAVID N. BALAAM**

*Professor of International Political Economy*

**MICHAEL VESETH**

*Professor of International Political Economy*

IN COLLABORATION WITH FACULTY
OF THE INTERNATIONAL POLITICAL ECONOMY PROGRAM
UNIVERSITY OF PUGET SOUND
TACOMA, WASHINGTON

PEARSON
Prentice
Hall

Upper Saddle River, New Jersey 07458

**Library of Congress Cataloging-in-Publication Data**

Balaam, David N.
    Introduction to international political economy / David N. Balaam, Michael Veseth.—
4th ed.
        p. cm.
    "In collaboration with Faculty of the International Political Economy Program,
University of Puget Sound."
    Includes bibliographical references and index.
    ISBN-13: 978-0-13-615563-8
    ISBN-10: 0-13-615563-4
1. International economic relations.    I. Veseth, Michael.    II. Title.
    HF1359.B33 2008
    337—dc22

                                                                    2007015475

**Editorial Director:** Charlyce Jones Owen
**Executive Editor:** Dickson Musslewhite
**Associate Editor:** Rob DeGeorge
**Editorial Assistant:** Synamin Ballatt
**Senior Marketing Manager:** Kate Mitchell
**Marketing Assistant:** Jennifer Lang
**Director of Operations:** Barbara Kittle
**Senior Managing Editor:** Lisa Iarkowski
**Production Liaison:** Jean Lapidus
**Composition/Full-Service Project
    Management:** Aptara, Inc.

**Production Editor:** Donna Leik
**Senior Operations Specialist:** Mary Ann
    Gloriande
**Cover Art Director:** Jayne Conte
**Cover Design:** Bruce Kenselaar
**Printer/Binder:** Courier Companies,
    Inc./Stoughton
**Cover Printer:** Courier Companies,
    Inc./Stoughton

This book was set in 10/11 Palatino by Aptara, Inc.

Pearson Education LTD.
Pearson Education Singapore, Pte. Ltd
Pearson Education, Canada, Ltd
Pearson Education–Japan
Pearson Education, Upper Saddle River,
    New Jersey

Pearson Education Australia PTY, Limited
Pearson Education North Asia Ltd
Pearson Educación de Mexico, S.A. de C.V
Pearson Education Malaysia, Pte. Ltd

10 9 8 7 6 5 4 3 2
ISBN 13: 978-0-13-615563-8
ISBN 10:    0-13-615563-4

# Contents

# Preface

*. . . the ideas of economists and political philosophers, both when they are right and when they are wrong, are more powerful than is commonly understood. Indeed the world is ruled by little else. Practical men, who believe themselves to be quite exempt from any intellectual influences, are usually the slaves of some defunct economist. Madmen in authority, who hear voices in the air, are distilling their frenzy from some academic scribbler of a few years back.*[1]

John Maynard Keynes

It is hard to make sense of a newspaper, a business investment, or a government policy without an understanding of the theories, institutions, and relationships found in international political economy (IPE). It is difficult, in other words, to understand our everyday lives without some understanding of IPE, so deeply are we now touched by international and ever more global political, economic, and social forces and events.

We believe that IPE is so important that all college students need to understand it in a fundamental way. Our conviction is that it is possible to present this material to undergraduates in relatively simple ways that retain the complexity of the global issues and intellectual problems we address, without making the discussion fit only for advanced undergraduate and graduate courses. In particular, our aim is to provide educational materials that will allow "beginners" (especially college freshmen and sophomores) to go from "zero to 60" in IPE in a single semester. Our hope is that these students will get excited about IPE as an element of life-long learning and in the process become better citizens and more knowledgeable individuals.

## OUTLINE OF THE BOOK

As in previous editions, the book begins with five chapters designed to set out some basic tools for studying IPE. Chapter 1 introduces the fundamental elements of the subject and some recent developments in what has become a very popular field of study. We begin with relatively simple tools and ideas, then we add layers and detail about different problems and issues to make IPE real. Chapters 2, 3, and 4 explore three dominant analytical approaches to studying IPE that reflect powerful forces in history and that remain influential today: mercantilism, liberalism, and Marxism or structuralism. Chapter 5 introduces four alternative but none the less important perspectives (rational choice, constructivism, feminism, and hegemonic theory) that offer students other theoretical concepts and ideas that can help them understand different IPE questions and events.

Part II of the text examines the web of relationships or structures that tie together a variety of international actors including nations and their citizens with international organizations, non-governmental organizations, and other groups. Students are linked to people and places around the world in a number of ways that need to be understood if they are to make good civic, business, social, and personal choices. Chapter 6 focuses on the production and international trade structure. Chapter 7 provides students with an outline of the international monetary and finance structure and problems that in Chapter 8 are applied to several recent global financial crises, including the problem of Third World debt. Chapter 9 focuses on a number of recent developments in the international security structure that includes a shift from national to individual security concerns, and Chapter 10 examines some of the ties among international actors influenced by knowledge and technology.

By the end of the first ten chapters, then, students should be able to imagine themselves as part of the international political economy and appreciate how they are connected directly to markets, states, and various societies around the globe. Readers should have a fundamental understanding of what these linkages are and an appreciation of the theories and perspectives that guide our understanding of them.

The second half of the book looks at specific regions and countries, focusing on a number of IPE problems that are essential to a sound understanding of the world today. In Part III, Chapters 11 and 12 examine many tensions among markets, states, and societies in the industrial nations of the European Union and Japan. Chapter 13 focuses on an array of issues generally associated with some of the newly industrialized countries (NICs) of Eastern Europe and China as they try to transform and incorporate a bigger role for markets in their national political economies. Chapter 14 is a new chapter that covers the Middle East and North Africa, regions fraught with what seem like insurmountable development and security problems.

In Part IV, on North–South problems and issues, Chapter 15 examines the problem of development and some of the different strategies that many of the less developed countries have used to "grow" their economies and modernize their political institutions. Chapter 16 examines human connections in the international political economy through tourism and migration issues. In Chapter 17 we examine the role of transnational corporations in the international political economy.

Finally, in Part V, as part of an effort to understand a number of important global problems and issues, Chapter 18 is another new chapter that examines illicit activity involving drugs and other items. Chapters 19 and 20 discuss global food and environmental problems, again employing many of the same analytical tools developed earlier in the book. As in the last edition of the book, the very last chapter, Chapter 21, asks, "Where do we go from here?" After reviewing basic concepts and examining the fundamental tensions that shape today's world, we consider a number of possible scenarios for the future of the international political economy and also render some advice to students.

We have written this text to help our students at the University of Puget Sound and elsewhere and to serve the needs of instructors and professors everywhere like ourselves. We hope all of you will find it a valuable educational resource.

## What's New in the Fourth Edition?

Against a backdrop of a great many changes that have occurred in the international political economy, we have retained the basic format of the book that has proved so successful: a survey of theoretical perspectives followed by an analysis of structural connections, leading to sections that explore state–market–society tensions, North–South issues, and a sampling of global problems. Within this structure, each chapter has been carefully revised or updated. The most significant changes in this edition compared to the last are the following.

- *Chapter 1* has been revised to deal directly not only with the effects of terrorism on the international political economy following the attacks of September 11, 2001, but also the status of globalization in relation to those events. These two phenomena have dominated the agenda of many IPE theorists and public officials alike since the end of the Cold War in the early 1990s. In many ways they now compete with one another for our attention. Suffice it to say they coexist and mutually affect one another, as will become clear throughout the book.

- In consideration of its connection to neoliberal ideas, *Chapter 3* provides more discussion of the nature of globalization along with its positive and negative effects. The chapter concludes with a discussion of the probable status of neoliberal thought in the near future. The effects of globalization on other issues and problems are also discussed throughout the book.
- The discussion of structuralism in *Chapter 4* has again been revised to introduce students to a broader sampling of more recent structuralist views and contemporary critiques of capitalism.
- *Chapter 5* includes new sections on constructivism and hegemonic theory and their significance to the study of IPE. Constructivism offers IPE another approach that gives needed attention to social values, beliefs, and other cultural factors and conditions. Hegemonic theory focuses on issues related to a state seeking to dominate the international political economy and the various roles associated with that position.
- Once again, *Chapter 7* has been revised slightly to provide students with a clear explanation of the basic concepts and vocabulary of exchange rates, balance of payments, and the International Monetary Fund. In this edition it reintroduces more history into the chapter, similar to the second edition of the book.
- *Chapter 8* again examines recent problems in international finance through case studies of the peso crisis, the Asian financial crisis, and the Argentine crisis, but also covers another type of crisis, namely, the debt crisis that many of the poorer states face. Recently, international finance organizations have been giving more attention to the poorer nations and their efforts to get beyond the first stages of development. Analytically, much of this effort comes on the heels of still more criticism of neoliberal (that is, market-oriented) development strategies and policies.
- In *Chapter 11* Hendrik Hansen delves more deeply into some European Union institutions and processes that are playing a major role in the integration of the European community.
- *Chapter 14* is a completely new chapter for the book. Written by Bradford Dillman, a specialist on the Middle East, the chapter looks at a variety of Middle Eastern and North African states and focuses on many of the distinct features of these states that do not make the front pages of newspapers. Dillman is also the author of *Chapter 18,* which has been recast to focus on illicit economies and activities involving drugs and strategic resources such as diamonds.
- Sunil Kukreja continues to revise *Chapter 15* on "The Two Faces of Development," maintaining focus on the dual problems of poverty and inequality but expanding the chapter to include discussion of more recent efforts to deal with long-term poverty, debt, and corruption in developing nations by international organizations and nongovernmental organizations. The New Millenium Project and UN goals are introduced and discussed.
- As one of the newer pieces of work in the last edition, *Chapter 16* on "The Human Connection," has been revised and updated by Monica DeHart and Nick Kontogeorgopolous. DeHart focuses on migration and immigration issues, whereas Kontogeorgopolous examines in more detail the political, economic, social, and environmental problems associated with travel and tourism, the world's largest industry.
- Throughout the book, readers will notice more emphasis on the status and ever-increasing role of China in the international political economy. They will also notice much more attention to social issues along with beliefs, values, and other cultural conditions.
- Likewise, throughout the book we continue to emphasize the role of international organizations and nongovernment organizations in the international political economy.
- Finally, for this edition we have added a list of Key Terms near the end of each chapter. These terms are also included, and defined, in the Glossary at the back of the book.

All the writers of the various chapters have made an effort to link issues of one chapter to those in another to demonstrate to students how IPE issues tend to be interconnected. It is these connections that make IPE topics so fascinating to study, but that also require a good understanding of a wide variety of analytical tools. It is this endeavor we take up in the first section of the book.

## ACKNOWLEDGMENTS

This textbook is truly a cooperative effort. We would like to thank all of the people at Pearson Education who have been so helpful to us, including our assistant editor, Jennifer Murphy, who, for this edition, was so supportive every step of the way. Lynne Lackenbach was a fabulous copyeditor and Donna Leik the production editor. We are also grateful to our colleagues at the University of Puget Sound (UPS), in the IPE program and elsewhere, who have either recently or in the past contributed to this work by writing chapters in their fields of expertise: David Sousa, Karl Fields, Elizabeth Norville, Ross Singleton, Patrick O'Neil, and Lisa Nunn. We would also like to thank and recognize our students and friends, Josh Anderson, Jessica Bruce, Kristine Kalanges, David Evans, Pamela Bess, Casey Dillon, Ryan Cunningham, Emily Knudsen, and Elizabetta and Shaun, for their comments and research assistance. Dave would also like to thank Dr. Michael Carey for his continued academic support and friendship. Most of all, Dave would like to thank his wife, Kristi Hendrickson, for her editorial assistance, patience, and loving support throughout the project.

Our thanks, also, to the reviewers of this edition: Terrence Casey, Rose Hulman Institute of Technology; Anthony Gadzey, Auburn University; Jill Crystal, Auburn University; Julie George, Queens College City University of New York; and Olufemi Babarinde, Thunderbird School of Global Management.

Dave would like to thank his colleagues and friends with whom he spent the spring of 2007 while working as a Fulbright lecturer in the Dipartimento di Politica, Istituzioni Storia, Università di Bologna, Bologna, Italy. Special thanks to Professors Tiziano Bonazzi, Pietro Manzini, and to the Direttore of the department, Fulvio Cammarano, and his staff, including Maria Pia Santarelli, Paola Malattia, and Massimo Francesconi, for their support, friendship, and often-requested Italian lessons. Thanks also to the Council of International Exchange of Scholars and the Italian Fulbright Commission for their assistance and support and who made it possible to be in Italy. Thanks also to the students in his graduate seminar, "Bubba vs. the Cowboy," and to Lucia, Dirce, Francesca, Carla, Marco, Paolo, Marco, and Luigi, who helped every day in dealing with and appreciating a beautiful culture. Finally, while in Bologna, Dave was also a research associate at the John Hopkins School of Advanced International Studies (SAIS) and would like to thank especially Professors Erik Jones, and the director of the SAIS Bologna Program, Professor Ken Keller, and the staff of the Bologna Center for all their support and friendship.

Finally, with this edition of the text Michael Veseth has decided to retire from his role as co-editor. With heartfelt thanks, all of us involved in the IPE program at the University of Puget Sound would like to recognize the time, energy, and enthusiasm that Michael put into the text since its inception in 1994. Michael was instrumental in founding the IPE program at UPS two years earlier and has since gone to great lengths to promote and nuture the program and the textbook project. For his leadership and for all that he has done for us and the IPE program, we are truly blessed and proud of Michael.

We both owe debts we can never repay to our families and mentors, past and present, whom we love very much. We dedicate this fourth edition to all our students everywhere, who through the years have made our classes and the IPE program at UPS the success that it is.

David N. Balaam and Michael Veseth
Seattle and Tacoma, Washington,
and Bologna, Italy

## NOTE

1. John Maynard Keynes, *The General Theory of Employment, Interest, and Money* (New York: Harcourt Brace Jovanovich, 1964), p. 383.

# PART I

# Perspectives on International Political Economy

✹✹✹✹✹✹✹

What is international political economy (IPE)? The first chapter of this book discusses the fundamental nature of IPE and some analytical issues related to its multidimensional character. The chapters that follow in Part I broaden and deepen this basic understanding. Chapters 2 through 4 are the core chapters of Part I and present ideas that are used everywhere in the text. These chapters explore the history of IPE through a discussion of the three main IPE perspectives—mercantilism, liberalism, and structuralism—and provide a basic vocabulary, some theoretical tools useful in understanding any IPE issue, and the ability to see more clearly IPE's relevance to the contemporary world. The first part of the text concludes with Chapter 5, which examines four popular alternative viewpoints of IPE thought that derive, in part, from the three main perspectives and that, depending on the issue under study, are quite useful.

# What Is International Political Economy?

## OVERVIEW

What is **international political economy (IPE)**? In simple terms, we define IPE as an analytical effort to break down the barriers that separate and isolate the disciplines of politics, economics, and sociology and their methods of analysis, seeking a comprehensive understanding of mainly international, if not global, issues and events. In doing so, IPE employs three major analytical perspectives and four international structures that combine elements of economics, politics, and sociology to describe and explain international and global problems and issues in a way that cannot adequately be addressed by each of those disciplines alone.

This chapter clarifies the nature of IPE as a field of study through an examination of several different definitions of IPE written by some well-known experts on the topic. Based on their views, we focus on its fundamental principles and multidisciplinary nature, along with reasons why we feel it is important and should be studied. Drawing on the topics of **globalization**—the intensive political, economic, and social connections between states and the people in them—and the dramatic events of September 11, 2001 (aka "9/11"), we examine how different disciplines would explain these phenomena, and why those explanations are inadequate, given the complex nature of issues and problems in the international political economy today. Because globalization and 9/11 continue to profoundly shape the lives of people not only in the United States but everywhere in the world, we argue that events like these are better understood from the interdisciplinary, multidimensional perspective that IPE provides, as opposed to a single disciplinary explanation. The same holds true for a great many other issues, including: the transformation of different national economic systems in Eastern Europe, Southeast Asia, the Middle East, and in other parts of the world; continued problems surrounding the development of some of the world's poorer nations; and efforts by states, international organizations (IOs), and nongovernmental organizations (NGOs) to solve a host of problems related to Third World poverty and debt, hunger, and global warming.

To provide more detail about the nature of IPE we explore some of the fundamentals of the three disciplines that form its core focus of study—economics, political science, and sociology—together with a number of analytical issues that result from efforts to splice together these disciplines.

We end the chapter by outlining several analytical tools used to describe, explain, and understand IPE problems and issues, including the three dominant IPE approaches or perspectives, the level-of-analysis problem, and the four IPE structures.

## THE ESSENCE OF IPE

The world is a complicated place characterized by a tremendous amount of **interdependence** (interconnectedness) among individuals, social groups, nation-states, and a variety of other actors in the international system. In the 1990s government officials, business people, academics, and the press alike constantly reminded people everywhere in the world about how interconnected and dependent they were on one another, in many ways and on many levels. As a reflection of this reality, in one sense IPE represents a return to the kind of analysis done by political theorists and social scientists *before* the study of human social behavior became fragmented into the discrete fields of economics, political science, and sociology, supported by history and a certain amount of philosophy. In an academic world full of analytical boundaries that enclose disciplines and limit interaction, Susan Strange, who helped establish the modern study of IPE at the London School of Economics and Politics, suggests that IPE represents a return to the idea that up until the twentieth century was

> . . . a vast, wide open range where anyone interested in the behavior of men and women in society could roam just as freely as the deer and the antelope. There were no fences or boundary-posts to confine the historians to history, the economists to economics. Political scientists had no exclusive right to write about politics, nor sociologists to write about social relations.[1]

It makes sense, then, that in today's complex world, the most important issues we all face have an international or multinational aspect to them that is best understood through an integrated study drawing on a variety of tools and analytical perspectives. Rowland Maddock puts it in a slightly different way:

> . . . international political economy is not a tightly defined and exclusive discipline with a well-established methodology. It is more a set of issues, which need investigating and which tend to be ignored by the more established disciplines, using whatever tools are at hand.[2]

Let us look first at the basic elements of the term *international political economy*. One way to understand its nature is to pick apart its name. First, IPE is *international* in scope, meaning that it deals with issues that cross national borders and with relations between and among nation-states. (A **nation-state** is a legal political entity that governs a geographically defined territory composed of one or more groups of people with different ethnic backgrounds and cultures.) Increasingly today, people talk about a *global* political economy because more and more problems and issues affect the whole world, not just a few nations, and require a universal perspective and understanding. This book will often use the terms *international* and *global* interchangeably, keeping in mind that the two words imply different degrees of spatial coverage related to a problem or issue.

Second, IPE involves a *political* dimension in that it usually focuses on the use of state power to make decisions about who gets what, when, and how in a society. Among other things, politics is a process of collective choice, drawing in competing and often conflicting interests and values of different actors, including individuals, nation-states on a bilateral and multilateral (i.e., between and among nation-states) basis, conflicts between states and international organizations, regional alliances, nongovernmental organizations, and transnational corporations (TNCs).

Third, IPE is about the *economy* or economics, which means that it deals with how scarce resources are allocated for different uses and distributed among individuals, groups, and nation-states through the market process, which is sometimes decentralized and other times quite centralized or controlled by state officials. Economic, political, and social analysis often look at the same questions, but economic analysis focuses less on issues of state power and national interests and more on issues of income, wealth, and individual interests.

Note that the term *IPE* does *not* capture enough of an important element of this multidimensional outlook, related to the effects of *society* and culture on politics and economics. As a reflection of this reality, perhaps the term IPE should give way to IPES. Despite the recent popularity of the idea that market forces have weakened both the state and society, the international political economy does not exist in a social vacuum. The social forces associated with class, ethnic, religious, and other cultural groups, along with their different beliefs and values, must also be considered in the IPE analytical formula. Likewise, the state, economy, and society are also affected by the historical development of important events and issues that cannot be ignored. IPE, then, attempts to understand the complex interaction of real people in the real world, along with their attitudes, emotions, and beliefs.

Finally, in an effort to combine important features and effects of politics, the economy, and society, Susan Strange makes the case that their relationship to one another can be viewed in the form of four distinct structures (discussed near the end of the chapter). In her words, IPE

> . . . concerns the social, political, and economic arrangements affecting the global systems of production, exchange, and distribution and the mix of values reflected therein. Those arrangements are not divinely ordained, nor are they the fortuitous outcome of blind chance. Rather they are the result of human decisions taken in the context of manmade institutions and sets of self-set rules and customs.[3]

We will develop in more detail the four arrangements or *structures* Professor Strange mentions here later in the chapter. Suffice it to say at this point that these structures can also be thought of as formal (institutional) arrangements and even understood bargains among any number of international actors that directly and indirectly decide outcomes or that shape the "rules of the game" on a particular international issue or problem. Strange also stresses that IPE is more than just the study of institutions or organizations; it is also the purposeful decisions that people make and the *values* they reflect.

## Why Study IPE?

Students should study international political economy for at least three reasons—because IPE is important, useful, and interesting.

*IPE is important.* IPE makes the front pages every day because many events affect us all as citizens of the world, residents of particular nation-states, and daily participants in societies and systems of markets that are increasingly international, if not global, in nature. It is crucial in today's world, in which events and conditions in one part can strongly affect conditions in other parts, that we analyze these conditions so as to understand what caused them and how they might be managed.

*IPE is useful.* Public and private employers increasingly seek out individuals who can think broadly and critically, and who can appreciate the effects of social conditions and alternative values. Real problems require solutions and policies that reflect a comprehensive analysis and understanding of complex and dynamic systems. In a global political economy and society in which so many things influence and affect one another, employers and government officials seek out those who can understand the international and global context of human activity. Indeed, a person needs to understand at least a little IPE just to be able to make sense of the plethora of information available in the nightly newscasts, in magazines, over the Internet, and in other forms of communication. IPE is the social science that most directly addresses these needs.[4]

*IPE is inherently interesting.* To paraphrase Samuel Johnson, a person who is bored with IPE is bored with life! IPE is all about life and the many actions and interactions that connect human beings around the globe. The study of IPE is the opportunity to study some of the most fascinating issues and questions of the past and present.

Globalization and the events of September 11, 2001, have not changed the world so much as they have made millions of people realize that the the world we live in is changing rapidly. This is so obvious that it hardly needs saying; nonetheless, it is important to say because it is the best reason to read the rest of this book. The best way to understand some of these changes and cope with some of their consequences is through the wide-open search for knowledge and understanding that defines international political economy.

## This Changes Everything: From Walls to Webs

Even if this textbook is your introduction to the formal study of IPE, it is unlikely that this is the first time you have confronted the sorts of issues that IPE studies. Every day the media are full of IPE because, in a way, the study of IPE is the study of modern life. Two issues in particular that have been high on the international agenda for public officials and IPE students since the end of the Cold War are globalization and the events surrounding September 11, 2001, when nineteen terrorists hijacked four commercial jet airliners and turned them from practical tools of civilian transport into weapons of mass destruction. According to those who have studied these phenomena and their effects on the international political economy, no one reading this text can escape their influence because they are so pervasive!

Shortly after the Cold War ended in the early 1990s, major newspaper headlines, journalists, and many academics alike proclaimed that security issues could finally take a back seat to the economy. In the early 1990s many of the economic ideas promoted by U.S. President Ronald Reagan and British Prime Minister Margaret Thatcher were about the need to free up markets both at home and internationally and to limit the state's role in the economy (see Chapter 3). Throughout the 1990s a good number of books that focused on globalization popularized the idea that—for good or for bad—through major economic and technological developments, people the world over were being interconnected in new, different, and profound ways. These changes in the international economy in the 1990s included new production technologies, new communication systems, and unexpected amounts of money moving quite freely throughout the international political economy in search of investment opportunities. Along with expected economic growth came the popularity of Western (read U.S.) products, including electronic goods, computers, and weapons technology, along with music, clothing, and food. The United States seemed to reap many of the economic rewards associated with globalization, namely, increased wealth and prosperity for large numbers of people, especially in the industrialized nations of the north, which led to record levels of product consumption and tourism, as well as record numbers of obese people.

Many state and international economic organization officials claimed that developing nations would also grow out of their debt and prosper if they too adopted neoliberal economic policies. In fact, many developing nations did experience tremendous national and per-capita growth, especially many of the Asian Tigers (Singapore, Hong Kong, Taiwan, and South Korea—see Chapter 15) and other southeast Asian economies such as Malaysia, Indonesia, and Thailand, to name only a few of the newly industrialized countries (NICs).

By the mid-1990s, however, a number of critics of globalization, including both academics and public officials, began to discuss and debate the positive and negative political, social, and economic effects of globalization (see Chapter 3). In the late 1990s a number of NGOs, international conference protestors, and in some cases anarchist groups, took to the streets of Seattle, among other cities in the United States and Europe, to protest many of the neoliberal economic policies promoted by the World Trade Organization (WTO), the International Monetary Fund (IMF), and the World Bank. Some of the critics charged the United States and other industrialized nations that supported globalization with fostering a new form of imperialism in developing nations.

One academic development of the early 2000s related to globalization has been the number of academics and public officials who have been increasingly more negative about what was supposed to be a positive thing for everyone. One's view of globalization seemed to depend on how much one benefited from it. The downturn in international economic growth in the early 2000s was related, in part, to the bursting of the technological bubble in the United States and quite possibly to the 9/11 terrorist attacks. At the same time, however, it also became clear that many developing nations were not growing out of poverty as expected. Aside from the damaging effects of the Mexican, Asian, Russian, and Argentinian monetary crises throughout this period (see Chapter 8), for many less developed countries, particulary the poorest ones, debts continued to mount along with disease, hunger, famine, and even civil, if not conventional, wars between them and what many regarded as "failed states" and other poor countries. With these developments have come increased doubts about, if not outright rejection of, economic liberal ideas and development strategies (see Chapter 15).

At the same time as many experts and state officials were raising doubts about the effects of globalization, these effects were felt on the level of personal security on September 11, 2001. Nearly all of us can recall where we were when we heard the news and witnessed the close-up television coverage of the collapse of the World Trade Center towers, the rubble and smoldering fire at the Pentagon, and the crash debris left in the field in Pennsylvania, which resulted in the deaths of nearly 3000 people. Almost as soon as the first plane hit one of the two towers in New York, people in Europe learned of the attack on television and on the Internet. One aspect of globalization—advanced communication systems—made it possible for some of the passengers on other hijacked planes to be notified on their cell phones by friends and loved ones of what had happened in New York. Amidst the chaos of that morning, the U.S. civil aviation system was shut down, top national leaders were hustled away to secure hideouts, and skyscrapers across the country emptied of their workers, while much of the world watched as horrific images of death and destruction filled the media round the clock.

Almost immediately following 9/11, television news channels carried footage of the noted terrorist Osama bin Laden. He was identified as the leader of al-Qaeda, a transnational terrorist network he had helped create and fund. In a number of his speeches, bin Laden had called for a *jihad* (loosely interpreted to mean a "holy war") against the United States for deploying its troops on Saudi soil during the Persian Gulf War, supporting the Saudi royal family, supporting Israel, and promoting a decadent Western lifestyle throughout the world that incorporates ideas about globalization but that (bin Laden argued) corrupts and destroys Islamic values.

The day after the attack on the United States, NATO allies adopted Article 5 of the NATO charter for the first time, making an attack on one an attack on all. Newspaper headlines quoted the French president as saying that "the United States is Us," implying that Europe and other NATO partners stood together and would cooperate to find bin Laden and break up his and other terrorist networks. Within a few months, troops from several NATO countries, including the United States, Great Britain, France, and Germany, invaded Afghanistan to defeat the Taliban government that supported al-Qaeda and to try and capture bin Laden. Within a few years the United States and some "coalition partners" would invade Iraq, in part for its alleged connection to al-Qaeda (see Chapter 9).

Regardless of the terrorists' motives, the front lines of the political battle shifted to U.S. soil and to some U.S. coalition partners such as England, Spain, and Italy, which supported the U.S.–British invasion of Iraq in 2003. Simultaneously, the old rulebooks were thrown out. In reaction to 9/11, the United States and other industrialized nations began reorganizing their defense agencies to deal with terrorist-related issues such as the protection of communication facilities and information, the deployment of military forces and protection of businesses and citizens abroad, and security for air travel and commerce. Germany tried to restrict access to the Internet by groups that support terrorism. And, in order to protect private and public financial transactions, the U.S. government froze the assets of organizations and individuals linked to al-Qaeda and began promoting a "key recovery" system that would permit law enforcement officials to have access to encrypted records or communications.

Indeed, after 9/11, many academic experts, journalists, and people the world over struggled to know what to say or think about 9/11 and the events that followed in Iraq. Many said something to the effect that "This changes everything—it is a whole new world," as a reflection of the political, social, and psychological effects of these events. For some people the problems of the world could no longer be viewed merely in terms of "foreign" or external affairs. More people than ever realized they were connected to developments in the international economy and to a new style of international terrorism that had been brought home in the most direct way possible. *New York Times* columnist Thomas Friedman captured these ideas very well in the preface to his book, *Longitudes and Attitudes: Exploring the World After September 11* (see Suggested Readings). According to Friedman:

> The world has become an increasingly interwoven place, and today, whether you are a company or a country, your threats and opportunities increasingly derive from who you are connected to. . . . We have

gone from an international system built around division and walls to a system increasingly built around integration and webs.[5]

Still another, broader political-economic development stemming from 9/11 was its effect on globalization. After the Cold War ended in the early 1990s, some thought that economic issues would trump security concerns on the international agenda. The events of 9/11, however, made security king once again, as the attacks proved that even the most powerful country in the world was vulnerable to terrorism. Analysts and policymakers once more had reason to suspect the possibility of a nuclear, chemical, or biological terrorist attack.

If there are lessons to be learned from the events of 9/11, one of them surely is that we do now live, and for a long time have been living, in a world-wide web of sorts—and not of just the computer type, but a web of international and in some cases global systems, structures, and networks (to be examined throughout this book). Sometimes these webs make us better off, but sometimes they expose us to new threats. And sometimes they do both. Just as international political economy makes the front page, as with globalization and the 9/11 tragedy, so these webs of interdependence are likely to generate more tensions in our lives. Friedman also said:

> Everyone in the world is directly or indirectly affected by this new system, but not everyone benefits from it, not by a long shot, which is why the more it becomes diffused, the more it also produces a backlash by people who feel overwhelmed by it, homogenized by it, or unable to keep pace with its demands.[6]

In any case, today we all confront a tightly interconnected, thoroughly multidimensional world that cannot be fully understood by examining any single element in isolation. It is a world that begs for the sort of complex and multidimensional analytical frameworks that IPE provides.

## Disciplinary Explanations of Globalization and 9/11

We have argued that the IPE approach synthesizes a number of methods and insights derived from economics, political science, and sociology as conditioned by an understanding of history and philosophy. This synthesis is necessary in part because of the tendency of separate academic disciplines to focus on only certain elements of complex problems while real-world issues expand beyond any particular set of physical and intellectual boundaries. Both globalization and the 9/11 attacks and the responses to them provide a good example of the relationship between IPE and different academic disciplines. A short list of the ways that some academic disciplines might address these conditions and events, each focusing on a particular element of this complex issue, includes the following:

- *International economics.* Many of the neoliberal policy recommendations that international economists make about international trade, finance, and development assume that a limited role of the state will benefit people everywhere with increased wealth and welfare. Thus, some international economists are concerned about 9/11 to the extent that international trade and finance played a role in President George W. Bush's response to the terrorist attacks. After the attack, President Bush announced that the United States would attempt to increase trade with Arab nations, on the premise that beneficial economic linkages would help forge stronger political ties among nations. Many governments also sought ways to build safeguards into the international financial system to prevent transfers of funds to terrorist organizations. Many experts are still debating the extent to which the same fluid system that made international investment possible on a massive scale (sometimes attributed to economic globalization) also permitted organized crime and terrorist groups to finance their operations efficiently.
- *Comparative politics.* A comparative political scientist might focus on the effect of globalization on different national political economies and their societies. Globalization has been quite beneficial for many industrialized nations, at least for certain sectors of the economy such as those involved in traded high-technology products. Many developing countries, however, have not fared as well and feel threatened by globalization. Although it is debatable to what extent the lack of benefit is a problem of corrupt governments or other issues, in some cases left-wing, pro-socialist governments have been making a comeback,

especially in Latin America. Likewise, comparative political scientists may study reactions to 9/11 based on different political systems, their cultures, and historical circumstances. After 9/11, President Bush, for example, stressed in some statements that one goal of his policies would be to foster democracy abroad. However, democracy is not a universally desired political system. Thus the effect of the President's proposals is likely to differ in different political systems, such as the dictatorships in many African nations, monarchies as in Saudi Arabia, and theocracies (rule by a religious organization) in places like Iran that are not likely to look with favor on the U.S. president's effort.

- *International relations.* International relations specialists often focus on nation-states and their relationships to one another in the international system (see Chapter 9). Many of them are concerned that the attacks were perceived as a response to the relationship of the United States to Iraq or to some other state such as Sudan or Afghanistan—where the terrorists might have been trained—or the United States's relationship to Saudi Arabia, home to many of the terrorists' families. Many sets of bilateral and multilateral relations between the United States and other countries were affected as well. For example, the United States has since tightened immigration rules in an attempt to prevent terrorists from entering the country secretly, an action that divided the U.S. populace and generated tensions with Mexico.
- *Sociology.* A sociologist might be concerned with how matters of class, race, ethnicity, and gender enter into the issues of globalization and terrorism. One effect of both globalization and the terrorist attacks has been to make some people more fearful of displaced immigrants and foreigners. Many sociologists study how people behave when confronted with "otherness." They might also be particularly concerned about how immigrant groups were treated in the aftermath of 9/11 and the effects of the attack on their families, communities, and their identities.
- *Anthropology.* An anthropologist might focus on the cultural differences between the United States and countries that are less diverse in terms of religion and ethnicity, and on how culture contributes to the debate about global problems such as globalization and 9/11. An anthropologist might view conflict as a clash of cultures or cultural values, not so much as a result of tensions between different nations or different economies. Anthropologists are usually sensitive to such issues as the status of women and how this might affect various policy responses. The Bush administration, for example, made equal treatment for women an important point in justifying a war on terrorism, yet has not been so keen on promoting equality for women in the case of globalization.
- *History.* A historian would also have a great deal to say about terrorism. For example, in the 1990s many political and economic historians considered the issue of globalization. The distinguished Princeton professor of Arab history, Bernard Lewis, wrote a book partly in response to the terrorist attacks titled *What Went Wrong? Western Impact and Middle East Response* (see Suggested Readings). Professor Lewis looked at a number of historical interactions between the West and Islam and made popular the argument that, among other things, Islamic influences were often integrated into Western life, but that the Islamic world had no similar record of readily accepting Western culture and values. Similar to many sociologists and anthropologists, his analysis suggests that culture and history matter, and an attempt by the West to liberalize or modernize Islamic peoples is necessarily problematic.

The point we want to make about these disciplinary specialties is that each makes an important but also incomplete contribution to our understanding of global events. Because IPE draws on elements of all of these fields, it has the potential to provide a more complete and meaningful analysis. An understanding of issues such as globalization and 9/11 necessitates that we use a variety of approaches that draw together methods and insights from several different disciplinary perspectives and from all four levels of analysis (individual, state, and international and global systems—discussed below), taking into account the many actors, institutions, and values of those involved in any situation as well as those of the analyst. As we have seen, the academic division of labor, in which scholars focus on a narrow range of methods and issues, allows for intellectual specialization and the analytical efficiency that goes with it, but also promotes a sort of scholarly blindness that comes from staring too long at just one side or set of issues of an analytically complex problem.

An international organization exists of physicians and medical professionals who volunteer their time and resources around the world wherever help is needed, called Médecins Sans Frontières, which is French for Doctors Without Borders. International political economy can be thought of as social science "sans frontières" because the IPE approach is not constrained by intellectual borders and walls, whether between countries or between academic disciplines. IPE adopts many of the methods and insights from separate disciplines and pulls them together into a more comprehensive analytical outlook.

## ANALYTICAL BUILDING BLOCKS: STATES, MARKETS, AND SOCIETIES

Much of the study of IPE focuses on the interaction of three highly important institutions—states, markets, and societies—and how their relationship to one another affects the behavior of a variety of different actors. A strict distinction between the state, the market, and society is quite arbitrary and imposed by disciplinary traditions. It is not always clear where the boundary lines between these analytical, but very real, entities are drawn, which is reflected in the three perspectives that dominate IPE studies (outlined below). If markets are yellow, the state blue, and society red, then most of the world is made up of the various shades of color that reflect the many degrees of relative influence of the state, market, and social forces. However, there are a few elements of each entity that should be taken into consideration when thinking about the nature of IPE.

### Politics and the State

International relations people like to emphasize that the **state** is a legal entity, or a relatively coherent and autonomous system of institutions that governs (i.e., makes important decisions) for a specific geographic territory and population. Since the mid-seventeenth century, it has become the dominant actor in the international community, based on the principle that is has the authority to exercise **sovereignty** (final authority) over its own affairs. Depending on the context for example, *France* refers to the state (government) and territory of the *nation* (its people) and their unique sociocultural qualities.

One political value that both states and markets value strongly is security. Feeling safe from physical threats, such as foreign invasion and physical violence or sickness, is a basic human need that people share as individuals but also collectively. People also seek security of their property, jobs, and the wealth they possess, along with preservation of their culture, religion, environment, and so forth. The search for security, therefore, is almost a never-ending job undertaken by the state, leading many international relations theorists to view the international system as exhibiting a potential state of anarchy or war at any time, given their differences in strength and weaknesses and their conflicting interests and values. In Chapters 2 and 9, we will examine some of the instruments, such as military weapons and wealth, that states often use to help secure themselves in a world where security cannot be guaranteed by any political actor.

Two issues add to the complexity of issues surrounding the goal of security. First, because it is intangible, some states, like some individuals, feel more insecure than others and put a higher priority on security than on other national goals and objectives. Likewise, the need for security sometimes drives states and markets in the same direction. At other times, these two spheres conflict. For examples, farmers in both the United States and the European Union (EU) are often threatened by poor market conditions for commodities that both overproduce. In order to maintain political support for their governments, state officials will provide their farmers with subsidy payments to not produce as many commodities, store them, or help them export them. These subsidies, however, create problems in international food markets, generating conflict between states and lessening security for farmers who face cutbacks in their level of support. Likewise, many developing nations are threatened by the amount of support that U.S. and EU farmers receive, especially when it means limiting developing-country food imports into those countries.

Realist-type international relations experts (see Chapter 2) also like to focus on how states "allocate and distribute power." The classical realist Hans Morgenthau (see Chapter 9) defined power as the ability to control the minds and actions of others. Susan Strange calls this **relational power**, or the ability of one actor to get another to do or not do something. Most of us normally think of this kind of power when it comes to using conventional force or even nuclear weapons to deter or punish an adversary. Theoretically, because a state has a monopoly on the means of violence over its territory and population, state officials usually choose where, how much, and on whom to employ these tangible instruments.

Increasingly, however, in an interdependent world, what is important in IPE, according to Professor Strange, is **structural power**, which she defines as "the power to shape and determine the structures of the global political economy within which other states, their political institutions, their economic enterprises and (not least) their scientists and other professional people have to operate."[7] These structures or networks (discussed later) are composed of bargains among a variety of actors such as states, including IOs, NGOs, TNCs, and others, whose relationship to one another help determine the "rules of the game" of a particular system, such as the security structure. Structural power is less direct than relational power, but can be even more effective in some situations, depending on who benefits from these bargains, as we will see in cases such as the international trade, finance, and knowledge and technology structures (discussed in Chapters 6, 7, and 10).

Still another way to think about power is the distinction Joseph Nye makes between soft and hard power.[8] **Hard power** refers to the application of military force and economic instruments to compel, coerce, influence, or persuade enemies, opponents, or other actors. **Soft power** incorporates the influence of culture, beliefs, values, and ideals and is less direct but perhaps more effective than hard power—at least in some cases. In the initial phases of the war on terrorism and the subsequent invasions of Afghanistan and Iraq, President Bush drew on both hard power and soft power: hard power to defeat physically the terrorists who were connected with the Taliban and supposedly with Saddam Hussein's regime in Iraq, and soft power to influence the cultures that tolerated or supported them. However, as the wars in Iraq and Afghanistan dragged on, it became clear that the Bush administration's reliance on hard power was not effective in establishing peace in the Middle East and that the gradual deemphasis on U.S. structural power came at a high cost in terms of cooperation with U.S. allies and management of international security (see Chapter 9) and other structures (see especially Chapters 6, 7, 8, and 10).

The state can also be viewed more broadly as the domain of collective political behavior that increasingly takes place at a regional geographic level. The EU, for instance, is not a single nation-state but a supranational organization of nation-states that "pools" some elements of sovereignty around a number of supranational institutions (see Chapter 12). To the extent that the EU makes choices or adopts policies that affect its entire membership of some twenty-seven nations and their citizens, it demonstrates the properties of a state. This raises the issue of the increasingly important role of IOs and NGOs in the international political economy.

According to realists (see Chapters 2 and 9), IOs are the creation of nation-states and, at their whim, serve their purposes. Most IOs, such as the United Nations, the North Atlantic Treaty Organization (NATO), the World Health Organization, and a number of economic organizations including the WTO, IMF, and World Bank, do not have much authority beyond what member states grant them. On the other hand, many idealists and political liberals (see Chapter 3) look to IOs to gradually acquire more authority as they accomplish institutional objectives by promoting cooperation between nation-states, and between nation-states and other actors. Likewise, as IOs benefit states, states will become more dependent on them to solve complex international problems and member states will be willing to grant them more decision-making authority—as EU members have done. As we will see in the various chapters of the book, many international and global issues are increasingly managed by not only nation-states but also by IOs. One obvious example is the role of the United Nations Security Council, which establishes and maintains peacekeeping operations all over the world (see Chapter 9). Increasingly under question is the extent to which the UN can intervene in the affairs of states that violate the human rights of their members. In such as Somalia, Rwanda, Congo, and Sudan, the principle of noninterference in the domestic affairs of states is increasingly at odds with the humanitarian rights of individuals, regardless of the state in which they live.

NGOs are perhaps the fastest-growing group of actors in the international political economy today. Their ranks include the Red Cross and the previously mentioned Médecins Sans Frontières, environmental organizations such as Greenpeace, and a host of other humanitarian, development, and human rights–oriented private groups. In many cases these humanitarian-oriented actors have been quite vocal in their opposition to globalization and to a variety of economic liberal (the so-called Washington consensus, see Chapters 7 and 8) trade, currency, and debt policies.

## Economics and the Market

Many people associate the **market** with economic enterprises and the institutions of modern capitalism, such as large capital-intensive and highly sophisticated industrial production (e.g., Boeing) and service industries (e.g., SYSCO), transnational manufacturing firms (e.g., Toyota) scattered the world over, large banks that loan and borrow money that finance these operations, and the intensive marketing and selling of these items. However, markets are essentially interchanges between real people, where one person exchanges something for something else. Although a market can be thought of as a geographic location (such as the New York Stock Exchange or the Pike Place Market in Seattle) where goods and services are exchanged and purchased, it can also be thought of as a *driving force* that shapes human behavior. For many economists, especially those of the popular economic liberal variety (see Chapter 3), markets have a sense of mystery about them—their so-called "hidden hand"—made famous in a single passage by the Scotsman Adam Smith.

Under pure market conditions (i.e., the absence of state intervention or social influences), people are assumed to behave rationally (see Chapter 3). That is, they will naturally seek to maximize their gains and limit their losses by producing and exchanging (selling) things. This desire to exchange is a strong motive behind their behavior, along with pressure to generate wealth by competing with others for sales in local and international markets. A value many people (should) strongly hold that is reflected in market activity is *economic efficiency,* the ability to use and distribute resources (and hence power) effectively and with little waste. Why is efficiency important? Efficiency requires that society's scarce resources be put to their highest and best use. When an economy is inefficient, scarce resources go unused or could be used in other ways that would be more beneficial. Society is assumed to sacrifice resources that could benefit education, health care, and so forth, that could have been used more wisely.

Theoretically, in a pure market society, human interchange results in a positive-sum game in which everyone benefits from what everyone else produces most efficiently. The prices of goods and their supply balance against one another as a reflection of individual choices, desires, and the ability to come up with enough resources to pay for purchased goods. Many neoliberal economists also argue that markets can be a highly decentralized and individualistic way to decide how scarce resources are used (allocation) and who benefits from them (distribution). In effect, individual consumer purchases and sales end up coordinating or directing society to produce the right amount of what people need and want.

The distinguished political scientist Charles Lindblom takes a different tack on markets. He argues that only *theoretically* does the market include the sphere of human action dominated by individual self-interest and conditioned by the forces of economic competition.[9] As other critics of the economic liberal market outlook suggest, the market reflects a good many political and social pressures and elements. Even Adam Smith recognized the need for certain functions only the state could provide in order to make a market economy work, including defense and laws related to curbing enterprises (monopolies) that could render the market unworkable. In many countries the state is often the biggest buyer of goods and services—military weapons, police, and other services. It also supplies the economy with educated people and tax monies for highway infrastructure and controls the banking system.

One of the main tenets of economic liberals is that for states that are democratic and capitalist in nature, the market *should* play a large role in a decentralized decision-making process (see

Chapter 3). Yet many neoliberals decry the more usual situation in which states do interfere in the market. The question then remains as to why they interfere as much as they do, at least in the minds of many neoliberals. As someone who has spent a great deal of time thinking about the relationship of markets to the state and society, Robert Gilpin suggests that, theoretically (and practically as well), open markets and free trade (the absence of protection for certain groups) creates a dilemma for the state. According to Gilpin:

> Whereas powerful market forces in the form of trade, money and foreign investment tend to jump national boundaries, to escape political control, and to integrate societies, the tendency of government is to restrict, to channel, and to make economic activities serve the perceived interests of the state and of powerful groups within it. The logic of the market is to locate economic activities where they are most productive and profitable; the logic of the state is to capture and control the process of economic growth and capital accumulation.[10]

While Gilpin stresses the conflicting goals between states and markets, we could go one step further and argue that, by definition, markets exist within some form of political arrangement or bargain whereby states or some other form of political unit helps maintain their existence and ultimately decides their primary function, whether it be which class interests they support most (the structuralist focus—see Chapter 4), how "open" they will be when it comes to trade policy (see Chapter 6), or the extent to which they will be used as some kind of weapon or strategic instrument (see Chapter 9). In other words, markets do not exist in a political, or for that matter, social vacuum. As some people who have bought shoddy goods or who have not received the items they purchased from eBay have discovered, modern capitalist systems require an effective legal system to enforce contracts related to purchased goods and deliveries. Aside from the need for national defense, Adam Smith recognized that markets would not work well without state establishment and maintenance of a common standard by which money is valued or, in the case of international trade, investment, and tourism, currencies are exchanged.

The noted economist J. Maynard Keynes argued that markets routinely fail, especially as a result of rational consumer behavior. In Chapter 3 we discuss some of Keynes's views and the recommendations he made to overcome the Great Depression of the 1930s through a compromise of the sort Gilpin refers to between states and markets that increases the role of the state in the economy. Yet another issue that concerned Keynes was that of equity or fairness, which markets do not guarantee. As we have seen in both developed and developing nations, market outcomes that affect public policies and relations between and among individuals can be unfair or unequal if the power that individuals exercise (either through states or markets) is distributed unequally.

In "mixed economies," then—such as the United States and England, among others—market forces influence a great many resource allocation and distribution decisions, but not all of them. In many nations, people prefer more state control or regulation over market activity in an effort to guide outcomes in directions that favor (or disfavor) certain people or groups. In "command economies" such as the former Soviet Union before 1989, for example, the state tried to make nearly all allocation and distribution choices based on the leadership's notion of society's and the national interest (which included anticapitalism). In this case, many critics of the Soviet Union and other socialist societies point out that the state overregulated the economy, resulting in huge inefficiencies when it came to the production of goods and services and to the overbureaucratization of the Soviet state. Achieving efficiency required a great deal of information about the availability of resources, their use, the benefits of alternative uses, and so on—more information than any centralized authority such as a state possibly could have accumulated at that time or even using the most powerful computers in the world today.

Since the end of the Cold War, a number of former Soviet-bloc countries in Eastern Europe and elsewhere (see Chapter 13) have been undergoing a transformation whereby markets play a decidedly bigger role—in contrast to the state—in deciding economic policies. In many cases, such as with some of the poorer developing countries and also China, shifting to a market economy and to a democratic government that will supposedly *limit* the state's role in the economy is not an easy process. In most societies the role of the state is not that circumscribed or constrained.

Many other factors go into determining or explaining the relationship of the state to the market. As mercantilists and structuralists are quick to point out (see Chapters 2 and 4), when states curb their interference in the market, it may reflect more of a conscious choice on the part of state officials, often acting in concert with private enterprises, to direct outcomes in one direction or another—a political decision—rather than the result of market forces alone. In most cases, markets are another tool that states use to achieve an array of political goals and objectives.

## Sociology and Society

To add still more complexity to an already complicated situation, society adds another element of tension to the state, market, and society mix, because different societal groups usually want to preserve and promote the history, culture, and values of their social system. It may take a good deal of money and effort to preserve what one writer refers to as *jihad* in the face of globalization ("McWorld") and its leveling effect on society.[11] There are usually many different social groups *within* a state, such as tribes, clans, and ethnic or other types of communities whose borders often cut across national boundaries. Even if academics and political officials tend to fold these groups into one nation-state or another, we need to account for cases such as Iraq, Iran, and many other Middle Eastern nation-states, for example, where tensions between different religious groups often play a major role in shaping social, political, and economic behavior, as well as the relationship of these states to others.

Once again it is Lindblom who makes a different and interesting case for the relationship of society to both the economy and state. He starts by suggesting that the economy is actually nothing more than a system for coordinating social behavior! Markets for certain items such as labor, agricultural and industrial goods, and services cannot be thought of as distinct from a **market system** in which these factors are necessarily linked to one another. In an age of increasingly growing globalization, market systems link people and their different values and interests with one another when they make products better, cheaper, or more attractive to people in other nations. Relatively unregulated markets can perform a social "coordinating without a coordinator" function, whereas, in more authoritarian systems, markets serve as a "cruel and harsh coordinator."[12]

Playing off of Gilpin's tension between the state and market, Lindblom suggests that the market is like a dance with an orchestra (the state). In this dance, markets diffuse participation and control, simplify decision patterns, and coordinate sets of preferences, helping consumers settle claims to an extent related to the amount of money people have. Think of the control the U.S. government has over the air waves, along with its influence, if not control, over the Internet. We could go one step further (no pun intended) and suggest that the standards used to judge the effectiveness or efficiency of markets and market systems always reflect the dominant ideas about society's values and beliefs. Robert Heilbroner outlines this argument in his work on past societies—whose major objective was usually to command, control, and distribute resources to limited numbers of people.[13] What we view today as market behavior would look strange, let alone be of little utility, in the early Mesopotamian societies. Thus, markets are a force, but not one that is easily separated from social and political forces that give them purpose and provide them with different functions.

This raises a fundamental issue—some say it is the essence of IPE—as to what should be the proper balance among the state, society, and the economy. Suffice it to say, even if economic liberals have suggested the market should take precedence over the state and society, there is no set formula for all nation-states nor for their societies. What is interesting are the *patterns of interaction* between the state, society, and markets that change over time and that shape local, national, and international institutions as well as individual behavior patterns in dynamic ways. At times the market may dominate more than the state or society, resulting in a shifting configuration of group and actor interests and values. This seems to have been the pattern of the 1990s when globalization became so prevalent.

As we will see in Chapter 13, in China, for example, changes in the economy have helped galvanize forces for political change in the state. In an attempt to improve the living standards of their people, in the late 1970s Chinese leaders began introducing free-market forces into some areas of China's economy. Free markets, profits, and private enterprise have since become quite popular and viewed as a means to speed growth and increase income levels, in addition to raising the standard of living and social status of the people. Yet these market forces have also generated problems for the Chinese state and many of its people. Many state industries have been privatized, their workers laid off, and their benefits cut in order to modernize the production process. Corruption and prostitution have become much more prevalent, according to some sources. And many migrants have left the countryside looking for better jobs, raising complaints against the migrants and increasing the efforts of those who would like to see stricter laws limiting their movement. As these developments continue, one has to wonder how long any of the egalitarian values of Mao's era can survive the changes that usually parallel the economic development of societies.

### State, Market, and Society Dynamics

Several points about the *relationship* of states, markets, and society to one another emerge from the discussion above about politics, economics, and society. First, because they embrace different basic values and prefer to work in different ways to achieve different ends, sharp *tensions* and *conflicts* often result within and between different nation-states and their societies. Second, most people live simultaneously in a state that exhibits certain types of political institutions, national market arrangements, and a distinct social system that differs from other nation-states that have their own political, market, and social arrangements and institutions. Therefore, it is not surprising that *change* in one sphere evokes change in another sphere and renders IPE to a constant state of transition. Robert Gilpin has focused on this issue and argues that the market greatly influences the creation and distribution of wealth both within and among nation-states.[14] Likewise, we know that the ideas and values of state officials and their societies often dramatically shape the role of markets in society.

Third, how well the collective choices of the state reflect the general will and the public interest depends on a large number of factors, such as voting rights, rules about representation, and the nature of political institutions in a country. The United States, for example, employs an extremely complicated system of public choice, with a great many elected and appointed executive and legislative officials, deliberative bodies, and administrative agencies. It remains a problem as to whether, as economic liberals tend to assume, decentralized markets with little to no state involvement in the economy serves society's best interests. In many states the distribution of resources is dominated or manipulated by a small group of "elites" or by the influence of special interests. The public interest can easily be sacrificed on the altar of narrow private interests.

To summarize, states, markets, and society seek different *goals* (such as security, efficiency, and the preservation of culture), employ different *means* (decentralized markets and voluntary bargains versus collective action and force), and reflect different *values* (justice, peace, equity, fairness). For many political, economic, and social reasons, and despite the popularity of neoliberal economic policies that would minimize the role of the state (see Chapter 3), in the international political economy at present, the state continues to play an important, and some argue vital, role in the economy, depending on economic conditions but also on society's demands and needs. Some state functions help the national and international market system work efficiently, whereas others are not helpful.

## ANALYTICAL TOOLS OF IPE

Several analytical dilemmas arise when it comes to explaining IPE problems such that they account for state, market, and society relations. Because each has its own unique character traits and motives, and reflects different values, establishing an approach to explain IPE problems seems nearly impossible. One way to approach IPE is to think about the different dimensions that important complex international problems exhibit in the same way that we think about the size, shape, color, and texture of multidimensional physical objects. This provides us with both a vocabulary to use in describing international issues and a set of analytical tools to increase our understanding of them. The most important dimensions of IPE, as we will discuss them in this textbook, are

- Three analytical perspectives: mercantilism, liberalism, and structuralism
- Four levels of analysis: the individual, the state, the international system of states, and the global level
- Four international structures: security, production, finance, and knowledge

## Three Interdisciplinary Perspectives and Sets of Values

A variety of approaches attempts to describe how global actors such as states should interact (based on certain normative theories that reflect a particular set of values) or how they really do behave (based on several positive theories). Three broad approaches act like lenses that can be used to view and interpret developments in the international political economy. Different people give different names to the main IPE approaches—a problem that results from the "wide open spaces" that are also the strength of IPE.

**Mercantilism,** or economic nationalism, is the IPE perspective most closely associated with political science, especially the political philosophy of *realism*, which looks at IPE issues mainly in terms of national interests and state struggles for wealth and power.

**Liberalism** (especially economic liberalism) is rooted in a focus on IPE issues mainly in terms of individual interests. Economic or neoliberalism is most closely associated with the study of markets and the behavior of different actors associated with them. As we discuss in Chapter 3, many liberal values and ideas are the ideological foundation behind globalism and the globalization campaign.

**Structuralism,** rooted in Marxist analysis but not limited to it, looks at IPE issues mainly in terms of how classes, class interests, and ultimately all of society are shaped by the dominant economic structures of society. Structuralism is most closely associated with the methods of analysis employed by many sociologists.

In many respects the analytical history of international political economy is a competition for dominance among opposing IPE approaches and theoretical perspectives, along with the values and beliefs they represent. The next three chapters examine them in some detail, exploring their development and their relationship to one another. These approaches provide us with a frame of reference to try to understand IPE and the connections among its many dimensions. Each viewpoint sheds light on some aspects of an issue particularly well but may cast a shadow on other important points. All IPE theories look at the same world of international problems, issues, and events, yet each approaches those issues from a different angle that reflects a different set of core beliefs, values, and solutions to problems. They guide the thoughts and actions of men and women in all sorts of ways, and so shape and condition a variety of international and global problems the world over.

Often a particular situation can be most revealingly understood from one perspective. Thus, while we encourage the consideration of many perspectives, we emphasize the right and obligation of individuals to make their own judgments about which view (or combination of perspectives) helps them best make sense of a topic or problem. Much of the time this will depend on the facts or data related to the issues, the questions asked about it, the applicability of any of the approaches, and the views of the analyst herself.

## Four Levels of Analysis

When it comes to explaining issues, most IPE problems involve all four different **levels of analysis**—the individual, state, international system, and what is increasingly recognized as a global level. In Kenneth Waltz's famous book on the causes of war, *Man, the State, and War* (see Suggested Readings), for example, he determined that international conflict was sometimes caused by conditions related to human nature (at the individual level), sometimes by aggressive characteristics of national governments (at the state level), and sometimes by a risky and unstable configuration of the distribution of power (at the international system level).[15] Increasingly, a number of students of IPE, and especially international relations, argue that there is a global level at which issues or problems exist and which share characteristics all their own. Combined with Waltz's classic three levels of analysis, these four levels help organize our thoughts about the different causes of issue conflicts as well as a good many of their solutions.

For example, in response to the security threats of September 11, 2001, strategies to increase security involved all four levels of IPE. At the actor level, Osama bin Laden and others may constitute a terrorist threat not only to the United States, but to states everywhere. At the level of internal characteristics of a state, some states tolerate terrorist organizations more than others for any number of reasons related to their economy, culture, type of government, and a host of other reasons that emanate from within the state. At the international level, states sometimes cooperate with other states to deal with the issue and at other times prefer not to cooperate. At the global level, many questions have been raised recently as to how much and why terrorism appears to have taken on a global (all over the world) dimension.

## Four Global Structures

The institutions, arrangements, and "rules of the game" that govern the behavior of states and markets in the international political economy can be analyzed as four networks, structures, or bargains that result in the production, exchange, and distribution of global wealth and power.[16] These bargains determine different patterns of production and exchange, along with the distribution of wealth and power all over the world. They can take many forms, including formal agreements that are signed, ratified, and enforced. Other bargains are merely conventions, understandings, or rules of thumb. These bargains tend to be far less formal, but just as important.[17] It is useful to think of these structures as networks, bargains, or linkages that connect individuals and states and that form international systems through which relational and structural powers are exercised by any number of actors in the international system.

These four **IPE structures** are described below.

The **Security Structure**. Security—from natural forces or, more important, from the threats and actions of other states and nonstate actors—is perhaps the most basic human need. When one person, state, or international organization contributes to or provides security for states and other organizations, a security network is created. The nature of this security structure depends on the kind of bargain that is struck among its participants. The international security structure was an important defining force in IPE in the twentieth century. The 9/11 attacks, and the many responses to them, illustrate vividly how complex security has become and how correspondingly complicated the security structure itself is. The Cold War looks frighteningly simple by comparison (see Chapter 9).

The **Production and Trade Structure**. Producing things is one element of generating value and wealth, and wealth is nearly always linked to power. The issue of who produces what for whom on what terms, therefore, lies at the heart of international political economy. Recent decades have witnessed dramatic changes in the production structure, with production of certain high-value items such as automobiles shifting from the United States to Japan and then on to other countries, such as Korea, Mexico, Brazil, and China. These structural changes affect trade and the distribution of wealth and power in the world and therefore affect the other IPE structures.

The **Finance and Monetary Structure**. This is perhaps the most abstract set of linkages between and among nations. One way to describe the finance and monetary structure is to say that it is the pattern of money flows between and among nations. That is, this structure defines who has access to money, how, and on what terms. This definition's simplicity covers up two important points. First, we are not really interested in money so much as in what money can buy—scarce resources. So, this structure is really a description of how certain resources are allocated and distributed between and among nations. In this respect, money is a means, not an end. Second, we are, at this point, interested in money mostly to the extent that it creates an obligation between people or states. International money flows pay for trade and finance investment. At other times the money movement takes the form of direct investment through which a foreigner gains control directly over the use of resources by, say, purchasing a factory or a farm. Financial bargains then create obligations, which join the interests of different nations. Other times, money moves from one nation to another in the form of loans, which must be repaid.

The global financial and monetary structure has recently been marked by the movement of "hot money" from one country to another, chasing quick profits. Unregulated financial markets were in part responsible for financial crises in the 1990s in Mexico, parts of Asia and Latin America, and Russia (see Chapter 8). Unregulated capitalism associated with increasing globalization may also be partly responsible for breeding both poverty and support for terrorists in some of the depressed areas of the world.

The **Knowledge and Technology Structure**. It is often said that knowledge is power. Knowledge is wealth, too, for those who can use it effectively. Who has knowledge and how it is used is therefore an important factor in IPE. Nations with poor access to knowledge in the form of industrial technology, scientific discoveries, medical procedures, or instant communications, for example, find themselves at a disadvantage relative to others. Increasingly in the world today, the bargains made in the security, production and trade, and finance and monetary structures depend on access to knowledge in its several forms.

The connection between technology and terrorism tightens by the day. Newspapers are full of stories about terrorist tactics and the array of weapons of mass destruction (WMD) that are available in the trade structure, such as nuclear, biological, and chemical weapons. New technology has also made many of these weapons obsolete to the extent that they are either too costly to make, too difficult to deploy or transport, or require people with sophisticated skills to maintain. On the other hand, new technologies have revolutionized the size of weapons and the effects they have when put to use. Many weapons can easily be transported in a backpack or a briefcase. The ultimate miniature weapon may no longer be an atomic bomb or other weapons of mass destruction, but a few grams of anthrax on a letter.

Taken together, these four IPE structures form the international system within which the interdependent relations of individuals and states occur. The international system is therefore composed of a set of bargains and relationships—human arrangements—that condition how states and individuals behave and determine in part the mix of values that result from their dynamic interaction. The most important thing about the bargains we study in IPE is that they are multidimensional. That is, they defy any attempt to oversimplify them—to make them simple one-dimensional issues. Today, we as individuals and as members of different nation-states are interconnected to the rest of the world in ways that also generate complex relationships, which can be described by words such as "web" or "network" of relations, that influence strongly the institutions and rules related to the flows of trade, finance, and technology—via a global network of multilayered security relationships. These connections are in fact linked to one another. As we have seen, determining the causes of terrorism for instance, and then dealing with it, forces us to reconsider, appreciate, and understand the increasingly tight linkages among these four different webs or networks.

Finally, what gets produced, exchanged, and distributed in the global political economy also affects other important aspects of life such as the distribution of power, security, culture, and people's status. Therefore, IPE structures are often filled with elements of tension—generated by spatial and time boundaries where differing and sometimes conflicting interests, points of view, or value systems challenge one another. A good example is that security issues that involve conflict or war often get the most press attention. However, economic and cultural issues have generated needed attention to the various dimensions of this issue (see Chapter 9). For example, the AIDS crisis, particularly in many poorer nations, has taken major economic and political tolls on these and other societies.

## CONCLUSION: LIVING IN INTERESTING TIMES AND WHY WE SHOULD STUDY IPE

In conclusion, this book is an introduction to IPE, written to help students understand the issues, forces, and problems that characterize today's interdependent world and also to help you appreciate where you fit into the "big picture" of the international political economy. IPE is not a single discipline but an effort to break down the walls between three different disciplines: politics, economics, and sociology. Drawing on each of these disciplines, IPE focuses on individuals, states, markets, and societies (along with other actors and institutions) all over the world and on institutional networks and arrangements or structures that have evolved to link them. These arrangements reflect culture, history, and values, and thus they generate tension and conflict. They can also be expected to evolve and change in the future.

This chapter used examples of globalization and 9/11 to illustrate the importance of IPE. Both of these issues have made millions of people realize that the world has changed and is changing around them. The very foundations of wealth, power, and security are revealed to be much more delicate and more important than we had imagined them to be, especially since the end of the Cold War. Toward the goal of explaining and understanding these and a host of other issues covered in this book, we outlined three approaches or analytical perspectives, four levels of analysis, and four international structures that students can use to analyze different problems and issues of IPE.

As we proceed in this book we hope you will find IPE as relevant, fascinating, and provocative a topic as we do.

## DISCUSSION QUESTIONS

1. Pick a recent news article that focuses on some international or global problem, and give examples of how and where state, market, and society interact and at times conflict with one another. How hard is it to determine the boundaries between the state, market, and society in this case?
2. How do states, markets, and society differ in terms of their values and goals and in the means different actors use to achieve goals related to each of them? Discuss this question both in general and with respect to the current event topic in Question 1.
3. In your view, which matters most in IPE; the state, the market, or society? Explain with reference to the reading.
4. Find a newspaper article and outline some elements in it that fit into any of the four IPE structures. If there is more than one, explain their connection.
5. Find a newspaper article and use the levels of analysis to explain the perspective from which the author explains the problem or issue under study. What can we conclude about understanding this problem from different levels of analysis?

## INTERNET LINKS

Each chapter of this textbook will include several suggested links to sites on the World Wide Web that can provide current information or greater depth for the interested reader. Internet addresses change frequently, however, so do not be discouraged if some of the addresses you find here are "broken" when you try them. An up-to-date set of Internet links as well as many other useful and interesting items can be found at the Internet home page for this textbook:

www.ups.edu/ipe/ipebook.htm

Home page for *The Lexus and the Olive Tree* by Thomas L. Friedman:
www.lexusandtheolivetree.com

The IPE Network (sponsored by the IPE section of the International Studies Association):
http://csf.colorado.edu/ipe

The International Studies Association website:
http://csf.colorado.edu/isa

*The Economist*, a British weekly magazine that is required reading for students of IPE:
http://economist.com

The *Financial Times*, a British daily newspaper in which IPE issues are discussed and debated:
http://news.ft.com

## SUGGESTED READINGS

Kenneth E. Boulding. "Is Economics Necessary?" and "The Relations of Economic, Political, and Social Systems," in *Beyond Economics: Essays on Society, Religion and Ethics*. Ann Arbor: University of Michigan Press, 1970.
Milton Friedman. Especially chap. 1 in *Capitalism and Freedom*. Chicago: University of Chicago Press, 1982.

Thomas L. Friedman. *The Lexus and the Olive Tree: Understanding Globalization.* New York: Farrar, Straus & Giroux, 1999.

Thomas L. Friedman. *Longitudes and Attitudes: Exploring the World After September 11.* New York: Farrar, Straus & Giroux, 2002.

Robert Gilpin. Especially chap. 1 in *The Political Economy of International Relations.* Princeton, NJ: Princeton University Press, 1987.

Bernard Lewis. *What Went Wrong? Western Impact and Middle East Response.* New York: Harper Collins, 2003.

Martin Staniland. *What Is Political Economy? A Study of Social Theory and Underdevelopment.* New Haven, CT: Yale University Press, 1985.

Susan Strange. *States and Markets: An Introduction to International Political Economy.* New York: Basil Blackwell, 1988.

Kenneth N. Waltz. *Man, the State, and War: A Theoretical Analysis.* New York: Columbia University Press, 1959.

## KEY TERMS

international political economy
   (IPE)
globalization
interdependence
nation-state
state
sovereignty
relational power

structural power
hard power
soft power
market
market system
mercantilism
liberalism
structuralism

levels of analysis
IPE structures
security structure
production and trade structure
finance and monetary structure
knowledge and technology
   structure

## NOTES

1. Susan Strange, ed., *Paths to International Political Economy* (London: George Allen & Unwin, 1984), p. ix.
2. Rowland Maddock, "The Global Political Economy," in John Bayless and N. J. Rengger, eds., *Dilemmas of World Politics* (New York: Oxford University Press, 1992), p. 108.
3. Susan Strange, *States and Markets: An Introduction to International Political Economy* (New York: Basil Blackwell, 1988), p. 18.
4. More and more colleges and universities are now giving undergraduate students the opportunity to study IPE, either as special courses or as an academic major. IPE has also become an important area of graduate education. A gateway to the world of IPE on the Internet can be found at www.ups.edu/ipe.
5. Thomas L. Friedman, *Longitudes and Attitudes: Exploring the World After September 11* (New York: Farrar, Straus & Giroux, 2002), p. 4.
6. Friedman, *Longitudes and Attitudes,* p. 5.
7. See Strange, *States and Markets,* pp. 24–25.
8. For a detailed discussion of soft power and its utility in the international political economy, see Joseph Nye, *Soft Power: The Means of Success in World Politics* (New York: Public Affairs, 2006).
9. See Charles Lindblom, "Market System Ascendant," in his *The Market System* (Yale Note Bene, 2002).
10. This is the definition used by Robert Gilpin in his influential book, *The Political Economy of International Relations* (Princeton, NJ: Princeton University Press, 1987), p. 8.
11. Benjamin Barber, *Jihad vs. McWorld* (New York: Ballentine Books, 1995).
12. See Lindblom, "Market System Ascendant," p. 14.
13. Robert Heilbroner, *21st Century Capitalism* (New York: W.W. Norton, 1993).
14. See Gilpin, *The Political Economy of International Relations.*
15. Kenneth N. Waltz, *Man, the State, and War: A Theoretical Analysis* (New York: Columbia University Press, 1959). Waltz wrote about three "images" rather than three "levels," and both terms are used in discussions of this concept. The recent focus on globalization has generated a good deal of attention on a global level of analysis.
16. See Strange, *States and Markets,* chaps. 3–6.
17. Ibid.

# Wealth and Power: Mercantilism and Economic Nationalism

## OVERVIEW

Mercantilism is the oldest and, from a historical viewpoint, perhaps the most important theoretical perspective in international political economy (IPE). The central focus of mercantilism is the problem of security and the role of the state and the market in providing and maintaining a nation's security in all its forms. This chapter begins by examining the three aspects of mercantilism: mercantilism as a period in world history, as a political philosophy or worldview that arose during that period, and as a set of state policies and actions that derive from that philosophy.

Mercantilism has changed over the years as the economy and the nature of the problem of national security have changed and as the tools that can be used to achieve security have also changed. This chapter traces the history of mercantilist thought from its origins, when it took the form of classical mercantilism; to its development as economic nationalism; to several of its forms as "neomercantilism" today.

As you read about mercantilism in its different stages and variations, try to keep clear in your mind the basic elements of each of its forms and why mercantilism is such an important IPE perspective.

*Anglo-American theory instructs Westerners that economics is by nature a "positive sum game" from which all can emerge as winners. Asian history instructs many Koreans, Chinese, Japanese, and others that economic competition is a form of war in which some win and others lose. To be strong is much better than to be weak; to give orders is better than to take them. By this logic, the way to be strong, to give orders, to have independence and control, is to keep in mind the difference between "us" and "them." This perspective comes naturally to Koreans (when thinking about Japan), or Canadians (when thinking about the United States), or Britons (when thinking, even today, about Germany), or to Chinese or Japanese (when thinking about what the Europeans did to their nations).[1]*

James Fallows (1994)

*Our economic rights are leaking away. . . . If we want to recover these rights. . . we must quickly employ state power to promote industry, use machinery in production, give employment to the workers of the nation. . . .[2]*

Sun Yat-sen (1920)

Mercantilism is a theoretical perspective that accounts for one of the basic compulsions of all nation-states: to create and sustain wealth and power in order to preserve and protect their national security and independence. Wherever you find a concern about foreign threats to security—whether military, economic, or cultural—you will find evidence of mercantilist thought. Typically, mercantilism is defined somewhat narrowly in terms of state efforts to promote exports and limit imports, thereby generating trade surpluses to create wealth and power.[3]

In IPE, we like to think of mercantilism in somewhat broader terms, as a theoretical perspective that puts security at the center of national concerns. A nation's security can be threatened in many ways: by foreign armies, but also by foreign firms and their products, by foreign influence over international laws and institutions, and even by foreign movies, magazines, and television shows. As noted in Chapter 1, for many people the 1990s marked a period of intensive globalization related to a number of developments that centered around changes in the nature of capitalism, the use of new technologies and communication systems, and the popularity of economic liberal ideas (see Chapter 3). Even so, during that decade and since then, a great many others have not looked with favor at intensive capitalist industrial economies and have come to view globalization as a threat to their group's or nation's social values, beliefs, and other cultural idiosyncrasies.[4] Likewise, since 9/11, new fears have arisen about individual security threats—apart from threats to states—related to international terrorism (see Chapter 9).

## MERCANTILISM AS HISTORY, PHILOSOPHY, AND STATE POLICY

The term mercantilism tends to be used in three different ways in IPE discourse. Sometimes it refers to a period of history. At other times it denotes an analytical perspective or philosophy of political economy. More recently the term has come to signify a set of state policies and actions aimed to secure and maintain a nation's security and independence, especially with respect to its economy. We will survey these three aspects of mercantilism and then move on to an examination of the ways that mercantilist thought and action have evolved and adapted over time to culminate in a persistent role for protectionist policies that states and other actors continue to pursue in today's global political economy. Contrary to the hopes of many neoliberals (see Chapter 3), globalization has not ended protectionism and actually may be helping entrench it.

The classical mercantilist period of history is inextricably linked to the rise of the modern nation-state in Europe during the fifteenth through eighteenth centuries.[5] This was a period when the idea of state building and intervention in the economy for the sake of making the nation-state secure dominated political economic thought. A **nation** is a collection of people who, on the basis of ethnic background, language, and history—or some other set of factors—define themselves as members of an extended political community.[6] As we saw in Chapter 1, the **state** is viewed as a legal entity, theoretically free from interference by other nations, which monopolizes the means of physical force of its society and exercises **sovereignty** (final political authority) over the people of a well-defined territory.[7]

From a mercantilist perspective, the new nation-states had many needs that could be secured through either violent or peaceful means. The threat of war and violence was always real, as the history of European wars in this period makes clear.[8] Territorial security was always considered the first priority of the state, because efforts to achieve prosperity, justice, or domestic peace were useless if the nation was not protected from foreign invaders or internal groups that might overthrow the state. Security was costly, however. Armies and navies were expensive to raise, equip, and maintain. Along with weapons and other instruments of power, wealth came to be regarded as one of the essential keys to achieving and preserving national security.

Because it bought weapons and financed armies, wealth was viewed as being intertwined with power and part of a *virtuous* cycle in which power generates wealth, which in turn increases power, which in turn leads to more wealth, which makes a nation more prosperous and thus more secure. At the same time, wealth and power were deemed to be part of a *vicious* cycle in which the policies adopted by a monarch or a group of officials to generate and protect their national wealth and security were often perceived to be at the expense of another state. Thus, most government officials viewed state power in terms of *absolute gains and losses;* more power could help protect the state, inadequate power could lead to disaster. The poorer the nation, the weaker and more vulnerable it might appear to be to others. Indeed, many officials felt that this vicious cycle of weakness and poverty, if left unaddressed by mercantilist action to protect the nation-state, would, and often did, lead to disastrous situations such as military defeat, economic bankruptcy, or the destruction of the society—its territory, culture, and language.

For mercantilists, then, as for their intellectual cousins the realists (discussed later), gains in economic wealth by one state, which were often perceived as losses by competing states, conferred on mercantilism a **zero-sum** (nobody wins) worldview. Dependency on other states would supposedly weaken a nation-state if imported provisions were cut off. The dependent state might also be vulnerable to the influence and power of the providing state. Therefore, in an increasingly economically competitive and politically hostile environment, states were motivated to generate wealth aggressively, especially through international trade and specifically by generating surpluses, limiting imports, and acquiring gold and silver bullion, much of it from colonies in the new world.

**Colonialism**, supplemented by state military power, was viewed as another important instrument in mercantilist efforts to control trade. Mercantilism has often been cited as one of the main driving forces behind colonialism and imperialism in developing regions of the world. Mercantilists established colonies to be exclusive markets for the goods of the mother country, a source of raw materials or goods bought from a competitive country, or a source of cheap labor. Thomas Mun, a successful trader and director of the East India Company, argued for "the overridding [sic] need for England to pursue a positive balance of trade."[9] In so doing the growing merchant class supported a strong state that would protect its interests, and in return the state sanctioned monopolistic merchant control over certain industries that profited merchants and the state via commercial trade.

**Classical mercantilism** then refers to a period of history when newly emerging nation-states faced the problem of using their economies as a means to achieve wealth and power for the sake of national security. The political philosophy of mercantilism suggested how national leaders could create a virtuous cycle of power and wealth that would allow them to prosper while making them more powerful. Mercantilist policies included the use of subsidies to generate exports and restrictions on imports, along with the development of colonial empires. These policies appeared to be very rational given the relatively insecure nature of newly established states to one another. States could look only to themselves, and mercantilist policies to help protect and sustain themselves.

## MERCANTILISM AND REALISM: COMPLEMENTARY PERSPECTIVES

Quite often the ideas of mercantilists and realists have been lumped together, because **realism** like mercantilism, accounts for many of the ways that politics, power, and the state affect the economy and markets. Realism has been the dominant *Weltanschauung* (worldview) of most world leaders and foreign policy officials since World War II.[10] In many ways these two approaches incorporate some of the same assumptions, yet in some ways they also differ. A brief sketch of realism reveals that many of the forces that drive the international political economy and that generate economic nationalism are the same conditions that compel states to seek security for themselves along with the groups within their jurisdiction.

For realists, as for mercantilists, the nation-state is the primary actor in the international system because it is regarded as the highest unit of sovereign political authority.[11] One of the tenets of realism is that the international system of nation-states is in a constant state of potential anarchy and war, given that conflicting national interests force states to compete with one another for limited amounts of resources. Relational power (i.e., the ability to get someone to do something he or she does not want to do) is the ultimate arbiter of conflict. Hard-power instruments or state capabilities derive from natural resources, geographic location, and national characteristics and traits that go into the production of wealth, military weapons, and other national capabilities. For many realists the capabilities of states and the global distribution of power determine the manner in which rival states deal with one another in a self-help international state system. Like mercantilists, realists also see state competition resulting in a zero-sum game in which relative gains for one state may be perceived as absolute losses by other states. Both realists and neomercantilists today assume that measures taken to enhance the security of one state necessarily detract from the security of others because of the relatively fixed amount of power resources in the world.

One difference between realists and modern neomercantilists is the stress that realists put on military instruments and similar state capabilities to achieve state security. When push comes to shove, realists feel strongly that military power and capabilities are more important than the economy if a state is to defend itself against the aggressive tendencies of other states or, if necessary, defeat its enemies. On the other hand, mercantilists and economic nationalist types of mercantilists stress not only that conflict is economically driven, but also that a viable economy is essential if a state is to be able to purchase the weapons necessary to secure itself.

The tension between the pursuit of wealth and the pursuit of power by the state is usually settled in favor of one or the other from time to time, or both simultaneously. Jacob Viner's often-cited dictum that "wealth and power are each proper and ultimate ends of national policy"[12] has become the credo of most economic nationalist and more recent neomercantilist-type state officials (see Chapter 12). Furthermore, in an international system in which states must ultimately rely on themselves for security, the economy remains one of several instruments the state can use to accomplish a variety of domestic and foreign policy objectives.

## ECONOMIC NATIONALISM

Mercantilist ideas have evolved over the years and adapted to changing conditions in the economic and political environment. An important example of this evolution is the development of economic nationalism as a form of mercantilism in the late eighteenth and nineteenth centuries. *Nationalism* is often defined as an identification or strong loyal sentiment toward a certain country that is shared with the people of that country. These sentiments are bound up in the history of that state; its culture, religion, and language; and its ideological outlook.

Whereas classical mercantilism focused on gaining wealth and power through unequal foreign trade, **economic nationalism** focused on the internal development of the national economy. In an important sense, economic nationalism was very much a reaction to economic liberalism, which had gained a good deal of popularity by the 1840s (see Chapter 3). As Great Britain grew more rich and powerful, other nations such as the United States and the German principalities grew concerned about their independence and adopted economic nationalist policies as a way to protect themselves from what they perceived as Britain's aggressive economic liberal politics.

Contributing to the rise of economic nationalism were improvements in production technology and transportation that gradually created economies that were truly national in scope (as opposed to local or regionally based). The political boundaries of the state and the economy began to coincide to a greater degree. To a certain extent, the line between wealth and power began to blur, too, because either one could be used to gain the other. To be an independent political power, some thought, it was necessary to be an independent economic power, too. However, markets, left to their own devices, naturally link up into domestic and international patterns of trade that were viewed by mercantilists as fearful webs of dependency. How could a nation be independent of, say, Great Britain, if it depended on it for manufactured goods and as a market for agricultural exports?

If, as mercantilists believed, unregulated markets fostered economic dependency, then it was up to the state to turn market linkages inward and develop the domestic economy as a strong and independent engine of wealth and power. The idea that the economic interests of the nation should be put ahead of the economic interests of the individual and fostered through strong state action, then, is the dominant theme of economic nationalism.

The most famous proponents of economic nationalism were the American Alexander Hamilton (1755–1804) and the German Friedrich List (1789–1846). In the United States, Hamilton[13] felt that a strong manufacturing and industrial base for the nation required an active state along with trade protection for the country's infant industries. In his *Report on the Subject of Manufactures* to the first Congress, he argued, in terms that are familiar even today, both for trade protection and for a strong role for the state in promoting domestic industries. Hamilton saw U.S. economic security threatened by the mercantilist policies of other nations and believed that strong state actions were necessary for the time being to beat back foreign economic competitors. He favored subsidies to make U.S. goods more competitive at home and abroad and to offset subsidies granted by foreign states. Hamilton reluctantly favored the use of tariffs to limit imports. He wrote that

> It is well known. . . that certain nations grant bounties [subsidies] on the exportation of particular commodities, to enable their own workmen to undersell and supplant all competitors in the countries to which those commodities are sent. Hence the undertakers of a new manufacture have to contend not only with the natural disadvantages of a new undertaking, but with the gratuities and remunerations which other governments bestow. To be enabled to contend with success, it is evident that the interference and aid of government are indispensable.[14]

The nineteenth-century German political economist Friedrich List was an even more vigorous proponent of economic nationalism. Exiled from his home—ironically, for his radical free-trade views—List came to the United States and, in a sense, saw the results of Hamilton's economic nationalist policies. Here was a nation that had built itself up and achieved independence and security, he thought. Writing in the 1840s, List came to believe that state action was indeed needed to promote productive power in the form of education, technology, and industry. According to List, "The *power of producing* is. . . infinitely more important than *wealth itself.*"[15] List also offered many reasons for believing that manufacturing, and not agriculture, was the most desirable basis for national wealth and power. His argument that manufacturing developed greater human skills and opportunities is still popular today. He wrote:

> If we regard manufacturing occupations as a whole, it must be evident at first glance that they develop and bring into action an incomparably greater variety and higher type of mental qualities and abilities than agriculture. Manufactures are at once the offspring, and at the same time the supporters and the nurses, of science and the arts.[16]

The writings of Hamilton and List incorporate a spirit of patriotic economic nationalism to the extent that they both support state policies that further the national interest by assisting in the industrialization of the economy. Their views tie together the important notions of **national interest** (states goals), a positive role for the state in the economy, and sacrifice for future gain. Many regard these ingredients as key elements in the classical formula for nation building. Indeed, more recently, Robert Reich, the ex-Secretary of Labor and Professor of Economics at MIT, has written that "the idea that the citizens of a nation shared responsibility for their economic well-being was a natural outgrowth of this budding patriotism."[17]

This kind of patriotic political economy is still found everywhere in the world today. For example, many officials in developing nations view development and nation-building as processes of "catching up" with the Western industrialized nations. To this end, quite often they look to the state to promote domestic industries and/or to protect their infant industries against the more mature industries and protectionist policies of the industrialized nations. In the 1980s and 1990s a popular academic trend was to contrast the economic success of Japan and some of the newly industrialized countries (NICs) with that of the United States and other industrialized nations. Economist Lester Thurow wrote that the Japanese secret was found in the fact that they "tapped a universal human desire to build, to belong to an empire, to conquer neighboring empires, and to become the world's economic power."[18] The ambition to protect one's industries, to get ahead of others, and to gain more and more security in an unpredictable world is one of the motives that drive mercantilism even today.

Although the goals of economic nationalism seem relatively benign—to build domestic economic power in order to gain security and independence—improvements in technology, communication, and transportation eventually changed the impact of these policies significantly. By the end of the nineteenth century a nation's ability to produce manufactured goods often far exceeded the ability of its domestic markets to absorb these items. The focus of economic nationalism turned from developing domestic **productive power** to finding foreign markets for the goods that productive power produced. The key to security changed from not only strengthening the domestic economy but also acquiring an extensive foreign economic empire capable of supplying scarce resources to the home country and purchasing the output of its industries. In short, as many structuralists point out (see Chapter 4), economic nationalism helped generate foreign imperialism.

As many different nations adopted similar policies to develop domestic industries and then to expand into foreign markets, it was inevitable that national interests would clash. It can be argued that to a certain degree the global conflicts of World War I and World War II had at their root the international competition among nations that economic nationalism promoted.[19]

## THE ENTRENCHMENT OF NEOMERCANTILISM

International organizations such as the General Agreement on Tariffs and Trade (GATT) and its successor, the World Trade Organization (WTO), along with many regional organizations such as the Asia-Pacific Economic Cooperation (APEC) and the North American Free Trade Association (NAFTA) have promoted free trade and open markets (see Chapter 6). The logic of this movement was that free trade and open markets would prevent the sort of mercantilist conflicts that had plagued the recent past and caused so much human suffering.

Despite the formal commitment to the international goals of opening up international trade and reducing trade barriers, members of these organizations and many other states remain concerned and quite protective of their own economic security and national independence. Simultaneously, they have continued to pursue ways to protect their particular industries and the whole domestic economy within an international political and economic environment that discourages classical mercantilist policies, especially tariffs and quotas. **Neomercantilism** is a more subtle form of protection that accounts for what are essentially mercantilist-defensive–oriented policies many individual nations feel compelled to adopt as a result of domestic pressure to protect certain industries from overseas competition and international economic integration. Likewise, domestic producers, if not the state itself, may initiate protectionist measures in an effort to "strike before the iron is hot" or, in other words, to dispel the fear that failure to do so will send a message of weakness or disinterest to competitors.

Contrary to the use of overt protectionist trade barriers such as import tariffs, after World War II neomercantilist policies were often craftily designed to appear to be less than protectionist in nature. Many of them such as nontariff barriers (NTBs) (see Chapter 6), reflected new and more subtle forms of political and economic advantage for national industries or private enterprises whereas other measures were employed to counter the advantages that other states gave their industries.

For an example of how economic interdependence has led to neomercantilism, look no further than your car, truck, or sport utility vehicle. In 1973 (and again in 1979 in the case of price hikes), the Organization of Petroleum Exporting Countries (OPEC) oil cartel raised the price of oil, embargoed oil shipments to the United States and the Netherlands, and reduced oil shipments to the rest of the world by 25 percent. The resulting increase in the price of oil and the transfer of massive amounts of currency to oil-rich countries was thought to have economically weakened the West and made OPEC a political economic power with which to reckon.[20] The dependence of the

West on oil imports, and on OPEC in particular, helped push the issue of *economic security* higher on the policy agenda of oil-importing nations everywhere in the world. In the United States, President Jimmy Carter went so far as to say that efforts to combat oil dependency were "the moral equivalent of war."

The result was a campaign by many of the industrialized states to decrease their dependence on oil imports in order to enhance economic security. The United States sponsored the development of a "strategic petroleum reserve" and promoted development of the North Slope oilfields in Alaska. Other national policies included tax breaks for people who adopted measures to cut home energy use, a 55-mile-per-hour automobile speed limit, and state funds for the development of alternative energy resources. Congress even imposed fuel mileage requirements on automobile manufacturers to push them to design more fuel-efficient cars.[21] In a sense, what you drive, how you drive it, and where the gas for your car or truck comes from today have all been conditioned by neomercantilist policies dating from the 1970s that were designed to reduce economic dependence on oil imports.

International economic interdependence also applies to a number of other natural resources and raw materials—often referred to as **strategic resources**—that have been in great demand in the industrialized nations such as special alloys and minerals used in aircraft production or uranium for atomic weapons. Both realist and neomercantilist explanations of IPE hold that, at some point, dependence on foreign suppliers for strategic resources is an unacceptable security risk.[22]

Realists (see Chapter 9) and neomercantilists also believe that interdependencies are not always symmetrical (felt equally) between states. The suppliers of oil and other needed resources or commodities tend to view their capacity and the resulting dependency as something positive that improves their power and security. In many cases, the relatively high cost of oil, coupled with supplier threats to cut it off to client states, makes the issue of dependence on any resource or vulnerability to a supplier of that resource synonymous with a national security threat.[23] Ideally, only complete self-sufficiency would make a nation-state politically and economically secure. In the real world, however, states are constantly trying to minimize their dependence on others while fostering conditions that make others dependent on them.

In the 1970s many states found themselves torn between their international obligation to promote and protect free trade and open markets and their natural desire to safeguard their nation's independence and economic security. In the face of this dilemma, another variety of new (neomercantilist) protectionist techniques emerged in the 1970s that were not covered by international trade agreements. Some states employed export subsidies to lower the price of goods, making them more attractive to importers. The United States still routinely subsidizes its agricultural exports—in order, it claims, to counter the subsidies the EU uses to increase its share of agriculture export markets (see Chapter 6).

Similarly, a number of methods have been developed to limit consumer spending on imports. Although the multilateral GATT negotiations after World War II successfully curtailed the use of import *tariffs* (taxes on imports) on industrial products, many nations have since resorted to the use of import *quotas* to steer consumers away from imported goods (see Chapter 6). These quotas specify the quantity of a particular product that may be sold locally. The United States still uses import quotas to limit the amount of sugar its consumers can buy from abroad, which helps its sugar producers compete with foreign sugar producers. Another way to limit imports from abroad is the Voluntary Export Agreement (VEA). This policy amounts to a negotiated quota or "gentlemen's agreement" between an exporter and an importer whereby the exporter "voluntarily" restricts sales of its products in the importing country. Exporters feel compelled to comply with the importer's request for fear the importer may impose some more costly form of protection on its exports. More sophisticated import barriers include an array of nontariff barriers. For instance, a series of complex government regulations pertaining to health and safety standards, licensing and labeling requirements, and domestic content requirements have been known to either block or distort the sales or distribution of imported goods. Many health and safety standards that restrict the import of certain food items have been designed to protect national industries (see the box "Bananas, Beef, and National Security").

## BANANAS, BEEF, AND NATIONAL SECURITY

Two examples of controversy about the intent behind trade policy are recent disputes between the United States and the European Union over bananas, and U.S. beef imports into Japan. The banana dispute began in 1993 when, in an effort to support a number of ex-British and French colonies in the Caribbean, the EU restricted imports of bananas into the EU from other areas of the world. The United States brought the issue before the World Trade Organization dispute panel in 1995 and again in 1997, and on both occasions the WTO found that the EU had illegally restrained imports of Latin American–grown bananas into Europe.[a]

Because the EU failed to comply with the WTO finding, in 1999 the Clinton administration took the step of imposing 100 percent duties on imports originating in the EU on items such as cashmere sweaters, pork, wine, cheese, fruit, and toys. The WTO eventually authorized the largest-ever trade sanction—$191 million annually on the EU (the amount the Chiquita and Dole corporations in Ecuador lost as a result of the EU's discriminatory policies). The dispute ended in 2001 when the EU agreed to implement new import trade rules that gave Ecuadorian and other banana growers a chance to sell their bananas in EU markets.[b]

In 2003 the United States experienced its first (known) case of "mad cow disease."[c] (The United States also banned beef imports from Canada when it was discovered that the diseased animal came from Canada.) Later, two other cases of the disease were discovered, leading to continuation of the ban by Japan on U.S. beef. This ban cost the United States an estimated $1.4 billion annually, as Japan had been one of the largest importers of U.S. beef.

During the ban, public officials such as Senator Chuck Hagel (R, Nebraska) insisted that "U.S. beef is the safest and highest-quality in the world."[d] In 2005 the Japanese reopened their border to U.S. beef imports, only to close it again two months later when they detected spinal cords in a shipment of East Coast veal. Asian countries consider backbones to be at risk of mad cow disease because inner organs of the animal are most likely to harbor the disease.

In June 2006 Japan decided to lift the ban on U.S. beef imports, but under the condition that it be allowed to inspect meat packing plants in the United States. A spokesman for the Texas and Southwestern Cattle Raisers Association remarked that "It's USDA's [the U.S. Department of Agriculture] job to regulate our processing industry, not Japan's."[e] Another cattlemen's group official argued that the United States was setting a precedent by allowing another country to inspect U.S. plants. The Japanese insist that the beef they import be from cows less than 20 months old, as these would be less likely to have the disease. They also reached an agreement with the United States to conduct surprise inspections of U.S. plants, accompanying U.S. inspectors. In return, Japan agreed that in the event of another case, it would target individual shipments rather than banning all beef imports. Tyson Foods, the world's largest beef processing company, accepted the terms of Japan's officials to inspect its plants, but other industry officials remained guarded about Japan's "empty promises and continued delays" in reopening the market.

To some degree these two cases (bananas and beef) blur the line between acceptable and unacceptable efforts to protect a state or a particular interest group. What they have in common is that the core issue for both the EU and Japan (as well as for many other nations) is their authority and capacity to control the types of goods they allow into their nations—an issue both countries view in terms of their sovereign right to protect their societies from possibly unhealthy foods and commodities, including genetically modified ones. These are also examples of one nation's political and business interests conflicting with the practices and interests of other states or international organizations. The loss of banana and beef sales to the EU and Japan did not make or break the balance of trade of the United States, Japan, or the EU, but because trade is closely linked to security, even relatively trivial issues like these have great symbolic importance and may set precedents. Other recent disputes have involved computers, steel, airplanes, and a variety of other goods and practices that governments feel are the basis of the state's wealth and power.

Where the cases differ is in the rationale for protection and acceptance of the motives behind the policies that banned bananas and beef. The banana dispute is not so much a health issue as it is about buyers, sellers, and WTO trade regulations. The EU and other states argue that genetically modified organisms are a danger to people's health, but as yet the scientific community has not substantiated that claim. On the other hand, both scientists and the general public accepted the evidence that mad cow disease is a serious health risk. The U.S. public, the USDA, and many U.S. beef interests accept (even if grudgingly) the Japanese claim that U.S. beef may pose a threat to their society. As in the case of bananas, however, it is harder to claim that the beef import ban was a conscious attempt to redirect trade to local producers or that the Japanese set out to damage or bring down the U.S. beef industry. Japan's insistence on inspections was more easily accepted as they opened the market once again.

*References*

[a] See "Banana Talks with Europe Turn Nasty," *The New York Times*, January 26, 1999, p. C6.

[b] See Anup Shah, "The Banana Trade War," at www.globalissues.org/TradeRelated.7.

[c] "Mad cow disease" is the common name for bovine spongiform encephalopathy (BSE), which is a slowly progressive, degenerative, fatal disease that affects the central nervous system of adult cattle. The exact cause of the disease is unknown, but it is suspected of being related to Creutzfeldt-Jacob disease, which is found in people, who acquire it by eating contaminated beef products from BSE-affected cattle. See "Commonly Asked Questions About BSE in Products Regulated by FDA's Center for Food Safety and Applied Nutrition," U.S. Food and Drug Administration, www.cfsan.fda.gov/~comm/bsefaq.html, September 14, 2005.

[d] Betsy Blaney, "Mixed Response as Japan Decides to Lift Beef Ban," *The Seattle Times*, June 22, 2006.

[e] Ibid.

Other neomercantilistic import measures are meant to overcome the dislocating effects of trade protection on society in subtle ways that were not offensive. A number of states support efforts to create comparative advantages in the production of particular goods and services in order to undercut other states. Many states routinely provide assistance to certain industries, such as relief to displaced workers, loans, regional infrastructure development programs, investment promotions, and even direct public ownership of some industries. Many governments also help selected companies market their products overseas. Most developed countries routinely employ embassy officials whose responsibility it is to monitor political and economic conditions in the country to which they are assigned and to assess their potential effects on the businesses of the home country, just as, in earlier days, they would have kept track of troop buildups and deployments.

For most modern neomercantilists, the capacity of the nation-state to generate wealth is as important as its capacity to produce military weapons. Many industrial policies that affect defense industries are viewed as neomercantilist in nature and benefit the state in at least three ways. First, they generate military weapons and defense-related technologies and products. Second, the effects of industrial production spill over into other parts of the national political economy, generating jobs and stimulating the production of consumer goods such as computers and lasers. Under pressure to make their businesses competitive internationally, many industries find it exceedingly difficult to be competitive without state assistance.

Finally, many neomercantilists today argue that, to accumulate and maintain their wealth and power, states are tempted more than ever to intervene in and influence developments not only in their domestic economies but also in the economies of other nations. In support of their own industries, many states try to restructure the international economy in their favor by one means or another. One way to do so is to influence or even control the political and economic rules of the game governed by the WTO and IMF, for instance, in such a way that efforts to open up certain international markets mask protectionist motives to support certain domestic producers. For many neomercantilists, as it was for classical mercantilists in the first part of the nineteenth century, economic liberalism is simply another tool that state officials can employ to protect their industries along with their wealth and power.

## Benign or Malevolent Mercantilism?

Robert Gilpin makes a useful distinction about many of the neomercantilist policies that states employed after World War II to assist their industries as well as increase their power and security.

According to Gilpin, **malevolent mercantilism** is a more hostile version of the economic warfare and expansionary economic policies associated with the practices of such countries as Nazi Germany and Imperial Japan. Malevolent nations employ a variety of measures intentionally to expand their territorial base and/or political and economic influence at the expense of other nations beyond what is regarded as reasonable to protect themselves. On the other hand, **benign mercantilism** is more defensive in nature, as "it attempts to protect the economy against untoward economic and political forces."[24] As demonstrated in the box "China versus Unocal," what one state regards as benign, another might regard as malevolent mercantilism, especially when the policies of the first state wreak havoc on the security and other political, social, and economic interests of the second.

---

### CHINA VERSUS UNOCAL[a]

The international oil and gas industry is a complicated web of independent firms, governments, and cartels that produce an average of over 80 million barrels of oil daily. As in any industry, firms frequently swap assets and production resources through sales, mergers, and acquisitions of subsidiary companies. The contested acquisition of Unocal Corporation by China in the summer of 2005, however, quickly became more than a routine business deal—it developed into a bilateral international trade issue between China and the United States and reveals many insights into the mercantilist motives, realist security concerns, and economic liberal rhetoric of each nation.

In April 2005, Chevron Corporation, the largest U.S.-based oil conglomerate, made a $16.5 billion takeover bid comprised of both cash and stock offerings to acquire a controlling stake in its smaller domestic rival, Unocal. While financial analysts and key players on all sides considered the offer, another multinational energy giant stepped into the game with an unsolicited counter bid. The Chinese National Offshore Oil Corporation (CNOOC), a firm in which the Chinese government holds a 70 percent stake, leveraged its strong fiscal reserves to make what was at first glance a significantly more compelling proposal: $18.5 billion for Unocal, paid entirely in cash.

For Unocal's shareholders, however, choosing the better option quickly became more complicated than a simple analysis of balance sheets. As word of the CNOOC bid spread, concern arose in the United States over the prospect of a foreign government taking control of critical resource production. The deal quickly became a national security issue. On June 27, 2005, key Republicans and Democrats on Congressional energy committees wrote a letter to President George W. Bush warning that China's "aggressive tactics to lock up energy supplies" threatened domestic interests.[b] More than forty members of Congress signed a similar letter to the Treasury Department, urging a review of the deal for security reasons, and former CIA Director James Woolsey publicly referred to the CNOOC offer as part of a "conscious long-term effort" to take control of U.S. energy resources.[c] Days later, the House of Representatives overwhelmingly (398 to 15) passed a resolution urging the president to block the deal as a threat to national security.[d]

Shortly after the Congressional resolution passed the House, the Chinese Foreign Ministry issued a harsh statement condemning the United States for erecting barriers in the face of business. The statement demanded that Congress "correct its mistaken ways of politicizing economic and trade issues and stop interfering in normal commercial exchanges between enterprises of the two countries."[e] The statement went on to essentially demand that Congress repudiate its vote on the blocking resolution.

Despite this tough rhetoric, CNOOC ended up dropping its bid. The U.S. government never took direct blocking action—the House resolution was nonbinding and never cleared the Senate—but ultimately the political barriers created by the controversy discouraged hopes for the efficacy of a CNOOC-operated Unocal. Fiscal advisors from top Wall Street firms, both those employed by the primary parties in the deal and those operating as commentators, came to a consensus that the extra $2 billion in cash wasn't worth the ongoing concern and tensions that CNOOC's bid incited.[f]

---

## Neomercantilism

The key to understanding and learning from the China/Unocal incident lies in the gap between incentives and rhetoric on each side of the debate. Both China and the United States operated under the fundamental principles of mercantilism in approaching the situation, but neither addressed these reasons directly in public discourse. The United States framed the issue under the guise of realism as a security concern, and China retaliated with classic economic liberal language about interfering in the market. Ultimately, these political factors became part of the economic equation that favored Chevron's offer.

Though Unocal was a small player in the global oil industry—producing less than 200,000 barrels daily worldwide—its most lucrative holdings were based largely in and around Asia, and it claimed to be the largest producer of geothermal energy on that continent. According to its last quarterly Securities and Exchange Commission (SEC) filing as an independent firm, only 32 percent of Unocal's revenue came from its North American operations (based largely in the Gulf of Mexico), while 57 percent of its revenue came from its Asian operations in Thailand, Indonesia, Myanmar, and Bangladesh.[g] China's incentive to control these regional energy resources is clear: for the first time in its history, the budding industrial nation has come to rely on foreign energy imports to meet its growing demand for oil. Acting through its controlling interest in CNOOC, the Chinese government was attempting to secure an oil supply line for its rapidly growing economy. This state action to advance the interests of commerce in a competitive global marketplace is a classic example of mercantilism at work.

The United States acted with equally mercantilist motivation in moving to block the deal. As the debate unfolded in the United States, many energy experts remained skeptical of the national security concerns ostensibly behind the controversy. They criticized the logic that the Unocal bid was part of a larger Chinese military supply strategy antagonistic to the United States, pointing out instead that the industrial growth inciting China's oil demand in the first place is dependent largely on the United States as a primary importer of Chinese industrial goods. Indeed, it is this trade situation that provided a much more genuine cause for U.S. concern: by the time CNOOC submitted its bid, the United States already had a $160 billion trade deficit with China.[h] Moving to correct this rapidly expanding trade imbalance and block China from acquiring a strategic commercial asset, Congressional leaders were clearly leveraging their political power in the name of national commercial interests.

This situation reveals an ongoing tension in the global political economy as commercial development and national security are increasingly wedded in the minds of policymakers, corporations, and regular citizens as well. Globalization is both helping change and encountering a changing security landscape wherein power dynamics are increasingly more complex. As nonstate actors such as terrorist groups exert control over the actions and ambitions of states and corporations, security concerns—whether founded or not—promise to play an increasing role in global commerce. Moreover, as this power landscape diversifies and nations such as China and India develop major industrial production economies, the battle for control of scarce energy resources will no doubt become more intense. The United States's actions in responding to the Unocal situation may well have set a new paradigm for international trade that is far more guarded and complicated than the economic liberal globalization of the past three decades.

*References*

[a]  Ryan Cunningham conducted the research and produced a draft for this topic. Our thanks to him.
[b]  Paul Blustein, "Many Oil Experts Unconcerned over China Unocal Bid," *The Washington Post,* July 1, 2005, p. D1.
[c]  John Tamney, "Unocal Hysteria," *The National Review,* June 30, 2005.
[d]  Peter S. Goodman, "China Tells Congress to Back Off Business," *The Washington Post,* July 5, 2005, p. A1.
[e]  Ibid.
[f]  "Why China's Unocal Bid Ran Out of Gas," *Business Week Online,* August 4, 2005. www.businessweek.com/bwdaily/dnflush/Aug 2005/nf20058084_5032_db0lb.htm?chan-search. Accessed 3/19/07.
[g]  Unocal Corporation Form 10-Q, Filed August 4, 2006, p. 29.
[h]  Goodman, "China Tells Congress to Back Off Business," p. A1.

After World War II, Japan adopted a carefully thought-out strategy of strengthening its domestic industry along the lines recommended by Alexander Hamilton and Friedrich List. Officials from the Ministry of International Trade and Industry (MITI) worked closely with corporate officials and Liberal Democratic Party (LDP) members to carefully guide the development of the economy (see Chapter 12). At first the United States willingly accepted Japanese import barriers as a cost of basing U.S. troops in Japan and using it as one of its geopolitical pillars in its campaign against communism. In a sense, Japan was able to adopt its own overt neomercantilist policies to promote its economic security, because a strong Japan complemented the military security interests of both it and the United States.

In the 1980s, however, relations between the United States and Japan changed because of the large U.S. trade deficits that resulted, in part, from Japan's aggressive export-led growth strategy, which limited imports from all countries into Japan. Much as it has been doing more recently in the case of China (see Chapters 6 and 7), the United States gradually put more pressure on Japan not only to lower its trade barriers but also to open its markets to more foreign (especially U.S.) competition. Since then the United States and Japan have repeatedly confronted one another in a series of trade disputes over a variety of items from rice and beef to semiconductors. As we saw, in the box "Bananas, Beef, and National Security" earlier in the chapter, the U.S. government continues to accuse Japan of engaging in malevolent mercantilism designed to weaken the economies of other nations, while Japan maintains that it seeks only to strengthen its own national security through benign mercantilist policies.

It is difficult to determine who is right; even the experts disagree. For example, Chalmers Johnson argued that Japan's state-dominated style of capitalism, which made use of an **industrial policy** whereby the government chose certain industries to receive state and bank subsidies to make them more competitive with U.S. and European firms, was essentially a benign effort.[25] Others, such as Clyde Prestowitz, added that Japan *also* employed a more aggressive **strategic trade policy** whereby, when it lacked a natural comparative advantage in the production of certain products, it used a combination of state assistance and industry efforts to *purposefully create* such an advantage in favor of its industries.[26] The result was a hostile reception to these policies in countries that felt it necessary to adopt protectionist measures of their own to defend themselves against Japan's policies. Not unexpectedly, neomercantilist policies tend to provoke retaliatory actions that can lead to trade tensions regardless of whether the "first shot" fired was benign or malevolent in its intent.

As discussed in Chapter 6 in particular, the problem of intentions behind trade policies, for example, tends to generate tension and conflict in multilayer trade negotiations such as those ongoing in the Doha round. This makes it difficult for developing countries to protect some of their "infant industries" or for other countries to adopt measures in consideration of efforts to support labor or improve the environment, for example, without raising suspicion that these sorts of policies mask protectionist support for inefficient industries at the expense of other nations. As we will see in Chapter 15, with emphasis on increased trade as an objective associated with the liberal development strategy in many developing nations, one reaction in some developed industrialized states has been increased support for trade protection along with other efforts to support domestic industries and society.

## GLOBALIZATION AND NEOMERCANTILISM

Neomercantilists themselves tend to be divided about globalization and its effects on both national and international security. Some neomercantilists, and realists in particular, support globalization to the extent that, as List pointed out almost 200 years ago, the openness associated with many globalization policies can work to the advantage of the nation-state by helping to generate wealth and power. As discussed in the box "Bananas, Beef, and National Security," globalization benefits some states that export and import bananas, and threatens others. On the other hand, although the EU has not been able to justify protection of some banana producers on the basis of its fear of genetically modified bananas, Japan has certainly been within its sovereign right to protect its consumers from mad cow disease.

Many of the negative effects of globalization have received a good deal of publicity (see Chapters 3 and 8). In her book, *World on Fire,* Yale Law School Professor Amy Chua goes to great lengths to document cases where many developing nations have adopted neoliberal development strategies (see Chapter 15) and opened their borders to the policies of neoliberal institutions such as the IMF and World Bank and investment by transnational corporations.[27] However, in an effort to control the profits of local enterprises, diamond or gold miners and oil producers, authoritarian regimes and officials in the Philippines, Indonesia, Sierra Leone, Cameroon, and Russia, for example, have consistently helped foster high levels of corruption, ethnic conflict, antidemocratic values and policies, and in some cases genocide. Globalization has weakened these nations, and it has not brought with it political, economic, and social stability and peace.

Thus, some neomercantilists go a step further and argue that globalization tends to *undermine* itself.[28] As more wealth and power are diffused around the world, more states and people have an investment in either protecting themselves from globalization's negative effects or sustaining its positive effects. Both situations require state power and instruments that in effect (re)invigorate states in danger of losing their power and authority.[29] Many of these cases involve the effects of globalization on a variety of national security interests. According to Moisés Naím, the lack of state regulation of the international economy makes it easy for illegitimate sectors of the economy (see Chapter 18) to thrive in the trade of drugs, arms trafficking, alien smuggling, money laudering, and pirating intellectual property.[30]

These sorts of situations have in effect helped weaken the popularity of neoliberal ideas, examined more thoroughly in the next chapter. They also have tremendous implications for the attractiveness of democratic ideas associated with capitalism in many developing nations. The growth of populist movements in Latin America[31] along with the entrenchment of authoritarian regimes in many parts of the world cannot be separated from issues of protection from globalization. As we will see in other chapters of this book, many neoliberal ideas have come under scrutiny as developing nations search for a more pragmatic and subtle mix of policies that accounts for the interests of the market but also those of society and the state.

### Globalism as Dogma

As with mercantilism itself, these ideas are not all that new. Recent criticisms of globalization reflect a much deeper critique and assessment of many of the economic liberal ideas and assumptions behind the trend. For example, more than a few IPE enthusiasts of late have discovered the work of Karl Polanyi (1892–1964). An Austrian political economic historian, his book, *The Great Transformation*, focuses on events and conditions surrounding the birth of the modern market in England and the development of economic liberal ideology from approximately 1600 until the Great Depression of the 1930s.[32] Polanyi's path-breaking work argued that the market is *not* self-regulating, but rather is a man-made construction employed by politicians in reaction to many of the changes in society connected to the Industrial Revolution. The belief that the market is self-regulating reached its peak of popularity by the mid-1850s and complemented England's stature as a political and economic hegemon in the world.

Polanyi found that until the 1800s, "gain and profit made on exchange never. . . played an important part in human economy."[33] Gradually, increasing the supply of wealth took priority over feeding and sheltering every person. As a market mentality arose, the utilitarian saying of the greatest good for the greatest number gained in popularity. By the mid-nineteenth century the idea of a self-regulated market had blossomed and was being promoted throughout the world by England, in particular, while its wealth and power helped institute and maintain a stable international economic order in the gold standard and political balance of power, which allowed Britain to dominate and influence other political and economically competitive states.

What is important about Polanyi's ideas today is that the free-market ideology has often resulted in a **countermovement** (much like the antiglobalization movement today) whereby many working-class groups have attacked economic liberal ideology for its severe negative effects on society. Because self-regulation did not protect workers from unfair management practices, social legislation helped soften the effects of the market. More important, at the same time, grave doubts were raised by *economic liberals themselves,* who sought protection and gained it in the form of trade protection and other policies designed to check the market and *prevent* the utopian idea of a self-regulating market. We will discuss this development in more detail in Chapter 21.

## CONCLUSION

Of the three ideological perspectives most often used to explain IPE, that is, mercantilism, liberalism, and structuralism, mercantilism is the oldest and arguably the most powerful. If Friedrich List were still around, he would likely argue that as long as states are the final source of political (sovereign) authority (and we believe they are), the economy and markets cannot be divorced from their connection to the effects that politics and the state, along with society, have on them. Realists would also note that by their very nature states *can* be expected to use the economy, either legally or illegally (see Chapter 18), as a means to generate more wealth and power.

As trade increased between nations, so did the opportunity for economic and political rivalry, contributing to the popular notion that mercantilism and today's neomercantilist policies are still responsible for a good deal of international conflict and hostility. Until World War II, mercantilism was often cited as a driving force behind colonialism and imperialism in developing regions of the world.

List would also likely argue that free trade is a myth. As long as states exist, they can be expected to give first priority to their own national security and independence, including economic security and independence. All nations have employed mercantilist policies and measures, as Great Britain did in the nineteenth century during the height of the popularity of economic liberal ideas about free trade. Likewise, the United States did throughout the twentieth century, even when it assertively advocated free trade. Today it continues to use a variety of protectionist measures to assist some of its industries and many agricultural products. The rise of neomercantilism is proof that states favor free trade when it benefits them and protection when it does not.

Responsibilities and objectives related to increasing and maintaining state wealth and power have proliferated since World War II as a result of the growing interdependence of nations and globalization of the international political economy. Managing the international economy remains a complicated task that befuddles politicians and academics alike. To a great extent the *success* of globalization has also helped undermine the openness of the international political economy when it comes to state economic interests as well. As states and national industries have become more dependent on external sources of revenue and markets, public officials have also felt more *vulnerable* to developments in the international political economy, leading to arguments that market forces have weakened state power and authority significantly. Yet protectionist trade, finance, and monetary policies have periodically proliferated as governments have attempted to reassert themselves and better macro- and micromanage their economies, along with the international economy as well. For mercantilists and realists, despite the popularity of economic liberal ideas discussed and developed in the next chapter, the world is not ready for the market to rule all.

## *DISCUSSION QUESTIONS*

1. Each of the IPE perspectives has at its center a fundamental value or idea. What is the central idea of mercantilism? Explain how that central idea is illustrated by the mercantilist period of history, mercantilist philosophy, and mercantilist policies.
2. Mercantilism has evolved and adapted to changing international political economic environments. Briefly explain how and why the following forms of mercantilism differ: classical mercantilism, neomercantilism, defensive mercantilism.
3. What is the difference between benign mercantilism and malevolent mercantilism in theory? How could you tell the difference between them in practice? Find a newspaper article that demonstrates the tensions between these ideas, and explain how the issue is dealt with by the actors in the article.
4. How much is economic globalization a threat to nation-states? Make a brief list of the positive and negative potential effects of a more integrated global economic system, and explain the basis for your opinion.

## INTERNET LINKS

Japan's Ministry of International Trade and Industry:
    www.miti.go.jp/index-e.html
Office of the U.S. Trade Representative:
    www.ustr.gov
The Banana Trade Wars:
    www.globalissues.org

## SUGGESTED READINGS

James Fallows. *More Like Us: Putting America's Native Strengths and Traditional Values to Work to Overcome the Asian Challenge*. Boston: Houghton Mifflin, 1990.

James Fallows. *Looking at the Sun*. New York: Pantheon, 1994.

Alexander Hamilton. "Report on Manufactures," in George T. Crane and Abla Amawi, *The Theoretical Evolution of International Political Economy: A Reader*. New York: Oxford University Press, 1991, pp. 37–47.

Eli F. Heckscher. *Mercantilism*. Rev. ed., 2 vols. New York: Macmillan, 1955.

Robert Kuttner. *The End of Laissez-Faire*. New York: Knopf, 1991.

Friedrich List. *The National System of Political Economy*. New York: Augustus M. Kelley, 1966.

Robert B. Reich. *The Work of Nations*. New York: Knopf, 1991.

Lester Thurow. *Head to Head: The Coming Economic Battle Among Japan, Europe, and America*. New York: William Morrow, 1991.

Jacob Viner. "Power Versus Plenty as Objectives of Foreign Policy in the Seventeenth and Eighteenth Centuries," *World Politics* 1 (October 1948), pp. 1–29.

## KEY TERMS

| | | |
|---|---|---|
| mercantilism | classical mercantilism | strategic resources |
| nation | realism | malevolent mercantilism |
| state | economic nationalism | benign mercantilism |
| sovereignty | national interest | industrial policy |
| zero-sum | productive power | strategic trade policy |
| colonialism | neomercantilism | countermovement |

## NOTES

1. James Fallows, *Looking at the Sun* (New York: Pantheon, 1994), p. 231.
2. Sun Yat-sen (1920), cited in Robert Reich, *The Work of Nations* (New York: Knopf, 1991), p. 30.
3. See, for example, the "Mercantilism" entry in Randy Epping, *A Beginner's Guide to the World Economy* (New York: Vintage Books, 1992), p. 139.
4. There is a plethora of literature on this subject. See, for example, Alexander Cockburn, Jeffrey St. Clair, and Allan Sekula, *5 Days That Shook the World* (London: Verso, 2001), Kevin Danaher and Reger Burbach, eds., *Globalize This!* (Monroe, ME: Common Courage Press, 2000), and Robert Wade, "Globalization and Its Limits: Reports of the Death of the National Economy Are Greatly Exaggerated," in Suzanne Berger and Ronald Dore, eds., *National Diversity and Global Capitalism* (Ithaca, NY: Cornell University Press, 1996), pp. 60–88.
5. The rise of the nation-state was very uneven. France was already a "nation-state" in the fifteenth century, whereas Germany and Italy were not consolidated into the national entities that we know today until the second half of the nineteenth century.
6. The concepts of *nation* and *nationalism* are the focus of the classic work by Hans Kohn, *The Idea of Nationalism* (New York: Macmillan, 1944) and of E. J. Hobsbawm's *Nations and Nationalism Since 1780,* 2nd ed. (Cambridge: Cambridge University Press, 1992).
7. The classic definition of the state is Max Weber's, which emphasizes its administrative and legal qualities. See Max Weber, *The Theory of Social and Economic Organization* (New York: The Free Press, 1947), p. 156.

8. See Charles Tilly, "War Making and State Making as Organized Crime," in Peter Evans, Dietrich Reuschemeyer, and Theda Skeeocpol, eds., *Bringing the State Back In* (Cambridge: Cambridge University Press, 1985), pp. 161–191.

9. Robert Heilbroner, *Teachings from the Worldly Philosophy* (New York: W. W. Norton, 1996), p. 25.

10. There are a variety of subdivisions within realist thought. Two of the classic works in the field are Hans Morgenthau, *Politics Among Nations: The Struggle for Power and Peace* (New York: Knopf, any edition), and Kenneth Waltz, *Theory of International Politics* (Reading, MA: Addison-Wesley, 1979).

11. See Waltz, *Theory of International Politics*.

12. Jacob Viner, "Power Versus Plenty as Objectives of Foreign Policy in the Seventeenth and Eighteenth Centuries," *World Politics* 1 (October 1948), p. 2.

13. For a detailed account of Hamilton's works, see Henry Cabot Lodge, ed., *The Works of Alexander Hamilton* (Honolulu: University Press of the Pacific, 2005).

14. Alexander Hamilton, "Report on Manufactures," in George T. Crane and Abla Amawi, *The Theoretical Evolution of International Political Economy: A Reader* (New York: Oxford University Press, 1991), p. 42.

15. Friedrich List, *The National System of Political Economy* (New York: Augustus M. Kelley, 1966), p. 144. Italics are ours.

16. Ibid., pp. 199–200.

17. Reich, *The Work of Nations*, p. 18.

18. Lester Thurow, *Head to Head: The Coming Economic Battle Among Japan, Europe, and America* (New York: William Morrow, 1991), p. 118.

19. See the discussion of John Maynard Keynes in Chapter 3 and V. I. Lenin's views in Chapter 4.

20. Kenneth Waltz argues that interdependence was actually greater after World War I than in the 1970s. See Waltz, *Theory of International Politics*, pp. 141–143. By other measures, however, economic interdependence reached a peak in the late twentieth century that has not yet been surpassed.

21. Ironically, this instead gave auto firms an incentive to design and market new trucks, minivans, and sport utility vehicles, which, because they are all classified as "trucks," were not covered by the fuel mileage requirement (nor by many auto safety rules). Until recently, when gas prices rose dramatically again, the best-selling vehicles in the United States were trucks and minivans—perhaps an unintended consequence of the OPEC-driven neomercantilism of the 1970s.

22. See, for example, Michael T. Klare, *Resource Wars: The New Landscape of Global Conflict* (New York: Henry Holt, 2002).

23. For a more detailed discussion of dependence and interdependence, see Robert Keohane and Joseph S. Nye, Jr., *Power and Interdependence* (Boston: Little, Brown, 1977).

24. Robert Gilpin, *The Political Economy of International Relations*, (Princeton, NJ: Princeton University Press, 1987), p. 33.

25. See, for example, Chalmers Johnson, "Introduction: The Idea of Industrial Policy," in his *The Industrial Policy Debate* (San Francisco: ICS Press, 1984), pp. 3–26.

26. See, for example, Clyde Prestowitz, *Trading Places: How We Allowed Japan to Take the Lead* (New York: Basic Books, 1988).

27. See Amy Chua, *World on Fire: How Exporting Free Market Democracy Breeds Ethnic Hatred and Global Instability* (New York: Doubleday, 2002).

28. See, for example, Tina Rosenberg, "Globalization: The Free Trade Fix," *The New York Times Magazine*, August 18, 2002.

29. See, for example, Linda Weiss, *The Myth of the Powerless State* (Ithaca, NY: Cornell University Press, 1998), and Robert Wade, "Globalization and Its Limits."

30. For a more detailed discussion of these threats, see Moisés Naím, "The Five Wars of Globalization," *Foreign Policy*, January/February 2003, pp. 30–36.

31. See, for example, Michael Shifter and Vinay Jawahar, "Latin America's Populist Turn," *Current History*, February 2005.

32. Karl Polanyi, *The Great Transformation: The Political and Economic Origins of Our Time* (Boston: Beacon, 1944).

33. Ibid., p. 45.

*3*

# "Laissez-Faire, Laissez-Passer": The Liberal IPE Perspective

## OVERVIEW

Liberalism, like many other terms in international political economy (IPE), suffers from something of a personality disorder. The term means different things in different contexts. In the United States today, for example, a *liberal* is generally regarded as one who believes in an *active* role for the state in society, such as helping the poor and funding programs to address social problems. Since the 1980s, what has become thought of more narrowly as *economic liberalism* means *almost* (but not exactly) the opposite. For economic liberals (also referred to as *neoliberals* and sometimes as *neoconservatives*[1]), the state should play a *limited*, if not constricted, role in the economy and society. In other words, today's economic liberals have much in common with people who are usually referred to as "conservatives" in the United States and many other countries.

This chapter outlines what has become the most popular of the three IPE perspectives. Liberalism, particularly economic liberalism, emphasizes individual economic freedom and growth, along with individual rights and unregulated, relatively free markets, to achieve those objectives. We trace the rise of and some important developments associated with economic liberalism from its historical roots in eighteenth-century France, through nineteenth-century England, to the United States and Europe in the twentieth century. Today these ideas serve as an ideological rationale (that is sometimes referred to as **globalism**) which supports liberal economic policies, global integration, and globalization. We also outline some of the basic features of the market and capitalism, two of the primary focal points of liberal thought. Throughout the chapter we discuss the various views about the relationship of the market to the state and to society of some of the most famous liberal political economists: Adam Smith, David Ricardo, John Maynard Keynes, Friedrich Hayek, Milton Friedman, and a variety of more recent supporters of globalization. We also introduce the important notion of hegemony—when a rich and powerful nation organizes the international political economy, as Great Britain did during the nineteenth century and the United States did during part of the twentieth century. At the end of the chapter, an appendix lays out the characteristics of a market model and develops the notion of efficiency, and then contrasts efficiency with equity.[2] Students are encouraged to review the model in some detail to understand the basic assumptions many economists make about the role of the market in a liberal society.

## ROOTS OF THE ECONOMIC LIBERAL PERSPECTIVE

The liberal perspective today reveals many insights about political economy that mercantilists miss or do not address. Essentially, the broad term **liberalism** means "liberty under the law."[3] Liberalism focuses on the side of human nature that is competitive in a constructive way and is guided by reason, not emotion. Although liberals believe that people are fundamentally self-interested, they do not see this as a disadvantage because broad areas of society are set up in such a way that competing interests can engage one another constructively. This contrasts with the mercantilist view, which, as we saw in Chapter 2, dwells on the side of human nature that is more aggressive, combative, and suspicious.

Today's economic liberalism is rooted in reactions to important trends and events in Europe in the seventeenth and eighteenth centuries. François Quesnay (1694–1774) led a group of French philosophers called the Physiocrats or *les Économistes*. Quesnay condemned government interference in the market, holding that, with few exceptions, it brought harm to society. The Physiocrats' motto was *laissez-faire, laissez-passer,* meaning "let be, let pass," but said in the spirit of telling the state "Hands off! Leave us alone!" This became the theme of Adam Smith (1723–1790), a Scottish contemporary of Quesnay, who is generally regarded as the father of modern economics. Admonishing politicians, Smith said:

> The Statesman, who should attempt to direct private people in what manner they ought to employ their capitals, would not only load himself with a most unnecessary attention, but assume an authority which could safely be trusted, not only to no single person, but to no council or senate whatever, and which would nowhere be so dangerous as in the hands of a man who had folly and presumption enough to fancy himself fit to exercise it.[4]

These views are reflected in the thoughts of many today, including Václav Havel, the former president of Czechoslovakia:

> Though my heart may be left of centre, I have always known that the only economic system that works is a market economy, in which everything belongs to someone—which means that someone is responsible for everything. It is a system in which complete independence and plurality of economic entities exist within a legal framework, and its workings are guided chiefly by the laws of the marketplace. . . . The attempt to unite all economic entities under the authority of a single monstrous owner, the state, and to subject all economic life to one central voice of reason that deems itself more clever than life itself, is an attempt against life itself.[5]

Both Smith and Havel display respect, admiration, almost affection for the market, juxtaposed with distaste for the state, or at least for the abusive potential of the state. Smith's state is dangerous and untrustworthy.[6] Havel's can be arrogant and "monstrous." Likewise they share affection for the laissez-faire world of individual initiative, private ownership, and limited government interference. Their fears and loathing, however, are directed toward very different sorts of states.

The state against which Adam Smith argued in 1776 was the mercantilist state of the eighteenth century, an institution established on the principle that the national interest is best served when state power is concentrated and used to create wealth, which produces more power. For Smith, the individual freedom of the marketplace represented the best alternative to potentially abusive state power when it came to the allocation of resources or organizing economic activity. Recently, Václav Havel lived under an authoritarian communist regime in Czechoslovakia before 1989 that suppressed the market and, for the most part, replaced most market activities with rigid and centralized state planning. The state owned the shops and factories and natural resources and ordered their use in ways that fit the planners' notion of the national interest. This centralized state market system proved to be terribly inefficient in its ability to create wealth. In embracing the marketplace, then, Havel sought to gain both individual freedom from state power and prosperity through the market's flexibility and dynamism.

Today's news is filled with stories of the transition from rigid communist states to flexible free markets. Mexico, India, and Russia have all adopted pro-market "reforms." Some communist states in Central and Eastern Europe are now members of the European Union's (EU) single market. And China has made headlines for using the market to infuse its political economy with the spirit of individual initiative. Taken together, over half of all the human beings on earth have come to terms with the economic liberal ideas of Quesnay, Adam Smith, Havel, and many others of their stripe.

## Smith, Capitalism, Self-Interest, the Invisible Hand, and Competition

Economic liberals, then, come down heavily on the side of the market when choosing sides among the state, market, and society, a fundamental tension that characterizes IPE in general. A free market is just one element of the liberal view, in which individuals are considered best equipped to make social choices. As a liberal, Smith believed in the cooperative, constructive side of human nature. For him, the best interest of all of society is served by (rational) individual choices, which when observed from afar appear as an "invisible hand" that guides the economy and promotes the common good. He wrote:

> He [the typical citizen] generally, indeed, neither intends to promote the public interest, nor knows how much he is promoting it. By preferring the support of domestic to that of foreign industry, he intends only his own security; and by directing that industry in such a manner as its own produce may be of the greatest value, he intends only his own gain, and he is in this, as in many other cases, directed by an invisible hand to promote an end which was no part of his intention.[7]

The oft-quoted but only one-time passing reference to the "invisible hand" in Smith's work has two tightly intertwined parts: self-interest and competition. Smith was writing at a time when the production system known as capitalism was replacing feudalism. For a description of capitalism, see the box "The Tenets of Capitalism." In a capitalist economy, self-interest drives individuals to make rational choices that best serve their own needs and desires. However, competition constrains self-interest and prevents it from becoming destructive to the interests of others. Producers face competition that forces them to charge reasonable prices and provide quality goods. Consumers face competition, too, from other consumers. Even if producers might want to push prices very high to satisfy their narrow economic interests, and buyers might want to push prices very low for the same reason, the force of competition keeps the pursuit of self-interest from going to the extreme.

---

### THE TENETS OF CAPITALISM

Humans have been making and exchanging things throughout history. Capitalism, however, has been around only since the eighteenth century. Before that time, the Egyptian and Roman empires bought and sold spices, gold, slaves, cloth, pottery, and foodstuffs produced locally or by slaves in parts of Asia and Africa. No "web of transactions" bound the production of goods with their distribution. During the Middle Ages the means of production was related mainly to the land, which was controlled by the rich and powerful. Peasants were not free, and the idea of economic freedom meant little. Lords decided production and distribution schedules; only leftovers were sold in small local markets, and moneymaking was not held in high regard—it was even considered a sin in some cultures. Moneymaking was also beneath people of nobility. With the exception of wars now and then, life was rather stable, as "the basic rhythms and techniques of economic existence were steady and repetitive."[a]

Since, then, many countries have experienced an economic, political, and social transformation from an agricultural-based economy to one characterized as industrial or service-based. Capitalism today connotes large manufacturing plants with long production lines. Much of the work is done by people who labor on assembly lines, or who may be controlling machines that can do the job of ten or more people, spitting out more varieties of a product, and at reduced cost to both the producer and consumer. Capitalism is clearly also associated with market forces that both reflect and influence consumers' demand for certain items along with how much of these items are produced (supplied). Capitalism spread far and wide over large parts of the world. Countries on every continent have introduced capitalist market-oriented reforms in pursuit of a better life for their citizens. And the free-trade paradigm at the heart of globalization is an integral component of this system of production and distribution.

So what are the fundamental tenets of capitalism? Capitalism means different things to different people. Structuralists, particularly Marxists, consider capitalism a dynamic and powerful economic system capable of creating unprecedented economic growth. Capitalism played a critical role in the evolutionary process from feudalism to communism. It also has a very dark underbelly, as exploitation and class conflict are inherent in the system. Capitalism contains the seeds of its own eventual destruction. Economic liberals also consider capitalism part of an evolutionary process, but from their perspective capitalism is the natural end result of that process. The competitive process and economic freedom inherent in capitalism, paradoxically, turn the most powerful human motive, the pursuit of self-interest, to the service of society's welfare.

According to leading economic historian Jerry Muller, capitalism can be defined as "a system in which the production and distribution of goods is entrusted primarily to the market mechanism, based on private ownership of property, and on exchange between legally free individuals."[b] Adam Smith was the first to develop a comprehensive portrait of capitalism. He, better than anyone before or after, captured the essence of capitalism in his famous book, *The Wealth of Nations*, originally published in 1776.[c] What follows is a rendition of the tenets of capitalism based in large part on Smith's work.

*Self-interest* motivates economic activity. One might at first conclude that life in a society in which the primary economic motivation is the pursuit of individual self-interest would be "nasty, brutish, and short." Not so, according to Smith. Rather, as if led by an "invisible hand," individuals in pursuit of their own self-interest serve society's interests. Smith famously said, "It is not from the benevolence of the butcher, the brewer, or the baker, that we expect our dinner, but from their regard to their own interest. We address ourselves, not to their humanity but to their self-love, and never talk to them of our necessities but of their advantages."[d]

In a market economy, income is based in large measure on the contribution one makes to national output. By maximizing your contribution to output, you provide more and better goods and services to others and in turn maximize your own income. The refuse collector who rattles down the alley like clockwork once a week is hardly motivated by my needs but rather by the relatively high incomes and benefits that many refuse collectors enjoy. The small business owner who succeeds and becomes wealthy obviously produces goods and/or services that consumers value. The article of faith represented here, that the pursuit of self-interest leads to enhanced social welfare, in turn relies on the regulatory force that competition provides. That is, the simultaneous competitive pursuit of self-interest leads to behaviors that benefit all of society. The pursuit of self-interest by a monopoly producer, however, leads to restricted output, the underallocation of resources to the monopolized good, and a consequent loss of social welfare. Absent competition, the "invisible hand" loses its grip.

*Private property* creates strong incentives to use resources efficiently. When resources are privately owned, they tend to be used efficiently. Private property creates a direct link between effort and reward. The owner of a resource is legally entitled to the income that flows from the resource. Consequently, the resource owner makes every effort to ensure that the resource is used efficiently. A privately owned tractor will be well-maintained and will be operated in an optimal manner. The farmer's hard work and ingenuity will be rewarded with more income. When property rights are less clear, the incentive to use resources efficiently is dulled, and waste and lethargy often become common. Private property—clear title to land, for example—also encourages the owner to make investments in improving the land and provides the owner the collateral with which to obtain the credit necessary to do so.

One of the first reforms that countries implementing capitalist policies undertake is to privatize firms operated by the state. *Privatization* has many desirable outcomes, the most significant of which is to introduce strong incentives to use (now privately owned) resources efficiently. It is in the self-interest of resource owners to maximize the productivity of those resources. When individuals pursue their self-interest, they ensure that resources are not wasted and are used in their most highly valued uses. An additional benefit (when privatization is handled correctly) is the creation of competitive markets in place of monopolized state-controlled markets, which results in less need for state subsidization of inefficient state-run firms.

*Competition* is the *sine qua non* of capitalism. Competition regulates economic activity. Competition disciplines the pursuit of self-interest. Competition for well-paying jobs requires individuals to acquire the necessary training, education, and skills, to accept a wage that reflects their productivity, and to perform at consistently high levels to hold those jobs. Suppliers of goods and services must compete for their customers. They must satisfy customers at least as well as other firms that offer similar goods and services. Competition prohibits an individual firm from raising prices above costs and from providing poor-quality service. Price competition results in the efficient allocation of resources among competing uses. Competition also requires firms to be production efficient, in the sense that it pays to adopt cost-saving innovations in the production of goods, the delivery of services, and the management of resources.

Competition among firms (both existing firms and potential competitors) also requires firms to remain on the cutting edge of product and process innovation. The leaders of even the most powerful firms must keep one step ahead of technologically audacious newcomers. *Only the Paranoid Survive*, the title of a best-selling book by Andy Groves, the chairman of Intel, reflects the intensity (and possibly the consequences) of this competitive pressure.[e] Competitive markets free from government intervention and from private manipulation successfully coordinate the interests of buyers and sellers in such a way that resources are allocated and reallocated efficiently. However, Smith was concerned that firms could conspire to reduce competitive pressure by agreeing to hold prices artificially high or to refrain from research and development. As he noted, "People of the same trade seldom meet together, even for merriment and diversion, but the conversation ends in a conspiracy against the public, . . ."[f]

Firms can also erect strategic barriers to entry (think of bundling an Internet browser with an operating system) in an effort to protect themselves from competitive pressures. And they often solicit the power of the state in an effort to contravene competitive pressures through the use of licenses, exclusive franchises, tariffs, and quotas, for example (see Chapter 2). These realities require capitalist economies to create and enforce competition policies and to exercise vigilance against rent-seeking by powerful business interests. (**Rent-seeking** is the manipulation of the state to create artificial shortages that reward the favored group with high prices and high profits.) Competition in the economic sphere reduces the power of any one supplier. Competition in the political sphere reduces the power of any one party.

*Markets* coordinate society's economic activity. In a capitalist economy, no one is in charge of how resources are allocated. Rather, market coordination entails a decentralized resource allocation process guided by the tastes and preferences of individual consumers. If, for example, gasoline prices rise and consumers' tastes and preferences turn in favor of smaller, more fuel-efficient cars, the demand for small cars will rise. Consequently, the price of small cars will rise and car makers will hire scarce resources away from competing uses to expand production of small cars. And, in the long run, more companies will enter the profitable small car industry, bringing resources with them, expanding supply, and causing prices to decline. More of society's scarce resources will be engaged in the production of small cars, but no central authority will have been responsible for this reallocation of resources.

Government intervention in the market generally distorts resource reallocation and frustrates the coordination function we have described. Had a price ceiling been imposed on small cars, there would have been no incentive for existing producers of small cars to step up production. Had a "windfall" profits tax been imposed on producers of small cars, there would have been no incentive for entry into this market. The quick response of producers to market signals and incentives reflects the economic freedom that producers enjoy in a capitalist economy.

*Economic freedom* consists of freedom of job choice and freedom of enterprise. When individuals are free to make their own career choices, they naturally prepare for and seek out careers or lines of employment in which they are likely to be most productive. (Recall the link between productivity and income.) And, as economic circumstances change, labor resources will be rapidly redeployed to growing sectors of the economy as individuals take advantage of new opportunities. Freedom of enterprise means that individuals are free to start up any new business enterprise without state permission. Freedom of enterprise permits individuals to enter profitable industries, thereby channeling resources to the production of goods and services that are in high demand while simultaneously intensifying competitive pressures in these industries.

Freedom of enterprise allows entrepreneurs to test new ideas in the marketplace and thereby fosters entrepreneurial activity. The economic world is in a constant state of flux. As tastes and preferences change, the availability of resources changes, and new technologies foment product and production process innovation. In such a dynamic environment, resources will be redeployed rapidly in response to changing circumstances when entrepreneurs are free to respond to new opportunities. Freedom of enterprise also entails the ability of firms to increase or reduce their labor force as necessary. Because firms can easily exit or contract, the risk associated with entry or expansion is thereby minimized and competition is consequently enhanced. Freedom of enterprise is, in turn, constrained by consumer sovereignty. Though entrepreneurs are free to develop new products and services, they must do so in a way that accords with the tastes and preferences of consumers.

*Consumer sovereignty* is Smith's idea that in a capitalist economy the consumer is king—the consumer dictates how resources will be allocated and reallocated through time. In his best-selling book, *The New Industrial State,* John Kenneth Gailbraith challenged the idea that the consumer remains sovereign in today's highly technological and large-scale industrialized capitalist economy.[8] Galbraith argued that in today's world the technological complexity of products and production processes requires large-scale firms with the ability to marshal the necessary resources and the power to control the markets for their new products. The risks of introducing new products, given the huge investments and time lags involved, could be mitigated if firms were able to guarantee consumer acceptance. Therefore successful firms invested in shaping and molding consumer tastes and preference via expensive, sophisticated, and sometimes subtle marketing campaigns. Consumers often became putty in the hands of Madison Avenue advertising executives. Consumers were carefully prepared for new products, which passed control of resource allocation into the hands of large corporations.

Shortly after the publication of Galbraith's book, however, one of the most powerful corporations in the world, Chrysler Corporation, came perilously close to bankruptcy when it continued to design, market, and produce gas-guzzling cars in the wake of the oil crisis of the mid-1970s. Consumers ignored Chrysler's marketing campaigns that promoted the power and comfort of their large vehicles, and instead, stuffed themselves into tiny Volkswagens, Honda Civics, and Fiats that delivered many more miles per gallon.

Even in the technologically complex, industrialized twenty-first-century version of capitalism, consumers appear just as powerful as in the simpler, more agrarian version of capitalism in Smith's day. According to Smith, then, in a capitalist economy, consumers determine how resources will be allocated; self-interest motivates entrepreneurs to develop, and firms and their workers to produce the goods and services consumers desire; the market coordinates economic activity by communicating the ever-changing tastes and preferences of consumers to producers; and competition ensures that the pursuit of self-interest serves social (consumer) interests. According to Smith, a capitalist economy is self-motivating, self-coordinating, and self-regulating. What useful role could the state play in such an economy? Again, according to Smith, the state plays a critical role, notwithstanding the dictum universally associated with Smith: laissez-faire.

*Laissez-faire* translates loosely from the French as "leave alone," reflecting a doctrine that suggests a capitalist economic system functions best when there is no intervention by the state. Smith believed that intervention by the state (in the form of tariffs, quotas, price controls, exclusive franchises, subsidies, etc.) was almost always motivated by and served the interests of some special-interest, rent-seeking group. The public at large was ill-served by state intervention. Tariffs, quotas, price controls, and exclusive franchises raise prices. Subsidies raise taxes. Smith also advocated a policy of laissez-faire because he understood that state intervention would undermine the self-motivating, self-coordinating, and self-regulating nature of the economy. However, he also believed that the state played a fundamental role in the success of a capitalist economy.

The state is responsible for creating the legal rules of the game and for ensuring national security. The rules of the capitalist game include property law and contract law. The state must define and enforce property rights. It must also define the terms on which property can be exchanged and enforce those contractual obligations. As noted earlier, the state must also guard against the use of private power to deter competition. Today, most economists also support the use of state power to mitigate market failures (the misallocation of resources) associated with externalities, public goods, and information problems. As will be discussed later in the chapter, most economists also support a broad role for the state in using fiscal and monetary policy to try to avert extended periods of unemployment or inflation or both.

Capitalism does not evolve without the state exercising some power. Absent property law, contract law, competition policy, and national security, the undeniable instinct to trade and barter will not of itself ignite the dynamism, risk taking, creativity, saving, investment, and wealth creation associated with capitalism.

However, if the state oversteps its bounds, using its power to alter market-determined outcomes, the rent-seeking associated with such intervention can paralyze the market process—killing (or at the very least making quite sick) the goose that lays the golden eggs.

*References*

[a] For a more detailed discussion of the history of capitalism, see Robert Heilbroner and Lester Thurow, "Capitalism: Where Do We Come From?" in their *Economics Explained: Everything You Need to Know About How the Economy Works and Where It's Going* (New York: Simon & Schuster, 1994), pp. 11–25.

[b] Jerry Muller, *The Mind and The Market: Capitalism in Western Thought* (New York: Anchor Books, 2002), p. XVI.

[c] Adam Smith, *The Wealth of Nations* (New York: The Modern Library, 1937).

[d] Ibid., p. 14.

[e] Andrew S. Grove, *Only the Paranoid Survive* (New York: Currency Doubleday, 1996).

[f] Smith, *The Wealth of Nations*, p. 128.

[g] John K. Galbraith, *The New Industrial State* (Boston: Houghton Mifflin, 1967).

Smith's works struck the right note at the right time and so gained a measure of respect and influence that is rare. The title of his book, *The Wealth of Nations*, makes it appear that liberalism is concerned only with economics and wealth, when in fact it is perhaps more profoundly a view of politics, power, and freedom. Even if many people associate Adam Smith with the liberal doctrine of laissez-faire, for him, the state had a number of *limited* tasks to perform in society that individuals cannot perform by themselves, such as establishing and maintaining a basic legal system and assuring national defense. Basically, the state's job is to help create an institutional environment that fosters individual action. Smith would likely agree with Havel as quoted earlier, when he says that the marketplace needs a legal framework around it. Smith expressed concern that "people of the same trade seldom meet together, even for merriment and diversion, but the conversation ends in a conspiracy against the public, or in some contrivance to raise prices."[8] For Smith, then, the state appears to have some necessary functions in society, especially with regard to keeping the market functioning and helping it to achieve individual rights. However, he is not clear about who would deal with potential abuse of their power, even by capitalists.

Adam Smith's economic writings were part of a broader intellectual movement that engendered not only economic but intensely political change in society. Liberals in general at the time are represented by the writings of John Locke (1632–1704) in England and Thomas Jefferson (1743–1826) in the United States. Economic theorists may think of laissez-faire in terms of markets. However, this philosophy also implies that citizens need to possess certain negative rights (freedoms *from* state authority, such as freedom from unlawful arrest), positive rights (which include unalienable rights and freedoms *to* take certain actions, such as freedom of speech or freedom of the press), and the right of democratic participation in government without which positive and negative freedom cannot be guaranteed.[9] If these liberal political ideas sound familiar, they should, as they are embedded firmly in the U.S. Declaration of Independence and the Bill of Rights, which were becoming well known at the same time as Adam Smith's notion of consumer freedom was becoming popular.

Mercantilists, on the other hand, tend to be ruled by the passion to pursue self-interest, even at the expense of foreigners (see Chapter 2). Competition among mercantilists also tends to be a cutthroat contest of passions, in which winners create losers. Liberals pursue their self-interest, but their passions are restrained by competition that prevents anyone from gaining too much power that could lead to coercion. Liberals, then, are ruled by their interests, not their passions, and their interests are often very enlightened. Serving one's own interests in a competitive society means competing to best serve the interests of others, to behave honestly, and to gain a reputation for fairness. In a world of intense competition, an honorable reputation is a powerful advantage.

## THE LIBERAL VIEW OF INTERNATIONAL RELATIONS

Economic liberals tend to focus on the domain in which nation-states show their cooperative, peaceful, constructive natures through harmonious competition. As we will see in Chapter 6, international trade is seen as being mutually advantageous, not cutthroat competition for wealth and power. What is true about individuals is also true about states. As Smith wrote, "What is prudence in the conduct of every family, can scarce be folly in that of a great kingdom. If a foreign country can supply us with a commodity cheaper than we ourselves can make it, better buy it of them with some part of the produce of our industry, employed in a way in which we have some advantage."[10] Smith generally opposed most state restrictions on free international markets. He condemned the tariffs that mercantilists used to concentrate wealth and power. "Such taxes, when they have grown up to a certain height, are a curse equal to the barrenness of the earth and the inclemency of the heavens."[11] However, Smith did support the Navigation Acts that required that British goods be shipped to its colonies in British vessels, an act of mercantilism.

David Ricardo (1772–1823) followed Smith in adopting the economic liberal view of international affairs. Ricardo pursued successful careers in business, economics, and as a Member of Parliament. Ricardo was a particular champion of free trade, which made him part of the minority in Britain's Parliament in his day. He opposed the Corn Laws (see the box "Britain's Corn Laws"), which restricted agricultural trade. About trade, Ricardo argued:

> Under a system of perfectly free commerce, each country naturally devotes its capital and labour to such employments as are most beneficial to each. The pursuit of individual advantage is admirably connected with the universal good of the whole. By stimulating industry, by rewarding ingenuity, and by using most efficaciously the peculiar powers bestowed by nature, it distributes labour most effectively and most economically: while, by increasing the general mass of productions, it diffuses general benefit, and binds together, by one common tie of interest and intercourse, the universal society of nations throughout the civilized world.[12]

---

### BRITAIN'S CORN LAWS

Britain's Parliament enacted the Corn Laws in 1815, soon after the defeat of Napoleon ended twelve long years of war. The Corn Laws were a system of tariffs and regulations that restricted food imports into Great Britain. The battle over the Corn Laws, which lasted from their inception until they were finally repealed in 1846, is a classic IPE case study in the conflict between liberalism and mercantilism, market and state.

Why would Britain seek to limit imports of food from the United States and other countries? The "official" argument was that Britain needed to be self-sufficient in food, and the Corn Laws were a way to ensure that it did not become dependent on uncertain foreign supplies. This sort of argument carried some weight at the time, given Britain's wartime experiences (although Napoleon never attempted to cut off food supplies to Great Britain).

There were other reasons for Parliament's support of the Corn Laws, however. The right to vote in Parliament was not universal, and members were chosen based on rural landholdings, not on the distribution of population. The result was that Parliament represented the largely agricultural interests of the landed estates, which were an important source of both power and wealth in the seventeenth and eighteenth centuries. The growing industrial cities and towns, which were increasingly the engine of wealth in the nineteenth century, were not represented in Parliament to a proportional degree.

Seen in this light, it is clear that the Corn Laws were in the economic interests of the members of Parliament and their allies. They were detrimental, however, to the rising industrial interests in two ways. First, by forcing food prices up, the Corn Laws indirectly forced employers to increase the wages they paid workers. This increased production costs and squeezed profits. Second, by reducing Britain's imports from other countries, the Corn Laws indirectly limited Britain's manufactured exports to these markets. The United States, for example, counted on sales of agricultural goods to Britain to generate the cash to pay for imported manufactured goods. Without agricultural exports, the United States couldn't afford as many British imports.

The industrialists embraced the economic liberal view that free markets and minimal state interference were in the nation's interest. (It was clearly in their interest to do so!) David Ricardo, the liberal political economist, grew wealthy enough from his financial affairs to acquire landholdings and a seat in Parliament, from which he railed against the Corn Laws.

Clearly, the industrialists favored repeal of the Corn Laws, but they lacked the political power to achieve their goal. However, the Parliamentary Reform Act of 1832 revised the system of parliamentary representation but also reduced the power of the landed elites who had previously dominated the government, and increased the power of emerging industrial–center representatives. The 1832 Reform Act began the political process that eventually abolished the Corn Laws by weakening their political base of support.

In an act of high political drama, the Corn Laws were repealed in 1846, which changed the course of British trade policy for a generation. Although this act is often seen as the triumph of liberal views over old-fashioned mercantilism, it is perhaps better seen as the victory of the masses over the agricultural oligarchy. Britain's population had grown quickly during the first half of the nineteenth century, and agricultural self-sufficiency was increasingly difficult, even with rising farm productivity. Crop failures in Ireland (the potato famine) in the 1840s left Parliament with little choice. It was either repeal the Corn Laws or face famine, death, and food riots.

The repeal of the Corn Laws was accompanied by a boom in the Victorian economy. Cheaper food and bigger export markets fueled a rapid short-term expansion of the British economy. Britain embraced a liberal view of trade for the rest of the century. Given its place in the global political economy as the "workshop of the world," liberal policies were the most effective way to build national wealth and power. Other nations, however, felt exploited or threatened by Britain's power and adopted mercantilist policies in self-defense.

The Corn Laws illustrate the dynamic interaction of state and market. Changes in the wealth-producing structure of the economy (from farm to industry, from country to city) led eventually to a change in the distribution of state power. The transition was not smooth, however, and took a long time—important points to remember as we consider states and markets in transition today. The case also illustrates that the market can be dominated by particular groups and is not apolitical or asocial, but reflects important social and cultural interests.

For Ricardo free commerce makes nations efficient, and efficiency is a quality that liberals value almost as highly as liberty. Individual success is "admirably connected" with "universal good"—no conflict among people or nations is envisioned here. The free international market stimulates industry, encourages innovation, and creates a "general benefit" by raising production. In IPE jargon, liberals think that outcomes of state, market, and society relations is a **positive-sum game**, in which everyone can potentially get more out of a bargain than he or she put into it. Market exchanges of goods or services are mutually advantageous to both parties. Mercantilists, on the other hand, tend to view life as a **zero-sum game**, in which gains by one person or group necessarily come at the expense of others.

Most important, perhaps, is the notion that these payoffs bind together, by a common thread of interest and intercourse, the nations of the world. As is often argued by those who support globalization today, free individual actions in the production, finance, and knowledge structures create such strong ties of mutual advantage among nations that the need for a tie of security is irrelevant, or nearly so. The nations of the world become part of a "universal society" united, not separated, by their national interests, weakening or entirely eliminating reasons for war.

## JOHN STUART MILL AND THE EVOLUTION OF THE LIBERAL PERSPECTIVE

Political economy is a dynamic field, and the liberal view has evolved over the years as the nature of state–market–societal interaction has changed to reflect changing cultural values and ideas. Liberalism today is more complex and interesting, reflecting a set of variations on Adam Smith's powerful themes.

A critical person in the intellectual development of liberalism was John Stuart Mill (1806–1873),[13] who inherited the liberalism of Smith and Ricardo. His textbook, *Principles of Political Economy with Some of Their Applications to Social Philosophy* (1848) (the same year Marx published *The Communist Manifesto*), helped define liberalism for half a century. Mill held that liberal ideas behind what had emerged as full-blown capitalism in Europe had been an important *destructive* force in the eighteenth century—even if it was also the intellectual foundation of the revolutions and reforms that weakened central authority and strengthened individual liberty in the United States and Europe.

He wanted a philosophy of social progress that was "moral and spiritual progress rather than the mere accumulation of wealth."[14] Mill doubted the extent to which the competitive process and economic freedom inherent in capitalism would turn the most powerful human motive, namely, the pursuit of self-interest, into the service of society's welfare. At the time, many people were working in factories and living in wretched conditons. Whole families worked six days a week for more than eight hours a day. Many were routinely laid off with little notice or without another job.

Mill proposed, therefore, that to achieve social progress, the state should take limited action to supplement the market, correcting for its failures or weaknesses. He advocated *selective* state action in some areas, such as educating children and assisting the poor, when individual initiative might be inadequate in promoting social welfare. In general, Mill supported as much decentralization as was consistent with reasonable efficiency; the slogan was "Centralize information, decentralize power." Parents had a duty to educate their children, and might be legally compelled to do so, but it was obviously intolerable to make them pay for this education if they were already poor. It was also dangerous for the state to take over education as a centralized activity. Thus Mill acknowledged the problems created by the market's inherent inequality of outcomes. Some state action—grants for people to pay for private school and the operation of "model schools," for example—was the suggested remedy.[15]

Mill's views on education and other social issues reflect the evolution of liberalism in his time. The guiding principle was still laissez-faire: When in doubt, state interference was to be avoided. However, within a political economy based on markets and individuals, some limited government actions were desirable. The questions, for Mill as for liberal thinkers since his time, are when, how, and how far government's *visible* hand is justified as an assistant to or replacement for the invisible hand of the market. How far can the state go before its interference with individual rights and liberties is abusive?

To understand many of the fundamental assumptions and principles in economic thought, this is a good place to encourage students and instructors who are not well versed in economics to read the appendix to the chapter, which develops the concepts of economic efficiency, and distinguishes between equity and efficiency.

## JOHN MAYNARD KEYNES AND THE GREAT DEPRESSION

One of the most influential political economists of the twentieth century was John Maynard Keynes (pronounced "canes") (1883–1946), who stands out in the evolution of liberalism for developing an interesting and subtle strain of liberalism called the **Keynesian theory** of economics, or sometimes **Keynesian political economy**. The Keynesian version of liberalism (though there are many liberals who would not include Keynes in their ranks!) combines state and market influences in a way that, while still in the spirit of Adam Smith, relies on the "invisible hand" over a *narrower* range of issues, and sees a *larger but still limited* sphere of constructive state action.

Like Mills, Keynes was critical of the single-mindedness of those in some political camps who preferred a limited role for the state in the economy. Keynes was influenced by the Great Depression of the 1930s, which he interpreted as evidence that the invisible hand sometimes errs in catastrophic ways. As early as 1926, he wrote:

> Let us clear from the ground the metaphysical or general principles upon which, from time to time, *laissez-faire* has been founded. It is *not* true that individuals possess a prescriptive "Natural liberty" in their economic activities. There is *no* "compact" conferring perpetual rights on those who Have or on those who Acquire. The world is *not* so governed from above that private and social interest always coincide. It is *not* so managed here below that in practice they coincide. It is *not* a correct deduction from the Principles of Economics that enlightened self-interest always operates in the public interest. Nor is it true that self-interest generally *is* enlightened; more often individuals acting separately to promote their own ends are too ignorant or too weak to attain even these. Experience does *not* show that individuals, when they make up a social unit, are always less clear-sighted than when they act separately.[16]

In Keynes's view, individuals and markets tend to make decisions that are particularly unwise when faced with situations in which the future is unknown and there is no effective way to share risks or coordinate otherwise chaotic actions. It is possible for individuals to behave rationally and in their individual self-interest, Keynes thought, and yet for the *collective result* to be both irrational and destructive—a clear failure of the invisible hand. The stock market crash of 1929 showed what can happen when investors are spooked and stampede.

A classic example of this problem is called the **paradox of thrift**. What is the rational thing to do when one is threatened by unemployment? One rational response to uncertainty about your future income is to spend less and save more, to build up a cushion of funds in case you need them later. This is fine for you, but what if everyone behaves rationally in this way? If everyone spends less, then less is purchased, less is produced, fewer workers are needed, and less income is created. The recession and unemployment that everyone feared *will* come to pass—*caused* by the very actions that individuals took to protect themselves from this eventuality. And, just as no individual caused the recession, no individual can reverse or prevent it either. Only collective action—through the state—can make a difference. Therefore, Keynes argued that the state should spend and invest when individuals will not, to offset their collective irrationality. He wrote:

> Many of the greatest economic evils of our time are the fruits of risk, uncertainty, and ignorance. . . . Yet the cure lies outside the operations of individuals; it may even be to the interest of individuals to aggravate the disease. . . . These measures would involve Society in exercising directive intelligence through some appropriate organ of action over many of the inner intricacies of private business, yet it would leave private initiative and enterprise unhindered.[17]

In other words, Keynes thought that the state could and should use its power to fortify and improve the market, but not along the aggressive, nationalistic lines of mercantilism, and not with the oppressive force of communism.

Keynes opposed mercantilism, and his experiences in and with the Soviet Union discouraged any thought he might have had of adopting a Marxist or communist point of view. He viewed Leninism as a religion, with a strong emotional appeal that capitalism lacked, and not as a theory of political economy. Keynes found the Soviet regime repressive and its disregard for individual freedom intolerable. He was, at heart, a liberal, who believed in the positive force of the market but also saw the need for state action when rational individual choices were likely to produce irrational collective outcomes. He wrote:

> For my part, I think that Capitalism, wisely managed, can probably be made more efficient for attaining economic ends than any alternative system yet in sight, but that in itself is in many ways objectionable. Our problem is to work out a social organization which shall be as efficient as possible without offending our notions of a satisfactory way of life.[18]

## The Keynesian Compromise: Balancing State and International Interests

Keynes's complex views shaped the world's outlook about state–market–society relations for a generation. For the most part he advocated free markets in a wide domain, including international trade and finance. As we have seen, he also believed that positive government action was both useful and necessary to deal with problems that the invisible hand would not set right. Beginning in the early 1930s and then after World War II, these problems ranged from the domestic macroeconomic diseases of inflation and unemployment to unemployment insurance, social security programs, and bank deposit insurance—and to international trade and finance.

Near the end of World War II, leaders of the Allied nations met at a hotel in Bretton Woods, New Hampshire, to forge global structures (often referred to as the **Bretton Woods system** of international political and economic arrangements and institutions) that would significantly change the war–depression–war pattern of the first half of the twentieth century. Keynes headed the British delegation to the meetings, and the institutional result, though not his plan, certainly reflected many of his ideas. The postwar Bretton Woods system has been called the **Keynesian compromise**, whereby a Keynesian version of liberalism was embedded (entrenched) in the international political economy.[19] This system envisioned a liberal or open international system, in which market forces and free trade policies would play major roles in each state's foreign economic policy objectives.

The Keynesian flavor of liberalism—markets swirled with a distinct state stripe—became the mainstream IPE view in the industrialized world from the 1930s to the 1970s, as many industrialized nations used state power to supplement, strengthen, and stabilize the market economy within the liberal Bretton Woods system of international institutions. In some places, such as Hong Kong, the market was emphasized to a greater extent, creating a dynamic, free-wheeling, free-market system. In other places, such as Sweden, the role of the state was emphasized to a greater degree, creating a more socialist system. In the United States after World War II, state policy became much more activist than in previous decades. The U.S. federal government played a very active role in the economy at home and abroad through such varied areas as space exploration, promoting civil rights and the "Great Society" antipoverty programs, helping the elderly with Medicare medical insurance, regulating business, and fighting the Vietnam War.

In the early days of the Cold War after World War II, the international economy remained relatively open, generating a tremendous amount of economic productivity and growth. Gradually, however, it became difficult to keep the international trade, monetary, and finance systems open, as states were driven by their domestic agendas to protect themselves in an international arena marked by increased interconnectedness and also intense competition. How could the international political economy be kept open without states sacrificing domestic interests and objectives?

## The Liberal View of Hegemony

In the 1970s and 1980s a number of researchers and officials alike focused on **hegemonic stability theory** to explain how international markets work best when a **hegemon**, a single dominant state, accepts the costs associated with keeping the international economy open for its friends and allies by providing them with certain international collective or **public goods** (see Chapter 5).[20] Examples include as a sound system of international payments and the U.S. defense of Western Europe after World War II. In this case the United States (the hegemon) covered many of the expenses associated with establishing and maintaining the monetary system and providing for the defense that each of the allies would have had to pay for alone. As a result, the allies in Europe could spend more for their recovery while benefiting from a system of opening up the trade system, sound money, and peace and security that stimulated the growth of markets everywhere.

Mercantilists and realists (see Chapter 2), however, would stress that when it comes to applying this theory to hegemonic behavior, sustaining liberal embeddedness in the system is more complex. Many political economists recognize three general international hegemons and hegemonic stability eras in modern history: the United Provinces (Holland) in the eighteenth century, Great Britain in the nineteenth century, and the United States in the post–World War II era.[21] Because they shared many mutual political and economic interests, the United States provided its allies and other countries with many public goods during the early days of the Cold War. As time went on, however, U.S. and European interests changed, and as they did, hegemony gradually became more expensive for the hegemon as well as for its allies. For example, the United States felt strongly that the costs of fighting the war in Vietnam were becoming prohibitive without more allied financial and political support; however, many allies no longer shared the same security objectives as the United States and cut back on their shares of security costs. Given that the United States could not *selectively* withdraw military protection from noncooperative allies without hurting those that did cooperate, noncooperative states in essence received a **free ride** in the form of uncompensated security coverage. Likewise, some allies no longer accepted the terms under which they cooperated with the hegemon, such as West Germany when it wanted to trade with the Soviet Union after 1968.

By the mid-1970s many experts posited that the United States had become a "hegemon in decline."[22] As we will discuss in Chapter 7 and in other chapters as well, liberal ideas and values were being undermined in the international economy at the time. In 1971, for instance, the United States abandoned fixed exchange currency rates of dollars to gold and no longer converted other currencies to gold. Not surprisingly, when the dollar came under attack, the United States acted in its own interest rather than absorbing the costs of providing confidence and stability (public goods) for the international economy.

Many questions remain about hegemony: under what conditions hegemons emerge, their viability, when and why their effectiveness wanes, and under what conditions they are challenged and replaced by other hegemons. One example is the George W. Bush administration's efforts to compel NATO countries and other states to share in the costs of the war in Iraq (see Chapter 9). Some countries made it clear they would not contribute personnel or funds to U.S. efforts, even if U.S. efforts in Iraq ultimately provided these countries with some amount of security.

## CONSERVATISM: THE RESURGENCE OF CLASSICAL LIBERALISM

As domestic and international economic protectionist measures increased in the 1970s and 1980s, the popularity of the Keynesian compromise gradually diminished. In its place, classical liberal ideas like those of the Austrian Friedrich Hayek (1899–1992) and the American Milton Friedman (1912–2006) became increasingly popular and powerful, laying the intellectual groundwork for what has become a distinct variation of liberalism, otherwise known as economic liberalism or neoliberalism.

The rising influence of the state in socialist countries and in "liberal" industrial nations stimulated a resurgence of "conservative" classical liberal (economic liberal) views. Hayek's most influential work was *The Road to Serfdom* (1944), in which he argued that socialism and growing state influence represented fundamental threats to individual liberty. In Hayek's view, the growing role of government to provide greater economic security was the first step on a slippery slope. A little economic security soon leads to demand for even more security, he wrote, and before you know it you've slid all the way—the role of the state has grown so large that individual freedom and liberty have disappeared, as in Fascist Germany. Looking at the world of the 1930s, he wrote:

> If we want to form a picture of what society would be like if, according to the ideal which has seduced so many socialists, it was organized as a single great factory, we have only to look to ancient Sparta or to [Hitler's] Germany. . . .
>
> In a society used to freedom it is unlikely that many people would be ready deliberately to purchase security at this price. But the policies which are now followed everywhere, which hand out the privilege of security, now to this group and now to that, are nevertheless rapidly creating conditions in which the striving for security tends to become stronger than the love of freedom. The reason for this is that with every grant of complete security to one group the insecurity of the rest necessarily increases. . . . And the essential element of security which the competitive system offers, the great variety of opportunities, is more and more reduced.[23]

Drawing on older theories of economic liberalism, Hayek argued that the only way to have security *and* freedom was to limit the role of government and draw security from the opportunity that the market provides to free individuals. Echoing Hayek's foundation, in *Capitalism and Freedom* (1962), Friedman reacted directly to the pro-government policies of President John F. Kennedy, who said in his Inaugural Address that citizens should "Ask not what your country can do for you—ask what you can do for your country." Friedman wrote:

> How can we keep the government we create from becoming a Frankenstein that will destroy the very freedom we establish it to protect? Freedom is a rare and delicate plant. Our minds tell us, and history confirms, that *the great threat to freedom is the concentration of power.* Government is necessary to preserve our freedom, it is an instrument through which we can exercise our freedom; yet by concentrating power in political hands, it is also a threat to freedom.[24]

Here Friedman consciously returned to the classical liberalism of Adam Smith. A state that takes its citizens' freedom through actions based on Keynesian ideas is no better than one that seizes their freedom guided by mercantilist, socialist, or fascist notions of security. Power naturally concentrates in the state, and the great threat to freedom is the concentration of power. Capitalism, with its free competitive market, diffuses power and so preserves freedom. Friedman's title, *Capitalism and Freedom*, stresses the classical liberal view that the market preserves and protects liberty.

## REAGAN, THATCHER, AND THE NEOCONSERVATIVES

In the 1980s the classical liberal view of IPE reasserted itself even more forcefully through a movement called **neoconservatism** (not to be confused with the neoconservatives of the George W. Bush administration—see Chapter 9). In Great Britain this movement was associated with the Conservative political party, but today it is almost universally termed **neoliberalism**. Prime Minister Margaret Thatcher of Great Britain and U.S. President Ronald Reagan were the chief practitioners of applied neoconservative ideas. Their neoconservative policies and views of state–market relations owed far more to Adam Smith, Friedrich von Hayek, and Milton Friedman than to J. Maynard Keynes.

To "free up the market and grow the economy," neoliberalism in the United States and Great Britain was designed to reduce state control of private-sector activities, cut taxes, and deregulate markets. The top income tax rate in the United States was cut in stages from 70 percent in 1980 to 33 percent in 1986. Telephone, commercial airline, and trucking industries were subject to dramatic deregulation, allowing greater competition and freedom to set prices. Deregulation in Great Britain was accompanied by a dramatic reduction in state ownership of business and assets. Publicly owned firms and publicly held housing were "privatized," reducing the size of government and its influence on individual decisions. For both popular leaders, the state was to interfere minimally in all spheres of activity, except security, where a strong anticommunist stand was advocated by both of them.

In their best-selling book, *The Commanding Heights*, Daniel Yergin and Joseph Stanislaw concluded that

> Thatcherism shifted the emphasis from state responsibility to individual responsibility, and sought to give first priority to initiatives, incentives, and wealth generation rather than redistribution and equality. It celebrated entrepreneurship. . . . By the 1990s it would turn out that Margaret Thatcher had established a new economic agenda around the world.[25]

The success of these economic liberal policies in the United States and Great Britain, combined with the collapse of communism in Eastern Europe, led to a dramatic renewal of economic liberal policies around the world. Many attribute the global economy recovery after 1992 to deregulation and privatization, which became widespread policies in places all over the world—from Africa to Europe, from South America to Asia. By the mid-1990s it became commonplace to read that the economic liberal perspective and neoliberalism were triumphant, both as a theoretical perspective and in practical policy terms. Francis Fukuyama, in *The End of History* and *The Last Man* and *New York Times* columnist Thomas L. Friedman, in *The Lexus and the Olive Tree* (see Suggested Readings), argued that economic liberalism's triumph was also based on the failure of any other political economic ideology, especially since communism in the Soviet Union had collapsed and Japanese-style mercantilism no longer seemed workable.

## GLOBALIZATION AND THE ECONOMIC LIBERAL HOUR

The "conservative revolution" of classical liberalism continued throughout the 1990s. Perhaps nowhere did neoliberalism gain a bigger voice (and was also criticized more) than in the globalization campaign of the late 1980s and 1990s.[26] During that time the United States in particular championed **globalization**, or the extension of economic liberal principles as a process that would expand the international economy, and by extension those nations linked to it. Emphasizing the role of unfettered (that is, unchained by the state) markets, globalization was expected to generate economic growth the world over, to enhance production efficiency, and to generate jobs in response to increased demand for a wide variety of new products and services. New technologies and communication systems were producing a quantum change in human affairs that connected people more intensely, faster, and in ways never before imagined. Through increased growth, an integrated global economy was also expected to benefit millions of people trapped in poverty in developing nations.

By the mid-1980s the term *globalization* began appearing in the IPE lexicon to describe and account for the interconnection of people and states in deeper and more complex ways achieved through new information and communication technologies. The reduction in ideological conflict that occurred after the end of the Cold War helped shift the attention of state officials away from security toward economic issues. With growing interdependence also came expectations that a mix of nation-states and international organizations (IOs) would have to deal with an array of issues such as development, debt, and the environment. At the same time, nongovernmental organizations (NGOs) were growing in number and stature, largely because certain segments of civil society were unsatisfied with the ability of states and IOs to deal satisfactorily with many social issues.

The following is a partial list of characteristics of globalization drawn from a wide variety of sources.[27] Reflecting many of the neoliberal ideas that gained popularity in the 1980s and 1990s, globalization is characterized as:

- An *economic process* that reflects accelerated and intense individual and state interconnections based on new technologies and communication systems and the mobility of trade and capital,
- The integration of national and regional markets into a single global market,
- A *political process* that weakens state and national borders, and
- A *cultural process* that reflects a densely growing network of complex cultural interconnections and interdependencies in modern society.

Some analysts further claim that globalization:

- Is an inevitable occurrence that is likely to produce a new form of capitalism,
- Requires global governance by a combination of states, IOs, and NGOs, because nobody is in charge of it,
- Benefits everyone, and
- Furthers the spread of democracy in the world.

It should be made clear that a relatively small number of academics and experts do not believe in the existence of globalization at all. Often referred to as "globaloney" types, they do not see the world as fully integrated, nor do they view the phenomenon as novel; instead, they view globalization as merely another marketing tool that globalist capitalists use to sell things.[28]

### Globalizaton Today: Is the Liberal Hour Waning?

In the late 1990s many researchers and journalists focused on globalization's social, economic, and political *positive and negative effects*, the tensions it produces in different societies, and the effect it has on various policy issues (some of which are explored in other chapters of this book). Most neoliberals support globalization because of its emphasis on values such as increased production efficiency, the free flow of currency (capital mobility), free trade, markets, positive-sum outcomes for actors, and individual empowerment. It is not surprising that globalization has remained quite popular with elites and large numbers of the masses in the developed industrialized countries as well as with the transnational elites in developing nations. Globalization is also expected to help transform the coming global society by compressing time and space and intensifying human relations. The increased flow of people across borders might lead eventually to better understanding between different groups of people and thus to a global culture with less conflict in the world.

Thomas Friedman and other neoliberals argue that globalization both reflects and fosters a new brand or phase of capitalism that drives individuals, states, and transnational corporations (TNCs) to continually produce new and better products in a hypercompetitive global atmosphere.

Consequently, individuals and their societies are better off. In his latest book, *The World is Flat*,[29] Thomas Friedman argues that new technological developments are *in the process of* leveling the relationship of individuals to their states and to one another. Leveling generates new opportunities for individuals to compete with people in their own society and with those in other countries. Sounding some of the neoliberal themes of the 1980s about competition, Friedman also argues that the continued diffusion of technology throughout the global market makes it easier for countries such as China, India, and others to challenge the supremacy of the U.S. and European economies. In short, despite a few shortcomings, globalization is here to stay and should be embraced.[30]

As globalization grew in popularity, so did local resistance (in some parts of the world referred to as *jihad*)[31] to many of its effects. In the 1990s, the antiglobalization movement gained momentum on a global scale. Many NGOs and other public-interest groups pitched their cause in newspaper articles, on their websites, and in journal articles. Much of their focus was directed at, among other things, sweatshop production conditions in many poor countries, damage to the environment, and income distribution issues.[32] Many of these groups formed coalitions with labor, environmental, and peace activists and held massive demonstrations that often turned violent in major cities such as Seattle, Washington, D.C., Salzburg, Genoa, and Prague. Protests were aimed at WTO, IMF, and World Bank policies that reflected support for the "Washington Consensus" (see Chapter 8) about the benefits of globalization. Issues surrounding globalization have decisively affected local, regional, and even national elections.[33] And, of course, as pointed out in Chapter 1, antiglobalization might have been a factor behind the 9/11 terrorist attacks on the United States.

While the severity of the protests against the effects of globalization subsided a bit in the early 2000s, even some intellectual *supporters* of globalization began to identify and address potential problems associated with rapid, unregulated globalization. In Chapter 8 we will discuss some of the work of Joseph Stiglitz, who is critical of IMF (and to some extent World Bank) policies that he believes have made it difficult for many developing nations to get out of debt and benefit from globalization.[34] Likewise, Jeffrey Sachs has experience dealing with this issue and has put forth a variety of proposals that might help the poorer developing nations realize economic growth.[35] Although these are only two of the most often cited works of a critical nature, there are many more, all of which attempt to challenge some of the more academic and critical assumptions of globalization as a set of ideas that represent certain values as opposed to being merely a process. It should also be noted that a good number of these critics are not opposed to globalization or economic liberal ideas. They merely want globalization to be managed better in today's international political economy.

## CONCLUSION: ECONOMIC LIBERALISM TODAY

This chapter has described and explained how the ideas and values associated with liberalism and more recently with economic liberalism have changed throughout history to reflect major historical, political, economic, and social changes. Beginning with Quesnay, Smith, and Ricardo, through thinkers such as Keynes, Hayek, and Friedman, these authors have appreciated the role of market forces in societies that have been in the throes of economic transformations whereby capitalism replaced feudalism. Going back to Smith, many of these writers recognize that markets have not always played as positive a role in society as supporters would either imagine or like them to. By the 1980s a split had occurred in liberal views, resulting in those who supported a positive role for the state in the economy and those who saw the state's role in the economy and society as potentially negative. Since then, neo- or economic liberalism has been more popular than the more political version of liberalism. However, the popularity of neoliberal ideals and neoliberal faith in markets have been unable to overcome the well-established political liberal idea that the state still has *some* role to play in the economy, especially when it comes to protecting some groups and countries from some of the negative effects of the market and redistributing income. For example, see the box,

"Ordoliberalism and the Social Market Economy." Many neoliberals recognize that some state actions may be necessary to preserve the environment, promote education and training, improve transportation and communication, and advance science and the arts.

---

### ORDOLIBERALISM AND THE SOCIAL MARKET ECONOMY

Economic liberalism had been largely discredited in Europe by the 1920s. Economic liberalism, particularly in Germany's post–World War I Weimar Republic, had come to be associated with economic chaos, political corruption, and the exploitation of the working class.[a] In response to this perception and to Hitler's consequent rise to power, a small group of academics at Freiburg University developed a new conception of liberalism they called *ordoliberalism.* Walter Eucken (1891–1950), Franz Böhm (1985–1977), and Hans Grossman-Doerth (1894–1944) founded this school of thought. Ordoliberals believe that the failings of liberalism resulted from the failure of nineteenth- and twentieth-century laissez-faire policymakers to appreciate Adam Smith's insight that the market is embedded in legal and political systems.

Ordoliberal thought reflects the humanist values of classical liberalism, including the protection of human dignity and personal freedom. Ordoliberals espouse the classical liberal notions that private decision making should guide resource allocation, that competition is the source of economic well-being, and that economic freedom and political freedom are inextricable. Like classical liberals, they also believe that individuals must be protected from excessive state power and that political power should be dispersed through democratic processes that maximize participation in public decision making. Ordoliberals also emphasize that individual freedoms must be protected from private power. Private economic power in the form of monopoly control of markets leads to the exploitation of consumers, who then face restricted choice and high prices. Private economic power can also subvert democratic processes as powerful firms wield undue influence over politicians and other policymakers—influence used to create special privileges that rig markets in favor of those dominant firms.

Ordoliberals believe that the market process will support and promote liberal values only if appropriate rules governing the market process (property law, contract law, trade law, competition policy, etc.) are established by the state. *Ordo*, from the Latin, means "order." The rules governing the market process should be "constitutional" rules immune from political manipulation that reflect the shared liberal values of society. With such a framework in place, the market process will reinforce the economic and political freedoms so central to the liberal conception of the good society. With such a framework in place, the efforts of powerful firms to subvert the market process (via price controls, import restrictions, subsidies, restrictive licenses, etc.) will be deemed "unconstitutional." Politicians will be in a strong position to resist the special pleadings of powerful interest groups, and the power of the state in general to influence market outcomes will be severely restricted. A privilege-free economy will be the highly desirable result.

Ordoliberal thought has had a profound influence on economic and political policy in the European Union. Current European competition policy clearly incorporates ordoliberal principles. Competition policy in Europe severely restricts the behavior of dominant firms—particularly, any practices that might inhibit the entry of small or medium-sized rivals. By maintaining open markets, European competition authorities hope to foster economic freedom in the form of freedom of entry, thereby enhancing economic opportunity, promoting competition, and diffusing economic and political power. Microsoft's antitrust problems in Europe can be better understood in this light.[b]

Ordoliberalism does have an inherent ethical stance. Market outcomes generated within an appropriate legal and political framework are nondiscriminating, privilege-free outcomes and are likely to be just outcomes.[c] Ordoliberals recognize, however, that some income redistribution will likely be called for, given the limited productivity of some individuals—often due to circumstances beyond their control.

Other German intellectuals, principally Alfred Müller-Armack (1901–1978), accepted key ordoliberal principles but challenged the ordoliberal notion that market outcomes are just outcomes. Müller-Armack argued that supplemental "social" policies are necessary to ensure that market outcomes will indeed be consistent with a "good" society. Further, these supplementary rules might indeed affect specific market outcomes so as to privilege certain segments of society. Müller-Armack is credited with developing the basis of the "social" market economy that characterizes many modern European states.[d] For some analysts, that these supplementary rules might erode "constitutional" market principles helps explain the current state of many European economies (including Germany's), where legislative and judicial manipulation of the "rules of the game" in the interest of "social" outcomes has arguably undermined the market economy.[e]

*References*

[a] The discussion of ordoliberalism in this and the following paragraphs is based largely on David J. Gerber, "Constitutionalizing the Economy: German Neo-Liberalism, Competition Policy and the 'New' Europe," *The American Journal of Comparative Law*, 42 (1994), pp. 25–88.

[b] "Microsoft on Trial," *The Economist*, April 28, 2006, www.economist.com/agenda/displaystory. cfm?story_id=E1_GRSDSRP.

[c] Victor J. Vanberg, "The Freiburg School: Walter Eucken and Ordoliberalism," Walter Eucken Institute, Freiburg Discussion Papers on Constitutional Economics, November 2004, p. 2.

[d] Ibid.

[e] Ibid.

Most of the current debate about neoliberalism centers around the issue of globalization. Although there are still many strong supporters of globalization, recently some of the main precepts and policies associated with this popular ideological campaign have come under attack, which we will also discuss in more detail in different chapters in this book.

## DISCUSSION QUESTIONS

1. Adam Smith and Václav Havel are both liberals in the sense in which this term is used in IPE. Explain what views Smith and Havel share regarding the market, the state, human nature, and power.
2. Explain Adam Smith's concept of the "invisible hand." What roles do self-interest and competition play in this concept?
3. Compare and contrast the liberal view of the outcome of competition, as found in Adam Smith's invisible hand, with the mercantilist view of the same topic. What accounts for the differences between the two views? Explain.
4. How do liberals such as David Ricardo view international trade? Why do they hold this opinion? Explain how the Corn Laws debate in nineteenth-century Britain illustrates the conflict between mercantilist and liberal views of international trade.
5. John Stuart Mill and John Maynard Keynes thought that government could play a positive role in correcting problems in the market. Discuss the specific types of "market failures" that Mill and Keynes perceived and the types of government actions they advocated. If Mill and Keynes favored some state action in the market, how can we consider them liberals? Explain.
6. Compare and contrast the liberal perspective on IPE with the mercantilist perspective in terms of the following factors: level of analysis, view of human nature, attitude toward power, notion of the proper role of government, and view of the nature of the international system.
7. Explain the relationships between liberalism and its more narrow form of economic liberalism. How are they similar and different in terms of values, ideas, and policies?
8. Explain the factors that have made economic liberalism such a popular ideological outlook. What factors would you suspect have contributed most to its waning popularity?
9. What factors accounted for the popularity of globalization in the 1990s, and what contributes most to the various criticisms of it today?

## INTERNET LINKS

WGBH website for *The Commanding Heights: The Battle for the World Economy:*

   www.pbs.org/wgbh/commandingheights/lo/index.html

This is an unusually rich website for the study of IPE in the twentieth century. The PBS documentary, *The Commanding Heights,* is a history of IPE in the twentieth century, with a focus on the tension between states and markets. The website adds useful depth and contrasting viewpoints to the video.

Stanford Encyclopedia of Philosophy "Liberalism":
   http://plato.stanford.edu/entries/liberalism
*Liberalism in the Classical Tradition* by Ludwig Von Mises:
   http://plato.stanford.edu/entries/liberalism
"A Short History of Neoliberalism" by Susan George:
   www.zmag.org/CrisesCurEvts/Globalism/george.htm
"The New Liberal Imperialism" by Robert Cooper:
   www.observer.co.uk/worldview/story/0,11581,680095,00.html

## SUGGESTED READINGS

Benjamin Barber. *Jihad vs. McWorld*. New York: Ballantine Books, 1995, 2002.
Milton Friedman. *Capitalism and Freedom*. Chicago: University of Chicago Press, 1962.
Thomas L. Friedman. *The Lexus and the Olive Tree*. New York: Anchor Books, 1999, 2000.
Thomas L. Friedman. *The World Is Flat: A Brief History of the Twenty-First Century*. New York: Farrar, Straus & Giroux, 2005.
Francis Fukuyama. *The End of History and the Last Man*. New York: The Free Press, 1992.
Friedrich A. Hayek. *The Road to Serfdom*. Chicago: University of Chicago Press, 1944.
John Maynard Keynes. *Essays in Persuasion*. New York: W. W. Norton, 1963.
Joel Krieger. *Globalization and State Power: Who Wins When American Rules?* New York: Pearson Longman, 2005.
Michael Mandelbaum. *The Ideas That Conquered the World*. New York: Public Affairs, 2002.
David Ricardo. *The Principles of Political Economy and Taxation*. London: Dent, 1973.
Adam Smith. *The Wealth of Nations*. New York: Dutton, 1964.
Manfred B. Steger. *Globalism: The New Market Ideology*. Boulder, CO: Rowman & Littlefield, 2002.
Martin Wolf. *Why Globalization Works*. New Haven, CT: Yale University Press, 2004.
Daniel Yergin and Joseph Stanislaw. *The Commanding Heights*. New York: Simon & Schuster, 1998, 2002.

## KEY TERMS

| | | |
|---|---|---|
| globalism | Keynesian political economy | public goods |
| liberalism | paradox of thrift | free ride |
| rent-seeking | Bretton Woods system | neoconservatism |
| positive-sum game | Keynesian compromise | neoliberalism |
| zero-sum game | hegemonic stability theory | globalization |
| Keynesian theory | hegemon | |

## NOTES

1. In this book the term *neoconservatives* or "neocons" also refers to George W. Bush administration officials who had a decidedly unilateral outlook about the world and U.S. power and capabilities to manage it (see Chapter 9).
2. Our thanks to Ross Singleton for preparing the appendix and the boxes "The Tenets of Capitalism" and "Ordoliberalism and the Social Market Economy," and for reviewing this and other chapters.
3. Ralf Dahrendorf, "Liberalism," in John Eatwell, Murray Milgate, and Peter Newman, eds., *The New Palgrave: Invisible Hand* (New York: W. W. Norton, 1989), p. 183.
4. Adam Smith, *The Wealth of Nations* (New York: Dutton, 1964), p. 400. *The Wealth of Nations* was first published in 1776, a noteworthy year in that the U.S. Declaration of Independence was written the same year.
5. Václav Havel, "What I Believe," in *Summer Meditations*, trans. Paul Wilson (New York: Knopf, 1992), p. 62.
6. Smith's "state" meant Britain's Parliament, which represented the interests of the land gentry, not those of the entrepreneurs and citizens of the growing industrial centers. Not until the 1830s was Parliament reformed enough to redistribute political power more widely. As a Scot without land, who therefore could not vote, Smith had some reason to question the power structure of his time.
7. Smith, *The Wealth of Nations*, p. 400.
8. Ibid., p. 117.
9. Michael W. Doyle, *The Ways of War and Peace* (New York: W. W. Norton, 1997), p. 207.
10. Smith, *The Wealth of Nations*, p. 401.
11. Ibid., p. 410.
12. David Ricardo, *The Principles of Political Economy and Taxation* (London: Dent, 1973), p. 81.

13. John Stuart Mill's dates place him between the life spans of Adam Smith and John Maynard Keynes, which is roughly where he falls, as well, in the development of liberal thought.

14. Alan Ryan, "John Stuart Mill," in Eatwell et al., eds., *The New Palgrave*, p. 201.

15. Ibid., p. 208.

16. John Maynard Keynes, "The End of Laissez-Faire," in *Essays in Persuasion* (New York: W. W. Norton, 1963), p. 312.

17. Ibid., pp. 317–318.

18. Ibid., p. 321.

19. For a more detailed discussion of embeddedness, see John Ruggie, "International Regimes, Transactions, and Change: Embedded Liberalism in the Postwar Economic Order," *International Organizations*, 36, 1982, pp. 379–415.

20. U.S. economist Charles Kindleberger is generally credited as the originator of the hegemonic stability theory. See his *Money and Power: The Economics of International Politics and the Politics of International Economics* (New York: Basic Books, 1970).

21. For another enlightening discussion of hegemonic theory, see Robert Gilpin, *War and Change in World Politics* (Princeton, NJ: Princeton University Press, 1981).

22. For a discussion of this argument and a counterargument, see Henry Nau, *The Myth of America's Decline: Leading the World Economy into the 1990's* (New York: Oxford University Press, 1992).

23. Friedrich A. Hayek, *The Road to Serfdom* (Chicago: University of Chicago Press, 1944), pp. 127–128.

24. Milton Friedman, *Capitalism and Freedom* (Chicago: University of Chicago Press, 1962), p. 2. Italics added.

25. Daniel Yergin and Joseph Stanislaw, *The Commanding Heights* (New York: Simon & Schuster, 2002), pp. 104–105.

26. See, for example, Edward Goldsmith and Jerry Mander, *The Case Against the Global Economy and for a Turn Toward Localization*, 2nd ed. (San Francisco: Earthscan, 2001).

27. For a good discussion of the topic of globalism, see Manfred B. Steger, *Globalism: The New Market Ideology* (Boulder, CO: Rowman & Littlefield, 2002).

28. See, for example, Michael Veseth, *Selling Globalization: The Myth of the Global Economy* (Boulder, CO: Lynne Rienner, 1998), and his aptly titled *Globaloney: Unraveling the Myths of Globalization* (New York: Rowman & Littlefield, 2005).

29. Thomas Friedman, *The World is Flat: A Brief History of the Twenty-First Century* (New York: Farrar, Straus & Giroux, 2005).

30. This is the thesis of Thomas Friedman's *The Lexus and The Olive Tree* (New York: Anchor Books, 1999, 2000).

31. The term is used in this broad manner by Benjamin Barber, *McWorld vs. Jihad* (New York: Ballantine Books, 1995, 2002).

32. See, for example, many of the articles in Robin Broad, ed., *Global Backlash: Citizen Initiatives for a Just World Economy* (Boulder, CO: Rowman & Littlefield, 2002).

33. See, for example, Jorge Castañeda, "Latin America's Turn to the Left," *Foreign Affairs*, 85 (May/June 2006), pp. 28–43.

34. See Joseph Stiglitz, *Globalization and Its Discontents* (New York: W. W. Norton, 2002).

35. See Jeffrey Sachs, *The End of Poverty: Economic Possibilities in Our Time* (New York: Penguin, 2005).

## Appendix:  The Market Model, Market-Based Resource Allocation, Economic Efficiency, Efficiency Versus Equity

### The Market Model

At the heart of the liberal perspective lies the market as the means of allocating scarce resources among competing uses. An appreciation of the market mechanism in this regard requires a basic understanding of the market as captured in the following market model. The *market model* consists of a demand model representing the consumers (buyers) and a supply model representing the producers (sellers).

The demand for a particular commodity (the willingness and ability of consumers to pay for the commodity) depends on the price of the commodity, the prices of related goods (substitutes and complements), the income of consumers, consumer tastes and preferences, the number of consumers, consumer expectations regarding future prices, and other considerations. The quantity of the commodity demanded increases when the price of the commodity decreases, holding other determinants of demand constant. This is depicted as a movement along the demand curve, from $P_1, Q_1$ to $P_2, Q_2$ in Figure 3–1. As the price of a commodity falls, consumers will substitute more of that commodity for other goods, which now cost relatively more. The inverse relationship between price and quantity demanded reflects the law of demand. So, the effect of a change in price is depicted by a movement along the demand curve. How about the effect of a change in any other determinant of demand? A change in any determinant of demand other than the price of the commodity itself will cause a shift of the entire demand curve. For instance, if consumer income increases, consumers will normally want to buy more of the commodity at each indicated price. Consequently, the entire demand curve shifts to $D'$ as in Figure 3–1. This is referred to as a *change in demand*—an increase in demand.

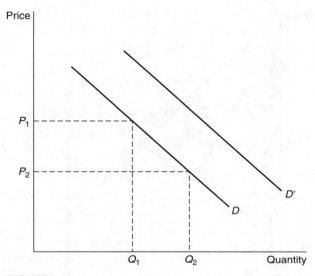

**FIGURE 3–1**

The supply of a particular commodity (the willingness and ability of producers to supply the commodity) depends on the price of the commodity, the prices of resources needed to produce the commodity, production technology, the number of producers, and other factors. The quantity of the commodity supplied increases when the price of the commodity increases, holding other determinants of supply constant. This is depicted as a movement along the supply curve, from $P_1, Q_1$ to $P_2, Q_2$ in Figure 3–2. The profit-maximizing response to a higher price is to expand production. The direct relationship between price and quantity supplied reflects the law of supply. A change in any determinant other than the price of the commodity itself will cause a shift of the entire supply curve. For instance, if the price of a resource needed to produce the commodity increases, producers will react by producing less of the commodity at each price. Consequently, the entire supply curve shifts to $S'$ as in Figure 3–2. This is referred to as a *change in supply*—a decrease in supply.

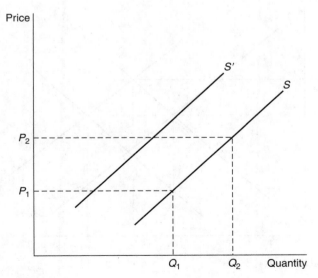

**FIGURE 3–2**

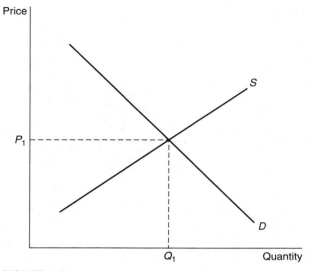

**FIGURE 3–3**

The market is in equilibrium at the price at which the quantity demanded and the quantity supplied are in balance. In Figure 3–3, $P_1$ and $Q_1$ are the equilibrium price and quantity, respectively.

## Market-Based Resource Allocation

Using this simple model, we can now describe how resources are allocated and reallocated via the market. Assume that consumer tastes and preferences turn in favor of the particular commodity, the market for which is depicted in Figure 3–4. The demand for this commodity will increase. The demand curve will shift to the right to $D'$. At price $P_1$, a shortage of the commodity ($Q_3 - Q_1$) will be created as the quantity demanded exceeds the quantity supplied. The

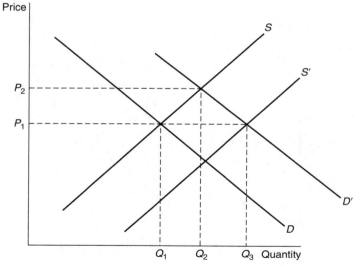

**FIGURE 3–4**

shortage in turn will cause the price of the commodity to rise, and as the price rises, consumers and producers will respond. Consumers will buy less of the commodity, moving up $D'$ from $Q_3$ to $Q_2$. Consumers will conserve on their use of the commodity and/or buy relatively less expensive alternatives. Producers will respond by increasing production (moving up the supply curve from $Q_1$ to $Q_2$). Producers increase production (in order to maximize profit) by hiring more labor, purchasing more raw materials, using more energy—acquiring more resources necessary to produce this commodity.

These resources will be bid away from other lesser-valued uses. Consequently, resources will be reallocated away from other uses and to this use in accordance with changing consumer tastes and preferences. No central agency or authority oversees this resource reallocation process; rather, this reallocation occurs in response to the incentives created by the higher price for the commodity. That is, producers increase production in an effort to increase their profitability, not out of concern for the well-being of consumers and not because they have been directed to do so by a central planning authority. Yet the producer's self-interested behavior ultimately serves consumers, who are able to enjoy more of the commodity. In the long run, the profits made by producers in this market will attract entry by new producers into this industry. When those new firms enter (bringing resources with them), the supply of the commodity will expand to $S'$ and the price will eventually fall to $P_1$ and the associated equilibrium quantity will expand to $Q_3$. In the long run, consumers will enjoy more of the product while paying only the original price. (Students of economics will recognize the implicit assumption that the market in question is a constant-cost market—a market in which entry has no effect on input prices.)

If, instead, consumers' tastes and preferences move away from a particular good, the demand for that good will decline—the demand curve will shift left. Consequently, there will be a surplus of the good at the original equilibrium price. This surplus in turn will cause the price to fall. As the price falls, producers will reduce production and will redeploy resources to other, more highly valued uses. In the long run, the lower price will mean economic losses, and firms will leave the industry (taking resources with them). Consequently, the supply of the commodity will decrease and the price will increase to the original level.

## Economic Efficiency

The concept of *economic efficiency* is central to the study of IPE. Public policies, and even entire economic systems, are evaluated based on their "efficiency." But what does this term mean? It is a slippery term, in part, because of the various meanings implied or intended by its use. Efficiency may mean one thing to an economist, another to a sociologist, and something else again to a political theorist.

Economists' conceptions of economic efficiency include allocative, production, and dynamic efficiency. *Allocative efficiency* concerns the allocation of scarce resources among competing uses—a fundamental task that every society must undertake in one way or another. We will use the market model we have developed to illustrate the concept of allocative efficiency in some detail in the following paragraphs. First, however, it is important to note, if only in passing, the additional meanings of this term as commonly used by economists. *Production efficiency* concerns how well resources are used in a particular use. How efficiently is steel produced? How efficiently are health care services delivered? When production efficiency exists, goods and services are produced at the lowest possible cost. *Dynamic efficiency* concerns the rate of technological progress in an industry or within an economy. Technological progress is, in large part, the result of investment in research and development (R&D). Dynamic efficiency exists when the current level of investment in R&D results in an optimal rate of technological progress. We will have more to say about dynamic efficiency in Chapter 10.

Resources are best allocated among various goods and services by the state (structural perspective) or by the market (liberal perspective) or by some combination of the two. Regardless of the mechanism, the goal is, presumably, to allocate scarce resources to their most highly valued uses in order to maximize social welfare.

Social welfare from the perspective of an economist has a very particular meaning. The social welfare that can be derived from a particular commodity (a good or service) is the total benefit derived from that commodity minus the total cost of producing that commodity. This idea of social welfare takes into account the dictum, "There is no such thing as a free lunch." Social welfare is a measure of not only the benefit of using resources in a particular way but also the costs of doing so.

The allocation process using the market is decentralized in the extreme—no one is in charge. Rather, the interactions of individual consumers and producers as reflected in demand and supply result in an efficient allocation of resources (absent the many well-known causes of market failure, including monopoly, externalities, public goods, and information problems). Recall that the demand curve represents the prices that consumers are willing and able to pay for additional units of a commodity. Economic theory suggests, in turn, that the price a consumer is willing and able to pay

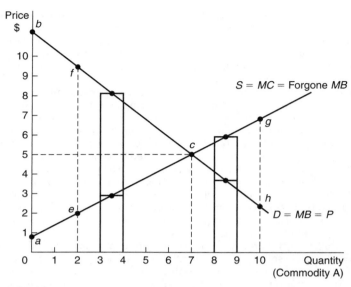

**FIGURE 3–5**

for an additional unit of a commodity reflects the additional or marginal benefit the consumer anticipates from consuming that unit. The demand curve, then, is a *marginal benefit curve*. The supply curve reflects the prices at which producers are willing and able to supply the commodity. Economic theory demonstrates that these supply prices reflect the additional or marginal cost of producing each additional unit of output—the supply curve, then, is a *marginal cost curve*. When the market for a particular commodity is in equilibrium—demand equals supply—the marginal benefit (*MB*) of the last unit produced exactly equals its marginal cost (*MC*), as in Figure 3–5 for commodity A.

The significance of this outcome can best be appreciated if we consider the notion of opportunity cost. The *opportunity cost* of using resources in one use is the benefit foregone of not using those resources in their best alternative use. For example, the opportunity cost of reading this paragraph is the benefit you otherwise would have realized from using your time (a very scarce resource) in its best alternative use (perhaps watching a rerun of Seinfeld, or working on a cure for malaria). The marginal cost of producing an additional unit of commodity A, say, the fourth unit in Figure 3–5, is $3. This implies that there is some other use for the resources necessary to produce this fourth unit of A that would yield a marginal benefit of $3. Should resources be allocated to produce the fourth unit of A? Yes! The marginal benefit of the fourth unit is $8. The foregone marginal benefit associated with the production of the fourth unit is $3. Clearly, allocating resources to this use rather than their next best use is appropriate. Social welfare (benefit minus cost) will increase by $5.

Producers acting from the profit motive will expand production (as long as price exceeds marginal cost) until marginal cost equals market price. Producers in this market will bid sufficient resources away from other uses to produce the equilibrium (and profit-maximizing) quantity of seven units. When the market is in equilibrium, every unit will be produced for which marginal benefit exceeds or (at equilibrium) just equals marginal cost. Area *abc* in Figure 3–5 represents the social welfare derived from this commodity. If fewer than seven units, say, two units, were produced, a social welfare loss equal to the area *efc* would be incurred from the underallocation of resources to this commodity. For example, the marginal benefit of the fourth unit is $8, and its marginal cost is $3. If resources are not allocated to the production of this unit, $5 in social welfare will be lost. If more than seven units are produced, say, ten units, a social welfare loss equal to *cgh* will be incurred from the overallocation of resources to this commodity. For example, the marginal cost of the ninth unit is $6 and the marginal benefit is $3.50. If resources are allocated to the production of this unit, a welfare loss of $2.50 will be sustained. Resources should have instead been allocated to their best alternative use, where $6 in marginal benefit would have been realized rather than the $3.50 in marginal benefit realized by the production of the ninth unit.

The magic of the market is that the equilibrium level of output is also the social welfare–maximizing level of output. The market process, then, results in an efficient allocation of resources.

## Efficiency Versus Equity

The question remains: Is an efficient allocation of resources necessarily an equitable (fair) allocation of resources? In fact, the concept of allocative efficiency is based on a very particular (some might say peculiar) definition of social welfare. Recall that social welfare is defined as total benefit minus total costs. Further, marginal benefit is reflected in the price that consumers are willing and able to pay. Unless a consumer is both willing and able to pay, his or her preferences regarding the allocation of resources will not be reflected in the market. Consumers "vote" (on resource allocation) with their dollars. The more dollars any individual possesses, the more votes she can cast. The particular allocation of resources to the production of various goods and services, then, reflects a particular distribution of income. If income is redistributed, then a different efficient allocation of resources will be realized. The question that opens this paragraph can then be answered: An efficient allocation of resources is also an equitable allocation of resources if income is distributed in an equitable manner.

The next logical question is: What constitutes an equitable distribution of income? There is, of course, no easy answer to this question. However, we can contrast the liberal perspective and the structural perspective in this regard.

Those in tune with the liberal perspective tend to think in terms of market justice. *Market justice* implies that the income each member of society enjoys (and therefore the votes he can cast in the market) equals the contribution each member makes to national output. Brain surgeons are rich (and deserve to be) because they render services that are highly valued—they contribute substantially to national output. Star athletes or entertainers are ultrarich because they provide entertainment services that many consumers value very highly indeed (You paid *how much* for those Knicks tickets?). Entrepreneurs are sometimes spectacularly rich (and deserve to be) because of astonishing innovations they pioneer and bring to the market. On the other hand, those of us with more ordinary skills, talents, training, education, or creativity make more ordinary contributions to national output and deserve more ordinary incomes. The liberal dictum might be, "From each according to his ability and to each according to his ability."

Market justice also means that those of us who might be disadvantaged regarding our ability to contribute to national output due to circumstances beyond our control (physical or mental disability, born to a drug-addicted single mom, discriminated against in the workplace based on race or religion, etc.) will earn very little income and therefore have little access to the goods and services produced within our own economy. We will be on the outside looking in. There are, of course, ways of taking the hard edges off market justice—income supplements to the poor or, better yet, enhancing economic opportunity via training, education, and public works programs, for instance. Perhaps this is what President George H. W. Bush meant by "compassionate conservatism."

While market justice can be harsh, it does undeniably create strong incentives to be productive. By establishing a direct link between effort and reward, individuals are rewarded for their hard work, their investment, their creativity, their drive, their dependability, their adaptability, and their willingness to take risks. Margaret Thatcher, the British Prime Minister who instituted liberal reforms in Great Britain, in effect argued that market justice would promote the "vigorous virtues" of individual initiative, deferral of gratification, personal responsibility, independence, and entrepreneurship. Attending to the needs of the poor is recognized, then, as something of a balancing act. Providing government income or housing or other supplements dulls incentives and undermines the "vigorous virtues" by severing the link between effort and reward.

Against the liberal notion of market justice stands the ideal of *distributive justice* as associated with structuralism. The essence of distributive justice is captured in Karl Marx's dictum, "From each according to his ability and to each according to his need." In a society that really adheres to the principle of distributive justice, income is determined by the needs of the various members of society. A worker who supports a large family receives more income than an unmarried worker. Both workers, however, contribute to national output based on their individual capabilities. An unmarried brain surgeon works long hours for relatively little pay, knowing that her services benefit the members of her community. The father of a large family works long hours in the steel mill, knowing his services benefit the members of his community and confident that his remuneration will be sufficient to provide for his family.

Or . . . does the would-be brain surgeon choose not to undertake the arduous years of necessary training, knowing that her efforts will not lead to commensurate monetary rewards? Does the mill worker fail to show up on Mondays and Fridays? Does the entrepreneur bother to innovate? Who invests? In other words, what about incentive? Also, how is relative need assessed, and by whom? The state? Who controls the state apparatus? Won't these interests have unchecked power? Won't growing dependency on the state wither the "vigorous virtues" and undermine the dynamism of the economy? Asking these obvious questions reveals some of the concerns about distributive justice that have been voiced by liberal critics. Nevertheless, the appeal of distributive justice is undeniable. It is a dream that has driven revolutions.

# Marx, Lenin, and the Structuralist Perspective

## OVERVIEW

Karl Marx is one of the most imposing figures in the history of political economy. With the collapse of communism in Russia and Eastern Europe, it is tempting to conclude that "Marx is dead" and to move on to other, easier pursuits. However, ideas that originated with Marx remain very much alive today. Theories that incorporate notions of class struggle, exploitation, imperialism, and technical change, to name just a few, remain important tools of analysis in international political economy (IPE).

This chapter explores a number of theories, ideas, and concepts whose roots are found in Marxist and Leninist thought. The general heading *structuralism* accounts for some of the more recent theories and concepts that incorporate a number of Marx's and Lenin's ideas.

Modern structuralists often ask questions that others tend to overlook or downplay. Indeed, there are many problems in IPE that cannot be understood or completely appreciated without considering Marx's viewpoint and the more recent structuralist perspectives he helped pioneer. The underlying notion uniting the ideas of what we will call structuralism is that structure conditions outcome. Because capitalism was primarily a national phenomenon in Marx's time, he focused most of his analysis on national economies and how the class structure resulted in exploitation, conflict, and crisis within nation-states.

V. I. Lenin expanded Marx's study to account explicitly for imperialism, manifest in the dominant and exploitative relationship of industrial countries with their colonial possessions. This analysis continued with subsequent work in dependency theory and modern world systems theory.

Another line of structuralist analysis is especially critical of its intellectual and cultural effects. We survey briefly some of the ideas of Weber, Gramsci, and Lukács in this regard. We conclude with a discussion of the significance of structuralism and Marxism today.

*The history of all hitherto existing society is the history of class struggles.*[1]

Karl Marx and Friedrich Engels

*Imperialism is capitalism in that stage of development in which the domination of monopolies and finance capital has established itself; in which the export of capital has acquired pronounced importance; in which the partition of all the territories of the globe among the great capitalist powers has been completed.*[2]

V. I. Lenin

*The Third World countries of today were drawn into the capitalist world market under regimes of formal and informal colonialism, as appendages of the metropolitan nations to supply raw materials and exotic commodities to the industrial center.*[3]

Joan Robinson

❁ ❁ ❁ ❁ ❁ ❁

On January 1, 1994, a small army of peasant guerrillas seized six towns in the poor Mexican state of Chiapas. The "Chiapas Awakening," as it was called by some, was a protest against a political and economic system that the peasants saw as fundamentally biased against them. The date of the revolt was carefully chosen for its symbolic value. New Year's Day 1994 was the date when the North American Free Trade Agreement (NAFTA) came into force, uniting Mexico with Canada and the United States in a huge open market. NAFTA, the rebels believed, would serve to increase their exploitation by the capitalist system. In revolting against the Mexican system of political economy, they were revolting against the inherent inequality of certain kinds of economic development.

The Chiapas Awakening clearly was neither liberal nor mercantilist in nature. The rebels protested against both the force of the market and the collective power of the state. The intellectual forefather of the Chiapas rebellion was Karl Marx, not Adam Smith or Friedrich List. The Chiapas Awakening reflected the third perspective on IPE, which we term **structuralism**.

This chapter explores the intellectual family tree of structuralism from its historical roots in the Industrial Revolution to its several branches in the world today. The quotations that opened this chapter, by Karl Marx, V. I. Lenin, and Joan Robinson, hint at where the discussion in this chapter will take us. We will first explore the early roots of the structuralist perspective in the writings of Karl Marx. Marx thought that power was rooted in the ownership of production capital (the means of production), which shaped the relationship among different classes within a nation. Lenin saw imperialism—the domination of industrializing nations over dependent colonial possessions—as a necessary stage of capitalism. Later in the chapter, we will explore a number of contemporary structuralist viewpoints that incorporate variations on these themes.

Some people tend to look at all of IPE from the structuralist perspective, rejecting as hopelessly biased the other viewpoints we have discussed so far. In the same way, economic liberals and mercantilists usually reject the structuralist view as fatally flawed.

In this book, we take a firm stand on middle ground. The structuralist perspective forces us to analyze problems, issues, and events that might be overlooked if we limited ourselves to the liberal and mercantilist viewpoints. For example, issues of class, exploitation, the distribution of wealth and power, dependency, and global aspects of capitalism take center stage in this perspective.

Moreover, this perspective is, at its roots, a critical one, raising challenges to the existing state of affairs. First, many see in structuralism not only the tools to conduct a scientific analysis of existing capitalist arrangements but also the grounds for a moral critique of the inequality and exploitation that capitalism produces within and between countries. Second, this framework of analysis is the only one that allows us to view IPE "from below"; that is, from the perspective of the oppressed classes and poor, developing Third World nations. In contrast to mercantilism and liberalism, it gives a voice to the powerless. Finally, structuralism focuses on what is dynamic in IPE, seeing capitalism and other modes of production as driven by conflict and crisis and subject to change. What exists now is a system and set of structures that emerged at a particular time and will eventually be replaced by a new and different system of political economy.

We should make it clear at this point that a good many of the more recent structuralists do not subscribe to Marx's or Lenin's views in a prescriptive sense—that is, they do not agree ideologically with many of the political implications that flow from Marxist or Leninist ideas. However, these structuralists base a good deal of their analysis of IPE on many of Marx's and Lenin's more well-known perceptions and arguments.

## MARX AND HISTORY

The first great scholar to pioneer a structural approach to political economy was Karl Marx (1818–1883). Born in Trier, Germany, Marx did his most important work while living in England, spending hours in research at the British Museum in London. Many of his views reflect conditions he and his collaborator Friedrich Engels observed in English mills and factories at the height of the Industrial Revolution. Adults and children often labored under dreadful working conditions and lived in abject poverty and squalor. Marx's theory of history, his notion of class conflict, and his critique of capitalism must all be understood in the context of nineteenth-century Europe's cultural, political, and economic climate.

A word of caution is in order concerning Marx and Marxism. Marx wrote millions of words; in so vast a body of work, he necessarily treated the main themes repeatedly, and not always consistently. What Marx "said" or "thought" about any interesting issue is, therefore, subject to some dispute. In the same way, Marxist scholars have interpreted Marx's writings in many ways. There is not, therefore, a definitive reading of Marx, any more than there is a definitive interpretation of the Bible or performance of a Beethoven sonata. Marxism is at once a theory of economics, politics, sociology, and ethics. For some, it is also a call to action.

Marx understood history to be a great, dynamic, evolving creature, determined fundamentally by economic and technological forces. Marx believed that through a process called **historical materialism**,[4] these forces can be objectively explained and understood just like any other natural law.

Historical materialism takes as its starting point the notion that the *forces of production* of society (i.e., the sum total of knowledge and technology contained in society) set the parameters for the kind of system of political economy, or *mode of production*, that is possible. As Marx put it, "the hand mill gives you society with the feudal lord, the steam mill society with the industrial capitalist."[5] The economic structure (what Marx called the *relations of production*, or class relations) that emerges from such a mode of production in turn determines the social and ethical structures of society.

It is in the contradictions or conflicts between the forces of production and the relations of production in a society that Marx sees the mechanism for evolutionary and revolutionary change. Marx sees the course of history as steadily evolving. The process of change from one system of political economy (or mode of production, in Marx's words) to another is rooted in the growing contradiction between the forces of production (technological development) and the class or property relations in which they develop.

Because class relations change more slowly than technological development, social change is impeded, fostering conflict between the classes. An example today is the development of computers, which open up possibilities for different class relations and more free time for workers. However, because capitalists control how technology is used, many of the computer's potential gains are not realized. When that class conflict becomes so severe that it blocks the advance of human development, a social revolution sweeps away the existing legal and political arrangements and replaces them with ones more compatible with continued social progress.

In this way, history has evolved through distinct epochs or stages: primitive communism, slavery, feudalism, capitalism, socialism, finally arriving at pure communism. In each of these modes of production, there is a dialectical process whereby inherently unstable and tortured opposing economic forces and counterforces lead to crisis, revolution, and to the next stage of history. And for Marx, the agents of that change are human beings organized in conflicting social classes.

## MARX AND CLASS STRUGGLE

"For Marx," according to economic historian John Kenneth Galbraith, "power was the inescapable fact of economic life; it proceeded from the possession of property and was thus the natural inevitable possession of the capitalist."[6] Caught in history's capitalist era, Marx tried to understand the nature of the political economy and the forces pushing toward crisis and for change. Marx did not approach the questions of political economy from the perspectives of either the liberals or the mercantilists. He did not frame his questions in terms of the individual (market) versus society (state). Rather, influenced by the human relationships that he saw in his factory visits, where the capital-owning **bourgeoisie**, or capitalists, seemingly exploited the laboring **proletariat**, or wage workers, Marx looked at social change from an angle that revealed deep class cleavages. For Marx, a **class** was a set of persons who stood in the same objective relationship to the means of production. According to Todd Buchholz,

> Each system of production creates ruling and ruled classes. Each epoch is marked by a particular way of extracting income for the rulers. In Roman times, whoever owned a slave owned a claim on output. In feudal times, lords owned a claim on the output of serfs. Under capitalism, owners of factories and land owned a claim on the output of their wage laborers.[7]

Critical for Marx is the fundamental imbalance of power between the classes. To a liberal, the bourgeoisie and proletariat should be capable of forming a peaceful and mutually advantageous relationship. To Marx, however, the bourgeoisie and the proletariat are trapped in a decidedly one-sided relationship, with an "unemployed army" of workers frustrating the ability of the labor force to organize itself, and giving the capitalists the upper hand in all negotiations.

The pressure of competition and profit maximization drive the bourgeoisie to ruthlessly exploit the workers they employ. According to Marx and Engels:

> Modern industry has converted the little workshop of patriarchal master into the great factory of the industrial capitalist. Masses of laborers, crowded into the factory, are organized like soldiers. As privates of the industrial army they are placed under the command of a perfect hierarchy of officers and sergeants. Not only are they slaves of the bourgeois class, and of the bourgeois state; they are daily and hourly enslaved by the machine, by the overlooker, and above all, by the individual bourgeois manufacturer himself. The more openly this despotism proclaims gain to be its end and aim, the more petty, the more hateful and the more embittering it is.[8]

Marx argued that the concentration of wealth in the hands of fewer and fewer capitalists leads to the impoverishment of greater numbers of laborers. At the same time, new technology gradually replaces labor, driving up the reserve army of the unemployed and driving down the pay that workers receive. Ultimately, this process results in a mass of proletarian misery, setting the stage for revolution. A popular saying attributed to Marx and Engels is that capitalism produces its own "gravediggers."[9]

Marx is critical of the bourgeoisie for the callous manner in which they treat the proletariat. In *The Communist Manifesto*, he and Engels assert that the bourgeoisie

> . . . has left no other bond between man and man than naked self-interest. . . . It has drowned the most heavenly ecstasies of religious fervor, of chivalrous enthusiasm, of Philistine sentimentalism, in the icy water of egotistical calculation. It has resolved personal worth into exchange value, and in place of the numberless indefeasible chartered freedoms, has set up that single, unconscionable freedom—Free Trade. In one word, for exploitation, veiled by religious and political illusions, it has substituted naked, shameless, direct brutal exploitation.[10]

## MARX AND THE CRISIS OF CAPITALISM

Marx's attitude toward capitalism and exploitation can be frustrating, even if you believe that his views are fundamentally correct. Although he points out the abuses of capitalism, he also finds merit in its effects. Capitalism is, for Marx, more than an unhappy stop on the road to socialism. It is also a *necessary* stage, which builds wealth and raises material living standards. For Marx, it is the dynamic nature of market capitalism that lies at the heart of political economy. Rational men, driven by fierce competition, assault the status quo where they find it, transforming the world.

According to Marxian analysis, capitalism has a historic role, which is to transform the world. In so doing, capitalism accomplishes two goals at once. First, it breaks down slavery and feudalism, which are its historical (and dialectical) antecedents. Second, it creates the social and economic foundations for the eventual transition to a "higher" level of social development.

> The bourgeoisie has through its exploitation of the world market given a cosmopolitan character to production and consumption in every country. . . . The bourgeoisie, by the rapid improvement of all instruments of production, by the immensely facilitated means of communication, draws all nations, even the most barbarian, into civilization. The cheap prices of its commodities are the heavy artillery with which it batters down all Chinese walls, with which it forces the barbarians' intensely obstinate hatred of foreigners to capitulate. It compels all nations, on pain of extinction, to adopt the bourgeois mode of production; it compels them to introduce what it calls civilization into their midst, i.e., to become bourgeois themselves. In a word, it creates a world after its own image.[11]

It seems, then, that the Marxian vision foresees the triumph of capitalism over other world orders.[12] In fact, Marx believes that capitalism is fundamentally flawed. As we discussed earlier, according to Marx, capitalism contains the seeds of its own destruction. The crisis of capitalism is inevitable. Marx identified three objective laws of this mode of production:

- *The law of the falling rate of profit* holds that as capitalists try to gain a competitive advantage by investing in new labor-saving and productive technologies, unemployment increases and the rate of profit decreases. Surplus value (or profit) can only come from living labor and not machines, and because production is increasingly based on less labor, even with very high rates of exploitation of those still working, the rate of profit tends to fall.
- *The law of disproportionality* (also called the *problem of underconsumption*)[13] argues that capitalism, because of its anarchic, unplanned nature, is prone to instability. For a variety of reasons, capitalism is subject to overproduction or, the obverse side of the same coin, underconsumption. That is, capitalists are not able to sell everything they produce at a profit, and workers cannot afford to buy what they make. This disproportionality between supply and demand leads to wild fluctuations in the history of capitalism, with periodic booms and busts. This increases the likelihood of social unrest and the prospects for revolution and change. In response, capitalist governments have often stepped in to smooth out the development of the economy by, for example, creating a large military-industrial complex.
- *The law of concentration* (or *accumulation of capital*) holds that capitalism tends to produce increasing inequality in the distribution of income and wealth. As the bourgeoisie continue to exploit the proletariat and weaker capitalists are swallowed by stronger, bigger ones, wealth and the ownership of capital become increasingly concentrated in fewer and fewer hands. This, then, makes more visible the inequalities in the system and exacerbates the effects of the law of disproportionality, because the mass of impoverished consumers lack purchasing power.

The curse of capitalism, seen in this light, is its deceptive logic. Workers and business owners are indeed all rational individuals, as Adam Smith would have us believe, acting primarily in their own self-interest. In this case, however, the invisible hand does not benignly guide everyone so that all of society benefits. Rather, individual rationality adds up to collective irrationality.

## THREE VIEWS OF COMPETITION: MARX, SMITH, AND THE MERCANTILISTS

The heart of Marx's critique of capitalism is a particular view of competition. Consider how Marx views competition, as compared with Adam Smith and with the early mercantilists. For mercantilists, as we pointed out in Chapter 2, competition is head to head, cutthroat, and zero-sum. Competition is a battle in which one either wins or loses.

Adam Smith, on the other hand, saw competition as a social control on passions and interests. Individuals pursue their own interests most of the time, Smith believed, but conflicting interests do not necessarily produce the brutal conflicts that mercantilists perceive. Rather, competition among sellers prevents any individual seller from having too much power. The seller's passions may drive him or her to take advantage of customers, but the seller's interests, in an environment of fierce competition, force him or her to treat customers honestly and fairly. Employers don't abuse their workers, according to Smith's view of competition, because workers can always seek employment elsewhere. So long as competition is a strong force among buyers and sellers and among workers and employers, the passions are controlled and self-interest is aligned with social interest.

Now let's turn to Marx. What distinguishes Marx's view of society is that he sees the market as a system that links buyers and sellers with workers and employers. Marx was perhaps the first thinker to attempt to understand the market economy as a system, rather than piece by piece. Mercantilists, for example, think of the individual buyer versus the individual seller, each with concentrated power. No wonder they see these relationships as conflictual! Smith and the liberals think of a market with thousands of buyers (or employers) and thousands of sellers (or workers), none of whom has much power because of competition. No wonder they see society as less conflictual and more reasoned than the mercantilists do!

Marx, on the other hand, sees a market system, wherein the mass of workers who produce goods are also, for the most part, the mass of consumers who purchase them. The markets for goods and for workers are therefore tightly linked. This link—the result of thinking in terms of a market system, not just individual markets or individual buyers and sellers—fundamentally changes the nature of competition in Marxian analysis.

The bourgeois factory owners are locked in fierce competition with each other, which drives each of them to try to gain market share by cutting costs, such as through labor-saving technology. As in Smith's world, their self-interest is increased efficiency, which should benefit them and their customers, too. The labor-saving machines, however, reduce the demand for workers. Workers could refuse to accept lower wages, but competition among the proletariat prevents them from doing so. Instead, the proletariat are driven to cutthroat competition for jobs, driving wages and working conditions down to shocking levels, trading even their children's youthful vigor for a little more money.

This would seem to benefit the bourgeoisie, but remember that workers are also consumers. Because they have lower wages now, the proletariat cannot afford to purchase as many goods as before. The demand for factory goods falls, threatening the bourgeoisie. The bourgeoisie react by cutting costs, which forces down wages and, in turn, shrinks market demand, and so on.

In Marx's analysis, the problem is competition. Competition among the bourgeoisie and competition among the proletariat create a system that is not zero-sum, as the mercantilists believe, nor positive-sum, as in liberal thought, but actually negative-sum. Competition ultimately makes both proletariat *and* bourgeoisie worse off. Competition among the proletariat causes them to drive down their own wages. Competition among the bourgeoisie, within the market system described here, systematically drives them out of business and into the ranks of the proletariat. No wonder Marx was so struck by the fundamental contradictions of the competitive capitalist system!

## SUMMING UP MARX

So far, we have just scratched the surface of Marx and Marxism, and a deeper analysis of Marx's work and its influence lies well beyond the scope of this text.[14] (See the box "Marx and Culture.") Let us pause, then, and briefly attempt to restate Marx in a way that will help us in later sections.

Marx's analysis finds a home under the general heading of *structuralism* (or perhaps **economic structuralism**) because he views the economic structure to be the strongest single influence on society.[15] Marx focused on the *production* structure inherent in capitalism, seeing in it a dynamic that produces classes, leads to class struggle, and generates crises that lead to revolution and the next stage in history. For Marx, it is the structure that dominates events, more so than ideas, nature, or military generals. Marx saw people trapped in a production structure that shaped them and that they could change only by acting collectively and heroically.

Marx, then, sees IPE in terms of class exploitation driven by market forces. Where is the state, in Marx's view? Whereas the state is a powerful force to mercantilists, and a dangerous force to liberals, to Marx it is *not* an *independent* force. In Marx's view, the state and the bourgeoisie are intertwined to such an extent that the two cannot be separated. The state exists to support and defend the interests of the dominant class of bourgeois capital owners.

---

### MARX AND CULTURE

Although Marx wrote about economics and class conflict, he was interested in something much larger: society, the social relations that comprise society, and the dynamic that drives it. Marx thought that the most important factors in understanding all of this were production and private property. The basic social relations, including, of course, class relations, were determined by the relationships established at the office, factory, or store. Certainly his classes, the bourgeoisie and the proletariat, are defined this way.

In general, Marx's influence on the study of culture takes the form of an understanding that what happens to individuals is a surface phenomenon, like the surface geology of the earth, that is conditioned by much deeper internal structures. Marxian cultural analysis looks through the surface of society to reveal the structural relationships, much as an X-ray looks through the skin to see the muscles, organs, and bones. Herewith are three admittedly shallow examples of Marxian cultural analysis.[a]

If you have taken an art history class, you have had a chance to see how Western art was transformed during the Italian Renaissance. In the Middle Ages, paintings and sculptures were more symbolic than representative of the natural world. Human figures were wooden and stylized, two-dimensional, and out of perspective. Figures standing together were given size and weight according to their symbolic importance, not according to their actual physical stature. A saint, for example, appears to be 11 feet tall when standing next to a 5-foot-tall feudal lord, who looks down on a 2-foot-tall shepherd. It is hard for untutored modern eyes to look closely at these works of art and appreciate them, even the great ones, because they are so alien to our everyday experiences. They are symbols, to be read like a visual code—not photographs. They are meant to display social and religious images, not the simple images you observe directly.

With the Renaissance, however, art began to display real people, presented in realistic perspective and proper proportion. You can feel the power in the muscles of Michelangelo's *David*, for example; he is *so* real.

Why did art change and become more realistic during the Renaissance? It changed, a Marxian scholar would say, because in Renaissance Italy the means of production changed from the feudal farm to the urban textile factory. The elite class changed, too, from the hereditary aristocracy to the newly rising class of bankers, traders, and factory owners—the early capitalists. The new bourgeoisie had "cruder" tastes—they wanted to see people like themselves in buildings like their own, and they wanted them to be something they could understand. They were not interested in visual codes. They wanted the Renaissance equivalent of photographs. The art did change, too, in just this way, as changing production structures shifted power relations between and among the classes. In a Marxian analysis of art, the answer is fairly clear. Art is expensive, and it is produced to please those who can afford to commission and buy it. Artists produce, generally, what art patrons want to buy. Who could afford expensive art during the Middle Ages? The answer is the elite landowners, who formed a hereditary and therefore nearly impenetrable aristocratic class. *They* were the big figures in those paintings—not as large as Christ or Saint Francis, maybe, but surely a lot bigger than a peasant or a shopkeeper. *They* had the leisure, as well, to study and interpret these art works. The great art of the Middle Ages is great because it served the purposes of the aristocrat class.

Marxian analysis of Renaissance art therefore focuses on how the rise of proto-capitalism in the Italian city-states and the fall of the feudal system changed the dominant socioeconomic class from feudal lords to people like the Medici—rich urban bankers and factory owners with "bourgeois" tastes. This fundamental change in the nature of production is the deep structural change that is important. The transformation of Western art is a surface phenomenon that could not have happened except through the influence of the deeper structural movements.

Let us shift to literature. Literature tells stories about people, and we usually focus on the characters and what they think, how they feel. It is no great leap, however, to consider that the characters are elements of classes, and that their place in society and what happens to them are determined by social structures. The stories of these people can be interpreted in the light of the structural forces and class issues that are revealed in the story. Thus we can read a story on two levels—the individuals in the story and the structures and classes they represent. This is not very hard to do in, for example, John Steinbeck's classic novel of the Great Depression, *The Grapes of Wrath,* or in Tom Wolfe's best-selling novel of the 1980s, *The Bonfire of the Vanities.* When you read these books for the first time, Fate seems to be the main character. In both cases the reader senses early on that a tragedy is in the works—even the book's characters seem to understand this. What is Fate to the people on the surface, however, is in Marxian analysis the force of the deep structures of production and finance, which condition the outcomes experienced by both the Dust Bowl "Okies" and the Wall Street "Masters of the Universe."

Third, films and theater can be subjected to Marxian-type analysis with interesting results. It is not so hard, for example, to see class struggle symbolically represented by the main characters in the movie *Titanic.* In fact, isn't that what the movie is really all about—not some icy boat-versus-iceberg confrontation? Although "Titanic: The Historical Event" is a complex tragedy that wraps together nature, technology, and human folly, "*Titanic:* the Movie" is a tragedy of class struggle. What separates the lovers and is the source of their tragedy is not an iceberg but social class, the difference between first class and steerage, bourgeoisie and proletariat.

What about *The Lion King,* the Disney animated classic? Deep structures are what are important here, too, not the surface tale of singing zoology. Is it difficult to see that the lions in this film are the feudal aristocracy class in the precapitalism era? Certainly they behave like feudal lords and ladies, relying on power to maintain power—they control the local geography, which is their means of production—and their society is even organized as a hereditary monarchy. You cannot get much more feudal than this.

This ruling class is inevitably brought into conflict with the rising capitalist class—played by the "lower" animals in the movie (after all, the lions *eat* them—peaceful class relations shouldn't be expected under these circumstances!). The hyenas, who have the least "refined" taste of all the animals in the film, are the future bourgeoisie. Marx would tell us that it is their role to rise up and destroy the feudal lion kingdom so as to make way for the next stage of history: capitalism. For Marx, deep structural forces make history a straight line of change: feudalism → capitalism → socialism → communism. The feudal lions, however, want to hold onto what they've got, so they sing about a "circle of life," which keeps coming back around, always with them on the top and the other animals on the bottom.

If Marx had written *The Lion King,* the lions would be overthrown, as the feudal lords were in real life, and the "lower" animals would take over. In the Marxian version, the melodious critters on the screen are just surface phenomena, and their individual stories aren't what's really important: The real story is about structural change and class conflict. In Marxian analysis, the hyenas inherit the earth, but then the story goes on. Soon a class-based hierarchy is established among these animals, based on ownership of the means of production, and the crisis of capitalism begins to loom over the African landscape. (Can you see George Orwell's *Animal Farm* falling into place at this point?).

In Marx's *Lion King,* lions lose, the king dies, the hyenas take their place, and history moves on to its next stage. The Disney studios wanted a happy ending, however, so the lions win, Simba becomes king, and the circle of feudal exploitation continues. This makes the lions happy, presumably, but it seems unlikely that Marx and Engels would give it "two thumbs up."

*Reference*

[a] In this box we discuss Marxian cultural analysis; some elements of this analysis are called structuralism, just as we call the overall IPE perspective discussed here structuralism, and often the general approach is the same: Structure conditions outcome. However, we intentionally avoid using the term *structuralism* in this box because its use in cultural studies is not consistently the same as or similar to its use in IPE. That is, some structuralist theories are based on different concepts of structure than those we consider in IPE.

## LENIN AND IMPERIALISM

V. I. Lenin (1870–1924) is best known for his role in the Russian Revolution of 1917 and the founding of the Soviet Union. Lenin symbolized for many people the principles and ideas of the 1917 revolution. In fact, in many ways, Lenin turned Marx on his head, placing politics over economics, when he argued that Russia had gone through its capitalist stage of history and was ready for a second, socialist revolution.

Here we focus on Lenin's ideas about imperialism more than on his revolutionary strategies. Lenin developed a perspective on IPE that took Marx's class struggle, based on the mode of production, and used it to explain capitalism's international effects as transmitted through the production and finance structures of rich industrial countries to the poorer developing regions of the world. Lenin's famous summary of his views is titled *Imperialism: The Highest Stage of Capitalism* (1917).[16]

Marx said that capitalism, driven by its three laws, would come to revolutionary crisis and suffer internal class revolt, paving the way for the transition to socialism. Lenin observed that capitalist nations had avoided this crisis by *expanding* the pool of workers they exploited. Capitalism, he argued, "had escaped its three laws of motion through overseas imperialism. The acquisition of colonies had enabled the capitalist economies to dispose of their unconsumed goods, to acquire cheap resources, and to vent their surplus capital."[17]

In short, Lenin added to Marx what Robert Gilpin has called a "fourth law" of capitalism, which we might call the *law of capitalist imperialism:* "As capitalist economies mature, as capital accumulates, and as profit rates fall, the capitalist economies are compelled to seize colonies and create dependencies to serve as markets, investment outlets, and sources of food and raw materials. In competition with one another, they divide up the colonial world in accordance with their relative strengths."[18]

To Lenin, imperialism is another portion of the capitalist epoch of history (referred to as the highest stage of capitalism) that the world must endure on the road to communism. According to Lenin, "Monopoly is the transition from capitalism to a higher system."[19]

The critical element fueling imperialism, in Lenin's view, was the decline of national economic competition and the growth of monopolies. Based on Marx's law of concentration, what emerged was an aggregation of market power into the hands of a few "cartels, syndicates and trusts, and merging with them, the capital of a dozen or so banks manipulating thousands of millions." Lenin goes on to argue that

> Monopoly is exactly the opposite of free competition; but we have seen the latter being transformed into monopoly before our very eyes, creating large-scale industry and eliminating small industry, replacing large-scale industry by still larger-scale industry, finally leading to such a concentration of production and capital that monopoly has been and is the result.[20]

The key for Lenin was that because monopolies concentrated capital, they could not find sufficient investment opportunities in industrial regions of the world. They therefore found it necessary to export capital around the globe to earn sufficient profits.

Lenin argued that imperialist expansion allowed capitalism to postpone its inevitable crisis and metamorphose into socialism. It also created new, serious problems for the world. Lenin viewed World War I as an imperialist war, caused by tensions that arose from the simultaneous expansion of several European empires. As nations at the core of capitalism competed to expand their exploitative spheres, their interests intersected and conflicted with one another, producing the Great War.

Lenin's role in the revolution of 1917 was to help defeat liberal political forces that sought to keep Russia within the European capitalist system. Under Lenin's leadership, Russia essentially withdrew from Europe and its imperialist conflicts, resolving to move quickly and on its own toward a communist system free of class conflict and imperialist wars.

## LENIN AND INTERNATIONAL CAPITALISM

Lenin's imperialist theory of capitalism has been very influential, so it is worthwhile considering briefly a few other aspects of his analysis. Lenin sought to explain how it was that capitalism shifted from internal to international exploitation, and how the inequality among classes had as its parallel the law of uneven development among nations.

For Lenin, profit-seeking capitalists could not be expected to use surplus capital to improve the living standards of the proletariat. Therefore, capitalist societies would remain unevenly developed, with some classes prospering as others were mired in poverty. The imperial phase of capitalism simply transferred this duality of wealth and poverty onto the world stage. Capitalists, seeking to maintain and even increase their profits, exported exploitation to what contemporaries of Lenin called "backward" regions of the world. These poor peripheral countries were now integrated into the world economy as the new "proletariat" of the world. According to Lenin:

> Monopolist capitalist combines—cartels, syndicates, trusts—divide among themselves, first of all, the whole internal market of a country, and impose their control, more or less completely, upon the industry of that country. But under capitalism the home market is inevitably bound up with the foreign market. Capitalism long ago created a world market.[21]

The uneven development of society within a nation now took place on an international scale.

Lenin saw imperial capitalism spreading through two structures of the IPE: production and finance. Both of these structures were so constituted, under capitalism, as to create dependency and facilitate exploitation. Cutthroat competition among poorer nations made them easy targets for monopolies in the production structure in the capitalist core. The same forces were at work within the finance structure, where the superabundance of finance capital, controlled by monopolistic banks, was used to exploit less developed countries.

The bottom line of **imperialism**, for Lenin, was that the rich capitalist nations were able to delay their final crisis by keeping the poorer nations underdeveloped and deep in debt, and dependent on the rich nations for manufactured goods, jobs, and financial resources. It is not surprising, then, that Lenin's theory of imperialism has been very influential, especially among intellectuals in the less developed countries, where his views have shaped policy and attitudes toward international trade and finance generally.

We include Lenin's theory of imperialism under the general heading of "structuralism," as we did with Marx's theories, because its analysis is based on the assumption that it is in capitalism's nature for the finance and production structures among nations to be biased in favor of the owners of capital. In theory, the relationship between capital-abundant nations and capital-scarce nations should be one of *interdependence*, because each needs the other for maximum growth, but in practice the result is *dependence, exploitation, and uneven development*. The same forces that drive the bourgeoisie to exploit the proletariat ultimately drive the capitalist core nations to dominate and exploit less developed countries.

No attempt to consider the IPE of relations between developed and developing countries is complete without taking theories of imperialism into account. To some extent, Lenin's ideas are the basis of the theories of dependency and of the modern world system, to which we now turn.

## MODERN WORLD SYSTEM THEORY

One fascinating contemporary variant of the structuralist perspective focuses on the way in which the global system has developed since the middle of the fifteenth century. This is the **modern world system (MWS)** theory[22] originated by Immanuel Wallerstein and developed by a number of scholars, including Christopher Chase-Dunn. Capitalist in nature, the world system largely determines political and social relations, both within and between nations and other international entities.

For Wallerstein, the world economy provides the sole means of organization in the international system. The modern world system exhibits the following characteristics: a single division of labor whereby nation-states are mutually dependent on economic exchange; the sale of products and goods for the sake of profit; and, finally, the division of the world into three functional areas or socioeconomic units, which correspond to the roles that nations within these regions play in the international economy.

From the MWS perspective the capitalist core states of northwest Europe in the sixteenth century moved beyond agricultural specialization to higher-skilled industries and modes of production by penetrating and absorbing other regions into the capitalist world economy. Through this process, Eastern Europe became the agricultural periphery and exported grains, bullion, wood, cotton, and sugar to the core. Mediterranean Europe and its labor-intensive industries became the **semi-periphery** or intermediary between the core and periphery.

It would be easy to define the core, periphery, and semiperiphery in terms of the types of nations within each group (such as the United States, China, and Korea, respectively), but the MWS is not based primarily on the nation-state. In this theory, the core represents a geographic region made up of nation-states that play a partial role in the modern world system. The force of bourgeois interests actually exists, in varying degrees, in every country. Every nation has elements of core, periphery, and semiperiphery, although not equally so. In common with Marx, then, the MWS theory looks at IPE in terms of class relations and patterns of exploitation.

According to Wallerstein, the core states dominate the peripheral states through unequal exchange for the purpose of extracting cheap raw materials instead of, as Lenin argued, merely using the periphery as a market for dumping surplus production. The core interacts with the semiperiphery and periphery through the global structure of capitalism, exploiting these regions and also transforming them. The semiperiphery serves more of a political than an economic role; it is both exploited and exploiter, diffusing opposition of the periphery to the core region.

Interestingly, on some issues, Wallerstein attempts to bridge mercantilism (and political realism) with Marxist views about the relationship of politics to economics. For instance, as a mercantilist would, he accepts the notion that the world is politically arranged in an anarchical manner—that is, there is no *single* sovereign political authority to govern interstate relations. However, much like a Marxist-Leninist, he proposes that power politics and social differences are also conditioned by the capitalist structure of the world economy.

According to Wallerstein, capitalists within core nation-states use state authority as an instrument to maximize individual profit. Historically, the state served economic interests to the extent that "state machineries of the core states were strengthened to meet the needs of capitalist landowners and their merchant allies."[23] Wallerstein also argues that, "once created," state machineries have a certain amount of autonomy.[24] On the other hand, politics is constrained by economic structure. He asserts, for instance, that strong (core) states dominate weak (peripheral) ones because placement of the nation-state in the world capitalist system affects its ability to influence its global role. As Wallerstein puts it, "The functioning then of a capitalist world economy requires that groups pursue their economic interests within a single world market while seeking to distort this market for their benefit by organizing to exert influence on states, some of which are far more powerful than others but none of which controls the world-market in its entirety."[25]

Wallerstein's conception of the modern world system has gained a good deal of notoriety in the last twenty years. He offers us a recipe composed of ideas and concepts that are relatively easy to understand and that account for a large part of the relationship of Northern (developed) to Southern (developing) nations. "Semiperiphery" also seems to fit the status of the newly industrialized countries (NICs). Furthermore, the MWS approach to structuralism sees exploitation as an inherent element of the capitalist structures both within and among core, periphery, and semiperiphery.

One problem with Wallerstein's theory is precisely what makes it so attractive: his comprehensive yet almost simple way of characterizing IPE. Many criticize his theory for being too deterministic, both economically and in terms of the constraining effects of the *global* capitalist system. Nation-states, according to Wallerstein, are not free to choose courses of action or policies. Instead, they are relegated to playing economically determined roles. Finally, Wallerstein is faulted for viewing capitalism as the end product of current history.

## DEPENDENCY THEORY

Another contemporary variant of the structuralist perspective is called **dependency theory**. A wide range of views can be grouped together under this heading. Their differences, however, are less important to us here than what they have in common, which is the view that the structure of the global political economy essentially enslaves the less developed countries of the "South" by making them dependent on the nations of the capitalist core of the "North."[26] Theotonio Dos Santos has written:

> By dependence we mean a situation in which the economy of certain countries is conditioned by the development and expansion of another economy to which the former is subjected. The relation of interdependence between two or more economies, and between these and world trade, assumes the form of dependence when some countries (the dominant ones) can expand and can be self-sustaining, while others (the dependent ones) can do this only as a reflection of that expansion, which can have either a positive or a negative effect on their immediate development.[27]

Dos Santos sees three eras of dependence in modern history: colonial dependence (during the eighteenth and nineteenth centuries), financial-industrial dependence (during the nineteenth and early twentieth centuries), and a structure of dependence today based on the postwar multinational corporations.

One dependency theorist in particular has focused a good deal of attention on the effects of imperialism in Latin America. Andre Gunder Frank rejects the Marxist notion that societies go through different stages or modes of production as they develop. However, he supports the imperialism thesis that connections between developed and developing regions of the world resulted in exploitation of peripheral regions by metropolitan capitalist countries.

Frank is noted for his "development of underdevelopment" thesis. He argues that developing nations were never "underdeveloped" in the sense that one might think of them as "backward" or traditional societies. Instead, once great civilizations in their own right, the developing regions of the world *became* underdeveloped as a result of their colonization by the Western industrialized nations. Along with exploitation, imperialism produced underdevelopment: "Historical research demonstrates that contemporary underdevelopment is in large part the historical product of past and continuing economic and other relations between the satellite underdeveloped and the now developed metropolitan countries."[28]

How are developing nations to develop if in fact they are exploited by the developed capitalist industrial powers? Dependency theorists have suggested a variety of responses to this trap. A number of researchers—Frank, for example—have called for peripheral nations to withdraw from the global political economy. In the 1950s and 1960s, the leadership of many socialist movements in the Third World favored revolutionary tactics and ideological mass movements to change not only the fundamental dynamic of both the political and economic order of their society, but also the world capitalist system.

More recently, dependency theorists have recommended a variety of other strategies and policies by which developing nations could industrialize and develop. Raul Prebisch, an Argentinean economist, was instrumental in founding, under the auspices of the United Nations, the United Nations Committee on Trade and Development (UNCTAD). The developing nations that have joined this body have made it their goal to monitor and recommend policies that would, in effect, help redistribute power and income between Northern developed and Southern developing countries. These and other dependency theorists, however, have been more aggressive about reforming the international economy and have supported the calls for a "new international economic order" (NIEO), which gained momentum shortly after the OPEC oil price hike in 1973.

The important point to make here is that dependency theories have served as part of a critique of the relationship of metropolitan to satellite, or core to peripheral, nations. Whether that relationship can—or even should—be equalized is a matter developed elsewhere. These theories will be important to our discussion of "the two faces of development" in Chapter 15.

## ANTONIO GRAMSCI AND INTELLECTUAL HEGEMONY

One of the most influential structuralists of the twentieth century—and one whose ideas are particularly relevant to the global political economy of the twenty-first—is the Italian Marxist Antonio Gramsci (1891–1937). Gramsci's work deepens our understanding of structuralism and provides a broader account of the nature of class relations both between core and periphery and within the core itself.

Gramsci lived in a time of tremendous economic and political tension, when the globalized world of the early twentieth century was torn apart by conflicts among nations and between classes. He proposed a philosophy of *praxis*—that we should demonstrate our beliefs through our actions—and both edited an intellectual journal, *Ordine Nuovo* (The New Order) and led worker protests in the Italian industrial center of Turin, especially against the manufacturing giant FIAT. His political and intellectual activities drew the attention of Italy's pro-industry fascist government, which imprisoned him. In his *Prison Notebooks*, Gramsci attempted to revise Marxist theory to account for changing conditions in the advanced industrial world. He died in prison at the age of 46.

The dominant class in society maintains its position, according to Gramsci, in two fundamentally different ways: through coercion and through consent. Coercion is an obvious mechanism, applying economic and political power directly to keep the subordinate class in line. In Gramsci's time, for example, government police and manufacturer-backed thugs employed violence against protesting workers. In contemporary times, one might substitute the images of police at antiglobalization protests such as the 1999 World Trade Organization meetings in Seattle, Washington.

Coercion is a powerful tool, Gramsci said, but ideas are even more powerful because they allow rule of the masses. Here's how **intellectual hegemony** creates consent. The dominant class produces and promulgates an ideology or worldview that supports and legitimizes its interests. These ideas permeate society through education and the communications media. Once the subordinate class accepts this worldview, whether intentionally or by osmosis, its thoughts and actions are brought into line with the interests of the dominant class. Police are not necessary because the idea of taking actions that oppose the dominant class is not part of society's accepted values and norms. Anyone who opposes the dominant class opposes society and so is by definition a criminal and lacks legitimacy. Thought organizes society more effectively than riot police because thought produces consent.

Some of the writings of George Orwell, such as *1984* and *Animal Farm*, suggest to us the power of ideas that Gramsci proposed. Both of these books stress the importance of official propaganda. The ruling class does not need police to organize society in its interests if it can do so through ideas—through its control of education and the communications media. Many contemporary writings, such as Benjamin R. Barber's *Jihad vs. McWorld* (see Suggested Readings), which oppose the increasing control of global media by an elite group of private owners, express a Gramscian-type concern about intellectual hegemony.

In Gramsci's vision there are no truly independent intellectuals. Traditional intellectuals, such as professors, like to "put themselves forward as autonomous and independent of the dominant group,"[29] but this self-image is inaccurate, as all intellectuals are products of particular historical events and social relationships. What is needed is for workers to develop, from within their class, **organic intellectuals** who remain connected to their class but give it organization, leadership, and a vocabulary that challenges the ideology of the dominant class and articulates a different vision of the future. If they can also win over many of the traditional intellectuals, the formulation of a counter-hegemonic ideology becomes all the more likely and legitimate. Schools, colleges, newspaper cartoons and editorials, political slogans, songs, and coffee shop debates will then reverberate with debate and demands for change.

Gramsci's theory of intellectual hegemony suggests that structural tensions are not limited to the areas of international trade and finance. Rather, they are built into our daily lives through the forces that condition what we think and don't think about the societies in which we live.

## THE STRUCTURALIST ANALYSIS OF MODERN SOCIETY

The notion that economic structures have a strong (some would say a determining) influence on social structures is a theme that runs from Marx to McDonald's. It is an important contribution to the structuralist critique of capitalist society. Marx observed that the structure of human relations determined by the factory (the creator of the proletariat and bourgeoisie classes) was reflected throughout society. If you had walked with Marx through the streets of London in 1848, you would have found it easy to tell the houses of the proletariat from those of the bourgeoisie, for example. Their clothes, their clubs, even the way their children talked and the games they played, were all different because of the unequal relations established on the factory floor. Economic structures are very powerful indeed.

The German sociologist and political economist Max Weber (1864–1920) was influenced by Marx, but believed that Marx was wrong to argue that economic structures determine society's path. Weber believed that religion and ethics are also important. Nonetheless, Weber's analysis of capitalism and its effects on society has been powerfully influential. Weber observed that it is the nature of capitalist production to rationalize and bureaucratize the factory, making it more and more efficient if less and less human. It follows, according to Weber, that it is the nature of capitalist society to also attempt to rationalize and bureaucratize. Thus, in structuralist analysis, Henry Ford's production-line technology of the 1920s became "Fordism"—the idea of a production-line society. The same is true of "Taylorism," named for Frederick Taylor, the author of *The Principles of Scientific Management* (1911) and the father of time–motion studies of worker efficiency. Ford and Taylor created a highly hierarchical production system with a rational, efficient division of labor. It is no accident, a structuralist would say, that soon other elements of society—schools, hospitals, and perhaps even churches—reflected these same rational organization principles. As production became more efficient and less personal, the structure of society followed suit, with consequences that are perhaps as pervasive as they are important.

The Hungarian Marxist Georg Lukács (1885–1971), for example, concluded that the unrelenting drive to rationalize and simplify production gradually dulled the minds of workers (a possibility that Adam Smith noted even before Karl Marx did). Lukács went further, however, concluding that it actually made the people stupid, unable to think clearly because their minds were as fragmented and bureaucratized as the offices and factories where they worked.

In a world defined by the division of labor, no one needed to understand the whole, only his or her rationally simplified particular job. In the same way, no one needed to (or, in the end, could) understand society or culture, either. People could not understand the system that ensnared them and could not, therefore, recognize their own (class) interests, as Lukács wrote in his famous essay on "Class Consciousness" (see Suggested Readings). Like Gramsci, Lukács looked to intellectuals to reveal the truth to the rest of society, especially through drama, art, and literature.

Austrian-American economist Joseph Schumpeter (1883–1950) was not a Marxist or a structuralist, but he also noted the rationalizing effect of capitalism. In his classic work, *Capitalism, Socialism, and Democracy* (see Suggested Readings), Schumpeter explained that capitalism would eventually crumble and make way for socialism, just as Marx had predicted, but for a very different reason. The workers of the world would not unite to revolt. Rather, capitalism would collapse inward upon itself as a result of its own rationalizing tendency. Schumpeter, you see, viewed capitalism as a process of "creative destruction" that was driven by the leadership of heroic entrepreneurs. Entrepreneurs took great personal risks, as great leaders often must do, and created new products, technologies, and industries (destroying the older products, processes, and industries they made obsolete). But rational calculation is the enemy of heroic risk taking. Eventually, Schumpeter wrote, the rationalizing tendencies of capitalism would eliminate the dynamic, risk-taking gene from capitalism's genetic makeup, leaving it a placid, stagnant creature that would easily make the transition to socialism.

Interestingly, Schumpeter believed that the same fate awaited democracy. He saw democracy as a dynamic market for leadership that helped society to progress because it rewarded heroic political entrepreneurs. However, as reason transformed society, he believed, real political leadership would be replaced by rational calculation, and democracy would also stagnate. Visionary leaders would be replaced by calculating elected bureaucrats who would make policy with a constant eye on voter poll results.

Recently, American sociologist George Ritzer and others have begun to study how the logic of production has begun to change the logic of consumption. Ritzer's best-selling book, *The McDonaldization of Society* (see Suggested Readings) extends Weber's theory to explain changing consumer behavior. Ritzer picked McDonald's as his key example because of how easy it is to see Ford and Taylor production-line influences on both sides of the counter. The efficient division of labor that produces the food is matched by the degree to which consumers behave like industrial robots, lining up to order, filling their own drinks, clearing their own tables, efficiently moving in and out through the doors. (The production-line metaphor is even stronger if we look at the "drive thru" line!)

More and more of society is coming to look like a McDonald's, Ritzer argues. And, of course, McDonald's looks like a factory custom-built for the efficient production and consumption of standardized food commodities. That the world looks this way derives fundamentally, in the view of structuralists, from the power of economic structures in society, which is why we present the **McDonaldization hypothesis** here in the chapter on structuralism. Through the work of Ritzer and others, the structuralist critique of capitalism and of capitalist society continues to evolve and remain relevant.

## STRUCTURALISM IN PERSPECTIVE

Some people ask whether studying Marxism or structuralism in the postcommunist era is worthwhile. The answer is yes (see the box, "Structuralism Today"). The structuralist perspective encompasses far more than the Soviet model of communism. This perspective on IPE is revealing and represents a powerful intellectual and political influence.

Indeed, noted historian Eric Hobsbawm observed, in his introduction to the one-hundred-fiftieth anniversary edition of Marx and Engel's *Communist Manifesto,* that it makes more sense to consider Marx's ideas now than at any previous time in history.[30] Marx looked ahead and saw what capitalism would do to the world, including the class conflicts that would unavoidably arise. The world of 1848, when the *Manifesto* was written, was not yet the world of the crisis of capitalism. However, Hobsbawm says:

> We now live in a world in which this transformation has largely taken place. . . . In some ways we can even see the force of the Manifesto's predictions more clearly than the generations between us and its publication. . . . In short, what might in 1848 have struck an uncommitted reader as revolutionary rhetoric—or, at best, plausible prediction, can now be read as a concise characterization of capitalism at the end of the twentieth century. Of what other document of the 1840s can this be said?[31]

---

### STRUCTURALISM TODAY: THE LOGIC OF GLOBAL CAPITALISM

It is commonplace today to say that Marx died with the fall of the Berlin Wall in 1989. The collapse of communism has put to an end the grand social experiment that began more than 150 years ago with *The Communist Manifesto* (1848). Although it is not the aim of this book to predict the future, it is almost certainly true that it is too soon to bury Marx. There are at least three good reasons to study Marx and the structuralist perspective built on his analysis of class struggle.

First, Marx presents us with powerful ideas that are worth studying as theory or philosophy or, as we saw earlier, cultural critique. Marx was the first political economist to present a theory of the dynamic development of society, which sought to explain not only politics and economics, but also the social relationships on which they are based. Serious students of political economy must study Marx to understand and appreciate the power of theory to shape our understanding of everyday events.[a]

Second, it is important to understand that communism is not the same as Marxism. Communism, as practiced in the former Soviet Union and elsewhere, was an economic, political, and social organization that, although rooted in the theoretical writings of Marx and Lenin, had relatively little to do with these ideas in practice. (See Chapter 14 for a more thorough analysis of the communist system of political economy.)

The practical problems of constructing a modern socialist state from the available feudal raw materials forced Lenin and then Stalin to institute many pragmatic policies that would surely have drawn scorn from Karl Marx. Marxian methods were sacrificed in an attempt to deal with critical short-term problems. The harsh international environment of World War II and the Cold War forced further deviations from Marx's goal of the withering away of the state. The bottom line is that communism had little to do in practical terms with Marxian philosophy. The collapse of communism should be seen as the rejection of a particular system of political economy and social relations, not necessarily as a refutation of Marx's ideas.

The third reason to study Marx and structuralism today is that some people believe that the process of globalization that we can see everywhere around us today is constructing a world that looks more and more like the world that Marx and Lenin wrote about. Two recent books, one by William Greider and one by Jeff Faux, illustrate this point in rather different ways (see Suggested Readings). In *One World, Ready or Not: The Manic Logic of Global Capitalism,* Greider writes that "Marxism is dead, the Communist system utterly discredited by human experience, but the ghost of Marx hovers over the global landscape, perhaps with a knowing smile. The gross conditions that inspired Karl Marx's original critique of capitalism in the nineteenth century are present and flourishing again. The world has reached not only the end of ideology, but also the beginnings of the next great conflict over the nature of capitalism."[b] Greider's analysis makes fascinating political economy. Keynesian economic policies (see Chapter 3) postponed the crisis of capitalism during the Great Depression of the 1930s. However, the renaissance of classical liberalism in the 1980s and the 1990s removed many of the state policies that had for fifty years tempered the "manic logic" of Marx's three laws of capitalism.

Now, unfettered capitalism is engulfing the world in the form of "globalization." The essence of globalization, Greider proposes, is the desire to produce more and more for less and less in search of profit. It is competition that is ultimately destructive to all parties, as Marx predicted.

What is the likely result of this vicious cycle of greater output, surplus, lower prices, lower wages, and falling profits? In the long run the crisis of capitalism looms as one possibility, Greider thinks. Faced with global recession, he believes that people will seek political solutions that could lead to the sort of radical nationalism that drove the fascist parties in Europe in the 1930s. Indeed, one doesn't have to look too hard to see early indicators of this trend in some nationalist and racist political movements around the world today.

In the short term, however, the exploitation of labor is the real problem. Thus Greider calls for a twenty-first-century version of "Workers of the World Unite" in the form of global unions. Only global unions would have the power to deal with global firms in global markets. Even so, there would still be the need for some sort of "global Keynesianism" to try to balance global demand with global supply and control capitalism's propensity to rational irrationality.

In the end, Greider cannot help but be a pessimist. Like Marx, he sees the forces driving the global economy to its own destruction as inevitable. Marx, however, accepted this as part of the great plan of history. Having seen the misery that nationalism, racism, and religious fundamentalism can produce, Greider cannot be as sanguine as Marx.

Jeff Faux, in *The Global Class War: How America's Bipartisan Elite Lost Our Future—And What It Will Take to Win It Back,* sees more human control behind the direction globalization is taking and is therefore more optimistic. What human beings have wrought, they can change. Using a structuralist framework, Faux paints a picture of the class struggle between capitalists and workers shifting from a national to a global arena. He claims that "as globalization integrates investors, managers, and professionals across borders, it merges their class interests across borders"[c] such that they increasingly put "class before country."[d] He calls this burgeoning global governing class the "Party of Davos," after the name of the exclusive Swiss resort where these elites meet to socialize and discuss the rules that should govern the process of globalization. To Faux, these rules ignore workers' rights and exacerbate inequalities within and among countries.

What is needed, Faux argues, are counterstrategies from those opposed to neoliberal globalization. Cross-border trade union collaboration would be a logical counterweight to global corporations, but in practice union movements in the developed countries are weak and on the defensive. Environmental, religious, university and other activists have been able to mount counterconventions to Davos in the Brazilian city of Porto Allegre. About 150,000 people attended in 2005. However, Faux believes that this opposition, which he calls the "Party of Porto Allegre," is "too diverse, too disconnected from the core culture of the global working class, and without a political vehicle to contest for global political power."[e] Faux advocates an interesting additional strategy: Citizens in the United States, Canada, and Mexico should campaign for a social democratic agenda within a North American Union modeled loosely on the European Union. Such a regional project, made more feasible because of the close economic, geographic, and cultural links among the three countries, would provide a more democratic and just model of economic integration.

*References*

[a] See Joseph Schumpeter, *Capitalism, Socialism and Democracy* (see Suggested Readings). Special attention should be given to "Part I: The Marxian Doctrine."

[b] William Greider, *One World, Ready or Not: The Manic Logic of Global Capitalism* (New York: Simon & Schuster, 1997), p. 39.

[c] Jeff Faux, *The Global Class War: How America's Bipartisan Elite Lost Our Future—And What It Will Take to Win It Back* (Hoboken, NJ: John Wiley, 2001), p. 157.

[d] Ibid., p. 112.

[e] Ibid., p. 175.

## DISCUSSION QUESTIONS

1. After reading the chapter, compare and contrast structuralism with mercantilism and liberalism in the following areas:
   a. The dominant actors
   b. Political versus economic motivation behind actor behavior
   c. The role of the state in the economy
2. Compare and contrast Marx's and Lenin's views of capitalism. How and why did their views differ? Be specific and give examples from the chapter.
3. What are the distinguishing features of imperialism in Lenin's analysis? Why did he call it "the highest form of capitalism"?
4. Outline the essential characteristics/features of Marxism, dependency theory, and the modern world system approach.
5. Explain Antonio Gramsci's theory of intellectual hegemony as a means of achieving social order and compare it with the liberal theory of hegemonic stability discussed in Chapter 3.
6. How does George Ritzer's analysis of the "McDonaldization" of society reflect the structuralist viewpoint?

## INTERNET LINKS

One Hundred Fifty Years of the Communist Manifesto:
    www.marxist.com/150years/index.html

Marxists.org internet archive and encyclopedia of Marxism:
    www.marxists.org

Fernand Braudel Center for the Study of Economics, Historical Systems, and Civilizations (Immanuel Wallerstein, Director):
    http://fbc.binghamton.edu

Antonio Gramsci Resources at Theory.org.uk:
    www.theory.org.uk/ctr-gram.htm

McDonaldization.com:
    www.mcdonaldization.com/main.shtml

The World-Systems Archives
    http://wsarch.ucr.edu

Dependency Theory: An Introduction:
    www.mtholyoke.edu/acad/intrel/depend.htm

## SUGGESTED READINGS

Benjamin R. Barber. *Jihad vs. McWorld*. New York: Ballantine, 1995, 2001.

Christopher Chase-Dunn. *Global Formation: Structures of the World Economy*. Cambridge, MA: Basil Blackwell, 1989.

Benjamin J. Cohen. *The Question of Imperialism*. New York: Basic Books, 1973.

Theotonio Dos Santos. "The Structure of Dependency," in George T. Crane and Abla Amawi, eds., *The Theoretical Evolution of International Political Economy*. New York: Oxford University Press, 1990.

Jeff Faux, *The Global Class War: How America's Bipartisan Elite Lost Our Future—And What It Will Take to Win It Back*. Hoboken, NJ: John Wiley, 2001.

Antonio Gramsci. *Selections from the Prison Notebooks*, Quintin Hoare and Geoffrey Nowell Smith, transl. and eds. London: Lawrence and Wishart, 1971.

William Greider. *One World, Ready or Not: The Manic Logic of Global Capitalism*. New York: Simon & Schuster, 1997.

V. I. Lenin. *Imperialism: The Highest Stage of Capitalism*. New York: International Publishers, 1939.

Georg Lukács. "Class Consciousness," in Arpad Kadarkay, ed., *The Lukács Reader*. Oxford: Blackwell, 1995.

Karl Marx. *Capital*, Friedrich Engels, ed. Chicago: Encyclopedia Britannica, 1952.

Karl Marx and Friedrich Engels. *The Communist Manifesto: A Modern Edition* (with an introduction by Eric Hobsbawm). New York: Verso, 1998. Be sure to read Hobsbawm's introduction.

George Ritzer. *The McDonaldization of Society*. Thousand Oaks, CA: Pine Forge, 1996.

Joseph Schumpeter. *Capitalism, Socialism, and Democracy*. New York: Harper & Brothers, 1942.

Max Weber. *The Theory of Social and Economic Organization*, A. M. Henderson, trans. and ed. Talcott Parsons, ed. New York: The Free Press, 1947.

## KEY TERMS

| | | |
|---|---|---|
| structuralism | economic structuralism | semiperiphery |
| historical materialism | imperialism | dependency theory |
| bourgeoisie | modern world system (MWS) | intellectual hegemony |
| proletariat | core | organic intellectuals |
| class | periphery | McDonaldization hypothesis |

## NOTES

1. Karl Marx and Friedrich Engels, *The Communist Manifesto*, Samuel Beer, ed. (New York: Appleton-Century-Crofts, 1955), p. 9.
2. V. I. Lenin, *Imperialism: The Highest Stage of Capitalism* (New York: International Publishers, 1939), p. 89.
3. Joan Robinson, "Trade in Primary Commodities," in Jeffrey A. Frieden and David A. Lake, eds., *International Political Economy*, 2nd ed. (New York: St Martin's, 1991), p. 376.
4. For a discussion of Marx's methodology, see Todd G. Buchholz, *New Ideas from Dead Economists* (New York: New American Library, 1989), pp. 113–120.
5. Karl Marx, *The Poverty of Philosophy* (New York: International Publishers, 1963), p. 122.
6. John Kenneth Galbraith, *Economics in Perspective* (Boston: Houghton-Mifflin, 1987), p. 133.
7. Buchholz, *New Ideas from Dead Economists*, p. 115.
8. Marx and Engels, *The Communist Manifesto*, p. 17.
9. Ibid., p. 22.
10. Ibid., p. 12.
11. Ibid., pp. 13–14.
12. See the comments by Václav Havel regarding the "cult of the market" in Chapter 3 for an indication of this viewpoint.
13. A more analytical definition of disproportionality and its place in Marx's theory can be found in Paul M. Sweezy, *The Theory of Capitalist Development* (New York: Monthly Review Press, 1970), chap. 5.
14. See the Suggested Readings on Marx and Marxism for this chapter.
15. We have used the term *structuralism* in a general sense here. At a more advanced level, "economic structuralism" is differentiated from "political structuralism." In economic structuralism, it is the structure of economic relations that influences society most. In political structuralism, it is the structure of political power that is most influential.

16. Lenin, *Imperialism*.
17. Robert Gilpin, *The Political Economy of International Relations* (Princeton, NJ: Princeton University Press, 1987), p. 38.
18. Ibid., p. 39.
19. Lenin argues that "this is a new stage of world concentration of capital and production, incomparably higher than the preceding stages." Lenin, *Imperialism,* p. 68.
20. Ibid., p. 88.
21. Ibid., p. 68.
22. Immanuel Wallerstein, "The Rise and Future Demise of the World Capitalist System: Concepts for Comparative Analysis," *Comparative Studies in Society and History,* 16 (September 1974), pp. 387–415.
23. Ibid., p. 402.
24. Ibid.
25. Ibid., p. 406.
26. Dependency theory is thus seen as an interpretation of North–South IPE relations.
27. Theotonio Dos Santos, "The Structure of Dependence," *American Economic Review, 60* (1970), pp. 231–236.
28. Andre Gunder Frank, *Capitalism and Underdevelopment in Latin America: Historical Studies of Chile and Brazil* (New York: Monthly Review Press, 1967), p. 9.
29. Antonio Gramsci, *Selections from the Prison Notebooks,* Quintin Hoare and Geoffrey Nowell Smith, transl. and eds. (New York: International Publishers), p. 7.
30. Eric Hobsbawm, "Introduction," in Karl Marx and Friedrich Engels, *The Communist Manifesto: A Modern Edition* (New York: Verso, 1998), pp. 3–29.
31. Hobsbawm, "Introduction," pp. 17–18.

# Alternative Perspectives of International Political Economy

## OVERVIEW

International political economy (IPE) is about states, markets, and society. It is also about *more than* these entities, as the analysis of the past four chapters should have made clear. Still, it is deceptively easy to oversimplify IPE: Liberalism is about laissez-faire, free markets, and greed; economic nationalism is about states, state power, and security; structuralism is about how capitalism pushes states and markets into class warfare. Each of these oversimplifications contains a kernel of truth, but much is lost in the process of simplifying, too. As Einstein said, it is important to make things as simple as possible, but no simpler.

An important intellectual initiative within IPE is the movement to expand the field to make it more inclusive of different ideas and to keep it from being oversimplified. This chapter presents four variations or critiques based on the mainstream IPE theories of economic nationalism, liberalism, and structuralism that, taken individually or together, expand IPE's domain and make it even more relevant and interesting: namely, rational choice theory, constructivism, feminism, and hegemonic stability theory. There are others, but for the sake of providing enough detail in a chapter-length study, we focus on these four.

We begin with rational choice theory, which applies what was originally an economic methodology to a variety of issues and problems in the social sciences. "Rat choice," as it is sometimes referred to, focuses on the way individuals and the aggregate units that represent them, such as states and other actors, make decisions. In so doing it attempts to reveal the political, economic, and social interests behind those choices. Constructivism is a newer and more controversial theory that focuses on the values, beliefs, ideas, and other intangible elements that shape the views of people, officials, and nation-states in the international system. More than the other alternative theories, constructivism focuses on society and culture and posits that policies change when people's values and their fundamental ideas about them change.

The feminist critique is concerned with the status of women and the role they play in relation to a variety of IPE issues, especially human rights and development. Along with constructivism, feminist theory focuses on the connection between gender and issues of wealth, power, authority, along with issues that are often overlooked, such as the importance of the family, family security, and reproduction in today's world. In the last twenty years in particular, a host of international organizations (IOs) and nongovernmental organizations (NGOs) have taken up the cause of promoting women's rights and improving conditions for women in all countries, but especially in developing nations. In many cases, IOs and NGOs have made end runs around states to accomplish these objectives.

Finally, hegemonic stability theory is used quite often to explain a variety of situations and issues in the international political economy. It raises fundamental questions about who organizes the different structures of the international political economy—who decides and enforces the rules. Since the war in Iraq began in 2003 it also regenerated a good deal of interest in empires and the extent to which the United States today is an empire—for good or for bad.

The world is a complicated place, characterized by elements of interdependence in many ways and on many levels. The international political economy manifests many boundaries and tensions due to conflicting interests, points of view, or value systems that increasingly come into contact with one another. The mainstream IPE theories of economic nationalism, liberalism, and structuralism frame IPE issues in particular ways that capture some of the most important elements of IPE today, but not all of them. One of the main intellectual projects of contemporary IPE is to expand its domain to include actors, frameworks, and ways of thinking that cannot easily be classified under the three main perspectives. One of the goals of this chapter is to highlight some of the ways in which IPE can be more inclusive—"without fences," as it were—when it comes to honestly confronting a broader range of important issues and theories in today's world without necessarily abandoning IPE's intellectual roots.

This chapter presents four alternative or variations of the mainstream IPE theories: rational choice theory, constructivism, feminist theory, and hegemonic stability theory. Each of these critiques asks us to think of IPE in a different and generally broader way. IPE in the twenty-first century, however it develops, will necessarily reflect and condition each of these views.

Before we begin, a word of caution is in order. Each of the four IPE critiques described and explained here is complex and controversial. As in the case of the three dominant IPE perspectives, many different viewpoints or variations exist within each critique. Thus, it is either bold or foolhardy to try to concisely and simply sum up any of these schools of thought. The analysis presented here, however, *is* concise and therefore intentionally incomplete, and also therefore necessarily superficial. This chapter was not written for experts of these theories as much as it was written for IPE students. Our aim is to acquaint students with a variety of other analytical tools and perspectives that may lead them to a deeper understanding of some of the issues surrounding IPE.

## THE RATIONAL CHOICE CRITIQUE

The three overarching IPE perspectives tend to frame questions in terms of states, markets, and class relations. States supposedly act in the national interest, markets are driven by the invisible hand of individual self-interest, and class conflict results from diverging interests of different socioeconomic groups (classes) of people.

**Rational choice analysis** is a methodology of economics that is used so frequently that it is an unconscious model of thought. Within the discipline of political science this methodology is referred to as rational choice theory; in economics it goes by the name **public choice analysis**. By either name, rational choice theory provides a model of decision making against which an analyst contrasts decisions that people (either as individuals or as aggregate actors such as nation-states) have made in relation to a single or a variety of economic, political, and social problems.[1] From this model the analyst attempts to discern, explain, or evaluate *why* a particular course of action, strategy, or solution to a problem was selected from among different options. Decision makers are assumed to have sufficient information to contemplate and logically calculate, in an unemotional manner, alternative courses of action or strategies and their consequences, such that decision makers' choices maximize the gains and minimize the costs of these choices for themselves or for the state or group of people they represent. Rational decision making also assumes that actors *weigh* their options based on the utility or importance attached to each option—something that cannot always be calculated on the basis of objective criteria.

In the study of international politics, for instance, realists often use rational choice theory to explain why, during the Cold War, the United States and the Soviet Union engaged in an arms race and threatened to destroy one another. Predictably, as one side built new weapons, the other side calculated that it was in its best interest to match those weapons, for fear that if they did not, the other side would have an advantage and therefore would be able to coerce them into surrender or defeat if they were to fight one another. In this case, each state was viewed as a rational actor (see Chapters 2 and 9) to the extent that it calculated the costs and benefits of matching the other's weapons or anticipating choices the other actor would make based on a rational calculation of their costs and benefits.

A more recent example occurred in 2003, when Great Britain joined with the United States and invaded Iraq. One might ask: Why did Britain make this choice? On the basis of rational thinking, some might conclude that it was not rational for the British to help the United States invade Iraq, if it meant that Great Britain supported the U.S. effort to promote a unipolar international system. Such a security order was likely to lead to opposition from the Iraqis and their allies and also opposition from other states that felt threatened by the U.S. desire to play a hegemonic role in the international system (discussed in more detail below).

In both these cases, rational choice theory casts light on the power capabilities of different states and the distribution of that power in the international system.[2] Despite preferences for different structures, most realists agree that unipolar systems (dominated by a single state or hegemon) are *not* conducive to international peace because the preponderance of power is aggregated in the hands of one state, which might rationally decide that as a hegemon it must impose peace on other states by force. Other states might necessarily react to this structure by either going along with the hegemon, if it is in their best interest to do so, or opposing it, which could result in conflict, if not war, with the hegemon.

Employing rational criteria to state behavior helps explain some things, but also presents an analyst with some fundamental intellectual problems. The first is that, in trying to explain state behavior, the analyst necessarily focuses on the reasons, motives, and calculations of, say, the British government that decided to send its troops into Iraq along with U.S. forces. Out of necessity, diplomats, historians, journalists, and many academics often describe and assess events in terms of state behavior. In effect, they treat the state as a living, breathing organism that thinks through problems, weighs alternatives, and arrives at the "best" option considering what is good for itself, if not for all of society.

As we pointed out in Chapter 1, in the levels-of-analysis problem, the state is assumed to be the dominant actor in the international system. As a sovereign entity, it makes life-and-death decisions that protect society. In doing so it requires and uses power to achieve a variety of ends related to its security. Even if what we think of as the state is actually a composite of foreign policy decisions made by many actors within its institutions, from the perspective of the 199 or so other states operating in the international political economy, the state must be viewed and treated by other states as a single ("unitary") actor. Likewise, state decision makers are also compelled to assume that other states (and their leaders) are rational actors. If they did not, they would be predisposed to think the worst of them, which could compel them not to negotiate (U.S. policy toward the Soviet Union until 1933), lead to war, and be more costly than assuming they were rational states that were only acting in their own interest.

A second problem is that, because so many individuals play a role in a state's foreign policy institutions, to focus on individual decision makers only makes arriving at an explanation more difficult and overly complicated. On the other hand, many rational choice theorists recognize that Britain's choice was actually made by Prime Minister Tony Blair, who at some point most likely consulted with his cabinet or other close advisers. Ideally, rational choice theorists would like to narrow their focus to the one decision maker (especially during a crisis) or group of people who ultimately "decided" to go on the mission to Iraq with the United States and then determine how they arrived at that decision—on what basis they determined that it served their (or Britain's) best interest.

This raises another issue, which is taken up in the classic book on this issue, *The Essence of Decision*, by Graham Allison of Harvard University.[3] Allison argues and demonstrates that foreign policy decision making is not a single rational decision-making process in and of itself, but a series of decisions. We may be tempted to focus on a nation's leader as a rational actor, but we also know that his or her views are shaped by his role as a leader, the information she receives from her advisors, and most important, by the information he receives from bureaucrats and other officials working in a variety of agencies under him. Information and decisions at these levels all have a bearing on a leader's "final" decision.

Thus, why did Tony Blair decide to send British troops into Iraq? What did he expect to gain or lose by doing so, in terms of either his own or Great Britain's interests? Furthermore, what did the British foreign ministry think about the Prime Minister's plan, likewise British intelligence? In many ways, to ask these sorts of questions is to open a can of worms when it comes to the rationality of decision making. In these situations, rationality explains some of the elements that are part of the decision-making process, especially questions related to specific individuals. In general, however, when applied to issues of international politics, rational choice theory tends to produce what amounts to, by definition, oversimplified answers. It assumes that decision makers have a certain amount of information or knowledge available to them, which, in the case of the run-up to the invasion of Iraq by the United States in 2003, was not the case. As noted in the Iraq War box in Chapter 9, President George W. Bush may have weighed some information as being more important than other facts, or he may simply have been wrong about the predicted consequences of his strategy to win the war.

State interests are constantly changing based on new sources of information or changed circumstances over which a state may have no control. Ironically, rational choice theory actually helps the analyst appreciate how much a decision does *not* fit the rational model of decision making, as the analyst can never know exactly what combination of political, social, and psychological factors played a role in producing a decision. Finally, it must be stated that what is rational to either the decision maker or to the analyst might not be to others in different cultures. Rational choice theory, then, is bound not only by time and specific questions but also by the culture that produces these questions and ultimately views them as satisfactory.

## Economics and Public Choice Analysis

Economists who use rational choice theory like to point out that *states* do not make choices; its leaders and political officials do. Government policies are set by elected officials and appointed bureaucrats who make choices in a world of scarce resources. These actors are influenced by each other, by their relations with foreign officials, and by voters, campaign contributors, political party leaders, and a variety of other individuals, including union officials, corporate executives, community leaders, and journalists, who have a direct or indirect stake in public policies. The political marketplace is comprised of the individuals who "demand" certain types of public policies and those who "supply" them.

For economists (and for some political scientists and sociologists as well), individuals are self-interested and motivated to make themselves better off. Stated in these simple terms, it is easy to assume that elected officials are corrupt and will sell their votes to the highest bidder or provide government benefits in exchange for campaign contributions or election endorsements. In fact, some government officials *are* corrupt—political corruption scandals are uncomfortably familiar news. However, the rational choice critique does not *assume* that government officials are corrupt generally. An elected official has a strong self-interest in being reelected, for example, and that self-interest may drive him or her to do an exceptionally good job of representing the interests of voters in the district.

The self-interest motive is complicated because the elected official may also be motivated by the need to raise funds for the next election campaign, the desire to please voters and to give them sound public service, a personal philosophy or set of beliefs about what is best for the nation, or perhaps even a yearning for a prominent place in the history books. According to the rational choice critique, public policy depends on these complex interests, not on simple images of the "national interest."

Likewise, public policy is also conditioned by the institutional structure of the political marketplace. The institutional structure is the "rules of the game," the guidelines that condition political choices. The structure of political decision making, combined with the interests of different actors and the resources they command, determines what government policies are enacted and how they are implemented. Thus, as we will see, *how* political choices are made influences *what* political choices are made.

The rational choice critique can shed light on many other issues that we study in IPE. For example, rational choice analysis helps us understand the debate between liberals and mercantilists regarding tariffs and quotas and other protectionist trade policies. Liberals since David Ricardo have argued that protectionism is generally counter to the national interest because it is inefficient, whereas mercantilists, in the spirit of Friedrich List and Alexander Hamilton, tend to argue that trade barriers promote the national interest by building domestic economic strength. The rational choice critique points out that national interest does not always determine government policy— individual interests can be far more powerful.

To see this, suppose that today the House of Representatives is considering a tariff on inexpensive imported sports shoes. Let us suppose that this tariff would benefit a small number of domestic shoemaking firms, their owners, and employees, but that it would harm the nation overall by reducing the real incomes of many millions of households by a small amount each. The protectionist gains are assumed to be very small in absolute amount and highly concentrated compared with the costs of protectionism, which are typically large but highly diffused. The winners gain a lot per person, and the losers each lose only a little. However, the number of winners is so small compared with the vast majority of losers that their voice is often drowned out by losers who might have lost a job compared to the winners who bought shoes for a few dollars less than they would have with protection in place. In other words, the tariff redistributes income from a large group in society to a much smaller one, but in a very inefficient way.

If we had a system of direct democracy, in which every voter cast a ballot on each issue, the shoe tariff might be very well voted down in an enormous electoral landslide. However, we have a system of representative democracy, in which elected representatives supposedly serve our interests. How will Congress vote on this issue? The "national interest" would seem to be served by a "no" vote in this example, because we have assumed that the total losses outweigh the total gains, yet rational choice analysis predicts a "yes" vote by Congress even if elected officials are not corrupt. Here is the logic behind this conclusion. In a representative democracy like ours, it is costly to attempt to follow what Congress is doing and to influence votes that affect our individual interests. We tend to remain rationally ignorant of most government actions, which have little direct bearing on our lives, and to pay attention to only the small number of items that are likely to impose high costs or provide high benefits to us. Your representative is therefore unlikely to get much mail opposing the shoe tariff, because most of the voters who would be harmed by it are rationally ignorant of the bill. Domestic shoe interests, however, have a much stronger incentive to lobby representatives, send them mail, make campaign contributions, and commission studies and reports that stress the jobs and other benefits that a protected domestic shoe industry would provide. Listening honestly to the "voice of the people," your busy representative might conclude that shoe tariffs are a good idea because the voices of those who would benefit are much louder than the voices of the (rationally ignorant) persons who would be harmed.

The bottom line of this rational choice analysis is that representative democracy is biased *in favor* of government policies that favor special interests and biased *against* policies that benefit society broadly, if they impose concentrated costs on some well-organized interest group. This bias may not result in government policies that are *always* undesirable, because political leaders and elected officials take into account many different factors in choosing how to vote. They are often too sophisticated to be influenced by a special-interest letter-writing campaign, for example. Representative democracy is not perfect, as this example indicates, and one should not always assume that the "national interest" that public policies reflect is actually the same as the interest of a majority of the nation's citizens.

One of the more useful aspects of rational choice analysis is its ability to help us understand change in the international political economy. Changing national policies, viewed this way, are not necessarily based on changing national interests but rather occur due to a combination of changes in *the actors, their interests,* and the *institutional environment* of the political marketplace. This provides a well-structured framework for analysis.

For example, how can one explain why the United States, which was highly protectionist during the Great Depression, became such a strong advocate of free trade after World War II and, in fact, was a leading force in the General Agreement on Tariffs and Trade (GATT) and World Trade Organization (WTO) negotiations that reduced tariff and quota barriers throughout the world? How and why did U.S. policy change so dramatically? Rational choice analysis asks us to look at the actors, their interests, and the institutional environment.

The implementation of the Bretton Woods agreements in the years immediately following World War II (see Chapters 6 and 7) had many important effects. In the *trade regime,* the GATT was established as a system of multilateral negotiations aimed at reducing protectionism. Although the GATT had no real enforcement powers, causing it to be dubbed by cynics "the Gentlemen's Agreement to Talk and Talk," it was still an important actor. This is because, in part, it is better to "talk, talk" than to "tariff, tariff" (to paraphrase Winston Churchill), and also because GATT rules altered the domestic political environment.

The GATT rules specified that each trade negotiation round be multilateral, with many countries participating, and that tariff reductions be reciprocal, so when the United States lowered tariffs on, say, the shoes that it imports, other countries would simultaneously reduce tariffs on, say, the wheat that the United States exports. Thus, if Congress were to vote against a GATT treaty in an attempt to protect domestic shoe firms and workers, it would also necessarily be voting to damage the interests of U.S. exporters in another sector.

This, clearly, had the effect of bringing new interests—the interests of exporting firms—into the political marketplace. Whereas before GATT the concentrated interests of protection-seeking firms often dominated the interests of the majority of consumers, the GATT environment had the effect of mobilizing countervailing export interests. Those seeking protection from foreign competition now had to contend with firms that wanted freer access to foreign markets. The GATT, the new actor that created a new political environment, allowed new interests to be represented and so changed national policy regarding trade.

It should be noted that many historians and political scientists contend that a major shift in the direction of U.S. trade policy in 1934 toward reduced protection reflected not so much the strength of different interest groups as a choice that President Franklin D. Roosevelt and other officials consciously made. A changing world economy but also an effort to recover from the Great Depression lead many in Roosevelt's administration to believe that a "free trade" policy was now in the U.S.'s best (national) interest.

One of the most important insights that rational choice analysis provides to IPE involves the concept of **rent-seeking behavior**. In economics, the term *rent* is often used to describe unearned income that a person or firm receives because of scarcity. If a monopolist is able to restrict supply and drive up prices, for example, the extra profits are called *rents*. David Ricardo used the term *rent* for the income that landlords received from their ownership of land—a scarce resource with fixed supply.

## RENT-SEEKING IN MEXICO

Rent-seeking behavior and the environment of corruption that it fosters comprise one of the most serious problems facing less developed countries today. A recent study by Paul Craig Roberts and Karen LaFollette Araujo has drawn attention to the role of rent-seeking in explaining Mexico's uneven path toward prosperity in the postwar era.[a]

Mexico has long been a paradox to those who study international affairs from narrow disciplinary perspectives. For a country to be prosperous, many people believe, you need abundant economic resources and political stability. Mexico has both. From the economic standpoint, it has many valuable natural resources, a talented and creative population, and access to foreign investment and technology. It also has had a stable political system, long dominated by the Institutional Revolutionary Party (PRI), which has held the reins of government power in Mexico for most years since 1929. And yet Mexico has failed to achieve self-sustaining economic growth. What holds Mexico back?

The answer, according to Roberts and Araujo, is at least in part the structure of government and the perverse incentives that structure created. Until recently, the PRI had very little competition from other political parties and enjoyed a virtual monopoly on domestic power. Within the PRI, power was concentrated at the top, in the hands of the president. Power was distributed like a pyramid, with the political elites holding most of the control and the masses having just a little (the power of the vote and sometimes—when elections were rigged—not even that).

The rational choice approach asks us to consider how this power structure affects the incentives of the people of Mexico. With small chance of being turned out of office, Mexican officials needed to pay only nominal attention to the voting masses. It was in their interests to use their power to enrich themselves. "Within the government, the modus operandi was 'robar pero obrar,' which means literally 'steal and build.' Someone would say 'PRI functionary so-and-so stole millions,' while another person would reply, 'Yes, but he built the municipal buildings and opened the local state-owned sugar mill.'"[b] It is estimated that President José López Portillo (1976–1982) accumulated $1–$3 billion via top-level robar pero obrar.[c] The total amount that was extracted at all levels by the political elites through bribes, corruption, and crime is uncounted, but it is surely an enormous sum, especially compared with the low living standards of many Mexican citizens.

This corruption has many roots (see Chapter 18). In part, the ethics of Mexico's government may reflect values and practices inherited from past colonial rule and administrations. "Like European aristocrats of former times, Mexican elites built mansions, the modern equivalent of castles, and felt few qualms about enriching themselves from public coffers. For the most part, they did not wear the look of the guilty. Indeed, they did not even regard themselves as wrongdoers. Plunder has always been the job of the Mexican ruling class."[d]

Roberts and Araujo, however, note that Mexico's constitution concentrates power in particular ways, without many checks and balances, creating a monopoly environment that encourages self-interested behavior that violates the public trust. Mexican presidents, for example, may serve only a single six-year term. Because they cannot gain through reelection, their self-interest necessarily drives them to gain through other means, some of them corrupt. Thus, in a way, the corrupt officials are only doing what the rational choice critique predicts they will do: rationally promote their self-interest given the incentives and constraints they face.

It would have been bad enough if Mexico's only problem was a corrupt government sector, but rent-seeking is contagious. As the government took over a larger and larger part of the economy, to increase its gains, rent-seeking and corruption became increasingly prevalent. Even in the nongovernment sector, rent-seeking became the surest way to individual prosperity. Business executives found it more important to keep up contacts and favorable relationships with the PRI than to invest in new factories and technology. The PRI could, perhaps, throw vast profits their way by enacting favorable regulations or import restrictions, whereas investing in the market economy was risky and—if someone else got to the PRI first with a gift or a bribe—perhaps even economically fatal.

"A fish rots from the head," it is said, and when rent-seeking begins at the top, as it did in Mexico, it eventually spreads all the way through the body politic. Crime, corruption, and bribery paralyzed Mexico, making it, in Roberts and Araujo's terminology, "the blocked society." Nothing much could happen to mobilize Mexico's vast resources and people with a bribe, so the wealth went to the crooks, not to the people.

Significantly, Roberts and Araujo are optimistic about Mexico's future. Mexico's severe debt crisis, which came to a head in the early 1980s, forced the government to reduce its influence in the country's economy. So perhaps these reforms can reduce rent-seeking in Mexico and change the blocked society and the culture of corruption, with elites skimming the cream, to a flexible and productive commercial and political culture that can benefit the masses.

*References*

[a] Paul Craig Roberts and Karen LaFollette Araujo, *The Capitalist Revolution in Latin America* (New York: Oxford University Press, 1997). See especially chap. 3, "The Blocked Society," pp. 52–101. Special thanks to Ross Singleton for suggesting this topic for treatment in this chapter.

[b] Ibid., p. 56.

[c] Ibid., p. 75.

[d] Ibid.

Some resources are scarce by nature, but other resources are scarce because of human action. Diamonds, for example, are really a relatively abundant mineral. They are expensive, however, because diamond cartels keep the supply of gem-quality diamonds artificially limited in order to keep prices and profits high (see Chapter 18). Some cartels try to intentionally create scarcity so that they can earn rents. Likewise, governments have the ability to create artificial scarcity of some items through the policies that they adopt. Individuals who wish to profit from a government-created scarcity are called "rent-seekers." When these individuals try to influence public policy to gain rents, they are engaged in rent-seeking behavior. Basically, they are looking for ways to use public policy to create private profits for themselves.

If the United States were to impose a quota on automobile imports, for example, imported cars would become scarce and their price would rise. The government would distribute import licenses to certain dealers, giving them the right to import cars and sell them at the higher price. Dealers not favored with import licenses would not be able to benefit directly from the import car shortage. This is how most import quotas work.

Rent-seeking behavior can occur at several points in the political system when an import quota is enacted. First, of course, politically well-placed auto dealers may begin to lobby members of Congress to impose a quota so they can receive rents—this is classic rent-seeking behavior. However, they may not get all the rents that would be available. Some elected officials are especially well placed to influence trade legislation because of their committee assignments and other factors. These officials, even if they are honest and upright, will end up collecting some of the rents available as they receive campaign contributions, gifts, or other favors from individuals seeking their influence over legislation.

Rents can also be dispersed within the bureaucracy. It may be that an Office of Auto Import Licenses is created, for example, to handle applications by various auto dealers for the right to bring cars into the country. In this case, some of the focus of rent-seeking behavior may fall on those who have some influence over the issuance of import licenses. A corrupt official may be able to demand bribes in exchange for considering an application for an import license. Even an honest official may get some benefits from the position in the form of favors, gifts, or discounts on car purchases. Individual rent-seeking behavior has the direct effect of distorting government policy and the indirect effect of creating an environment in which corruption is possible, profitable, and therefore more likely to exist.

In summary, the rational choice critique reminds us that public policies are made by a variety of actors ranging from individual consumers to corporate entities, to states, and even to organizations as large as some international organizations. The public interest always reflects the private interests of at least some persons. Different actors, their interests, and the institutional environment in which they operate must also be considered if we are to understand how decisions are made in the international political economy.

## CONSTRUCTIVISM

Many students find the constructivist perspective interesting and exciting because it focuses on arrangement of issues and actors that are often overlooked in typical studies that are labeled "the IPE" of something or other. **Constructivism** involves "deconstructing" something—to take it apart. Most IPE theories have a one-way view of causality to the extent that institutions such as the state, market, or even society are assumed to determine behavior, without paying much attention to the social contexts that "construct" or make up these institutions. Recently, a number of theorists, such as Alexander Wendt[4] and others, have focused on the way ideas and beliefs shape people and even states' identities as well as their self-interests.

Operating more on the second and first levels of analysis (see Chapter 1), constructivists contend that state preferences reflect different social values and belief systems. States are not only political actors, they are also social actors to the extent that they adhere to rules, norms, and institutional constructs that reflect society's values and beliefs. Why do some people or states cooperate more than others? Is it because they are threatened by a more powerful state? Perhaps! More often than not, though, states cooperate because they are predisposed to work with other states. Their societies value cooperation and prefer cooperative tactics to more violent means of solving common problems. A good example of this is the states in the United Nations that tend to have reputations for "neutrality," or that act assertively to promote diplomatic or peaceful settlements of disputes, or that volunteer troops for UN peacekeeping missions—Canada, Norway, Sweden, Denmark, Beglium, and the Netherlands, to name only a few. Many of these states are also the first to sign on to arms control treaties or human rights conventions because of strong personal and public views in their nations about the nature of international relations and foreign policy.

Another difference between constructivism and the three dominant IPE perspectives is in the fundamental assumptions that realism and liberalism make about the structure of the IPE and its ability to condition state or individual behavior. Whereas realists (see Chapters 2 and 9) argue that the balance of power conditions states' behavior, constructivists suggest that conflict between two or more actors is a product of the different values, beliefs, and interests of those actors. One of realism's central assumptions is that a potentially anarchic "self-help" world forces all actors to make security their first priority, lest they be killed or overtaken by other states. Questions of identity and interest formation are considered to be analytically irrelevant. Social factors such as beliefs and values do not have causal power, because they will always be overwhelmed by the structural realities of a self-help world.[5]

Likewise, liberals share the realist assumption of an anarchic world, but hold that well-designed institutions can create the possibility for positive-sum gains. Like the realists, liberals have a rational view of the world, in which institutions such as capitalism help to order the international political economy. Institutions act on society, shaping actors' identities and interests. Social factors have no direct effect on institutional structures or processes.

On the other hand, Alexander Wendt argues that "structure has no existence or causal power apart from processes. Self-help and power politics are institutions, not essential features of anarchy. Anarchy is what states make of it."[6] In other words, the structure of anarchy is not sufficient to produce a self-help world. A combination of social processes associated with different actors' assorted identities and subjective interests causes us to view anarchy in terms of a world of potential chaos and disorder. For Wendt, we do live in a self-help world, only because over time we have come to "believe" that self-help is a consequence of anarchy. The international system is quite orderly; most of the time, states act in accordance with formal and informal rules and norms.[7] The fact that some states are now regarded as "rogue states" is testimony to the idea that they are "deviant" in some fashion (see Chapter 9), because they have not behaved in a way acceptable to the community of nations.

Another feature of constructivism is that it often focuses on change or the transformation of an idea or set of beliefs about something. Examples abound, such as the increasing importance of human rights, a variety of environmental issues (see Chapter 20), and the importance of debt relief (see Chapters 8 and 15). As discussed in the box "Landmines," the Treaty to Ban Landmines was signed and ratified faster than almost any other treaty in history. Among the factors that led to its quick ratification were the efforts of treaty supporters to change the beliefs and views about the need for landmines of people everywhere, along with the views of the security establishments of different states. World public opinion was swayed dramatically by information and photos about the effects of landmines, which often meant the loss of a leg or arm by civilian noncombatants, especially in developing nations. Peoples' values and beliefs were also challenged by the background studies of many NGOs that were easily transferred around via the Internet and by rock stars and famous dignitaries such as Princess Diana of England.

---

### LANDMINES[a]

The case of antipersonnel landmines (APLs) directly connects the issue of personal security to the growing role of NGOs in the new global security structure. Landmines have a long history of use in conventional wars as well as in guerrilla and low-intensity conflict settings. APLs were particularly popular during the 1970s and 1980s, when insurgent groups took advantage of their inexpensive and simple use. They are hockey-puck-size containers buried in the ground that explode when someone steps on them or drives over them, and they cost approximately $3 each to make.

After the Cold War, APLs were considered by many to be unreasonable weapons because they "do not distinguish between civilians and combatants; indeed, they probably kill more children than soldiers."[b] This new realization of the detriment of APLs motivated a worldwide effort in the early 1990s to eliminate them completely. With worldwide support of the issue, including publicity from such celebrities in the British spotlight as Princess Diana and Linda McCartney, the International Campaign to Ban Landmines (ICBL) gained rapid popularity after its founding in 1992. Current estimates put the number of remaining APLs at around 70 million,[c] most of them in developing countries such as Angola, Afghanistan, Cambodia, and Mozambique, which injure an estimated 25,000 people (a third of them children) every year.

The ICBL is an umbrella organization pulling together a number of NGOs into an antilandmine advocacy campaign co-sponsored by the Vietnam Veterans of America Foundation and Medico International.[d] Beginning with six core organizations, the ICBL has since expanded to include about 1400. The Campaign gained prominence in 1995 at the Review Conference of the Convention on Conventional Weapons (CCW), when a number of states and individuals abandoned the CCW's effort to control the use of landmines because its treaty contained too many loopholes. In a very short time the ICBL produced a comprehensive treaty that completely bans the use of landmines. Created under the auspices of the UN, the treaty calls on signatories to "never under any circumstances" "use," "develop, produce, otherwise acquire, stockpile, retain or transfer to anyone" antipersonnel mines. Each party also undertakes the duty "to destroy or ensure destruction of all anti-personnel mines." In Canada in December 1997, some 122 nations signed the treaty, officially named the Convention on the Prohibition of the Use, Stockpiling, Production and Tranfer of Anti-Personnel Mines and on Their Destruction, but known more commonly as the Ottawa Treaty. As of September 1998, some forty nations had ratified the treaty, bringing it into international law in March 1999.

An interesting feature of the campaign itself was the method the NGOs used to further their cause. The International Committee of the Red Cross (ICRC) commissioned an analysis of the military utility of APLs by a retired British combat engineer, who found them to be unnecessary and not as useful as has often been assumed. A number of NGOs also conducted extensive education campaigns to inform the public and state officials of the horrible effects of APLs, all the while lobbying, and also, in some cases, shaming state and military officials who resisted their discontinuation.

The Clinton administration claimed to support the treaty, but the United States did not sign it, for reasons related to the use of APLs as a defense mechanism in South Korea near the Demilitarized Zone (DMZ). The United States did give $7 million to assist in de-mining fourteen countries, including Afghanistan, Angola, Cambodia, Eritrea, Ethiopia, Laos, Mozambique, Namibia, and Rwanda, along with $15 million for de-mining efforts in Bosnia-Herzegovina. Russia and Japan have signed the treaty, but China, Poland, Spain, and Kuwait have not. China has been a major supplier of cheap landmines, especially to African nations.[e] Russia finally signed the treaty in 2003, but China and the United States still hold out.

Thus far the ICBL is credited with the destruction of about 40 million antipersonnel mines[f] and has been awarded the Nobel Peace Prize for its efforts. Its work is done primarily through advocacy networking through NGOs, and so it is important to credit those organizations working on the ground. The HALO Trust in particular, a British de-mining organization, has been at the forefront of this effort since the beginning.

Founded in 1988, the Hazardous-Life Support Organization, or HALO Trust, remains the largest de-mining NGO worldwide. It operates with 7000 personnel in about twenty-five countries, working on full clearance programs in some areas and survey and assessment programs in others. Unlike other organizations, HALO focuses particularly in the field, physically de-mining as opposed to providing publicity and advocacy about the issue; their mission statement is simple: "Getting mines out of the ground, now."

As a result of rampant violence and long-standing insurgency, Afghanistan is believed to be one of the most heavily mined, dangerous countries in the world. However, working between the legacy of Soviet occupation and consistent Taliban rebellion, HALO has maintained projects in Afghanistan. Doubling efforts in Afghanistan since the official disbandment of the Taliban in 2001, HALO has in total decreased the number of landmines by 50 percent and plans for a landmine-free nation by 2013.[g]

Slowly, de-mining goals are being met. Most urgent for the cause is not new technology, as the most basic developments have proven to be the most reliable. De-miners typically use a standard metal detector in the field. HALO also uses modified British hedge trimmers to clear fields before de-mining can take place, and dogs to seek out mines by detecting the scent of explosive vapors.

Most urgent for the international community to address in the war against APLs is increased cooperation of states and other international organizations to help move the process along, particularly their willingness to share information and allow de-mining forces into their countries. In Afghanistan alone, HALO estimates there are still about 640,000 landmines, and although progress is slow, there is a foreseeable end to the blind violence.

*References*

[a] Many thanks to our students Meredith Ginn and Lauren Whaley, who helped research this issue.

[b] Warren Christopher, "Hidden Killers: U.S. Policy on Anti-Personnel Landmines," *U.S. Department of State Dispatch 6* (February 6, 1995), p. 71.

[c] http://landmines.org.uk.

[d] For an excellent discussion of the politics of the ICBL, see Richard Price, "Reversing the Gun Sights: Transnational Civil Society Targets Land Mines," *International Organization, 52* (Summer 1998), pp. 613–644.

[e] http://landmines.org.uk.

[f] Zabz, Deh. "Mines Still Kill or Maim 100 People a Month in Afghanistan," *Agence France Presse*, April 3, 2006.

[g] Ibid.

Some constructivists like to trace change through speeches or the works of important officials or actors on the state or international level. For this reason, many constructivist studies have been labeled "postmodern" to the extent that researchers deconstruct or take apart pieces of literature or a document to discern hidden meanings or the intentions of the writer, or the state associated with a particular policy. Often, op-ed pieces in newspapers are mini-deconstructions. Why did UN Secretary General Kofi Anan pursue a particular objective? How much of the objective reflects his own values and beliefs as opposed to those of the member states he represents? Answers to this question might conflict with one another, but for constructivists, it is important to get behind the headlines or inside the mind of Kofi Annan, as opposed to assuming that his views reflect only those of the membership of the United Nations.

In sum, then, the five basic assumptions of constructivism applied to IPE are that:

1. Ideas, beliefs, values, and identities of individuals and groups are the key to understanding IPE.
2. Ideas, values, beliefs, and identities are socially constructed.
3. Ideas, values, etc., are social forces that are more important than military or economic factors.
4. Conflict and cooperation are products of values and beliefs.
5. Change can be explained by examining changes in the values and beliefs of individuals and other actors over time.[8]

Critics of constructivism like to argue that it is a very inexact analytical devise or theory. Interpreting what people believe or their values is not easy, nor is it regarded as valid by many researchers. In most cases there also is not a lot of concrete (i.e., quantifiable) evidence that beliefs or values influence anyone's views or outlook. Of course, it can be argued that most quantitative studies have the same problem and contain many subjective elements to them, such as weighted answers or even numbers. Another criticism of constructivism is that state beliefs and values may not register a sum of each member of society's beliefs and values. Quite often, state officials act as delegates and decide things apart from the views of their populace. Two things should be noted here in response to these criticisms. First, realists also have a hard time determining theoretically what the state's interests are. Most often it is simply assumed that they are what the leaders say they are. However, we know that there is often a great disconnect between state leaders and society's values and beliefs. Also, most leaders like to assume they know society's views or that at least they can influence or change them. As many philosophers and political theorists note, this is one of the main criticisms of modern democracies—that they often do not register the "people's will."

As all perspectives have their strengths and weaknesses, constructivism sheds light on factors that many agree influence or shape distinctive features and issues in IPE. Depending on the topic students study and the questions they ask, constructivism can provide enlightenment about some dimensions of an issue that are not captured in other perspectives. That alone makes it worth knowing something about.

## THE FEMINIST CRITIQUE

The feminist critique (**feminism**) invites a gendered analysis of IPE issues. Whereas sex is the anatomobiological difference between men and women, gender accounts for societal norms and expectations related to what is appropriate for males and females. Until recently, in many Western states women were expected to stay at home and take care of the house and children, while men were expected to be the main breadwinners in the family. These roles for men and women were defined by their gender. In the 1980s some feminist scholarship sought to describe and explain many of the hidden assumptions about gender in mercantilism and realism, liberalism, and structuralist studies. Until that time the role of the female in international relations and economics, more so than in studies of different social systems and societies, was largely overlooked.[9]

Most "traditional feminists" argue that male patterns of thought and action are so deeply rooted in most social science theories that we often accept them without thinking or realizing their existence. For example, international relations theorists are predominantly males, who emphasize war, conflict, military weapons and power, and many other power- and security-oriented subjects that are important to men.

At the same time, many "neofeminists" feel that the study of women's roles in the international political economy has been overlooked because women are trivialized. Female experiences are deemed not as important as male experiences. In international relations studies, according to many feminists, patriarchy (male dominance) is a ubiquitous element of nearly every issue. As opposed to war and peace, women are supposed to be naturally more concerned with education, health, poverty, justice, and the environment. Many realists might say that women are not physically capable of wielding powerful weapons or choosing war over diplomacy when necessary. And many of those who appear to do so, such as Margaret Thatcher of Great Britain, are merely trying to imitate men. Neofeminists like to argue that women should be valued for being more coopera-tive, sensitive, intuitive, and nurturing than men.

"Postmodern feminism" emphasizes how gender-laden language and concepts about women are.[10] Quite often these theorists and researchers deconstruct primary resources and journal and newspaper articles, searching for subtexts or unstated views or biases about women in the litera-ture or written presentations. Finally, Marxist feminists challenge the idea that capitalism benefits women in almost any context. Many NGOs working on a variety of development and women's is-sues subscribe to this and other views of feminism at the same time. Special efforts are needed to promote the rights of women and to secure a better life for them in countries that are poor but also where values reflect both the superiority of the female over the male, as well as development strate-gies that support men before or even to the exclusion of women.

Feminism, then, is an approach to IPE that focuses on how gender influences a variety of po-litical, social, and economic issues. Some feminist IPE theorists seek to highlight the degree to which IPE studies are dominated by male gender attitudes and stereotypes. They would like to see this change and point out that male dominance is built into most state and international institutions such as IOs, NGOs, and transnational corporations. They note that females who do head lead agen-cies tend to run the World Health Organization (WHO), the United Children's Fund (UNICEF), or the UN Development Fund for Women (UNIFEM).[11]

Other feminists seek to build the female gender element into the study of IPE. They suggest that the International Monetary Fund and the World Bank, for example, conduct more studies of how their policies specifically affect women in developing nations. Economic analysis focuses on self-interested individual choice, drawing on the methods of scientific inquiry to produce simple cause-and-effect narratives. Neoclassical economics also focuses on production and accumulation. However, the feminist critique argues that economic analysis tends to ignore important issues of reproduction and provisioning. In many assessments, only paid work is valued, and economic de-velopment success is measured by the ability of states and markets to create jobs. These jobs, until relatively recently, were men's jobs, and the emphasis given them reflects the structural power of men in states and markets.[12] Unpaid jobs, such as raising children, growing and cooking food, providing services to family and community, have not been included in measures of production, reflecting the lower social status of the women who perform them. The feminist critique sounds similar to con-structivist theory when it suggests that we need to rethink the idea of production and the concept of social value so that we perceive the worth of women's work and not just the money that men make.

One of the most important structural changes in IPE over the last twenty years has been the rise of the market and the expansion of market forces. Some countries are experiencing a transition from state to market, other countries from traditional social arrangements to market-driven relationships. This transition to the market has many effects. An important element of this is the transition from the production of goods ("men's work") to greater production of services ("women's work"). Greater fe-male participation in the labor force, combined with the need for a more "flexible" labor force (which women often provide) goes hand in hand with economic development. The growth of the market therefore often affects change in the status and power of women and can help affect social and cultural change in countries that are transitioning to market economies or even in less developed nations.[13]

On the other hand, globalization has not always been a good thing for many females. When a 21-year-old woman who worked in a clothing factory in India returned late to her home in the slums one evening, her rickshaw-driver husband was waiting for her. He was furious that there was no food on the table. He stalked out, but returned later with a vial of sulfuric acid, which he threw on her as she slept, severely burning her face, arms, and chest. This story is repeated over and over again in Dhaka. *The Economist* found that sixteen women in a hospital burn unit all suffered from acid burns, and all told just about the same story.[14]

One theory for this behavior is that the trend toward acid burns is a backlash against the ris-ing status of women in this part of the world. The globalization of economic activity creates new opportunities for women in factories and shops, draws them out of the home, gives them increased independence, and generally shakes up traditional gender roles. *Microlending* schemes (see Chapter 15), which provide start-up loans for women's cooperative enterprises, also provoke male backlash. "Progressive" economic development initiatives can have unexpected, and often tragic, consequences when they are mixed with rigid attitudes in a previously male-dominated society.

In conclusion of this section, a few IPE theorists claim that feminism lacks good scholarship, mainly because it presupposes that females are purposefully devalued by researchers along with political institutions. Many of the ideas and values that feminists stress cannot be measured or studied rigorously. However, by focusing largely on states and markets, traditional IPE analysis overlooks the *differential* effect of economic, political, and social change on men and women. This is a great mistake. Often, what is left out of economics, and therefore left out of IPE studies, are ways to account for intuition, emotion, feeling, belief, and the complex and ambiguous senses that we usually associate with the humanities or that cannot be easily measured objectively. These senses are not coldly rational, but they are hardly irrational either. They are human feelings, but they are more often associated with women than men, and therefore they are dismissed as unimportant by (mostly male) economists and others more attuned to a male-conditioned mode of thought.

The solution to problems like those reported here begins with the quest to understand them, as the feminist critique encourages. As the noted political neorealist and advocate of the power politics Kenneth Waltz suggested in his discussion of the level-of-analysis problem (see Chapter 1), attitudes such as aggression are not "natural"; they are socially constructed, and we do not have to accept them. What can be socially constructed can be socially changed.

## HEGEMONIC STABILITY THEORY

The notions of hegemony and hegemonic cycles are among the most durable and powerful ideas in IPE. As we saw in Chapter 3, mercantilists, liberals, and structuralists all have their own versions of the hegemony and the role of hegemons in the international political economy. Much has been written in recent years built on premises inspired by the idea of hegemony or domination. Some worry that the United States might be weakening—that it is a hegemon in decline—and speculate as to whether it can maintain or regain its strength, whether some other country could rise up to take its hegemonic crown, or what kind of chaos might result if no country is a hegemon.[15] Others have spilled ink crowing that the United States is as strong as ever and that the world is in good order because a hegemon is in place. When President George H. W. Bush sent U.S. troops into Kuwait and then into Iraq in the early 1990s, he was fulfilling his role as a hegemonic leader, conditioned by hegemonic theory. The same was often said about the President George W. Bush when he invaded Afghanistan and Iraq after the 9/11 attacks.[16]

**Hegemonic stability theory** posits that one country that is unusually rich and powerful dominates other states or the entire international system for a length of time during which it establishes and enforces a set of rules that regulate various elements of the international political economy. Economic liberals emphasize that this nation-state, if it assumes the rights and responsibilities of the hegemon, will supply **public (collective) goods** such as sound money while absorbing the costs associated with promoting free trade and other economic benefits to other members of the system. In essence, hegemons have to accept a certain amount of "**free riding**," or letting other states not have to pay for system maintenance, in exchange for their cooperation and letting the hegemon rule.

Thus, mercantilist-realists emphasize the extent to which the hegemon provides a good deal of security for other members of the system in return for their cooperation (see Chapters 7 and 9) and whatever benefits it gains from its position at the center of the world system. Some have argued that, in effect, that is what the United States did after 9/11 by taking on terrorism and covering the expense of promoting democracy and stability the world over.[17]

Finally, structuralists tend to think of hegemons in a pejorative sense. Because hegemons dominate others, they impose either their ideals or rules that favor the hegemon at the expense of others. The imperial bourgeois states of the West, especially Great Britain and the United States, have filled this bill. For modern world system theorists (see Chapter 4), hegemons come from the ranks of core states that exploit others. Hegemony, then, is not something that is required, nor is it necessarily something to be proud of. It is merely another means of domination and subjugation of the weak by the strong.

As the reign of a hegemon goes on, its power and influence tend to recede, for a variety of reasons. In some cases hegemons become overextended in terms of their ability to pay for expenses associated with pursuing their interests in the international system. U.S. security interests and costs during the Cold War increased over time related to U.S. assistance to Europe and other allies in the campaign against communism along with the costs of the Vietnam War (1964–1973). All the while, President Lyndon Johnson also tried to pay for the Great Society program at home, which sought to eradicate poverty. Too many obligations may overwhelm the resources available to pay for these ventures and goals. The hegemon then has trouble making ends meet. Historian Paul Kennedy, for example, made this argument in his influential book, *The Rise and Fall of the Great Powers*.[18]

At some point the hegemon becomes selfish or more interested in achieving domestic objectives as opposed to pleasing others or paying for expensive international objectives. In so doing it becomes perceived as weak by officials both within and outside the nation—to the extent that it no longer pursues maintaining order over its sphere of influence. In cases such as the United States towards the end of the Cold War, its economic and security objectives came directly into conflict with those of its (former) allies. As Robert Gilpin likes to argue, with a change in the distribution of wealth and power in the international economy, both the interests of the hegemon in preserving order and that of its allies in buying into that structure, shift.[19]

Another argument about hegemony made by Robert Gilpin is that in some cases hegemons find themselves challenged by other powers that seek to become the dominant power.[20] For a variety of reasons, they challenge the hierarchical order of the international system. In the eyes of the hegemon, as others gradually increase their wealth and power, others may intentionally or unintentionally challenge the hegemon, which could possibly result in a hegemonic war. Such was the case of Nazi Germany and Imperial Japan before World War II. Today some fear that China may do so in the near future, based on its growing economy but also on its increasing political and military influence in Asia and the world over.[21]

Another interesting take on hegemony was discussed in Chapter 4. Antoni Gramsci, the Italian Marxist, posited that hegemons often dominate others simply because people or states consent to go along with the dominant power. Constituents may agree with the hegemon's beliefs and values or are pleased with what it provides to system members. Hegemony then is not so much imposed as it is chosen and even valued.[22] When the hegemon is in decline, its moral authority to rule is undermined and its ideals challenged.

Based on hegemonic stability theory, two issues in particular have recently been raised in relation to management of the international political economy in the early 2000s. One is the extent to which the United States viewed itself as a hegemon when the Cold War ended about 1990 and then accepted the responsibilities that came with it—especially when it came to providing for the security of the international system after 9/11 (see Chapter 9). Others wonder how much the supposed hegemonic power of the United States was based on a overestimation of U.S. military strength,[23] overestimation of U.S. influence, or simply a miscalculation on the part of the George W. Bush administration. As the war in Iraq came to a standstill in 2006 and the Bush administration's policies were met with resounding disapproval in mid-term elections, many wondered if the administration would continue along the path of unilateralism based on hegemonic precepts, or pull back and seek to cooperate with others on a more equal multilateral basis so as to share the costs of fighting terrorism.

Finally, for many academics, including historians, classicists, psychologists, political scientists, and religious officials, assertion by Bush administration officials of a unilateralist outlook after 9/11 based on hegemonic stability theory led to much concern that the United States was either consciously or subconsciously seeking to become a global empire (see Chapter 9).[24]

What's wrong with hegemonic stability theory? For many realists it makes a good deal of sense and history confirms it. Others argue that it is a grand theory of history although history does not obey grand theories. The theory looks for cycles where there are none. There may be times when the world system is peaceful and times when it is chaotic. But there is no single world system, so the whole point of a hegemon organizing the world system makes very little sense. Likewise, hegemonic stability theory also posits that the world system reaches some sort of stable equilibrium, a balance of forces that leads to peace and prosperity. However, some critics charge that equilibrium is a useless concept in the social sciences, where things constantly change and are transformed. Equilibrium might usefully describe two weights sitting on opposite sides of a scale, but it is just plain wrong to think of society in the same way. The world is fragmented, and relationships are unstable. For these critics the world also does not have a center or a single organizing principle. It is aimless to try to understand the world as if it did.

On the other hand, many economic liberals would assert that the neoliberal principles behind globalization might in fact be a single organizing principle.[25] And that for now a good deal of the world is pursuing the Western, if not the U.S. version of those ideals (see Chapter 3). The U.S. brand of hegemony, then, might not be effectively sustained by military power as it was during the Cold War, but is promoted and accepted to a great extent by the "soft power" that comes with economic and cultural influence.[26] Hegemonic stability theory suggests that the global antiglobalization campaign is as much about opposition to an ideology as it is opposition to U.S. global influence. More important, if the world is as integrated as neoliberals assert that it is or soon will be, but also exhibits a great deal of fragmentation, conflict, tension, and war, then it is all the more important that we understand hegemonic stability theory.

## CONCLUSION

Ideas are very powerful and *should* be taken seriously. The rational choice, constructivist, feminist, and hegemonic stability theories *all* challenge us to think about IPE in new and different ways. As John Maynard Keynes noted famously in the closing pages of his *General Theory*,

> the ideas of economists and political philosophers, both when they are right and when they are wrong, are more powerful than is commonly understood. Indeed the world is ruled by little else. Practical men, who believe themselves to be quite exempt from any intellectual influences, are usually the slaves of some defunct economist. Madmen in authority, who hear voices in the air, are distilling their frenzy from some academic scribbler of a few years back.[27]

## DISCUSSION QUESTIONS

1. How does the rational choice critique explain the existence of tariffs and other mercantilist policies? How does this critique explain liberal policies such as efforts to reduce trade barriers?
2. Do you support the idea that nations as a single entity can be liberal or mercantilist in outlook? Why? Why not? Explain.
3. Do you think constructivism should get more attention as a social science theory? Why? Why not?
4. How would the feminist critique of IPE approach mercantilism, liberalism, and structuralism? Explain.
5. Based on your knowledge of hegemonic stability theory, would you be inclined to support or oppose the idea that the United States became a hegemon after the end of the Cold War? After 9/11? Explain?

## INTERNET LINKS

The Canadian Electronic Feminist Network:
    www.unb.ca/web/par-l/index.html
People-Centered Development Forum:
    http://iisd1.iisd.ca/pcdf
Positive Futures Network:
    www.futurenet.org

## SUGGESTED READINGS

Michael Allingham. *Rational Choice Theory: A Very Short Introduction.* New York: Oxford University Press, 2002.

Graham Allison and Philip Zelikow. *Essence of Decision: Explaining the Cuban Missile Crisis,* 2nd ed. New York: Longman, 1999.

Dale C. Copeland. "The Constructivist Challenge to Structural Realism: A Review Essay," *International Security, 25* (Autumn 2000), pp. 187–212.

Barbara Ehrenreich and Arlie Russell Hochschild. *Global Woman: Nannies, Maids, and Sex Workers in the New Economy.* New York: Henry Holt, 2002.

John Elster. *The Cement of Society: A Survey of Social Order.* Cambridge: Cambridge University Press, 2003.

J. K. Gibson-Graham. *The End of Capitalism (As We Knew It): A Feminist Critique of Political Economy.* Oxford: Blackwell, 2002.

Phillip I. Levy. "A Political-Economic Analysis of Free-Trade Agreements," *The American Economic Review, 87* (September 1997), pp. 506–519.

Julie A. Nelson. "Feminism and Economics," *The Journal of Economic Perspectives, 9* (Spring 1995), pp. 131–148.

"Not Quite a New World Order, More a Three Way Split," *The Economist,* December 20, 1997, pp. 41–43.

Mancur Olson. *Power and Prosperity: Outgrowing Communist and Capitalist Dictatorships.* New York: Basic Books, 2000.

Paul Craig Roberts and Karen LaFollette Araujo. *The Capitalist Revolution in Latin America.* New York: Oxford University Press, 1997.

Steve Smith, Alexander Wendt, and Thomas Biersteker. *Social Theory in International Politics,* Cambridge: Cambridge University Press, 1999.

J. Ann Tickner. *Gendering World Politics: Issues and Approaches in the Post Cold War Era.* New York: Columbia University Press, 2001.

Georgina Waylen. "Gender, Feminism and Political Economy," *New Political Economy, 2* (July 1997), pp. 205–220.

Alexander Wendt. "Anarchy Is What States Make of It: The Social Construction of Power Politics," *International Organization, 46* (Spring 1992), pp. 391–425.

## KEY TERMS

rational choice analysis
public choice analysis
rent-seeking behavior

constructivism
feminism
hegemonic stability theory

public (collective) goods
free riding

## NOTES

1. A classic application of this approach to IPE can be found in Bruno Frey, *International Political Economics* (New York: Basil Blackwell, 1984).
2. For an application of rational choice theory to international relations, see J. Goldstein, *International Relations,* 4th ed. (New York: Longman, 2001), pp. 75–78.
3. Graham Allison and Philip Zelikow, *Essence of Decision: Explaining the Cuban Missile Crisis,* 2nd ed. (New York: Longman, 1999).
4. Goldstein, *International Relations.*
5. See Kenneth N. Waltz, *Theory of International Politics* (Reading, MA: Addison-Wesley, 1979).
6. See Alexander Wendt, "Anarchy Is What States Make of It: The Social Construction of Power Politics," *International Organization, 46* (Spring 1992), pp. 391–425.
7. Steve Smith, Alexander Wendt, and Thomas Biersteker, *Social Theory in International Politics* (Cambridge: Cambridge University Press, 1999).
8. Wendt, "Anarchy Is What States Make of It."
9. See, for example, Georgina Waylen, "Gender, Feminism and Political Economy," *New Political Economy, 2* (July 1997), pp. 205–220; and Julie A. Nelson, "Feminism and Economics," *The Journal of Economic Perspectives, 9* (Spring 1995), pp. 131–148.
10. The classic read of this sort is Helen Caldicott, *Missile Envy* (New York: Bantam Books, 1985).
11. See, for example, J. Ann Tickner, *Gendering World Politics: Issues and Approaches in the Post Cold War Era* (New York: Columbia University Press, 2001).
12. Nelson, "Feminism and Economics," p. 134.

13. This is one of the themes of Barbara Ehrenreich and Arlie Russell Hochschild, *Global Woman: Nannies, Maids, and Sex Workers in the New World Economy* (New York: Henry Holt, 2002).

14. "Acid Horrors," *The Economist,* January 17, 1998, pp. 35–36.

15. See, for example, Niall Ferguson, *The Rise and Fall of the American Empire* (New York: Penguin, 2005).

16. Charles Krauthammer, "The Unipolar Moment Revisited," *The National Interest, 70* (Winter 2002/2003), pp. 5–17; and Max Boot, "The Case for American Empire," *Weekly Standard, 7* (October 15, 2001), pp. 27–31.

17. Ferguson, *The Rise and Fall of the American Empire.*

18. Paul Kennedy, *The Rise and Fall of the Great Powers* (New York: Random House, 1987).

19. Robert Gilpin, *War and Change in World Politics* (Cambridge: Cambridge University Press, 1983).

20. Ibid.

21. See, for example, Jed Babbin and Edward Timperlake, *Showdown: Why China Wants War with the United States* (Washington DC: Regency, 2006). For a more insightful read, see Ted. C. Fishman, *China Inc.* (New York: Simon & Schuster, 2006).

22. Antonio Gramsci, *Selections from the Prison Notebooks,* Quintin Hoare and Geoffrey Howell Smith, transl. and eds. (London: Lawrence and Wishart, 1971).

23. Christopher Layne, "Impotent Power?," *The National Interest, 85* (September/October 2006), pp. 41–47.

24. See, for example, Andrew Bacevich, *The Imperial Tense: Problems and Prospects of American Empire* (New York: Ivan R. Dee, 2003).

25. This is one of the themes of the work of Thomas Friedman. See his *The Lexus and the Olive Tree* (New York: Knopf, 2000).

26. See Joseph Nye, *Soft Power: The Means to Success in World Politics* (New York: Public Affairs, 2005).

27. John Maynard Keynes, *The General Theory of Employment, Interest, and Money* (New York: Harcourt Brace Jovanovich, 1964), p. 383.

# PART II

# *IPE Structures: Production, Finance, Security, and Knowledge*

❋❋❋❋❋❋❋

The first five chapters of this book have provided an intellectual foundation on which to build a sophisticated understanding of the international political economy. In them we addressed many of the basic ideas and fundamental assumptions about international political economy (IPE), the three principal IPE perspectives that are most often used to analyze and interpret IPE interactions, and several variations on some of the themes outside those principal IPE perspectives. The next five chapters examine the relationships or "structures" that tie together nation-states and other actors and that link national and global markets in the IPE. Professor Susan Strange, a leading IPE thinker, has proposed that the main elements and arrangements of the international political economy can be organized into four core structures or systems: production and trade, finance and monetary issues, security, and knowledge and technology.

A word of explanation is useful at this point concerning our use of the term *structure* and its relationship to *structuralism* as discussed in Chapter 4. Each of the four main IPE structures is a network of bargains, agreements, institutions, and other relationships that connect the people of the world in various ways. A computer network or system is a structure, for example, in the sense that people are connected in particular ways by the "hardware" (institutions and their structural power) and the "software" (individual bargains and personal arrangements with their relational power) that make up the network. We propose to study how the four main structures of IPE connect the people of the world and condition the behavior of states, markets, and society.

On the other hand, many of those who subscribe to the structuralist (Marxist-based) perspective (see Chapter 4) believe that the best way to understand IPE is to focus specifically on the capitalist elements of the international political economy. According to this perspective, the economic structure of capitalism conditions or determines the outcomes of IPE.

Each of the four network structures consists of a set of relationships or arrangements and distinct rules (if not tacit understandings) between and among different political, economic, and social actors in each of these areas. In examining the characteristics of these four structures or systems, Strange also encourages us to ask the simple question, *"Cui bono?"* ("Who benefits?"). This question forces us to go beyond description to analysis—to identify not only the structure and how it works, but what benefit it provides to those who founded it or to those who manage it today. What sources of power were used to create the framework, and how has it been managed since? Strange also encourages us to ask questions about the relationship of one structure to another. An interesting thing about IPE is the fact that states, markets, and society, along with an increasing number of other important actors, are generally involved in a number of simultaneous structural relationships, often on different terms, and usually with different partners. A good example is the way many officials promote trade (an element of the production structure) as an "engine to growth" and at the same time often attempt to use it as a means or tool of foreign policy to punish another nation (an element of the security structure) by withholding trade from that nation.

This section's information will be especially useful in the second half of the text, when we tackle international and global problems. In these later sections, we will build on the foundation of the IPE perspectives and structures to construct a clear yet sophisticated understanding of some of the most important issues of yesterday, today, and tomorrow.

We begin by examining the production and trade structure, which accounts for who produces what, where, and under what conditions, and how it is sold, to whom, and on what terms. Some scholars have characterized the production structure as the international division of labor, but it means much more than simple categories of nations that produce different types of goods given their local resources and labor conditions. In IPE, the production structure also includes issues involving international trade. In Chapter 6 we explain why production and trade are so controversial related to who gains as a result of this production, and what terms or conditions prevail when it comes to the sale or exchange of these goods. Because of their connection to earning income and development, these issues are politically charged and some of the most controversial in IPE.

Our study of the finance and monetary structure is covered in two separate chapters. Chapter 7 examines in some detail the history, vocabulary, and basic concepts everyone needs to know about finance and the workings of various international monetary systems. Chapter 8 is a discussion of recent events surrounding several international finance crises, especially their causes, effects, and some of the measures put forth by the International Monetary Fund to address them. The rest of Chapter 8 examines the ongoing debt problems of many of the poorest developing nations and explores some of the World Bank's policies on debt. It ends with a discussion of the increasing role of nongovernmental organizations (NGOs) and even individuals in dealing with what many refer to as the "debt crisis."

In Chapter 9 we examine and define the sets of relationships and rules of behavior that affect the safety and security of states, groups, and individuals within the international political economy. Some parts of the security structure are easy to recognize, such as the role of the major powers in affecting war and peace and formal security alliances such as NATO (North Atlantic Treaty Organization). Other aspects, such as the role of terrorists, for example, are less visible or certain, but, as the events of September 11, 2001 ("9/11") demonstrated, of equally critical importance.

Finally, states, markets, and society are also linked by a set of relationships involving knowledge, ideas, and technology. In Chapter 10 we explore who has access to knowledge and technology, and on what terms—a question of growing importance and fascination in the study of IPE today. More and more, knowledge and technology represent the ability "to make and do things" that dramatically affect the balance of power between and among actors in the finance, production, and security spheres of life. Knowledge is power, as the saying goes, but who has this power, and how will it be used and for what purposes?

# 6

# *International Production and Trade*

## OVERVIEW

International production and trade is one of the international political economy's most controversial subjects. To review, the production and trade structure is the set of relationships between and among states, international organizations (IOs), international businesses, and nongovernmental organizations (NGOs) that together influence and manage international rules and norms related to what is produced, where, by whom, how, for whom, and at what price. Together with the international financial, technological, and security structures, trade links nation-states and other actors, furthering their interdependence, which benefits but also generates tension between and among these actors and different groups within them. Controversies about production and international trade stem from the compulsion of nation-states (rich and poor alike), as well as business enterprises, to capture the economic benefits of production and trade while limiting their negative political, economic, and social effects on producer groups and society in general.

This chapter surveys a variety of developments and changes that have occurred primarily in the post–World War II production and trade system. Over that period the production process has been transformed dramatically, such that some experts argue that recent changes in how things are made are greater than those that occurred leading up to the Industrial Revolution. Concurrently, many trade experts and officials in the Northern industrialized developed nations have sought ways to liberalize (open) the international trade system—that is, to reduce the level of protectionist barriers that limit or distort trade. The United States and its allies created the General Agreement on Tariffs and Trade (GATT) in 1947 to promote liberal trade values and objectives commensurate with U.S. political and military strategic objectives. In an effort to further liberalize world trade, in 1995 the World Trade Organization (WTO) replaced the GATT. Despite some successes these organizations have had in promoting free trade, the result is an impasse of sorts whereby many developing nations and a growing number of other actors with an interest in trade policy have sought "fair trade" or a mix of protectionist and free-trade policies.

The chapter concludes with a survey of other important trade problems and issues, namely, the growing number of regional trade blocs or alliances; North–South trade relations and their effects on issues of production economic development but also human rights and the environment; and the use of trade as an instrument of foreign policy. These and other issues make trade one of the most complex and politically contentious areas in the international political economy.

*In the absence of a world government, cross border trade is always subject to rules that must be politically negotiated among nations that are sovereign in their own realm but not outside their borders.*[1]

Robert Kuttner

Trade is *always* political, Robert Kuttner tells us. The economics of trade cannot be separated from its political aspects. In fact, many IPE theorists believe that no topic is more quintessentially IPE than trade. If anything, Kuttner's words understate the issue: Trade has become one of the most debated topics in IPE. Not only does it continue to be very important for national officials, the number of political actors and institutions outside the nation-state that shape international trade and manage the international production and trade structure have proliferated significantly since the end of the Cold War in the late 1980s.

In this chapter we outline some of the basic features and issues that are part of the international production and trade structure. By the end of the chapter it might appear that describing and explaining this structure is much like the blind men touching different parts of the elephant and describing what they think they feel, which are quite different from the parts others are touching. Using the three IPE perspectives, we will highlight many of the different parts of this structure—one whose management reflects the recent adoption of a common set of rules and principles. In many ways, the debate about who makes these rules and whose interests they reflect has only just begun.

## Production

Because of its direct connection to trade, the international production structure has fascinated and been increasing in significance to students of IPE. The **production and trade structure** accounts for what is produced, how, by whom, for whom, and on what terms. A recurring theme in Thomas Friedman's work is the transformation in the production process associated with globalization. In his earlier work, *The Lexus and the Olive Tree*, Friedman focused on how people the world over, but mainly in the developed industrialized nations, are using sophisticated technology and communication systems in the form of multifunctional, "postindustrial" age products, goods, and services.[2] The Internet connects people all over the world in ways previously unthought of—for both good and for bad. New lines of cars and clothing are mass-produced, but also produced massively in custom styles and shapes. Compared to before the Industrial Revolution, the nature and pace of innovation and production have changed radically, occurring in quantum leaps and at an exponential rate. The production process has also shifted from one based largely on assembly lines to the use of computers and sophisticated technologies that can develop virtual worlds and languages.

While all this has been happening, the production process has also been becoming much more fragmented, resulting in vertical **specialization** and **outsourcing**. As in, for example, the case of Boeing commercial jets, many production plants do not make their own component parts, but assemble them after the components are produced somewhere else. In his latest work, *The World Is Flat*, Friedman focuses on the continuing transformation of the production process whereby, in just a few short years, production techniques and processes have not only spread rapidly throughout much of the world (most recently to India and China), they have advanced to the point of empowering individuals to collaborate and compete globally. As anyone who has waited on the phone while speaking to a company "representative" in India can appreciate, the lever that enables individuals and groups to go global so easily and so seamlessly is a wireless, satellite network that makes it easier to outsource parts production or services related to those products.

According to Friedman, "every new product—from software to widgets—goes through a cycle that begins with basic research, then applied research, incubation, development, testing, manu-

**TABLE 6–1    Net Inflows of Foreign Direct Investment (in millions of $)**

| REGION/CLASSIFICATION | 2004 | 2002 | 2000 | 1990 | 1980 |
|---|---|---|---|---|---|
| Asia (excluding Middle East) | 146,607.1 | 95,157.1 | 146,156.2 | 18,920.7 | 2,971.6 |
| Central America and Caribbean | 23,273.3 | 20,129.7 | 21,524.9 | 3,608 | 2,876.3 |
| Europe | 277,058.2 | 436,551.7 | 866,982.9 | — | 21,367.2 |
| North America | 113,115.1 | 102,244.3 | 387,418.2 | 56,070.6 | 22,743.3 |
| Oceania | 44,773.6 | 18,457.2 | 17,139.4 | 10,116.2 | 2,162.3 |
| South America | 37,948.8 | 28,523 | 57,864 | 4,757.4 | 3,523.8 |
| Sub-Saharan Africa | 11,308.9 | 9,517.9 | 6,496.9 | 1,209.2 | 178.1 |
| Developed Countries | 454,003.8 | 573,409.2 | 1,287,513 | — | 46,489.5 |
| Developing Countries | 210,986.8 | 145,016.7 | 227,209.7 | 28,642.9 | 10,941.6 |

*Source:* World Resources Institute, Earthtrends: Searchable Database, October 17, 2006.

facturing, support, and finally continuation engineering in order to add improvements."[3] Friedman's "flat world" is one of giant video screens and call centers; the outsourcing of tax returns and market research, and flight reservations made in places such as India, but also in other countries around the world, wherever workers, as individuals, are anxious to become part of the global economy and to affect it in some unique way. The transformation and globalization of the production process is not unique to the manufacturing of goods and the development of services but has also occurred in agriculture and food production, other basic commodities such as cotton for textiles, along with military weapons and sophisticated new private and national security systems.[4]

The World Bank reports that in 2005 the world's gross domestic product (GDP) totaled $44.3 trillion—with the high-income countries producing $34.5 trillion or 78 percent of the total. Middle- and low-income countries produced only $9.9 trillion or 22 percent of the total, while low-income countries by themselves produced $1.3 trillion or just 4 percent of the world's total output.[5] One way to think about production is in terms of foreign direct investment (FDI) connected to where production takes place. Andrew McGrew reports that production has become much more diffuse but also more intense, reaching a peak of $1.2 trillion or four times the level of only five years earlier.[6] As Table 6–1 demonstrates, most FDI (68 percent) remains concentrated among the developed nations, though investment is slowly spreading out to every continent. Within the developed regions, most FDI is concentrated between and within the United States, Japan, and the European Union (EU). After that, the Asian newly industrialized countries (NICs), Central and South America, and the transition economies of Eastern Europe are where most investors deposit their funds. The share of total world FDI for developing nations did jump from 20 to 32 percent between 1980 and 2004, yet the share of investment in the least developed countries has remained stagnant, while ten developing nations receive almost 80 percent of FDI in developing countries.

According to McGrew, these patterns of investment have contributed to the mobility of capital (see Chapter 7) and to economic restructuring whereby industries tend to leave the industrialized nations in search of new markets, cheap labor, or other production advantages by transnational corporations (TNCs) in developing parts of the world (see Chapter 17). As expected, many mercantilists and structuralists note that these trends have important consequences for the distribution of the world's wealth and power through international trade as well as for issues related to labor conditions, the environment, and many other issues in developing nations that we will discuss later (see also Chapter 15).

## International Trade

International trade is a process that occurs when goods and services cross national boundaries in exchange for money or the goods and services of another nation. Although most of the goods and services produced locally are consumed in confined markets, international trade has grown dramatically as a reflection of increased demand for goods and services that do not exist or cannot be produced locally. Increased international trade also reflects the growing internationalization or globalization of production. During the period from 1953 to 2004, for example, world trade in merchandise and services increased from a total of $84 billion to more than $76 trillion (both figures in constant 1995 dollars).[7]

Trade, then, ties countries together, and in so doing, generates significant economic, political, and social interdependence. However, it also generates a good deal of tension and conflict between and among different states. For most states, trade can be an easy way of generating income and jobs. For many developing nations, it is often a critical component of development plans. More than ever, therefore, states are compelled to regulate trade in order to maximize its benefits and limit its costs to their economies. Concurrently, without a set of international rules and procedures in an international political economy that is becoming more global in nature, domestic-oriented trade policies would undermine and conflict with one another.

The international trade structure pulls national leaders, IO and NGO officials, and the public in three directions at once. It is possible to support and espouse the principles of all three IPE perspectives of production and trade at the same time. Economic liberals tend to emphasize that the rational thing for states to do (see Chapters 3 and 5) is to agree on a common set of international rules and regulations that will maximize the gains from trade, in a competitive, interdependent, if not globalizing, international political economy. Likewise, without these rules, many states and groups they represent in society are likely to incur substantial economic losses. Mercantilists and structuralists agree that there are economic gains to be made from trade, but a variety of other issues related to how trade contributes to national wealth and power (mercantilism) and how it benefits some groups more than others (structuralists) makes trade a much more complex and controversial topic.

What follows is a brief overview of trade history and discussion of how the three perspectives view trade and their reasons for doing so.

## THREE PERSPECTIVES ON INTERNATIONAL TRADE

From the sixteenth through the eighteenth centuries (see Chapter 2), there were no international trade rules as we know them today. Early European states aggressively sought to generate trade surpluses as a source of wealth for local producers, for royalty, and later for the bureaucratic state. To help local industries get off the ground, imports of intermediate goods were discouraged if they meant people would purchase imports instead of buying locally produced goods. For mercantilists, trade was one instrument that states tried to use to enhance their wealth, power, and prestige in relation to the wealth, power, and prestige of other states.

### Economic Liberals

Many economic liberal ideas about trade are rooted in the late-eighteenth-century views of Adam Smith and David Ricardo, who were reacting to what they viewed as mercantilist abuses at the time. They proposed a distinctly liberal theory of trade that dominated British policy for more than a hundred years and is still influential today. Smith, of course, generally advocated laissez-faire policies (see Chapter 3). Ricardo went one step further; his work on the **law of comparative advantage** demonstrated that free trade increased efficiency and had the potential to make everyone better off. It mattered little to economic liberals who produced the goods, where, how, or under what circumstances, as long as individuals were free to buy and sell them on open markets.

The law of comparative advantage suggests that when people and nations produce goods and services, they give up something else they could have produced, but that would have been more expensive to make than the goods they actually created. This is what economists call **opportunity cost**. The law of comparative advantage invites us to compare the cost of producing an item ourselves with the availability and costs of buying it from others, and to make a logical and efficient choice between the two. In Ricardo's day, as we saw in Chapter 3, the law of comparative advantage specified that Great Britain should import food grains rather than produce them at home, because the cost of imports was comparatively less than the cost of local production.

For many economic liberals in the late 1800s, the world was supposedly becoming a global workshop, where everyone could benefit from trade, guided by the "invisible hand" of the market. As we will see later in this chapter (and in Chapters 7 and 8), these ideas remain quite influential and popular today and are the basis of free-trade and other policies (commonly referred to as the **Washington consensus**) promoted by the United States, other nations, and by a host of international economic institutions such as the World Trade Organization (WTO), the International Monetary Fund (IMF), and the World Bank. A large (but far from universal) consensus exists that the benefits of a liberal or open international trade system far outweigh its negative effects.[8] States should do what they can to limit or control demands for trade protection in order to realize the gains that come from production efficiency related to each state's comparative advantages in natural and human resources.

## Mercantilists

Many neomercantilists and structuralists are critical of the economic liberal view of trade. As we outlined in Chapter 2, Alexander Hamilton and Friedrich List, among others, challenged what became accepted economic liberal doctrine about trade. From their mercantilist perspective, liberalism and free-trade policies were merely a rationale for England to maintain its dominant advantage over its trading partners on the Continent and in the New World. For Hamilton, supporting U.S. infant industries and achieving national independence and security required the use of protectionist trade measures.[9] Likewise, List argued that in a climate of rising economic nationalism, protectionist trade policies such as import tariffs and export subsidies were necessary if Europe's infant industries were to compete on an equal footing with England's more efficient enterprises.[10] More important, List also maintained that in order for free trade to work for all, it must be preceded by greater equality between states, or at least a willingness on their part to share the benefits and costs associated with it.

Many neomercantilists today challenge the assumption that comparative advantage unconditionally benefits both or all of the parties engaged in trade. People employed in different industries or sectors of any economy can be expected to resist being laid off or moving into other occupations as comparative advantage shifts to different nations. In many cases, states can intentionally *create* comparative advantages almost overnight in the production of new goods and services simply by adopting **strategic trade policies** that invest heavily in those projects. New technology, skills, and other resources such as cheap labor can easily help one state's new industries gain a comparative (competitive) advantage over the industries of another state. This has been the case of many industries, including auto, steel, and textile producers,[11] along with farmers, who continually seek trade protection for their commodities and products.

Another political reality that does not easily square with free trade is that, in democratic nations with representative legislatures, it is the state's *duty to protect* society and its businesses from the negative effects of trade. When many domestic groups and industries appeal to the state for protection, they are likely to receive help because legislators are threatened when these constituents face layoffs or competition from cheaper imports. In many cases, protection is a built-in feature of many democratic systems. Those who benefit from a small savings on the price of an imported article of clothing or new car, for instance, usually do not register their support for free trade as loudly as workers displaced by those policies and who seek protection.

Trade protection is also associated with a fear of becoming too dependent on other nations for certain goods, especially food and items related to defense. In some cases, states such as Japan worry that too much dependency on another state for certain items such as energy resources can lead to either economic or political exploitation of the dependent state. Such was the intention of the United States when it exported soybeans to Japan in the early 1970s and then cut off those exports when U.S. mothers complained of high meat prices and used soy as a replacement for meat.

Finally, some neomercantilists are concerned that the protectionist trade policies of a regional trade alliance such as NAFTA or the European Union (EU) (discussed later), which are designed to help local industries, might either intentionally or unintentionally disrupt another country. Often, this disruption is followed by an assortment of defensive or retaliatory neomercantilist policies (see the box, "The Vocabulary of International Trade Policy") that counter the original measures or "even the score" with the other state.

---

### THE VOCABULARY OF INTERNATIONAL TRADE POLICY

Some of the more important and most often used protectionist measures include the following.

- *Tariffs:* A tax placed on imported goods to raise the price of those goods, making them less attractive to consumers. Tariffs can be used to raise government revenue (particularly in less developed countries) or, more commonly, as a means to protect domestic industry from foreign competition.
- *Import quotas:* A limit on the quantity of an item imported into a nation. By limiting the quantity of imports, the quota tends to drive up the price of a good at the same time it restricts competition.
- *Export quotas:* International agreements that limit the quantity of an item a nation can export, with the effect of limiting the number of goods imported by another country. Examples include Orderly Marketing Arrangements (OMAs), Voluntary Export Restraints (VERs), or Voluntary Restraint Agreements (VRAs). For example, the Multifibre Agreement (MFA) established a system of textile export quotas for less developed countries.
- *Export subsidies:* Any measure that effectively reduces the price of an exported product, making it more attractive to potential foreign buyers.
- *Currency devaluations:* The effect of making nation's currency worth less (or more of other currencies) makes exports to other countries cheaper and imports from abroad more expensive. Currency depreciation thus tends to achieve the effects, temporarily at least, of both a tariff (raising import prices) and an export subsidy (lowering the costs of exports). However, currency changes affect the prices of all traded goods, whereas tariffs and subsidies generally apply to one good at a time.
- *Nontariff barriers (NTBs):* Other ways of limiting imports, including government health and safety standards, domestic content legislation, licensing requirements, and labeling requirements. Such measures make it difficult for imported goods to be marketed or significantly raise the price of imported goods.
- *Strategic trade practices:* Efforts on the part of the state to *create* comparative advantages in trade by methods such as subsidizing research and development of a product, or providing subsidies to help an industry increase production to the point at which it can move down the "learning curve" to achieve greater production efficiency than foreign competitors. Strategic trade practices are often associated with *state industrial policies,* that is, intervention in the economy to promote specific patterns of industrial development.
- *Dumping:* The practice of selling an item for less abroad than at home. Dumping is an unfair trade practice when used to drive out competitors from an export market with the goal of generating monopoly power.
- *Countervailing trade practices:* State defensive measures taken to counter the advantage gained by another state when it adopts protectionist measures. Such practices include antidumping measures and the imposition of countervailing tariffs or quotas.
- *Safeguards:* Another defensive measure, used when, after tariffs are reduced, a product is imported in quantities that threaten serious injury to domestic producers of like or directly competitive products.

As many mercantilists see it, economic liberal theories about trade cannot account adequately for the real political world, in which states manipulate production and trade for a host of social, political, and economic reasons. As in the analogy of the Prisoner's Dilemma (see Chapter 8), because there is no guarantee of security in the international security structure (see Chapter 9), there is no guarantee that, even when states say they prescribe to free trade, they will not engage of protectionism in one form or another. Therefore, the rational thing for states to do is to be prepared to act in their own interest by protecting themselves.

### Structuralists

Structuralists label the early mercantilist period as one of classical imperialism. The drive to explore and to colonize undeveloped regions of the world by the major European powers originated in their own economies. Mercantilist policies that emphasized exports became necessary when industrial capitalist societies experienced economic depression. Manufacturers overproduced industrial products, and financiers had a surplus of capital to invest abroad. Colonies served at least two purposes: They were a place to dump these goods, and a place where investment could be made in industries that profited from cheap labor and access to plentiful (that is, inexpensive) quantities of natural resources and mineral deposits. Trade helped colonial mother countries dominate and subjugate the people and economies of the colonial territories (see Chapter 4). Lenin argued that national trade policies benefited most the dominant class in society—the bourgeoisie. In the period of **modern imperialism** toward the end of the nineteenth century, capitalist countries used trade to spread capitalism into underdeveloped regions of the world. The "soft" power of finance as much as the "hard" power of colonial military conquest helped generate empires of dependency and exploitation.

During the early colonial period, developing regions of the world remained on the periphery of the international trade system and provided their mother countries with primary goods and mineral resources along with markets for manufactured products. Structuralists argue that industrializing core nations converted these resources and minerals into finished and semifinished products, many of which were sold to other major powers and back to their colonies. To this day, trade plays a key role in helping the imperialist industrialized nations subjugate the masses of people in developing regions of the world. Although particular sectors (enclaves) of core economies have developed, political and economic conditions for the masses of people within peripheral nations and regions *have become underdeveloped* since contact with the industrialized nations through trade.[12]

Immanuel Wallerstein stresses the linkage between capitalist core countries and periphery and semiperiphery regions of the world.[13] Today, patterns of international trade are determined largely by an **international division of labor** between core, semi-peripheral, and peripheral states that accompanies and drives capitalism to expand globally. The integration of global markets and free-trade policies associated with globalization are an extension of the same economic motives of imperial powers of the nineteenth and twentieth centuries.

In sum, all three IPE perspectives on trade also contain a variety of different ideological outlooks about trade and different trade issues. Even though today a majority of academics and policy officials favor an economic liberal international trade system, within a system that is supposed to gradually be liberalizing or opening up, most nations tend to behave in a mercantilist fashion when their national interests are threatened. And as we will see in the next section, there is also a good deal of concern in both developing and industrialized nations that trade may be more exploitative than mutually advantageous.

## GATT AND THE LIBERAL POSTWAR TRADE STRUCTURE

Until after World War II, trade rules largely reflected the interests of the dominant states, especially Great Britain. Despite a few decades in which economic liberal ideas prevailed, protectionism was the order of the day. Trade rules were enforced at the point of a gun—or cannon, as in the case of the United States forcing Japan to open its doors to U.S. trade in the 1860s.

The post–World War II structure of much of the capitalist world's political economy was established in 1944 at the Bretton Woods conference in Bretton Woods, New Hampshire. There, Allied leaders, led by the United States and Great Britain, created a new economic order based on numerous liberal ideas they hoped would prevent many of the interwar economic conflicts and problems that had led to World War II. By the turn of the twentieth century, protectionist trade policies had been on the rise as the major powers raced to stimulate industrial growth. During the Great Depression of the 1930s, protectionism spiraled upward while international trade decreased significantly, by an estimated 54 percent between 1929 and 1933, strangled in part by the Smoot-Hawley tariffs in the United States and onerous trade barriers enacted elsewhere. According to some historians, the trade situation and the depressed international economy helped generate the bleak economic conditions to which ultranationalist leaders such as Mussolini and Hitler reacted. It is important to note that, in contrast to the common assumption that the United States has always supported free trade, it was not until 1934 that it officially adopted a free-trade policy, until then routinely protecting most of its traded items.

In conjunction with this effort, the United States promoted the establishment of an **International Trade Organization (ITO)** that was to oversee new liberal trade rules that would gradually reduce tariffs, subsidies, and other protectionist measures, offsetting domestic protectionist and mercantilist tendencies. The ITO never got off the ground because a coalition of protectionist interests in the U.S. Congress forced the United States to withdraw from the agreement, effectively killing it. President Harry Truman advanced a temporary alternative structure for multilateral trade negotiations under the **General Agreement on Tariffs and Trade (GATT)**. In 1948, the GATT became the primary organization responsible for the liberalization of international trade[14] through a series of multilateral negotiations, called *rounds,* at which the world's main trading nations would each agree to reduce their own protectionist barriers in return for freer access to each others' markets.

The GATT was based on the principles of **reciprocity** and **nondiscrimination**. Trade concessions were reciprocal—all member nations agreed to lower their trade barriers together. This principle was conceived as a way to discourage or prevent nations from enacting unilateral trade barriers. The loss in protection of domestic industry was to be offset by freer access to foreign markets. Designed to prevent bilateral trade wars, the principles of nondiscrimination and the **Most Favored Nation (MFN)** trading status required that imports from all countries be treated the same whereby imports from one nation could not be given preference over those from another. Theoretically, the GATT's membership was open to any nation, but until the 1980s most communist countries refused to join it, viewing it as a tool of Western imperialism.

The principles of reciprocity and nondiscrimination would prove to be potent during the early years of GATT negotiations in a series of trading rounds, as members began slowly to peel away the protectionist barriers they had erected in the 1930s and allowing international trade to expand dramatically. In many cases, however, it was not possible to divorce politics from trade, even under GATT rules. Some nations were not always willing to grant reciprocity to their trading partners automatically, but granted it selectively to those they favored politically or wanted to assist, while for any number or reasons withholding it from other states. Later in the chapter we will discuss the case of the United States using trade as a strategic instrument by withholding MFN status from China to achieve a variety of U.S. foreign policy objectives.

Keep in mind that the GATT was not a set of rules that could be enforced by the organization but depended on the members to fulfill multilateral trade obligations with one another. Policy decisions were made on the basis of consensus, and thus implementation of polices often reflected a combination of political and economic interests. Written into the GATT were a series of exceptions from generalized trade rules for certain goods and services, including tariffs and quotas on textiles and agricultural products along with regional trade agreements (RTAs), discussed below. At first these exemptions allowed many of the war-ravaged nations to resolve balance-of-payments shortages.

In the case of agriculture they also reflected food shortages in Europe and the need for financial assistance to farmers and other groups.

## Mercantilism on the Rebound

During the 1960s and early 1970s the pace at which the Western industrialized economies had grown after the war began to slow appreciably. The OPEC (Organization of Petroleum Exporting Countries) oil crisis began in 1973 and soon resulted in economic recession in many of the Western industrialized nations. Throughout this period international trade continued to grow, but not at the rate at which it had earlier. Under increasing pressure to stimulate economic growth, many nations reduced their tariff barriers. At the same time, however, they devised new and more sophisticated ways of protecting their exports and otherwise limiting imports. By the time the Tokyo round of the GATT (1973–1979) got underway, the level of tariffs on industrial products had decreased to an average of 9 percent. The Tokyo GATT round tried to deal with a growing number of **nontariff barriers (NTBs)** that many believed were stifling world trade. Rules or codes covered a range of discriminatory trade practices, including the use of export subsidies, countervailing duties, dumping, government purchasing practices, government-imposed product standards, and custom valuation and licensing requirements on importers. Some new rules were also devised that covered trade with developing nations.

Many liberal trade theorists at the time argued that the Tokyo round did not go far enough, especially in dealing with the growing problem of NTBs or with enforcing GATT rules. In the 1970s and 1980s, the industrialized nations were encountering a number of old and also new kinds of trade problems. Trade among the industrialized nations quadrupled from 1963 to 1973, but increased only two and one-half times in the next decade. Meanwhile, trade accounted for increasingly higher percentages of gross domestic product (GDP) in the industrialized nations in the 1980s: around 20 percent for the United States, 20 percent for Japan, and an average of 50 percent for members of the European Union. To put it mildly, trade policy continued to be a serious source of tension and disagreement among the industrialized nations, reflecting their increasing dependence on trade to help generate and maintain economic growth.

Japan, the quintessential mercantilist nation during this period, benefited from the liberal international trade system while erecting domestic trade and other protectionist policies (see Chapter 12). By the 1970s, Japan's export-led growth trade strategy began to bear fruit. Its **Ministry of International Trade and Industry (MITI)** helped pick corporate winners that it and other government officials felt would prosper in the international economy from state assistance. Most of these industries were high-employment, high-technology firms whose future looked bright. Working closely with their national firms, the Japanese and the newly industrialized countries began assisting their firms in ways that would put them in a strong competitive position.

The term *strategic trade policies* became synonymous with state efforts to stimulate exports[15] or block foreign access to domestic markets and included "the use of threats, promises, and other bargaining techniques in order to alter the trading regime in ways that improve the market position and increase the profits of national corporations."[16] In the United States, for instance, the Omnibus Trade and Competitiveness Act of 1988 produced **Super 301**, which required trade officials to list "priority" countries that unfairly threatened U.S. exports. Aside from export subsidies and the use of a variety of import-limiting measures, proactive strategic trade policy measures included extended support for "infant industries" complemented by import protection and export promotion measures. Some states went out of their way to form joint ventures with firms in the research and development of new technologies and products. An example was U.S. government assistance to the Microsoft Corporation in an effort to crack down on Chinese computer software pirates.[17]

With the acceptance of some amount of trade protection, a more liberal (open) GATT system seemed compromised. **Free trade** was slowly replaced as the central principle by the notion of **fair trade** or a "level playing field," where states sought to enact policies to counteract as much but not more so than those of their trading partners. Trade policy moved from the multilateral arena of

GATT to a series of bilateral discussions, as between the United States and Japan and between the United States and the European Union. Under conditions of increasing protectionism but also in an effort to benefit more from trade, it was the United States during the Reagan administration that first sought to reassert the liberal vision of free trade. Thus was born the Uruguay round of the GATT.

## The Uruguay Round

The eighth GATT round—the Uruguay round—began in 1986 in Punta del Este, Uruguay, and was completed on December 15, 1993. Generally speaking, economic liberals tend to view this round as a success because of the effect it had on the volume and value of international trade. Many import quotas were eliminated, and export subsidies were brought under control. Foreign direct investment surged alongside growth in trade, further connecting national economies into an interdependent international trade network.

Specifically, the Uruguay round established new rules and regulations related to limiting protectionist measures such as "dumping" (selling goods at below fair market prices) and the use of state subsidies. The round went beyond previous trade rounds and established fifteen working groups that covered such items as market access for textiles and agricultural goods; trade-related intellectual property rights (**TRIPs**) that include such items as copyrights, patents, and trademarks on computer software; trade-related investment measures (**TRIMs**); and the complicated issue of trade in services. TRIMs and service issues reflected recognition that as the nature of production changed and spread to different parts of the world, it affected both the amount and kind of international trade.

For the first time, GATT trade negotiations dealt in a comprehensive manner with the contentious issue of agriculture. All of the major producers and importers of agricultural products routinely employ subsidies and other measures that, according to economic liberal critics, distort agricultural trade. Agricultural issues had been intentionally absent from previous GATT rounds because they were politically too contentious and would have prevented progress in areas where agreements were possible. This time, trade officials made the issue of agricultural assistance and reform one of the main objectives of the Uruguay round.[18] The United States, the Cairns Group (composed of Australia and seventeen other pro–free-trade countries) led a politically radical effort to phase out all agricultural subsidies. After resistance by some U.S. farm groups and government officials, the United States agreed to *gradually* eliminate its domestic farm programs and agricultural trade support measures. EU efforts to significantly reduce their agricultural subsidies were complicated by the EU's Common Agricultural Policy (CAP)—a community-wide farm program that reflected the combined interests of its fifteen member states, with France most critical of efforts to decrease agricultural support. Bringing the EU's farm program in line with GATT reform proposals would be a politically difficult and complicated process that took almost five years to complete.

Many U.S. exporters expected a new multilateral agreement to produce 20,000 jobs for every $1 billion increase in exports and access to overseas markets for U.S. semiconductors, computers, and a variety of U.S. agricultural commodities.[19] However, agricultural trade remained one of the major sticking points of the negotiations, deadlocking the entire negotiations on several occasions. Eventually, at the eleventh hour, in November 1993, an agreement on agriculture was reached that opened the way for agreement on all other issues.

In order to arrive at a consensus, the new agreement reflected numerous "deals" or compromises between nations or blocs of nations. Under the new agreement, all countries were to reduce their use of agricultural export subsidies and domestic assistance *gradually* over a period of years. The new rules allowed states to convert nontariff import barriers into tariff equivalents, which were then to be reduced in stages. However, because of the strength of farm lobbies and the importance of agricultural exports in many of these countries, the method for calculating tariff equivalents in most cases actually set new tariff levels *higher* than they had been, effectively nullifying efforts to reduce farm support.

It is important to note that the Uruguay round did produce some sixty or so agreements on a host of other issues, including safeguards, TRIPs, rules of origin, technical barriers to trade, and textiles and clothing.[20] The Uruguay round also became famous for creating the **World Trade Organization (WTO)** and for institutionalizing what would become a set of global trade rules and regulations. GATT rules and a number of procedures became a legal element of the WTO. Trade officials claimed that progress was made toward liberalizing agricultural trade in the Uruguay round, but in reality, protectionism remained a key feature of agricultural trade. Many delegates intended that problems remaining in agriculture, establishing a services code, and developing nation concerns about how TRIPs gave advantages to developed states, would be dealt with more directly in the next round of trade negotiations.

### The WTO

The final agreement of the Uruguay round launched the new World Trade Organization, comprised of 146 members at the time.[21] The WTO is headquartered in Geneva, Switzerland, and accounts for over 90 percent of world trade. Its primary job is to implement the latest GATT agreement and to act as a forum for negotiating new trade deals, to help resolve trade disputes, to review national trade policies, and to help developing nations deal with trade policy issues through technical assistance and training programs. Theoretically, WTO decisions are still to be made by a consensus of the members. The WTO's decision-making structure includes a secretariat (administrative body), a ministerial conference that meets at least once every two years, and a general council composed of ambassadors and delegation heads that meets several times a year in Geneva. Numerous specialized working groups focus on the environment, development, TRIPs, membership applications, regional trade agreements, the relationship of trade to investment, the interaction between trade and competition policy, and transparency in government procurement.

The WTO has a **Dispute Settlement Panel (DSP)** that rules on trade disputes, giving the WTO an enforcement mechanism, something the GATT did not have. An impartial panel of experts oversees cases submitted to it for resolution, and members can appeal their findings. The DSP can impose trade sanctions on member states that violate trade agreements. Several cases have gained significant press attention, including a judgment against the EU's attempt to limit imports of hormone-fed U.S. beef into the EU. Likewise, the WTO ruled against the EU's banana import program, which tried to curtail imports of bananas produced by U.S. companies in the Caribbean. (See the box, "Bananas, Beef, and National Security," in Chapter 2.) Another case was the transatlantic conflict over the production and use of genetically modified foods and organisms (GMOs) (see the box, "GMOs," in Chapter 19).

For the most part, since the founding of the WTO, trade disputes have become more complex and politicized. Some nations have even threatened to withdraw from the WTO when DSP decisions go against them. In some cases, state officials are accused of "losing state sovereignty" to the WTO when they lose a dispute. So far, however, most states have either accepted the board's findings or arrived at a satisfactory resolution, because so much is at stake economically or politically or because they feel compelled to participate in the rule-making exercise rather than be left out of it.

### The Doha "Development Round"

The next round of multilateral trade negotiations was to begin in 1999, but the WTO's ministerial talks in Seattle ended in deadlock, with riots in the streets and antiglobalization protestors blocking delegates from entering the negotiations. The "Battle of Seattle" became a rallying cry for many antiglobalization NGOs concerned about the violations of human rights in sweatshops, the large tracts of land farmed by agribusinesses in developing countries, the effects of large capitalist enterprises on the local environment, the lack of transparency in decision-making processes of the WTO, and a host of ethical issues.[22] Critics of all ideological persuasions, including President Bill Clinton, questioned the WTO's ability to deal with these popular issues as well as with institutional issues such as the connection between trade and such topics as investment, competition policy, and WTO decision making.

After the events of 9/11, many trade officials pushed to restart multilateral trade talks. At the 2001 ministerial meeting (far away from protestors), the next multilateral trade round began in

Doha, Qatar. From the beginning, many developing countries complained openly that many of the agreements reached at the Uruguay round had not resulted in significant gains for them. As expected, they also argued that before new trade agreements could be reached, including those unresolved in the Uruguay round, the developed nations would have to make a concerted effort to include developing nations in the negotiation process and to integrate them in the global economy. In recognition of this goal, the Doha round was nicknamed "the Development Round," to reflect the growing importance of developing nations in the international trade system.

At Cancun, Mexico, in November 2003, ministerial talks broke down once again. U.S. Special Trade Representative Robert Zoellick blamed developing nations and NGOs (especially those associated with the antiglobalization campaign) for resisting efforts to reach a new agreement. Many developing countries blamed the WTO for failing to fulfill promises it had made in the Uruguay Round. Some countries claimed to be suffering more poverty, along with environmental, social, and economic damage, after implementing the WTO's new rules. Outside the talks, many developing countries were resisting efforts by the United States, the EU, Japan, and others to implement the "Washington consensus" or one-size-fits-all strategy of economic development that included trade liberalization. The Group of 20 (G-20), headed by Brazil, India, South Africa, and China, focused on cutting the farm subsidies of the rich countries. As a bloc, they dismissed 105 changes in WTO rules that would provide more access to their markets by the developed states.[23]

To restart the talks, the United States offered to cut subsidies if others did the same. Meanwhile, the 2002 U.S. farm bill passed by Congress had *increased* U.S. farm and agribusiness support by $70 billion, making the U.S. commitment to trade liberalization seem hollow because it insulated farmers from fluctuations in world market prices. The result, many critics point out, has been more overproduction and a distortion of world commodity prices, leading to the dumping of excess commodities onto world markets. This displaces local production in developing countries' markets, disrupts the local food infrastructure, and depresses prices received by local farmers. Even President George W. Bush recognized that continued subsidies of farm commodities in the United States and the EU hurt poorer farmers in developing nations.[24] For many developing countries, however, the United States was always "demanding too much liberalization while offering too little itself."[25]

Late in 2005, India, China, Brazil, and the rest of what became the G-20 pushed the United States and the EU to cut domestic agricultural support significantly. However, many U.S. and EU farmers consistently balk at losing their income protection measures. A sideshow throughout the round was sniping between the United States and the EU, at times almost as if they were unaware of or did not care about the effects of their policies on developing nations and international trade. The EU was not scheduled to reform (cut) its CAP policy for another three years.[26] Meanwhile, the United States claimed that the EU's tariffs were twice as high and EU subsidies three times more than those of the United States, to which an EU spokesman responded, "the favorite blood sport of trade negotiators is to go after the EU on its agricultural policy."[27]

In response, WTO Director-General Pascal Lamy put forward a **20/20/20 deal** whereby the United States would limit its subsidies to $20 billion, the EU would agree to the G-20's proposal to cut farm tariffs, and developing countries would limit their industrial tariffs to 20 percent.[28] The EU and Brazil leaned toward accepting the proposal while India did not, saying that these kinds of changes in their policies would hurt the poor in their country. The United States still wanted *deep* cuts in tariff barriers all around and did not want to compromise further without them.

At the G-8 meeting in the summer of 2006 in St. Petersburg, Russia, the major powers made yet another effort to come to an agreement that would end the Doha round talks. WTO Director-General Lamy chaired talks in Geneva between the G-6 nations of Australia, the United States, the EU, Japan, Brazil, and India. Only days later, however, the Doha round reached an impasse, and as in the Uruguay round, agriculture was again the major sticking point, blocking agreements on all other trade-related issues.

Issues other than agriculture also remain on the Doha agenda. In the case of TRIPs, many developing countries argue that their lack of access to medicines, especially in generic form, is a result of patents held mainly by U.S. companies and compromises their ability to fight disease and epidemics (see the box, "Patent Rights Versus Patient Rights" in Chapter 10). Most of the poorer developing nations, especially those in Africa, lack the infrastructures necessary to compete with U.S. firms. The United States retorts that allowing developing nations to produce cheaper generic drugs would hurt (the profits of) major drug manufacturers. After some negotiation, U.S. drug companies agreed to allow certain developing nations to produce a limited number of drugs used in the fight against AIDS and other diseases in developing nations.

The WTO has also failed to reach consensus on specific measures regarding the movement of "cultural products" (such as movies), insurance companies, security firms, banking across national borders, and protectionist "local content" legislation. Other potential stumbling blocks have been negotiations over trade in manufactures and services, accession issues for potential new members, and special and differential treatment (S&DT) rules. These rules define market access to individual developing countries with a *unique* approach in terms of trade policy for each country.

### Doha in the Dumps

Contrary to past stalemates, however, no new deadline has been set for completion of the Doha round. On the whole, it has proven to be quite difficult to integrate two-thirds of the world's population into an international set of trade rules and regulations. Without an agreement on agriculture and some of the other contentious issues, many economic liberal commentators and trade officials fear that the Doha round will never be successfully concluded. Some believe that the inclusion of the developing nations in the WTO has created an agenda that is now too large to find consensual positions. Another result could be "**Doha lite**"—or a watered-down compromise that does not require nations to give up too much out of fear that not reaching an agreement will undermine the WTO as an institution. Some also argue that a stalemate in these sorts of talks is part of the process, and that, because so much is at stake, negotiators will eventually arrive at a political compromise at the eleventh hour.

Other experts fear that the failure of the United States to compromise further signals a "pox on multilateral trade agreements" in general and quite possibly on the WTO as well. It also remains to be seen if the WTO can bring down trade barriers, codify the terms of global competition, and administer a unified package of agreements to which all members are committed—without a national hegemon (see Chapter 3) imposing order on the trade system or internalizing the costs of adjustment associated with freer trade. Without an assertive hegemon, globalization of trade may have made it too difficult to reconcile economic liberal objectives with domestic pressures to limit the dislocating effects trade has on the economy and various societal groups.

## REGIONAL TRADE BLOCS

Some mercantilist and economic liberal critics of the Doha round suggest that, instead of multilateral talks, the United States and other states ought to pursue bilateral and regional trade agreements with different nations. In fact, the United States has already agreed to more than 300 bilateral agreements with other countries, with more on the way. It also belongs to a number of **regional trade agreements (RTAs)** such as NAFTA and APEC (see below), where it is easier for the United States to dictate terms and not face pressures from some pro–free-trade businesses to complete the Doha round, which in most cases has a bigger payoff than an RTA. RTAs also have less bureaucracy and more room to account for the idiosyncracies of partner states or to reconcile conflicting interests on a geographically regional level.

**Regional trade blocs** are defined as a formal intergovernmental collaboration between two or more states in a geographic area.[29] They promote a mix of economic liberal and mercantilist trade policies, reducing barriers within the trade bloc while retaining trade barriers with nonmember nations. Ravenhill notes that RTAs number well over 300 and have grown prodigiously since the end of the

Cold War. They are estimated to have controlled 43 percent of world trade in 2000. The most well known regional trade blocs are the European Union (EU) and the North American Free Trade Agreement (NAFTA). Others include the Latin American Free Trade Association (LAFTA), the Central American Free Trade Association (CAFTA), Mercosur, the Association of Southeast Asian Nations (ASEAN), the Economic Community of West African States (ECWAS), and the Asia-Pacific Economic Cooperation (APEC). APEC is an **intraregional trade bloc** that attempts to integrate eighteen Pacific and Asian nations into a nonbinding arrangement that would gradually remove trade barriers among members by 2020. As a promoter of the agreement, the United States hopes to further liberalize trade among the members while accelerating economic growth in the Pacific–Asia region.

Finally, speculation continues that the Bush administration would like to see a Trans-Atlantic Free-Trade Zone (TAFTZ) and that possibly Germany may be interested in such a development. Aside from the economic advantages of merging the United States and the EU, failure to make progress in the Doha round motivates some officials, while for others a mega-market merger is needed to meet the challenge of growing Asian economies.[30]

Why so many RTAs, and are they good for trade? Technically, RTAs violate the GATT and WTO principle of nondiscrimination, but they are nonetheless legal entities. Article XXIV of the GATT and Article V of the General Agreement in Trade and Services (GATS) exempt them, as long as they make an effort to liberalize trade within the bloc. In some cases RTAs generate more efficient production within the bloc, either while infant industries are maturing or in response to more competition from outside industries. In other cases they attract FDI when local regulations and investment rules are streamlined and simplified. For many economic liberals, regional trade blocs are stepping stones toward the possibility of a global free-trade zone as they gradually spread and deepen economic integration.

Not all economic liberals support RTAs. The noted pro–free-trade economist Jagdish Bhagwati is concerned that bilateral and regional agreements are likely to generate a "spaghetti bowl effect" of multiple tariffs and preferences, making it harder to eventually reduce trade protection measures significantly.[31] Other liberals believe that RTAs undermine the WTO process and the ultimate goal of *world* free trade, because protectionist measures tend to beget more trade protectionism and neomercantilist practices on the national, regional-bloc, and global levels. The prime example here is the case of imports of U.S. bananas and hormone-fed beef into the EU, which nearly resulted in trade wars between the U.S. and EU (see Chapter 2).

Mercantilists tend to focus on the political rationale behind RTAs as well as the way in which they serve a variety of political and economic objectives. For some states they are essentially bargaining tools used to prevent TNCs from playing one state off against another. For example, one of the arguments President Clinton made in support of U.S. efforts to help organize NAFTA was that the United States should be able to penetrate and secure Mexican markets before the Japanese did.[32] If the United States did not quickly bring Mexico into its trade orbit in 1993, Japanese investments in Mexico would negate U.S. influence over Mexico's future trade policies.

## North–South Trade Issues

Tensions between the Northern industrialized and Southern developing nations over trade issues are not new. However, G-20 resistance to some of the measures of the Doha round that resulted in a deadlock does reflect the increasing importance and influence of Southern developing nations in the international production and trade structure.

In 1973, when the OPEC nations dramatically raised the price of oil for the first time (see Chapter 18), a coalition of developing nations in the UN called the Group of 77 (G-77) demanded an entirely new international economic order (NIEO).[33] Based on complaints about the terms of trade favoring the developed states, part of the G-77's demands included major changes in trade policies that permitted more access of their primary commodities into the heavily protected markets of the Northern industrialized regions of the world. The G-77 also demanded a TNC "Code of Conduct" to assure developing nations control over their own resources along with a stronger voice in GATT decision making.

Consistent with the political environment at the time, these demands produced no fundamental change in GATT, IMF, or World Bank policies. The United States and other states responded that, rather than trying to change system rules and procedures, developing nations should become more integrated into the international economy. Because trade is an "engine to growth" and an essential element of development, developing nations would benefit from efficiencies gained from trade if they brought down their tariff barriers on their commodities and products and opened their economies to FDI.

In the 1980s these same economic liberal ideas became the basis of Northern nation solutions to the debt crisis that emerged early in the decade when many developing countries borrowed heavily from Western banks and some international finance agencies (see Chapter 8). Again, instead of changing the fundamentals of the international production and trade and monetary structures, the Northern industrialized nations recommended what was essentially the same set of policies they had suggested a decade earlier when it came to trade, this time packaged as what became referred to as the "Washington consensus" (see Chapter 15). Developing nations should grow their way out of debt by, among other things, liberalizing their trade policies and opening up their economies to FDI. Many of these economic liberal ideas also served as justification for the **structural adjustment policies (SAPs)**—conditions the IMF and World Bank required developing nations to adhere to if and when they borrowed money from these institutions to overcome their long-term debt or short-term financial crises (see Chapter 8).

In the 1990s these same economic liberal ideas about trade also served as an ideological justification for the globalization campaign (see Chapter 3), and they are still quite popular today. The WTO and the World Bank support the views of many trade experts who argue that countries that have experienced strong export growth have lower levels of import protection than countries with declining exports.[34] They contend that much of the economic growth that has occurred in many developing nations since the 1970s is due, for the most part, to an emphasis on manufactured goods produced for export (see Table 6–2), especially in the Southeast and East Asian economies. In some cases, developing countries have also benefited from joining RTAs.

**TABLE 6–2   World Merchandise Exports, by Region**

| REGION/COUNTRY | VALUE (BILLIONS OF $) 2004 | GLOBAL SHARE (%) | | | |
|---|---|---|---|---|---|
| | | 2004 | 2000 | 1995 | 1990 |
| **World** | **8907** | **100.0** | **100.0** | **100.0** | **100.0** |
| North America | 1324 | 12.9 | 19.5 | 17.1 | 16.6 |
| United States | 819 | 9.2 | 12.5 | 11.7 | 11.6 |
| South and Central America | 276 | 3.1 | 3.1 | 3.0 | 3.1 |
| Brazil | 96 | 1.1 | 0.9 | 0.9 | 0.9 |
| Europe | 4031 | 45.2 | 42.0 | 46.5 | — |
| European Union (25) | 3714 | 41.7 | 38.9 | — | — |
| Commonwealth of Independent States (CIS) | 266 | 3.0 | 2.3 | 2.2 | — |
| Russian Federation | 183 | 2.1 | 1.7 | 1.6 | — |
| Africa | 232 | 2.6 | 2.3 | 2.2 | 3.1 |
| South Africa | 46 | 0.5 | 0.5 | 0.6 | 0.7 |
| Middle East | 390 | 4.4 | 4.3 | 3.0 | 4.1 |
| Asia | 2388 | 26.8 | 26.4 | 26.0 | 21.8 |
| China | 593 | 6.7 | 4.0 | 3.0 | 1.8 |
| Japan | 566 | 6.4 | 7.6 | 8.8 | 8.5 |
| Six East Asian traders | 860 | 9.7 | 10.4 | 10.3 | 7.8 |

*Note:* The Six East Asian traders are Hong Kong, Malaysia, Singapore, South Korea, Taiwan, and Thailand.
*Source:* World Trade Organization, *International Trade Statistics 2005.*

Today, many economic liberals continue to support the objectives of the Doha trade round, especially trade policies that include and ensure the success of developing countries. The WTO continues to suggest that if developing nations remain committed to the new trade rules, they are likely to attract new foreign and domestic investors. Likewise, the Uruguay round included special provisions that allowed developing nations longer time periods for implementing agreements and commitments; provisions requiring WTO members to safeguard the interests of developing nations; and several measures to help developing countries build their infrastructures, handle disputes, and implement technical standards.

## Some Structuralist and Mercantilist Reactions to Economic Liberal Trade

Many structuralists (and some mercantilist-realist types) are critical of these ideas about trade and their effects on North-South relations. Some mercantilists do support economic liberal ideas and globalization to the extent that they serve state interests—usually those of the major powers. For others, though, the numbers quoted to demonstrate the gains from trade do not reflect a clear understanding of the consequences of economic liberal trade policies. In the 1960s, 1970s, and even into the 1980s, many structuralists would have recommended that developing countries do as China did, and separate or insulate themselves from the inherently exploitative capitalist international trade system and economy. At the end of the Cold War, however, many hard-core Marxist structuralists seemed to accept the necessity of trade but continued to criticize the international trade system and shifted their attention to reforming it.

Today many structuralists argue that the Uruguay round and efforts by the WTO since then perpetuate the exploitative relationship of the North to the South. Northern trade and development policies result in economic growth for many states, but not for the greater number of people within the poorer ones. Recently, Robert Hunter Wade carefully calculated that, while trade has resulted in economic growth, it has also generated significant inequality between and especially within the developing nations.[35]

Other numbers for developing nations do not look good either. Trade accounts for as much as 75 percent of the foreign exchange earnings of many developing nations (see Table 6–3). Likewise many developing nations quadrupled their percentage share of world merchandise exports, from 7 percent in 1973 to 29 percent in 2001.[36] However, the vast majority of developing nations still account for only about one-fifth of the world's trade in manufactured goods. Some 40 percent of those exports came from the NICs (especially the Asian Tigers) in the last quarter-century (see Table 6–2). During this same period, the share of developing nation trade in agricultural and mining products and fuel declined. Many states, especially the least developed ones in Africa along with some in Latin America, suffer chronic trade deficits and the effects of large international debt (see Chapter 8).

**TABLE 6–3   Global Trade as Percent of Gross Domestic Product by Region**

| REGION | EXPORTS | | IMPORTS | |
|---|---|---|---|---|
| | *2004* | *2000* | *2004* | *2000* |
| East Asia and the Pacific | 42.9 | 36.1 | 39.5 | 31.8 |
| Europe and Central Asia[a] | 41.4 | 40.7 | 41.3 | 39.4 |
| Latin America and Caribbean | 25.6 | 20.6 | 22.7 | 21.6 |
| Middle East and North Africa | 33.8 | 28.4 | 33.5 | 26.0 |
| South Asia | 18.9 | 14.2 | 21.2 | 15.9 |
| Sub-Saharan Africa | 32.1 | 32.1 | 31.3 | 31.3 |

[a] *Note:* Does not include the European Monetary Union nations.

*Source:* World Bank, *World Development Indicators* database, April 2006.

Aside from these numbers, some structuralists and mercantilists focus more on the effects that trade has on specific societies and the people within them, instead of on general trends that provide distorted pictures of consequences. For example, Walden Bello claims that new trade rules for agriculture have hurt small rice farmers in Malaysia and rice and corn farmers in the Philippines. Liberalization better serves the interests of the U.S. agricultural "dumping lobby" and a "small elite of Asian agro-exporters."[37] Jeff Faux argues that the effect of NAFTA on Mexican small farmers has been devastating. After cutting farm subsidies of all types in Mexico, 85 percent of remaining subsidies go to agribusinesses, while between 1993 and 2002, two million small farmers were driven off the land.[38] According to economic liberals, this consequence flows naturally from the transformation of economies that accompanies the shift from an agricultural to a manufacturing-based economy. Yet the problem for many structuralists and some mercantilists is that the outcome is usually not what that society would chose for itself but is imposed on it as a result of a dependent relationship to the Northern states.

As we saw in the case of agriculture in the Doha round, many developing countries accuse the developed nations of hypocrisy when it comes to living up to the principles and ideals of the liberal international trade system. Some mercantilists note that countries such as the United States have favored free trade when it benefits them but not when it might benefit producers in developing nations at the expense of U.S. producers. As pointed out earlier in the chapter, the developed states have an extensive history using protectionist trade measures to promote their own economic growth at the expense of other states. After World War II, the United States and its allies used the GATT and are now employing the WTO, along with other trade and finance organizations, to lower tariff barriers and thereby expose the infant industries of developing nations to competition with the more mature industries of the industrialized nations.

Even a supporter of managed globalization such as Dani Rodrik points out that many of the world's faster-growing economies, such as China, Vietnam, and Malaysia, insulated themselves from the international economy during the recent Asian crises (see Chapter 8). They also have a history of state intervention in the economy. According to Rodrik, in the past, high-tariff countries grew *faster* than those without tariffs.[39] Now the developed states want to "kick away the ladder" (take away protection) from under the developing nations who have every reason and right to employ protectionist trade measures.[40] Walden Bello also makes the case that protection serves a variety of "socially worthy objectives such as promoting food security for society's low income people, protecting small farmers and biodiversity, guaranteeing food security, and promoting rural social development."[41]

### NGOs and Economic Liberals Criticize the WTO

Two other recent developments have influenced North–South relations. The first routinely makes headlines. In the 1990s a growing number of NGOs, many with structuralist views and closely connected to the antiglobalization movement, have focused attention on the connection between trade and issues such as the environment, global labor conditions, drugs, and even terrorism. NGOs such as Oxfam, Global Trade Watch, and Global Exchange, to name only a few, attempted to acquire first-hand information about the effects of Northern trade policies on developing nations and publicized it in speeches, newspapers, journals, and on their websites.[42] Production and trade activities affect the environment in ways that states and businesses possibly never anticipated, as the demand for more energy resources increasingly makes the true cost of trade incalculable. To some extent, constructivist theorists (see Chapter 5) posit that these civil groups are responsible for changing the way the general population of developed countries thinks about globalization and "free trade."

Polls in the United States indicate that support for free trade has gradually decreased without a consensus about its benefit to the U.S. economy.[43] One factor that contributes to this shift is the large number of jobs in industrialized states that have been outsourced to countries such as India. Even though a good case can be made that outsourcing generates more jobs globally than it takes away, the plight of a middle-aged hard-working U.S. citizen losing her job to a poorly paid Indian is politically hard to swallow.

This issue is closely related to the **"race to the bottom"** problem that nations encounter when TNCs move out of one country as increased labor costs and regulations lead international enterprises to look elsewhere for lower-wage labor and fewer regulations.[44] For outsourcing and job displacement when factories move elsewhere, NGOs have played a role in monitoring the effects of TNCs on various societies, casting light on many of the ethical, moral, and judicial dimensions of these issues. In some cases NGOs have been a source of information for WTO dispute hearings. In other cases they have been locked out of these cases for fear that they might prejudice a case.

Finally, a growing number of NGOs have played a critical role in developing alternative trade strategies. One such effort is the "fair trade" movement that seeks to earn higher prices for certified goods such as coffee, timber, and a host of other products of workers in developing countries. Large numbers of students in the United States, Europe and parts of Latin America and Asia have joined such groups, which have extensive websites and which collect large amounts of reports and articles on a variety of traded products. In a few cases, some activist groups have also produced their own documentaries on fair-trade coffee, timber, and other rainforest products.[45]

A second recent interesting development is the criticisms of economic liberal trade policies and the IMF by economic liberals, who question the appropriateness of these theories and trade policies for developing nations. In his best-selling book, *Globalization and Its Discontents*, Joseph Stiglitz, the former chief economist of the World Bank, took the WTO to task for trying to make the Washington consensus fit the unique situations of developing countries in debt.[46] In his new book, *Making Globalization Work,* Stiglitz devotes a whole chapter to arguing that free trade should be converted into "fair trade."[47] He argues that globalization has been oversold and that, in order for it to work, states must be more willing to accept some of the costs associated with its negative effects (some of the issues we will take up in the conclusion, and in Chapter 8). What Stiglitz suggests, however, is that if states had the "political will" to do so, they could overcome this problem. However, in most democracies the state is too weak to hold off private interests and usually acts as a gatekeeper between domestic and international interests.

## TRADE AS A FOREIGN POLICY TOOL

Finally, many state officials over the years have attempted to use trade as an instrument or weapon to achieve any combination of political, social, and economic objectives. If wealth is power, then trade is both—a fact as old as history. Athens may have sparked the Peloponnesian wars when it tried to restrict imports from one of Sparta's allies, Megara.[48] Trade sanctions take many forms, including boycotts, import restrictions, and embargoes that prohibit exports to another country. These and other sorts of sanctions are one kind of penalty that states use to reward certain states, coerce a competitor, or punish an enemy.

In the 1980s, the Reagan administration applied a series of economic sanctions including trade restrictions to nations it felt were either supporters of communist revolutionary movements (for example, Vietnam, Cambodia, and Nicaragua), sponsors of terrorism (Libya, Iran, Cuba, Syria, and the People's Democratic Republic of Yemen), or states such as South Africa, which was reluctant to give up the practice of *apartheid* (racial segregation). The objective was to impose an intolerable hardship on a society that would break the will of its people and leaders to carry on the unacceptable behavior.

After the first Persian Gulf War, the UN sponsored sanctions against Iraq to punish it for invading Kuwait and to compel it to stop producing weapons of mass destruction (WMD). By the mid-1990s many states came to view these sanctions as morally repugnant because of the pain they inflicted on the Iraqi people and not on Saddam Hussein's regime itself. Since then the use of sanctions has lost popularity as a tool of foreign policy. Most critics of trade sanctions have not focused on interference in the market or the loss of trade so much as the inability of sanctions to affect any real change in state policy.[49]

Many experts suggest that the effectiveness of economic sanctions requires a number of conditions to be present. Governments must be able to control their own businesses or prevent certain goods from being shipped to the targeted country via third-party nations that will find it profitable to provide the targeted country with boycotted goods. Often both businesses and governments can get around trade sanctions because goods produced in one country are hard to distinguish from those produced in another. It is also difficult to determine how the target state will react and adjust to an embargo or boycott. In cases such as Nicaragua in the 1980s, Iraq in the 1990s, and North Korea in 2006, economic sanctions helped generate popular support for the government to resist the "imperial aggressors" who imposed the sanctions.

In some cases, sanctions have been deemed to have worked, but policy changes were not immediate nor were sanctions always clearly connected to specific actions taken by the state that imposed them. One such case was the attempt by the United States to change China's human rights record. Early in the Cold War the United States cut off trade with China but reopened it in the late 1970s when China adopted its modernization program and began importing large amounts of goods from the Western industrialized nations. After the Tiananmen Square massacre in 1989, the first Bush administration found itself caught between the proverbial rock and hard place when it tried to reconcile its displeasure over the way the Chinese government handled the pro-democracy movement with its objective of promoting trade with China. In 1993, the U.S. Congress imposed on the Clinton administration the requirement that China make significant progress on a number of issues, including human rights, if it were to be granted MFN status. In spite of critical reports on China's human rights record, in 1997 the Clinton administration granted China MFN status, and in 2003 China officially joined the WTO.

In this case, instead of using trade as a weapon, most U.S. officials thought of trade more as a carrot that would draw China *into* the world market system. The Clinton administration's "commercial diplomacy" advanced a liberal economic policy that complemented mercantilist objectives by benefiting U.S. businesses while helping to eventually change China's political institutions. Clinton's advisors felt that while human rights violations certainly should not be overlooked, there was more for the United States to gain by fostering trade with China than by punishing it with a trade embargo. In this case the administration's decision was not one of economics over politics, but of economics and one political objective over another political objective that would hurt trade.

Recently some Bush administration officials were suspicious of China's intentions in the region and as a global power.[50] They felt that China might be using some of the sophisticated technology it imports to modernize, if not significantly increase, the size of its nuclear arsenal. Ironically, many U.S. political leaders, but also business leaders who supported increased trade with China, had to argue that trade is *not* connected to politics by way of U.S. security interests and that security considerations and trade should be separated from one another.

In an even more recent case, trade was used as a weapon and not as a carrot. In the fall of 2006 the UN Security Council was once again pressed by some of its Permanent Members to apply trade and other sanctions against North Korea for its failure to stop producing and testing nuclear and other WMDs.[51] These sanctions included inspections of goods coming into and out of North Korea (by boat, plane, or train), which had been problematic for China in particular—it supported the UN resolution but is also North Korea's neighbor and ally. South Korea, the United States's ally, was divided over continuing to support joint ventures with North Korea dealing with tourism and an industrial complex that manufactures garments and kitchen utensils. Meanwhile, North Korea's nuclear tests also threatened South Korea's "sunshine policy" with the North, which promotes political reconciliation and economic cooperation.[52] Some officials wanted to stop these programs and other forms of aid to North Korea for fear they would only help North Korea build more weapons or that sanctions would end up hurting the North Korean people more than Kim Jong Il's government. Others felt that, as in the case of China more than twenty years earlier, engagement was the best policy if North Korea was to change without forcing it to do so.

These cases demonstrate that there is more to the use of sanctions than simply using trade to punish or reward a state. When it comes to which trade sanctions to use in a given situation, tensions often reflect conflicting domestic and foreign policy objectives and the interests of different interest groups and foreign policy officials. Businesses often have vested interests in trade policy to the extent that international economic conditions can either constrain or provide them with new opportunities. For the most part, however, states are reluctant to use trade and other sanctions because they do not always work and often have unintended side effects. In some sitautions states feel that the use of military instruments is unwarranted or could have worse consequences than losing some trade. For the most part then, trade remains a tool many states use to help discipline or send a distinct message to another state. In the case of North Korea, even the pro–free-trade policy journal *The Economist* recommended that the UN *should* employ trade as a weapon to try to change North Korea's behavior.

## CONCLUSION: THE ELEPHANT OF INTERNATIONAL TRADE

Many economic liberal objectives of the production and international trade structure have been achieved since World War II, resulting in a dramatic shift in production both within developed states and into less developed regions of the world. This has helped and reflects increases in the volume and value of international trade. However, a number of countertrends coexist within this liberal trade order, demonstrating that its popular economic liberal values are not shared by all states, especially by many developing nations and NGOs.

Through a series of multilateral negotiation rounds, the industrialized nations have pushed for the liberalization of international trade and regulations related especially to manufactured goods but also to many goods and services associated with information and communication systems and new technological products. Many trade experts contend that economic liberal trade rules that are part of the U.S.-backed globalization campaign will further integrate the global economy but also help developing nations grow and develop economically. However, in the new Doha round, for example, many developing nations have resisted these policies that they claim leave them vulnerable to exploitation by developed nations. Some mercantilists and structuralists maintain that the United States and other developed nations have supported multilateral talks, to the extent they do, for fear of losing export markets for semifinished and finished products, such as telecommunication technology and services, and for fear of losing greater access to resources and raw materials in developing nations.

From the perspective of many trade experts of all ideological stripes, what was supposed to have been a "sweetheart" deal for developing countries has become an issue of political sensitivity for the Northern industrialized states, which are reluctant to decrease protection for their agriculture and other commodities and products. Lack of agreement also reflects the extent to which trade issues have become increasingly complicated. Negotiations have been drawn out over a variety of technical problems associated with the use of new technologies in global telecommunication systems, information products, pharmaceuticals, TRIPs, and in clarifying the nature of services. Likewise, trade negotiation difficulties also reflect the connection between trade and other structural issues such as monetary, finance, and national security.

Difficulties in multilateral negotiations also reflect, and continue to generate, tensions between the North and the South. The WTO's economic liberal trade policy objectives, regulations, and procedures reflect predominantly the interests of the richest and most powerful Northern industrialized nations. Developing countries now have increasing influence in multilateral negotiations, based on their importance to developed states as markets and sources of labor for TNCs. Many free-trade and economic liberal ideals have come under attack from antiglobalization groups and NGOs that have mounted campaigns to challenge the assumed benefits of free trade and other policies associated with globalization. Likewise, a number of pro-economic liberal academics and experienced trade officials have criticized many of the WTO's procedures that lead to more support for selective protectionist trade policies rather than overcoming some of the negative effects of globalization.

One reaction by some of the more developed states to these developments is to shift attention away from the multilateral trading system and the WTO toward more bilateral and regional trade agreements. RTAs simultaneously embrace both the principle of free trade and the practical need for protectionism, making them popular if not acceptable to both mercantilists and economic liberals. Even if economic liberals are uncomfortable with the idea, in a world of insecure states and a changed international security environment since 2001, trade has been and is likely to serve as a policy instrument that can sometimes be an effective tool to achieve any number of political and economic goals.

What does the production and trade structure elephant look like? For economic liberals the liberal trade structure appears to be giving way to fair trade (a mix of liberal and protectionist policies and ideals). A **managed trade system** best describes and accounts for the mixture of liberal, mercantilist, and sometime structuralist trade practices that have become the objectives of most of its state members. For some economic liberals, RTAs might be the most integrated the production and trade structure can become given this mix of state political, economic, and social objectives. In order for WTO talks to go forward, some degree of protection must be reconciled with the political and social realities that demand such protection.

For both mercantilists and structuralists, politics and society still trump economics. Mercantilists support resumption of the Doha round to the extent that it reflects the interests of states. For stucturalists, the production and trade structure needs major reform, paradoxically without which it will continue to be undermined by economic forces and policies that will only generate *more* demand for protection, inside both the developed and developing nations. For now, the straightjacket of globalization, as Thomas Friedman likes to refer to it,[53] has not been strong enough to either push or pull states and their economies into a truly integrated global production and trade network.

## DISCUSSION QUESTIONS

1. Discuss and explain the roles of production and trade in the international production and trade structure. Why is trade so controversial?
2. Outline the basic ways that mercantilists, economic liberals, and structuralists view trade. (Think about the tension between the politics and economics of trade.)
3. Outline and discuss some of the basic features of the GATT and WTO and issues related to the Uruguay and Doha rounds. Are you hopeful the Doha round WTO will be able to continue? Why? Why not?
4. Outline the basic features of RTAs. Do you see them as being primarily liberal or mercantilist in nature? Explain. Of what consequence is it that officials view them as primarily one or the other?
5. Which of the three IPE approaches best accounts for the relationship of the Northern industrialized nations to the Southern developing nations when it comes to trade? Explain and discuss.
6. How have the United States and other nations used trade as a tool to achieve foreign policy objectives? Be specific and give examples. Research some other examples.

## INTERNET LINKS

World Trade Organization:
    www.wto.org

Institute for International Economics:
    www.iie.com

Office of the U.S. Trade Representative:
    www.ustr.gov

United States APEC Index:
    www.apec.org

Jagdish Bhagwati's home page:
    www.columbia.edu/~jb38
Archive of Robert Kuttner's articles:
    www.prospect.org/columns/kuttner
Buyer Be Fair video:
    www.buyerbefair.org
Bilaterals.org (specific criticism of many bilateral trade and investment agreements):
    www.bilaterals.org
Oxfam home page:
    www.oxfam.com
FLO International (standards and certification body for the Fairtrade movement):
    www.fairtrade.net
Transfair USA (the fair trade certifying organization in the U.S.):
    www.transfairusa.org
Oxfam America's Coffee Campaign:
    www.oxfamamerica.org/whatwedo/campaigns/coffee
United Students for Fair Trade:
    www.usft.org

## SUGGESTED READINGS

Jagdish Bhagwati. *Protectionism.* Cambridge, MA: MIT Press, 1991.
Jorge G. Castaneda. "NAFTA at 10: A Plus or a Minus?" *Current History*, February 2004, pp. 51–55.
Ha-Joon Chang. "The Dangers of Reducing Industrial Tariffs," *Challenge*, 48 (November–December 2005), pp. 50–63.
Thomas Friedman. *The Lexus and the Olive Tree: Understanding Globalization.* New York: Anchor Books, 1999.
Thomas Friedman. *The World Is Flat.* New York: Ferrar, Straus & Giroux, 2005.
Brian Hocking and Steven McGuire, eds. *Trade Politics: International, Domestic and Regional Perspectives,* 2nd ed. London: Routledge, 2004.
Douglas A. Irwin. *Free Trade Under Fire,* 2nd ed. Princeton, NJ: Princeton University Press, 2005.
Anne Krueger. *Trade Policies and Developing Nations.* Washington, DC: Brookings Institution, 1995.
Robert Kuttner. *The End of Laissez Faire.* New York: Knopf, 1991.
Tina Rosenberg. "Globalization: The Free-Trade Fix," *The New York Times Magazine*, August 18, 2002.
Joseph Stiglitz. *Making Globalization Work.* New York: W. W. Norton, 2006.
Gilbert R. Winham. "The Evolution of the Global Trade Regime," in John Ravenhill, ed., *Global Political Economy.* Oxford: Oxford University Press, 2005, pp. 87–115.

## KEY TERMS

production and trade structure
specialization
outsourcing
law of comparative advantage
opportunity cost
Washington consensus
strategic trade policies
modern imperialism
international division of labor
International Trade Organization (ITO)
General Agreement on Tariffs and Trade (GATT)

reciprocity
nondiscrimination
Most Favored Nation (MFN)
nontariff barriers (NTBs)
Ministry of International Trade and Industry (MITI)
Super 301
free trade
fair trade
TRIPs
TRIMs
World Trade Organization (WTO)

Dispute Settlement Panel (DSP)
20/20/20 deal
Doha lite
regional trade agreements (RTAs)
regional trade blocs
intraregional trade bloc
structural adjustment policies (SAPs)
race to the bottom
managed trade system

## NOTES

1. Robert Kuttner, *The End of Laissez Faire* (New York: Knopf, 1991), p. 157.
2. Thomas Friedman, *The Lexus and the Olive Tree: Understanding Globalization* (New York: Anchor Books, 1999).
3. Thomas Friedman, *The World Is Flat* (New York: Farrar, Straus & Giroux, 2005), pp. 3–47.
4. Eliot Cohen, "A Revolution in Warfare," *Foreign Affairs*, 75 (March/April 1999), pp. 37–54.
5. See World Bank website, www.WorldBank.com.
6. Anthony McGrew, "The Logics of Globalization," in John Ravenhill, *Global Political Economy*, 2nd ed. (Oxford: Oxford University Press, 2005) p. 212.
7. See World Trade Organization, *Annual Report* (Geneva: World Trade Organization, 2005), p. 9.
8. A good summary of this argument is given by Douglas A. Irwin, *Free Trade: Under Fire* (Princeton, NJ: Princeton University Press, 2005).
9. See Jacob E. Cooke, ed., *The Reports of Alexander Hamilton* (New York: Harper & Row, 1964).
10. See Friedrich List, "Political and Cosmopolitical Economy," in *The National System of Political Economy* (New York: Augustus M. Kelley, Reprints of Economic Classics, 1966).
11. See, for example, Pietra Rivoli, *The Travels of a T-Shirt in the Global Economy* (Hoboken, NJ: John Wiley, 2005).
12. Andre Gunder Frank, *Latin America: Underdevelopment or Revolution* (New York: Monthly Review Press, 1970).
13. Immanuel Wallerstein, "The Rise and Demise of the World Capitalist System: Concept for Comparative Analysis," *Comparative Studies in Society and History*, 17 (September 1974), pp. 387–415.
14. Technically, the GATT was not an international organization but rather a "gentlemen's agreement" whereby member parties (nation-states) contracted trade agreements with one another.
15. For a sophisticated account of strategic trade policy, see Paul Krugman, *Strategic Trade Policy and the New International Economics* (Cambridge, MA: MIT Press, 1986).
16. Robert Gilpin, *The Political Economy of International Relations* (Princeton, NJ: Princeton University Press, 1987), p. 215.
17. "U.S. Aids Microsoft in War on Software Piracy by Chinese," *Tacoma News Tribune*, November 22, 1994, p. E5.
18. For a more detailed discussion of agriculture's role in the Uruguay round, see David N. Balaam, "Agricultural Trade Policy," in Brian Hocking and Steven McGuire, eds., *Trade Politics: International, Domestic, and Regional Perspectives* (London: Routledge, 1999), pp. 52–66.
19. "U.S. GATT Flap Reverberates Around the World," *The Christian Science Monitor*, November 23, 1994, p. 1.
20. See www.wto.org. See also Irwin, *Free Trade: Under Fire*.
21. For a more detailed discussion of the Doha round of the WTO, see Aileen Kwa and Fatoumato Jawara, *Behind the Scenes of the WTO* (New York: Zed Books, 2004).
22. See, for example, Janet Thomas, *The Battle in Seattle, The Story Behind and Beyond the WTO Demonstrations* (New York: Fulcrum, 2003).
23. Lori Wallach, "Trade Secrets," *Foreign Policy*, 140 (January/February 2004), pp. 70–71.
24. See www.whitehouse.gov/news/releases/2005/11/20051106-3.html for the text of a speech by President Bush given in Brazil. See also www.whitehouse.gov/news/releases/2005/09/20050914.html for President Bush's speech to the United Nations.
25. See "World Trade Under Attack," *The Economist*, July 8, 2006.
26. Ibid.
27. See Bradley S. Klapper, "5 Years of WTO Talks Crash Amid Bickering," *Seattle Times*, July 25, 2006.
28. See "World Trade Under Attack."
29. For a detailed discussion of regionalism and Free Trade Agreements, see John Ravenhill, "Regionalism," in John Ravenhill, *Global Political Economy*, 2nd ed. (Oxford: Oxford University Press, 2005), pp. 116–147.
30. See, for example, Gabor Steingart, "An Argument for a Trans-Atlantic Free-Trade Zone," Spiegel Online, October 20, 2006, www.spiegel.de/international/0,1518,druck-443306,00.html.
31. Jagdish Bhagwati, *In Defense of Globalization* (Oxford: Oxford University Press, 2004).
32. See John Dillin, "Will Treaty Give U.S. Global Edge?" *The Christian Science Monitor*, November 17, 1993.
33. For a detailed discussion of the NIEO, see Jagdish Bhagwati, ed., *The New International Economic Order: The North South Debate* (Cambridge, MA: MIT Press, 1977).
34. See, for example, Irwin, *Free Trade Under Fire*, especially chap. 2.
35. Robert Hunter Wade, "The Rising Inequality of World Income Distribution," *Finance and Development*, 38 (December 2001), pp. 37–39.

36. Scott Newton, *The Global Economy: 1944–2000* (London: Arnold, 2004).
37. See Walden Bello, "Rethinking Asia: The WTO's Big Losers," *Far Eastern Economic Review,* June 24, 1999, p. 77.
38. Jeff Faux, *The Global Class War* (Hoboken, NJ: John Wiley, 2006), pp. 133–134.
39. Dani Rodrik, "Goodbye Washington Consensus, Hello Washington Confusion?" *Journal of Economic Literature,* XLIV (December 2006), pp. 973–987.
40. See Ha-Joon Chang, *Kicking Away the Ladder: Development Strategy in Historical Perspective* (London: Anthem, 2002).
41. See Bello, "Rethinking Asia," p. 78.
42. See, for example, the Oxfam International website, www.maketradefair.com.
43. See, for example, "Analysis: The Complicated Politics of Free Trade, Unrestricted Trade Makes for Strange Bedfellows," The Pew Research Center for the People and the Press, January 4, 2007.
44. For a good discussion of the concept of the race to the bottom, see Rivoli, *Travels of a T-Shirt*.
45. See, for example, Christopher Bacon, "Confronting the Coffee Crisis: Can Fair Trade, Organic, and Specialty Coffees Reduce Small-Scale Farmer Vulnerability in Northern Nicaragua?" *World Development, 33* (2005), pp. 497–511.
46. Joseph E. Stiglitz, *Globalization and Its Discontents* (New York: W. W. Norton, 2002).
47. Joseph E. Stiglitz, *Making Globalization Work* (New York: W. W. Norton, 2006).
48. Cited in David Baldwin, *Economic Statecraft* (Princeton, NJ: Princeton University Press, 1985).
49. See Richard Haas, "Sanctioning Madness," *Foreign Affairs, 76* (November/December 1997), pp. 74–85.
50. Dan Blumenthal, "What Didn't Happen When Bush Met Hu," *The Weekly Standard*, May 1, 2006.
51. See "Security Council Slaps Sanctions on North Korea," *Seattle Times*, October 15, 2006.
52. See "South Korea Grapples with Competing Pressures as It Weighs Its Response to North Korea," *The New York Times*, October 13, 2006, p. A10.
53. See Friedman, *The Lexus and the Olive Tree*.

# The International Monetary and Finance Structure

## OVERVIEW

The intricate workings of the international monetary and financial structure matter to us as individual tourists exchanging currencies on vacation and as individual consumers buying imported goods. These relationships matter to us as workers and investors because currency exchange rates and transnational financial flows affect the success of many businesses and industries. They also affect us as citizens because the particular rules, regulations, and conventions governing international monetary and financial relationships affect our ability to attain a variety of political, social, and economic objectives. These relationships matter to states as they affect their wealth and power. Finally, this structure matters to us as citizens of the world because issues such as development, international peace, and prosperity are also influenced by how well this system works.

Discussion of monetary and finance issues has long been dominated by economists, but since the 1970s and the rebirth of international political economy (IPE) (see Chapter 1), other academics and state officials have realized and acknowledged the political and social dimensions of money and finance. As one expert notes, "In all modern societies, control over the issuing and management of money and credit has been a key source of power, and the subject of intense political struggles."[1] Today, cross-border flows of capital overshadow international trade, while the integration and globalization of the international political economy enhances the speed and extends the reach of legal tender. The increasing importance of the international monetary and finance structure to nation-states and other actors in an increasingly integrated world makes it difficult for states to reconcile a variety of domestic political, social, and economic objectives with the necessity for a common set of international principles and rules for monetary and investment policies. In many countries, voters and national leaders must wrestle with foreign exchange and investment problems that they may or may not be able to completely control. Like the other three international structures, at times the monetary and finance network is embroiled with tension and even hostility that renders it difficult to manage effectively and efficiently.

This chapter describes and explains a number of fundamental elements of the international monetary and finance structure, including its basic institutions and who manages them, who determines its rules, why and how these rules change, and finally, *Cui bono?*, or who benefits from its framework. These issues make the news every day but are usually located deep inside the newspaper or may not appear on the major news channels. Additionally, this subject has its own specialized vocabulary that can present a formidable barrier to understanding some of its intricate elements. Students will quickly realize that one element of the structure affects another and that it is a challenge to understand how all the different elements are related. However, once you understand and appreciate the significance of some of the basic elements of this structure, a whole new world of IPE will open up to you, making it easier to grasp other important concepts and ideas in other parts of this book.

The international monetary and finance structure is a complex web of political and economic agreements, understandings, institutions, and relationships that help determine two things in particular. One is a set of institutions that establish values for different national currencies in terms of other currencies. The second is a set of rules as to how much, how often, and under what terms money (in the form of finance) moves into and out of national economies. Because currency exchange rates and cross-border flows of money significantly affect national wealth and power through international trade, investment, and access for credit (borrowing money), states pride themselves on being able to control money and finance. Too much money in the national economy generates inflation, causing the national currency to decrease in value such that less can be purchased with it. However, if there is not enough money (liquidity), businesses cannot expand and economic growth and trade is stifled. Another problem that many states share today in the global economy is that there are tremendous amounts of "hot" (uncontrolled by any state) money in the international system, with which states tend to have a love–hate relationship. Initially this money is attractive to states, because investments bring with them new jobs and other benefits. However, many investments can just as quickly leave a state with little or no notice, putting thousands of people out of work.

When introducing this subject in our classes we often hear students say that the world's international monetary and finance system operates on the basis of laissez-faire, economic liberal (see Chapter 3) principles and polices. Although elements of this picture are certainly true, for the most part it is oversimplified. There is so much more to know and understand about money and finance. In this chapter we will explore some of the other motives and ideological outlooks that influence the monetary and finance system's actors, institutions, and processes.

We begin by explaining the role of exchange rates in the international political economy. We then describe and discuss three distinct international monetary and finance structures that have existed since the nineteenth century. Each reflects a different set of national and international circumstances, dominant political-economic ideologies, and the interests of the states that constructed and tried to maintain the structure. We inquire into who the major actors were, how market forces, state political, and social objectives shaped policies, what accounts for shifts from one structure to another, and how effectively and to what ends the international monetary and finance structure is being managed today.

The chapter concludes with a brief discussion of different views about the weakness of the U.S. dollar in the international political economy today. Some experts are concerned that confidence in the U.S. dollar could easily deteriorate, given a number of economic indicators that point to excessive consumer and state spending. This discussion pulls together some themes developed earlier in the chapter. This discussion is also a conduit to a more detailed discussion of the International Monetary Fund (IMF) and the World Bank's role in helping developing countries deal with currency crises and other debt problems. Chapter 8 goes into more detail about several monetary crises and global finance problems including long-term international debt—both hotly debated topics. As is our practice throughout the book, we use parts of the three major IPE perspectives to help us understand some of the more controversial aspects of this structure.

The thesis of this chapter is that both states and markets greatly influence the development of institutions, rules, and processes that constitute the international monetary and finance structure.

Even though market forces currently play a bigger role in the monetary and finance structure than they did in the past, using the three major approaches to IPE will help us to realize and explain how and why our present system reflects predominantly the political interests of the major powers, especially the United States. Since World War II the monetary and finance network has gradually been deregulated, but not as much as many economic liberals would prefer. Despite the popularity of economic liberal ideas, global integration, and globalization, states are caught between a rock and a hard place when it comes to money and finance. Some states want to integrate into the international economy to gain many of its benefits, but they also want to manipulate currency exchange rates and control the mobility of capital into and out of their borders to preserve their autonomy and independence.

## FOREIGN EXCHANGE RATES[2]

Before discussing the basics of the three international monetary and finance structures, let's examine some of the economic principles behind currency exchange rates. Just as people in different nations speak different languages (requiring translation to understand one another), they also do business in different currencies, requiring exchange rates to convert one type of money to another. Most people are exposed to exchange rates when traveling abroad and face a purely practical problem: How much of one currency will it cost to buy pesos, pounds, euro, or yen needed to buy things or invest in another country? Some people quickly become accustomed to the math of exchange rates—using official exchange rates to convert from one currency into another and back again. For example, if the yen–dollar exchange rate is ¥100 per 1 US$, then a ¥1000 caffé latte at the Tokyo airport costs a U.S. tourist in Japan $10 (¥1000 ÷ ¥100 per $ = $10).

Table 7–1 shows the exchange rates in terms of how many foreign currency units it took to purchase a U.S. dollar on three different dates. On August 27, 2006, for example, one US$1 was worth 0.53£ (British pound) or 0.78€ (euro). The exchange rate converts values from one country's unit of measurement to another, and it does not really matter what units are used. What matters is that the measurement is acceptable to the actors exchanging their currencies.

What factors determine the *value* of one country's currency relative to other currencies? In unfettered market conditions (when the state does not interfere in the market), *flexible or market-based exchange rates* are theoretically determined by the interaction of demand and supply in foreign exchange markets. For example, let's examine the Mexican–U.S. exchange rate and what factors influence its value. As of June 21, 2006, the value of one U.S. dollar was 11.456 pesos, and the reciprocal value was 0.087, or 1 peso equals 8.7 cents.

The demand for dollars in our example reflects the desire of Mexican households, businesses, and government entities to buy U.S. goods and services, to buy U.S. assets (stocks and bonds and real estate, etc.), and to travel in the United States, where they will spend dollars. The quantity of

**TABLE 7–1   Foreign Exchange Rates for Selected Countries, Various Dates**

| COUNTRY | CURRENCY UNIT | FOREIGN EXCHANGE PER US$ | | |
| --- | --- | --- | --- | --- |
| | | *8/16/2006* | *7/19/2006* | *7/20/2005* |
| Great Britain | Pound sterling (£) | 0.53 | 0.54 | 0.58 |
| European Eurozone | Euro (€) | 0.78 | 0.80 | 0.83 |
| Canada | Canadian dollar | 1.12 | 1.13 | 1.22 |
| Japan | Yen (¥) | 116.00 | 117.00 | 114.00 |
| Mexico | Peso | 10.80 | 10.90 | 10.60 |
| China | Yuan | 7.99 | 8.00 | 8.28 |
| Argentina | Peso | 3.08 | 3.08 | 2.86 |

*Source: The Economist,* various issues.

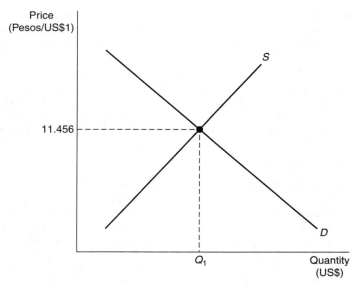

**FIGURE 7–1**   Foreign Exchange Market

dollars demanded is inversely related to the price of dollars—the demand curve slopes downward. (See Figure 7–1.) As the price of the dollar increases (and the dollar *appreciates*), fewer dollars will be demanded. Why? This relationship reflects the law of demand. Yes . . . but why?

Consider the Mexican (peso) price of Windows Vista, Microsoft's new operating system. If the U.S. price is $300, what is the Mexican (peso) price? That clearly depends on the exchange rate. If the exchange rate is 11.456 pesos per dollar, the Mexican (peso) price will be 3436.8 pesos—that is, a Mexican company will have to pay 3436.8 pesos to import Vista. However, if the dollar appreciates to 20 pesos per dollar, the Mexican peso price will be 6000 pesos. Clearly, as the dollar *appreciates*, U.S. goods and services become *less* competitive (attractive) and Mexican purchases of Vista decrease. Consequently, the quantity of dollars demanded *decreases* as the price of dollars rises. The movement along the demand curve *D* in Figure 7–2 reflects such a decrease in quantity demanded.

The demand for dollars is also affected by a number of other variables, particularly interest rates in the United States relative to interest rates in Mexico, the price level in the United States relative to the price level in Mexico, business expectations in the United States relative to business expectations in Mexico, national income in Mexico, and so on. If interest rates in the United States rise relative to interest rates in Mexico, Mexican investors will find U.S. interest-earning assets highly desirable, and more dollars will be demanded at every price level—that is, the demand for dollars will increase. The shift in demand in Figure 7–2 from *D* to *D'* reflects this increase in demand. If the price level in the United States increases less rapidly than the price level in Mexico, U.S.-made goods and services will become more competitive and the demand for dollars will increase. If business expectations in the United States are strong relative to business expectations in Mexico, Mexican investors will find U.S. assets highly desirable because of anticipated capital gains (the price of stocks of U.S. companies rising) and higher dividend payments. If national income in Mexico rises, Mexican households, businesses, and government entities will likely increase their purchases of U.S. goods and services and perhaps increase travel in the United States. Consequently, the demand for dollars will increase.

Now we switch to the *supply* side. The supply of dollars reflects the desire of U.S. households, businesses, and government entities to buy Mexican goods and services, assets, and to travel in Mexico. Dollars are supplied to the foreign exchange market in order to acquire the pesos necessary

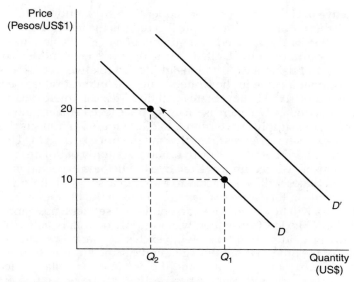

**FIGURE 7–2**   The Demand for Dollars

for these transactions. The quantity of dollars supplied is related directly to the price of dollars—the supply curve slopes up, as shown in Figure 7–3. As the price of the dollar rises (as the dollar appreciates), the quantity of dollars supplied rises. To see why this is so, consider the U.S. (dollar) price of a men's suit made in Mexico that costs 1500 pesos there. If the exchange rate is 10 pesos per dollar, the U.S. (dollar) price will be $150. If the dollar appreciates to 20 pesos per dollar, the U.S. price will be $75. As the dollar appreciates, Mexican goods and services become less expensive for U.S. citizens

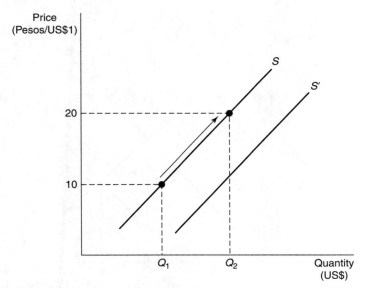

**FIGURE 7–3**   The Supply of Dollars

and thus more attractive to U.S. customers. Consequently, the quantity of dollars supplied increases. The movement along the supply curve in Figure 7–3 reflects the increase in quantity supplied.

The supply of dollars is also affected by a number of other variables, including interest rates in Mexico relative to interest rates in the United States, the price level in Mexico relative to the price level in the United States, business expectations in Mexico relative to business expectations in the United States, and national income in the United States. As interest rates rise in Mexico relative to the United States, investors in the United States will find Mexican interest-earning assets highly desirable, and the supply of dollars will increase at every price level—that is, the supply curve will shift to the right. The shift in the supply curve from $S$ to $S'$ in Figure 7–3 reflects this increase in supply. As the price level in Mexico increases less rapidly than the price level in the United States, Mexican-made goods and services become more attractive, and the supply of dollars consequently increases. As business expectations in Mexico improve relative to business expectations in the United States, investors in the United States will be attracted to Mexican assets and the supply of dollars will increase. As national income in the United States rises, household, businesses, and governmental entities in the United States will buy more Mexican goods and services, buy more Mexican assets, and travel more frequently in Mexico. Consequently, the supply of dollars will increase.

It should already be evident that this foreign exchange market can also be viewed in reverse, from the perspective of the other nations engaged in the same kinds of transactions. The supply of dollars in fact reflects the demand for pesos, and the demand for dollars reflects the supply of pesos. If we view the market from this reverse perspective, the price on the vertical axis will be the dollar price of 1 peso, and the demand for and supply of pesos will be illustrated.

The demand and supply curves for dollars that we have developed can be used to illustrate how the value of the dollar will change relative to that of the peso in various situations. Consider the following. How will the value of the dollar change if national income in the United States increases? An increase in U.S. national income will increase the supply of dollars as U.S. households, businesses, and government entities buy more Mexican goods and services, purchase more Mexican assets, and increase travel to Mexico. The effect of rising national income in the United States on the value of the dollar is illustrated in Figure 7–4. As the supply of dollars increases, from

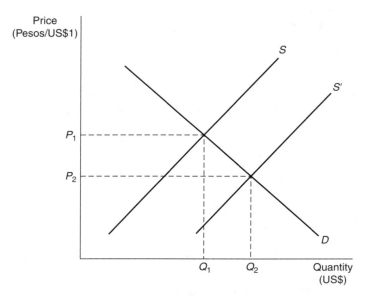

**FIGURE 7–4**   Effect of Increasing National Income in U.S.

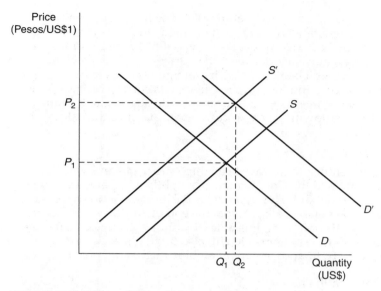

**FIGURE 7–5**    Effect of Rising U.S. Interest Rates

*S* to *S'*, the value of the dollar decreases (the dollar depreciates). (Can you, using this model, explain why the dollar will appreciate if national income increases in Mexico?) Here is another example. How will the value of the dollar change if interest rates in the United States increase relative to interest rates in Mexico? The effect of rising U.S. interest rates relative to those in Mexico is illustrated in Figure 7–5. The demand for dollars will increase from *D* to *D'* (as U.S. assets become more attractive to Mexican investors) and the supply of dollars will decrease from *S* to *S'* (as Mexican assets become less attractive to U.S. investors). Consequently, the dollar will appreciate.

**Speculation** also plays an important role in foreign exchange markets. If those who invest in currencies (speculators) hoping to capitalize on changes in exchange rates believe (based on their understanding of the foreign exchange market model and anticipated changes in the various determinants of demand and supply) that the peso will appreciate in the future, they will want to buy pesos now. However, the increase in demand for pesos will raise the peso price as a direct result of speculation. **Hot money** (foreign investment in stocks and bonds, etc., not regulated by the state) can move in and out of a country very quickly. As we will see in Chapter 8, in the late 1990s and early 2000s, speculation and hot money contributed to financial and monetary crises in Mexico, Asia, Argentina, Russia, and other countries. It has also caused many to ask whether states and the IMF should not do more to regulate capital movements (especially relative to investment) around the world.

This model demonstrates how market conditions affect foreign exchange rates. Changes in foreign exchange rates have profound political and social implications. As currency values change, there are always winners and losers. For example, as a nation's currency appreciates, companies that export goods and services will be hurt as their products become less competitive internationally. However, importers in the same country (consumers of foreign goods and services and companies using foreign inputs in their production processes) will benefit as those imports become cheaper. Thus, for any number of political and social reasons, governments quite often attempt to influence their currency's value relative to other currencies by controlling interest-rate changes, tax laws, domestic inflation rates, and a variety of other domestic factors.

As we will see in our discussion of different monetary and finance systems, sometimes governments intervene directly in currency markets, buying up their own currency or selling it in an attempt to alter its exchange value. The government (through its **central bank**) intervenes in the foreign exchange market, buying (demanding) and selling (supplying) its own currency as necessary to alter the exchange rate. In order to affect the value of its currency, a country's central bank must maintain foreign exchange reserves—reserves of foreign currency. If, for example, the demand for the country's currency declines, the currency will depreciate unless the state's central bank intervenes. The central bank will use its foreign reserves to buy (demand) its own currency, thereby stabilizing the demand for and the value of its currency. On the other hand, if the demand for the country's currency increases, the currency could appreciate too much unless the central bank intervenes by selling (supplying) its own currency to stabilize the value of its currency.

## FOREIGN EXCHANGE RATE SYSTEMS

Since the nineteenth century, there have been three structures and sets of rules related to foreign exchange rates.[3] The first was the Gold Standard, a tightly integrated international order that existed up until the end of World War I. The second was the Bretton Woods fixed-exchange-rate system created by the United States and its allies before the end of World War II and managed by the IMF. The current system is the "flexible" or adjustable (floating) exchange-rate regime. As we explore some of the basic features of these systems we will also highlight an issue that is related directly to currency exchanges, namely, finance or capital mobility across national borders.

### The Classic Gold Standard: Phase I

Although we tend to think of the related issues of interdependence, integration, and globalization as post–Cold War phenomena, many who study these subjects note that, from the end of the nineteenth century up until the end of World War I, the world was even more integrated (interconnected) than it is today. Cross-border flows of money increased in response to, among other things, interest rates in other countries. The leading European powers also invested heavily in their colonies. The currencies of these nations were part of a fixed exchange-rate system that linked currency values to the price of gold, thus the "gold standard." Similar to the European Union today, some countries created "monetary unions," in which their currencies would circulate in different geographic regions of the world.[4]

Some unique features of this particular structure were that, under the prevailing liberal economic doctrine of the time, in theory, the system was a *self-regulating* international monetary order. Different currency values were each pegged (fixed) to the price of gold. If a country experienced a balance-of-payments deficit—that is, it spent more money for trade, investments, and other items than it took in via those same sorts of activites (discussed in more detail later)—corrections occurred almost automatically in the domestic economy via wage and price adjustments. Known as the "price–specie flow mechanism," a country's gold would be sold to earn money to pay for its deficit. This resulted in tighter monetary conditions that curtailed the printing of money, raised interest rates, and cut government spending in response to a deficit. In turn, higher interest rates were supposed to attract short-term capital that would help finance (pay for) the deficit. In effect, domestic monetary and fiscal policy was "geared to the external goal of maintaining the convertibility of the national currency into gold."[5] The measures of the Gold Standard had a stabilizing, equilibriating, and confidence-building effect on the system.

By the end of World War I the Gold Standard had died, though it was temporarily resurrected again in the early 1930s during the Great Depression. Why? What happened? Some experts focus on changes in the role of Great Britain as the economic hegemon at the time. Among other things, before the war the pound sterling was the world's strongest currency. As the world's largest creditor, Great Britain loaned money (a collective good) (see Chapter 3) to other countries when economic growth slowed, to compensate them for not being able to buy other countries' exports. After World War I, Britain became a debtor nation and the U.S. dollar took the place of the pound sterling as the world's strongest and most trusted currency. The United States might have stepped into the hegemonic vacuum left by Great Britain, but isolationism and strong domestic interests prevented it from doing so. For many hegemonic theorists, the Gold Standard folded because of a power shift in the international system, in which the United States acted more in its own interest and failed to meet the international responsibility commesurate with its economic and military power.

Another argument is that the Gold Standard ended, not because Britain lost power, but because domestic forces within member states forced it to. It had been the elites who in particular were committed to economic liberal values, but public policies more often reflected the interests and growing influence of labor unions, the poor, and foreign investors, who often controlled monetary policy in the colonies. The extension of the electoral franchise (vote) produced more government intervention, pressuring governments to avoid the automatic policy adjustments the Gold Standard required in order to meet domestic needs. In many cases, states preferred to depreciate their currencies to generate trade rather than slow the growth of their economies or cut state spending. Many states and experts began considering or supporting the idea of flexible exchange rates, whereby currency values would fluctuate in response to market conditions and insulate the state from external economic pressures. In a move to insulate their economies further, many states adopted capital controls (limits on how much money could move in and out of the country). John Maynard Keynes supported these measures and was quoted as saying, "Let finance be primarily national."[6]

An important point to make here is that many states gradually found that the "embedded" economic liberal ideas of a self-regulating economy did not work. For hegemonic theorists (see Chapters 3 and 5), Britain could no longer afford to keep the system open by providing public goods to other members. For others, the Gold Standard's automatic disciplinary measures were too painful for society. At the same time, because the states under the Gold Standard were not yet very democratic, large numbers of people could not express their discontent with it via the vote.

Karl Polanyi wrote of this period that, by the end of World War I, one hundred years of relative political and economic stability ended when economic liberal ideas no longer seemed appropriate given world events and conditions.[7] As European and the U.S. economies were transformed into industrialized capitalist economies and became more interdependent (even more so than today), they were willing to cooperate with one another in order to live under the rules of a fixed exchange-rate system. However, the negative effects of capitalism generated demands for more and different types of protection in various states. Many societies sought relief from a brand of capitalism that failed from time to time, as evidenced during the Great Depression.

## The Bretton Woods System: The Qualified Gold Standard and Fixed Exchange Rates: Phase II

During the Great Depression the international monetary and finance structure was in a shambles. Reflecting policies that put national ahead of international interests, "beggar thy neighbor" trade policies resulted in some of the highest tariffs in history (see Chapter 6). The nonconvertibility of currency was also blamed, in part, for increasing the hostility among the European powers that ultimately resulted in World War II.

In July 1944 the United States and its allies met in Bretton Woods, New Hampshire, to devise a plan for European recovery when the war ended and to create new postwar international monetary and trade systems that would help growth and development. One aim of the meeting was to set policies in an atmosphere of cooperation, to avoid the nationalist pressures that had led to two world wars in a single generation. Most of the countries of the world in 1944 (about fifty-five of them) had only a decade earlier been in the throes of the Great Depression, during which as much as half their workforce had been unemployed. National delegates to the conference very much wanted to avoid the *competitive currency devaluations* of the 1930s, which were perceived as malevolent in their intent and thus often generated tit-for-tat retaliation measures. For Keynes and some others, efforts to gain at the expense of their competitors, instead of taking coordinated action that might benefit all states, eventually hurt them all.

## The Early Years

At the Bretton Woods conference the Great Powers created the International Monetary Fund, the World Bank, and what ultimately became the General Agreement on Tariffs and Trade (GATT) (see Chapter 6). More than a few people argue that these institutions were empty shells that represented only the values and policy preferences of the major powers, especially the United States.[8] Located across the street from one another in Washington, D.C., the IMF's primary role was to facilitate a stable and orderly international monetary system and investment policies,[9] whereas the World Bank was mainly concerned with economic recovery immediately after the war and then development issues (see Chapters 8 and 15). It is still the IMF's role to facilitate international trade, stabilize exchange rates, and to help members with balance-of-payments difficulties on a short-term basis (see the box, "The IMF and the Balance of Payments"). However, a newer role the IMF actively pursues today (discussed in Chapter 8) is to prevent and resolve currency and finance crises that have recently occurred in developing countries.

---

### THE IMF AND THE BALANCE OF PAYMENTS

The International Monetary Fund is the central bankers' central bank. It tries to create stable and responsive international financial relations among nations, just as central banks seek to create a favorable financial climate within the borders of each country. Currently (as of July 2006), it has a membership of 184 countries, a staff of 2716 from 165 countries, and a reserve of $317 billion.[a] It has loans out to seventy-four countries worth $28 billion. The IMF director is currently Rodrigo de Rato from Spain, who previously served as Spain's representative to the WTO and, among other positions, as the EU's representative to the G7 meeting in 2002. He heads a board of directors made up of twenty-four members from different countries who meet twice a year. Although members try to reach consensus on policy, major policy decisions are decided on a weighted voting basis. The weight of a state's vote is related to how much it contributes to the IMF's reserve. Currently the United States has the most votes, with 17.8 percent of the vote. Japan is a distant second at 6 percent, with Great Britain and France both at 5 percent.

The balance of payments is a statistic the IMF and national officials watch carefully because it registers an accounting of all the international monetary transactions between the residents of one nation and those of other nations in a given year, measured in current dollars. It indicates how much a state owes other states. The balance of payments also reflects what a nation produces, consumes, and buys with its money. If a state takes in enough money from other states to cover what it owes other states for imports, investments, and other items, we say that it has a balance-of-payments *surplus.* Likewise, if it does not take in enough to cover those items, it has a *deficit.* For national finance officials the biggest concern is having a deficit (or even a surplus) for too long, because that may require changes in the economy and society that they prefer not to make.[b]

You can think of your checkbook register as your own personal balance-of-payments account. Like a checking account, the *current account* (named after what a checking account is called in Great Britain, where the terminology of international finance originated) records "deposits" or money inflows. For a nation these deposits are derived from sales of currently produced goods and services, receipts of profits and interest from foreign investments, plus unilateral transfers of money or income from other nations, which include foreign aid a nation receives, private aid flows, and money that migrants send home to friends and families from abroad (see Table 7–2). According to the IMF, these receipts should equal money outflows related to the purchase of goods and services from other countries, payments of profits and interest to foreign investors, and unilateral transfers to other nations.

If a state has a *current account surplus,* its receipts or earnings are greater than its "withdrawals" or expenditures, so that on net these international transactions have increased national income, measured in dollar terms. However, when a nation has a *current account deficit,* outflows or withdrawals are greater than inflows or deposits in a particular year, and the net effect of these international transactions is to reduce the national income of the deficit country.

**TABLE 7–2   Elements of Balance-of-Payments Accounts**

|  | *CURRENT ACCOUNT* | *CAPITAL AND FINANCIAL ACCOUNT* |
|---|---|---|
| Current account surplus examples: Japan, China | Foreign receipts for exports, receipts of investment income (interest and profit), and unilateral transfers are greater than equivalent foreign payments. | Increase in domestic ownership of foreign assets; "creditor" nation. Technically termed a capital and financial account deficit to balance the current account surplus. |
| Current account deficit examples: United States, Mexico | Foreign payments for imports, payments of investment income (interest and profit), and unilateral transfers are greater than equivalent receipts. | Increase in foreign ownership of domestic assets; "debtor" nation. Technically termed a capital and financial account surplus to balance the current account deficit. |

Note that what is commonly referred to as the *balance of trade* is usually defined and analyzed separately from other items in the current account. The balance of trade registers a nation's payments and receipts for the exchange of goods and services only—essentially receipts for exports minus payments for imports. Therefore the balance of trade is only a *partial* indicator of what is happening in a nation's current account, and so provides only a glimpse of a nation's financial position or how much it is changing. The trade balance receives a lot of attention in the news media because of its direct effect on people in the large number of jobs that rely on trade in various countries.

The other IMF account—the *capital and financial account*—includes money that, in our checking account analogy, you might have borrowed or acquired as interest payment on an investment. For states these are longer-term economic transactions related to foreign investments, borrowing and lending, and sales and purchases of assets from other states such as stocks and real estate. Thus, the capital account (see Table 7–2) is an indicator of the effect of international transactions on changes in a nation's holdings of assets or wealth with respect to other countries. If there is an overage (surplus) or net inflow of money to the capital and financial account, foreigners are net purchasers of a country's assets. If there is a net outflow (deficit) of funds, on the other hand, the country has increased its net ownership of foreign assets.

It is easy to confuse the technical language of the balance of payments. It is a common practice to say that a nation has a "balance-of-payments" deficit. Normally, a surplus in one account must be offset by a deficit in another—establishing an accounting balance of 0. What people usually mean by a balance-of-payments deficit or surplus is shorthand for a current account deficit or surplus, with payments for goods, services, and transfers exceeding the corresponding receipts.

State officials tend to regard the current account as being more important than the capital account as an indicator of whether in the short term their state is running in the red and going into debt. A nation with a current account deficit must either borrow funds from abroad or sell off assets to foreign buyers to pay its international bills and thus achieve an overall payments balance. A current account deficit therefore requires a capital account surplus. Likewise, a current account surplus generates excess funds to purchase foreign assets. There are many political consequences of any nation's balance-of-payments status. If a state has a large foreign debt, for instance, it will need to increase output at home to generate more exports, decrease consumption (especially of imports), or perhaps do some combination of all these things.

Economically, but also politically and socially, these are not easy choices for states and their societies to make. Increasing output, for instance, might mean asking workers to accept lower wages, giving tax incentives to business firms, or removing regulatory roadblocks to more efficient production. It might also involve raising consumer taxes, reducing government subsidies, cutting government programs, or increasing interest rates to discourage consumption, attract savings, and encourage foreign investment in the home economy. In these circumstances it is easy to see why currency devaluation is so attractive to states, as it can quickly generate more exports by making goods less expensive. As we noted earlier, however, such a move is also likely to invite retaliatory "defensive" moves by other states, negating the economic gains of the first state but also generating more tensions between states, as was the case during the interwar years.

Japan and China tend to have a current account surplus, which means that each receives more foreign receipts from exports, investment income payments, and unilateral transfers than it spends for these items. Their current international transactions generate net income that they can use to purchase foreign assets (Japan has been a large international investor, and China is becoming more so all the time) or to pay off foreign debts incurred in the past. The United States and Mexico tend to have current account deficits. They pay out more for imports, investment income to foreigners, and unilateral transfers than they receive for these items. In order to pay these bills, they need to raise funds on the capital and financial account by increasing their foreign debt or by attracting investment funds from abroad by, say, raising bank interest rates.

Ideally, the IMF would like to see an equilibrium in a state's balance of payments. Theoretically, nations should spend only as much as they take in. On the other hand, this might not necessarily be a good thing. In order for businesses to expand and the economy to grow, banks lend out more than they have on deposit to back their loans. So the international economy needs a source of liquidity (money) for new investments and production that comes when a country runs a balance-of-payments deficit, which the United States did for all but two years under the Bretton Woods monetary and finance system. Countries that perform this collective good for the rest of the system are usually hegemons, and in these circumstances they are often referred to as a "locomotive." When the hegemon's economy heats up, it helps generate growth that benefits (pulls along) other members of the system.

On the other hand, if the United States cut its deficit by buying fewer automobiles, for example, then Japan would probably produce fewer autos and Saudi Arabia would probably produce less petroleum. One state's falling deficit would be another's decreased surplus. In a global political economy, our political and economic tensions would become their tensions. As we noted in Chapter 3 and will see in other sections of this chapter, economic hegemonic functions are difficult to separate from the political costs and benefits the hegemon must deal with as part of its system management functions.

*References*

[a] See the IMF website at www. IMF.org.

[b] For a detailed description of the balance of payments and its relationship to political-economic conditions in the fixed-exchange-rate Bretton Woods system, see Robert Warren Stevens, *A Primer on the Dollar in the World Economy* (New York: Random House, 1972).

Two distinct IPE perspectives give primary responsibility for the institutional design and mission of the IMF to different players. From the economic liberal perspective (see Chapter 3), the noted economist (and British representative at the meeting) John Maynard Keynes was instrumental in convincing the Allied powers to construct a new international economic order based on important new liberal ideas being proposed at the time. Pursuant to what has become known as the "Keynesian compromise," the postwar system of international finance would allow individual nation-states to continue regulating domestic economic activities within their own geographic borders. In some nations, these regulations were mercantilist in their intent, if not in their outcome. In the international arena, however, in order to avoid another Great Depression, the IMF would collectively manage financial policies. Global financial crisis and collapse were to be avoided by isolating each nation's financial system and then regulating it in consideration of international conditions and developments.

At the Bretton Woods conference, Keynes worked on setting up the World Bank and was also committed to creating an institution that could provide generous aid to both the victors and the vanquished nations after World War II. Keynes wanted to prevent a repeat of the brutal and ultimately destructive terms that the winners had imposed on the losers at the end of World War I. He was also adamant that creditors should help debtors make adjustments in their economies when it came to international payments and finance.

Meanwhile, U.S. Treasury official Harry Dexter White pushed through a distinctly U.S. vision for the IMF. White's plan for the IMF was to put nearly all of the adjustment pressure on debtor countries, without any symmetric obligation for creditors to make sacrifices. This was in the best interest of the United States, which came out of World War II as the world's biggest creditor nation, and with no plans to relegate that role. The U.S. Congress would not have approved a treaty that forced the United States to make more sacrifices just because Britain or some other debtor country could not pay its bills. (In fact, the United States was adamant about Great Britain honoring its wartime debts to the United States once the war was over.) The IMF, then, was designed to provide *temporary* assistance to all debtor countries while they adjusted their economic structures to the emerging international economy. The burden of adjustment ultimately fell on them, the debtors, not on both debtors and creditors as Keynes had intended.

According to many realists (and some economic liberals as well), immediately after the war, the United States was an *emerging but reluctant* major power, unwilling to assume the hegemonic role that Great Britain had played in the nineteenth century. For the United States, by virtue of the fact that it had the most votes when it came to policy decisions (based on holding 31 percent of the IMF reserve at the time), its major role in the IMF was to use it as an indirect way to promote an orderly liberal financial system that would lead to nondiscrimination in the conversion of currencies, confidence in a new order, and eventually more liquidity (money) in the system—which without a doubt it eventually did. These goals also complemented U.S. liberal values, beliefs, and policy preferences at little cost to the United States.

For mercantilists, and especially for realists, the IMF's institutional structure and monetary rules also reflected the interests of the Great Powers (as they were called at the time) along with the political and economic environment of 1944. Under pressure from the United States, the IMF adopted a modified version of the former Gold Standard's *fixed exchange-rate system* that was more open to market forces but not divorced from politics. At the center of this modified Gold Standard was a fixed exchange-rate mechanism based on an *unchangable* rate of US$35 for an ounce of gold.[10] The values of other national currencies would fluctuate against the dollar (and only indirectly to gold) in reflection of changes in the supply and demand for those currencies. Additionally, governments agreed to intervene in foreign exchange markets to keep the value of currencies within 1 percent above or below par value (the fixed exchange rate) on any given day.

Figure 7–6 represents this arrangement. As supply and demand conditions for other currencies changed, the trading bands established by the IMF defined limits within which exchange rates

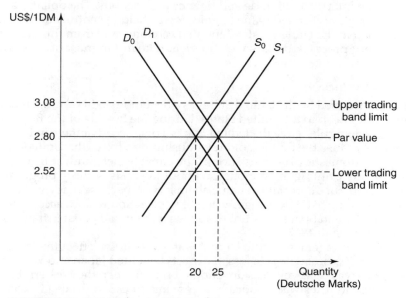

**FIGURE 7–6**   IMF Exchange-Rate Trading Bands

could fluctuate. If the value of any currency increased above or fell below the band limits, the national central banks behind those currencies were required to step in and buy up excess dollars or sell their own currency to return its value within the trading bands, which represented an established range of supply–demand equilbrium (par value). As in the earlier system, central banks could also buy and sell gold to help settle their accounts, which the United States often did. What officials liked about this system was that the quasi-self-adjusting mechanism allowed for diverse levels of growth in different national economies.

Confidence in the system relied on the fact that dollars could be converted into gold at a set price. This pleased the French, in particular, who preferred gold to anything else as scarce resource on which to ultimately base currency values. At the end of World War II, the United States started with the largest amount of gold backing its currency. This arrangement politically and economically stabilized the monetary system, which desperately needed the members' confidence and a source of liquidity (funds) if recovery in Europe and then economic growth and development were to be realized.

This arrangement worked fairly well from 1947 until the late 1960s because, as Benjamin Cohen argues, a political bargain was struck between the United States and the nations of Western Europe.[11] Once the Cold War began in 1947, the United States consciously accepted its hegemonic role of providing the collective good of security for its allies. As part of an effort to contain Soviet expansionism, the Western European nations provided the United States with forward bases where the United States staged an array of conventional and strategic weapons such as bombers and, later, nuclear weapons as part of a strategy to deter the Soviet Union from attacking U.S. NATO allies.

Many mercantilist-realists point out that in the bipolar world (see Chapter 9) of the Cold War, this arrangement boosted Western European and Japanese recovery from the war and preserved an environment for trade and U.S. and other foreign investment in Western Europe. These policies also helped tie together the allies into a liberal-capitalist U.S.-dominated monetary and finance system that also complemented U.S. efforts to *divide* the West from the Soviet-dominated Eastern Bloc. Capital movements into and out of the communist nations were severely limited.

As a hegemonic currency, the U.S. dollar played the role of **top currency**, one in great demand that was often used in international trade and finance transactions. The dollar was also the **reserve currency** in that, because of its fixed value to gold, it was held in central banks as a reserve. It was no small coincidence that the United States benefited economically from this arrangement because, as part of the recovery processs, dollars were in great demand in most of Western Europe and in other parts of the world.

## The Bargain Comes Unstuck

What were the costs incurred by the United States as a hegemon in this arrangement? On the whole, hegemony came quite cheap to the United States. During the heyday of the Bretton Woods system, from 1956 to 1964, system rules gave the United States a distinct advantage in U.S.–Western Europe monetary relations. Because the dollar–gold relationship was fixed, the United States could spend freely for a variety of domestic programs such as the Great Society and, at the same time, fund the Vietnam War by merely printing more money, without the costs of those programs weakening the dollar. The dollar could not depreciate in value against gold, because that would undermine one of the primary features of the fixed exchange system. Depreciation would, according to some U.S. officials, also make the United States look politically weak, as it had Great Britain when it finally devalued the pound sterling in 1967.

One cost of this arrangement to the United States was in the effect that an articially overvalued dollar had on U.S. exports. The U.S. loss of exports benefited Japan and Western Europe. Given that the United States was relatively less dependent on trade than the Western Europeans, the loss of business from these policies was politically acceptable to U.S. officials in exchange for successfully achieving other political and economic objectives. However, the United States would complain that the Europeans were "free riding" on U.S. defense spending by not providing the personnel they had promised for NATO.

Because the United States was free to continue spending and running a deficit in its balance of payments, in effect, it exported its inflation (an oversupply of dollars) abroad through the monetary system. Western European banks were committed to buying up those surplus dollars to bring their currency values back inside the trading bands to par value, which was against their best interests. Thus, the more the United States invested in Europe and spent for the Vietman War, the more it came under pressure to sell more of its gold to repurchase some of those surplus dollars in Europe or to cut back on government spending at home or abroad.

At one point, French President Charles DeGaulle complained that by France holding weak dollars in its banks instead of converting them to gold, which would have nearly emptied the U.S. gold reserve, it was underwriting the U.S. war in Vietnam. (DeGaulle was also being ironic, if not sarcastic, as France had been defeated in Vietnam a decade earlier and had warned the United States not to take on the war.)

By the early 1970s there were not enough U.S. gold reserves to cover all the dollars already in the international system. In these trade-dependent economies, a U.S. dollar that could not be devalued translated into an increase in the value of Western European currencies, thereby raising the price of European goods and leading to fewer exports. To generate more trade, West Germany pressured the United States to lift its restrictions on trading with the Soviet Union. The Western European economies had recovered sufficiently that they no longer needed as many dollars. U.S.-dominated monetary policy was restricting their economic growth and limiting their choices in politically unacceptable ways.

By the late 1960s, then, it was becoming clear that the political bargain between the United States and Western Europe was unravelling as their political and economic interests gradually changed and diverged from one another. All the major actors were less willing to live under an arrangement that only a few years earlier had seemed to satisfy both.

The success of the fixed exchange-rate system eventually undermined the value of the dollar, the monetary structure's institutions and rules, and U.S. leadership of the Bretton Woods monetary structure. By the early 1970s that structure had become too rigid, making it difficult for states to grow at their own pace and to promote their own interests and values. To prevent a recession (a slowdown in the domestic economy) at home, in August 1971 President Richard Nixon *unilaterally* decided to make dollars nonconvertible to gold. The United States devalued the dollar, and, to help make up its deficit in the balance of payments, imposed a 10 percent surcharge on all Japanese imports coming into the United States—a slight the Japanese would not soon forget. The United States abandoned its role of benevolent hegemon for the sake of its own interests. Both the United States and Western Europe accused one another of not sacrificing enough to preserve the fixed exchange-rate system. From the U.S. perspective, Western Europe needed to buy more goods from the United States to help correct the balance of trade and thus help the United States solve its balance-of-payments problem. The Europeans argued that trade was not the issue; instead, the United States needed to get out of Vietnam and cut back on domestic spending.

In any case, growing interdependence was uncomfortable to both parties. Europe's response to the U.S. actions was limited to verbal complaints, because no other state was politically or economically strong enough to lead a counterhegemonic campaign against the United States. In terms of the Keynesian compromise, domestic considerations weighed more heavily than international ones. U.S. hegemonic responsibilities and obligations became too expensive both financially and politically. The United States could no longer force other nations to absorb such costs as the loss of jobs, fewer exports, and slower economic growth, which resulted from its exported inflation.

### Finance and Capital Controls

In the early stages of the Bretton Woods system, investment funds could not move easily among countries to take advantage of possible higher returns on interest or investments. However, the obstacles were placed for explicit reasons. Fixed exchange rates and capital controls were manipulated to allow states to respond to domestic political forces without causing exchange-rate instability. Policymakers also intentionally limited finance and capital mobility for fear that global financial linkages like those in the 1920s and 1930s would easily spread a financial crisis in one country to many others.

Certain countries had specific reasons for limiting capital flows. To diminish the number of dollars leaving the United States in 1965, for instance, U.S. President Lyndon Johnson proposed limiting U.S. capital flows by the Interest Equalization Tax accompanied by "voluntary restraints" on foreign loans and investments. To say the least, these measures were not popular in Congress. Western Europe and Japan also limited capital movement as a way of controlling speculation on some of their currencies and the yen as they increased in value. France considered restricting dollar investments that purchased many European businesses.[12]

In 1971 the United States began pressuring its allies to relax their capital controls. However, by the time the Bretton Woods system ended in 1971, widespread currency convertibility (achieved by 1958), the large numbers of dollars pumped into the international economy via U.S. current account deficits, and the expansion of U.S. transnational corporation (TNC) investments greatly expanded business in Western Europe. These developments shifted the distribution of wealth and power among the allied member nations of the Western financial structure at the time. Capital controls had restricted international capital mobility to allow states to control the rate of investment in their economies, along with the direction and pace of economic change. However, expanding economies were now turning many of the allied economies in another direction—outward. Once capital controls were relaxed such that finance could move more freely throughout the new structure, the door (some would say floodgates) to an intense period of financial growth and investments was opened. Flexible exchange rates would soon add sources of financial liquidity to the international economy, including growth in markets for borrowers, investors, and speculators alike.

## The Float or Flexible Exchange-Rate System:
## Phase III and the Changing Economic Structure

In 1973, after a brief attempt to reinstate the formal Bretton Woods system failed, another version of it emerged to replace it—the float or flexible exchange-rate, or *managed float* system. The United States unilaterally devalued the dollar and rejected the idea that it would again be made convertible to gold. The major powers authorized the IMF to widen the trading bands (see Figure 7–6) so that changes in currency values could more easily reflect the supply and demand of currencies. They also independently floated their currencies, while many of the countries that joined the European Economic Community (EEC) sought regional coordination of their policies, and in the 1990s produced the European Monetary System (EMS). States still had to deal with an array of balance-of-payments issues, but the new rules were meant to be less constraining on public officials and their societies, while maintaining a framework of collective (as opposed to U.S.-dominated) management. Ironically, as the rules were relaxed, many states tried even harder to control the pace of economic growth and adopted monetary and fiscal policies (spending for domestic programs) that were more in line with their own national interests.

On the surface, the flexible exchange-rate system reflected several influential political and economic developments, namely, the recovery and growing influence of the Japanese and West European economies, the economic growth of the newly industrialized countries (NICs), and the advent of the Organization of Petroleum Exporting Countries (OPEC). Beginning in the 1970s, Japan began to experience rising living standards and high rates of economic growth that dramatically changed its status in the world economy. Along with the increasingly prosperous nations of the European Community, Japan soon became a major economic player in international monetary and finance issues.

Undoubtedly, the rise of OPEC and tremendous shifts in the pattern of international financial flows that followed dramatic oil price increases in 1973–1974 and then again in 1978–1979 helped further transform the international into a global financial network. Almost overnight, billions of dollars moved through previously nonexistent financial channels as OPEC states demanded dollars as payment for oil. This increased the demand for dollars in the international economy, which helped maintained its status as top currency. Many of these OPEC "petrodollars" were deposited in Western banks and then recycled in the form of loans to developing countries, which were increasingly viewed as good investment risks because of their natural resources and growing demand for consumer goods. However, between 1973 and 1979, the debt of developing nations increased from $100 billion to $600 billion.[13] As we will discuss in more detail in Chapter 8, this soon turned into a "debt crisis" when scores of indebted developing countries threatened to follow Mexico and Brazil's lead and declare bankruptcy.

In the early 1980s, continuing current and trade imbalances in the developed countries contributed to *stagflation* or slow economic growth accompanied by rising prices—two phenomena that do not usually occur together. When the dollar weakened in value, U.S. officials focused on fighting domestic inflation by raising interest rates to tighten the money supply, further contributing to global recession. At this time too, the pattern of financial regulation, already strained by the structural economic changes mentioned earlier, gave way to a change in political philosophy. In Britain and the United States, the prevailing Keynesian orthodoxy was swept aside in favor of a return to the classical liberal laissez-faire ideas of Adam Smith, but also Frederick Hayek and Milton Friedman (see Chapter 3).

In later 1982 British Prime Minister Margaret Thatcher, and a short time later, U.S. President Ronald Reagan, began promoting economic neoliberal ideals that meant, among other things, privatization of national industries, deregulation of financial and currency exchange markets, tax cuts at home, and liberalization of trade policy. Theoretically, this was supposed to produce increased savings and investments that would stimulate a return to economic growth. Beginning in 1983, economic recovery did begin, especially in the United States, stimulated by higher rates of consumption, a less restrictive monetary policy, and attention to fighting inflation—all policies that benefited mainly wealthier people. Some experts have suggested that, more than anything else, a drop in world oil prices helped stimulate economic growth, particularly in the industrialized nations.

In a number of cases, market forces alone did not determine state policies, but they did shape state responses to a series of issues associated with increased interdependence. Despite the laissez-faire rhetoric, Reagan's defense budget was the biggest since World War II, aimed at renewing the West's effort to contain the Soviet Union, a.k.a. the "Evil Empire." These expenditures and a strong dollar led to increased prices for U.S. exports and lowered import prices, which in turn led to record trade deficits, especially with Japan. Much like the hegemonic role the United States had played under the Bretton Woods system, rather than cutting back on government spending or raising taxes, the Reagan administration pressured Japan to adopt a variety of adjustment measures, including revaluing the yen, in order to shrink the U.S. trade and current account deficits. A number of mercantilist U.S. trade officials "bashed"[14] Japan for not playing fair when it came to lowering its import barriers. As economic liberals pointed out at the time, high interest rates in the United States helped attract Japanese investments in the United States, which in turn helped the United States balance its current account deficit while sustaining the value of the dollar as well. Ironically, then, while the U.S. economy went through an "adjustment" that led to a restructuring of its industries (higher than usual unemployment and decreased exports), Japanese purchases of U.S. property and other foreign direct investment (FDI) measures actually helped sustain the U.S. economy and maintain the strength of the dollar.

By the mid-1980s, however, corrective market measures such as these did not work as well for countries such as Mexico and Brazil, who threatened to declare bankruptcy because they could not pay back the debt that had accumulated on the money they had borrowed in the 1970s. Concerned about communism becoming more popular in poor Latin and Central American states, the Reagan administration responded by promoting measures that would help these countries reschedule their debt. The IMF and World Bank, under U.S. pressure, offered indebted developing nations new sources of income to finance their debts provided they agreed to economic liberal structural adjustment policies (SAPs) that emphasized cutting back domestic spending while opening themselves up to FDI and promoting international trade, which we also discuss in more detail in Chapter 8.

In the 1990s Mexico, Brazil, and a number of Southeast Asian nations also experienced a series of financial crises that some experts blamed on deregulated capital and currency markets. Unfettered portfolio investments of stocks and bonds moving quickly into and out of a country caused investors to lose confidence in many of these economies. This drove down the demand for that country's currency and resulted in riots, many deaths, and severe damage to these societies and to their economies.

Unexpectedly, by 1985 the United States had become the world's largest debtor nation, owing the world some $5 trillion.[15] Many countries and U.S. businesses connected to trade complained that the dollar was overvalued. Rapid capital flows were contributing to volatile exchange rates, which interfered with FDI and international trade. As it had twenty years earlier, the United States again resisted making hard choices about adjustments in the U.S. economy that could threaten its economic recovery or lead to cutbacks in defense spending. Instead, in 1985 the United States pressed the other G5 states (Great Britain, West Germany, France, and Japan) to meet in New York, where they agreed to intervene in currency markets to *collectively manage* exchange rates. The **Plaza Accord** committed the G5 to work together to "realign" the dollar so that it would depreciate in value against other currencies. For the Europeans and Japanese, however, by only devaluing its currency and not cutting back on its spending, the United States was merely avoiding making politically sensitive adjustments to its domestic economy.

## The Roaring Nineties and a Weak Dollar

By the end of the Cold War in the early 1990s, some of the remaining barriers to international transactions and capital flows had been removed, and private capital flows dwarfed official flows. FDI investment increased dramatically, especially in Southeast and East Asia (see Table 7–3). Emerging market economies receive private and official capital flows. **Private capital flows** take four forms: direct investments by TNCs, portfolio investments (such as purchases of foreign stocks by international mutual funds), commercial bank lending, and nonbank lending. **Official capital flows** include lending by states and loans by the IMF, World Bank, and a number of regional banks. In 1996, to take an extreme example, net private capital flows amounted to $327 billion, compared to net official flows of only $4.7 billion.

This capital helped underwrite the technological and communication revolution of the 1980s and 1990s in electronics, superfast computers, instantaneous worldwide satellite communications, and especially the Internet, linking people and machines in networks of economic power and efficiency, and thus contributing greatly to the integration of national economies and to the globalization of finance.[16] Today, equipped with a notebook computer in a wi-fi café, anyone can easily access financial markets around the world. Global finance has also accelerated the tendency toward global production and frag-

**TABLE 7–3    Net Inflows of Foreign Direct Investment (in millions of $)**

| REGION/CLASSIFICATION | 1980 | 1990 | 2000 | 2002 | 2004 |
|---|---|---|---|---|---|
| Asia (excluding Middle East) | 2971.6 | 18920.7 | 146156.2 | 95157.1 | 146607.1 |
| Central America & Caribbean | 2876.3 | 3608 | 21524.9 | 20129.7 | 23273.3 |
| Europe | 21367.2 | — | 866982.9 | 436551.7 | 277058.2 |
| North America | 22743.3 | 56070.6 | 387418.2 | 102244.3 | 113115.1 |
| Oceania | 2162.3 | 10116.2 | 17139.4 | 18457.2 | 44773.6 |
| South America | 3523.8 | 4757.4 | 57864 | 28523 | 37948.8 |
| Sub-Saharan Africa | 178.1 | 1209.2 | 6496.9 | 9517.9 | 11308.9 |
| Developed Countries | 46489.5 | — | 1287513 | 573409.2 | 454003.8 |
| Developing Countries | 10941.6 | 28642.9 | 227209.7 | 145016.7 | 210986.8 |

*Source:* World Resources Institute, Earthtrends: Searchable database, 17 October, 2006.

mentation of the production process (see Chapters 6 and 17). It has also helped generate tremendous increases in both the volume and the value of international trade (see Chapter 6).

Many experts attribute these developments to the success of economic liberal policies adopted in the 1980s. Aside from generating more wealth and business, financial integration and globalization have benefited some states—particularly the newly industrialized countries, which have enjoyed increasing levels of income and consumption. The liberalization of finances also helped change the relationships of states to businesses as they have incentives to form partnerships that promote business opportunities and economic growth.[17]

At the same time, these changes also made it more difficult to coordinate policies within the finance and monetary structure. Whether politically motivated or the result of market forces, changes in currency values tended to unleash a series of changes in both domestic and external economic relations, some positive and some negative. International economic policy options were increasingly limited by what has come to be known as the *Mundel trilemma*. States desire three things: (1) the ability to respond to domestic political forces (sometimes called monetary autonomy), (2) international capital mobility (necessary for efficient international finance), and (3) stable exchange rates (desirable for smooth international trade and investment). The problem is that only any two are possible at the same time. The third option always cancels out the effectiveness of the other two.

The United States and Japan, for example, tend to have large international trade sectors in absolute terms that are in fact relatively small compared with the domestic economy. Thus, it is more important for them to have a free hand in domestic economic policy, and to have access to international capital markets for financing, than it is to have stable exchange rates. On the other hand, Argentina and Hong Kong, for instance, which were more dependent on the international economy, chose to accept stable exchange rates in exchange for domestic autonomy. Both Argentina and Hong Kong pegged (fixed) their currencies to the U.S. dollar. This made their exchange rates more stable but limited their ability to respond to domestic economic and political problems.

Taiwan made other choices related to its large current account surpluses that fuel FDI abroad. Taiwan is the home base for a number of transnational enterprises, including Compal Electronics, AU Optronics, Quanta Computer, and Acer. All these Taiwan-based electronics and computer firms are among the largest in their respective global markets and increasingly invest Taiwan's current account surplus abroad, buying assets and building factories in many countries, including China.

In some quarters, however, globalization has *not* been well received when it comes to finance and monetary issues. In Chapter 8 we will discuss the argument that economic liberal–style capitalism and globalization have not worked well for everyone, especially when it comes to finance and long-term debt.

## The Dollar Versus the Euro

In the early 1990s, EU members established the European Monetary Union (EMU) and a European Central Bank (ECB) in conjunction with an effort to deepen the integration process and to help insulate European currencies from the U.S. dollar and its effects on the international political economy. A common currency benefited intra-European trade by helping investors save tremendous amounts of money on the cost of currency exchanges.

When the euro was introduced in 2002, it was valued at almost one for one against the U.S. dollar. Since then the euro has gradually increased in value against other currencies. Meanwhile, the dollar has been steadily declining in value since the early 2000s. In the fall of 2006, $1 was worth 0.78 €. Some political economists attribute U.S. dollar weakness to the increased consumption of imported goods, increased spending for domestic entitlement programs such as health care and welfare, the war in Iraq, and the war on terrorism in other countries. In 2005 the U.S. trade deficit was $716.7 billion, with a total current account deficit of $808 billion (see Table 7–4), which represented 6.6 percent of U.S. gross domestic product (GDP), accompanied by a record U.S. budget deficit of $342 billion. A weak dollar is also blamed on the huge trade and current account deficits,

**TABLE 7-4    Current Account Balances, Selected Countries**

| G-7 COUNTRIES | CURRENT ACCOUNT ($ BILLIONS) | | |
| --- | --- | --- | --- |
| | *AUGUST 26, 2006* | *AUGUST 26, 2000* | *AUGUST 25, 1990* |
| United States | −808.5 | −367.2 | −105.3 |
| Canada | +31.8 | +2.2 | +4.2 |
| Japan | +164.6 | +117.7 | +63.6 |
| Great Britain | −52.3 | −18.3 | −34.1 |
| France | −33.4 | +35.1 | −6.4 |
| Germany | +106.2 | −21.9 | +75.0 |
| Italy | −34.7 | +3.2 | −12.5 |
| **Emerging Market Countries** | | | |
| Argentina | +6.7 | −12.0 | |
| Brazil | +12.5 | −24.0 | |
| Chile | +0.8 | | |
| China | +160.8 | +15.7 | |
| India | −10.6 | −4.2 | |
| Mexico | −1.2 | −14.9 | |
| Poland | −4.2 | −12.2 | |
| Russia | +91.4 | +31.4 | |
| South Korea | +7.8 | +15.0 | |
| Taiwan | +20.6 | +4.3 | |
| Thailand | +2.7 | +10.7 | |
| Turkey | −28.7 | −6.6 | |

*Note:* Current account balance is for previous 12 months of available data. Dates given are dates of source. 1990 data for Germany is actually for West Germany.
*Source: The Economist,* various issues.

which have grown over time. As was the case in the 1960s, this spending pumps huge amounts of U.S. dollars into the market, leading to an oversupply of dollars and pushing down the value of the dollar. Finally, some U.S. officials blame China for purposely holding down the value of the yuan to make Chinese goods more attractive in trade markets, thereby artificially adding to the U.S. trade deficit. (See the box, "The Tangled Web of China's Currency Manipulation.")

---

**THE TANGLED WEB OF CHINA'S CURRENCY MANIPULATION[a]**

From 1994 to July 2005, China pegged its currency—known as the yuan (also called the renminbi)—to the U.S. dollar at a fixed rate of 8.28 to 1. The People's Bank of China, which is China's equivalent of the U.S. Federal Reserve, maintained this exchange rate by using yuan to buy up U.S. dollars that entered the Chinese market as investment expenditures and export earnings. After swapping yuan for dollars, the dollars were placed in China's foreign reserves. This policy made the yuan relatively abundant and the dollar relatively scarce, artificially decreasing the yuan's value. By undervaluing its currency, China hoped to aid its development by making its exports cheaper. To illustrate, consider how a revaluation of the yuan (meaning an increase in its value) affects the export price of Chinese T-shirts:

| Yuan/Dollar | Price of T-Shirts in Yuan | Price of T-Shirts in Dollars |
| --- | --- | --- |
| 8.28/1 (undervalued yuan) | 100 yuan | $12.08 |
| 4/1 (revalued yuan) | 100 yuan | $25 |

As you can see, undervaluing the yuan makes China's goods cheaper in U.S. markets. Another effect is to make U.S. imports into China more expensive. Consider how the yuan's value affects the price of American computers imported into China:

| Yuan/Dollar | Price of Computers in Dollars | Price of Computers in Yuan |
|---|---|---|
| 8.28/1 | $1000 | 8280 yuan |
| 4/1 | $1000 | 4000 yuan |

Theoretically, an undervalued yuan puts Chinese producers at an advantage by making Chinese goods cheaper in the United States and U.S. goods more expensive in China.

In July 2005, in the face of pressure from a variety of sources, China officially abandoned the yuan–dollar peg in favor of a peg to a basket of currencies. By the end of April 2006, however, the yuan had risen only a modest 3 percent in value, demonstrating that China continues a *de facto* policy of undervaluing the yuan relative to the dollar.

China's currency manipulation has incensed many U.S. manufacturers and unions, who claim that U.S. products cannot compete against Chinese goods that are unfairly cheap in U.S. markets, nor can they compete in Chinese markets because U.S. goods are too expensive there. Many U.S. politicians, confronted with a massive $202 billion trade deficit with China in 2005 (an all-time high for any one country), have also demanded that China take steps to increase the yuan's value. Senators Lindsey Graham (Rep., South Carolina) and Charles Schumer (Dem., New York) have several times threatened to introduce a bill placing a 27.5 percent tariff on all Chinese goods unless China stops its currency manipulation.

Opponents of the Schumer-Lindsey bill argue that China's blame for the trade deficit with the United States is overstated. They point to evidence that the yuan is undervalued by only 10 to 15 percent, rather than the 15 to 40 percent claimed by Schumer and Lindsey.[b] They also argue that even a big revaluation would do little to shrink the U.S.–China trade deficit.[c] With a stronger currency, Chinese imports of raw materials would get cheaper, lowering production costs of many goods and thus offsetting the expected rise in export prices. A depreciation of the yuan might encourage Chinese producers to cut costs in other ways, such as transferring production to the Chinese interior or to other developing countries where labor costs are low enough to offset the lost export competitiveness.

Even if applying tariffs on Chinese goods did successfully shrink the U.S. trade deficit with China, many have questioned whether this is in fact desirable. Driving up the price of Chinese goods could trigger rapid inflation, given the dramatic U.S. dependence on Chinese imports.[d] Inflationary pressures would force the U.S. Federal Reserve to increase interest rates, decreasing the affordability of investment in the United States. According to the economic liberal view, China has become the world's factory for the time being, and U.S. business should acknowledge China's comparative advantage in labor-intensive goods and increase specialization in capital- and knowledge-intensive production, rather than demanding protection from more competitive producers.

Another complicating element in this debate is China's role in financing U.S. government spending. China's foreign reserves—the depository for U.S. dollars after they are pulled out of Chinese markets—were on track to exceed $1 trillion in value by the end of 2006.[e] About three-quarters of these reserves are held in the form of U.S. Treasury Bonds, which are purchased by the People's Bank of China after they are issued by the U.S. Treasury Department. The U.S. government issues these bonds in order to raise the money needed for deficit spending—the result of the government spending in excess of its tax revenue. There are several motivations for holding Treasuries as opposed to cash. U.S. Treasuries are perhaps the safest investment in the world, as the U.S. government is very unlikely to default on its debt. Treasuries are also highly liquid (meaning they can be easily turned into cash), and pay interest, which ensures that China's reserves are flexible in composition and don't decrease in value over time. Another supposed motivation is that China wishes to facilitate U.S. consumption to boost its own exports.[f]

This creates a form of co-dependency, in which the United States relies on China to finance its deficit spending and China relies on the United States to buy its goods.[g] If China floated its currency (allowed currency markets to freely determine the yuan's value), it might no longer need to accumulate dollars and would therefore have less to invest in U.S. Treasuries. A decreased accumulation of Treasuries would force the United

States to raise interest rates, stunting investment and hurting consumption by driving up the price of credit. Others contend that this is not a serious problem because China would remain dependent on U.S. markets and would thus be deterred from deliberately worsening the financial situation in the United States.[h]

This debate speaks to the importance of global financial linkages. Many questions remain unanswered. Does China's currency manipulation harm the U.S. economy? If so, what if anything should U.S. policymakers do to alleviate the U.S. trade deficit? What seems certain is that the relationship between the U.S. and China is highly interdependent, making the resolution of these controversies vital to both countries' long-term economic health and political relationship.

*References*

[a] Our thanks to Josh Anderson for helping research and draft the material in this box.

[b] "Gently Towards the Heavens," *The Economist*, April 1, 2006.

[c] Ira Kalish, "Economist's Corner: What Does China's Currency Revaluation Mean?" *Deloitte Research*, July 2005. www.deloitte.com

[d] "From T-Shirts to T-Bonds," *The Economist*, July 30, 2005, pp. 61–63.

[e] Jane McCartney and Gary Duncan, "Chinese Foreign Reserves to Exceed $1 Trillion," The Times Online, March 29, 2006. http://business.timesonline.co.UK/tol/business/markets/China/article698289.ece

[f] The relationship between the U.S. budget deficit and U.S. consumption, as well as the danger posed by America's large trade deficit, is explored in Menzie D. Chinn, "Getting Serious About the Twin Deficits" (*Council on Foreign Relations*, September 2005). www.cfr.org/content/publications/attachments/Twin_DeficitsTF.pdf also, it is Council Special Reports no. 10.

[g] For both sides of the deficits debate, see Brad Setser, Nouriel Roubini, David Levey and Smart Brown, "How Scary Is the Deficit?" *Foreign Affairs* July/August 2005, pp. 194-200.

[h] Josh Anderson, "American Profligacy and Chinese Patronage: The Alleged Peril of a Post-Pegged World," unpublished paper, University of Puget Sound, Tacoma, WA, December 2005.

As would be expected (see the box, "The IMF and the Balance of Payments"), to settle its balance-of-payments account the United States continues to sell off more of its industries and property. The United States has a record-setting national debt of $8.3 trillion (as of May 2006). Many experts note that Americans do not save enough to offset these expenditures. This worries those concerned that China, Japan, Great Britain, South Korea, and other countries that invest heavily in U.S. Treasury Bonds, which helps underwrite the U.S. deficit, could stop investing in the United States or sell their bonds. The United States would have to raise interest rates to make U.S. bonds more attractive, which could stifle domestic investment and consumption based on credit. In the worst-case scenario the result would be the bankruptcy of the U.S. economy, which would undoubtedly spread throughout the global economy.

However, many economic liberals are adamant that a weak dollar is *not* a significant problem and that "the weight of history suggests that the trade deficit, a symptom of investment inflows, is a sign of national economic strength."[18] Instead, the current trade deficit reflects heavy investment in U.S. high-tech and high-productivity industries, fueling the U.S. economy. The United States continues to grow much faster, even if at a relatively slow rate, than many states with trade surpluses, such as Germany and Japan. A weaker dollar also means more exports of U.S. manufactured products. For these experts, currency exchange rates are *not* as tightly connected to national debt and spending as many people think. Instead, "speculators and emotional momentum appear to dominate exchange markets."[19]

Other experts and officials *are* gravely concerned about a weak U.S. dollar, but for different reasons. They wonder what a wobbly dollar means not only for international trade, finance, and monetary policy, but also whether it could eventually destabilize the international finance and monetary structure and spill over to undermine U.S. military power and the global security structure as well. Gabor Steingart of *Der Spiegel* magazine in Germany makes an interesting argument that many countries have been willing to invest in the United States, not only for economic reasons, but because "one can almost completely rule out the possibility of political unrest in the United

States. . . . Given the size of the currency's spread and the quantity of dollars circulating worldwide, speculators have no cause to get overly anxious about the dollar."[20] Steingart notes that in 2005, 20 percent of all currency reserves held in the world were euros but more than 60 percent were U.S. dollars. Thus the U.S. dollar remains "the world's currency anchor."

What worries these mercantilist-realists the most is that this situation might not last *if* investors should lose confidence in the dollar. A weakening dollar usually causes investors to sell off some of their dollars. However, investors continue to buy dollars precisely because "if they were to stop buying dollars tomorrow, suspicion about the currency would spread and insecurity would grow."[21] To not buy dollars then could seriously undermine their own investments. In essence, "the dollar is strong because that's the only thing that can prevent it from growing weak. . . . Behaving irrationally has become rational behavior."[22] Steingart likens the U.S. economy to an "economic giant on steroids." The shots the United States takes are investments from countries such as Japan, South Korea, China, Great Britain, and the Netherlands, along with those from private enterprises from many nations. Everyone is caught in a "dollar trap" of sorts. Because things are so interconnected in terms of their effects on investors' trust and confidence in the U.S. dollar, the wrong signal from the U.S. Federal Reserve, for example, could easily push investors to sell off their investments and dollars before they are sharply devalued. A dollar crisis *could* easily translate into a domestic economic crisis that would affect U.S. industries, businesses, and households but could also spread to other countries within days. The U.S. economy could expect massive layoffs, reduced consumption, a decline in real estate prices, and decreased imports that would hurt developing countries.

This argument runs counter to those of economic liberals, who see a weak dollar as nothing to get too worried about. Although continued consumer spending in the United States and debt in fact produces growth rates that justify trust, at some point Japanese or Chinese banks will be tempted to dump their dollar holdings. What troubles realists especially is sudden *fear,* which could spark a herd instinct to dump the U.S. dollar before other investors do. The basis of this fear is not clear, but it could be political or social in nature.

This problem has important implications for policymakers and in terms of IPE theory. Because the dollar has been so strong politically since World War II, it would be hard to imagine another currency as strong or that investors would trust as much, given the role of the United States in managing the finance and monetary structure, along with the international security structure. Today, because economic and political-military issues are so tightly interconnected (see Chapter 9), we must ask how does a weak U.S. dollar affect the capability of the United States to promote international peace and stability?

As we discussed earlier in this chapter, during the Cold War the United States used a strong dollar and pursued "hegemony on the cheap," while incurring huge balance-of-payments deficits that the Europeans and Japan accepted in exchange for U.S. security guarantees. At some point, however, might U.S. debt and the balance-of-payments deficit undermine U.S. defense expenditures on behalf of a variety of common international political and economic objectives, or public support for those goals? One also has to wonder if, more so than any other economic indicator, a weakening of U.S. military capabilities, power, and resolve might be a factor that causes emotional investors to shift away from the dollar.

On the other hand, if mercantilist-realists are correct that confidence in the U.S. dollar could easily be reversed, could U.S. efforts to combat terrorism and security in various parts of the world *continue* to instill confidence in the dollar? Another way of asking the question is, if investors do abandon the dollar, is another state or group of states prepared to assume security structure management responsibilities? Much as in the 1960s, then, an implicit bargain does seem to exist between the United States and states that support its security interests. The United States plays a large role in managing the international security structure, but this time it is in exchange for foreign investment in the United States. So far neither the EU nor any other state or group of states wants or even desires that responsibility. As history has demonstrated, however, all this could easily change!

## CONCLUSION

In the United States and Western Europe, post–World War II financial policies were heavily influenced by the experience of financial collapse during the Great Depression of the 1930s. By isolating each nation's financial system and then regulating it, policymakers wanted to avoid global financial crisis and collapse. Under the Bretton Woods system (1947–1971), investment funds could not move easily among countries to take advantage of higher returns, and currency discrimination continued until 1958. The IMF limited exchange-rate fluctuations to narrow trading margins in consideration of U.S. and its allies' efforts to stabilize the Western capitalist economies and, among other things, contain the Soviet Union.

When the financial system did not keep up with underlying changes in different national economies and their changing interests and goals, the Bretton Woods fixed exchange-rate system gave way to a flexible exchange-rate system and to less control over capital transfers. Since the early 1970s, in an era marked by increasing interdependence and more recently by globalization, three forces led to increased growth and income and helped to integrate international markets: changes in different national economies that reflected different national of international interests, the increasing popularity of neoliberal ideas, and dramatic changes in technology. These forces helped produce a finance and monetary structure that has become increasingly less regulated but also integrated and global in nature. In so doing the structure has become increasingly much more difficult to manage and requires a good deal of cooperation to maintain.

By the late 1980s and throughout the 1990s, the idea that markets (as opposed to the state) influenced developments in the international finance and monetary structure became quite popular in academic and official circles. This idea also became one of the ideological justifications behind the globalization campaign (see Chapter 3). Market forces were also weakening nation-states and their ability to control or manage finance and currency markets.

However, in this chapter we have seen that although it may *appear* that states have been weakened, the emergence of a more market-oriented and global financial structure does *not* mark the triumph of the markets over the state. Dani Rodrik and Linda Weiss, among others, reject the argument that globalization has weakened the state.[23] Yet because currency values and capital mobility dramatically affect domestic employment and investment in many industries and services, states feel more than ever compelled to assert themselves in order to achieve an assortment of national objectives.

At the same time, the Mundel trilemma demonstrates that nations that attempt to retain political autonomy while intervening to preserve some measure of exchange-rate stability, for example, inevitably run into a myriad of problems. Globalization and the economic liberal market ideology also make it increasingly difficult for states to reconcile domestic with international interests that require cooperation and maintanance of some sort of international finance and monetary structure.

If anything, a **paradox of globalization** permeates the finance and monetary structure just as it does the production and trade structure. Although globalization certainly compels states to aggressively compete with one another on an economic basis, in so doing the liberalization of finance and currency markets has also generated enthusiasm for protection or insulation of national economies from one another. At the same time, economic logic alone is not enough to sustain investor trust and confidence in an economy like that of the United States, which continues to run large deficits that, in effect, help stabilize international markets. Much investor confidence expresses genuine appreciation and support for U.S. values and institutions along with implicit support for U.S. efforts to manage the international security structure. Likewise, once again a bargain exists between the United States and those states that subscribe to and benefit from U.S. international security policies. And, as in the 1960s, that is likely to change!

This chapter also demonstrated that issues of wealth and power cannot be separated from one another. Today's international political economy is much more integrated than it was only twenty years ago. Interdependence and globalization have redistributed large amounts of wealth and, with it, political power. This has made it exceptionally difficult to manage the finance and monetary structure in ways that reflect the interests of other than the major powers. This is likely to change soon, as we will discuss in Chapter 8. For now it is clear that deregulation of exchange rates and capital movements have certainly benefited the wealthier industrialized states and many successful TNCs, along with banks and other sources of private capital. It has certainly helped people in developed parts of the world produce and consume more. Likewise, many economic liberals contend that it has likewise benefited the developing nations.

As we will see in the next chapter, the role of developing countries in the international finance and currency structure is changing and remains quite controversial. Because so much money is now beyond state control, numerous financial institutions did not hesitate to launch speculative attacks that generated currency crises in Mexico, Thailand, Russia, Argentina, and a number of other countries. This raised much controversy surrounding the IMF's role today in the poorer countries in terms of the IMF and World Bank's efforts to solve a series of problems related to both financial crises and long-term debt. More important, it has raised issues about who makes the rules of this structure and whose interests they reflect.

## DISCUSSION QUESTIONS

1. Outline the basis of the political, economic, institutional, and procedural features of the gold standard, the fixed exchange-rate, and the flexible exchange-rate systems. What are some of the political and economic advantages and disadvantages of each?
2. Outline the institutional features of the IMF and its role in settling current account deficits.
3. The U.S. dollar depreciated dramatically relative to the Japanese yen in 1995. What effect would this event likely have had on consumers and businesses in each country? Is a falling dollar good or bad for the United States? Explain.
4. Suppose that the Japanese yen were to appreciate relative to the U.S. dollar. How would this event affect each of these people:
   - Japanese and U.S. auto workers (making cars to sell in the United States)
   - U.S. and Japanese farmers
   - A Japanese business that has a dollar-denominated loan from a U.S. bank
   - A U.S. investor who has a yen-denominated investment (such as a Japanese government bond)
5. The United States has recently experienced huge current account deficits along with capital and financial account surpluses. What specific political and economic factors contributed to this condition? What role does it play in the weak U.S. dollar? If you were an international investor, would you be investing in the United States? Why or why not?

## INTERNET LINKS

Currency Converter:
   http://cnnfn.com/markets/currencies
The International Monetary Fund:
   www.imf.org
IMF Survey (biweekly report):
   www.imf.org/external/pubs/ft/survey/surveyx.htm
The IMF explained:
   www.imf.org/external/pubs/ft/survey/sup0998/contents.htm
Rolf Englund's Debt Crisis page:
   www.international.se/ldc.html

## SUGGESTED READINGS

Paul Blustein. *The Chastening: Inside the Crisis That Rocked the Global Finance System and Humbled the IMF.* New York: Public Affairs, 2001.
David Calleo. *The Imperious Economy.* Cambridge, MA: Harvard University Press, 1982.
Benjamin J. Cohen. *The Geography of Money.* Ithaca, NY: Cornell University Press, 1998.
Oswaldo De Rivero. *The Myth of Development: The Non-viable Economies of the 21st Century.* New York: Zed Books, 2001.

Barry Eichengreen. *Globalizing Capital: A History of the International Monetary System.* Princeton, NJ: Princeton University Press, 1996.

Guilio M. Gallarotti. *The Anatomy of an International Monetary Regime.* New York: Oxford University Press, 1995.

Scott Newton. *The Global Economy: 1944–2000.* London: Arnold, 2004.

## KEY TERMS

| | | |
|---|---|---|
| speculation | top currency | private capital flows |
| hot money | reserve currency | official capital flows |
| central bank | Plaza Accord | paradox of globalization |

## NOTES

1. Eric Helleiner, "The Evolution of the International Monetary and Financial System," in John Ravenhill, ed., *Global Political Economy* (Oxford: Oxford University Press, 2005), p. 152.
2. The "Foreign Exchange Rates" section of this chapter was written by Ross Singleton. We would like to thank him for his role in producing not only this section, but for reviewing and commenting on other parts of the chapter as well.
3. For a more detailed discussion of the history of the monetary and finance structure, see Eric Helleiner, "The Evolution of the International Monetary and Financial System," in John Ravenhill, ed., *Global Political Economy* (Oxford: Oxford University Press, 2005), pp. 151–175.
4. Two examples of these unions were the Latin American Union (LMU), which in 1865 included France, Switzerland, Belgium, and Italy; and the Scandanavian Union, which in 1873 included Sweden, Denmark, and later Norway. See Helleiner, ibid., p. 153.
5. Ibid., p. 155.
6. Cited in ibid., p. 156.
7. See Karl Polanyi, *The Great Transformation: The Political and Economic Origins of Our Time* (Boston: Beacon Press, 1944).
8. See, for example, Oswaldo De Rivero, *The Myth of Development: The Non-viable Economies of the 21st Century* (New York: Zed Books, 2001), pp. 54–61.
9. See www.imf.org.
10. For a more detailed discussion of the early Bretton Woods period that focuses mainly on economic factors, see Robert Warren Stevens, *A Primer on the Dollar in the World Economy* (New York: Random House, 1972).
11. Benjamin Cohen, "The Revolution in Atlantic Relations: A Bargain Comes Unstuck," in Wolfram Hanrieder, ed., *The United States and Western Europe: Political, Economic and Strategic Perspectives* (Cambridge, MA: Winthrop, 1974), pp. 106–133.
12. See, for example, Jean Jacques Servan Schreiber's *The American Challenge* (New York: Avon Books, 1968).
13. Reported in Thomas Lairson and David Skidmore, *International Political Economy: The Struggle for Power and Wealth*, 3rd ed. (Belmont CA: Wadsworth, 2003), p. 104.
14. At the time it was common to refer to those who were critical of Japan's protectionist trade policies as being engaged in "Japan bashing," for failing to account for the social and cultural factors behind Japan's political and economic policies. See Michael Donnelly, "On Political Negotiations: America Pushes to Open Up Japan," *Pacific Affairs, 66* (1993), p. 427.
15. See Robert Gilpin, *The Challenge of Global Capitalism* (Princeton, NJ: Princeton University Press, 2000), p. 6.
16. For a recent version of this argument, see Thomas Friedman, *The World Is Flat* (New York: Farrar, Straus & Giroux, 2005).
17. See, for example, Susan Strange and John Stopford, *Rival States, Rival Firms: Competition for World Markets* (Cambridge: Cambridge University Press, 1991).
18. See Tim Kane, "The Brutal Price of a Dollar," The Heritage Foundation, Washington, DC, http://heritage.org/Research/TradeandForeignAid/bg1855.cfm.
19. Ibid.
20. See Gabor Steingart, "Playing with Fire," Spiegel Online, www.spiegel.de/international/0,1518,druck-440054,00.html.
21. Ibid.
22. Ibid.
23. See, for example, Dani Rodrik, "Sense and Nonsense in the Globalization Debate," *Foreign Policy* (Summer 1997), pp. 19–37; and Linda Weiss, *The Myth of the Powerless State* (Ithaca, NY: Cornell University Press, 1998).

# The IPE of International Debt

## OVERVIEW

As we saw in Chapter 7, global financial markets and monetary issues now transcend national borders; they are the form and substance of the global financial structure. In the cases of both capital mobility and currency exchange rates, since the 1980s a good deal of deregulation has occurred that reflects the interests of the industrialized developed states, some of the international organizations they sponsor such as the International Monetary Fund (IMF) and World Trade Organization (WTO), transnational corporations (TNCs), investment banks, and others. Global finance now goes on 24 hours a day. As economic liberals are quick to point out, these developments produced record levels of economic growth in both developed and developing nations, especially in the 1990s, that was aided by an ideological outlook that served as the ideological underpinning of what has become an intensive form of globalization.

However, this growth has not prevented a large number of developing nations from needing and even being encouraged to borrow money and remaining in debt. Debt, then, is another important aspect of the international finance and monetary structure and is the focus of this chapter. Three aspects of international debt concern us most in this chapter. First, since the early 1980s many less developed countries (LDCs) have experienced a series of debt problems that have not been easy to solve, and that in many cases act as barriers to economic development. Second, and more dramatically, in the late 1990s some of the newly industrialized countries (NICs) in Asia and Latin America experienced speculative attacks on their national currencies that compelled many of them to borrow from the IMF and World Bank.

Finally, in many of the poorest countries in Africa and elsewhere, long-term debt, together with HIV/AIDs and other major problems, continue to plague what are essentially already impoverished nations. Recently, a number of international organizations and relief agencies, together with vast numbers of nongovernmental organizations (NGOs), have launched a campaign to do more than wait for the **heavily indebted poor countries (HIPCs)** to work themselves into the global economy and out of debt. Debt relief or cancellation of the debt altogether has been one of the major goals of what has become an international movement.

Many of the issues surrounding debt have raised a number of fundamental questions about globalization and the global political economy. How much have lending policies that benefited the richer states hurt the countries that borrowed from them? How much of the debt problem is the

151

fault of the borrowers? John Maynard Keynes argued that lenders have an obligation to help borrowers solve their debt problems. Given a number of recent issues connected to debt, in this chapter we explain the roles that states, international organizations (IOs), and NGOs play in dealing with a variety of debt problems. As we will see, the three main theories of international political economy (IPE) help us describe, explain, and propose some solutions to various aspects of debt and finance problems.

**S**ince World War II, the international financial system has undergone rapid and dramatic change. The *globalization* of finance is the single most important trend in finance today. Many economic liberals in particular tend to believe that global markets today are dominated less by states and more by banks and other agencies and private capital flows, for whom national borders and regulations are relatively unimportant. Indeed, the global financial system does have a great deal of money to manage. An estimated $8 trillion of foreign exchange is traded *per day* on global markets; so foreign exchange market activities are by far the largest financial flows in the world, dwarfing even the vast economy of the United States.

The 1990s were relatively good years for many of the major industrialized nations and foreign investors, who rode a wave of globalization and hype about its benefit to everyone and especially to LDCs that integrated into the new global economy. In Chapter 7 we also saw how an emerging global economy still exhibits a good deal of volatility for the developed nations related to a series of agreements over the years to deregulate finance and currency exchanges. However, for many mercantilists, an integrating international political economy is not one from which many states can easily insulate themselves. Although the major industrialized nations have not experienced anything like a Great Depression, many LDCs feel that they have or continue to be in one. For them, debt continues to be something of a double-edged sword, something that makes a certain amount of economic sense in the short term, while at the same time something that does not make sense in the long term.

Drawing on some of the themes we introduced in Chapter 7, this chapter examines three recent interrelated financial debt issues that some claim to be of crisis proportions. For many, especially Marxist-structuralists, these problems indicate how (un)successful management of the finance and currency exchange structure has been. The first part of the chapter covers the IMF and the role it played in overcoming debt problems in the early 1980s, when outright default on Mexico and Brazil's debt seemed imminent. More recently, in an era of unfettered capital and currency exchange markets, the IMF has worked in conjunction with the World Bank to deal with a second series of financial problems in Mexico in 1994, Asia in 1997, and Argentina in 2001, brought on by financial investment bubbles and currency speculation. Many economic liberals are likely to say that the IMF and World Bank have been successful in a few cases, but more often than not, some mercantilists and many structuralists along with some economic liberals believe they have not.

The third part of the chapter deals specifically with long-term debt issues related to perpetual poverty in the world's poorest countries. Here we focus on World Bank, United Nations, and NGO efforts to help developing nations relieve their debt and develop. We also outline some of the recent proposals made by a number of experts to solve a problem that raises serious issues about the emerging finance and monetary structure.

The thesis of this chapter is that the events of the 1990s and the early years of the twenty-first century indicate that, contrary to first impressions, many parts of the global financial and monetary structure are quite fragile, subject to debt crises, financial bubbles, speculative attacks, and currency crises. Some system of global governance is needed to promote greater stability in this structure in ways that accounts for LDCs, and in particular for the world's poorest people. An efficient international financial system provides many benefits, but the lack of such a system is a real threat to what has become a global network of finance and money.

## THE DEBT CRISIS OF THE 1980s

By most accounts, the first LDC debt "crisis" began in 1982, when Mexico announced that it would default on its bank debt, generating a good deal of fear that other countries that had accumulated substantial debt, such as Brazil, would follow Mexico's lead.[1] This crisis was a consequence, in part, of the early stages of the globalization of finance in the 1970s. As financial flows became more global in scope, powered by market deregulation and technological change, financial centers in the industrial North increasingly sought new investments possibilities and higher returns wherever they could be found. As noted in Chapter 7, many banks were flush with recycled OPEC petrodollars that were reinvested back into the industrialized nations and their banks. These banks and other financial institutions turned their attention to LDCs in the South, which were receiving less financial assistance from government—Official Development Assistance (ODA)—sources. U.S. foreign aid to developing nations, in particular, decreased after the Vietnam War, when the United States trimmed assistance to many of its Third World allies who had received U.S. support in the war against communism.

Northern finance ministers and state policymakers actually encouraged LDCs to borrow some of this money, especially because inflation rates were running ahead of interest rates on loans—creating negative *real* rates, which traditionally favor borrowers.[2] In theory, from a liberal perspective these loans should have resulted in economic growth and higher returns for both borrower and lender. Many LDCs had resources (including oil), the prices for which in a scarce market were unusually high. Many developing nations also looked promising in terms of new investment opportunities related to low-cost labor and favorable LDC economic development policies (see Chapter 15). In practice, however, the uncoordinated actions of the market generated a "debt trap"[3] for both debtor states and their creditors. In restrospect, too much was loaned to too many.

International banks continued to make additional loans to states with growing debt as a way to provide more resources for economic development but also to sustain interest payments on earlier loans. However, the debt continued to grow exponentially, generating a major burden on LDCs and risking the solvency of the financial institutions involved. As would have concerned Keynes, with so much debt outstanding, the banks were in as much trouble as the debtor nations. Debtor nations owed more than they could reasonably be expected to repay, yet they continued to borrow more and more in order to meet their short-run obligations. IMF debt management policies at the time included austerity measures (cutbacks in state spending), debt rescheduling with commercial banks, and new public and private lending. In essence, debtor states only refinanced their loans and stretched out the period of time to pay back the loan. Most states restrained imports and promoted exports to generate income. Eventually, economic growth in these countries slowed down and the situation grew worse. Only Korea and Turkey recovered; others went deeper into the red.

U.S. Treasury Secretary James Baker initiated a plan—the Baker Plan—to implement market-oriented structural changes to debtor economies combined with efforts to coax commercial banks into providing $20 billion in new loans over three years. The World Bank was also expected to increase its lending capacity by $3 billion per year. These efforts continued to focus on enabling debtor nations to "grow" their way out of the debt. However, the plan did not work. As countries tried to expand their exports all at once, commodity and oil prices collapsed, leaving many nations (especially African countries) worse off than before the loans. This problem was exacerbated by a recession that slowed down economic activity throughout the industrialized North, shrinking the market for LDC exports. In some cases loan money was used in unprofitable projects or was siphoned off by corrupt leaders.[4] Political tensions in many countries prevented them from pursuing structural reforms. Most countries could barely afford to service their debt. Finally, new sources of credit from banks and the World Bank were ill-timed and slow in coming.

By the late 1980s many debtor states faced "donor fatigue," whereby social and political tensions related to policies adopted to relieve the debt grew and dissatisfaction with international debt management festered. A number of Latin and Central American states unilaterally suspended all or part of their debt service payments. In response to these and other signs of opposition, other industrialized nations put pressure on the United States to come up with other measures to relieve the debt. Opposed by the Reagan administration at first, *debt swaps* were employed in some cases. Some amount of debt could be swapped with a bank in exchange for land or valuable properties in debtor countries.

Debt relief at this point would obviously have helped debtor nations, by reducing their international obligations, and it might also have helped creditor banks, by clearing their books of bad loans and reducing the risks they faced from default. However, the banks found themselves unable to pursue grant debt relief in this manner because they were caught in a situation often referred to as the **prisoner's dilemma** (see the box, "The Prisoner's Dilemma"). Each bank or state wanted others to forgive the debt but were unwilling to do so themselves, for fear (rationally speaking) that those who cooperated to grant relief would bear a cost that would not be shared by those who paid nothing to solve the problem. Each state and bank, then, had an incentive to be a "free rider" (see Chapter 3) and let someone else bear the burden of debt relief. It was not surprising, then, that given the high stakes and the intensely competitive nature of international finance, no one state or bank was willing to forgive LDC debts, and the vicious cycle of LDC debt continued.

---

### THE PRISONER'S DILEMMA

Why are some countries or businesses reluctant to "stick around and pick up the pieces" when things go wrong? The analogy of the Prisoner's Dilemma emphasizes the rational thinking that goes into the preferences of the actors involved, which results not in the best outcome for each actor, but one that costs them both, but less than they would have had to pay if one of them acted alone.

In one statement of the Prisoner's Dilemma, two burglars are captured by the police near the scene of a theft. The police are certain that the two worked as a team to commit the robbery, but the only evidence they have is some of the loot, which the crooks did not have time to sell or hide. The prisoners are put into separate cells. Each is told: "We have enough evidence to charge you with possession of stolen merchandise. It is certain that you will go to jail for six months, but we'd like to make a deal. If you will give evidence against your partner so that he can be convicted of the more serious crime of burglary, and if no other evidence against you appears, we will recommend that you be released on probation, a very minor punishment, while your partner spends three years in jail. However, if he accuses you of the crime, we have no way of telling who lied. Therefore, each of you will get three months in jail."

Which do you choose: six or three months in jail, or probation? Most people would rather go free than go to jail, and a short jail term is preferable to a long one. This is a situation, therefore, in which it is in the individual interest of each prisoner to give evidence and try to get a lighter sentence. It is clearly better to be free on probation than to spend six months in jail. However, if *both* prisoners give evidence and the police have no way of knowing who actually committed the crime, they *both* receive a lighter punishment of three months. It might appear logical for both prisoners to keep quiet (each hoping the other does not defect or accuse the first of the crime)—that is, to *cooperate*. However, given that each does *not* know what the other will do, it is in their individual interests to *defect* and take action that benefits one and harms the other. Because of the nature of the situation and the incentives that the prisoners face, it is likely that they will choose the actions (defect/defect) that leave them both with the second worst possible outcome.

In some IPE situations the dismal logic of self-interest seems to rule. Many LDCs have experienced dramatic deforestation in recent decades (see Chapter 20). Trees are cut and forests destroyed for fuel to heat and cook and sometimes to sell as hardwood lumber. As forests are destroyed, the resource base shrinks, land erodes, farming productivity falls, and wood for heat and cooking becomes even harder to find. It would clearly be in the collective interest of the population to limit tree cutting and stop the loss of the forest. But to each individual, cutting another tree is beneficial personally, because the loss, which is shared with the rest of society, is more than offset by the personal gain.

Can cooperation be assured, or at least encouraged? Or are defection and disaster the general fate of people and nations? Political economists have studied the prisoner's dilemma in some detail because of its important role in many aspects of life. Several lessons have been learned. The first is that cooperation is more likely when the persons involved are part of long-term relationships, where they will face the consequences of their actions again and again. Such is the situation of international debt. Loaning and borrowing money, for whatever reason, is a major feature of the international finance and monetary system. The prisoner's dilemma teaches us that banks are compelled to free-ride and defect for fear that if they assume responsibility for dealing with the debt, others will free-ride or defect.

On the other hand, cooperation can be encouraged by "side payments," by which potential gainers bribe likely defectors to go along. Such side payments are most likely to succeed if one participant is so large (and its share of the gains from cooperation so great) that it is always in its interest to promote cooperation. This "player" becomes, in essence, a hegemon, willing to bear the costs of organizing a cooperative effort because its share of the resulting gains are so great. As we will see, the United States came to play the role of hegemon in dealing with the international debt crisis of the 1980s to the extent that it pressured the IMF to adopt certain policies to help LDCs overcome their debt.

In 1989 President George W. H. Bush initiated another program—the Brady Plan—whereby old debt was exchanged for new bonds that could be exchanged for new bank loans. Negotiations for these bonds were carried on between the banks and each debtor state. Under the Brady Plan, in hegemonic fashion, the United States offered to refinance Mexico's external debt, provided all lenders accepted specific measures of debt relief, including interest-rate cuts, payment rescheduling, and some measure of forgiveness. Private banks exchanged their Mexican debt for a lesser amount of U.S. government securities—Brady Bonds—backed by Mexican obligations. Mexico would pay the United States, which paid the creditors. Under this scheme, Mexico benefited from some debt relief, the banks reduced the risk of default, and the U.S. government avoided increasing international financial instability. In the late 1980s, net flows of IMF funds to debtor states declined.

Banks went along with these and similar measures because they feared financial disaster if debtor countries defaulted. Table 8–1 shows that external debt was still a very serious burden for many LDCs in 1991. Brazil's total debt was 36.9 percent of its national income, for example, and the annual interest burden amounted to over 17 percent of its export earnings. Although Brazil and Mexico had the largest debts, Argentina, Nigeria, Chile, and Nicaragua faced perhaps the greatest debt burdens relative to the size and strength of their economies.

**TABLE 8–1    Financial Indicators of Selected Debtor Nations, 1991**

| NATION | TOTAL EXTERNAL DEBT | DEBT AS PERCENT OF GNP | DEBT SERVICE AS PERCENT OF EXPORTS |
|---|---|---|---|
| Brazil | $116 billion | 36.9% | 17.3% |
| Mexico | $101 billion | 28.8% | 15.4% |
| Indonesia | $ 73 billion | 66.4% | 13.2% |
| India | $ 71 billion | 29.3% | 13.6% |
| Argentina | $ 63 billion | 49.2% | 25.1% |
| China | $ 60 billion | 16.4% | 5.3% |
| Poland | $ 52 billion | 68.5% | 3.3% |
| Turkey | $ 50 billion | 48.1% | 12.8% |
| Nigeria | $ 34 billion | 108.8% | 16.8% |
| Chile | $ 17 billion | 60.7% | 24.3% |
| Nicaragua | $ 10 billion | 153.5% | 62.4% |

Source: World Bank, *World Development Report 1993*.

Creditors also feared the consequences to the international political economy if LDCs were to do what was necessary to repay the loans in full. To honor such huge debt and interest burdens would have required harsh mercantilist policies to restrict imports and expand exports, generating problems in the industrialized nations that rely on LDCs to import some of their manufactured goods. The discipline and sacrifice necessary for LDCs to service their debt also often generated much social and political unrest that included strikes and even riots.

## Debt Crises and a New Role for the IMF

For a short while many states came around to support the idea of debt forgiveness. In the early 1990s countries such as Brazil were judged to have overcome their debt problems (despite the evidence in Table 8–1). During the mid-1980s, however, the United States had pushed the IMF to work closely with the World Bank to focus on solving LDC debt problems. During this period the *Washington consensus* on development (see Chapter 15) gradually emerged as the best strategy for developing nations to grow and develop. Debt would be overcome as economies opened up and integrated into the growing global economy.

Recall in Chapter 7 that we discussed how the architects of the postwar Bretton Woods system of international finance gave the IMF responsibility to help member states deal with balance-of-payments problems by providing liquidity (money in the form of accumulated currencies and gold from member states) on a short-term basis to states that for some reason were running balance-of-payments deficits. In the 1980s some experts and officials believed that the IMF could play another role in the international economy as a **lender of last resort** or institution that that could help debtor nations overcome their debt.

World Bank and IMF loans were made subject to **structural adjustment policies (SAPs)**, which are a series of conditions or actions to which the borrowing government must agree before receiving a loan. If these conditions were violated, IMF or World Bank assistance could be withdrawn. IMF **conditionality** is controversial to the extent that IMF terms reflect the economic liberal ideas behind the Washington consensus policies and interests of the United States and not the individual needs of the borrowing nation. A typical IMF debt plan involves a number of politically unpopular SAPs designed to restore economic balance, including *currency devaluation* to generate trade export, policies that encourage *price stability* to control inflation and encourage savings, *fiscal austerity* to cut state spending and subsidies while privatizing national industries, *tariff liberalization* to encourage imports, *higher interest rates* to attract investment in the short run, and *sound social programs* in reaction to higher import prices, reduced subsidies and programs, and higher taxes.

The logic of the IMF's policies is to reduce the current account deficit (see Chapter 7) in the short run by increasing exports and reducing imports and simultaneously help finance the capital account by stemming capital flight and limiting new borrowing needs. In the long run, these policies are also intended to encourage economic growth, creating a situation in which the nation can repay its old debts and be less dependent on credit in the future. In the short run, austerity policies tend to create tremendous political pressures because the debtor-nation government must enact policies that at first lower living standards and impose hardship, especially on the poor. Thus, the stronger (more authoritarian) the state, the more likely it will be able to enforce these measures.

In essence, the government must sacrifice domestic autonomy for the sake of its international financial stability. Austerity measures are never popular and generally hurt the poor the most, in some cases leading to violence and civil unrest. The influence of special interests on government policies is particularly problematic, as high government subsidies or payments often benefit special interests and political supporters. When fiscal austerity becomes necessary, special interests may be protected by their friends in government so that the burden of the cuts is borne disproportionately by the poor and others who lack political connections. According to many critics, quite often these measures weaken the debtor's ability to achieve its goals, which in turn can lead to domestic political crisis, exacerbating and deepening the economic crisis and leading to other financial problems.[5] Some neoliberals also fear that a debt crisis can be a cyclical political and economic nightmare, undermining the IMF as an important international financial institution.

Although in theory the IMF and the debtor-nation government supposedly work together to deal with the debt crisis, in practice their relationship can be conflictual, with the IMF responsible for international financial stability while the debtor-nation government must respond to domestic political forces. Bilateral negotiations require some diplomacy, because a strong state is needed if IMF-approved austerity policies are to be implemented. Given the political and social turmoil these policies generate, resolving a debt crisis is thus a delicate matter, with international economic stability balanced against domestic political realities.

As we will describe and explain shortly, by the mid-1990s, in what became volatile international economic conditions, both the IMF and World Bank found themselves responding to another source of debt. In this case a series of financial crises often took the form of speculative attacks on local currencies brought on by what economists refer to as a balance-of-payments crisis; these cases included the manic behavior of foreign direct investors and speculators in Mexico in 1994, in parts of Asia in 1997, and in Argentina in 2001, among other places. Foreign investors flooded these countries with huge amounts of funds—more money than could prudently be invested. When the investment bubble burst, of course, many of the investments went bust and their currencies collapsed. The result was that these and many other countries accumulated large international debts that were very difficult to repay.

### A Balance-of-Payments Financial Crisis

Before describing these financial crises in depth, we need to provide a little more detail about what economists mean by a **balance-of-payments crisis**. As we have already noted, in some cases states have borrowed too much money to use for development projects, or they cannot export enough to pay for imports. These states may lack foreign investment that could help offset a current account deficit. Just knowing about these conditions often results in **capital flight**, when investors transfer their bank accounts out of the country to "safe harbor" nations. This often creates an extreme shortage of funds in the debtor-nation banks, which sends national interest rates shooting up, which could gradually attract more investment down the road. For the time being, however, a nation might be unable to borrow under favorable terms and international trade is disrupted because needed imports may be impossible to obtain.

What worries officials a good deal is that debt problems related to a balance-of-payments crisis brought on by speculation and capital flight can disrupt and distort trade and international finance relationships. Conceivably, a crisis in one nation, along with that nation's attempts to deal with its problems, could spawn additional crises elsewhere, as it did during the Great Depression of the 1930s. Although a financial crisis is, fundamentally, an economic problem, it also quickly translates into a political problem, because it usually falls to the state and its political leadership to propose and implement the frequently harsh policies necessary to bring international payments back into balance.

### The Seven Stages of Financial Crisis

Financial crises do not appear overnight. Seven common features or stages occur in the development of a financial crisis: displacement, expansion, euphoria, distress, revulsion, crisis, and contagion. Imagine for a moment a market for investments that has reached some sort of equilibrium, in which investment flows are consistent with the information known to and the expectations held by the market's participants. Financial crises can appear and then develop through the following phases.

**Displacement** refers to an external shock or some "news" that fundamentally alters the economic outlook in a market, shifting expectations concerning future profits in some significant way. In this case, some asset or financial instrument becomes the focus of investors and speculators, based on news about a new technology or the worth of real estate, for example. **Expansion** is the stage in which the boom is fed by an increase in liquidity (investment money), which provides the means for the boom to grow, perhaps becoming a bubble. There are many potential sources of liquidity, including bank credit, financial innovations, increased leverage, margin buying, and other techniques that can stretch more buying power from a given monetary base. Perhaps the most obvious form of expansion is the widening of the pool of potential investors or speculators, from a set of "insiders" to a larger group of "outsiders." Walter Bagehot, the great nineteenth-century political economist, suggested that panics form when an object of speculation (rationally!) attracts the greed of ordinary people—authors, rectors, and grandmothers.

Expansion becomes **euphoria** when the purpose of buying becomes to sell and take a capital gain as the price rises higher and higher. The new buyer's motives are the same, and this euphoria continues as long as expectations do not change and liquidity holds out. Adam Smith called this "over-trading" and Kindleberger, "pure speculation"—that is, speculation on the basis of rising prices alone. A bubble (that will burst) or a mania (driven by wild-eyed investor maniacs) is often the result.

**Distress** is the stage between euphoria and revulsion, when there is concern that the strength of the market may be fragile or that the limits of liquidity may be near. Distress is an unsettled time, and the reactions to this unsettled environment often deflate the bubble and defuse the mania. Distress can persist for lengths of time until the crisis is averted, or it can turn sharply into revulsion. **Revulsion** is a sharp shift in actions and expectations caused by new information or a significant event. "Insiders" (cf. Martha Stewart!) realize the importance of the news and sell first, perhaps at the top of the market, while "outside" authors and rectors are still buying. Liquidity dries up, especially bank lending, causing *discredit*. Revulsion and discredit lead to crisis, as outsiders join insiders in selling off their interest in the item or service. Kindleberger proposes the image created by the German term **Torschlusspanik**—gate-shut panic—to describe how falling prices feed on themselves, creating self-fulfilling prophecies.[6] The result is a crisis, which may also be a crash (a collapse in price) or a panic (sudden needless flight).

A crisis can spread from nation to nation through international linkages such as capital, currency, money, and commodity markets, trade interdependence effects, and shifting market psychology. Paul Krugman reserves the term **contagion crisis** for a financial crisis that spreads internationally to the extent that it causes a worldwide depression.

What brings the crisis to an end? According to Kindleberger, there are three possibilities. The crisis may turn into a "fire sale," with prices falling until buyers are eventually brought back into the market. Or trading may be halted by some authority, limiting losses. Or, finally, a lender of last resort, in this case the IMF, may step in to provide the liquidity necessary to bring the crisis to a "soft landing." In some cases this can help banks defend their currency and restore confidence in their economy. As we shall see, however, in some cases (labeled "moral hazard") it can help investors earn a return they might not otherwise have received had the IMF not stepped in to loan these countries more money to restore confidence in their currencies.

### The Peso Crisis and the Tequila Hangover[7]

Mexico's peso panic followed this pattern fairly closely. Mexico's entrance into the North American Free Trade Agreement (NAFTA) may have been the displacement that started the bubble in this case. Certainly NAFTA altered the views of many regarding Mexico's prospects for political stability and economic growth. Capital began to flow into Mexico to take advantage of the new opportunities people thought were about to open up. However, a financial crisis drove down the peso's value, drove up interest rates, and created a short but very deep recession.

By the 1990s financial markets were well organized to mobilize the funds of authors, clergymen, and grandmothers to invest in foreign countries that many would be hard-pressed to find on a map. The era of "global" and "emerging markets" mutual funds was here, creating the conditions for a classic speculative bubble. A modest recovery in economic prospects from the dismal 1980s led to large capital gains for those few investors who had been willing to put money into Third World markets. Their success led other investors to jump in, driving prices up still further. And by 1993 or so, "emerging markets funds" were being advertised on television and in the pages of some popular magazines. As speculation on price alone took off, even fund managers became uncritical of their investment decisions, driven as they were to invest the huge sums coming in from authors and clergymen every day. "We went into Latin America not knowing anything about the place," one of them noted after the Mexican crisis. "Now we are leaving without knowing anything about it."[8] One can see how disconnected investment became from any analysis of the realities involved.

Euphoria came next. "During the first half of the 1990s," according to Paul Krugman, "a set of mutually reinforcing beliefs and expectations created a mood of euphoria about the prospects for the developing world. Markets poured money into developing countries, encouraged both by the capital gains they had already seen and by the belief that a wave of reform was unstoppable."[9] Distress can be pinpointed to March 1994, with the assassination of the ruling party's presidential candidate, Donaldo Colosio, which raised significant doubts among foreign investors about the political stability of Mexico. The era of political stability and economic expansion that President Carlos Salinas had engineered was suddenly threatened. Insiders began to shift funds out of Mexico.

Revulsion came in November 1994, as Mexican authorities found themselves in a position in which they had to choose between their international financial responsibilities and their domestic political survival at a time when pressure was rising both inside and outside the country. They wanted to keep their exchange rate fixed to the dollar, but that required raising domestic interest rates to keep capital from fleeing. But raising domestic interest rates would have been damaging both to Mexican borrowers and to their banks and would also have created a political crisis just as the presidential vote was taking place. It was too much to risk. Inevitably, domestic issues were found to be more important, and the peso was allowed to fall in value. Insiders caught the scent of a crisis and ran for the closing gates.

Contagion occurred both within Mexico and between Mexico and other countries. The effects of peso depreciation, domestic inflation, and higher interest rates caused Mexico to experience a severe recession. Unemployment rose sharply, from just 3.2 percent in December 1994 to 7.6 percent in August 1995, before falling somewhat to about 6.0 percent in 1996. Inflation, as measured by monthly changes in the national consumer price index, rose from 3.8 percent per month in January 1995 to 8.0 percent in April, then fell back to 2–3 percent per month in 1996. Interbank interest rates soared, reaching 86.03 percent in March before falling back, although they remained above 40 percent until April 1996.

Although the peso-crisis recession in Mexico turned out to be relatively short, it was also relatively deep, and its effects may be long-lasting. Mexico's gross domestic product (GDP) fell dramatically in 1995, effectively wiping out the short-run gains from the NAFTA boom and leaving Mexico's citizens not much better off, if at all, than in the old days before market reforms. Recovery was highly concentrated in the export sector, which benefited from the peso's lower value. Mexico's internal economy, that part not directly affected by exports, remained deeply depressed by a combination of high interest rates, credit shortages, and general poverty.[10] International contagion also occurred, notably to other "emerging market" nations that suffered from the "tequila hangover" effect. Krugman took a pessimistic view that because "the 1990–95 euphoria about developing countries was so overdrawn, the Mexican crisis is likely to be the trigger that sets the process in reverse."[11] Krugman, however, overestimated the memories of international investors. Within a couple of years they were back into emerging markets again, but in Asia this time. The bubble they created there was a major factor contributing to the Asian financial crisis of 1997–1998.

## The Asian Financial Crisis

The next financial crisis was much larger and threatened for a time the financial stability of the entire globe. Even today, years after the initial crisis, its effects linger in East and Southeast Asia.[12] The

Asian financial crisis shows that crises can happen to states, even those with otherwise sound economic policies, if they make commitments that global market actors consider questionable or unsustainable. Then they fall under the guns of a speculative attack.

The whole event started on July 2, 1997, when Thailand's currency, the baht, suddenly collapsed in value, an event that is called a **currency crisis**. This event, which was initially reported only on the back pages of the financial sections of world newspapers, started a chain reaction of economic, political, and social effects that together are termed the *Asian financial crisis* because its contagion spread to Indonesia, Malaysia, Taiwan, Hong Kong, South Korea, and elsewhere in the region.

The Thai government had guaranteed that the exchange rate between the Thai baht and the U.S. dollar would be held at a rate of 25 baht per dollar. That meant that if you had 25 baht you could reasonably expect to exchange them for a U.S. dollar, and vice versa. The Thai government did this because it wanted to encourage trade with and investment from the United States and other countries to help Thailand's economy grow. It seemed natural that this would occur, given the government's guarantee, because interest rates were lower in the United States than they were in Thailand. The government's pledge of a stable currency value encouraged Thai finance companies to borrow U.S. dollars on global markets, convert them to Thai baht at the fixed exchange rate, and then lend them out, at a higher interest rate, in Thailand, stimulating investment of one sort or another there.

Imagine that you are a Thai finance company executive who borrows a million dollars (at, say, 10 percent interest) and converts this sum into 25 million baht, which you expect to lend in Thailand at an interest rate of 15 percent. With the Thai government's exchange-rate promise in force, this appears to be a good deal for everyone. The U.S. lender gets 10 percent interest. You (the Thai borrower) get access to funds for business investment that might not be available if you didn't borrow abroad. And you stand to gain the difference between the 15 percent interest you will collect and the 10 percent interest you will owe. If everything works out as planned, you stand to make $50,000 on this deal (5 percent of $1 million) from the difference in interest rates. Very nice! Thai banks borrowed a lot of dollars and other hard currencies, which were lent and invested in business expansions, property purchases, and speculation on Thai stocks, among other things. Bubbles began to inflate in Thailand and in some other countries in the region.

Then problems began to appear. Thai banks were found to have a lot of bad loans on their books—loans that were unlikely to be repaid on time and that perhaps could never be repaid at all. Some of these bad loans were blamed on a type of corruption often called **crony capitalism**. Some of the Thai finance companies received favorable treatment from the government in return for financial considerations sometimes given under the guise of loans. When the bad loans were revealed, international investors became concerned about both the health of the Thai banks and the government's ability to honor its exchange-rate pledge. So these investors began to pull their funds out of Thailand.

Foreign investors who withdrew their funds wanted to convert them back into dollars, naturally. This meant that for every 25 baht withdrawn, the Thai government had to stand ready to give one U.S. dollar in return. As the flow of funds out of Thailand increased, the Thai government's supply of dollar reserves was drawn down. Speculation began that the government would not be willing or able to keep its promise—what would it do when it ran out of dollars or nearly so?

This speculation caused a panic, which is a kind of self-fulfilling prophecy. Because people worried that the Thai government could not keep its exchange-rate promise, they pulled their funds out of Thailand. When everyone did this at once, it was of course impossible for the Thai government to pay everyone dollars at once. It might have been able to pay, and the currency crisis might have been avoided, had it not been for a speculative attack that was launched against it.

### A Speculative Attack!

A **speculative attack** is essentially a confrontation between a central bank, which pledges to maintain its country's exchange rate at a certain level, and international currency speculators, who are willing to wager that the central bank is not fully committed to its exchange-rate goal. Speculators attack the currency by borrowing huge amounts of it and then selling them on the currency market. The central bank can keep its pledge by using its currency reserves to buy up the currency that the speculators are selling. If the central bank keeps its pledge, the speculators stand to lose very little because they can buy back the currency to repay their loans at about the same rate at which they sold it. If, however, the central bank is not willing to intervene to keep its currency stable, or if it runs low on the reserves it needs to do this, then the currency will fall. The speculators will be able to buy back their currency at a lower price and have great profits left even after they've paid back their loans.

Suppose, for example, that you borrowed 25 million baht and sold them at 25 baht per dollar (the government-guaranteed rate) to receive a million U.S. dollars. If your action, along with those of other speculators, succeeded in breaking the Bank of Thailand, then the baht's foreign exchange value might fall to 50 baht per U.S. dollar. At that exchange rate, it would take only $500,000 to purchase the 25 million baht you owe. The other $500,000 would be your profit. This is a strong incentive to treat the financial market like a casino—in Keynes's terminology, to bet against the house rather than investing in a productive enterprise.

Central banks are serious economic institutions that typically have billions of dollars of reserves and access to considerably more funds through agreements with other countries' banks. How, then, is it possible to "break the bank" with such apparent ease? The answer is that the global financial markets, when focused on a single country or industry, have even greater resources.

One type of business that is particularly suited to a speculative attack is called a hedge fund. A **hedge fund** is an investment instrument that attempts to make a profit from the fact that an asset such as a stock or bond might be trading at different prices in different places or have some similar pricing imperfection. The hedge fund bets that the prices will converge and earns a profit if they do. Because such pricing anomalies are typically very small, a hedge fund must be able to mobilize vast sums of money—hundreds of millions or even billions of dollars—with each dollar invested earning a small but quick return. Small profits multiplied by vast amounts equals tidy profits.

Usually the activities of hedge funds are uncontroversial, but they can be controversial when the focus of hedge fund speculation is a currency that appears to be trading at a higher price than is justified by political and economy conditions. Then the hedge fund's vast potential is used in a speculative attack, as described above, and considerable damage is done. Hungarian-American hedge fund investor George Soros pocketed $1 billion in profits in 1992 by betting that the Bank of England would not maintain the pound's value relative to European currencies.

Speculative attacks were responsible for the collapse of the Indonesian rupiah and the Malaysian ringgit in 1997–1998, as well as the British pound and the Italian lira in a different crisis during 1992–1993. As long as investment capital is freely mobile between countries, the sorts of currency crises that are caused by speculative attacks and investment bubbles are likely to occur. Exchange rates, therefore, can be expected to display a variety of patterns over time, including stability, cycles, booms, and crashes.

## Crisis and Contagion

On July 2, 1997, the situation in Thailand reached a boiling point. So many baht were leaving the country that the Thai government was forced to abandon its pledge of a 25-baht-per-dollar exchange rate. The baht's value collapsed, falling from 25 baht per dollar to about 30 baht per dollar in a matter of days (as the baht's value falls, it takes more baht to buy a dollar). The baht continued to fall in July and August. The crisis in Thailand had a contagion effect on similar currency crises in other Asian countries. Seeing the crisis in Thailand, investors "sold Asia," pulling their funds out of other countries in the region.

The currency crises continued through the summer and into the fall. When the dust settled, the new exchange rate was about 50 baht per dollar, with similar collapses in other Asian countries. This had a number of serious effects. For Thai citizens, the most direct effect was that foreign goods were suddenly more expensive. A $10 bottle of a U.S.-made prescription drug that used to cost 250 baht was now priced at about 500 baht. This was bad news both for Thai people who needed imported medicines (and other goods) and also for the U.S. firms and workers that made these items.

U.S. citizens were also affected by the exchange-rate change. A 100-baht sack of Thai jasmine rice, which used to cost $4.00, now had a price of just $2.00. This benefited U.S. consumers of Thai goods, but of course put pressure on U.S. rice farmers to match the lower Thai prices. The currency crisis caused a major change in relative prices between the United States and Thailand. Thai goods were about 50 percent cheaper to U.S. buyers, and U.S. goods were 100 percent more expensive to Thai buyers. These changes created many winners and losers in both countries.

However, the biggest effects were in the financial sectors, and to see this you need to think about yourself as a Thai banker again. Recall that great investment you made just a few paragraphs back. You borrowed $1 million at 10 percent interest in the United States, which you converted into 25 million baht. You lent the baht in Thailand at 15 percent interest. Your reward? The difference between the two interest rates, or about $50,000 per year. Not bad for a few minute's work. However, this profit was based on your assumption that the government would honor its pledge to keep the exchange rate fixed at 25 baht per dollar. Here's where you stand after the currency crisis.

You borrowed $1 million and you lent 25 million baht. If your loan is repaid on time and with all the 15 percent interest you are due, you should get back about 28,750,000 baht. At the post-crisis exchange rate of 50 baht per dollar, this sum is worth only $575,000—much less than the $1 million you borrowed. You owe $1 million (plus interest) and you have no prospects to repay it. Although you have made good business decisions—perhaps you have lent the money efficiently and will get repaid in full and on time (in baht)—you cannot possibly repay your U.S. dollar loan because to do so requires twice as many baht as you expected you would need.

You are bankrupt (deep in debt beyond your means to repay), but because you are a banker this problem affects many more people than just yourself. Your depositors will become concerned about their funds and may stage a run on the bank. You will be less able to give new loans to Thai borrowers. You may have to call in existing loans, forcing current borrowers to liquidate their investments, perhaps even forcing them into bankruptcy. This is the bottom line for the Thai currency crisis. Thai citizens who were acting rationally suddenly found themselves bankrupt—deep in debt, the savings of a lifetime often wiped out, with few prospects for short-term recovery.

Table 8–2 suggests the magnitude of the economic losses that citizens of these countries suffered. The losses in Thailand were enough to lower the per-capita income average of the entire country by about 25 percent in one year alone. Of course, the losses were not suffered equally or on average, so a great many people experienced even greater hardship than this figure suggests. This sort of economic collapse was indeed like something out of the 1930s, the era of the Great Depression. Indonesia's 210 million citizens experienced perhaps the worst of the crisis. As Table 8–2 indicates, the average per-capita income fell by almost 50 percent in a single year. As shocking as these numbers were, they did not reflect the social and political dimensions of the crisis.

Although the worst effects of the Asian crisis were felt by the citizens of these countries themselves, the world is sufficiently interlinked that some of the effects were felt around the world. The

**TABLE 8–2    Effects of the Asian Crisis**

| | PER-CAPITA INCOME (US$) | | |
| --- | --- | --- | --- |
| *COUNTRY* | *1997* | *1998* | *1999* |
| Thailand | 2,700 | 2,020 | 1,940 |
| Indonesia | 1,120 | 580 | 690 |
| Malaysia | 4,600 | 3,250 | 3,330 |
| South Korea | 11,400 | 9,010 | 9,460 |

*Source:* World Bank online country profiles, selected countries.

depressed economy in Thailand, for example, caused the Thai airlines to cancel orders for Boeing airplanes, leading to economic problems in the United States and other countries. If anyone thought that a crisis in a faraway part of the world could not affect them at home, the Asian financial crisis proved them wrong indeed.

## The IMF and the Asian Crisis

The IMF's actions in the wake of the Asian crisis were widely criticized. These Asian countries really experienced two crises at once as a result of the currency collapse: an internal crisis of lower incomes, higher unemployment, and rising social tensions; and an external crisis in the form of a current account deficit and rising foreign debt. To many, the IMF seemed to be more concerned about the external crisis than the internal one, that is, more concerned about investors than about impoverished citizens. To many economic liberals this criticism seemed unfair, but the image stuck. For many structuralists, in pressuring these countries to reduce tariffs, cut government programs, and raise interest rates, the IMF actually made the internal problems worse.

Part of the problem, it must be said, was that the IMF is a creature of the system of nation-states, and many of the key actors in the Asian crisis were not nation-states. At one point in the crisis, for example, IMF officials in South Korea realized that a number of foreign banks were about to pull out massive amounts of funds, which would surely have made the crisis even worse. A huge bailout would have been necessary, and even then great damage would have been done. An alternative was what is called a "bail-in," whereby lenders try to protect their investments by extending additional credit rather than pulling funds out of the country. South Korea was a good possibility for a bail-in because its main creditors were a small number of big banks, not thousands of investors and funds as was the case elsewhere in Asia. The IMF tried—and succeeded—in negotiating with the international banks to keep their funds in place, but it was not an easy task. Banks are not members of the IMF, and the IMF has little direct power over them. The IMF had to persuade the banks to bail-in, using a variety of tools including veiled threats, implicit promises, and what is called "moral suasion."[13]

The problem that the IMF faced is another example of a prisoner's dilemma. In the case of South Korea the bankers all knew that their losses would be minimized if they all kept their investments in South Korea. In this case the bankers' interests were aligned with those of South Korea and the IMF. Instead of this situation being a case in which participants broke ranks and rushed to save themselves, the IMF was able to stare down the bankers and limit the number that exited.

## The Argentine Financial Crisis

What can a country do to protect itself from financial crises like these? Argentina is an example of a country that made a serious effort to configure its political economy to maximize growth potential and minimize the risk of financial crisis. These efforts were ultimately unsuccessful, however.

In Chapter 7 we noted that when it comes to economic policy, Japan and the United States prefer to have a free hand in domestic economic policy, and to have access to international capital markets for financing, than to have stable exchange rates. Like some other countries, Argentina chose stable foreign exchange rates and free capital mobility, giving up domestic economic independence. In 1991, Argentina fixed its exchange rate at one peso per U.S. dollar. This was seen by many as a good choice at the time, because Argentina had a history of corruption and political influence in its domestic economic policy that had resulted in cripplingly high rates of domestic inflation. Taking the policy levers out of domestic political hands and trusting in international markets for economic growth seemed a prudent policy in 1991.

However, there was an unforeseen problem. For the decade that Argentina pegged its peso to the U.S. dollar, the U.S. dollar appreciated dramatically against most other currencies, pulling the Argentine peso along with it. Argentina found its currency overvalued compared to economic competitors such as Brazil. The high-valued peso crippled Argentina's export industries and induced a flood of imported items. Argentina soon fell deep into debt.

In retrospect, Argentina could have broken the peso–U.S. dollar link and benefited from a depreciation of the peso. Argentina did not do this for several reasons. First, there was concern that the old corrupt political economy would return, with high inflation and economic stagnation. Argentina did not want to go back to that. Second was the problem that most of Argentina's foreign debt, and a great deal of its domestic debt, was denominated in U.S. dollars, and so the debt burden was affected by the exchange rate. If Argentina cut the peso's value from $1 to 50 cents, for example, then the debt burden, in peso terms, would double.

Eventually Argentina found itself trapped. If it maintained the exchange rate, its debt would grow bigger and bigger (so long as the U.S. dollar's foreign exchange value remained high). An economic crisis would slowly build up before *eventually* bursting forth. If it devalued its currency, the debt crisis would be *immediate,* because the sudden increase in the debt burden would overwhelm the economy. There seemed to be no escape and, as policymakers waited and hoped for some sort of relief, the problem got worse and worse. Finally, in January 2002, Argentina was forced to abandon its fixed exchange rate, with disastrous economic and political consequences.

In the end, Argentina's sacrifice of domestic economic independence produced neither the external stimulus nor the internal stability that it had hoped for. Instead, Argentina suffered from a new form of dependency as it essentially "imported" economic policy from the United States. The strong U.S. dollar, which was beneficial for the United States, proved disastrous to Argentina. The United States, with its hard currency and enormous borrowing power, could afford the current account deficits that the strong dollar created. Not so for poor soft-currency Argentina. The U.S. dollar went from being a symbol of hope and prosperity to one of crisis and debt in this part of the world.

## Lessons from These Crises

The Asian financial crisis has three important lessons for us. The first is that economic crises can happen anywhere. It is always possible to blame a crisis on unwise domestic political choices, but studies of financial crises suggest that sound policy is no guarantee of safety from unregulated "mad money." Crises hit countries with sound policies as well as those with policy problems.

A second lesson is that little was learned from the Mexico peso crisis. Mexico demonstrated that neither the U.S. government nor the IMF was a lender of last resort that could prevent crises from happening. Instead, investors in the "Asian miracle" economies behaved almost as if there were no risk at all. They suffered **moral hazard**, which is the problem that people will take on more and more risk if they believe that someone will bail them out of any loss they incur. The investors in Asia behaved as if someone—the Thai government, the U.S. government, the IMF—would cover their losses. So they raised their bets and took on more and more risk.

Finally, we learned that global finance creates the possibility of a global financial crisis. At the height of the crisis, there was concern that Hong Kong would suffer a successful attack, that Japan might be next, and the United States after that. There was serious concern that the global financial system might collapse as it had in the 1930s. No one was really surprised when the crises in Asia were followed, in the next few years, by financial emergencies in Russia, Brazil, and elsewhere.

Another question remains: What about the IMF and its role as the lender of last resort? Are IMF Washington consensus–based SAPs the right way to deal with the problem of debt and balance-of-payments crises? Should not the role of the IMF be reconsidered now that finance is less a *domestic* matter, caused by internal actions and remedied by internal reforms, and more a *global* problem? How can bubbles be prevented? The classical solution, which Walter Bagehot presented over a hundred years ago, is an international lender of last resort that will lend when no one else will, that will hold open the shutting gate and so stop the panic.[14] We can imagine that the IMF could be an international lender of last resort, based on its central role in the international monetary system, but in fact that has not been the case. Much of that is the doing of the United States, which greatly influences IMF policy. At this writing the United States has 17.4 percent of the IMF's total votes, while Japan is a distant second with 6.24 percent, Germany has 6.09 percent, and Great

Britain and France each has 5.03 percent.[15] The IMF lacks the resources and institutional commitment to perform this task effectively. Although the United States did help Mexico deal with the aftereffects of its crisis, it did not really play the role of lender of last resort, which is to try to prevent economic collapse, not just soften the aftershocks.

At this point it is not at all clear that traditional IMF austerity programs are the most effective policies in these cases. Elements of the IMF's "architecture" have proven to be quite controversial today for a number of reasons. Politically, of course, as many structuralists and social critics point out, the IMF has become a bully, picking on the poor and the weak to protect the interests of the rich and powerful.[16]

Economic liberal observers such as Joseph Stiglitz argue that in some cases, international investment and capital mobility controls, along with policies to improve **transparency**, or the public's ability to see how decisions are made within the IMF, would provide more information to investors to make better decisions. As opposed to austerity measures, in so doing transparency could also serve as part of an early warning of another bubble.[17] These policies might prevent a crisis from forming, not just sweep up the debris afterward.

## LONG-TERM DEBT AND THE HIPCs

A third type of debt problem has been around since the 1950s but has recently gained a good deal of international attention as many NGOs and the UN focus on forty-one of the world's poorest (HIPC) countries, primarily in Africa. Many of these states face high incidences of poverty and HIV/AIDs (see Chapter 15). Many of them have also endured long-term debt resulting from a variety of sources over the years, including money borrowed from the World Bank, the IMF, and some international banks. Table 8–3 highlights the value of debt as a percentage of gross national income for the ten poorest HIPC states. Today, some of these states complain about **odius debt**, or obligation incurred by a former corrupt regime that left a new government owing billions to outside agencies. Iraq's Saddam Hussein, Ethiopia's Megistu Haile Mariam, and Chile's Augusto Pinochet allegedly fit in this category.[18] For the most part, poorer states feel that debt-relief mechanisms of the global finance and monetary structure were not designed with them in mind, and they have not been effective.

Since the late 1990s the UN and many NGOs, along with the IMF and World Bank officials, a variety of development experts, rock stars, and other celebrities have been campaigning to rectify this problem. In 1996, under pressure from popular movements in both the North and South, creditors launched the **HIPC Initiative** under the direction of the World Bank. The goal was to

**TABLE 8–3   Debt of the Poorest Countries**

| COUNTRY | PRESENT VALUE OF DEBT AS PERCENT OF GNI (2004) | GNI (2004, MILLIONS OF $) | GNI PER CAPITA (2004) |
|---|---|---|---|
| Burundi | 15 | 666 | 90 |
| Congo, Dem. Rep. | 36 | 6366 | 110 |
| Liberia | 760 | 3777 | 120 |
| Ethiopia | 30 | 9311 | 130 |
| Malawi | 60 | 2051 | 160 |
| Guinea-Bissau | 326 | 241 | 160 |
| Eritrea | 53 | 808 | 190 |
| Sierra Leone | 37 | 1106 | 210 |
| Rwanda | 15 | 1872 | 210 |
| Niger | 25 | 2810 | 210 |

*Note:* Countries shown are the world's ten poorest, ranked by gross national income (GNI) per capita.

**TABLE 8–4    Total External Debt of Developing Countries (in billions of dollars)**

| COUNTRY | 1998 | 2000 | 2002 | 2004 |
|---|---|---|---|---|
| All developing countries | 2321.8 | 2283.9 | 2359.0 | 2755.7 |
| China | 144.0 | 145.7 | 186.4 | 248.9 |
| Indonesia | 151.2 | 144.4 | 132.2 | 140.6 |
| Russia | 177.8 | 160.0 | 147.4 | 197.3 |
| Turkey | 97.1 | 117.3 | 131.2 | 161.6 |
| Argentina | 141.4 | 147.4 | 149.9 | 169.2 |
| Brazil | 241.7 | 243.4 | 233.1 | 222.0 |
| Mexico | 159.0 | 150.3 | 140.2 | 138.7 |
| India | 97.6 | 99.1 | 104.8 | 122.7 |
| South Africa | 24.8 | 24.9 | 25.0 | 28.5 |

*Source:* World Bank, *Global Development Finance 2006: The Development Potential of Surging Capital Flows*, Table A.21.

push all the players in the finance and debt structure to accept debt cancellation. By 1999 it was clear that this effort had failed. With only four countries receiving debt relief, the rise in interest payments owed on the debt wiped out any gains of the four. Total debt for HIPC countries remained at $216 billion from 1996 to 1998, while debt service rose by $3 billion during that time. Table 8–4 highlights the total debt for *all* developing countries, which in 2004 reached an estimated $2.7 trillion.

Many structuralist critics complained that the IMF and World Bank measures for qualifying for debt relief still required adopting an IMF austerity program for three years before receiving relief. Meanwhile, the two agencies responded with yet another economic measure—called a Poverty Reduction Strategy Paper (PRSP)—that required consultation with civil society before action could be taken on the debt.[19]

In 1999, during massive demonstrations at the G7 meeting in Cologne, Germany, supporters of Jubilee 2000 targeted the inadequacy of neoliberal development policies and, in particular, IMF and World Bank practices related to debt relief. Jubilee 2000 is an effort by a coalition of development-oriented NGOs, churches, and labor groups to, among others things, pressure the industrialized nations into canceling the debt of twenty countries by 2000. Jubilee 2000 framed its rationale for debt cancellation in terms of fairness and global justice, a message intended to cut across disparate political, economic, and social boundaries. Other groups and some public officials have connected debt to concerns about terrorism eminating from poorer countries such as Sudan and Afghanistan. At that G7 meeting, state leaders in fact pledged to write off $100 billion of poor-country debts. By 2005, twenty-eight countries had been granted debt relief of $56 billion.[20]

Joseph Stiglitz reports that conditions to obtain relief are less onerous than in the past and are more focused on alleviating poverty.[21] In some ways this reflects a continuing shift in World Bank policy away from support for neoliberal "one size fits all" policies to more of a grab-bag approach to development in general[22] (see Chapter 15). Stiglitz and others also complain that things are not moving fast enough. Some countries that could use relief, such as Indonesia, do not qualify as being poor enough, while others, such as Moldova, are not eligible because they were in the former Soviet bloc of nations. At the June 2005 G8 meeting (now including Russia) in Gleneagles, Scotland, members agreed to fund 100 percent debt relief for eighteen of the world's poorest countries (fourteen of which are in Africa).

Structuralists such as Walden Bello contend that the IMF and World Bank are both in crisis over how much and how to reform the agencies.[23] The Bank has suffered a loss in borrowers' fees and investments. China, Indonesia, Mexico, and Brazil are looking elsewhere for loans. The IMF is essentially still in denial about the Asian crisis and disdains the politics that comes with its programs. Bello also charges, with regard to both the World Bank and the IMF, that "Having completed doctorates in economics or finance, the staff are ill-equipped for the complex and messy work of the political systems in which they work." One study suggests that the IMF responds by being less visible in public, while the World Bank spends a good deal of time and money ($30 million a year) on public relations—to put on a good face.

Meanwhile, as discussed in Chapter 15, in 2000, the UN, the IMF, and the World Bank,[24] as well as many NGOs and celebrities, have made debt relief an important goal and an instrument of the UN's Millenium Development Goals (MDG). In an effort to target poverty at the local level, MDG goals include the eradication of extreme hunger and poverty, universal primary education, gender equality and the empowerment of women, reduction in child mortality, improvement of maternal health, efforts to combat HIV/AIDs, malaria, and other diseases, efforts to ensure environmental sustainability, and development of a global partnership for development. In July 2004 Harvard economist Jeffrey Sachs, who is a special adviser to the UN secretary general, said that African nations should refuse to pay their debts and that "the money would be better spent on urgent social investment in health, education, drinking water, control of AIDS and other needs."[25]

## CONCLUSION

Each of the three IPE perspectives interprets recent developments in the finance and monetary structure quite differently. We can contrast their views about different issues and actors using many of the points and concepts of this chapter and Chapters 6 and 7.

### Liberals

Most economic liberals favor increased international trade and investment opportunities, which have been made available by flexible exchange rates and capital mobility. Increased trade generates income that moves more easily within a nation or worldwide, creating new factories, processing facilities, and stores. More income generates new technologies and communications networks, reinforcing integration and globalization. Market-oriented policies reflect pressure from domestic businesses and TNCs that seek profits from opportunities to conduct banking and other services in countries that deregulate capital transactions. Elites in the United States and Great Britain, in particular, have favored market forces playing a bigger role in determining exchange rates and capital markets as part of their ideological commitment to economic liberal ideas and the benefits of globalization.

From a noeliberal perspective, the IMF and the World Bank have played positive roles in promoting economic liberal goals and policies. Lately, even if both have been criticized for several financial crises in the 1990s and continuing debt problems of the poorer states, both have also helped developing nations integrate into the world economy.[26] Although globalization has clear negative effects on some states and subgroups, most states and businesses feel that they cannot, and should not, miss the opportunities afforded by the liberalization of the finance structure.

Not everything is sanguine for economic liberals, however. Many are concerned about the weakness of the U.S. dollar, and at the same time, how much the liberal principles and ideas that led to wide currency fluctuations remain embedded in the finance and monetary structure. As the U.S. dollar weakens, will the United States become more protectionist? Might it be less likely to provide (hegemonic) leadership for the finance and monetary structure? More fundamental is the growing problem of speculation, which, as we saw in the case of Mexico, Asia, and Argentina, can quickly destabilize markets and severely punish honest and hard-working people.

If John Maynard Keynes were alive today, he would likely be bothered that the Northern industrialized states that make the rules have allowed speculation to play a major role in the new network of money and currency. As we saw in Chapter 7, speculation flows from deregulated currency and finance markets, generating great profits to increasingly larger numbers of people and states.

At the same time, the globalization (freeing of markets) of this structure has an undermining effect on these economies to the extent that it threatens to destabilize the entire international economy. Today more than ever, most foreign exchange transactions are *not* tied to any solid economic purpose. Rather, they are part of elaborate financial speculation strategies designed to extract profit from changes in exchange rates, interest rates, stock returns, political events, or other activities. Rationally speaking, investors could just as easily lose confidence in the Northern economies as they did in the South. This worries those who feel that confidence in the North is related to the ability of U.S. consumers to continue spending for large quantities of goods and services in order to sustain economic growth, all the while generating large trade and current account deficits and national debt.

Keynes would argue that it is dangerous to allow such an important part of a nation's political economy to be subject to speculative forces. During the Great Depression he warned against the possibility of what he called "casino capitalism": "Speculators may do no harm as bubbles on the stream of enterprise. But the position is serious when enterprise becomes the bubble on a whirlpool of speculation. When the capital development of a country becomes the by-product of the activities of a casino, the job is likely to be ill-done."[27]

Under these circumstances it is easy to understand why some experts feel that, when combined with growing concern about a gradually weakening dollar, among other indicators, volatile finance and currency markets, not only in LDCs but everywhere, could easily lead to a financial crisis of global proportions. Some even suggest that today's finance and monetary conditions are similar to those just before the Great Depression of the 1930s, when high levels of interdependence, trade protectionism, and competitive devaluations shook the economic world and helped pave the way to World War II.

Other Keynesian economic liberals direct their attention to debt and development issues. In the groundbreaking works of Joseph Stiglitz, Dani Rodrik, and Jeffrey Sachs (see Suggested Readings), among others, globalization is viewed as something that can be made to work. As economic liberals, they and others have attacked and criticized some of the basic precepts of globalization and its application to developing nations in particular. In the finance structure, where the market ideology has been so popular, developing countries must protect themselves to some extent, at least until they can compete with the industrialized states on a more equal basis. Sounding like mercantilists at times, many have noted that China and India have not integrated into the international economy as much as others and yet have achieved high rates of growth. What they have done is to "cherry-pick" the policies that work best for them.

If the job of the IMF is to facilitate a stable and orderly international financial system, then it is hard to conclude that in recent years it has been successful (although matters might have been even worse without the IMF). The world seems to have lurched from monetary crisis to monetary crisis, with the IMF often blamed for making bad problems worse. Most important, however, is the fact that debtors and creditors share interests in resolving payments problems. The IMF is not and cannot be the global lender of last resort. Either the governance structure must expand to match market forces—a bigger IMF with more resources and more power over more actors—or the markets could collapse, as they did in the 1930s.

## Mercantilists

As already noted, mercantilists occasionally share *some* of the views of economic liberals, especially if exchange rates and capital mobility correspond to or enhance state objectives that increase its wealth and power. As we saw in Chapter 7 in the case of the early Gold Standard, the Bretton Woods system, and the current flexible exchange-rate systems, it is difficult to separate the economic elements of these systems from their use by states as instruments to accomplish a variety of political and social objectives. Shifts in exchange rates always invite political manipulation. Because they change the terms of international trade and investment between nations, they necessarily alter conditions for business firms, affect individual workers and citizens, and thus are important to nations in terms of their foreign policy goals and relationships with allies.

As discussed in Chapter 6, there is always considerable temptation for a mercantilist nation (or a political leader facing an important election) to either devalue or overvalue its currencies to satisfy some combination of domestic and international objectives. These policies most often reflect the interests of wealthy elites and their demand for protection or cheaper imports. On the other hand, agriculture, for example, is especially sensitive to this problem. Some developing countries with overvalued currencies unintentionally destroyed their agricultural sectors and became dependent on artificially cheap foodstuffs.

The global security structure is changing under the influence of global finance. Global investment opportunities are channeling resources to China and Vietnam, for example—countries that for many years the United States tried to isolate for security reasons. The United States and other states continue to use financial controls as tools or even weapons in different situations, as Chapter 9 points out in the case of efforts to impose economic sanctions on North Korea, Iraq, and Iran.

Many states have supported the globalization campaign as part of a strategy to compete with other states for foreign investment, enhancing their wealth and power.[28] Not unexpectedly, some mercantilist-realists worry about system volatility to the extent that it does or could influence their domestic and international interests. The Mexican, Asian, and Argentinian crises, for example, did not make the United States, nor its democracy, nor capitalism in general, any more popular in those societies. These crises and antiglobalization sentiments may have played a large role in the electoral success of populist-socialist leaders in Venezuela, Bolivia, Brazil, Chile, and Nicaragua. As well, they are likely now playing a role in violent reactions to the reemergence of the left in these and some Central American societies (Mexico, Guatemala, and El Salvador). Even more in the news is the extent to which many state leaders are concerned that continued poverty and debt for so many of the world's poor generates conditions that foster terrorism. These and other concerns have left many state officials with tough decisions about how much more they want to push neoliberal objectives at WTO meetings for example, when the cost may be increased threats to their economic and political security.

However, it will not be easy to build a global consensus for reform of the IMF and World Bank. Japan and the United States have made Mundel trilemma choices—embracing global financial markets—that suit their particular needs very well but that would not suit most other nations. Meanwhile, the European nations that adopted the euro in 2002 (see Chapter 11) have taken matters into their own hands and created their own system, which reduces (but does not eliminate) their exposure to global financial risk but does not create momentum for global regulations. The other countries of the world face uncomfortable choices and the threat of contagion. It is difficult to see who would take the lead in creating a new international financial system or how the interests of different groups can be reconciled.

## Structuralists

Many structuralists are not surprised that the finance and monetary system is not as stable as neoliberals would like to think it is. Increased integration has freed markets for capital, trade, and FDI. However, the market's invisible hand has clearly failed many of the poor in LDCs—or even whole states in the cases of the HIPCs. The emerging global financial market continues to reward the rich capitalist states and select TNCs. Many structuralists focus on the ways in which the finance structure encourages exploitation and even imperialism.[29] Much of the antiglobalization literature focuses on the extent to which capital mobility contributes to debt, hunger, environmental problems, and a host of other issues that in some cases not only prevents development but also fosters underdevelopment. Others focus on more subtle means of neo-imperialism in the foundations of the financial and monetary structure that help the United States and other developed nations dominate developing nations.[30]

These and other policies that promote globalization only ensure that the United States and other industrialized states will politically and economically subjugate another nation or people, leaving them dependent on the developed states and vulnerable to their more forceful means of domination. For structuralists, reforms of the IMF and World Bank are virtually meaningless, because the two agencies represent the interests of the rich, who are not seriously interested in redistributing the world's wealth and power. *Cui bono?* Always the bourgeoisie and rich of the developed states who believe they have a vested interest in an open liberal economy.

It is our view that the smooth running of all four IPE structures requires an efficient and smoothly running finance and monetary order. The world clearly needs a stable finance and foreign exchange system that is able to adapt effectively to changing structural conditions. Lack of such a system is a real threat to economic and political stability. Yet the current financial structure continues to manifest many unresolved issues and unsolved problems. Global financial crises are an inherent aspect of the global financial system as it is currently constructed. However, financial regulations (the "adult supervision" that financial markets need to work smoothly) are still mainly domestic, not international or global, and are therefore uneven, incomplete, and difficult to enforce. The major industrial states, together with the IMF and World Bank, should be able to bring together major creditors and debtors, both public and private, so as to shore up the more volatile elements of the finance and monetary structure, especially when it comes to many of the poorer developing nations.

Although the need for change in the IMF and World Bank architecture is widely agreed on, there has been little consensus on what specific changes should be considered. The clash of national interests makes change difficult to achieve. Even technical changes in their rules and procedures have considerable political implications that impinge on the interests and policies of creditor and debtor nations. What appears to be emerging lately, however, is a view by many experts and civil society (NGOs) that poverty has to be dealt with head on. It will be interesting to see if the industrialized North, which seems primarily concerned with system confidence and stability, can reconcile its interests with those in the South, who are concerned about fairness, equity, and social justice.

## DISCUSSION QUESTIONS

1. Compare and contrast the three different types of debt problems that were discussed in this chapter in terms of (a) the source of the debt, (b) the major actors in each situation and their interests, and (c) how the situation was resolved, if it was.
2. Why so much fuss over speculation? Why do you supposed Keynes would be concerned about it today? Use Chapter 7 to help you answer this question.
3. What are the seven stages of a bubble, and how do they apply to the Mexican peso panic? Discuss the relationship between bubbles and speculation in the Mexican, Asian, and Argentine economies.
4. Explain the role of the IMF in helping to solve these balance-of-payments crises.
5. The Prisoner's Dilemma illustrates an important conflict between individual and group interests. Discuss the meaning and significance of the Prisoner's Dilemma and explain how it applies to any of these crises.
6. Why do you suppose the latest debt crisis has received so much press and attention? Are you optimistic or pessimistic that it can be solved? How?

## INTERNET LINKS

IMF *World Economic Outlook:*
    www.imf.org/external/pubs/ft/weo/2003/01/index.htm
Commanding Heights WGBH website:
    www.pbs.org/wgbh/commandingheights
Nouriel Roubini's Argentina Crisis Page:
    www.stern.nyu.edu/globalmacro/countries/argentina.html
The IPE of the Asian Crisis home page:
    www.ups.edu/ipe/asiacrisis
"The Crash," Frontline Public Broadcasting System Video: pbs.org, 1999.

## SUGGESTED READINGS

Robert M. Axelrod. *The Evolution of Cooperation.* Jackson, TN: Perseus, 2006.

Paul Blustein. *The Chastening: Inside the Crisis That Rocked the Global Financial System and Humbled the IMF.* New York: Public Affairs, 2001.

William Easterly. *The Elusive Quest for Growth: Economists' Adventures and Misadventures in the Tropics.* Cambridge, MA: MIT Press, 2002.

Barry Eichengreen. *Globalizing Capital: A History of the International Monetary System.* Princeton, NJ: Princeton University Press, 1996.

Susan George. *Debt Boomerang: How Third World Debt Harms Us All.* Boulder, CO: Westview, 1992.

Charles P. Kindleberger. *Manias, Panics, and Crashes: A History of Financial Crises.* New York: Basic Books, 1978.

Richard O'Brien. *Global Financial Integration.* New York: Council on Foreign Relations, 1992.

Eswar Prasad, Kenneth Rogoff, Shang-Jin Wei, and M. Ayhan Kose. *Effects of Financial Globalization on Developing Countries: Some Empirical Evidence.* Washington, DC: IMF, 2003. Available at www.imf.org/external/np/res/docs/2003/031703.htm.

Dani Rodrik, "Goodbye Washington Consensus, Hello Washington Confusion?" *Journal of Economic Literature,* XLIV, December 2006, pp. 973–987.

Jeffrey Sachs. *The End of Poverty: Economic Possibilities for Our Time.* New York: Penguin, 2006.

George Soros. "The Capitalist Threat." *The Atlantic Monthly,* vol. 279, Feb. 1979.

Joseph E. Stiglitz. *Globalization and Its Discontents.* New York: W. W. Norton, 2002.

Joseph E. Stiglitz. *Making Globalization Work.* New York: W. W. Norton, 2006.

Michael Veseth. *Selling Globalization.* Boulder, CO: Lynne Rienner, 1998.

## KEY TERMS

heavily indebted poor countries (HIPCs)

prisoner's dilemma

lender of last resort

structural adjustment policies (SAPs)

conditionality

balance-of-payments crisis

capital flight

displacement

expansion

euphoria

distress

revulsion

*Torschlusspanik*

contagion crisis

currency crisis

crony capitalism

speculative attack

hedge fund

moral hazard

transparency

odius debt

HIPC Initiative

## NOTES

1. For a good overview of the 1980s debt crisis, see Benjamin Cohen, *In Whose Interest?* (New Haven, CT: Yale University Press, 1986); especially chap. 8, "Latin Debt Storm."
2. Negative real interest rates exist when inflation rates exceed the interest rate over the term of a loan. This benefits the borrower, because loan repayments have less purchasing power (lower real value) than the amount borrowed.
3. Susan George, *A Fate Worse Than Debt: The World Financial Crisis and the Poor* (Berkeley, CA: Grove Press, 1988).
4. See Carole Collins, Zie Gariyo, and Tony Burdon, "Jubilee 2000: Citizen Action Across the North–South Divide," in Michael Edwards and John Gaventa, eds., *Global Citizen Action* (Boulder, CO: Lynne Rienner, 2001).
5. See, for example, Chris Jochnick and Fraser A. Preston, eds., *Sovereign Debt at the Crossroads. Challenges and Proposals for Resolving the Third World Debt Crisis* (Oxford: Oxford University Press, 2006).
6. A good background piece on currency and financial crises is Charles P. Kindleberger, *Manias, Panics, and Crashes: A History of Financial Crises* (New York: Basic Books, 1978).
7. This section is based on Michael Veseth, *Selling Globalization: The Myth of the Global Economy* (Boulder, CO: Lynne Rienner, 1998), chap. 4.
8. Quoted by Moisés Naím, "Latin America the Morning After," *Foreign Affairs,* 74 (July/August 1995), p. 51.
9. Paul Krugman, "Dutch Tulips and Emerging Markets," *Foreign Affairs,* 74 (July/August 1995), p. 39.
10. Lesley Crawford, "Survey of Latin American Finance and Investment: Only Zedillo Optimistic," *The Financial Times,* March 25, 1996, p. 4.
11. Krugman, "Dutch Tulips and Emerging Markets," p. 43.

12. See, for example, David Vines, Pierre-Richard Angenor, and Marcus Miller, *Asian Financial Crisis: Causes, Contagion, and Consequences* (Cambridge: Cambridge University Press, 2004).

13. See Paul Blustein, *The Chastening* (New York: Public Affairs, 2001), pp. 186–196.

14. Walter Bagehot, *Lombard Street: A Description of the Money Market* (Philadelphia: Orion Editions, 1991), p. 8.

15. See the IMF website, www.imf.org.

16. Jeffrey D. Sachs, "How to Run the International Monetary Fund," *Foreign Policy*, July/August 2004.

17. Joseph Stiglitz, *Making Globalization Work* (New York: W. W. Norton, 2006); see chap. 8, especially pp. 208–209.

18. Ibid., pp. 228–229.

19. See Joseph Hanlon and Ann Pettifor, "Kicking the Habit," Jubilee 2000, www.jubileeresearch.org/analysis/reports/habitfull.htm.

20. Stiglitz, *Making Globalization Work*, pp. 226–228.

21. Ibid.

22. See Dani Rodrik, "Goodbye Washington Consensus, Hello Washington Confusion," *Journal of Economic Literature*, XLIV, December 2006, pp. 973–987.

23. See Walden Bello, "Critics Plan Offensive as IMF-World Bank Crisis Deepens," www.50years.org/cms/updates/story/325.

24. Both the IMF and World Bank websites discuss in some detail the efforts both agencies are making to further what has become a very popular movement in many parts of the world.

25. See Jeffrey Sachs, "Africa 'Should Not Pay Its Debts,'" http://news.bbc.co.uk/2/hi/business/3869081.stm.

26. See, for example, Jhagdish Bhagwati, *In Defense of Globalization* (New York: Oxford University Press, 2004).

27. John Maynard Keynes, *The General Theory of Employment, Interest, and Money* (New York: Harcourt, Brace, 1936), p. 159.

28. See, for example, Joel Krieger, *Globalization and State Power: Who Wins When America Rules?* (New York: Pearson, 2005).

29. See, for example, Oswaldo De Rivero, *The Myth of Development: The Non-viable Economies of the 21st Century* (New York: Zed Books, 2001).

30. See Robert Hunter Wade, "The Invisible Hand of the American Empire," *Ethics and International Affairs, 17* (September 2003), pp. 77–88.

# The Global Security Structure

## OVERVIEW

The security structure may be the most important structure in the international political economy (IPE) because trade, finance, and technology networks and linkages matter little if nation-states, businesses, and other actors do not have a stable and secure foundation on which to operate. This chapter outlines key elements since the end of the Cold War in 1989 that developed into a multi-layered network of arrangements significantly different from the international security arrangements that had existed during the Cold War (1947–1989).

From a realist (mercantilist) IPE perspective, we view the security structure as a three-tiered, pyramid-like order composed of the stronger nation-states on the top level, international organizations and minor states on the second, and weaker nations on the lowest level. Nongovernmental organizations, subnational groups, international businesses, the media, and other actors interact with these actors on all levels. Together these players produce and manage the formal and informal rules that result from agreements, treaties, conventions and practices that determine how secure societies and individuals will be from threats or risks.

**A Vee**

at dusk visible
through a tall window.

A dozen geese
flying West
comes a blast and another,

loud explosions of daisy cutters
and mighty ordinance,

fuel air bomb concussions
and sharp reflected flashes.

Din of destruction
Drowning the turbine howl
From the low flock of F-16s
or Tornadoes that
moments before imitated geese.

Michael J. Carey[1]

Since the end of the Cold War, a significant shift has occurred in the way academics and government officials think about the global security structure. More than anything else in the second half of the twentieth century, tensions and hostility between the United States and the Soviet Union during the **Cold War** (1947–1989) framed most of the important security issues of the day.[2] In the late 1940s and 1950s the United States and the Soviet Union mirrored each other in ways that helped entrench a **bipolar balance of power**, or security arrangement under which the two superpowers organized international political, military, and economic alliances in opposition to each other. The sources of tension and conflict between the two superpowers (so designated because of their nuclear capabilities) were based mainly on ideological (democracy versus communism) and geopolitical (East–West territorial) differences. Developing nations were prized as members or potential members of each superpower's political and ideological sphere of influence. Nuclear weapons played a key role in promoting hostile and dangerous relations between the two superpowers. In zero-sum fashion, incremental increases in military or economic power by one were perceived as losses in power by the other.

Ironically, many security experts viewed the period as quite stable, because of the interaction between only two political economic hegemons (dominant powers). Because nuclear weapons are so destructive, they proved to be of little or no utility when it came to fighting frontier wars in places such as Asia, Africa, South America, and the Caribbean. Instead, the battle was joined in proxy wars like those in Vietnam and Nicaragua for the United States, and Afghanistan for the Soviet Union in the 1980s. One superpower and its surrogate state conducted conventional or guerrilla warfare against a proxy of the other superpower, avoiding direct confrontation for fear of initiating a nuclear war.

The defeats of the United States in Vietnam in 1973 and of the Soviet Union in Afghanistan in the late 1980s also weakened the security order by demonstrating that small, weak nations could defeat large, strong nations—or at least weaken their resolve. The collapse of the Soviet Union in 1989 was the watershed event that broke the foundation of the Cold War security structure and, ironically, resulted in a good deal of violence and war in the world.

For many state officials in the developed regions of the world, however, the 1990s was the decade of *globalization* when security issues seemed to no longer preoccupy world leaders. Many of these same officials were rudely awakened by developments surrounding the September 11, 2001, attacks on the U.S. World Trade Center and then the U.S. invasion of Iraq. Issues of national and global security once again grabbed headlines and seemed to preoccupy leaders of especially the major powers. For many of them, terrorism has since replaced nuclear war as the greatest physical and military threat to global peace. Meanwhile, incidents of bloodshed and violence related to civil war, long-standing ethnic and religious conflicts, and genocide, among other causes, occur routinely in the Middle East and parts of Africa. Except in a few cases, the major powers have been reluctant to involve themselves directly in these situations.

Paradoxically, as we will see, the economic part of globalization (see Chapters 3 and 15) has emphasized economic growth, wealth, and power based on the spread of capitalism along with new technologies and communication systems. In so doing, globalization has also helped to both generate but also solve a growing number of security issues. Thus, the new global security structure exhibits a broader agenda all the time, due in part to the expanding number of physical and psychological threats to states, but also to different groups within those states and to individuals as well.

In this chapter we make the following arguments about the security structure that replaced the Cold War framework. First, these appears to be a very low threat of *total war* between the major military powers, due in part to a variety of economic issues related to globalization replacing national security as the primary preoccupation of the wealthier states in particular. Second, as realists argue, nation-states remain the dominant actors in the global security structure, with territorial security their main priority. However, *geopolitics,* which emphasizes protecting national borders, is becoming less important today than it once was. Third, a growing number of actors, with many conflicting interests—such as international organizations, nongovernmental organizations, international businesses and sub- and transnational groups such as terrorists—share global security management responsibilities with the major powers. The result is an order that lacks the clear structural framework of the Cold War but also exhibits a broader agenda than the previous order, unclear rules, and many informal practices.

Fourth, the globalization campaign of the 1990s accounts for some of the increase in the number of potential physical and psychological threats to individuals as human beings, human rights violations, the spread of diseases, and environmental damage. Other threats are more endemic to society, especially in developing nations, where increases in violence and conflict are the product of domestic sociocultural, religious, economic, and political factors.

Fifth, and finally, is the *means* that states and other actors use to deal with security threats. During the Cold War, conventional and strategic (nuclear) weapons were designed specifically to fight and win largely conventional forms of war. These may not work on the many subnational conflicts. In many situations this makes "soft" power instruments—economic, technological, and other nonviolent means to achieve security—more important than ever. Meanwhile, globalization has also played a role in helping make available to almost any nation a vast array of both expensive and inexpensive weapons to defend states but also threaten them.

All of these elements make for a security structure that is in dynamic flux and very difficult to manage. Despite efforts to do so, national, and increasingly personal security, is not something that can be guaranteed.

## THE MULTILAYERED SECURITY STRUCTURE

To help describe and understand many of the major features of the new global security structure and some of the political-economic linkages between the actors within that framework, we use a realist characterization of a three-tiered arrangement of the most powerful and influential actors. The top layer of the security structure is made up of the United States—the world's remaining superpower—and a relatively small number of militarily powerful states such as Great Britain, France, and Russia, which until recently have thought about security issues primarily in terms of "great power" wars in which vast armies draw on the their state's resources and engage one another in conventional, or more recently, nuclear warfare.[3] Other states at the top are the great majority of minor powers or middle-income developing nations, including the more successful newly industrialized countries (NICs) such as Brazil, Indonesia, and China. Although the security agendas of these powers are likely to have been and still are shaped by the major ex-colonial powers of the top level, states such as India and Pakistan are more likely to be concerned about traditional regional conflicts among themselves and, on occasion, between themselves and the major powers.

Second-tier actors such as **international organizations (IOs)** often reflect the interests of minor-state powers and, as in the case of the UN Security Council and the North Atlantic Treaty Organization (NATO), are important to the extent that they serve the interests of their creators—the major powers in particular—and from which they also draw their authority. The minor powers themselves often play important roles in, and look to, IOs such as the UN, NATO, and transnational corporations (TNCs) to establish new global security standards and rules. Similarly, these states are also likely to be open to the influence of these actors along with **nongovernmental organizations (NGOs)**. Yet because security issues are so sacred to the major powers, minor powers, IOs, transnational corporations and NGOs find it difficult to influence security issues at this level, although there are clear signs that their influence is increasing.

The third tier of the security structure represents the great majority of poorer developing nations and weak states that lack the hard- and soft-power resources to deal with territorial and border issues and a wide variety of security problems concerning refugees, immigrants, minorities (see Chapter 16), human rights abuses, epidemic diseases, environmental problems (see Chapter 20), and a host of other wealth and welfare issues. UN peacekeeping forces and NGOs such as Amnesty International are also quite active and play major roles at this level. Because of their power, influence, and global interests, some states such as the United States are involved in problems at all three tiers, whereas other states are involved in one type or another.

Connecting actors at all three levels of the structure are a number of formal treaties, conventions, and other arrangements, rules, and informal norms meant to protect people from various kinds of threats. Many threats are political and military in nature; others are rooted in economic factors such as underdevelopment, weapons technology, production, and trade. Other economic issues that connect actors include the way in which the major powers use international economic institutions and policies to advance their security objectives and the effects they have on targeted nations. When it comes to protection, in many cases IOs and NGOs play important roles in managing the consequences of these policies. Finally, the structure of the global economy itself has recently proven to be a major security issue to the extent that terrorist organizations benefit from its lack of rules and regulations.

## THE TOP LAYER: POWER POLITICS AND STATE-SYSTEM ORDER

A relatively small group of the most powerful nation-states and minor powers continue to focus on traditional security interests that require fighting wars, or being prepared to fight wars, to protect national borders and the population within them. Strongly influenced by realist[4] ideas and concepts, most defense ministers and military officials consider the state the source of sovereign (final) authority in determining the nation's interests and objectives. The same is true of the instruments or means, strategies, and policies used to protect the nation and solve other security-related issues. To many realists, in a *potentially* anarchical international system in which absolute security cannot be guaranteed, security must be the primary objective—beyond all other state goals.[5] Likewise, many realists are committed to the idea that peace results when power is relatively balanced or distributed between two or more nations. The economy is simply another tool in the state's arsenal to achieve any number of national objectives (see Chapter 2). Even when states pursue economic liberal objectives, they do so ultimately for their own benefits.

One problem common to all the major powers is finding the best distribution of power structure. Given a nation's national and international interests, is **unilateralism**, **multilateralism**, or **isolationism** the best strategy?

### Unilateralism

Many unilateralists argue that even if Russia still possesses some nuclear weapons, at the end of the Cold War there remained just one superpower—the United States—which now had the opportunity to act as a liberal (benevolent) hegemonic power and impose a set of rules and regulations for peace and security on other nations.[6] According to the theory of liberal imperialism that was popular with some neoconservative members of the Bush administration (discussed below) and neoconservative pundits such as Charles Krauthammer and Max Boot,[7] the only way to achieve global stability and for the United States to secure its global interests was to promote—by force if necessary—the liberal values of freedom, democracy, and individual rights. The United States should try to impose order over uncivilized, undemocratic, and poor countries such as Haiti, Sierra Leone, and the Balkan states. Some pundits say the United States *should* also exercise power with restraint and benign intent, thus making its principles and values more likely to be tolerated by others.

The attacks on the World Trade Center of September 11, 2001, provided the opportunity for the second Bush administration to test this controversial idea. After 9/11, in 2002, the United States and Great Britain invaded Afghanistan to overthrow the Taliban, the Islamic fundamentalist government, which was helping al-Qaeda, the terrorist organization headed by Osama bin Laden. After defeating the Taliban (but not al-Qaeda), the administration linked al-Qaeda terrorism with Iraqi President Saddam Hussein's less than perfect willingness to cooperate with the UN. The United States then asked for, but was denied, UN Security Council authority to use force to compel Saddam to allow UN officials to inspect a variety of his facilities for biological and, especially, nuclear weapons. Adopting a go-it-alone policy, the United States, backed only by Great Britain, invaded Iraq on May 1, 2003, and after limited fighting removed Saddam Hussein from power.

A number of factors account for the administration's adoption of a unilateralist outlook. First, many U.S. officials, especially the neoconservatives around the President, felt strongly that the 9/11 attacks necessitated that the U.S. fight terrorism proactively, given the extent to which the nation and its interests abroad had proved to be vulnerable to both conventional weapons and quite possibly to **weapons of mass destruction (WMD)**, which include nuclear, biological, and chemical weapons.[8] Their argument quickly extended to include subnational groups that use terrorism as a tactic. Governments in Afghanistan and throughout the Middle East, and in many other places around the world, have fallen under suspicion.

Second, the Security Council split over the invasion of Iraq generated a rift between the United States and its Atlantic partners on the Security Council and in NATO. If the rest of Europe, plus Russia and China, were not going to join with the United States and Great Britain to fight in Iraq, the argument went, then someone must step up to the task, lest the terrorists go free and Iraq export its WMD. While he was in Europe, U.S. Secretary of Defense Donald Rumsfeld called France and Germany "old Europe" and implied that these states were weak for not supporting the invasion, whereas "new Europe," comprising many ex–Soviet-bloc nations, was strong for joining the coalition of states that invaded Iraq and stood up to terrorism. Of major concern to the administration was what it called **rogue states** (those that did not adhere to the norms of the international system), including the authoritarian and hostile governments of Iran, Iraq, and North Korea—three countries President Bush labeled the "axis of evil" along with Syria and Cuba—which either supported terrorist groups or had or might acquire the *potential* military capability to develop WMD.

When the U.S. invasion of Iraq did not go well, the administration's unilateralist policy bumped hard against reality. The administration had expected that the war in Iraq would turn out much the same way the Persian Gulf War had—largely a success and worth the price of lives and dollars. Now (in the spring of 2007) the Iraq war has become a quagmire. With U.S. military dead numbering 3150, more than 19,500 U.S. wounded, and Iraqi civilian deaths estimated at between 39,000 and 44,000, a civil war is also underway. An insurgency made up of ex-military and guerrilla forces from a variety of Middle Eastern countries have stood off U.S. and coalition forces. The box, "Iraq War: Why the Quagmire" examines some of the explanations for this quagmire, and ranks the success of the Bush administration's unilateralist political outlook and military strategy.

**THE IRAQ WAR: WHY THE QUAGMIRE?**

The level-of-analysis approach (see Chapter 1) is a useful explanatory tool that highlights multiple causes behind many situations while underscoring the extent to which institutional behavior reflects individual tasks, procedures, and values. Each level usually plays a role in policy decisions, thus levels of analysis are pragmatic.

## The Global Level

Although the war in Iraq does not cover the globe, for some experts and officials the quagmire that exists there at this time (March 2007) reflects a potential global issue, namely, the tension between Christians in the West and Islam in much of the rest of the world. Professor Samuel Huntington made popular the idea that the next great conflict (not necessarily war) would be a dispute between civilizations as they tried to preserve their culture, values, and religions.[a] An example is the period after 9/11, when Muslims in the United States and other countries were singled out and made to feel responsible for the actions of al-Qaeda and other Islamic fundamentalists. The economic liberal Thomas Friedman went so far as to suggest that the 9/11 attacks, in reaction to globalization, manifested a new form of international conflict and signaled the beginning of World War III.[b]

Realists, on the other hand, view the Iraq war as an extension of U.S. strategic political objectives to contain the influence of Iraq and Iran in this region, support Saudi Arabia and Israel (for different reasons), and control the supply of oil exported from the region.

## The Systemic Level

From a systemic or interstate perspective, several factors have contributed to the quagmire and to much criticism of the U.S.'s unilateralist military strategy. One set of factors involves the rationale for invading Iraq in the first place. Before the invasion the Bush administration argued that there was hard evidence that Saddam Hussein was developing a variety of weapons of mass destruction (WMD) that could be used against the United States, its allies, or Israel. Furthermore, on numerous occasions, administration officials appeared on national television and said that Iraq's WMD capabilities could be given to al-Qaeda terrorists. Hence Saddam Hussein's regime had to be forcibly removed from power.

Early on, U.S. officials clearly felt that the lone superpower had *hyperpower* capabilities and *could not* lose a war in Iraq. With its sophisticated weapons, the United States would simply finish what had been left unfinished in the Persian Gulf War by removing Saddam Hussein. After the invasion, however, no WMD were found. Some UN inspectors argued that since the end of the Persian Gulf War, Iraq had not restarted its weapons production processes, calling into question the quality of U.S. intelligence agencies, their information-gathering techniques, or at least the interpretation of that information.[c] U.S. leaders and military officials then made a variety of moves that in hindsight contributed to the quagmire. Some U.S. military generals complained that there were not enough forces to maintain control of the cities, let alone the rest of the country. Looting stripped the national museum of most of its artifacts, and, for example, copper wire from electricity facilities, while coalition troops protected the oil ministry. The chief of the Coalition Provisional Authority, Paul Bremer, disbanded the Iraqi army and national police. Between 30,000 and 50,000 Baathists then went underground; and without jobs, many joined the insurgency.

There is some evidence that Saddam Hussein knew he could not win a conventional war against the United States, so he planned on a guerrilla insurgency to gradually weaken U.S. resolve. When the war started, U.S. Defense Secretary Donald Rumsfeld was in the midst of trying to reconfigure the U.S. force structure and to pursue strategies he believed appropriate for the kinds of war the United States would face in developing regions of the world in the new century.[d] Indeed, the reduction in the level of U.S. forces and improved mobility seemed to pay off during the invasion. However, the administration was warned that invading Iraq would likely lead to insurgency by many different ethnic and religious groups. At first Rumsfeld denied there was an insurgency. Before long, however, coalition forces in Iraq were engaged in what many experts feared most—urban warfare, for which the U.S. troops in particular had little experience.

The Iraqi insurgency received various types of assistance from groups in Iran, Saudi Arabia, Syria, Yemen, and Sudan.[e] Some of these groups were well organized and connected to either Sunni or Shiia religious sects in Iraq, whereas others joined the insurgency as part of an effort to liberate Iraq from what they all view as an imperial power trying to maintain a footprint in the Middle East. The limits of a counterinsurgency strategy that included fighting in cities such as Fallujah, Ramadi, Samarra, and Mosul soon became clear. These battles were often followed by the U.S. troops rounding up young males to be interrogated in prisons such as Abu Ghraib, where some were tortured.[f] U.S. presitige diminished nearly everywhere in the world when the Bush administration argued that it was not bound by Geneva Convention rules regarding the treatment of combatants because these prisoners were terrorists, not soldiers. The United States was also accused of exporting detainees (called *rendition*) to Egypt, Eastern Europe, and elsewhere outside the United States, where laws against torture are ignored. This also weakened U.S. power and public support for the war at home and abroad.

Many experts raised issues about the nature of the strategy to prevail in Iraq along with the nature of the terrorist threat and the strategy to eliminate it. First, many doubted a connection between al-Qaeda and Saddam Hussein. Terrorism is a tactic that is usually employed to achieve political ends and is not something that can easily be countered by fighting a broad war against it in a country like Iraq. Insurgents in Iraq may employ terrorist methods, but their cause is not necessarily the same as al-Qaeda's. Thus, U.S. military strategies did not specify enough the nature of the threat. Some experts argue that civilian and military officials also did not focus enough on the rebuilding of Iraq. U.S. and other national military officials were unprepared to provide the Iraqis with basic needs in water, food, and medicine. The administration expected postwar operations to be relatively short-lived. Many blame bureaucratic turf wars between the State and Defense departments for the lack of postwar planning.[g]

Based on some of the lessons of the Vietnam War, some critics argue that the United States did not devise an overall joint military–political strategy to win over the "hearts and mind" of the Iraqi people.[h] Such a strategy would use small counterinsurgency special forces and target civilian acceptance of the United States and its partners instead of trying to defeat guerrilla forces. Under the guidance of U.S. military advisers, the Iraqis have been slow to field an army to take over the fighting from the coalition. The Iraqis did finally elect their own government. However, the combination of government ministers, who reflect a politically acceptable ratio of Sunnis, Shiites, and Kurds, is impossible to balance. Not unexpectedly, either, religious clerics and *mullahs* in Iraq may have more power and authority than secular leaders, raising more questions about the applicability of democracy in Iraq.

At the system level, Robert Jervis also takes the Bush administration to task for confusing preemption with a preventative war, the two terms often being used synonymously.[i] *Preemption* means initiating a conflict because it appears that an enemy is about to strike, and Saddam Hussein was not. *Preventative* war is not a reaction to an immediate threat; rather, it is a war based on fear of long-term measures that add up to a major threat sometime down the road. Korb and Wadhams also fault the Pentagon for ignoring the roles of deterrence and containment, which they believe are still useful concepts.[j] Might Saddam Hussein have cooperated more with the UN if the United States had threatened to use nuclear weapons against Iraq?

The U.S. unilateralist strategy generated disappointment, suspicion, and animosity between the United States and some of its allies. As payback for not supporting the invasion, the United States was reluctant to share contracts for rebuilding Iraq with other countries, especially France. The United States's attempt to be the world's policeman contributed to a reputation for arrogance and uncooperative behavior with other states. Lost were political and financial assistance, technical information, and diplomatic help from both old and new allies.

Unsurprising to realists, after no WMD were found in Iraq, the Bush administration switched to the idealistic goal of establishing democracy in Iraq and elsewhere throughout the Middle East "with the ultimate goal of ending tyranny in the world."[k] This Wilsonian vision of the world seems to have backfired in the Middle East as well as among Muslims the world over. The United States also looks hypocritical because it supports financially a number of authoritarian states that in turn support the U.S. counterterrorism campaign.

## The Subsystemic Level

Explanations of the quagmire are also related to policymaker and public support for U.S. goals in Iraq. Since the invasion of Iraq, the cost of the war for Americans alone has exceeded an estimated $300 billion, while 3430 U.S. military and coalition partner forces have been killed. By March 2007, public opinion in support of the Iraq war had dropped to an all-time low of 64 percent disapproval.[l] Some administration officials continue to argue that, essentially, in Iraq either things are not that bad or that the United States "will stay as long as it takes." Recent polls also show that the U.S. public is turned off to either party's solution to the problem and generally confused.[m]

More than anything else, lack of a victory or clear progress has undermined both the credibility of the Bush administration and domestic support for the war. Part of this can be attributed to not finding nuclear or any other WMD, after the administration went to great lengths to demonstrate that it had evidence of them. This argument was crucial in selling the U.S. public and Congress on the idea of an invasion, which Congress authorized in October 2002. Even though many experts pointed out that there was no connection between secular Iraq and religious al-Qaeda, the White House found it easy to sell this connection to the public and Congress as well, based largely on fear of another terrorist attack on the United States. Most simply, once the administration could no longer sell the fear of WMDs or a Saddam–bin Laden connection, the security threat from Iraq was punctured and has slowly leaked ever since.

Another source of problems has been the turf wars, won largely by the Defense Department, over other agencies as Defense Secretary Rumsfeld secured more authority for himself and for his department.[n] The administration's credibility was also hurt by several scandals directly or indirectly associated with the war, namely, the awarding of postinvasion contracts without open bids and overcharging by Halliburton Corp., which has ties to Vice President Dick Cheney; extended press coverage and graphic photos of the prisons at Abu Ghraib and Guantanimo Bay, Cuba; the alleged massacre and rape of civilians on more than one occasion; and efforts by the Defense Department to squelch information. Shortly after 9/11, the administration successfully pushed Congress to pass the controversial Patriot Act, which provided more domestic measures to track terrorists but also limited the freedoms and liberties of Americans. Later the administration went so far as to seek legal authority to gain access to library and banking files and to eavesdrop on people's phone calls, raising objections that it intentionally violated people's civil liberties and further undermined many of the democratic principles it claims to support.

In the midterm elections in November 2006, the Republicans lost control of both the U.S. Senate and the House of Representatives. Along with the public, many Republicans had become more critical of the President. A majority of Democrats supported the invasion—but came to feel that they had been lied to about the existence of WMD in Iraq. Representative John Murtha (D, Pa.), a conservative, a Vietnam War veteran, and former chair of the House Defense Appropriations Committee, was one of the first to call for the withdrawal of U.S. troops from Iraq. Senator John McCain (R, Ariz.) another Vietnam War veteran and former prisoner-of-war in Vietnam, protested the treatment of prisoners and pushed for hearings on their status while he has generally supported the war. More than a few Republicans have also expressed concern that the President seeks to enhance his own authority at the expense of Congress. Overall, neither party is clear about what the President should do about the quagmire, thus leaving him some wiggle room. Both Congress and the President want to see the Iraqis take over the war, but neither can articulate a policy or time frame to achieve that.

## The Actor Level

For realists, the actor level of analysis is crucial because the President plays a major role in determining U.S. interests and represents U.S. interests in the world arena. Much controversy surrounds President Bush as a decision maker, his personality traits, his outlook on the world, and his relationship to a select few advisors who have provided him with information and ideas.[o] During his first term, many argued that the President behaved much like a cowboy—for example, when he appeared at the World Trade Center after 9/11 ready to take charge, ride out, and take on the "evildoer" terrorists. Some link the Iraq war to his tough-guy wannabe outlook, which may be related to childhood feelings of inadequacy and weakness.[p] Finally, some analysts speculate that for the President himself, winning the war in Iraq may be part of a larger effort to carry out God's message to him by defeating terrorism the world over.[q] These motives may explain the President's missionary zeal to defeat the new "axis of evil" and his black-and-white outlook that anyone who is not with us is against us.

Much controversy has surrounded the President's immediate advisors Cheney, Rumsfeld, Paul Wolfowitz, and a number of other neoconservatives or "neocons" who were members of PNAC (the Project of the New American Century), which in the 1990s pressured the Clinton administration to remove Saddam Hussein. Mixing realism, idealism, and ideology, their views are reflected in the 2002 and 2006 National Security Strategy statements that the United States should reassert its role as a unilateralist-hegemonic actor, especially when it comes to leading an antiterrorism campaign, and by adopting militaristic measures to deal with balance-of-power conflicts in the Middle East.[r] Many are convinced that the views of the neocons account for an overestimation of U.S. power and military capabilities in dealing with the insurgents, and also in assuming that the Iraqi people would quickly choose democracy and capitalism over (where the ends justify the means) Islam and an authoritarian government. Their views have also made the United States look Machiavellian, often hypocritical, and not serious about human rights, democracy, and other ideals. Finally, the neocon outlook might have made it difficult if not impossible for the President and his advisors to consider and choose other options in order to win the war, or even to withdraw if necessary.

The levels of analysis demonstrate that the Bush administration consciously chose to act unilaterally in Iraq, when weak systemic conditions offered it a variety of other options to deal with Iraq. The Bush administration has a good deal invested in its unilateralist outlook and military strategy, and seems reluctant to change course even in the face of many systemic and subsystem factors such as the strength and durability of the insurgency and the lack of interest in democracy that have undermined U.S. efforts. Up to now the coalition has failed to win the hearts and minds of the Iraqi people. Subsystemically, the quagmire highlights the many different nations, individuals, subnational groups, and religious sects in Iraq whose interests and goals conflict with those of the U.S.-led coalition. Likewise, it highlights many of the bureaucratic problems behind the military strategy, efforts to manage the peace, and maintaining public support for the war effort. The President's close advisors and his own ideological and religious views may also play a role in sustaining the quagmire.

To change course at this time might be very difficult politically for the President and his advisors, who face the upcoming elections and are reluctant to admit mistakes. For the Bush administration it has been easier to change policy around the margins while waiting for the Iraqis to take over the war. In reaction to much criticism, both Wolfowitz and Rumsfeld have left the administration. Since the last U.S. election in 2006, and as the intensity of the insurgency continues to result in large numbers of civilian deaths and low morale among U.S. and coalition forces, the administration has reluctantly showed signs of shifting to a more multilateralist strategy by pressing other states and some IOs to share some responsibility and costs of the war. As the United States learned in Vietnam, strategies that states adopt to not only defeat an insurgent army but also to fundamentally change another society are usually ineffective and inappropriate.

*References*

[a]    For a more detailed discussion of this idea, see Samuel Huntington, "The Clash of Civilizations," *Foreign Affairs, 72* (Summer 1993), pp. 22–49.

[b]    Thomas Friedman, "Foreign Affairs; World War III," *The New York Times*, September 13, 2001, p. A27.

[c]    For a detailed account of the inspection issue, see Hans Blix, *Disarming Iraq* (New York: Pantheon, 2004).

[d]    Donald Rumsfeld, "Transforming the Military," *Foreign Affairs, 81* (May/June 2002), pp. 20–32.

[e]    See, "Guide: Armed Groups in Iraq," BBC News, August 15, 2006, http://news.bbc.co.uk/2/hi/middle_east/4268904.stm#background1.

[f]    See Maggie Farley, "Report: U.S. Is Abusing Captives," *The Los Angeles Times*, February 13, 2006.

[g]    See David Rieff, "Blueprint for a Mess," *The New York Times*, November 2, 2003.

[h]    See Thomas Ricks, "In Iraq, Military Forgot the Lessons of Vietnam," *The Washington Post*, July 23, 2006, p. A1.

[i]    Robert Jervis, *American Foreign Policy in a New Era* (New York: Routledge, 2005), pp. 84–86.

[j]    See Lawrence Korb and Caroline Wadhams, "A Critique of the Bush Administration's National Security Strategy," A Policy Analysis Brief, The Stanley Foundation, Muscatine, IA, July 2006, p. 2.

[k]    Ibid., p.3.

[l]    See "Iraq," CBS News/New York Times Poll, August 17–21, 2006, www.pollingreport.com/iraq.htm.

[m]    See, "On Iraq, U.S. Public Trusts Neither Party," *The Christian Science Monitor*, August 23, 2006.

[n]    See Rieff, "Blueprint for a Mess"; and Alan Sipress, "Powell vs. the Pentagon," *The Washington Post National Weekly Edition*, May 6–12, 2002.

[o]    See, for example, David Rothkopf, "Inside the Committee That Runs the World," *Foreign Policy, 147* (March/April 2005), pp. 30–40.

[p]    See, for example, John P. Briggs, M.D., and J. P. Briggs II, Ph.D., "Why Bush's Inner 'Reality' Has Poisoned His Own Troop Plan," *Truthout*, February 7, 2007, www.truthout.org/docs_2006/printer_020707R.shtml.

[q]    See, for example, Hans Hoyng and Gerhard Spörl, "War Out of Compassion," *Der Spiegel Online*, August 2003, www.spiegel.de/Spiegel/English/0,1518,236692,00.htm.

[r]    See, "The National Security Strategy of the United States of America," September 2002, http://whitehouse.gov.nsc/nss.html.

Simultaneously, to counter a possible ballistic (long-range) missile attack on the United States or its allies by a rogue nation, against the advice of many of its allies and Russia, the United States also proposed and continued to upgrade and deploy a new version of the **National Missile Defense (NMD)** program. New defensive antiballistic missiles (ABMs) would, it was hoped, find and destroy incoming ballistic missiles before they hit their targets—a feat that required new and advanced technology, research, and substantial amounts of funding. The Bush administration also came under fire for unilaterally withdrawing from the long-standing 1972 **Anti-Ballistic Missile (ABM) Treaty**, which outlawed the development of a space-based missile defense system. More important, many critics noted that even if an antiballistic missile could knock down an incoming missile, terrorists or rogue states were not likely to use that kind of weapon to attack the United States or its allies. Instead, they would be more likely to hide a low-grade nuclear device in a ship in harbor or build it in the target nation. Finally, among other examples, the Bush administration also acted unilaterally when it withdrew support for the Kyoto Treaty (see Chapter 20) and the International Criminal Court, and hesitated to support new efforts to enforce the Biological Weapons Treaty of 1972.

Overall, some realists take issue with many of the specifics of the Bush administration's "primacy" outlook. Some argue that preemption has always been a *de facto* reality of international politics, but to announce it as a cornerstone of U.S. defense policy puts the United States in the arrogant position of deciding too broadly what constitutes a military threat to itself, without considering international norms or the interests of other states. Effectively controlling rogue states might necessitate that the United States take over other governments, eventually producing an empire or raising the costs of sustaining what empire the United States already has. Either way, the political and economic costs are likely eventually to weaken and perhaps ruin the United States.[9]

At a fundamental level, however, these realists doubt the extent to which the benefits of unilateralism outweigh multilateralism—or isolationism for that matter. The United States might feel that the threat of international terrorism *should* compel other nations to follow the U.S.'s lead when it comes to control and maintenance of the international security system, but unilateralism always ends in a "prison camp" mentality whereby hegemony, if not imperialism, become justified at the economic and political expense of other states. The others must either agree to live within that structure or actively oppose it when it no longer serves their interests. Likewise, the hegemon must be willing to accept the political and economic costs associated with hegemony (see Chapters 3 and 5), something that inevitably undermines support for unilateralism from the citizens who ultimately bear its costs.[10]

## Multilateralism

Multilateralists want the United States to lead some alliance or coalition of partners in a multipolar (more than two) balance-of-power configuration that would produce a security environment favorable to the interests of the major powers. Bipolarity has some structural advantages, but the world's only superpower must still operate alongside a number of major powers, because even if the United States believes it has a monopoly on military power, the ability to use that power effectively is limited to specific situations, as demonstrated in Iraq.

According to Joseph Nye, a strong supporter of multilateralism and a multipolar security structure, hard-power instruments such as nuclear weapons are costly and can make the United States "musclebound."[11] With a broad range of interests, and international economic interdependence, Nye believes the United States and others should give more attention to soft-power instruments such as improved information and communication systems, the benefits of globalization, and multilateral cooperation rather than unilateral action. Hard power alone can no longer assure security for the United States and other states. Terrorists and suicide bombers, for example, can threaten and strike even in highly militarized places such as occupied Iraq and Israel's West Bank settlements. Hard power gains territory and destroys military hardware, Nye maintains, but soft power affects people more intimately and is a surer long-run road to security.

If hard weapons are designed chiefly to kill, soft ones perform a variety of functions that also enable hard instruments to work more effectively. For example, most experts agree that efforts both to counter terrorism by subnational groups and to curb the proliferation of WMD necessitate sharing information by major powers. This means information from police and from spies, no matter how good or bad relations with them are. Military expert Eliot Cohen argues that soft-power sources such as electronic communication and intelligence-gathering systems now play a greater role in the military strategies of the major powers, in part because some are less costly than the standard weapons of the Cold War.[12] On the battlefield, radio waves, radar, and infrared systems help soldiers see into the dark and illuminate the battlefield, while electromagnetic signals help improve soft-power communication systems. Similarly, Cohen notes that a revolution has been occurring in the use of digital communication systems, which compress data, while global positioning systems (GPS) make more exact guidance and navigation possible.

There are a few downsides to these developments. One is that the major powers have become increasingly dependent on sophisticated information and communication systems. This problem was demonstrated in the controversy surrounding the accuracy of U.S. and British intelligence about Iraq's possession of WMD as a rationale for attacking Iraq. More important, the Persian Gulf War and Somalia in the early 1990s, and then 9/11 and the recent antiterrorism campaigns that led to the U.S. invasion of Iraq, demonstrate that possession of both hard- and soft-power weapons does not always produce decisive victories. Superpower and major-power weapons are likely to be most effective when applied to a situation for which they were designed and in which opponents do not possess adequate countermeasures. In the case of 9/11, terrorists from mainly third-layer countries used relatively unsophisticated weapons (the Internet and commercial airlines), in contrast to what many experts envisioned they would use against a major power like the United States.

Cohen worries that future wars will not be fought on battlefields as we know them but will be *virtual wars* in which a virus or some countermeasure disrupts communication systems and severely weakens a state's military capabilities. Another problem, then, is that as military and civilian technology has become more sophisticated, it has generated issues related to access to information and communication systems. For example, the Internet was originally conceived as a communications system to help scientists conduct national defense research. As it has expanded both in terms of the information available on it and the number of persons who have access to it, its access has become a national security issue for many of the major powers.

Finally, a major problem in the role of soft power in the security structure today is the tension between realists who want to control both hard and soft measures in the name of national security and businesses' contrasting view from an economic liberal perspective, hence preferring less government regulation in this area. The selling of arms and military technology is a big business. Strong business interests within the United States and the major powers lobby for higher levels of defense spending, both in the name of national security and to promote the economic security of the firms that supply weapons and defense systems. Among the U.S. companies often involved in these transactions have been Vector Microwave Research, Electronic Warfare Associates, Science Applications International, Loral, McDonnell Douglas (now part of Boeing), and GM Hughes Electronics. Many of these companies utilize former U.S. defense officials to help them sell and acquire new technologies. Many structuralists point out that a "feeding frenzy" by both importing nations and corporations exists for weapons and technology, often reinforcing tensions or negative views of an enemy to justify sales.[13]

The point here, though, is that if U.S. companies can purchase these weapons and technologies, so can others. Thus, the goal of achieving military security through the use of secure, technically sophisticated defense systems often conflicts with the state's other goal of promoting economic growth through the production and sale of technically sophisticated industries. Although there is no general rule to follow in choosing one type of security over the other, many states are making a national technology policy part of their foreign policy—in the realization that mistakes in either area can have monumental consequences for defense.

The economic liberal policies of the International Monetary Fund (IMF), the World Trade Organization (WTO), and the World Bank are essentially another kind of instrument the major powers use to achieve security-related objectives. A commitment to open borders, free trade, floating exchange rates, and the magic of the "invisible hand" in the market, when combined with the globalization campaign, are expected to economically "grow" less developed countries (LDCs), invest them in the international economy and democratic institutions, and make them less interested in fighting wars. Thomas Friedman and others have helped popularize the idea that no two states with a McDonald's in them (that is, espousing democratic and liberal political-economic values and ideas) ever went to war with each other.[14] However, as we will discuss in the next section, most experts agree that interdependence and the interlocking political and economic interests of globalization generate a variety of security problems. These are such that the United States and other major powers increasingly feel pressured to manage them in cooperation with IOs, NGOs, international businesses, and even the media.

Finally, multilateralists confront a difficult problem in trying to determine how many and which powers can or should make up the multipolar system. Germany and Japan are not noted for their military capabilities so much as for their economic and political influence. Some have suggested that it may be time to include a few of the developing countries, such as Brazil or India, in big-power considerations. Although some of these states (China, for example) may see themselves as potential great powers, others, such as Japan, do not want the associated responsibilities. Security system management, then, is not a given, but a role states must actively attend to.

## Isolationism

Finally, isolationists prefer that the United States and other major powers disengage militarily from the international system and use force only when they are directly attacked. Attempts to balance power may overcommit and involve the United States and its allies in financially costly or "blowback" situations. The latter make the United States seem more like an occupying than a liberating force.[15] For realist-oriented isolationists, unless the state's core national interests are at stake in a threatening situation, the United States should focus more on itself and less on assisting others. Some isolationists would have the United States withdraw its bases from Western Europe and Asia, especially South Korea, and abrogate any security treaties that require the United States to go to war immediately.

Some isolationists argue that war is no longer worth its financial costs. Others believe that the "total war" version of conflict that results in the deaths of many soldiers and civilians has become morally and ethically unacceptable in the international political economy as it already is in international law. And finally, one version of isolationism is that the United States is actually *not* an all-powerful nation, given its unsuccessful record of dealing with conflict, especially in developing nations. Although military power has helped to overthrow some regimes, as in Afghanistan and Iraq, it has not led to an acceptance of liberal values and principles but has only bred resentment in those nations.[16]

Relative isolation appeared to be the position of the Bush administration during the first presidential election campaign when it claimed that "nation-building" by UN peacekeeping operations in places like Africa was not in the interest of the United States. The attacks of 9/11 changed that along with the administration's antiterrorism campaign and its invasion of Iraq. The United States and some of its traditional allies remain deeply divided over security objectives at the second and third levels of the security structure. At this writing the United States and other national forces are still bogged down in Afghanistan and Iraq. France has offered to assist in the pacification of former regime supporters and the rebuilding of Iraq, provided the UN takes over much of the postwar recovery operation. Meanwhile, the United States has agreed to supply assistance to UN peacekeeping forces in Sierra Leone, while renewing efforts to support a number of African countries economically.

In conclusion of this section, William Eckhardt found that from the end of World War II until 2000, at least thirty-five major wars were fought, involving the major powers and a number of LDCs, many of which were the former colonies of the imperial European and U.S. powers. Many of these wars were ideological struggles between supporters of one superpower or another, decolonization efforts (or "wars of national liberation"), religious and ethnic-based wars, or—the biggest increase in the cause of war—civil wars. In 2002 alone, at least twenty-two major wars occurred in the world, mainly in Africa, South Asia, and the Middle East.[17] It seems clear, then, that for the major powers at the top level, security issues are sacrosanct. However, their political and economic interests make it difficult for them to confine these issues to this tier.

## THE SECOND LAYER: THE CHANGING ROLE OF INTERNATIONAL ORGANIZATIONS

In this section we discuss the role of NATO, UN peacekeeping, and the International Criminal Court (ICC) as examples of some of the ways in which institutions and both major and minor powers manage a wider variety of security issues than at the first level. In short, its outlook reflects primarily a realist attitude about IOs that coincides with views about them during the Cold War—that in the case of security issues, IOs and regional organizations are the creation of and derive their authority from a few of the major powers. They are only as strong or effective as states allow them to be, and it is up to states to decide if or when IO-sponsored treaties or protocols are to be adhered to.

### IOs: The UN

Until the early 1970s, the lack of UN security treaties and conventions reflected U.S. and Soviet emphasis on expanding their arsenals and deterring one another from initiating an attack. As U.S. and Soviet relations improved toward the end of the Vietnam War, both superpowers looked to the UN to help establish a number of conventions, treaties, and protocols related especially to problems of nuclear weapons proliferation and control over the arms race. Many developing countries had purchased conventional weapons from one of the two superpowers or major powers, or were trying to build nuclear power plants of their own, ostensibly to generate domestic energy.

Active at this level are the major powers in the UN Security Council but also the less powerful (minor) states that cannot successfully address most of their security issues by themselves. Countries such as Italy, Spain, the Netherlands, and Belgium, along with middle-income developing nations such as Brazil, Indonesia, Malaysia, Poland, Hungary, and the Czech Republic, often join alliances with major power and IOs. As in the case of India and Pakistan, many of these states have some hard-power capabilities, but most cannot protect themselves with these instruments alone. They tend to look more positively than the United States does at international and regional organizations to generate norms, rules, or international standards that will defend and protect them.

The UN first played a decisively important but indirect role in promoting peace and security by serving as a forum for negotiations that resulted in several treaties covering different security issues. The **Non-Proliferation Treaty (NPT)** of 1968 obligated states with nuclear weapons not to transfer them to other states, and non-nuclear states not to receive nuclear weapons or devices from any other state. The NPT also created the *International Atomic Energy Agency (IAEA)*, based in Vienna, to inspect nuclear power facilities in member states and to guard against secret military diversions. Today the NPT has been signed by 180 parties. Its supporters argue that it has been quite successful in limiting the spread of nuclear weapons to developing nations. Japan and Germany, but also Brazil, Argentina, and several ex–Soviet-bloc countries, have chosen not to develop their nuclear weapons capabilities.

Some realist critics are quick to point out that without major or superpower support and willingness to enforce all these treaties, they demonstrate only the good intentions of states. A number of nuclear states, including India, Pakistan, Israel, Iran, Iraq, Libya, and North Korea, have either not signed the NPT or have failed to declare that they have nuclear weapons. North Korea withdrew from the treaty in 1993 and resorted to bargaining (some would call it extortion) with the leaders of the major powers for financial assistance in exchange for cooperation on inspections of its nuclear facilities. More recently, it and Iran have restarted their nuclear development programs, signaling their desire to join the club of states with nuclear weapons. Critics also charge that rogue states and terrorists could acquire these weapons via the expanding sources of suppliers willing to market them.

Another major treaty area is the *Biological and Toxic Weapons Convention (BWC)*, which was easily endorsed by more than 100 nations at the time of its inception in 1972. The signers included the United States and the Soviet Union, both of whom recognized the lethality of biological weapons and feared their ability to control them during a war. The BWC restricts research on biological weapons to defensive measures, but makes no provisions for inspection because biological weapons are easy to hide. The UN Special Committee (UNSCOM) was charged by the UN Security Council in 1991 with inspecting Iraqi facilities for evidence of anthrax and other biological materials. Iran, Syria, Russia, and at least sixteen other countries have been suspected of either producing biological weapons or conducting research in this area.

Other UN-sponsored treaties include the *Comprehensive Test Ban Treaty (CTBT)*, signed in 1996, which outlaws the testing of nuclear weapons under any conditions but does not take effect until all forty-four states that are capable of building a crude nuclear weapon have signed and ratified the treaty. The United States, France, and China, but also India and Pakistan, have been slow to come to terms over the CTBT because they have been developing a new generation of ballistic missiles and have wanted to test them in order to catch up with the other nuclear powers. In 1999 the U.S. Senate voted against ratifying the treaty and the CTBT, a move supported by the new Bush administration. Supporters of the treaty charge that it is basically a moot point, given that many weapons do not need to be tested or can be tested under laboratory conditions.

The *Chemical Weapons Convention (CWC)* of 1992 went into effect in 1997, when some 157 countries pledged to eliminate all chemical weapons by the year 2007 and never to develop, produce, stockpile, or use chemical weapons. Critics of the treaty are suspicious that nations such as Russia, Israel, Egypt, Syria, Libya, North Korea, and, until recently, Iraq have not signed the treaty, and may try to develop chemical weapons as a relatively cheap way of countering U.S. conventional and nuclear superiority. Finally, since 1987, countries capable of producing long-range missiles have worked on a convention to prohibit the export of missiles and related technology—the *Missile Technology Control Regime (MTCR)*. Iran, Israel, Saudi Arabia, Pakistan, India, North Korea, but also Argentina and Brazil, have been developing short- and medium-range ballistic missiles. China has also come under pressure to adhere to this agreement and has, despite selling missiles to Pakistan and possibly to Iran.

Finally, one of the ways in which developments in the technology and production structures influence security issues at this level is the issue of arms sales. Many security experts are concerned about the extent to which many states, including some rogue states, can easily acquire weapons through commercial and noncommercial channels. The bulk of the arms trade is in the export and purchase of conventional weapons.[18] LDC imports make up two-thirds of all arms sales, with about half of those in the Middle East, where oil export revenues help fund the purchase of arms. The rest of the imports are spread among Latin America, South Asia (India and Pakistan), East Asia (especially China), and Africa. The United States provides half of all arms exports, while Russia and France account for two-thirds of the rest. Spending for arms peaked in 1987 at $70 billion. In the 1990s, spending for arms decreased because of a drop-off in Russian arms production, Iraq's inability to purchase arms after its defeat in the Persian Gulf War, and budget difficulties in general. However, they have grown again since 1997—to roughly $800 billion a year.

A number of conditions make it difficult to implement agreements to limit the proliferation of weapons. First, this objective often conflicts with the economic liberal objective of states to market missiles and other technologies that can be used to produce weapons. Some recipient developing nations may resent attempts to limit their ability to acquire such weapons. Similarly, sellers are reluctant to place any kind of sanctions on violators because it is too hard to condition the buyer's behavior via these sales, or for fear that buyers will purchase from other producers.

Supporters of weapons conventions argue that since the late 1960s the majority of second-tier states, acting through the UN, have been engaged in assertive efforts to create new rules and conventions related to conditions surrounding the production, deployment, and sale of conventional weapons and, more recently, WMD and their component parts. These efforts increase awareness about programs and their transparency, thereby enhancing political and security conditions. Supporters also argue that these agreements help generate new norms and promote cooperation that in many ways involve soft power and make states feel secure without spending for or engaging in war.

## NATO and UN Peacekeeping Efforts

An important development on the second level for IOs on the regional security front since the mid-1990s has been regional peacekeeping efforts handled by NATO in some cases and by the United Nations in others. In 1999 Poland, Hungary, and the Czech Republic—three former allies of the Soviet Union in Central and Eastern Europe—formally joined NATO, bringing the number of members to nineteen.[19] In 1994 NATO also enrolled twenty-five small Eastern European and Balkan states in its Partnership for Peace (PfP) program, with the intention of increasing confidence and reinforcing stability throughout Europe. These twenty-seven PfP members routinely held joint exercises to deal with such common regional problems as peacekeeping, arms control, defense economic issues, civil emergencies, scientific and environmental issues, and mine action. Today, NATO has a total of twenty-six members, seven having been in the PfP program.

Despite the criticisms of NATO discussed above, its role in Kosovo (a small semiautonomous region of Serbia) in the late 1990s gave it new life when it became the basis of cooperative security actions among the United States, Great Britain, and some of the other major powers. NATO authorized air strikes on Serbian military targets in October 1998, when Serbian forces refused to withdraw from Kosovo. With reports of "ethnic cleansing" and other atrocities, an estimated 750,000 refugees sought asylum in Macedonia and Albania. After peace talks between Kosovo Albanians and Serbs failed in late March 1999, NATO began bombing Serbian targets in Kosovo, and later targets in Serbia itself, until early June, when Serbia finally agreed to withdraw its troops from Kosovo.

Since the end of the Cold War, many critics have questioned NATO's utility and cost in a changing security atmosphere. Some unilateralists have renewed the attack on NATO, charging that it is simply too expensive in view of the more subdued East–West environment that currently exists. They maintain that the United States should decouple itself from the costs and political burdens associated with defending—and extending nuclear deterrence over—a bigger Europe. Some also question NATO's willingness to act as a coherent unit under military duress and its resolve to protect newer (Eastern European) members in dealing with situations such as the one in the ex-Yugoslavia in the mid-1990s that deteriorated into so much bloodshed.

In the early stages of this conflict, NATO was criticized for not having a clear military strategy and clear political objectives. The preponderance of public opinion seemed to support NATO's bombing strategy in response to alleged atrocities, but allied national leaders were reluctant to send ground forces into Kosovo proper. Clearly, no one nation or small group of nations could manage this and the earlier Balkan conflicts, nor were the United States and Europe willing to let the UN play a role greater than sanctioning the actions and policies of the major powers.

Questions linger about NATO's role as many issues remain to be settled, including who pays for it and how much, its relationship to the European Union's new defense organization and army, and the relationship of the United States to both organizations. Other issues NATO must be able to deal with include nationalism and ethnic and religious rivalry in member states such as Turkey or nations on its eastern borders that are in line to become NATO members. And what strategy should NATO adopt to deal with civil wars and other forms of unconventional warfare that have become more prevalent since the end of the Cold War? It remains to be seen whether NATO can deal adequately with drugs, terrorism, weapons proliferation, and immigration issues, just to name a few other pressing security threats its members face.[20]

As we discuss with regard to the third layer of the security structure, UN peacekeeping efforts involve the periodic use of member-state troops to help settle disputes and resolve conflicts. Early in the Cold War, when the Security Council was deadlocked about when to use force, the UN created peacekeeping forces as a mechanism for dealing with aggression and conflict in situations that would *not* directly involve the superpowers or other permanent members of the Security Council. UN peacekeepers serve largely as a neutral force between warring states, policing cease-fires, enforcing borders, and maintaining order when states request their presence. Most of the forces in some fifty-nine operations over the life of the UN have been made up of specially trained soldiers from "neutral" countries such as Canada, Ireland, and Sweden, but some have also come from developing countries such as India and Pakistan.

Toward the end of the Cold War the UN's role in peace and security began to change markedly in accordance with efforts by the major powers to give it more authority. In the first four years after the end of the Cold War (1989–1993), UN peacekeeping operations were authorized. After the Cold War ended, the first President Bush proposed that in a "New World Order" the UN would play a bigger role managing security issues, and that the United States would no longer be the world's policeman. In 1992, UN Secretary-General Boutros Boutros-Ghali tried to break new ground by suggesting that UN peacekeeping forces should play a more assertive and proactive role in *peacemaking* to deal with nationalistic, ethnic, and religious conflict, poverty, disease, and environmental problems. This meant that to enforce the peace, blue-helmeted UN peacekeeping missions needed to include soldiers from the United States, Great Britain, France, and Russia, and from more developing countries. They would be authorized to defend themselves when fired on. Including big-power troops in the UN peacekeeping operations would help pressure combatants into cooperating with the UN.

The UN secretary-general also recommended that an "on call" force of 100,000 troops and support equipment be made available to be quickly dispatched to world hot spots if needed. More important, Boutros-Ghali wrote that "while respect for the fundamental sovereignty and integrity of the state remains central, it is undeniable that the centuries-old doctrine of absolute and exclusive sovereignty no longer stands, and was in fact never so absolute as it was conceived to be in theory."[21]

However, the UN Security Council failed to establish a significant presence in Somalia and in the Balkans during the conflict in the early and mid-1990s, because the major powers each sided with different national groups involved in the fighting. Two rather small UN peacekeeping contingencies were eventually deployed in the Balkans to protect several war-free zones and airports. Apart from sanctioning NATO's efforts, the UN played only minor roles in conflicts in Rwanda, Kosovo, East Timor, and, most recently in Iraq. It has also played only a minor role in Darfur where once again the major powers are reluctant to label the situation one of genocide.

### Human Rights and the ICC

The connection between security and human rights issues has become stronger in the new global security structure. Many UN members who cherish their right to self-defense have also gradually felt more willing, even compelled, to transfer some authority to the UN to manage a variety of human rights issues dealing with "war crimes" and "crimes against humanity." This movement dates back to the Nazi war crimes trials in Nuremburg, Germany, after World War II. In the 1990s, the UN established two truly international war crimes tribunals to deal with atrocities in the Balkans and Rwanda, and later added a tribunal that focused on atrocities in Sierra Leone, reflecting some amount of agreement about the conduct of nations and even individuals in war. Located in The Hague, the Netherlands, Kenya, and Sierra Leone, these tribunals have lacked both funding and the authority to arrest suspects.

However, a number of indictments for war crimes have been handed down against various soldiers and citizens. Several soldiers, officers, and even Serbian President Slobodan Milosevic have been indicted for crimes against humanity and other war crimes in Kosovo since the beginning of

1999. Milosevic was turned over for trial by the new Serbian government and was on trial for war crimes when he died in 2005.[22] The former prime minister of Rwanda, Jean Kambanda, was sentenced to life in prison for genocide in that country in 1994.

By 2000, 138 nations had signed a treaty to create a permanent **International Criminal Court (ICC)** to hear cases on genocide, war crimes, and crimes against humanity from anywhere in the world after July 1, 2002. The Clinton administration signed the treaty, but the second Bush administration opposed it on the grounds that U.S. officials could be accused of war crimes for any act of war. ICC officials argue that their concern is conduct in war, not involvement per se. Britain, France, and Germany are helping to finance and contributing staff to the new court. Yet the U.S. Republican-controlled Senate refused to ratify the treaty, even though some 100 nations have either ratified or acceded to the treaty at this writing (March 2007). The U.S. Senate went so far as to threaten that U.S. troops would not be allowed to serve in UN peacekeeping forces, and to link late payment of UN dues with whether the UN would exempt the United States from the treaty. In 2003, for a second time, the United States was exempted for one year from ICC provisions, generating much disappointment and tension between itself and its European allies, if not most UN members. This move, however, did not result in a change in U.S. views about the ICC.

Several realist critics point out that the new tribunals lack the authority to compel compliance to international laws and conventions that deal with the conduct of war, given that they have no real power when it comes to punishing nations or groups within them for violating these laws. Establishment of the tribunals, on the other hand, signifies that the issues of conduct during war, and also justice, have moved up on the agenda of states and shifted some authority beyond nation-states to IOs that deal with a relatively new security issue—the rights and treatment of individuals.

In conclusion, at the second layer of the security structure, IOs such as NATO and the UN play an increasingly important role in a number of security issues beyond protecting borders. Even if some of these organizations are still dependent for their authority on the major powers, they have gradually acquired more clout, in reflection of big-power interests but also because of their ability to confront and deal with certain issues. The ICC demonstrates that these organizations also help change the security environment around them by establishing new rules, norms, and expectations that are supported by many different nations.

## THE THIRD LAYER: THE COMING ANARCHY?

What sets apart states on the third tier from the other two are at least four elements. First, most of these states are relatively weak and therefore are not as capable as actors on the other two tiers of dealing with many internal and external threats to their security. In fact, many of them are labeled "failed" states because they exhibit a good deal of domestic violence and conflict and have not been able to develop economically because of persistent poverty, a host of other intractable internal problems related to the leftover remnants of colonialism, and continued big-power involvement in their affairs. The most noted cases of intense regional and ethnic conflicts since the end of the Cold War have occurred in what the press routinely labels "war-torn" countries in South Asia (India and Pakistan in particular), Southeast Asia (especially Indonesia, East Timor, and the Philippines), the Balkans, some of the former Soviet republics after 1989, the Middle East (especially Israel and Palestine, Lebanon, Iran, and Iraq), and large parts of sub-Saharan and southern Africa (especially Sudan, Sierra Leone, and Congo). Finally, one of the clearest trends in third-tier states is their growing dependence on UN peacekeeping forces and NGOs such as the Red Cross and Red Crescent, Amnesty International, and Worldvision to help them solve many of their security problems.

One such problem is the continuing global AIDs crisis, which since 1981 has left 25 million people dead and 40 million more infected. One half of those deaths and two-thirds of those infections have occurred in sub-Saharan Africa, with poverty, ignorance, and lack of political leadership most often cited as its main causes.[23] Globally, only one in five people gets the drugs needed to deal with the disease, with new but expensive medicines coming out all the time.

## Security and Development

The relationship of security to development in poor nations is a hotly debated issue. To Western economic liberal development experts, security problems either prevent or delay economic development by wasting resources. National leaders cannot generate the goods and services that people desperately need until they overcome the low economic growth rates that accompany poverty, a lack of resources, heavy debt to international banks and finance institutions, overpopulation that puts stress on government agencies, poor infrastructure, high incidence of disease, and an array of other economic and environmentally threatening issues that slow development and exacerbate tensions between poor nations and the industrialized nations.

Many security experts focus on the extent to which internal problems are a source of conflict and tension in weak or failed states. Thomas Homer-Dixon and Robert Kaplan, among others, have popularized the idea that, more than anything else, poverty in LDCs is the biggest threat to all nations because of the damaging effect it has on the environment.[24] Many poor states also adopt drastic measures in an attempt to make their economies grow, and in so doing violate human rights by forcing groups of people to migrate to undeveloped parts of the country (for example, the indigenous Indians in Nicaragua and Brazil) or pushing them out of the nation altogether, as happened in East Timor.

States on the bottom of the development ladder often have large slums around their cores. Even nations that are climbing the ladder, with modern cities such as Rio de Janeiro, are havens for urban violence. This can spill over into other states. Many terrorism experts contend that failed states like Afghanistan are hotbeds for both subnational groups and transnational terrorist groups such as al-Qaeda, which look there to find support for their cause. Thomas Friedman, for one, suggests that many potential terrorists can be found among the unemployed and bored young men in many Middle Eastern countries who find consolation in religious-ideological struggles.[25]

For many Western-trained development experts, trade, foreign investment, and the development of new technologies and communication systems are expected to help generate economic growth in developing economies (see Chapter 15) and also reduce tension and conflict. Yet many structuralists (see Chapter 4) argue that the past and present search by developed nations and transnational corporations for oil and other resources along with markets and wealth in developing regions have led to exploitation, poverty, imperialism, and repressive forms of neocolonialism.[26] The effects of economic liberal policies of international finance and trade institutions and the globalization campaign on states in the second and third tiers have on balance had a disastrous effect on their chances for development. The Asian financial crisis that began in the summer of 1997 (see Chapter 8) was part of an effort to reform what had up until then been some rather successful economies in Southeast Asia. The IMF imposed rather stringent fiscal and monetary constraints on, among others, Thailand, Indonesia, South Korea, and the Philippines. One outcome of these measures was large demonstrations and rioting in many cities. In some cases, ethnic and minority groups such as the Chinese, who had done well before the crisis started, became targets of disgruntled people.[27]

As discussed earlier, in an effort to stimulate trade and generate income, many first-tier states and international companies that produce conventional weapons and sophisticated technologies have been eager to sell these systems to some of the poorest developing nations. While the developed states account for roughly 92 percent of total arms exports (the United States alone accounted for over 50 percent of the market in the late 1990s), by the mid-1990s developing nations—especially in the Middle East and East Asia—accounted for nearly 80 percent of all arms imports. These weapons are not the only source of conflict and tension, but in places such as Sierra Leone, Liberia, and parts of the Middle East, they generate grave concern and fear in neighboring states and often result in more intense warfare and higher numbers of both civilian and military deaths.

In almost all third-tier states, poverty or underdevelopment exacerbates tensions between different ethnic and religious communities, resulting in human rights violations and in some cases genocide (efforts to wipe out a whole people or nation). The conflict between the Tutsis and the Hutus in Rwanda; between Shiites, Sunnis, and Kurds in Iraq; also the Kurds in Iran, Turkey, and Syria; and Muslims versus Hindus in India and Pakistan are only a few examples of situations where the UN and some NGOs have made some progress moving beyond the problem of border defense to protecting the basic rights and freedoms of people.

In the late 1980s and early 1990s, under Secretary-General Boutros Boutros-Ghali, the UN increased its operations in third-tier states including Angola, Liberia, Rwanda, Haiti, Tajikistan, Georgia, Bosnia, Croatia (two operations), Macedonia, Iraq/Kuwait, Somalia, and Cambodia, to name only a few of the more well-known efforts at proactive peacemaking. In a few cases (such as Cambodia) these missions were deemed successful; in most, they were not well received. Increasingly, critics questioned the UN's ability to produce peace in a civil war environment.[28] UN operations in Somalia, Bosnia, and Rwanda,[29] in particular, generated criticism that the UN often arrived too late to make a difference in many of these internal conflicts. Furthermore, the cost of operations often exceeded estimates, while member states used the UN to substitute for their more expensive campaigns. Because of the complex conditions and factors that generated these regional conflicts, UN peacekeepers could not easily find political, let alone military, solutions to them, all of which contributed to a diminishment of the UN's reputation.

Since the late 1990s, fifteen peacekeeping missions (seven of them in Africa alone) have been limited to focus on multidimensional problems where military, civilian police, and other civilian personnel can work alongside local governments and groups and NGOs "to provide emergency relief, demobilize former fighters and reintegrate them into society, clear mines, organize and conduct elections and promote sustainable development practices."[30] Authorized to "use all necessary means," most of the peacekeeping forces come from developing countries in South Asia and Africa, while the United States, Japan, and Germany help defray expenses the most.

The UN has also been criticized for its efforts to deal with terrorists, both locally and with the transnational groups that play an increasingly more demonstrative role in the new security structure. Centered in one particular location or scattered throughout the world, organizations using terrorist methods are usually not controlled by any particular state; an example is the provisional IRA in Northern Ireland in the 1970s–1990s. So-called state-sponsored terrorists are often financed or otherwise supported by governments seeking to affect the behavior of another nation. Iran, Iraq, North Korea, Sudan, and Syria, among others, have earned reputations as sponsors of terrorism. Religious terrorists make up one-fourth of all terrorist groups but often find it hard to separate religious from ideological sources of opposition such as the right to self-determination. A mix of religion and politics are behind Hezbollah, Hamas, Islamic Jihad operations in Lebanon and Palestine, and al-Qaeda's transnational operations.[31]

Recently, many states, international organizations, and NGOs have recommitted themselves to dealing with terrorism in a cooperative manner, largely because the weapons that are available to terrorists are so lethal, sophisticated, and easy to acquire. UN bodies have passed a series of resolutions to study and deal with terrorism by denying financial support and safe havens for terrorists, sharing information with others states about terrorists, and encouraging states to become party to terrorism conventions and protocols. The UN's *Counter-Terrorism Committee (CTC)* was created to monitor implementation of these resolutions but has encountered problems related to defining terrorism, sovereignty, and the interests of arms manufacturers and bankers with investments in weapons manufacturing and trade. Not surprisingly, when it comes to inspecting nuclear facilities to prevent the spread of nuclear weapons and their acquisition by terrorists, the IAEA is underfunded and understaffed. Six hundred and fifty inspectors must cover 900 facilities in some ninety-one countries.[32] Still, the UN has been sharply criticized for failure to do more about these sorts of problems. According to many terrorism experts, the industrialized states should cooperate with IOs and recommit themselves to economically develop and modernize the poorer economies via more aid, better terms of trade, and direct investment in these states.[33]

One of the clearest trends in third-tier states is the growing importance of NGOs. The Red Cross and Red Crescent, Amnesty International, Greenpeace, and Worldvision are motivated by a variety of humanitarian, ideological, and practical concerns and are gaining greater influence in the global security structure. A good example of the effect of NGOs on the security structure is the *International Campaign to Ban Land Mines (ICBL)* (see the box, "Landmines," in Chapter 5), which grabbed international headlines in 1997 when Jody Williams, head of ICBL, won the Nobel Peace Prize.[34] This case demonstrates the effect some NGOs have had when it comes to managing one particular issue area, in this case the security of individuals who feel they have been abandoned by nation-states.

Finally, one factor that accounts for the success of some NGOs has been the continuing, and even dramatic, effect of the media, especially visual images, on issues *at all levels* of the security structure. The media clearly generated much interest in landmines and their effect on individual human lives, which helped shape public opinion and lent support to NGOs bent on changing this aspect of global security policy. What motivates people to take an interest in these and other issues is sometimes referred to as the **CNN effect**. When NATO bombs fell in Belgrade in 1999 or when terrorists attacked the Twin Towers and the Pentagon, the world witnessed firsthand their effect on personal lives on CNN, the BBC, and other global news networks. The CNN effect has also put a compelling human face on problems such as AIDS, hunger, and genocide and made them personal issues that raise questions about the ability of states to resolve them.[35]

## CONCLUSION: THE TIMES ARE THEY A CHANG'N?

For many realists, what was especially good about the Cold War bipolar balance of power between the United States and the Soviet Union was its much more defined arrangement, which conditioned and limited the behavior of many states and actors. Since the end of the Cold War, however, the United States as the world's only superpower, and for many of the other major powers at the first level of the global security structure, traditional issues of territorial integrity and balance-of-power politics are still the issues that concern them most every day. Who and how will the security structure be managed—collectively or by one or even by no major powers, remains an important question to the major powers. There is a good deal of evidence, though, to suggest that the unilateralism of the Bush administration has not been very successful in dealing with terrorism.

Beginning with the Vietnam War but more recently demonstrated by 9/11 and the invasion of Iraq, top-layer states now have a hard time insulating themselves from many of the other security issues faced by second- and third-level actors every day. In fact, most of the security problems in all three tiers of the new security structure stem from developments in the other layers. New technologies produce more sophisticated conventional weapons along with nuclear, biological, and chemical weapons, while technological developments and the openness of the global economy have led to the proliferation of these weapons. Many of the major powers also assumed that economic liberal policies would result in democracy and peace in developing nations, yet it is quite clear that political and economic stability is not as institutionalized a norm in developing regions of the world as it is in the developed world.

The new global security structure is no longer managed by first-level powers alone, and its rules and norms are not as clear as they were in the previous structure. To protect against a growing number of threats to their societies but also to people as individual members of society, many states have intentionally chosen, while others have been compelled to share, security-structure management functions with IOs, NGOs, and to some extent with international businesses.

Another important development is the extent to which the public response and even outcry against genocide and other personal security issues such as landmines, along with support for the new conventions for some of these issues that have been generated in a relatively short period of time, highlights how much "personal security" has chipped away at the sanctity of "national security" and how much private organizations have successfully challenged the authority of public institutions. Related to this development are the powerful images of war and human rights violations that are easily recorded on videotape and communicated via broadcast and satellite around the world, helping to personalize these issues.

Realists tend not to be too surprised at many of these developments. Remember that for them the essence of the international security structure does not change fundamentally. Whether it is the nation-state or another actor, by nature we are all insecure. Economic wealth and development are positive things, but alone cannot guarantee society's security.

## DISCUSSION QUESTIONS

1. Outline and discuss some of the main structural features of the new global security structure.
2. Outline and discuss the way in which economic forces such as technology and different economic policies generate but also help solve security problems at each level.
3. Outline and discuss what you think the global security structure will look like in the next decade in terms of:
   a. Polarity (the number of regional or global hegemons and their allies)
   b. What types of military, economic, or social issues will generate security problems
   c. How much nation-states will manage this structure alongside other political and economic actors
4. Outline the more recent developments of the Iraq war such as those in the box "The Iraq War: Why the Quagmire?" and discuss:
   a. Which factors at the different levels of analysis best explain the quagmire
   b. Whether the administration is as constrained as it often argues it is when it comes to alternatives
5. Outline some of the security threats and issues that international organizations deal with and discuss:
   a. Why IOs do not have more success in these sorts of issues
   b. What it would take for them to be more successful
   c. Choose a security threat of your own and examine the IOs dealing with that issue and why they are or are not successful
6. Choose a security threat situation to examine in the developing nations and examine:
   a. The primary political, economic, and social causes of the conflict
   b. The extent of other state and IO involvement in the issue
   c. Some possible solutions to the problem

## INTERNET LINKS

### Government Organizations

Department of Homeland Security:
www.dhs.gov/dhspublic

U.S. Senate Committee on Foreign Relations:
foreign.senate.gov

CIA:
www.cia.gov

Western European Union:
www.weu.int

NATO:
www.nato.int

UN Security Council:
www.un.org/Overview/Organs/sc.html

Interpol:
www.interpol.int

### Security Think Tanks and/or Information Clearinghouses

Carnegie Endowment for International Peace:
www.ceip.org

Center for Strategic and International Studies:
   www.csis.org
Foreign Policy Association:
   www.fpa.org
Council on Foreign Relations:
   www.cfr.org
U.S. Institute for Peace:
   www.usip.org
Landmine Home Page:
   www.vvaf.org/htdocs/landmine/freeworld.html

## SUGGESTED READINGS

Michael Barnett. *Eyewitness to Genocide: The United Nations and Rwanda*. Ithaca, NY: Cornell University Press, 2000.
Edgar Bottome. *The Balance of Terror: Nuclear Weapons and the Illusion of Security 1945–1985*. Boston: Beacon Press, 1986.
Amy Chua. *World on Fire: How Exporting Free Market Democracy Breeds Ethnic Hatred and Global Instability*. New York: Anchor Books, 2003.
Robert Jervis. *American Foreign Policy in a New Era*. New York: Routledge, 2005.
Chalmers Johnson. *Blowback: The Costs and Consequences of American Empire*. New York: Henry Holt, 2000.
Walter Laqueur. *The New Terrorism: Fanaticism and the Arms of Mass Destruction*. New York: Oxford University Press, 1999.
Michael Mann. *Incoherent Empire*. London: Verso, 2003.
Brigette Nacos. *Terrorism and Counterterrorism: Understanding Threats and Responses in the Post-9/11 World*. New York: Pearson Longman, 2006.
Joseph Nye. *The Paradox of American Power: Why the World's Only Superpower Can't Go It Alone*. New York: Oxford University Press, 2002.
Clyde Prestowitz. *Rogue Nation: American Unilateralism and the Failure of Good Intentions*. New York: Basic Books, 2003.

## KEY TERMS

Cold War
bipolar balance of power
international organizations (IOs)
nongovernmental organizations
   (NGOs)
unilateralism

multilateralism
isolationism
weapons of mass destruction
   (WMD)
rogue states
National Missile Defense (NMD)

Anti-Ballistic Missile (ABM) Treaty
Non Proliferation Treaty (NPT)
International Criminal Court (ICC)
CNN effect

## NOTES

1. Michael J. Carey, "A Vee," in *Chronograph* (Portland, OR: Viviano Design, 2004), p.11.
2. For an overview of the dynamics of the Cold War, see Edgar Bottome, *The Balance of Terror: Nuclear Weapons and the Illusion of Security 1945–1985* (Boston: Beacon Press, 1986).
3. See John Mearsheimer, *The Tragedy of Great Powers* (New York: W. W. Norton, 2001).
4. The classic study outlining the principles of realism is Hans Morgenthau, *Politics Among Nations: The Search for Power and Peace* (New York: Knopf, any edition). For an insightful article that discusses possible security configurations since the end of the Cold War, see Charles W. Kegley, Jr., and Gregory A. Raymond, "Great-Power Relations in the 21st Century: A New Cold War, or Concert-Based Peace?" in Charles W. Kegley, Jr., and Eugene R. Wittkopf, eds. *The Global Agenda*, 5th ed. (Boston: McGraw-Hill, 1998), pp. 170–183. Noted security expert Samuel P. Huntington labels the current security structure a "strange hybrid, a *uni-multipolar* system with one superpower and several major powers." See his "The Lonely Superpower," *Foreign Affairs, 78* (March/April 1999), p. 36.
5. See Kenneth N. Waltz, *Theory of International Politics* (Reading, MA: Addison-Wesley, 1979).
6. See Robert Kagan, "The Benevolent Empire" *Foreign Policy, 111* (Summer 1998), pp. 24–49.
7. Charles Krauthammer, "The Unipolar Moment Revisited," *The National Interest*, Winter 2002/2003, pp. 5–17.
8. Technically, some experts claim that biological and chemical weapons do not as yet have the capability of nuclear weapons to kill massive numbers of people. Others include some conventional weapons as WMD because under the right circumstances they could kill massive numbers of people.

9. There is a plethora of books about empire building with this as one of its themes. Just a few are Clyde Prestowitz, *Rogue Nation: American Unilateralism and the Failure of Good Intentions* (New York: Basic Books, 2003); Chalmers Johnson, *The Sorrows of Empire: Mililtarism, Secrecy, and the End of the Republic* (New York: Henry Holt, 2004); and Michael Mann, *Incoherent Empire* (London: Verso, 2003).

10. A good overview of this theme is in Robert Gilpin, *War and Change in World Politics* (Princeton, NJ: Princeton University Press, 1981).

11. See Joseph Nye, *The Paradox of American Power: Why the World's Only Superpower Can't Go It Alone* (New York: Oxford University Press, 2002).

12. See Eliot Cohen, "A Revolution in Warfare," *Foreign Affairs, 75* (March/April 1996), pp. 37–54; and Douglas Jehl, "Digital Links Are Giving Old Weapons New Power," *The New York Times*, September 7, 2003.

13. See, for example, William Hartung and Michelle Ciarocca, "The Military-Industrial-Think Tank Complex," *Multinational Monitor,* January/February 2003.

14. For a more detailed discussion, see Thomas L. Friedman, *The Lexus and the Olive Tree* (New York: Farrar, Straus & Giroux, 2000).

15. See Chalmers Johnson, *Blowback: The Costs and Consequences of American Empire* (New York: Henry Holt, 2000).

16. See Immanuel Wallerstein, "The Incredible Shrinking Eagle: The End of Pax Americana," *Foreign Policy, 131* (July/August 2002), pp. 60–68; and Johnson, *Blowback,* ibid.

17. William Eckhardt, cited in Joshua Goldstein, *International Relations,* 5th ed. (New York: Longman, 2003), p. 211.

18. See "The Arms Trade Is Big Business," *Global Issues,* at Globalissues.org/Geopolitics/arms trade/bigbusiness. asp#ArmsSalesTrends1997-2004.

19. See the NATO website at NATO.int/home.htm.

20. This issue is discussed at some length in Moisés Naím, "The Five Wars of Globalization," *Foreign Policy, 134,* (January/February 2003), pp. 29–39.

21. See Boutros Boutros-Ghali, "Empowering the United Nations," *Foreign Affairs, 71* (Winter 1992/1993), pp. 98–99.

22. See "At the Hague, It's a Leader on Trial, Not a People," *World in Review, 27* (February 2003), p. 3.

23. See Terry Leonard, "25 Years on, AIDs Still Ravages," *The Seattle Times,* June 4, 2006.

24. See, for example, Thomas Homer-Dixon, "On the Threshold: Environmental Changes as the Cause of Acute Conflict," *International Security, 16* (Fall 1991), pp. 76–116; and Robert Kaplan, *The Coming Anarchy: Shattering the Dreams of the Post Cold War* (New York: Vintage, 2001).

25. Thomas Friedman, "The Global Economy and U.S. Foreign Policy," public address at the University of Puget Sound, Tacoma, WA, September 17, 2002.

26. A classic study of the subject is Richard J. Barnet and Ronald E. Muller, *Global Reach: The Power of the Multinational Corporations* (New York: Touchstone, 1974). See also William Greider, *One World, Ready or Not: The Manic Logic of Global Capitalism* (New York: Simon & Schuster, 1997).

27. This is one of the themes of Amy Chua, *World on Fire: How Exporting Free Market Democracy Breeds Ethnic Hatred and Global Instability* (New York: Anchor Books, 2003).

28. See David Rieff, "The Illusions of Peacekeeping," *World Policy Journal, 11* (Fall 1994), pp. 1–18.

29. An excellent read on the UN's role in Rwanda is Michael Barnett, *Eyewitness to Genocide: The United Nations and Rwanda* (Ithaca, NY: Cornell University Press, 2000).

30. See "Peacekeeping: An Evolving Technique," at www.un.org/Overview/Organs/sc.html.

31. For a more detailed overview of terrorism in general, see Brigette Nacos, *Terrorism and Counterterrorism: Understanding Threats and Responses in the Post-9/11 World* (New York: Pearson Longman, 2006); and Bruce Hoffman, *Inside Terrorism* (New York: Columbia University Press, 2006).

32. Charles Ferguson, "Tackling the Risks of Nuclear Terrorism," *The Seattle Times,* April 26, 2006.

33. See, for example, "Terrorism: The Price We Pay for Poverty," *New Statesman, 132* (February 3, 2003), p. 20.

34. For an excellent discussion of the International Campaign to Ban Landmines, see Richard Price, "Reversing the Gun Sights: Transnational Civil Society Targets Land Mines," *International Organization, 52* (Summer 1998), pp. 613–644.

35. See, for example, Norman Solomon, "Mass Media: Aiding and Abbetting Militarism," in Carl Boggs, ed., *The Masters of War* (New York: Routledge, 2003).

# 10

# *Knowledge and Technology: The Basis of Wealth and Power*

## *By Ross Singleton*

## OVERVIEW

Throughout history, but particularly in today's world, wealth and power flow from access to and control of knowledge and technology. In this chapter we examine the creation and diffusion of knowledge and technology. Who controls this process and how?

We begin by defining terms. What is technology? What is the nature of technological innovation? We then consider the notion of dynamic comparative advantage—the idea that countries can *create* comparative advantage given sufficient access to knowledge and technology.

The role of intellectual property rights, which control access to knowledge and the diffusion of technology, will be considered from the liberal, mercantilist, and structuralist perspectives. Do these rights further the development of the world market, thereby enhancing the benefits of specialization and trade? Do these rights provide a basis for national advantage in a struggle for wealth and power among nations? Or do these rights limit the transfer of technology to developing countries, thereby deepening their dependency?

The efforts of the United States to control the flow of technology beyond its borders using trade laws and the General Agreement on Tariffs and Trade (GATT, now the World Trade Organization) processes are examined in detail. These efforts include enhancing the international protection of intellectual property rights (patents, trademarks, and copyrights).

Efforts to harmonize the treatment of intellectual property rights across national boundaries and conflicts among developed countries regarding this process will also be considered. Finally, we will analyze the important process of the transfer of technology from developed to developing countries.

*The power of machinery, combined with the perfection of transport facilities in modern times, affords to the manufacturing State an immense superiority over the mere agricultural State. . . . in a manufacturing State there is not a path which leads more rapidly to wealth and position than that of invention and discovery.*[1]

Friedrich List

*Economic change and technological development, like wars or sporting tournaments, are usually not beneficial to all. Progress, welcomed by optimistic voices from the Enlightenment to our present age, benefits those groups or nations that are able to take advantage of the newer methods and science, just as it damages others that are less prepared technologically, culturally, and politically to respond to change.*[2]

Paul Kennedy

Students of international political economy (IPE) today find themselves in the midst of a technological-information revolution that will have political, economic, and social effects, many believe, even more profound than the Industrial Revolution of the nineteenth century. Scientists and engineers have made it possible for us to do things that were not just impossible a few years ago; they were absolutely unimaginable. Science fiction barely keeps ahead of science fact.

The Industrial Revolution had enormous effects on the international political economy because it altered global patterns of wealth and power. This makes the current revolution in science and technology an even more important factor in IPE because, compared to the Industrial Revolution, the changes in science and technology today are broader—affecting more aspects of life, faster, and more globally. What happens to IPE in the future depends increasingly on how the world's states and markets accommodate scientific and technical changes today.

The common notion that "knowledge is power" has therefore taken on profound significance. Individuals, business firms, and nations that control access to knowledge in the form of scientific understanding and technological innovation can often enjoy a clear competitive advantage in the world market, allowing them to dominate political and economic processes.

Three important trends have become apparent over the last twenty years.

1. First, knowledge and technology have become increasingly important as determinants of wealth and power. Economic success and political influence increasingly require technological prowess more than just natural resources.
2. Second, the pace of technological change has quickened. Computers and machines have long physical lifetimes but very short economic lives, given the speed with which more powerful and useful replacements are produced.
3. Finally, knowledge and technology are increasingly dispersed. The computer and communications revolutions make it possible for complex data and ideas to move instantaneously from desk to desk within a business and from country to country around the world.

These three trends mean essentially that knowledge is wealth and it is power—for those who have access to it and can control it. Those individuals, firms, and nations that are unable to acquire advanced technology, or that cannot innovate at a competitive rate, will necessarily fall behind. In his book, *The Work of Nations,* Robert Reich imagines a world in which knowledge and technology create an international class system.[3] Persons and nations are "haves" or "have-nots" based on how they "plug in" to the "global web" of the future. One needn't go so far as Reich in order to understand the importance of knowledge and technology in the future.

## THE INTERNATIONAL KNOWLEDGE STRUCTURE

The **international knowledge structure** is the set of relationships that govern access to knowledge and technology around the world. It is a web of rules, practices, institutions, and bargains that determines who owns and can make use of knowledge and technology, where, how, and on what terms. This structure is rapidly growing and changing, which adds an exciting dynamic element to its nature.

The knowledge structure establishes a set of linkages between and among states and markets in just the same general way as the production, finance, and security structures that have been discussed in this part of the textbook. To an important extent, a nation's position in the international political economy is determined by where it falls in the overlapping web that these four structures create.

What makes the international knowledge structure especially important today is the extent to which it interacts with the other IPE structures and thus conditions all IPE relationships. Indeed, it would be hard to overstate the importance of knowledge and technology today. The role of knowledge and technology in the security structure was noted in Chapter 9. To an important extent, the IPE of the Cold War was driven by technology. The strategy of nuclear deterrence was chosen by the United States in the early postwar years in part because technology made nuclear weapons appear to be a less costly strategy than conventional weapons. The high costs of the arms race, which was also a technology race, contributed to the pressures that brought the Cold War to an end in the 1980s. It seems likely that knowledge and technology will continue to influence the security structure in the years to come.

Knowledge and technology have had huge effects on the international financial structures discussed in Chapters 7 and 8. Advances in computer and communications technology have resulted in a global financial system that makes national borders and regulations almost irrelevant. As technology continues to advance, it will no doubt influence the financial structure in new ways. Today, for example, financial markets increasingly trade complex instruments called *derivatives* (because their value is derived from movements of other financial items, such as interest rates and exchange rates). Derivatives can be so complex that supercomputers, such as those used to track missiles, must be used merely to calculate their value. Technological change has made markets in these financial instruments possible; further advances are sure to shape financial relationships in future years.

The effects of knowledge and technology on international trade and the production structure (see Chapter 6) is especially significant and will therefore be the focus of most of the rest of this chapter. The **production structure** is the set of relationships that determine what is produced, where, how, for whom, and on what terms. Each and every aspect of the production function is now affected in important ways by technology and technological change. Advances in science and technology mean that new goods and services are being produced, in new and unexpected places, in ways different from the past, and distributed in new ways to new patterns of consumers. The knowledge structure and the production structure are now so intertwined that it is almost impossible to separate them in practice as we do here for analytical purposes.

Consider some of the consequences of rapid technological change in the production structure. Individuals who have the educational background and ability to understand and use sophisticated technologies—those whom Robert Reich has christened the "symbolic analysts"—are in great demand wherever they are located.[4] Motorola, Digital Equipment, and other U.S. corporations have recently located software development subsidiaries in India to take advantage of the plethora of software engineers that country's universities produce.

Because of their global reach and their control of knowledge and technology, business firms in some respects now rival states for command of scarce resources and for control of wealth and power. Firms in today's competitive world market find themselves on an innovation treadmill. Success requires the constant development of new product and process technologies. The ability to protect technological innovations from immediate imitation is therefore critical. Without patent, trademark, and copyright protection, firms would find it difficult to recoup investment in new technologies.[5] Firms that are able to develop and control technology can produce and market their products and services throughout the world. Revolutions in data processing, transportation, and communications have made global reach a reality. Firms have become paramount actors in the international political economy arena.

Nations also struggle to become or remain competitive in the new world economy. Countries as diverse as El Salvador, China, Hungary, Russia, and the United States share the common desire to grow and prosper by competing in the world market. Power in international relations now depends in large measure on a nation's ability to generate technological innovation and wealth.[6] The name of the economic and political game for governmental leaders and the managers of firms is winning and maintaining a large market share of high-value-added goods and services.[7] Clearly, winning or even holding their own in this game will require nations to develop or have access to the newest and best technology.

## THE NATURE AND EFFECTS OF TECHNOLOGICAL INNOVATION

**Technology** is the knowledge of how to combine resources to produce goods and services. Technological innovation comes in two varieties—product and process innovation. **Product innovation** is the development of new or better products. Product innovation can create entirely new markets and bring enormous benefits to consumers. The personal computer, ATM (cash) machines, cell phones, and a whole range of pharmaceutical products come readily to mind as recent examples of product innovation. **Process innovation** is the development of more efficient, lower-cost production techniques. The robotics revolution led by Japanese producers and managerial innovations (also by Japanese producers) are perhaps the most dramatic recent examples of process innovation.

Technological innovation is largely the product of investment in research and development by individual firms. However, governments can clearly also play an important role in the process. Governments recognize that technological growth has historically been a key determinant of economic growth. For example, "advances in knowledge" accounted for an estimated 68 percent of the increase in labor productivity and 28 percent of the growth in U.S. income between 1929 and 1982.[8] Governments also recognize the significance of technological innovation in the creation of comparative advantage. Therefore, governments have attempted to encourage technological growth in a variety of ways. Governments often subsidize basic science research at universities or research institutes. They sometimes subsidize research and development by firms or encourage the formation of research consortia among firms. And governments provide protection for intellectual property in the form of patents, trademarks, and copyrights.

Rapid technological change has many important effects in the world around us. Three that are worth special mention here are the product life cycle, which illustrates how technological change leads to globalization of production, the nature of high-tech (knowledge) industries and of competition within these industries, and the ability of a nation to *create* comparative advantage through strategic investment in knowledge and technology.

### The Product Life Cycle

The **product life cycle** was described in the 1970s by political economist Raymond Vernon (see Chapter 17 for further discussion of this topic). Vernon observed that some products the United States once produced and even exported were eventually produced abroad and became imports. This life cycle (from export to import) is in part based on the interaction of product and process innovation. The United States, with its individualistic, liberal IPE perspective, has for years been especially strong in product innovation. U.S. firms invent new products, develop them for the home market, and eventually export some of their production to other countries with similar needs.

Other nations, however, such as Japan, have shown greater success in process innovation. They find better ways to make existing products, often improving the basic goods in the process. As process innovation is applied, production is shifted abroad from U.S. factories. The new producer may be an especially innovative firm in Japan, or it could be a low-cost producer in a newly industrialized country (NIC) or a less developed country (LDC), especially if innovation has standardized the product and simplified its construction. The United States then imports at low cost the item it once exported.

One of the most famous examples of the product life cycle is the videocassette recorder (VCR). VCR technology was invented by a U.S. firm to provide recording facilities for television stations. European and Japanese firms took this product, designed for a limited market, and used process innovation skills to create the mass-market electronic device we know today. A similar process unfolded with DVD technology. Today the vast majority of DVD players are produced in China. Chinese manufacturers pay patent fees to U.S., European, and Japanese firms that hold the patent rights to DVD technology.

Once upon a time, it was probably enough to be successful in product innovation—new products could be produced, supplying profits and jobs for years and years. Today, however, with the rapid pace of technological change and the speed with which new ideas are diffused around the globe, process innovation has become perhaps the more important technological advantage.

## Schumpeterian Industries

High-tech (knowledge) industries have been termed **Schumpeterian industries**—after Joseph Schumpeter (1883–1950).[9] Schumpeter, an academic economist, who lived and worked primarily in the United States, gained renown for his ideas about technological innovation. Schumpeter believed that only firms with some degree of monopoly power would likely have the *incentive* (a large payback resulting from a long imitation lag) and the *ability* (in the form of monopoly profits) to invest in risky, expensive, and long-term research and development projects. Consequently, many key industries were likely to be monopolistically structured. However, over time, technologically audacious newcomers would displace once-dominant firms. "Gales of creative destruction" would destroy established monopolies and create new dominant firms. For Schumpeter, the kind of competition that mattered was not price competition among many firms producing nearly identical products but rather, "competition which commands a decisive cost or quality advantage and which strikes not at the margins of the profits and the outputs of existing firms but at their foundations and their very lives."[10]

Because of economies of large scale (including network economies), competition in many industries today is not for market share but for the market itself—competition becomes a "winner take all" or at least a "winner take most" proposition. For example, a single computer operating system now dominates the market (but will eventually be displaced by systems developed by rival entrepreneurs motivated by the high profit potential in this industry). This reality has obvious political economic implications, particularly from a mercantilist perspective, in which the location of that dominant firm is of paramount concern. In order to foster the development of national champions that dominate Schumpeterian industries, mercantilist-minded policymakers will put in place industrial policies that marshall the resources and power of the state to this end. President Jacques Chirac of France announced in April 2006 that the French and German governments would invest $750 million in several high-tech projects including Quaero ("I search" in Latin), an Internet search engine intended to compete with Google.[11] Even liberal-minded policymakers will recognize the importance of creating conditions within their countries that will promote the development of entrepreneurs capable of competing in Schumpeterian industries—conditions described in Michael Porter's best-seller, *The Competitive Advantage of Nations*.[12] The ability to acquire, create, and control technology has become central to international competition in the twenty-first century and has provided many developing countries with a new avenue into the world economy.

## Creating Comparative Advantage

The post–World War II Japanese experience and the more recent experience of the Asian "Tigers"—Hong Kong, South Korea, Taiwan, and Singapore—demonstrate the ability of nations to create comparative advantage in the production of **high-value-added goods**—products that generate substantial income flows for the firms and workers that produce them. Unwilling to accept their "natural" role in the world economy as producers of unskilled labor-intensive goods, these nations have, through partnerships between government and business, developed their technology base sufficiently to become producers and exporters of high-technology goods and services. These countries have all invested in the educational infrastructure necessary to support high-tech production. They have also acquired technology from foreign sources and have developed their own capability to create new process and, to a lesser extent, product innovation. Firms in these countries now compete head to head for world market share in high-value-added goods with U.S. and European firms.[13]

The transfer of technology from developed-country firms played a key role in the success of Japan and the Asian Tigers. Many developing countries are eager to follow this same path to development. Whether this model will succeed in Latin America, Africa, and Eastern Europe remains to be seen, but the transfer of technology will be a dominant issue in international political economy for some time to come. Clearly, firms in the developed countries own and control most of the technology that is so vital to international competition and the future of less developed countries. As a technological leader among developed nations, the United States has, understandably, taken the lead in defining the terms and conditions under which the transfer of technology will occur.

## THE IPE OF TECHNOLOGY AND INTELLECTUAL PROPERTY RIGHTS

If we stop for a moment and look back over the last few pages, an interesting dilemma appears. Knowledge and technology have become increasingly important in the international political economy in many ways. With the rapid pace of technological change, new products and new processes are especially valuable to individuals, business firms, and nations because of the wealth and power that derive from them. To gain the maximum advantage, however, one needs to control access to new knowledge and technology—to keep others from using the products of research and innovation without paying in full for the right. At the same time, however, the computer and communications revolutions are making it easier and more efficient to move information around, making the control of access harder and harder. In short, precisely when the control of technology is of greatest value, it has become much more difficult and cumbersome.

It is unsurprising, given all the potential wealth and power that are at stake here, that the control of information has become a very important issue in international political economy. The vocabulary of this part of IPE is somewhat technical, but the issues are important enough to make learning the new terms worthwhile. What is at stake, after all, is the technological future.

The key concept in the IPE of the knowledge structure today is **intellectual property rights (IPR)**. **Property rights** (generic term) are the rights to control the use of something, such as a house, or a car, or a book. It is possible to make markets in these things because their property rights are well defined and well enforced. That is, it is possible to determine who owns a house and who doesn't, and a person who uses a house that belongs to someone else without first concluding a bargain will be punished. We can feel secure in our ownership of everyday goods because this system of property rights works relatively well.

Intellectual property rights are the rights to control use of intellectual property—an invention or a creative work such as a novel or poem. Patents, copyrights, trademarks, and other systems of intellectual property rights are the mechanisms normally used to control access to new ideas. **Patents** are issued by a government and confer the exclusive right to make, use, or sell an invention for a period generally ranging from fifteen to twenty years (counted from date of filing). **Trademarks** are signs or symbols (including logos and names) registered by a manufacturer or merchant to identify goods and services. Protection is usually granted for ten years and is renewable. **Copyrights** protect the *expression* of an idea, not the idea itself. Copyright protection is provided for original works of authorship, including literary, artistic, and scientific works. Copyrights are also issued for software and databases in a growing number of countries. Copyrights prohibit unauthorized reproduction, distribution (including rental), sale, and adaptation of original work. Protection lasts for the life of the author, plus fifty years.

Intellectual property rights are most effective when the state defines and enforces them strictly. This creates a problem, however, because there are many different states, which may have many different rules regarding intellectual property rights. The inventor of a new process may be unable to stop a firm in another country from using his or her ideas if that country has less strict rules regarding patents, for example.

Intellectual property rights have thus become a critical issue both for those nations that own patents, copyrights, and so on, and for those nations that seek to use them to produce goods and earn incomes. One goal of the Uruguay round of the GATT negotiations (see Chapter 6) was to reach some agreement regarding intellectual property rights. The Trade Related Aspects of Intellectual Property Rights (TRIPS) agreement, which requires some minimum level of IPR enforcement for all members of the World Trade Organization (WTO) resulted from those negotiations. During the Doha round of trade negotiations, discussions regarding intellectual property continued. Key controversies include the access of poor countries to patented medicines and the desire of poor countries to include protection of biological resources and traditional knowledge.

## THREE PERSPECTIVES ON INTELLECTUAL PROPERTY RIGHTS

In the liberal view, property rights are fundamental to the functioning of a market system. Property rights create a powerful incentive to use resources efficiently. Property rights establish a direct link between effort and reward.

A privately owned farm, for example, is operated efficiently because the owner of the farm is legally entitled to all of the income that farm generates. The farmer strives to maximize the productivity of his land in order to maximize his own income. Now imagine a farm where property rights are not private and individually held, as in the farm above, but are collective or socially owned. On this farm there is no direct link between effort and reward. A farm worker who is very diligent and hard-working does not have the right to any more of the farm's output than another worker who shirks and is a *free rider*.

Clearly, there is less incentive for individuals to work hard under a system of collective property rights than under a system of private property rights. The private farm will be much more productive and efficient. Similarly, individuals and firms have a powerful incentive to innovate and invent when they are legally entitled to the income associated with that process. Intellectual property rights—patents, trademarks, and copyrights—create the link between effort and reward.

Invention and innovation (commercialization of an invention) involve the creation of knowledge. And knowledge, by its nature, is *nonrival*—that is, the knowledge one firm uses can also be used by other firms. (By contrast, the ton of steel that one firm uses cannot also be used by other firms. Steel is a *rival* good.) The knowledge that one firm develops in the form of product and process innovation can also be used by other firms. Consequently, unless firms can legally deny the use of newly created knowledge to other firms, rapid imitation will eliminate the profits from innovation necessary to recoup the original investment in research and development (R&D) that created the new knowledge. The efforts necessary to develop new technology would not be rewarded. Without intellectual property rights, insufficient resources would be devoted to R&D, and far fewer new and lower-cost products would be available to consumers.

From the liberal perspective, then, international protection of IPRs is essential if the world market economy is to enjoy the extraordinary benefits of rapid technological growth. International IPR conventions should be strengthened to guarantee the effective protection of technological innovation. The winners in this process will ultimately be consumers the world over, who will enjoy the availability of an astonishing variety of new products—from genetically engineered foodstuffs and medicines to educational and entertainment multimedia software. The only real losers will be those firms and individuals that will no longer profit from copying the creative, innovative efforts of others.

Mercantilists see the process of technological innovation in a much different light. Knowledge is a source of national wealth and power. Recall that, according to this school of thought, as discussed in Chapter 2, production, not consumption, is critical to the national interest. The ability to produce is the true measure of a nation's wealth and power. Technology, then—the knowledge of production—largely determines a nation's place in the world. Nations must develop and then closely guard their own technology, and technology controlled by other nations must be acquired. Technological dependence must be avoided.

The protection of IPRs for *domestic* firms is clearly appropriate in order to foster domestic technological innovation. Equal protection for technology owned by foreign firms, however, is unlikely to be in the national interest. Rather, government policy in this area should facilitate the acquisition of foreign-owned technology at the lowest cost possible. Increased international protection of IPRs is, then, not necessarily in the national interest. Protecting intellectual property of national firms in domestic and foreign markets is appropriate, but reciprocal protection for foreign firms in domestic markets should be resisted—recall that trade is, according to this view, a zero-sum game. One nation's gains in international market share come at the expense of some other nation's losses. The battle for markets will be won by the nation that can best exploit its technological advantages.

An additional insight provided by mercantilist thought considers imbalances in stages of national development. List and Hamilton, early mercantilists, argued that free trade benefits the most developed manufacturing nation(s) at the expense of less developed nations. Similarly, international conventions that protect intellectual property rights will benefit those nations with the most advanced technological capabilities at the expense of less technologically developed nations. In this regard, mercantilist and structuralist thought is similar.

Structuralists contend that IPRs increase the dependency of the periphery on the core (see Chapter 4). IPRs are tools of dependency. The developed nations use IPRs to maintain their technological advantage over Third World countries. Patents, trademarks, and copyrights are used to monopolize Third World markets, to extract and repatriate excessive profits from Third World countries, and to deepen and legitimate dependency.

From the point of view of dependency theorists, then, the winners from more stringent international enforcement of IPRs are clearly the developed countries and their firms. The losers are the people of Third World countries, who pay monopoly prices for many goods and services and who receive the benefits of technological transfer only on terms dictated by firms of the developed world. We will consider further the North–South aspects of IPRs in a later section of this chapter. First, it is appropriate to review the efforts of the United States to protect IPRs and then consider the degree of cooperation and conflict among developed countries regarding IPRs. See the box for a review of efforts to harmonize intellectual property protection of new knowledge related to biotechnology— knowledge of critical importance to the health and well-being of virtually everyone.

---

### INTERNATIONAL HARMONIZATION OF BIOTECHNOLOGY PROTECTION

In April 1988, a white mouse made history by becoming the first animal ever to be patented in the United States. The "Harvard mouse," as it is known, was developed by Philip Leder of Harvard University and his colleague Timothy Stewart, now at Genentech, Inc., using genetic engineering. They "invented" the extraordinary mouse by inserting a human cancer gene into mouse egg cells. The mouse satisfied the requirements for protection as an invention under U.S. patent law because of its novelty and its usefulness in cancer research.

Microbes, plants, and, lately, other animals have also received patent protection from the U.S. Patent Office. In response to pressure from the United States and from its own biotechnology industry, the European Union is currently considering proposals to create comparable biotechnology protection. Developing countries are also being pressured by the United States to extend IPR protection to biotechnology via bilateral negotiations and multilateral negotiations under the GATT agreement.[a] Because it may be impossible to get unanimous agreement on rules governing biotechnology protection, a more realistic goal is "harmonization." Harmonization in this context means that national laws can be different to reflect national priorities and viewpoints, but should be based on a common basic framework. Such laws would be in "harmony" with one another as compared to the present general dissonance.

Many countries offer very limited protection, if any, for biotechnology because the agricultural, pharmaceutical, and medical products and processes that result from biotechnological innovation are considered fundamental rights and needs of the people. About thirty-five countries offer no patent protection for food products, among them Brazil, China, Colombia, Denmark, Egypt, Finland, New Zealand, and Venezuela. Animal and plant varieties are excluded from patent protection in forty-five countries, including the EU member countries, Brazil, Canada, Colombia, Cuba, Ghana, Israel, Kenya, Malaysia, Nigeria, South Africa, Switzerland, and Thailand.[b] Many countries offer only process patents for pharmaceutical products, intending to create a powerful incentive for rival firms to develop different processes to produce the new and unpatented product. The reduced level of patent protection for biotechnology in many countries also reflects to some degree their greater reliance on government-sponsored, university biotechnology research, which does not require patent incentives.

The efforts of the U.S. government to increase the international protection of biotechnology arises from political pressure brought to bear by U.S. biotechnology firms that want to protect their competitive advantage in international markets. Governments in many other developed and developing countries are also beginning to feel the same pressures from their own budding biotechnology industries. However, there are many thorny issues associated with the protection of biotechnology that must be resolved before international harmonization can occur.

The primary controversy has been about whether living organisms are patentable. In the 1980s, the U.S. Supreme Court handed down several key decisions (in 1980 for an engineered microorganism, in 1985 for a maize plant and its components, and in 1988 for the aforementioned mouse) that set new precedents in this regard. The issue, according to the Court in the 1980 case, is not living versus nonliving but rather products of nature, living or not, versus human interventions.[c] Presumably, products of nature are not patentable, whereas products of human intervention may be. Although this legal issue appears to be resolved in the United States, many other controversial legal, technical, economic, and ethical issues remain.

If the international harmonization of biotechnology protection can be accomplished, great benefits might be forthcoming. A farmer anywhere in the world might buy a seed that has a U.S. company's disease resistance gene, an Egyptian company's drought resistance gene, and a Brazilian company's nutritional enhancement gene. Of course, the consequences of harmonization will likely be very different when viewed from a mercantilist or structuralist perspective.

*References*
[a] John A. Barton, "Patenting Life," *Scientific American, 264* (March 1991), p. 41.
[b] Paolo Bifani, "The International Stakes of Biotechnology and the Patent War: Considerations after the Uruguay Round," *Agriculture and Human Values, 10* (March 1993), pp. 47–59.
[c] Ibid., p. 50.

## U.S. EFFORTS TO PROTECT INTELLECTUAL PROPERTY RIGHTS

*The increased significance of technological diffusion and the increasingly arbitrary nature of comparative advantage as well as military security concerns are causing the United States to make the protection of its high technology industries an important priority. In addition to its own effort to slow down the outflow of industrial know-how, the U.S. has placed the international protection of intellectual property rights on the agenda of trade negotiations.*[14]

Robert Gilpin

U.S. firms have played a major role in elevating the protection of IPRs to the status of a major U.S. foreign policy issue. The Intellectual Property Committee, an *ad hoc* coalition of twelve major U.S. corporations representing the entire spectrum of industries, was established in 1986 with the goal of increasing the international protection of IPRs.[15]

The Intellectual Property Committee contends that there is a direct link between the protection of IPRs and U.S. international competitiveness. Without adequate protection of IPRs, U.S. firms would find it difficult to profit from product and process innovation. Foreign firms that infringe on IPRs have lower development costs, because they are merely copying original technological innovations. Consequently, these infringing firms can underprice the U.S. firms that incurred the original development costs. A new generation of semiconductors can cost $100 million or more to develop, and yet these same chips can be copied for less than $1 million. A popular software package that sells for $500 in the United States has been copied and sold for as little as $7.50 in other countries.[16] Piracy of U.S. entertainment media, including tape recordings and videotapes, has become epidemic in many parts of the world. The U.S. International Trade Commission has estimated that the overall loss to U.S. business from foreign infringement of IPRs in 1986 alone was between

$43 billion and $61 billion.[17] Responding to pressure from U.S. businesses, the U.S. government has attempted to increase the international protection of IPRs through unilateral, bilateral, and multi-lateral means.

Under U.S. trade law, the government can impose unilateral retaliatory trade sanctions against countries that fail to protect IPRs adequately. Special Section 301 of the 1988 Omnibus Trade and Competition Act, generally called **Super 301**, requires the United States Trade Representative (USTR) to retaliate against countries that "deny adequate and effective protection of intellectual property rights" or "deny fair and equitable market access to United States persons that rely upon intellectual property protection."[18] Super 301 requires the USTR to create a list every year of priority foreign coun-tries that have failed to protect IPRs adequately. After investigating the acts, practices, and policies of the offending country, the USTR may institute immediate trade sanctions, including the elimination of trade concessions and the imposition of import restrictions or duties. Or the USTR may choose to negotiate a bilateral agreement with the offending country to eliminate the cause of the action.

In 1989, the USTR identified no priority countries. Instead, a "watch list" was created, in-cluding twenty-five countries "whose practices deserve special attention." Eight countries—Brazil, India, the Republic of Korea (South Korea), Mexico, the People's Republic of China, Saudi Arabia, Taiwan, and Thailand—were placed on a "priority watch list" as countries that formally met the criteria of priority foreign countries, but that were making satisfactory progress in bilateral and multilateral negotiations to address shortcomings in the protection of IPRs.[19]

The 2006 Special 301 Report includes an assessment of the adequacy and effectiveness of in-tellectual property protections in eighty-seven countries. Of those countries, forty-seven were placed on the priority watch list, the watch list, or were singled-out for special monitoring. Concerns regarding IPR protections in China and Russia received special attention in the report, as did heightened concern for "rampant" counterfeiting and piracy. In remarks about the report, USTR Rob Portman said, "Safeguarding our creations and innovations is a key element of our trade com-petitiveness, but it is also in the interest of our trading partners to strengthen their IPR regimes." To see the USTR's rationale with respect to the suspect practices of each listed nation, see the Internet address given in note 20.

Section 337 of the Tariff Act of 1930 as amended by the Omnibus Trade and Competitiveness Act is designed to eliminate the importation into the United States of goods that infringe on IPRs. Under the amended Section 337, the complainant must merely demonstrate that an infringement of an IPR occurred, rather than substantial injury, as the original law required. The International Trade Commission can issue an exclusion order or a cease-and-desist order in response to complaints.[21]

The unilateral trade sanctions made possible by U.S. trade laws have been criticized by its trading partners as violations of GATT provisions. In 1989, a GATT panel concluded that Section 337 was inconsistent with GATT nondiscrimination provisions in that it "accords to imported prod-ucts challenged as infringing United States patents treatment less favourable than the treatment ac-corded to products of United States origin similarly challenged".[22] U.S. efforts to negotiate bilateral agreements to improve the protection of IPRs are also controversial.

With the stick of unilateral trade sanctions firmly in hand, the United States has been quite successful in negotiating bilateral agreements with many countries to improve the protection of IPRs. Negotiated changes in the treatment of IPRs have occurred in several countries, including Singapore, Malaysia, Thailand, the People's Republic of China, Taiwan, and South Korea. Bilateral disputes and negotiations continue between the United States and Brazil, India, Thailand, Japan, and the European Union.[23]

In 1991, while negotiating the North American Free Trade Agreement (NAFTA) with the United States, Mexico enacted comprehensive patent and copyright laws. The final NAFTA agree-ment "locks in" these Mexican reforms. As a result of the NAFTA negotiations, Mexico will now give copyright protection to software programs, satellite transmissions, and audio and video recordings. Better patent protection and protection of trade secrets and proprietary information in

Mexico and Canada are also major accomplishments of NAFTA.[24] On June 6, 2003, the USTR announced the signing of a free-trade pact with Chile—a pact that included unprecedented protections for U.S. intellectual property.[25] On August 5, 2004, the USTR signed CAFTA-DR, a trade pact incorporating strong IPR protections with the Dominican Republic, Costa Rica, El Salvador, Guatemala, Honduras, and Nicaragua.[26]

In 1986, the twelve U.S. firms that constitute the Intellectual Property Committee urged U.S. trade negotiators to place the protection of IPRs on the agenda for the Uruguay round of the GATT negotiations. The multilateral approach (described below) to the international enforcement of IPRs had, in the opinion of these U.S. firms, largely failed to provide adequate protection. More effective enforcement of IPRs, it was hoped, could be negotiated by linking the protection of IPRs to multilateral trade negotiation.

Multilateral agreements to protect IPRs include the Berne Convention, concluded in 1886 to define copyright protection, and the Paris Convention signed by the United States in 1887, which ostensibly provides protection for patents, trademarks, and industrial designs. In 1967, the World Intellectual Property Organization (WIPO), a UN agency, was created to monitor adherence to the Berne and Paris conventions. WIPO has been roundly criticized by firms in developed nations because its defined minimum standards of protection are inadequate and because it lacks effective enforcement and dispute-resolution mechanisms. Developed-country firms are pessimistic that WIPO will ever provide meaningful IPR protection because the policy and agenda of this organization are controlled by developing countries that, arguably, generally oppose IPR reforms.[27] We will explore developing-country attitudes toward IPR protection later in this chapter.

The GATT agreement concluded in 1993 did include, at the insistence of the United States and other developed nations, provisions regarding **trade-related intellectual property rights (TRIPs)**. TRIPs require countries to provide a defined minimum level of intellectual property protection.[28] TRIPs have become part of the fundamental structure of the WTO, which succeeded the GATT as the forum for multilateral trade negotiations. Special concessions were also negotiated for developing countries that need time to create or amend IPR laws in order to conform to the minimum standards that will be required as a condition for their continued participation in the WTO's multilateral trade negotiations.[29]

The developed nations of the world have, not surprisingly, supported the efforts spearheaded by the United States to enhance the international protection of IPRs, including the inclusion of TRIPs. Current discussions are underway within WIPO to enhance protection of performers, producers of sound recordings, and broadcasters. A new treaty to enhance trademark protection, called the Madrid Protocol, has been completed.[30] There has also been a concerted effort among these nations to reach agreements to "harmonize" IPR laws across national boundaries.

One example of the need for harmonization involves the issue of "first to file" versus "first to invent" with respect to the awarding of patent rights. The United States finds itself at odds with most other countries by granting patents on a "first to invent" basis. In Japan, Sankyo, a Japanese firm, was granted a patent on a new anticholesterol drug, whereas in the United States, Merck, a U.S. firm, was granted a patent on the same drug. Merck was able to verify prior invention even though Sankyo had been the first to file in both countries.[31] This kind of conflict will be avoided when developed countries succeed in "harmonizing" IPR laws.

In December 1996, a diplomatic conference convened by WIPO produced two new treaties that harmonize the protection of IPRs on the Internet and thereby promote international electronic commerce. The WIPO Copyright Treaty supplements the Berne Convention by clarifying that the digital transmission and distribution of literary or artistic works will receive copyright protection. This treaty also reconciles differences between the United States and European copyright protection systems. A second treaty, the WIPO Treaty on Performances and Phonograms, represents the first global efforts to protect sound recordings from exploitation by means other than simple physical reproduction.[32]

Although developed countries are cooperating in important ways, conflict between and among them over IPRs still exists to a significant degree. The basis of competitive advantage among developed countries in high-technology industries is knowledge.[33] Patterns of trade reflect the success that national firms have had in developing new products and processes. And the success of national firms depends in large measure on the national organization of competition and policy toward knowledge creation.[34] Disputes among developed nations involving the treatment of intellectual property are to be expected, given the centrality of knowledge and technology to competitive advantage. See the box for a discussion of the changing nature of the conflict between the United States and China over patent, trademark, and copyright protections.

---

### CHINA: COMING OF AGE?

China's rapid rise as an industrial power has transformed the international production and knowledge structures.[a] China has become the world's center for counterfeiting and piracy. The routine infringement of patents, trademarks, and copyrights by Chinese firms continues to be a major source of conflict between China and the United States. The most recent report by the U.S. Trade Representative (USTR) regarding Special 301 provisions highlights growing U.S. concerns over continuing piracy and counterfeiting in China. See Note b for the USTR's full report. By placing China on its "priority watch list," the United States is attempting to bring unilateral pressure on China to increase its enforcement of IPRs. The United States is also engaged in ongoing bilateral negotiations with China regarding IPRs and is working through WTO processes to bring multilateral pressure on China in this regard.[c]

Though China has recently tightened its enforcement of intellectual property laws, the effect on piracy and counterfeiting has been negligible. Chinese officials have been unwilling to this point to seriously crackdown on plants that produce illegal copies because those plants are often major employers in towns and cities across China. Although some Chinese courts have awarded monetary damages to foreign firms that have been victimized by piracy, the U.S. Federal Bureau of Investigation calculates the losses to U.S. firms from illegal copying in China at $250 billion annually.[d] Chinese piracy that limits the flow of U.S. exports to China also exacerbates the U.S. trade deficit with China.

Inadequate protection of trademarks is probably the most important violation of intellectual property.[e] A trademark is a sign or symbol (including logos and names) registered by a manufacturer or merchant to identify goods and services. Protection is usually granted for ten years and is renewable as long as the trademark is effectively used.

In a broader sense, trademarks are essential for the efficient functioning of the market. Trademarks convey information and protect investments in the production of quality goods and services. Trademarks help consumers select products of high quality and reliability. Consumers come to rely on trademarked products. Consequently, search costs are reduced. Trademarks also motivate producers to maintain quality standards. Producers who do so know they will be rewarded with repeat purchases by consumers who have come to trust their trademark. Without adequate trademark protection, then, consumers will necessarily spend more hours attempting to discern quality differences, and producers will be discouraged from investing in the production of quality goods and services.

Copyrights protect the expression of an idea, not the idea itself. Copyright protection is provided to authors of original works, including literary, artistic, and scientific works. Software and databases are also afforded copyright protection in a growing number of developed and developing countries. Copyrights generally allow the owner to prevent the unauthorized reproduction, distribution (including rental), sale, and adaptation of original work. Protection lasts for the life of the author plus fifty years.[f] Copyrights, like patents, are necessary to encourage innovation. Without this protection, rapid reproduction by rivals would diminish the return on investment in the creation of new computer software, computerized databases, literary, artistic, or scientific work.

As China develops its own capacity to produce and export products and services incorporating new technologies, its interest in promoting the protection of IPRs should naturally increase. In April 2006, the Chinese government promulgated a new order requiring all computers sold in China to come with legitimate pre-loaded operating-system software. Shortly thereafter, Lenovo, the Chinese computer maker that recently bought IBM's PC business, announced a deal to purchase $1.2 billion of Microsoft's Windows software. Lenovo's Chairman Yang Yuanqing noted that in order for the growing number of Chinese technology companies to compete around the world, China must implement better protection of intellectual property at home in order to provide the incentive to innovate.[g]

*References*

[a] See "How China Runs the World Economy," *The Economist*, July 30, 2005, for a detailed account of China's growing economic influence.

[b] www.ustr.gov/assets/Document_Library/Reports_Publications/2006/2006_Special_301_Review/asset_upload_file180_9335.pdf.

[c] "U.S. Perfecting WTO Case Against China IPR Violations—Commerce Undersecretary," Forbes.com, July 26, 2006 (www.forbes.com/markets/feeds/afx/2006/07/26/afx2904774.html).

[d] "Handbags at Dawn," *The Economist,* April 21, 2006, www.economist.com/agenda/displaystory.cfm?story_id-E1_GRQQPTG.

[e] Carlos M. Correa, *Intellectual Property Rights and Foreign Direct Investment,* Publication ST/CTC/ERS.A/24 (New York: United Nations, 1993), p. 14.

[f] Ibid., p. 8.

[g] "Chinese PC Giant Takes on Big Role in Piracy Fight," *The Seattle Times,* April 18, 2006, p. C1.

## NORTH–SOUTH CONFLICTS OVER INTELLECTUAL PROPERTY RIGHTS

Many developing nations opposed the TRIP provisions of the WTO. They argued that WIPO was the appropriate forum for discussing the norms and standards of IPRs. And, more fundamentally, they argued that the efforts by the United States and other developed countries to strengthen the international protection of IPRs has focused on the enhancement of the proprietary aspects of IPRs, thereby reinforcing monopoly privileges, while weakening the aspects of IPRs that promote the prompt and widespread diffusion of new technology.[35] For example, the TRIP provisions broaden the scope and duration of patent protection and therefore of monopoly privilege, while enervating working requirements that foster technological diffusion.

The basic premise of developing nations in granting a patent is that the firm that is granted the patent will produce the patented product or use the patented process in the country granting the patent.[36] When the patent is "worked" locally, technological spillovers are generated. Scientists, technicians, and engineers in the patent-granting country become familiar with the technology. And domestic firms may be called on to supply inputs into the production process, thereby upgrading their technological sophistication. As the technology is diffused throughout the domestic economy, it may become the basis for *domestic* technological innovation.

This premise is certainly consistent with the fundamental rationale for patents in any context. Patents represent a trade-off. The innovator is granted an exclusive right to produce the new product or use the new process. In exchange, the new knowledge the innovator has created is disclosed and made public in the patent application process so that others have access to this knowledge and can thereby create additional new knowledge. If patent rights were not available, innovators would attempt to keep new knowledge secret to avoid imitation. Patents and the working of patents facilitate the diffusion and creation of new knowledge.

The Paris Convention states that failure to work a patent is an abuse of patent rights. A compulsory license can be issued to another firm to guarantee local production. Firms from developed countries have argued that imports of the patented product or the product made with the patented process constitute working the patent. Developing countries have long opposed this notion. From their point of view, imports do not generate the same spillover benefits that domestic production would. Imports do not result in the transfer of technology—only local production accomplishes that.[37] Some analysts have gone so far as to oppose the creation of patent systems in developing countries on this basis. The granting of patents by developing countries, they argue, is akin to granting exclusive import rights to certain foreign firms, allowing them to monopolize the local market and eliminate other (especially local) firms.[38] However, against the protests of many developing nations, the United States and other developed nations prevailed. The WTO rules expressly permit imports to constitute the working of a patent.[39]

The South Commission argued forcefully, but ultimately unsuccessfully, that the inclusion of IPRs under the GATT would have "significant adverse effects on the pace of generation, absorption, adaptation and assimilation of technical change in the developing countries."[40] C. Niranjan Rao summarized the sentiment of many critics of the TRIPs provisions of the WTO/GATT agreement as follows:

> By asking for a GATT based agreement on IPRs, the developed countries are seeking to bring in a system which fits into their trade strategies and preserves their technological superiority. These proposals are much tougher and pro-patentee than the Paris Convention. Such an agreement, given the concentration of ownership of patents in large multinational corporations from highly developed countries, will make the third world a free playground for the trade and investment decisions of these MNCs.[41]

An additional area of contention between developed and developing countries concerns copyright protection. The developed countries, led by the United States, have recently been demanding stronger international copyright protection. The mindset of developing countries in this regard can be best understood by considering the historical role of the United States in international copyright protection. Early on, the United States was more a consumer of works produced by foreign authors than a producer for foreign markets. Consequently, the United States refused to sign the Berne Copyright Agreement or even respect foreign copyrights until forced to do so by the growth of its own artistic and literary community. In fact, the United States did not sign the Berne Agreement until 1989. The United States, then, is a "Johnny-come-lately" when it comes to the international enforcement of copyright protection.[42]

Even though most developing countries are also consumers of works by foreign authors and artists more than producers of these works for other countries, they are being pressured by the United States and other developed countries to respect foreign copyrights.

There are no guarantees that developing countries will benefit from strengthening their systems of IPR protection. However, for those countries attempting to follow outward-oriented development strategies, the risk of trade retaliation and the need to attract foreign direct investment provides strong incentives to comply with developed-country demands for stronger IPR protection.[43]

Many development agencies are highly critical of the TRIPs provisions. For example, Great Britain's secretary of state of international development, Clare Short, commissioned a major investigation of the effects of the TRIPs provisions on the development prospects of poor nations. The report of this commission of international experts on development and intellectual property rights, issued in September 2002, is highly critical of efforts to enforce developed-country IP standards in developing countries. They conclude:

> Standards of IP protection that may be suitable for developed countries may produce more costs than benefits when applied in developing countries, which rely in large part on knowledge generated elsewhere to satisfy their basic needs and foster development.[44] . . . Developed countries should pay more attention to reconciling their commercial self-interest with the need to reduce poverty in developing countries, which is in everyone's interest.[45]

The commission urges that developing countries be granted an extended period of transition for implementation of the TRIPs requirements until at least 2016, with possible extensions beyond that date depending on indicators of economic and technological developments in the various countries.[46]

The Doha round of trade negotiations, ostensibly devoted to promoting economic development for the have-nots of the world, bogged down in part over disagreements regarding intellectual property. Many developing countries want the WTO to provide protection for biological resources and traditional knowledge. Brazil, Cuba, Ecuador, India, Peru, Thailand, and Venezuela, among others, want the TRIPs provision revised to require the company seeking a patent or copyright to disclose the origin of biological resources and traditional knowledge and to prove that they have "prior informed consent" from the owners. This provision is designed to ensure that the indigenous people who hold this knowledge receive compensation for these ideas. Industrialized countries counter that patents and copyrights are designed to protect newly created knowledge—not traditional knowledge.[47]

Jeffrey Sachs, director of the Center for International Development at Harvard University, argues that today's world is less divided by ideology than by technology.[48] Many regions, particularly the poorest tropical countries, are technologically excluded regions. The technologies to prevent or cure infections disease, to enhance agricultural productivity and to mitigate environmental degradation are either not developed because of a lack of incentives for research and development or are available abroad but are unaffordable. (Sachs lauds the work of the Gates Foundation in enhancing access to already-available vaccines.)

Sachs points out that the scarcity of capital in poor countries results in high rates of return on new capital investments. Consequently, poor countries should be able to develop domestic savings (and investment) and attract inflows of capital from abroad. Over time, capital accumulation in areas where capital had been scarce results in a "convergence" of rates of return on capital. Unfortunately, according to Sachs, no such equalizing market forces are at work when it comes to technology. The process of technological innovation entails increasing returns to scale (and scope). Consequently, regions that already enjoy advanced technologies are in the best position to develop new innovations.

To promote innovation in technologically excluded areas, Sachs recommends a fundamental change in World Bank policies: a move away from a country-based model entailing conditionality provisions to a broader focus on the creation and dissemination of knowledge for development. The United States, Sachs argues, "the meanest donor of all," needs to become the "technological leader and beacon of hope for much of the world" by dramatically increasing its aid assistance and by exercising restraint regarding the use of intellectual property rights, especially regarding human and plant genetic sequences, chemical compounds in herbal medicines, and basic computer codes.[49] See the box for a discussion of the controversial role played by patent protection in the AIDS crisis in Africa.

---

### PATENT RIGHTS VERSUS PATIENT RIGHTS

In 1998 about one in five adults living in South Africa was infected with HIV/AIDS. Unfortunately, the patent-protected antiretroviral drug "cocktail" that holds the disease in check costs about $15,000 per patient per year in the United States. Consequently, only the richest South Africans can afford the treatment. Government subsidization of the drugs, at these prices, would overwhelm the budget. Generic versions of the drug cocktail produced in India cost only $200. Because India does not issue patents on pharmaceuticals (or on any other product), this allows the development of a competitive generic drug industry. (India will have to offer such patents in the near future, because of the TRIPs provisions.) South Africa, on the other hand, has long had very strong patent laws.

Faced with this tragic public health crisis, South Africa's government voted in 1998 to permit "parallel imports" and "compulsory licensing" of these drugs. Parallel imports are products produced in another country where companies are legally licensed to produce the patented product. Compulsory licenses are issued by a government to local producers in order to create generic alternatives to the patented drug. Compulsory licensing is allowable under the TRIPs provisions if the government first negotiates with the patent holder or, in the case of a national emergency, without consulting the patent holder. During the recent anthrax scare, the U.S. Congress threatened to issue compulsory licenses for the production of Bayer's Cipro—a life-saving patented antibiotic drug that is effective against anthrax. Bayer responded by agreeing to radically reduce prices and expand production.

The U.S.–led pharmaceutical industry responded to South Africa's new law by instigating a lawsuit. Thirty-nine pharmaceutical companies were party to this suit, which attempted to block South Africa's action. Activists around the world, incensed by this legal action, rallied against the lawsuit with the slogan, "Patient Rights over Patent Rights." When the lawsuit finally reached the courtroom in March 2001, the pharmaceutical companies withdrew the suit under mounting public pressure in an effort to avoid a public relations debacle.[a]

Developing countries then successfully pressured the WTO officials at their ministerial meetings in Doha in November 2001 to affirm their right to parallel imports and to issue compulsory licenses. Some countries, however, do not have companies with sufficient technological capacity to produce generics under compulsory licenses. And generics produced in other countries under compulsory licenses must be produced primarily for the domestic market. WTO officials agreed to find a solution to the plight of these least developed countries by the end of 2002. This due date was not met. The United States, pressured by the powerful U.S. pharmaceutical lobby, blocked a compromise resolution intended to permit the importation of generics by these least developed countries. However, after prolonged, intensive negotiations, the United States eventually agreed to accept the resolution, and on August 30, 2003, the WTO announced the terms of the accord. Poor countries would be allowed to import generic versions of patented medicines from countries such as India and Brazil without violating trade laws.[b]

Pharmaceutical companies have also responded to the AIDS crisis in more sophisticated ways. Abbott, Bristol-Myers Squibb, Merck, and Pfizer have pledged $275 million for HIV/AIDS assistance in developing countries, most of it in cash, exceeding the foreign aid contributions of several G7 nations.[c] GlaxoSmithKline, the largest manufacturer of AIDS drugs, lowered the price of its combination pill, Combivir, to poor countries to $1.70 per day. Under continuing criticism suggesting that this price was still excessive, Glaxo announced in April 2003 that it would reduce the price to sixty-three poor countries still further, to 90 cents per day. This price is roughly equivalent to the price of some generic versions of the AIDS drugs. Glaxo sells Combivir in the United States for $18 per day.[d] This further price reduction fulfills Glaxo's pledge to provide drugs at no profit to impoverished nations. As a sad postscript to this story, in 2002, Belgian officials discovered that one-third of the Combivir sold by Glaxo to African countries at the original discounted price was diverted to European markets by profiteers.[e]

*References*

[a] The description of these events in this and the following paragraph was drawn from Amy Kapczynski, "Strict International Patent Laws Hurt Developing Countries," *YaleGlobal*, December 16, 2002, yaleglobal.yale.edu/display.article?id=562.

[b] Elizabeth Becker, "Poor Nations Can Purchase Cheap Drugs Under Accord," *The New York Times*, August 31, 2003, p. 14.

[c] Michael A. Friedman, Henk den Besten, and Amir Attaran, "Out-Licensing: A Practical Approach for Improvement of Access to Medicines in Poor Countries," *The Lancet*, January 25, 2003, pp. 341–344.

[d] Redd Abelson, "Glaxo Will Further Cut Prices of AIDS Drugs to Poor Nations," *The New York Times*, April 28, 2003, p. C2.

[e] S. Boseley and R. Carroll, "Profiteers Resell Africa's Cheap AIDS Drugs," *The Guardian*, October 4, 2002, p.1.

## CONCLUSION

The issues surrounding the development and control of knowledge and technology clearly play a central role in international political economy. Whether viewed from a liberal, mercantilist, or structuralist perspective, knowledge and technology form an increasingly critical basis of wealth and power. In this era of global competition, individuals, firms, and nations understand that knowledge and technology confer competitive advantage. That the protection of intellectual property rights has risen to the status of a major foreign policy concern for the United States and many other countries is not surprising. The knowledge structure, like the production structure, the finance structure, and the security structure, clearly constrains the options and conditions the behavior of individuals, firms, and nations, and therefore affects the wealth and power they enjoy.

Key questions concerning the knowledge structure include: How will the forces of globalization affect the creation, control, and dissemination of knowledge? Will new alternative energy and conservation technologies be developed and deployed in time to avoid environmental crises associated with global warming? Who will develop and control these new technologies? Will stricter enforcement of IPRs enhance or hinder development among the poorest nations of the world? Will piracy and counterfeiting undermine the incentive to innovate in much of the world? Will new weapons technologies make the world a safer place? Or will increasingly widespread access to advanced weapons technology threaten world security? Will the dominance of the United States in science and technology continue, or will it be severely eroded by developments in China and India and other emerging economies? Will competition among nations for new technologies lead to a new era of economic nationalism? The answers to these questions will have profound effects on the lives of present and future generations.

## DISCUSSION QUESTIONS

1. What are intellectual property rights, and why are they important in today's global markets? Briefly compare and contrast the mercantilist, liberal, and structuralist views of IPRs.
2. What is a Schumpeterian industry? Characterize the nature of competition in Schumpeterian industries. What are the implications of Schumpeter's insights regarding the nature of global competition in high-technology industries?
3. Describe the nature of the TRIPs provisions. Provide arguments both for and against stronger IPR protections in poor countries.
4. Provide two examples of piracy and/or counterfeiting. What countries have been identified as major sources of pirated or counterfeited products? How has the United States attempted to influence these countries?
5. Have patents rights helped or hindered the plight of those suffering from AIDS? Explain.
6. Describe any two elements of the U.S. trade law that the United States uses unilaterally to enforce intellectual property rights.

## INTERNET LINKS

WTO Intellectual Property Page:
    www.wto.org/wto/intellec/intellec.htm
World Intellectual Property Organization:
    www.wipo.org
United States Trade Representative:
    www.ustr.gov

## SUGGESTED READINGS

Thomas Friedman. *The World Is Flat*. New York: Farrar, Straus & Giroux, 2005.
"Integrating Intellectual Property Rights and Development Policy," Report of the Commission on Intellectual Property Rights. London, September 2002.
John T. Masterson, Jr. "Intellectual Property Rights: A Post Uruguay Round Overview." Office of the Chief Counsel for International Commerce, U.S. Department of Commerce, April 20, 1998. Available at www.ita.doc.gov/legal/ipr.html (August 26, 1998).
Anne McGuirk. "The Doha Development Agenda," *Finance and Development*, September 2002, pp. 4–8.
Robert Reich. *The Work of Nations*. New York: Knopf, 1991.
W. E. Siebeck, ed. *Strengthening Protection of IP in Developing Countries: A Survey of the Literature*. World Bank Discussion Paper No. 112, Washington, DC: The World Bank, 1990.
Laura D'Andrea Tyson. *Who's Bashing Whom?: Trade Conflict in High-Technology Industries*. Washington, DC: The Institute for International Economics, 1992.

## KEY TERMS

international knowledge structure
production structure
technology
product innovation
process innovation
product life cycle

Schumpeterian industries
high-value-added goods
intellectual property rights (IPR)
property rights
patents
trademarks

copyrights
Super 301
trade-related intellectual property
rights (TRIPs)

## NOTES

1. Friedrich List, *The National System of Political Economy* (New York: August M. Kelley, 1966), pp. 201–202.
2. Paul Kennedy, *Preparing for the Twenty-First Century* (New York: Random House, 1993), p. 15.
3. Robert Reich, *The Work of Nations* (New York: Knopf, 1991).
4. Ibid., pp. 177–180.
5. For more detailed descriptions of these and other intellectual property rights, see Carlo M. Correa, *Intellectual Property Rights and Foreign Direct Investment*, Publication ST/CTC/SER.A/24 (New York: United Nations, 1993), pp. 8–9.
6. Thomas D. Lairson and David Skidmore, *International Political Economy* (Orlando, FL: Harcourt Brace Jovanovich, 1993).
7. Susan Strange, "An Eclectic Approach," in Craig Murphy and Roger Tooze, eds., *The New International Political Economy* (Boulder, CO: Lynne Rienner, 1991).
8. Edward F. Denison, *Trends in American Economic Growth, 1929–1982* (Washington, DC: Brookings, 1985), p. 30.
9. Richard Schmalensee, "Antitrust Issues in Schumpeterian Industries," *American Economic Review Papers and Proceedings*, May 2000, pp. 192–196.
10. Joseph Schumpeter, *Capitalism, Socialism and Democracy*, 3rd ed. (New York: Praeger, 1981), p. 84.
11. "Charlemagne: The Perils of Project Mania," *The Economist*, July 15, 2006, p. 53.
12. Michael Porter, *Competitive Advantage of Nations* (New York: The Free Press, 1990).
13. This is one theme of Lester Thurow's best-selling book, *Head to Head: The Coming Economic Battle Among Japan, Europe, and America* (New York: William Morrow, 1991).
14. Robert Gilpin, *The Political Economy of International Relations* (Princeton, NJ: Princeton University Press, 1987).
15. Carol J. Bilzi, "Toward an Intellectual Property Agreement in the GATT: View from the Private Sector," *Georgia Journal of International and Comparative Law, 19*(2) (1989), p. 343.
16. Ibid., p. 345.
17. Richard A. Morford, "Intellectual Property Protection: A U.S. Priority," *Georgia Journal of International and Comparative Law, 19*(2) (1989), p. 336.
18. Omnibus Trade and Competitiveness Act of 1988, tit. I, subtit. C, pt. 1, §1303, Pub. L. No. 100–418, 102 Stat. 1179–81 (codified at 19 S.S.C. §2242 [1992]).
19. Brent W. Sadler, "International Property Protection Through International Trade," *Houston Journal of International Law, 14*(393) (1992), p. 416.
20. See www.ustr.gov/assets/Document_Library/Reports_Publications/2006/2006_Special_301_Review/asset_upload_file180_9335.pdf.
21. Sadler, "International Property Protection Through International Trade," p. 408.
22. See the following Internet address for the GATT Panel's Report entitled "United States—Section 337 of the Tariff Act of 1930 (BISD 36S/345)": www.wto.org/English/tratop_e/dispu_e/gt47ds_e.htm.
23. See the International Trade Administration's (U.S. Department of Commerce) trade agreement database for succinct summaries of the many bilateral and multilateral trade agreements the United States has negotiated over the last two decades, www.mac.doc.gov/tcc/treaty.htm.
24. Gary Clyde Hufbauer and Jeffrey J. Schott, *NAFTA: An Assessment* (Washington, DC: Institute for International Economics, 1993), p. 85.
25. See www.ustr.gov/releases/2003/06/03-37.htm.
26. See www.ustr.gov/Trade_Agreements/Bilateral/CAFTA/Briefing_Book/Section_Index.html.
27. Critics of the TRIPs proposal argued that the effort to impose new international uniform standards at higher levels for IPR protection contradicts the GATT's traditional commitment to the principle of national treatment. By

requiring reciprocity, the TRIPs proposal would violate existing GATT provisions that refer to the nonreciprocity of trade relationships between developed and developing countries. See Paolo Bifani, "The International Stakes of Biotechnology and the Patent War: Considerations After the Uruguay Round," *Agriculture and Human Values, 10* (March 1993), p. 56.

28. See the WTO's discussion of TRIPs at www.wto.org/english/thewto_e/whatis_e/tif_e/agrm7_e.htm.
29. Bilzi, "Toward an Intellectual Property Agreement in the GATT," p. 346.
30. See www.wipo.int/treaties/en/registration/madrid_protocol for the text of this treaty.
31. Dennis W. Carlton and Jeffrey M. Perloff, *Modern Industrial Organization,* 2nd ed. (New York: HarperCollins, 1994), p. 675.
32. *Chair's Bulletin,* American Bar Association Section of Intellectual Property Law, Vol. 1, No. 5, January 1997.
33. Laura D'Andrea Tyson, *Who's Bashing Whom?: Trade Conflict in High-Technology Industries* (Washington, DC: Institute for International Economics, 1992), p. 18.
34. See Michael E. Porter, *The Competitive Advantage of Nations* (New York: The Free Press, 1990), for a discussion of how differences in national organization of competition and policies toward knowledge creation affect competitive position in international trade and investment.
35. Bifani, "The International Stakes of Biotechnology and the Patent War," pp. 55–56.
36. C. Niranjan Rao, "Trade Related Aspects of Intellectual Property Rights; Question of Patents," *Economic and Political Weekly, 13* (May 1989), p. 1053.
37. Ibid., p. 1055.
38. See R. Vayrynen, "International Patenting as a Means of Technological Dominance," *International Social Science Journal, 30* (1978), pp. 315–337.
39. John T. Masterson, Jr., "Intellectual Property Rights: A Post-Uruguay Round Overview," Office of the Chief Counsel for International Commerce, U.S. Department of Commerce, April 20, 1998, available at: www.ita.doc.gov/legal/ipr.html (August 26, 1998).
40. Rao, "Trade Related Aspects of Intellectual Property Rights," p. 1056.
41. Ibid.
42. Lewis Shapiro, "The Role of Intellectual Property Protection and International Competitiveness," *Antitrust Law Journal, 58* (1989), p. 577.
43. C. A. Primo Braza, "The Developing Country Case for and Against IPP," in W. E. Siebeck, ed., *Strengthening Protection of IP in Developing Countries: A Survey of the Literature,* World Bank Discussion Paper No. 112 (Washington, DC: The World Bank, 1990).
44. "Integrating Intellectual Property Rights and Development Policy," Report of the Commission on Intellectual Property Rights (Executive Summary) (London, September 2002) p. 2.
45. Ibid., p. 3.
46. Ibid., p. 21.
47. W. Bradnee Chambers and Alphonse Kambu, "Stop Exploitation of Indigenous Knowledge," available at: http://update.unu.edu/archive/issue30_19.htm.
48. Jeffrey Sachs, "A New Map of the World," *The Economist,* June 22, 2000, pp. 81–83.
49. Ibid.

# PART III

## State–Market Tensions Today

❀❀❀❀❀❀❀

Part III presents four case studies of international political economy (IPE) analysis: the European Union (EU), Japan, nations in transition from communism to capitalism, and the Middle-Eastern and North African states. Although these studies are informative about four important sets of nations, they are intended to have broader application. Each study poses a particular question or explores a particular theme that applies around the globe. Students are challenged to master the specific applications and at the same time appreciate the more general themes that derive from them.

Chapter 11 examines regionalism, one of the most important political and economic trends in contemporary IPE, with specific emphasis on the EU. Our survey of the history of the EU lets us examine the relationship between economics and politics in a complicated world. In the end we ask the question: What is regionalism? The answer may surprise you.

Readers will learn a lot about Japan and the global IPE in Chapter 12. This chapter's discussion of the capitalist developmental state, however, raises broader questions about the roles of states and markets in national development strategies. Japan's rapid growth and recent prolonged stagnation raise many questions about that country's political and economic institutions. Should Japan change? Can it? Will it? In trying to answer these questions we examine the issue of institutional stability in a period of rapid change and also Japan's changing political role in Asia.

Chapter 13's analysis of states and markets in transition focuses specifically on Russia, Central Europe, and China—three regions that are moving from systems of classical socialism to more market-oriented and, in the case of Russia and Central Europe, more democratic systems of political economy. How do such fundamental changes in states and markets interact? Do political reforms encourage economic change or hinder it? How do economic reforms affect political decisions? These questions are critical in Russia, Central Europe, and China but are equally so in a long list of other nations around the world.

Finally, in Chapter 14 we explore many of the patterns of political, social, and economic relations in several Middle Eastern and North African states. These states exhibit some common institutions, religions, and cultural traits. At the same time, these states differ from one another in ways that are usually not communicated in press and television news accounts. Thus, this chapter goes a long way toward dispelling some of the many myths about this region.

# The European Union and the IPE of Regionalism

## OVERVIEW[1]

This chapter examines the political economy of regionalism, which is one of the most powerful dynamics of this era in world history. Increasingly, nations are driven to unite their economies for greater efficiency and growth. Integrated markets do not necessarily mean integrated states, however. The fundamental tension between economics and politics is revealed in high relief in the process of integration. This chapter examines the international political economy (IPE) of regionalism by looking at its most important example, the integration of Europe.

The **European Union (EU)** formally began life in 1957 as the **European Economic Community (EEC)**, often called the **Common Market**. Its predecessor was the **European Coal and Steel Community (ECSC)**, which had been established in 1952. In 1967 the EEC and the ECSC merged (together with EURATOM, the European Atomic Energy Community) to form the **European Community (EC)**, often just called "the Community." In 1993 the name was changed again, to *European Union*, in order to emphasize that integration was spreading from the economic sphere to the political and social spheres of European life.

The EU is the product of fifty years of political and economic activity aimed at creating a prosperous and cooperative environment for Europe. It is, on one hand, arguably the largest and richest unified market in the world—a postwar success story. It is, on the other hand, arguably the weakest of political alliances imaginable, ever on the verge of collapse. The fundamental question that the EU seeks to answer today is whether economics is more important than politics. That is, do the dynamic individualistic motives of the market matter more than the unifying social values of the nation or state? Significantly, this is still an unanswered question at the start of the twenty-first century.

**R**egionalism is a distinctive feature of IPE in the twenty-first century, and that this is so comes, perhaps, as a bit of a surprise. We are living in an era when IPE seems to be pulled in two directions at once. On one hand, security concerns make the state as important now as it has ever been from a political standpoint, which means that it is very important indeed. The need to look after "homeland security" in all its forms and the ability to decisively pursue national interest are strong forces drawing our attention toward the importance of the nation-state.

At the same time, however, the forces of economic globalization are blurring the distinction between home and abroad. From an economic standpoint, the world is defined by markets, not state boundaries, and many of those markets—especially financial markets—are global, or nearly so. The force of economic globalization pulls IPE away from the nation-state, toward global markets.

This chapter seeks to understand twenty-first-century regionalism through an examination of the most important case of regionalism in the twentieth century, the EU. The EU can be thought of as the world's largest science experiment, testing the hypothesis that nations with a long history of conflict can solve the puzzle of peace and prosperity more successfully as a group than as separate autonomous nation-states. If and how the EU has solved the puzzle—and the potential lessons the experiment provides for other nation-states—are the questions this chapter explores.

## THE ECONOMICS AND POLITICS OF REGIONALISM

**Regionalism** in IPE refers to the process by which groups of nation-states, usually in the same geographic region, agree to cooperate and share responsibility to achieve common goals. Regional groups are "clubs" formed by nation-states to accomplish objectives that require coordinated or collective action. The goals may be very narrow and specific, such as developing an ecotourism industry along the Mekong River—a regional initiative sponsored by the Asian Development Bank. Or the goals may be very broad and somewhat ambiguous, such as the goals of the European Union.

Regionalism takes as many forms in IPE as there are possible shared goals among nation-states. There are regional environmental agreements, regional economic development programs, regional scientific and health regimes, and regional security arrangements. Regionalism is a logical response to problems that are too big for one state to solve by itself or problems caused by the actions of one country having effects in another, as with issues such as flood control, fisheries management, or pollution abatement. There is even a movement, sometimes dubbed the *new regionalism*, that looks for cooperative solutions to common problems at a more grass-roots level than the nation-state, through regional initiatives by local governments, nongovernmental organizations, and activist individuals in different countries.

Regionalism is not a new thing; it has always existed in the international political economy. What is new is the strength of regionalism as an organizing force, due, to a great extent, to the increasing importance of economic integration and the rise of regional **trade blocs** such as the European Union, the North American Free Trade Area (NAFTA), and similar groups around the world (see Chapter 6). Economic integration—making one large market out of several smaller ones—is the shared goal of these regional groups.

### Economic Integration

**Economic integration** is the process by which a group of nation-states agrees to ignore their national boundaries for at least some economic purposes, creating a larger and more tightly connected system of markets. Nations can commit to several different degrees of economic integration. A **free-trade area (FTA)** involves a relatively small degree of integration. Nations in an FTA agree to eliminate tariff barriers to trade for goods and services they produce themselves. Each nation, however, retains the right to set its own tariff barriers with respect to products from outside the FTA. The fact that some goods are tariff-free in FTA transactions, but other goods are still subject to differential trade barriers, complicates intra-FTA trade and therefore limits the effective degree of integration.

The **North American Free Trade Agreement (NAFTA)** is an example of an FTA. When NAFTA is fully implemented, goods from the United States, Canada, and Mexico will be traded freely within the NAFTA borders. Goods from other countries, however, will be subject to the differential tariff barriers of these three countries. If, for example, Canada has a lower tariff on French wine than does the United States, then any shipments of French wine that happen to flow through

Canada to the United States will be subject to an additional tariff upon entering the United States. To be sure that proper tariffs are collected, all goods will be accompanied by some sort of certificate of origin.

The next level of economic integration is called a **customs union** ("customs" is another word for tariff). In a customs union, a group of nations agree both to tariff-free trade within their collective borders and to a common set of external trade barriers. If NAFTA were to evolve into a customs union, for example, the United States, Canada, and Mexico would need to agree to a unified set of tariff barriers that would apply to products from other countries. The Treaty of Rome, which created the original European Economic Community, was based on the idea of a customs union.

The movement to a customs union is an important step in terms of economic integration because of the greater degree of political cooperation that is required. The nations involved give up some degree of sovereignty or national political autonomy, because they can no longer set their own trade barriers without consulting their economic partners. What they gain is a far greater degree of economic integration. Products flow more easily within a customs union, with no need for border inspections or customs fees because of the unified trade structure. In practice, of course, the elimination of trade barriers is not as complete as theory suggests, because member nations retain the right to impose some nontariff trade barriers, such as health and safety standards, for example. Still, a customs union is an effective means of increasing market size and stimulating growth and efficiency.

An **economic union** is the final stage of economic and political integration. In an economic union, nontariff barriers are eliminated along with tariff barriers, creating an even more fully integrated market. The degree of integration in an economic union goes further than this, however. Member nations in an economic union agree to four "freedoms" of movement: of goods, services, people, and capital. These four freedoms represent significant limitations on national sovereignty, but they can also have significant effects on economic activity. The EU, when its current plans are fully implemented, will become an economic union.

The free movement of goods is more complicated than it may seem, for it goes beyond the elimination of tariff barriers. Free movement of goods requires a variety of governmental health, safety, and other standards and regulations to be "harmonized" so that, at least in theory, a product that can be sold anywhere in the economic union can, in fact, be sold everywhere in it (aside from obvious technical barriers that can prevent sale, such as differences in electrical systems among nations, or the differences between left-hand-drive and right-hand-drive automobiles).

Free movement of services is also more complex than it may seem. The service sector of international trade includes many industries, such as banking and finance, that are traditionally subject to heavy regulation that varies considerably among nations. Free movement of people requires a unified immigration policy, because a person who is free to enter and work in one member of the economic union can, in theory, live and work anywhere in the union. Finally, free movement of capital means that individual nations give up their ability to regulate investment inflows and outflows. Many nations have traditionally imposed capital controls to encourage domestic investment, promote financial stability, or reduce foreign exchange variations. These controls are not eliminated in an economic union, but they must be "harmonized" so that national regulations are similar enough that they do not become a barrier to economic activity.

The most successful economic union in the world is the United States, if we consider it as an alliance of the separate states. Consider how freely goods, services, people, and capital move from one state to another. This gigantic single market has been remarkably flexible and dynamic, making it a model for other developed nations. Consider also, however, the degree of political complexity that is inherent in such a system as that of the United States. The elaborate system of economic and political federalism that characterizes the U.S. political economy is much different from relations that typically exist among and between autonomous nation-states. Economic integration is thus as significant politically as it is economically.

## Effects of Economic Integration

Economic integration is appealing because it is a way for nations to achieve greater *efficiency* in their use of scarce resources and higher rates of economic *growth.* In the lingo of economics, integration produces **static efficiency** gains and **dynamic efficiency** gains.

Economic integration promotes greater static efficiency for two main reasons. First, with completely free trade within the area, each member nation is able to specialize in producing the goods and services in which it is most efficient. Protective barriers that preserve inefficient industries and promote redundancy are eliminated. Economists believe that these gains from efficient specialization are significant. Second, the creation of a larger, integrated market promotes efficiency in certain industries in which large-scale production or long production runs are possible. These gains from *economies of scale* make products cheaper and more competitive.

These static gains are important, but they tend to reach their potential fairly soon after economic integration occurs. The more important economic benefit of integration occurs in the long run, as dynamic efficiency promotes economic growth. The logic is that a larger and more competitive market is likely to be more innovative. As internal trade barriers are removed, previously protected firms are forced to compete with one another. Firms become more efficient and "nimble."

If economic integration is successful, economic growth rates tend to increase, which raises living standards. Even a small rise in growth can be significant. If, for example, economic integration causes the long-term rate of economic growth to rise by one or two percentage points, the long-run effect will be that at the end of a single generation, the living standard could be double what would have occurred without integration! Thus, economic integration need produce only a little extra growth to have a considerable long-term effect on people's lives.

## The Trade Diversion Effect

Regional trade blocs became important and also controversial in the 1990s because of the **trade diversion effect** of a free-trade area, customs union, or economic union. By dropping internal trade barriers, members create more trade between and among member nations. Some of that trade is indeed "created" by the new opportunities that are provided by barrier-free trade, with no losses elsewhere. However, some of the trade is in fact diverted from other countries. For example, when Mexico joined NAFTA, its exports to the United States increased (trade creation), but exports from some other developing countries to the United States fell (trade diversion).

Being a member of NAFTA gave Mexico an edge over producers of some products in non-NAFTA countries, which were still subject to U.S. tariffs. Although entrepeneur and Presidential candidate Ross Perot famously predicted a "giant sucking sound" as U.S. jobs moved to Mexico as a result of NAFTA, the bigger effect was on other developing countries, not the United States. High-wage U.S. jobs did not move to lower-wage Mexico in significant numbers, but some low-wage jobs in Thailand, for example, moved to Mexico, where wages were also low and products could enter the United States tariff-free.

Trade diversion is a twofold problem. It is first an economic problem, because it means that economic integration is not as efficient as it may first seem. Trade blocs may be economically beneficial for the nations that form them, but they create inefficiency and economic loss for other countries that suffer the trade-diversion loss. And because the losers are by definition nonmembers of the trade bloc, they lack any way to seek compensation for their losses.

This economic problem creates a political problem. As more and more countries enter into regional economic groups, nonmembers find themselves locked out and vulnerable. They have a strong motivation to gain membership in an existing bloc to get the trade-creation effects, or to form their own bloc with other countries in the same boat. The threat of trade diversion and of being left out means that as trade blocs expand in size and number, it becomes more and more important for countries to gain membership. This economic imperative, however, raises the political concerns that we turn to next.

## Political Regionalism

Much of the discussion of regionalism tends to focus on the economic logic of a larger market, but many political economists believe that the political arguments for regionalism are even stronger. The economic focus is due in part to the fact that the promise of economic benefits is often used to justify regional political arrangements that might be difficult to achieve on the basis of their political benefits alone. This was certainly true in Europe, as we will see later in this chapter, and was true in North America as well. Although most of the discussion of Mexico's entry into NAFTA concentrated on its economic effects, politics was probably a more important factor in this decision. Free trade between the United States and Mexico was perhaps the economic means to achieve political goals: to consolidate democracy in Mexico and to improve U.S.–Mexico relations.

The fundamental political problem posed by regionalism is the loss of sovereignty that occurs when nations form regional blocs. These pluralistic organizations necessarily place constraints on the actions of sovereign nation-states. At some point, each member state risks being forced to ignore national interests—political, economic, social, or cultural—as a consequence of maintaining its regional obligations. This tension between national interest and international obligations is fundamental to multinational institutions and poses a severe dilemma for states, which tend to value security and autonomy above all else.

One aspect of this political problem is the so-called *democracy deficit* of political regionalism. To the extent that important political decisions are reached at a regional rather than national level, they are made outside the normal mechanisms of representative democracy. Regionalism weakens the link between voters and political decisions, it is argued.

Given the importance of these political issues, the extent of regional integration we observe in the world today should perhaps surprise us more than it does. Why would a nation sacrifice its sovereignty and risk the democracy deficit to join a regional organization, especially an economic one? Several arguments present themselves.

As global markets have become more important, the nation-state has been caught in a dilemma. States are too limited (by their territorial definition) to manage many economic forces and to regulate transnational corporations, but political deadlock prevents the emergence of effective global regulatory institutions (this is discussed in Chapter 17 with respect to transnational corporations and foreign direct investment, and in Chapter 6 in relation to the World Trade Organization). Regionalism presents an effective middle ground. Regional blocs, such as the EU and NAFTA, have the potential to provide a foundation of political governance to match expanding market forces.

Although deadlock seems to characterize many global negotiations, agreement on at least some regional issues may be easier to reach. Regional groups have a limited number of members, so it is sometimes easier for them to reach agreement than it is for much larger global organizations such as the World Trade Organization. And exceptions to various rules or laws are more common in regional negotiations than they are in global regimes. In short, regional political discussions have greater flexibility and, although this is not a guarantee that compromise can be reached on every issue, this does perhaps speed agreement on those points about which compromise is possible.

Another school of thought holds that regionalism is appealing because it represents a way of controlling domestic special-interest groups. A nation might choose to join a regional group in part to break the hold of special interests on domestic policies. A democracy deficit may be tolerable, this argument goes, if domestic special interests have already hijacked the democratic process. Suppose, for example, that the interests of heavy industry prevent adoption of environmental laws in a country. If the responsibility for environmental regulation is shifted to the regional level, it is possible that environmental voices may have more influence, especially if other countries in the regional bloc have strong "green" party organizations.

There is also the view that regionalism can actually be sovereignty-enhancing and that some individual nations may gain political power, especially in relations with other nations, by being members of a powerful alliance. This is the argument that Belgium, for example, is a more potent political presence as a leading nation of the EU than if it were simply a small but autonomous European nation making its own way in international politics. It is argued that smaller countries are far more powerful as members of a larger group than they would be as separate, unaffiliated individual nations.

## EUROPE AND THE MIRROR OF REGIONALISM

Regionalism is a complicated balancing act. There are many advantages in terms of politics and economics, but many potential problems as well. What explains regionalism's rapid advance as a force in IPE? One explanation is that, because regionalism is so complex, it can be attractive to many different political and economic actors for many different reasons. A coalition in favor of regionalism can be formed even if the members of that coalition support it for very different reasons. Some may seek the benefits of larger markets, for example, whereas others wish to control domestic interest groups or advance a regional security agenda. Because regionalism is relatively vague, it can be seen to serve many purposes at once. Politics, it is said, makes strange bedfellows—a remark that may apply especially to regional politics.

If we look at the origins of regionalism in post–World War II Europe, for example, we find that the image of a united Europe was like the Mirror of Erised in J. K. Rowling's book, *Harry Potter and the Sorcerer's Stone*. In the book, the Mirror of Erised does not reflect reality; rather, it shows each viewer's greatest hopes and fears. Reading the history books, this seems to be what people saw when they looked at European regionalism in the early postwar period:

- The United States supported postwar European regionalism because it saw in the mirror of regionalism the image of a strong anticommunist ally. The United States actually initiated the first postwar European regional project when it enacted the Marshall Plan in 1948. The **Marshall Plan** provided European nations with nearly $12 billion in aid (equivalent to more than $90 billion today) for the reconstruction of infrastructure and industries on the condition that these nations cooperate in their use. The motivation for the Marshall Plan was both humanitarian and strategic: Suffering masses in Europe needed to be helped both for their own sake and to prevent the spread of procommunist sentiment.
- Many Europeans supported regionalism in part because they wanted to see a solution to "the German problem"—a way to live with this mighty nation without being dominated by it. This was especially the perspective of the French, who had seen that the humiliation of Germany through the Treaty of Versailles after World War I had been a main cause of the next conflict. The new strategy was to accept Germany's political and economic power, but to embed it in supranational institutions. France looked at the mirror of regionalism and saw Germany tied to the rest of Europe but unable to dominate it.
- Germany, on the other hand, was seeking to become reintegrated into the international community after the moral disaster of National Socialism (Nazism). Therefore it perceived the transfer of sovereignty to supranational institutions as a mean of creating trust in the German effort to overcome nationalism. In addition, West Germany suffered greatly from the Cold War because the "Iron Curtain" divided its territory and threatened its existence. The "West-integration" was therefore the main purpose of Chancellor Konrad Adenauer's foreign policy in the 1950s.
- Inspired by the philosophy of Immanuel Kant (1724–1804), some saw a European federation of democratic republics so experienced at settling their disagreements peacefully that it could be the basis for perpetual peace (in stark contrast to the experiences of the two World Wars). The mirror of regionalism showed them a Europe finally at peace with itself.
- British Prime Minister Winston Churchill saw a "United States of Europe" that could balance U.S. influence (and possibly prevent U.S. dominance) in the postwar era. Churchill's mirror revealed his own fears of U.S. dominance and his hope for a European balance to U.S. power.
- French President Charles DeGaulle, on the other hand, envisioned a "Europe of States" in which the structure of regionalism would enhance the sovereignty and status of all its members—especially France, of course. DeGaulle's mirror focused on Europe, whereas Churchill's kept glancing at the United States.

Considering the diversity of fears and hopes, one might wonder how the Europeans were able to achieve close cooperation. What finally brought them together was the need to find a political solution after the catastrophe of World War II, which was perceived largely as the result of excessive nationalism. The European system of coexisting sovereign nation-states had failed because it had proved unable to prevent the two World Wars that devastated the continent. This fact and the resulting regionalism has to be seen in a larger historical context, however.

The system of sovereign European states had been established in reaction to the religious wars of the sixteenth and seventeenth centuries. A major step in its establishment was the Peace of Westphalia (1648), which ended the Thirty Years War and granted to all states the right to decide about their religion. This treaty acknowledged that the coexistence of European states could no longer be grounded in a common Christian belief, as it had been in the Holy Roman Empire of German nations that had dominated Europe politically in the Middle Ages under a fragile balance of power between political and ecclesiastical institutions. However, although the sovereignty of states did end the religious wars, it did not end wars caused by economic and political conflicts.

The interaction of European states after the Peace of Westphalia and until World War II can be summarized in three phases, each characterized by a specific model of state interactions.

- *The laissez-faire model* (1648–1815): The first phase was characterized by open striving for domination by all major European powers of the time.
- *The balance-of-power-model* (1815–1914): French Emperor Napoleon attempted during 1803–1815 to impose his rule over Europe. When he was defeated in 1815, Austrian Foreign Minister Prince Metternich, who was one of the leaders of the anti-Napoleon coalition, organized a peace conference. The Congress of Vienna led to the establishment of a security regime based on the idea of balancing the power and interests of the major European states. This model gave rise to nearly a hundred years of peace (with only few interruptions such as the war between Germany and France in 1870–1871). Its success was due mainly to the skillful diplomacy of some politicians such as Metternich and, later, Otto von Bismarck (prime minister of Prussia and then Germany).
- *The consultation model* (1918–1939): World War I, which caused 8.5 million deaths, was understood as a failure of the balance-of-power model and led to a twofold reaction: First, the winners of the war (especially France, Great Britain, and the United States) reduced Germany's sovereignty as well as its military and economic capabilities by the Treaty of Versailles (1919); and second, established mechanisms of consultation among the states to achieve better coordination of their foreign policies. The most important of these mechanisms was the League of Nations.

After World War II most European politicians agreed that closer cooperation among the (Western) European states was necessary to establish European peace and security. It was a widely shared conviction that the nation-states had to give up some sovereignty to supranational institutions in order to achieve stability in the interactions among the states. Regionalism was therefore the fourth model, the answer to the political challenge caused by World War II. The Cold War and economic interests acted as accelerants. The advantages of free trade among partners of a similar level of economic and technological strength were certainly an important incentive for regionalism. However, the main motive was political: the promotion of security, peace, and political freedom—in opposition to the totalitarian security structure established by the Soviet Union in Eastern Europe.

For the founding nations of the European Economic Community (France, West Germany, Italy, Belgium, the Netherlands, and Luxembourg), economic integration was therefore a means to achieve closer political integration. Cooperating to solve problems that were too big for one state was a way to solve the major problem of peaceful coexistence of sovereign states. This is obvious from the preamble of the **Treaty of Rome** (the document that established the EEC in 1958), in which the signatory states express their determination "to lay the foundations of an ever closer union among peoples of Europe." This is also evident from the institutional design of the EEC, which included not only the European Commission as the main executive body ("guardian of the treaties") but also a Common Assembly of national deputies, named from 1962 on the European Parliament

**TABLE 11–1    Chronology of the European Communities/European Union**

| YEAR | MONTH | EVENT |
|------|-------|-------|
| 1948 | May | A Congress in The Hague by leading supporters of a European federalism urges the establishment of an economic and political union. |
| 1950 | May | French foreign minister Robert Schumann proposes placing French and German coal and steel production under a common authority. |
|  | October | French Prime Minister René Pleven proposes creation of a European Defence Community (EDC). |
| 1951 | April | The treaty establishing the European Coal and Steel Community (ECSC) is signed by the Benelux states (Belgium, the Netherlands, and Luxembourg) France, Germany, and Italy, and goes into effect in July 1952. |
| 1952 | May | The European Defence Community (EDC) treaty is signed in Paris by the six member states of the ECSC; the treaty is rejected in August 1954 by the French National Assembly. |
| 1957 | March | The Treaty of Rome, establishing the European Economic Community (EEC) and the European Atomic Energy Community (EURATOM), is signed by the six member states of the ECSC; it goes into effect in January 1958. |
| 1960 | January | Agreement to establish a European Free Trade Association (EFTA) is signed by Austria, Denmark, Norway, Portugal, Sweden, Switzerland, and the United Kingdom. The EFTA goes into effect in May 1960. |
| 1963 | January | French President Charles de Gaulle announces his veto against membership of the United Kingdom in the EEC. |
| 1965 | April | The Merger Treaty that establishes a single Council and a single Commission for the European Communities (EC) is signed; it goes into effect in July 1967. |
|  | July | Until January 1966, France (led by President de Gaulle) boycots the European institutions to protest various proposed supranational developments. |
| 1968 | July | Customs Union completed: all internal customs duties and quotas are removed, and a common external tariff is established. |
| 1970 | October | The European Political Cooperation (EPC) (precursor of Common Foreign and Security Policy, CFSP) establishes a mechanism of regular consultation in foreign policy affairs among the members of the EC. |
| 1973 | January | Accession of Denmark, Ireland, and the United Kingdom to the EC. |
| 1974 | December | At a summit meeting in Paris, the heads of state and government of the EC agree to institutionalize their meetings (European Council) and to meet at least twice a year. The summit also decides that from 1979 on, the European Parliament will be elected in direct elections. |
| 1981 | January | Accession of Greece to the EC. |
| 1984 | January | Establishment of a free trade area between the EC and the EFTA. |
| 1985 | December | The European Council agrees on the Single European Act (SEA), which goes into effect in July 1987. |
| 1986 | January | Accession of Spain and Portugal to the EC. |
| 1989 | September–December | Collapse of communist regimes in Central and Eastern Europe. |
| 1990 | October | Reunification of Germany: East Germany becomes part of Germany and the EC. |
| 1992 | March | The European Council signs the Treaty on European Union (EU) in Maastricht, establishing the European Union and (as a part of it) the European Monetary Union. |
| 1995 | January | Accession of Austria, Finland, and Sweden to the EU. |
|  | March | Schengen Agreement (which abolishes all border controls) implemented by seven EU member states: Germany, France, the Benelux states, Spain, and Portugal. |
| 1997 | June | The European Council agrees on the Treaty of Amsterdam, which strengthens the institutions of the EU. |
| 1999 | January | The euro goes into effect with eleven of the fifteen EU members participating. |

**TABLE 11–1    Chronology of the European Communities/European Union (continued)**

| YEAR | MONTH | EVENT |
|------|-------|-------|
| 2000 | December | The European Council agrees on the Treaty of Nice, which fails to prepare the EU for enlargement. |
| 2002 | January | Euro coins and banknotes enter circulation and replace the national currencies. |
|      | March | The Convention on the Future of Europe opens under the chairmanship of former French President Valéry Giscard d'Estaing. |
|      | June | The Treaty on the ECSC expires after fifty years. |
| 2003 | July | The Convention on the Future of Europe presents the Draft of a Constitution for Europe. |
| 2004 | May | Accession of ten new members to the EU: Cyprus, the Czech Republic, Estonia, Hungary, Latvia, Lithuania, Malta, Poland, Slovakia, and Slovenia. |
|      | October | The European Council signs the treaty establishing a Constitution for Europe. |
| 2005 | May | The treaty establishing a Constitution for Europe is rejected in referenda in France (54.5 percent "no") and the Netherlands (61.6 percent "no"). |
| 2007 | January | Accession of Bulgaria and Romania to the EU. |

*Sources:* Neill Nugent, *The Government and Politics of the European Union* (Durham, NC: Duke University Press, 2006); website of the European Commission, www.europa.eu.int.

(directly elected since 1979 for a five-year term) and a European Court of Justice. These institutions were constructed with the hidden agenda of a future growth of functions; the expectation was that sooner or later the economic cooperation would "spill over" and lead to strong political cooperation.

### The First Steps of European Regionalism: Coal and Steel and the Community

Many Europeans have contributed to design a vision of European regionalism, but it was Jean Monnet, a French political economist, who provided the key to moving from imagination to reality.[2] Monnet believed that political divisions and disagreements could be overcome, in some cases, by the uniting force of economics. The promise of economic benefits could at least at times cause nations to set aside political disagreements and cooperate. The fact that regionalism today is very much focused on economic integration is due, perhaps, to the success of Monnet's strategy of using the promise of economic gains to overcome fear of political losses.

Although Monnet dreamed of a United States of Europe, he proposed a much narrower alliance along functional economic lines: a zone of free trade uniting the heavy-industry regions that spanned the French–German border. This plan, for the European Coal and Steel Community, was implemented by Robert Schuman, a French statesman, in 1950. The ECSC was the critical test case for economic and political cooperation between France and Germany. It was, by all accounts, a great success and thereby provided a model for further efforts toward integration in Western Europe. (For an overview of the development of European integration, see Table 11–1.)

A fuller measure of economic integration was achieved in 1957 when the Treaty of Rome created the European Economic Community (EEC), a customs union that brought together the markets of Italy, France, Belgium, Luxembourg, the Netherlands, and West Germany. This union of "the Six" was a great success because these nations were natural trading partners that could benefit from the static and dynamic benefits of economic integration. Indeed, it would be hard to find a group of nations that might be more suited, economically, to open markets.[3] Their limited but still very important economic union also benefited, however, from global trends of the time. Postwar recovery soon gave way to a global economic boom, which strengthened the ties of prosperity uniting Europe against the political and social forces that always act to drive nations apart.

Great Britain participated in the negotiations for the Treaty of Rome but decided in the end to stand apart from the EEC. There were many reasons for this decision, which was eventually reversed at some cost to Britain. The British were concerned, first of all, about the loss of political and economic autonomy that necessarily accompanies economic integration. British politicians (and probably most British citizens) were hesitant to cede decision-making power to others or to share it with the French and the Germans. Britain was forced to weigh the trade-off among self-determination, domestic democracy, and economic growth, which presented a constant tension in economic integration. Britain was also unwilling to give up either its "imperial preferences"—preferential trading relations with the Commonwealth nations—or its "special relationship" with the United States that it so highly valued.

Britain balked, therefore, at its first opportunity to enter the EEC, but it dared not be isolated from free trade in Europe. It therefore organized a weaker alliance of trading nations called the **European Free Trade Area (EFTA)**. The EFTA brought together Denmark, Sweden, Norway, Austria, Switzerland, Portugal, and the United Kingdom. A free-trade area, as noted earlier in this chapter, imposes fewer restrictions on national policy than does a customs union like the EEC, but it also provides fewer opportunities for economic gain. In fact, the EFTA offered only limited opportunities for the static and dynamic gains that the EEC experienced. Geographic separation, deep cultural divisions, huge economic gaps between rich nations (Switzerland, Great Britain) and poor ones (Portugal) all combined to limit trade and growth. The EFTA never was and never would be the engine of economic growth that the EEC promised to be. It was inevitable, then, that EFTA members would eventually seek EEC membership.[4]

Despite its remarkable success in gaining political cooperation among nations that had engaged in two world wars, it would be wrong to paint an overly rosy picture of the EEC. Trade among member nations was never entirely free. Nontariff barriers to trade abounded, and sometimes nations simply refused to accept imports of any items from another member, in open violation of the Treaty of Rome, because of domestic political or economic concerns. It was also necessary to create an elaborate and expensive system of agricultural subsidies across the EEC to defuse political opposition from powerful farm groups. The **Common Agricultural Policy (CAP)** provided for a complex pattern of payments to farmers in all EEC nations, although not equally to each (see the box). A unified system of farm payments was an improvement over the pattern of destructive competition in subsidies that might otherwise have resulted.

---

### THE COMMON AGRICULTURAL POLICY

The Common Agricultural Policy (CAP) is one of the most controversial and divisive elements of economic and political integration in Europe. The CAP is an EU-wide system of agricultural subsidies, financed through taxes imposed by EU member nations. The CAP has been far and away the largest item of expenditure of the European Union and has been a point of contention both within the EU and in its relations with other nations.

The origins of the Common Agricultural Policy reach back to the very beginnings of postwar European regionalism. As soon as the guns of World War II had cooled, European governments met to discuss the "farm problem," which was really two problems in one. The first problem was food security—the need to guarantee adequate supplies of agricultural foodstuffs. The second problem was farmer incomes, which suffered tremendously from the Great Depression, World War II, and postwar economic conditions. Because of the high level of interdependence in Europe, one country's farm policy affected all the others. No single country could solve these problems on its own. So a coordinated action was logical, but it proved impossible. All the nations agreed that something needed to be done, but they disagreed about the right collective policy. As a result, each state enacted its own plan to stimulate production and to support farm incomes.

The signing of the Treaty of Rome was a golden opportunity for the original six EEC members to establish a common farm policy. They agreed on a system of price supports, which guaranteed farmers high prices, and protective barriers against foreign agricultural produce. Protection plus high prices seemed to solve both farm problems in one stroke. High prices encouraged farmers to produce more and more, which addressed the food security concern. And the combination of high prices plus trade barriers guaranteed farmers higher incomes. It would be expensive, they believed, but affordable.

Over the years, however, the CAP's guarantees encouraged European farmers to expand production to a vast degree, creating "mountains" of surplus dairy products and "lakes" of surplus wine and olive oil, for example. These mountains and lakes owed their existence entirely to the CAP, because without it, prices would decline and surplus production would be eliminated.

By the 1990s the CAP was under fire from all sides, criticized in particular on four counts.

- First, the CAP was no longer affordable—it had become very expensive, costing more than 40 billion euro in 2001 or almost half of the total EU budget. And these costs would only increase as EU membership expanded.
- The CAP was also criticized on environmental grounds because the vast and uneconomic subsidy-driven overproduction of the farm sector was as hard on the environment as it was on the budget. Some farmers cut too many corners to expand subsidized output. Food quality, food safety, and especially environmental sustainability all suffered.
- The third criticism was that the EU's policy harmed poor farmers in other countries, especially less developed countries (LDCs). Farm trade barriers limited LDC access to EU export markets, of course, but the subsidized surpluses were the real problem. What happened to the EU's surplus farm goods? In many cases they were sold off or "dumped" on foreign markets, driving down farm prices there and in some cases driving indigenous farmers out of business. Poor farmers starved in some LDCs and food security suffered, it was said, so that the EU's far richer farmers could lead an even more comfortable life. This is a problem of farm subsidies generally, not just EU farm subsidies, but the EU's unwillingness to reduce CAP subsidies made it difficult to address this global problem.
- Finally, the CAP was blamed in part for the breakdown of global trade talks, which were stalled by disagreement between the United States and the EU over subsidies. As long as the EU kept its CAP, it was unlikely that the United States would reduce subsidies either, and the stalemate would continue, much to the displeasure of taxpayers in these countries and poor farmers in the developing world.

Although the arguments against the CAP were many and strong, they were matched by an equal number of obstacles to reform. Most important was the political clout of farmers within each EU member nation and especially, perhaps, in France. France received the most subsidies of any CAP nation, about 9 billion euro, and French farmers were vocal, visible, and politically powerful. For many years it looked as if CAP reform was an impossible dream.

Under great pressure from all sides, and perhaps especially mindful of the CAP's impact on LDC farmers, EU farm ministers agreed on a plan to reform the CAP in June 2003. The plan does not do away with farm subsidies—that would be politically explosive—but it reconfigures the payments in several useful ways.

The most important change is that quantity-based subsidies are replaced, in most instances, with fixed payments to farmers. Farmers keep their subsidies but lose the incentive to overproduce. This change promises to reduce substantially the wasteful and destructive surpluses that the old CAP produced. Moreover, the fixed payments require EU farmers to make progress on issues such as environmental sustainability and food safety (a particular concern since the spread of "mad cow" disease). The reforms include other items, such as rural development program funding and fiscal safeguards to prevent cost increases.

Will the CAP reforms achieve their ambitious goals of supporting farmers without damaging the environment, LDC farmers, and the EU budget? It is too soon to tell. However, that these reforms were agreed to at all is an indication that things are changing in the EU as it adapts to a changing world and steps tentatively into a new role.

*Suggested Readings*

"CAP Reform—A Long-Term Perspective for Sustainable Agriculture," EUROPA, website of the European Union: http://europa.eu.int/comm/agriculture/mtr/index_en.htm

"From Bad to Worse, Down to the Farm," *The Economist*, March 3, 2001, p. 45.

"Let Them Eat Foie Gras," *The Economist*, June 21, 2003, pp. 45–46.

## THE BICYCLE THEORY: BROADER, DEEPER, EVER CLOSER

The EEC changed its name in 1967, becoming the European Community (EC). The EEC formally joined with the ECSC and EURATOM, another pan-Europe organization, to create an institution with broader responsibilities. The change in name signaled an intention to move beyond purely economic issues, although economic concerns continued to dominate EC discussions.

This move to expand the political agenda reflected the prevailing wisdom in Europe that is sometimes summed up as the **bicycle theory** of European regionalism. A bicycle is stable so long as it keeps moving, but once it stops, its stability disappears and it tends to fall over. In the same way, according to Walter Hallstein, first president of the **European Commission**, European unity could be sustained only if European nations constantly strived for an "ever closer union." One way to think of the bicycle theory of European regionalism is that European nations are best able to set aside their differences if they must work together to overcome some common challenge or achieve some common goal. Jean Monnet proposed the economic goal of prosperity through a unified market, and that was indeed enough to get European regionalism's bicycle moving. In the years that followed, Europe sought to keep its momentum going by accepting a series of challenges.

The EC broadened its geographic vision in several stages. Table 11–1 traces the expansion of European regionalism to the current twenty-seven members of the European Union. Great Britain (the United Kingdom) finally entered the EC on January 1, 1973, along with Ireland and fellow EFTA member Denmark. Britain took the plunge only after two controversial referenda and a series of painful negotiations. By all accounts, Britain entered in 1973 on terms that were distinctly inferior to those offered in 1957. Britain's status as a European nation was determined, but its ambivalence about its relationship to Europe remained.

Greece entered the EC in 1981, followed by Spain and Portugal in 1986. In all three cases, EC membership was in part a reward for the triumph of democratic institutions over authoritarian governments. Free trade and closer economic ties were intended to solidify democracy and protect it from potential communist influences.

The broader market was not in all respects a better market, however. The entry of the poorer nations of Ireland, Greece, Spain, and Portugal (at the time they were called "the poor four") magnified a variety of tensions within the EC. These less developed nations were less clearly a part of the pan-European market. Lower living standards limited the extent of their trade with richer member states. Lower wage structures threatened some jobs in EC industries. Finally, the addition of four largely agricultural nations to EC institutions, including the CAP, put severe fiscal strains on the other nations. The broader market was surely in the long-run interest of the EC, but it imposed great stress on cooperative relationships in the short run.

These economic and political stresses reached a peak in the mid-1980s. Higher and higher EC program costs, imposing a disproportionate burden on Great Britain, precipitated a split in the EC. Jacques Delors, the newly appointed president of the European Commission, traveled from capital to capital seeking ways to reunite the governments and peoples of the EC in some common enterprise. What could restore a measure of unity and cooperation and keep the bicycle moving forward? A common defense and foreign policy? A common monetary system? In the end, Delors concluded that international trade, which Monnet had used to bring the EC together in the first place, was the force most likely to reenergize Europe. In 1985, therefore, Delors issued a "white paper" proposing the creation of a single integrated market by 1992. The **Single European Act (SEA)** formalized this grand experiment in market deepening—and kept the bicycle upright.

It might seem that the EC was already a single market—in theory no tariff barriers separated EC markets, and in practice goods flowed fairly freely across national borders. If, however, a single market is defined according to the principles observed in the United States (the world's largest single market and often its most dynamic one, too), then Europe was still a long way from its goal. Under Delors's leadership, the EC identified 200 general areas where agreement on "directives" was needed to achieve the goal of a unified market. The 1992 Single Market plan was off and running.

The goals of Europe in 1992 might be characterized as "four freedoms": free movement of goods, of services, of capital, and of people. Each of these freedoms is much harder to achieve in practice than to imagine in theory. Free movement of goods, for example, requires much more than the absence of tariff and quota barriers if the freedom is to mean very much. There are hundreds of nontariff barriers to the free production and sale of goods that must be addressed. Health, safety, and technical standards, each of which plays a constructive role, can all discourage imports from other countries (by raising the cost of selling) and encourage the purchase of domestically produced goods. These standards must be leveled (or *harmonized,* in the jargon of the trade) to allow, to the maximum possible extent, a good that can be sold anywhere in the group to be sold everywhere. In many industries, the cost of satisfying these standards and proving regulatory compliance far exceeded any imaginable tariff barrier to trade.

Services represent an increasing proportion of world trade. Achieving free movement of services, such as financial and insurance services, is a tricky task, given the complex systems of financial regulations that each nation has in place. Free movement of money or capital requires the dismantling of capital controls and investment regulations, which affect flows of funds into and out of a nation. Finally, free movement of people requires agreement on many points, most especially the adoption of a common immigration policy. Once a person has entered one EU nation, he or she is free to enter any other.

However, the SEA went beyond improvement of economic freedom in the EC. It also strengthened the political integration and prepared in many respects the big step forward that was made in the early 1990s with the Treaty of Maastricht. One of the major changes of the SEA was to change the requirement of a unanimous vote to approve most legislative decisions concerning the single market. The "unanimity vote" had made decisions on European legislation very difficult to make, because it essentially gave a veto to every single member of the Council of the European Community (the meeting of the national ministers of the member states). The SEA introduced a qualified majority rule, meaning that a decision was taken if a majority of 62 of 87 votes was in favor of a proposal (= 71.26 percent; the 87 votes were given to the 12 member states in relation to their size). In addition to its practical advantages, the qualified majority vote had great symbolic value. It meant that, at least with respect to single-market legislation, the European institutions were gaining in importance; that is, from then on it was possible to take decisions against the will of some opposing members. In addition to establishing the qualified majority vote, the SEA gave more power to the pan-European institutions: The competences of the European Commission were enlarged, the European Parliament was granted more rights to participate in European legislative processes, and the European Court of Justice was strengthened by the establishment of a Court of First Instance, in response to the increasing number of legal proceedings on the European level.

Delors's single-market initiative posed a real challenge to the EC member states. The year 1992 promised the creation of a larger, more dynamic market, with the wealth and political power that would flow therefrom. To achieve this big goal, however, required each nation to sacrifice its interests on hundreds of smaller issues, many of which had important domestic political effects, before the four freedoms could be achieved.

National sovereignty and economic growth were often in conflict. Germany, for example, desired to see its own high environmental standards applied to all EC vehicles. Environmentalism is an important social value in Germany, and the Green Party is a potent political force on some issues. These environmental regulations are costly, however, and were opposed on economic grounds by poorer countries such as Greece and Portugal. To a certain extent, at least, the four freedoms for the EC as a whole actually required sacrifice of some domestic freedoms, such as the right to self-determination of environmental and safety standards.

The years 1989 and 1990 brought about an unexpected turn to European politics. With the fall of the Berlin Wall and the collapse of socialist regimes in Central and Eastern Europe, the Western European countries faced a double challenge: German reunification (the formerly socialist German Democratic Republic joined the Federal Republic of Germany on October 3, 1990); and applications for membership from most of the Central and Eastern European countries. The **Treaty of Maastricht**, which established the European Union in 1992, was mainly a result of negotiations during the process of German reunification. Both Great Britain's Prime Minister Margaret Thatcher and France's President François Mitterand were reluctant to accept a unified Germany, which brought back memories of German domination in Europe. In this situation, two ambitious plans were proposed by France and Germany. France proposed monetary union—a single currency. In one respect, this was a continuance of the theme of this chapter. In theory, monetary union was thought to be able to solve several pressing problems in a single stroke. A single currency would make European markets more efficient and Europe's economies more dynamic. This would provide economic gains to offset the costs of eastward enlargement. The German problem would be solved because Germany would be chained to the rest of the EU by the strongest possible link—money—and it would have to give up the most powerful symbol of its economic strength, the Deutsche Mark. The second plan, proposed by Germany and France together, was to move further in European regionalism by promoting political integration. France supported the idea of the European Union in order to gain more control over Germany—and was ready to accept in exchange that it would itself have to give up sovereignty. Germany, on the other hand, was ready to give up national sovereignty in exchange for trust in its reunification.

The conference of Maastricht in December 1991 realized both plans. The heads of state and government of the twelve member states decided to establish a monetary union at the latest on January 1, 1999, and to replace the national currencies with one common currency: the euro (however, the name of the currency was chosen only in December 1995). Two decisions were made in Maastricht to strengthen the new currency. First, the European Central Bank (ECB) was to be independent in its monetary policies from other European institutions and from national governments, and it was committed only to the objective of price stability. Second, only those countries were meant to join the "Euro-zone" that were fulfilling the so-called convergence criteria: a low inflation rate, low interest rates, and a low state debt. A third decision to strengthen the Euro was taken by the European Council in 1997 by agreeing on the "Stability and Growth Pact," which forces the members of the Euro-zone, after joining the Euro, to respect a certain discipline in government spending. Since then, a high state debt—which risks causing inflation in the whole Euro-zone—can be penalized by the European Council.

Although the criteria for nations to be part of the single currency were thought to be very strict, in fact twelve of the fifteen countries in the EU in 1998 were set to enter into monetary union. Denmark, Great Britain, and Sweden elected to remain outside the Euro-zone. The ECB took control of the Euro-zone's monetary policy on January 1, 1999, and three years later the new banknotes and coins were introduced.

The second plan that was realized in Maastricht was to finally make the step from an economic community to a political union—a step that had already been prepared by the SEA in 1986. The union brings together three areas of cooperation into one legal and institutional structure:

- The **Single Market**, which was started with the EEC treaty in 1957 and accomplished by the SEA in 1986; in addition (but of minor importance), European cooperation in civil use of nuclear energy (EURATOM).
- Cooperation in foreign and security policy, which began in 1970 with the establishment of a process of regular consultation (European Political Cooperation, EPC). Cooperation in this area remains very difficult even today. Although all members realize that the EU would have more weight in world politics if it spoke with one voice, the national interests of the bigger members are often highly diverging. This can be seen quite well in the differences among the European states regarding the war in Iraq: some countries, including Great Britain, Italy, and Poland, joined the United States in invading Iraq, whereas France and Germany opposed the invasion.

- Cooperation in "Justice and Home Affairs" has developed since the 1970s for mainly two reasons. First, to establish the free movement of persons and goods, it appeared desirable to abolish border controls between the countries; and second, the rising number of immigrants to Europe was calling for European solutions. One of the important steps toward cooperation in these areas was the *Schengen Agreement* (named after the town in Luxembourg in which the agreement was reached in 1985), which determined to open the borders between most of the European countries and defined new forms of police cooperation (both realized from 1995 on). As of 2006, this agreement had been signed by Germany, France, Belgium, the Netherlands, Luxembourg, Austria, Italy, Spain, Portugal, Greece, Denmark, Finland, and Sweden. Great Britain and Ireland have not joined the agreement; Iceland and Norway joined it without being members of the EU.

Two models were discussed in Maastricht about how to integrate these areas of cooperation into the EU. According to the *tree model*, "Common Foreign and Security Policy" (CFSP) and "Justice and Home Affairs" (JHA) are added like branches to the existing trunk of economic integration. This meant expanding the supranational institutions of the Single Market to the new areas (with the European Commission being the dominant actor). The competing model was the *temple model*, according to which the CFSP and JHA are added as new pillars to the existing pillar of the Single Market, therefore allowing more intergovernmental provisions for the decision-making processes and leaving the main decisions to the European Council and to the Council of the EU (Council of Ministers). France and Great Britain, especially, were pushing for the temple model, which was finally decided on in Maastricht.

Figure 11–1 shows the structure of the European Union after the changes made by the Treaty of Amsterdam in 1996, which moved large parts of Justice and Home Affairs to the supranational pillar and left in the intergovernmental Pillar 3 "Police and Judicial Co-operation in Criminal Matters" (PJCCM). Cooperation in Pillar 3 has gained considerably in importance since September 11, 2001, because it is here that the member states are deciding about measures to fight Islamic terrorism within the borders of the EU.

The process of "deepening" the European way of regionalism was followed by "broadening": the big enlargements of 2004 (from fifteen to twenty-five members) and 2007 (with Bulgaria and Romania, to twenty-seven members). During the discussions about the accession of the new members

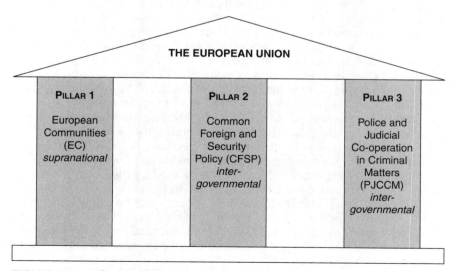

**FIGURE 11–1**  The Structure of the European Union in 2007

it was clear that a need for preparation existed not only on the part of the new members, but also on the part of the EU. Institutional design in 1957 reflected six members and would hardly work for twenty-seven. Some examples can illustrate the issues: Every state sends one commissioner in the European Commission, the main executive body of the EU; from 2007 on, there are therefore twenty-seven Commissioners, plus the president of the Commission. The presidency of the EU rotates every six months among the governments of the member states; since the enlargement, every state waits 13½ years before it is again its turn. In the European Council, discussions are usually opened with a *tour de table*, a brief statement by each of the heads of states and governments. With twenty-seven members, a single *tour de table* can take several hours. All these issues make institutional reforms necessary.

However, two attempts at such reforms have failed. In 2000, the European Council met in Nice, France, and drafted a treaty that was meant to prepare the EU for enlargement. But the conference did not produce strong results; the changes made by the Treaty of Nice are of relatively minor importance. A second effort was made in 2002, when the EU established the European Convention and gave it the task of drafting a constitution for Europe. The association of the name was clearly to the U.S. Constitutional Convention of Philadelphia; for many politicians the idea was to pave the way toward a "Unites States of Europe." For eighteen months, 105 deputies of the EU member states (including the states that would join in 2004 and 2007) discussed the institutional future of the EU. In 2004 the president of the convention, former French President Valéry Giscard d'Estaing, presented the result: the draft of a constitution that reflected a compromise between the need to streamline the decision-making processes, the desire for more political integration, and the fear of giving up too much sovereignty to the EU. In Summer 2005, the draft failed in the referenda in France and in the Netherlands; in both countries, a large majority, about 54.5 percent in France and 61.6 percent in the Netherlands, rejected the constitution. Since then, the EU has been in a process of "reflection," meant to give time to search for new solutions for reconciling both "deepening" and "broadening" of European regionalism.

## THE DEVELOPMENT OF POLITICAL INSTITUTIONS

European regionalism is always political, even if its appearance is economic. As we have stated before, the purpose of economic integration in the 1950s was to move further toward political integration, and this was the reason for designing an impressive set of political institutions to make policy, to settle disputes, and to provide leadership for Europe. The most important political institutions of the EU today are the European Council, the Council of the EU (also called the Council of Ministers), and the presidencies of the Councils; the European Commission; the European Parliament; and the European Court of Justice. Each of these institutions plays a specific role, first in setting the delicate balance between national interests of member nations and second in balancing power and interests on the European level. All of these institutions are characterized by a mix of intergovernmental and supranational qualities, combining the representation of national interests with promoting the emergence of a European perspective (see Table 11–2).

The **European Council** is the meeting of the heads of state and government of all member states. The European Council and the Council of Ministers are headed by the EU presidency, which rotates among the members every six months, allowing each nation in turn a chance to shape the agenda of the EU in important ways. The European Council was not among the original institutions that were established in 1957. It evolved out of informal meetings of the heads of state and government, which were institutionalized at the Paris summit in 1974 and made a formal part of the European treaties only with the Treaty of Maastricht (1992). The functions of the European Council can be described as strategic decision making. It negotiates the treaties that are shaping European integration, it is responsible for Pillar 2, the Common Foreign and Security Policy (this became formally the function of the European Council with the Treaty of Amsterdam), it nominates the president of the European

**TABLE 11–2   Political Institutions of the European Union**

| *POLITICAL INSTITUTION* | *FUNCTION* |
|---|---|
| President of the European Commission | Head of state of the European Union (EU). Leads the European Commission and represents the EU to other nations. |
| European Commission | The executive branch of the EU, serving much the same function as the cabinet in the United States or the United Kingdom. The Commission proposes legislation to the Council of Ministers, administers EU programs, and represents the EU in economic relations with other countries or international organizations. |
| Council of the European Union | The main lawmaking body of the EU, composed of a single representative from each member nation. It is also the body charged with implementing EU foreign and security policy. |
| European Council | Meetings of EU heads of state and government are called the European Council. Summit meetings of the Council are called at least once every six months by the country holding the presidency of the Council of Ministers. |
| European Parliament | The only body of the EU whose members are directly elected by the citizens of its member states. Formerly only a consultative body, the Parliament gained new influence under the Treaty on European Union. European Parliament committees review legislation proposed by the European Commission and may propose amendments to the legislation before submitting it to the Council of Ministers. The Parliament may veto a proposal after it reaches the Council of Ministers if it disagrees with the council's position. |
| European Court of Justice | The "Supreme Court" of EU law. Composed of 15 judges who are appointed to six-year terms. The court deals with disputes between member governments and EU institutions and among EU institutions, and with appeals against EU rulings or decisions. |
| European Central Bank | The EU's central bank (chief monetary authority), created after the decision to adopt the euro was made. There is an executive board, appointed for eight-year terms, and a government board, which includes the executive board and the heads of all EU member nation central banks. |

Commission (formally since the Treaty of Nice), it breaks deadlocks that occur on the ministerial level, and it decides the budget of the EU and strategic issues such as enlargement of the EU. The European Council meets at least twice a year for two or three days, accompanied by more than 1000 journalists, who report not only the formal decisions but also the general atmosphere of cooperation among the heads of state and government, which is decisive for moving further toward European integration.

The **Council of the EU (or Council of Ministers)** is subdivided into (currently) nine "formations" of different specialization, in which the respective ministers of national governments gather.[5] The most important are the General Affairs Council (GAC, meeting of the foreign affairs ministers), the Council of Economic and Financial Affairs (Ecofin, meeting of the ministers of finance and economics to coordinate fiscal policies and economic policies aimed at maintaining a strong euro and promoting economic growth), and the meeting of the ministers of agriculture. The main functions of the Council are to decide European legislation and to make policy decisions. Cooperation with the Commission and the Parliament varies with the pillar under which the respective decision has to be taken. Under Pillar 1 the Commission has the exclusive right to take the initiative for a legislative process, and the most important decisions have to be approved by the European Parliament in the so-called co-decision procedure. However, the Council can ask the Commission to take a legislative initiative, which relativizes the Commission's power in Pillar 1 legislation. Under Pillars 2 and 3 the role of the Council is more important: Under Pillar 2, the meeting of foreign affairs ministers serves to prepare decisions of the European Council; under Pillar 3, the Council of Ministers initiates and decides European legislation (in cooperation with the European Parliament). Under Pillars 2 and 3, decisions are mostly taken by unanimity; under Pillar 1 they are mostly taken by qualified majority vote (QMV). However, even if QMV is theoretically possible, it is rarely used: Both the European Council and the Council of Ministers are characterized by a strong desire for consensus. To prepare the decisions of the Council of Ministers, each member state of the EU has a number of Permanent Representatives in Brussels (the "capital" of the EU), who meet on a regular basis in the Committee of Permanent Representatives (COREPER). In contrast to the ministers, who represent their national governments in the Council and often take a firm national point of view, the Permanent Representatives live in Brussels in a "European environment," which shapes their approach to European politics. This helps in finding solutions for policy or legislative issues below the ministerial level and in preparing the agenda for the ministers in such a way as to ease negotiations.

The **European Commission** acts as the EU's executive cabinet. The membership of the Commission (called the "College of Commissioners") includes twenty-seven commissioners (one for every member state) and the president of the European Commission.[6] Each commissioner has a specific "portfolio" of responsibilities, such as competition policy, trade, or agriculture, making her or his responsibilities equivalent to those of a cabinet minister or department secretary in a nation-state. Decisions are taken *de jure*, by absolute majority (with a strong tendency to achieve a *de facto* consensus) and according to the "principle of collegiality," which implies that all commissioners are responsible for the final decisions. The president of the Commission and the commissioners are nominated by the European Council, the latter on the basis of nominations by the member states. Nominations have to be approved by an absolute majority of the European Parliament; the appointment is for a five-year term. The main functions of the Commission are to design policy programs, legislative proposals, and budgetary proposals. Under EC Pillar 1, it sets agendas and proposes new legislation to the Council, which decides about these proposals together with the European Parliament. Under the two other pillars, the Commission can also formulate policy programs and legislative proposals, but the main power remains on the side of the Council of Ministers and the European Council. A second important function of the Commission is to be the guardian of the treaties. Most EU legislation is implemented in the nation-states by the national governments. This process of implementation of EU laws is monitored (and, if necessary, sanctioned) by the Commission, which has earned a reputation as the European watchdog. A third important task is to represent European interests in international organizations such as the World Trade Organization.

The **European Parliament (EP)** has taken on over the years many of the functions of traditional parliaments. It was originally established in the ECSC and EEC treaties as the Common Assembly, with deputies nominated by the national parliaments of the six member states. Since 1962 the Assembly has been called the European Parliament, and since 1979 it has been elected in direct elections by European citizens for five-year terms. However, because of a general lack of awareness of the role and functions of the EP, election campaigns are often dominated by national issues and not by European politics. Also, election turnouts are significantly lower than in national elections.[7] This has often been attributed to the fact that the EP is not perceived as being representative of a European people, because European citizens do not feel that they are one people in the way that Americans do. The EP, which had 732 deputies in 2006, is organized along political party lines and not according to national citizenship. Socialists from all EU nations act together, for example, as do conservatives and other party groups. The EP's main political functions are, first, to participate in the process of drafting policy programs and European legislation; second, to cooperate with the Council of Ministers in European legislation; third, to vote on the EU budget, which is negotiated by the Council; and fourth, to approve and control the European Commission.

The **European Court of Justice (ECJ)** and the **Court of First Instance (CFI**, established by the SEA and functioning since 1989) are made up of one judge from each member state of the EU and a number of advocates-general. The Court of Justice adjudicates legal conflicts between EU institutions and between the EU and member states. The decisions of both courts usually emphasize the priority of European law over national legislation, and the courts are therefore important promoters of European integration.

Among other institutions of the EU, the most important in the IPE context is the **European Central Bank (ECB)**, which is responsible for monetary policy and price stability in the Euro-zone. It also conducts foreign exchange operations, manages the foreign reserves of the member states, and promotes the smooth operation of payment systems in the Euro-zone.

These EU institutions provide a comprehensive if somewhat unwieldy organization for setting policy and making decisions that affect the entire EU. In the early days of the EU, this political superstructure had more form than substance—its political powers were relatively limited and symbolic. As political and economic integration progressed, however, these political institutions have grown in importance. In a way, the broader and deeper EU has "grown into" its political clothing in the decades since the Treaty of Rome.

The broadening and deepening of the EU over the past twenty-five years has created real political problems that daily test the strength of the EU's political institutions. Deepening necessarily forced each member state to cede some economic and political powers to EU institutions, as more and more policies and regulations became EU-wide, not national, in scope. This has lead over time to a very complex relation between European and national legislation, which is confusing even for specialists. Broadening has also posed political problems, because any increase in the size of the Union necessarily reduces the clout of existing members, who find their votes reduced in relative importance. These threats to nation-state sovereignty pose threats to EU unity. In 1994, Spain briefly threatened to try to block negotiations to admit Sweden to the EU, for example, because Spanish leaders feared their nation would lose political power and economic benefits from EU widening. The most important issue created by the enlargement is that the EU has so far not been able to adjust its institutions to the large number of twenty-seven members.

## THREE CHALLENGES FOR THE EUROPEAN UNION

As the fiftieth anniversary of the Treaty of Rome approaches, the EU faces many challenges. The most obvious problem is the expansion of the group from fifteen to twenty-seven members. The new entrants are very diverse, as Table 11–3 suggests. In terms of population, they range from the island

**TABLE 11–3   New EU Member States (Expansions of 2004 and 2007)**

| COUNTRY | ESTIMATED POPULATION (JULY 2006 EST.) | ESTIMATED GROSS DOMESTIC PRODUCT PER CAPITA (2005) IN $ |
|---|---|---|
| Bulgaria | 7,385,367 | 9,600 |
| Cyprus | 749,200 (2004) | 21,500 |
| Czech Republic | 10,235,455 | 19,500 |
| Estonia | 1,324,333 | 16,700 |
| Hungary | 9,981,334 | 16,300 |
| Latvia | 2,274,735 | 13,200 |
| Lithuania | 3,585,906 | 13,700 |
| Malta | 400,214 | 19,900 |
| Poland | 38,536,869 | 13,300 |
| Romania | 22,303,552 | 8,200 |
| Slovakia | 5,439,448 | 16,100 |
| Slovenia | 2,010,347 | 21,600 |

*Source:* The World Factbook (www.cia.gov/cia/publications/factbook), August 17, 2006. Data for Cyprus are only for the Republic of Cyprus (for 2004, excluding the northern part, which is occupied by Turkey), website of the government of Cyprus: www.mof.gov.cy/mof/cystat/statistics.nsf/All/4E24598BFC64594AC22570BD0035F021?OpenDocument&sub=1&e, September 14, 2006.

of Malta, with 400,000 citizens, to Poland's 38 million. From an economic standpoint, only Cyprus and Slovenia have per-capita incomes that are roughly comparable to previous EU members such as Greece or Portugal.

Taken as a group, these countries are much poorer, and they do not have very much successful experience with the institutions of capitalism, democracy, and rule of law that are necessary for them to achieve successful union with their European neighbors. They are years behind in some areas, but it will not take years for them to catch up.

Why did the EU expand to encompass these nations if doing so is so troublesome? There are many theories, but in the end the best answer is that the bicycle theory still applies. The EU must accept challenges to give itself a mission and to prevent internal disagreements from boiling over. What if the EU did not take them in? What good would the EU be then? To keep itself upright and maintain its legitimacy, the EU must keep moving ahead, and this meant expanding by ten states in 2004 and two more in 2007 and adding perhaps a dozen more in the next decade.

The 2004 expansion of the EU certainly gave it lots of problems to solve, which should keep the bicycle wheels rolling; but the problem of more members is not the only challenge that the EU faces today. Three political challenges confront the European Union in the immediate future: the challenge of the euro, the challenge of a EU constitution, and a final challenge that we call "Pinocchio's dilemma."

## The Political Challenge of the Euro

On January 1, 2002, twelve of the fifteen members of the EU gave up their national currencies (and the ability to influence their individual values) and entered into a monetary union with a single currency, the euro. The twelve countries are Germany, France, Italy, Spain, Portugal, Belgium, Luxembourg, the Netherlands, Austria, Finland, Greece, and Ireland. Sweden, Denmark, and the United Kingdom elected to retain their national currencies, at least for the time being, and are not part of the "Euro-zone."

Table 11–4 highlights the members of the Euro-zone. The stated goal of monetary union was to give the EU's bicycle the ultimate economic push—a huge single market, with a single currency to drive it. It would be easy to conclude that the euro is all about economics, efficiency, and growth, but in fact the most important aspects of the euro are political.

Indeed, everything about the euro is political. Its name, for example, was chosen because it means nothing in any European language. For a time the name "ecu" (for European Currency Unit)

**TABLE 11–4   Population and Income for Euro-Zone EU Member States (2006)**

| COUNTRY | ESTIMATED POPULATION (JULY 2006) | ESTIMATED GROSS DOMESTIC PRODUCT PER CAPITA (2005) IN $ |
|---|---|---|
| Austria | 8,192,880 | 32,700 |
| Belgium | 10,379,067 | 31,400 |
| Finland | 5,231,372 | 30,900 |
| France | 60,876,136 | 29,900 |
| Germany | 82,422,299 | 30,400 |
| Greece | 10,688,058 | 22,200 |
| Ireland | 4,062,235 | 41,000 |
| Italy | 58,133,509 | 29,200 |
| Luxembourg | 474,413 | 55,600 |
| Netherlands | 16,491,461 | 30,500 |
| Portugal | 10,605,870 | 19,300 |
| Slovenia | 2,010,347 | 21,600 |
| Spain | 40,397,842 | 25,500 |

*Source:* The World Factbook (www.cia.gov/cia/publications/factbook), August 17, 2006.

was considered, but this was rejected as "too French," because a coin called the *ecu* once circulated in medieval France. Scenes on euro currency appear to be classic European images, but none of them is authentic. Putting any *real* European scene on the currency would cause political disagreements, so every euro image is created by artists to look European without representing any specific—national—monument. Even the euro symbol (€) has been tested for political problems. The symbol looks like a C with an equal sign running through it, perhaps to suggest common currency and the equality of all Europeans. In fact, it means nothing, for fear that anything else would cause political divisions.

Ironically, although the euro itself is politically neutral, its implications are politically explosive. In order to qualify for entry into the Euro-zone, for example, each nation had to meet a number of economic stability targets, such as low inflation, low interest rates, and low government debt. To achieve these goals was a great domestic political challenge, because raising taxes or cutting government spending or benefits is never popular. The fear of being left out of the Euro-zone's prosperity, however, motivated domestic political change, though not without creating tensions that linger today.

Once the euro was launched in 2002, the member nations faced a transformed political environment. Their ability to influence domestic economic conditions was much reduced, because interest rates are now set by the European Central Bank, not by policymakers in each country. This puts national leaders in a very awkward position: Their citizens might still hold them accountable for national economic conditions, but there is little that they can do to affect these conditions using traditional economic policy tools. The Spanish government cannot spend its way out of a recession, for example, or print money to pay unemployment benefits, because it does not have the full fiscal autonomy it had when the peseta was its sovereign currency. It might have to lower the minimum wage or reduce welfare benefits to attract business and create jobs—policies that would be politically divisive indeed. This will indeed be a new world of politics in Europe.

The euro is economic "superglue"; it binds together the nations of the Euro-zone and gives them good reason to try to work out differences in national interest and opinion as the EU expands. However, the cost is that domestic political differences and disagreements are magnified. Dealing with this issue will be a significant political challenge for EU members both old and new. One way to address this problem might be to clarify the relationship between domestic policy and EU policy generally, by writing a constitution for the European Union. That is the second challenge.

## The Constitutional Challenge

The EU has broadened, expanding its membership to twenty-seven with more in line, and deepened, through the single currency. The next step in the movement toward an "ever closer union," in the words of Walter Hallstein, is political union and a EU constitution. This is a tricky step, because it raises delicate issues of national sovereignty. Any attempt at large-scale political unity has been postponed—until now—because of the likely political disagreement. Adoption of the Treaty of Nice, however, was a signal that Europe was ready at last to confront the big, explosive political questions.

The Convention of Europe, chaired by former French President Valérie Giscard D'Estaing, began meeting to draft a constitution for the European Union in early 2002 and issued its report in the summer of 2003. The draft treaty establishing a constitution for the EU is an attempt both to summarize the current EU political system, by bringing various treaties and agreements together in one document, and to lay out a system of regional governance that would serve the needs of the EU and its citizens and their national governments well into the future. This is a delicate task. No wonder the draft treaty is 263 pages long!

Because the Constitutional Treaty was rejected in referenda in France and the Netherlands in summer 2005, it is currently unclear where the reform process will lead. At the time of this writing, the German government has announced that it will adopt a new initiative for the constitution during its presidency in the first half of 2007. It has also been pointed out by the Commission that there is no possibility for any further enlargement before a reform of the EU's institutions has come into effect. However, the current discussions in Europe emphasize that one reason for the failure of the referenda has been a growing gap between the growing importance of Brussel's politics for everyday life and a lack of identification with the European integration process among European citizens. Apparently, the main issue in moving forward from economic to political integration is not only that the nation-states have to give up parts of their sovereignty, but also that in a democratic system the citizens have to identify with the new political entity. The fate of the European reform process will depend mainly on Europeans' ability to deal with these issues of economic and political regionalism.

## Pinocchio's Dilemma

Pinocchio was the wooden puppet, carved by Geppetto, who became a real, live boy in the famous story written by Carlo Collodi in 1883. Most people who are familiar with the story (or the Disney cartoon or Roberto Benigni film versions) imagine that Pinocchio's dilemma is that his nose grows whenever he tells a lie—a memorable image indeed. However, the real problem, as Susan Strange has pointed out, is an ethical one. Once the puppet's strings were cut and Pinocchio became a real boy, he had to decide what to do, what to believe, how to act, and how to live a meaningful life.

This is the ultimate challenge facing the European Union as it confronts the problems of monetary union and political union head-on. It is not enough to centralize economic and political power. Europe must decide what this power will mean, what values it will champion, and how it will be used both domestically and in global affairs. This is exactly Pinocchio's problem, although on a much bigger scale.

One of the first questions that the EU will have to confront, once its constitution is set and it becomes a real, live boy, so to speak, is: What does it mean to be European? And is the European Union really about Europe, or is it more about Union and the values that unite? These questions will be posed by Turkey, one of the countries that is knocking on the door seeking membership. Turkey is a large country with a population that is mainly Islamic. It is also an intentionally European country with a European-style government and a capitalist market system; it is a member of NATO, the Western security alliance, and an original Marshall Plan nation.

Turkey's application for membership would shift the EU's center of gravity decisively south and east and force it to confront a range of social and cultural issues, in addition to the economic ones that are always present. It will be an interesting test of the EU's ability to envision itself as an independent actor more than a regional collection of states.

## CONCLUSION

The European Union today is, in many respects, in the same situation it was fifty years ago. Like Walter Hallstein's bicycle, it lurches forward if only to avoid falling down. Like Susan Strange's Pinocchio, it seeks meaning for its existence. Should we be optimists or pessimists about Europe's future? As with the Mirror of Erised, viewers look at the EU and see their own fears or hopes.

Johns Hopkins Professor David P. Calleo is an optimist who sees what he hopes. He is drawn to the image of the EU as a force for peace and civilization, advancing the general will of its citizens. It is tempting, he says,

> . . . to see a unifying Europe as the harbinger not only of a more plural world but also of one with better hopes for peaceful stability. In this vision, a strong, cohesive Europe joins in a rejuvenated alliance with America. Together they embrace Russia in a larger pan-European system—not to make a common front against an alien non-Western world, but to keep their own balance and their own relations in order across Europe and the Atlantic. Such a Europe becomes a model for reasonable behavior among states.[8]

This may not be good news for everyone, Calleo notes, thinking of Churchill and DeGaulle (and perhaps George W. Bush):

> And, of course, a European Union that does flourish in the twenty-first century will be a problem as well as a solution. . . . For those who have grown fond of the idea of a seamless global world, with only one superpower, this is a disquieting prospect.[9]

Editor Bill Emmott of *The Economist* is less optimistic. He looks at the EU and sees what he fears. He asks whether the EU could become a world power, like the United States. It could, he thinks, if it wanted to.

> But there's a crucial question: does it want to? . . . It does not seem to want to be unified as a single state or as another entity capable of speaking with a single voice. There are plenty of symbols of European identity to be seen throughout the Union, from flags to coins, but most people's primary sense of identity—and certainly their prime source of political engagement—remains national.[10]

Emmott is dissatisfied with the EU's vision of itself. It keeps the bike upright, but where is it going?

> The European Union is a success measured by the continued desire of countries to join it, and by the failure of any member so far to leave. But it is a muddle, chronically lacking a clear direction, for reasons that are likely to endure. Its muddles are not the sort to pitch nation against nation, to threaten dissolution, or breakup; but short of a mind-concentrating crisis, they are likely to keep the EU as an envious but fragmented force.[11]

Perhaps the secret of the European Union, and of regionalism in general, is that it is not one thing in particular, as Emmott might like, but many things muddled together, as Calleo seems to appreciate. It will always fail to be clearly defined and always succeed, we can hope, in muddling through.

## DISCUSSION QUESTIONS

1. What is the European Union? How has it evolved over the last fifty years? Discuss both its broadening and its deepening. What is its importance today?
2. The theme of this chapter is the tension between economic and political integration. Discuss ways in which economic and political integration are related.
3. Explain the difference between static efficiency and dynamic efficiency. How is each important to the integration process?
4. The widening and deepening of the EU has increased economic gains but intensified political pressures. Discuss the political problems, citing specific examples when possible.
5. What is the Common Agricultural Policy (CAP)? Explain how and why the CAP illustrates the theme of this chapter and also how it creates tensions both among EU members and between the EU and its international trading partners.
6. Discuss the political economy of the euro. What are the likely economic effects of the euro? What are its likely political effects? How is the euro supposed to solve the EU's political problems? Explain.
7. Do you think that Europe can be united? Explain what it would mean to be united and explain your position.

## INTERNET LINKS

The European Union:
    http://europa.eu

European Commission:
    http://ec.europa.eu

European Council:
    www.consilium.europa.eu

The European Parliament:
    www.europarl.europa.eu

European Central Bank:
    www.ecb.de/home/html/index.en.html

The European Convention:
    http://european-convention.eu.int

BBC News on Europe:
    http://news.bbc.co.uk/2/hi/europe/default.stm

This Week in Europe:
    http://europa.eu.int/unitedkingdom/press/the_week_in_europe/latest_en.htm

## SUGGESTED READINGS

"An Awfully Big Adventure: A Survey of EMU," *The Economist* (Special Section), April 11, 1998.
David P. Calleo. *Rethinking Europe's Future*. Princeton, NJ: Princeton University Press, 2001.
Bill Emmott. *20:21 Vision: Twentieth-Century Lessons for the Twenty-First Century*. New York: Farrar, Straus & Giroux, 2003.
Timothy Garton Ash. *Free World: America, Europe and the Surprising Future of the West*. Random House, 2004.
Harold James. *Europe Reborn: A History, 1914–2000*. New York: Pearson/Longman, 2003.
Kathleen R. McNamara. *The Currency of Ideas: Monetary Politics in the European Union*. Ithaca, NY: Cornell University Press, 1998.

## KEY TERMS

European Union (EU)
European Economic Community (EEC)
Common Market
European Coal and Steel Community (ECSC)
European Community (EC)
regionalism
trade blocs
economic integration
free-trade area (FTA)
North American Free Trade Agreement (NAFTA)

customs union
economic union
static efficiency
dynamic efficiency
trade diversion effect
Marshall Plan
Treaty of Rome
European Free Trade Area (EFTA)
Common Agricultural Policy (CAP)
bicycle theory
European Commission

Single European Act (SEA)
Treaty of Maastricht
Single Market
European Council
Council of the EU (or Council of Ministers)
European Commission
European Parliament (EP)
European Court of Justice (ECJ)
Court of First Instance (CFI)
European Central Bank (ECB)

## NOTES

1. Michael Veseth was the author of this chapter in earlier editions of the text. In this edition of the text Hendrik Hansen edited the chapter and updated several parts of it. Our thanks to Professor Hansen for his contributions to this chapter and his input on others.
2. Monnet served as deputy director of the League of Nations in the 1920s, a position that no doubt taught him both the need for cooperation among European nations and the tremendous difficulty of achieving that cooperation.
3. These nations were not, of course, natural political allies, which has created many difficulties, but one of the aims of economic integration has been to overcome political divisions.
4. Not all nations could enter the EEC, however. Recall that one goal of economic integration was to create a capitalist democratic barrier to communism. EEC members were required, therefore, to be democratic members of the Western alliance. This kept neutral nations (Switzerland) or nations with authoritative governments (Austria at this time) from joining.
5. It is important to distinguish the European Council, the Council of the EU (Council of Ministers), and the Council of Europe. The last one is not part of the EU institutions, but was founded in 1949 in the midst of the Cold War in an attempt to promote a security structure for Europe. In 2006 the Council of Europe had forty-five members and was concerned mainly with human rights issues.
6. Before Bulgaria and Romania joined the EU in 2007, the number of commissioners was twenty-five.
7. The voter turnout for EP elections has been constantly declining since the first election. In 1979, 62.4 percent of all persons eligible to vote participated in the election, whereas in the last election in 2004, the turnout was only 45.7 percent.
8. David P. Calleo, *Rethinking Europe's Future* (Princeton, NJ: Princeton University Press, 2001), p. 10.
9. Ibid.
10. Bill Emmott, *20:21 Vision: Twentieth-Century Lessons for the Twenty-First Century* (New York: Farrar, Straus & Giroux, 2003), p. 122.
11. Ibid., p. 143.

# 12

# Japan at the Crossroads

## OVERVIEW[1]

Rising from the ashes of World War II, Japan achieved an economic growth "miracle" that made it the envy of many other countries. One factor that contributed to Japan's dramatic rise was a particular set of close state–market relationships that is sometimes called "Japan, Inc.," but may more appropriately be termed the *developmental state*. Working as a team, Japan's state and market actors led their nation to become the second largest economy in the world. However, the "**iron triangle**" of Japanese political economy that links business, politicians, and the bureaucracy remained constant while the world inside and outside Japan changed. The system that once dominated does so no longer.

In the first edition of this book, written when Japan's influence was at its peak, we asked what Japan would do with its great wealth and increasing power. Would it take a more active leadership role in international affairs or would it continue its inward focus on national concerns? Events of the last decade now make these questions seem premature. In the second edition, we sought to understand Japan's political and economic malaise. During the 1990s Japan suffered a series of political upheavals and economic crises that taxed its wealth and sapped its power. Significantly, the developmental state that built Japan seemed unable to guide it to a recovery.

As this edition is being prepared, Japan remains mired in political and economic institutions that seemingly must change but have not. There is a growing sense, however, that Japan is now at a crossroads and that it must soon abandon the path that has brought it to this point and choose a new direction. Like a phoenix from the ashes, within a single generation, Japan rose from military defeat and economic devastation to become a world-class producer, exporter, and financier. The Cold War was good for Japan, but the years since 1989 witnessed a decline in Japan nearly as amazing as its dramatic rise. Taken together, Japan's rise and decline present a puzzle to students of IPE.

This chapter is therefore a discussion of the puzzle that Japan's postwar history presents. How did the developmental state contribute to Japan's economic miracle? How and why did Japan fall from the heights? Why has Japan been so slow to recover? And if Japan is now at a crossroads, what can it do? It is also a case study of how continuity and change can intersect in international political economy (IPE), with surprising and important consequences.

Japan has employed a version of "developmental capitalism" that allows for a much greater government role in promoting the country's international competitiveness than is typical in Anglo-American liberal capitalism. This unique system was often given credit for Japan's dramatic rise. Today, however, it is often blamed for Japan's sudden and prolonged fall. Does the developmental state deserve either the credit or the blame? The iron triangle that links its politicians, bureaucrats, and large businesses is rusty and old, ready to collapse but somehow still standing. Will Japan abandon it? Can Japan change? To begin to answer these questions about Japan's present and future, we must know a little about its past.

## PATTERNS OF CONTINUITY AND CHANGE IN JAPANESE HISTORY

Former U.S. Undersecretary of State George Ball once remarked that Japan's history has never been charted by the same kind of wavering curve that has marked the progress of other countries; instead it resembles more a succession of straight lines, broken periodically by sharp angles, as the whole nation, moving full speed, suddenly wheeled like a "well-drilled army corps" to follow a new course. There is nothing else in all human history to match it.[2]

These abrupt pivots took Japan from centuries of xenophobic isolation to open-armed welcome and emulation of the West in the last decades of the nineteenth century, from militarist imperialism to pacifist commercialism in the first half of the twentieth century, and from a position as an economic straggler to one of the most important national economies in the world.

Despite these remarkable turnabouts, Japan's association with the world has also been marked by several continuities. The first of these is Japan as emulator. Throughout history, Japan has borrowed liberally from the ideas, institutions, and technologies of those cultures and societies it has seen as having something superior to Japan's own. The Japanese, however, have in no way felt compelled to maintain the purity of these borrowings from abroad, adapting them to fit their own needs and, in the course of this process, often improving or enhancing the original.

Many of us are aware that VCRs and corporate "quality control circles" were both adopted from the United States and then adapted to Japan (and subsequently reintroduced to the United States), but the same can also be said for Zen Buddhism and chopsticks, which were borrowed from China. Japan was introduced to Confucianism via Korea, and to Western science and technology via the Dutch. It copied its first national constitution from that of the Prussians (postwar U.S. occupation forces literally wrote Japan's current constitution) and also adopted the German school system. When a local Japanese militia was soundly defeated by British gunships in the 1860s, the militia leaders surrendered and immediately requested to come on board the British man-of-war to see (and learn from) what had defeated them.

Second, the Japanese have always viewed the world in terms of hierarchy. International entities (countries, empires, races), like internal entities (family members, classes, companies), are seen and ranked in stair-step fashion. For most of Japan's history, the Japanese have viewed their nation as inferior to its powerful neighbors—China, Russia, Britain, and the United States. However, as Japan rose in stature and these neighboring countries declined either relatively or absolutely, Japan frequently shifted from idolizing to disdaining these countries.

A final continuity is Japan's national **corporatism**. Japan's island status and the relative homogeneity of its people have given the Japanese a very strong and sharply delineated sense of nationalism. This sense of tribe has often led the Japanese to adopt a mercantilist view of the world, with zero-sum gains and losses accruing either to Japan or to its competitors. It has also inspired the Japanese to great sacrifice on behalf of their nation, again often acting as Ball described—a well-drilled army corps—in both former military exploits and more recent economic campaigns. Although there have been important voices of opposition to national marching orders of both the imperial and commercial variety, the Japanese have strong social and cultural incentives to comply and co-operate. We need to keep these continuities in mind as we trace the "sharp angles" of Japan's modern history.

## HISTORY: FROM ISOLATIONIST TO IMPERIALIST

When European traders and missionaries first began arriving on Japan's shores in the mid-sixteenth century, they found a Japan that, for all its cultural differences, had a social and political economy strikingly similar to that of feudal Europe some 300 years earlier. At the end of the sixteenth century, one family emerged as the most powerful among these feudal lords and was able to name its successive patriarchs as the *shogun*, or dominant overlord, of Japan.

Over the next two-and-a-half centuries, this dynasty led Japan from decentralized martial anarchy to increasing national unification under the guidance of a highly capable bureaucracy, staffed by members of the former warrior or *samurai* class. This legacy of a skilled, disciplined, and highly respected bureaucracy intensely loyal to its political leaders gave Japan a very valuable asset in its modernization drive during the last century and a resilient capacity for enduring rapid change.

This *shogunal* government also severed Japan's ties with the rest of the world through a "closed country" policy of almost total seclusion. During the first half of the seventeenth century, the government expelled all foreign missionaries, virtually cut off foreign trade, and made travel abroad (or at least the return therefrom) punishable by death.

Two-and-a-half centuries of seclusion were brought to an abrupt end with the arrival of Commodore Matthew Perry and his squadron of four U.S. warships in 1853 with a presidential mandate to open trade negotiations with Japan. Well aware of China's failed efforts to resist Western gunboat diplomacy a decade earlier, the Japanese government acquiesced to a series of unequal treaties over the next few years, which opened certain Japanese ports to foreign trade.

This forced opening threw Japan into a quandary about how to react to this Western threat and the superior technology behind it. Although there was general consensus about the need to strengthen Japan's national defense, the role of foreigners and foreign learning was much debated. In the short run, xenophobic *samurai* terrorists succeeded in both angering the foreigners and weakening the government. In the long run, a group of forward-looking moderate reformer *samurai* prevailed, crushing the terrorists, ousting the crumbling feudal government in a near-bloodless coup, and establishing a new revolutionary government in 1868 in the name of the youthful *Meiji* emperor.

### Mercantilism and the Postal Savings Bank

This group of young *samurai*-turned-bureaucrats presided over a revolutionary overhaul of the Japanese political economy and its foreign policy. These leaders were witnessing the literal carving up of neighboring China at the hands of Western colonial powers and realized that quick action would be necessary to avoid a similar fate. As good mercantilists, Japan's leaders were convinced of the intimate relationship between economic development and industrialization on one hand, and military and political power in the international arena on the other. They promoted a mercantilist national policy of simultaneously building a "rich country and a strong army" (*fukoku kyoohei*).

Japan's "well-drilled army corps" of public bureaucrats, militarists, and private industrialists succeeded remarkably well on both counts of this national policy, establishing in the same broad stroke Japan as the first non-Western industrial capitalist economy and the first non-Western imperialist power. The state bureaucracy, staffed by able former *samurai*, played a crucial role in this Meiji industrialization, working hand in hand with huge private conglomerates known as *zaibatsu*.

In 1875, for example, Japan established a **Postal Savings Bank** system that channeled much of Japan's private wealth into government hands, especially in rural areas that city banks did not serve. Citizens trusted their savings to the local postmaster, who transferred them to the state bureaucracy, which made sure that these resources were used to build infrastructure and industry to strengthen Japan. The *zaibatsu* and other large businesses benefited from their access to these funds.

The Postal Savings Bank is in many respects the perfect example of the Japanese political economy. Japanese leaders learned of this system when the first contingent of *Meiji* reformers—the "Iwakura mission"—traveled on a British merchant marine vessel in their odyssey to learn from the West from 1871 to 1873, with stops in the United States and Europe. They learned about the Postal Bank system from the British Navy, which used the savings system to pay its sailors and, in classic form, they emulated the successful system they observed. Japan's Postal Savings Bank became an important part of the system that drove postwar Japanese growth. It is a key link in the iron triangle that connects politicians, bureaucrats, and big businesses. It is today, well past Japan's economic zenith, the world's largest bank, with more than $2 trillion in total deposits. To put this figure in perspective, the Postal Savings Bank has about six times the deposits of Citibank, the largest U.S. bank. In fact, the Postal Savings Bank has about as large a deposit base as the top ten banks in the United States put together. We will refer back to the Postal Savings Bank at several points in this chapter to illustrate key points about Japan's rise, fall, and current plight.

## The 1940 System in War and Peace

In less than fifty years, Japan went from a position of backwater isolation to that of the first non-Western world power in the international political economy. Over the next several decades, Japan industrialized at a frenetic pace, defeated both China and Russia in decisive military victories, and began a systematic imperial expansion throughout Asia. Inspired by both a perceived destiny to unite its Asian neighbors under its influence in a "Greater East Asian Co-prosperity Sphere" and the growing demands of a ravenous military-industrial complex, Japan saw its relations with both its Asian neighbors and the Western powers spiral downward during the 1930s as the Japanese empire expanded. Budding democracy within Japan during the 1920s gave way to rising militarism and ultranationalism, propelling Japan into war first with China and then with the United States and its Western allies.

In fact, many of the distinctive aspects of Japan's political economy today—such as high savings rates, protective trade barriers, lifetime employment, seniority-based wages, and close government ties with industry—are direct or indirect results of policies that Japan adopted in 1940 to help prepare the country for war.[3] The **1940 System**, as it has been called, maximized the military and industrial resources at the state's command by squeezing consumers and smaller businesses. The United States adopted its own system of rationing and resource allocation during World War II but abandoned it at war's end. Japan's system survived.

Like its nineteenth-century policy of seclusion, Japan's twentieth-century imperial expansion ended abruptly as the result of foreign pressure. In this case it took the form of military defeat and U.S. military occupation of Japan for seven years. And like Commodore Perry before him, General Douglas MacArthur forced processes of change in Japan that ultimately proved beneficial and that Japan would likely have been unable to make for itself. General MacArthur and his reform-minded administrators remained in Japan from the time of its surrender in 1945 until 1952, launching sweeping changes in the country's political, social, and economic institutions that were designed, in part, to break up the 1940 System.

Initially planning to remake Japan as a prosperous but neutral "Switzerland of Asia," MacArthur and his staff purged the military, the ultranationalist societies, and most wartime political leaders and *zaibatsu* business leaders. This purge destroyed the military class, replaced entrenched politicians with technocrats, replaced *zaibatsu* families with professional managers, and, most significantly, left the bureaucracy intact and in a position of overwhelming power relative to the other groups. MacArthur also presided over the rewriting of the Japanese constitution (including a clause renouncing forever the use of war or offensive military force), the breaking-up of the *zaibatsu*, extending the vote to all men and women, and guaranteeing to Japanese citizens civil rights similar to those in the United States.

Upon the "loss of China" and the onset of the Cold War, however, MacArthur and the U.S. government began to fear that Japan too could fall to communism. This led to an about-face in occupation policy beginning in 1947. The earlier emphasis on Japan as a "Switzerland" gave way to one of Japan as a full, albeit still unarmed, ally of the West with the full support and protection of the United States as patron. Conservative politicians who supported the alliance (many of whom had previously been purged) were rehabilitated and came to dominate Japanese politics. The broken-up *zaibatsu* reemerged as more loosely organized and professionally managed *keiretsu* and quickly regained their dominance of the Japanese economy.

The political economy system that was created to prepare Japan to win the war was restored, in modified form, to enable Japan to win the peace. With the elite bureaucracy at the helm and as a favored client of the United States, Japan was ready for its remarkable postwar catch-up.

## MULTIPLE EXPLANATIONS OF JAPAN'S ECONOMIC SUCCESS

Within a single generation, Japan rose from the ashes to become a world-class producer, exporter, and financier. How was this economic "miracle" achieved? This question has been the subject of a great deal of scholarly debate. Understanding what makes Japan "tick" is particularly important for Japan's trading partners, which must compete with Japan in the international political economy.

Analysts have identified a wide range of reasons for Japan's economic success. The popular notion of "Japan, Inc." reflects the belief that the Japanese people are simply a more cooperative bunch than the rest of us. Unlike prototypical "individualistic" Americans, who thrive amid dissent, the Japanese tend to favor group solidarity and consensus. The argument runs that the government, corporate management, and workers in Japan all agree on the primacy of economic development as a societal goal and have worked together to achieve this end. In this, as well as in more specific ways, Japanese cultural traits have translated into high economic growth.

Others have discovered the roots of Japan's success in unique features of its domestic economy, notably the "three sacred treasures" of semi–lifetime employment, seniority wage scales, and company-wide (as opposed to industry-wide) unions. These institutions, which were introduced in the prewar 1940 System, are said to contribute to employee loyalty and to a high degree of harmony between workers and management.

Economists as a rule have focused on the primacy of market forces in Japan.[4] They highlight the role of individual and corporate initiative in a mostly open marketplace as the central drive behind economic development in Japan. According to this line of reasoning, there is nothing exceptional about Japanese-style capitalism, and noneconomic factors have played a negligible part in Japan's economic development. To the extent that the government has positively influenced economic growth, it has been through wise macroeconomic policies. For example, Japan's tax system has historically been conducive to high investment rates. The country's lack of antitrust regulations has also been a boon to business. Japanese companies are allowed to pool their resources in the pursuit of joint research and development.

Those who emphasize the role of private initiative in Japan's development are particularly critical of the view that government-promoted "industrial policy" is relevant to understanding Japan's remarkable economic performance. They are skeptical about the ability of economic bureaucrats to devise a coherent national economic plan that anticipates the "winner" and "loser" industries of the future, and they see Japan's more recent downturn as vindication of their position.

A final argument about the roots of Japanese economic success after World War II nonetheless focuses on the role of the government or the state in fostering Japan's economic development. Advocates of this **developmental state capitalism** argument take issue with both the cultural perspective (that Japanese behavior can be reduced to the society's "Japaneseness") and the economics perspective (that Japan operates according to free-market principles). According to this perspective, the various "unique institutions" found in Japan are not isolated phenomena but rather are best understood as parts of a larger political and economic system. During the postwar period, the Japanese government set its sights on catching up with the West industrially and pursued this goal with single-mindedness.

Because it challenges conventional "liberal" understandings of how capitalism functions, and because the view has been propounded as a potential model for development elsewhere, we will take some care to delineate the developmental state argument. The following discussion elaborates on the nature of the Japanese state and its methods of intervening in the Japanese economy to promote industrial development.[5]

## MERCANTILISM MEETS CAPITALISM: THE DEVELOPMENTAL STATE

Those subscribing to the developmental state capitalism explanation depict Japan as possessing a distinct variant of capitalism, one that contrasts dramatically with the Anglo-American model. Three major factors distinguish laissez-faire capitalism from this neomercantilist type of capitalism.[6] The role of the state, the general code of economic conduct, and its underlying philosophical assumptions will be discussed in turn.

### The Role of the State

The factor that perhaps most distinguishes the developmental state capitalism from laissez-faire capitalism is the function of the state in the economy. This makes sense if, as William H. Overholt and others argue, the policies that we associate with the developmental state are for the most part elements of Japan's 1940 Plan. During a war, or the preparation for it, private interests are necessarily subordinated to the security needs of the state. The state must lead, not sit on the sidelines.

Where laissez-faire capitalism is practiced, as in the United States, the state functions as a referee in the marketplace (see Chapter 3), making sure participants in the free enterprise system observe the rules of the game. The government's major regulatory functions include maintaining an open and competitive market and protecting consumers.

In Japan's developmental capitalist system, by contrast, the state exchanges referee garb for a player's jersey. An actual market player itself, the government does not obsess about rules and procedures but rather preoccupies itself with substantive social goals, most especially with promoting the international competitiveness of industry. The state's industrial policy is geared toward this end.

### Codes of Economic Conduct

Beyond the central role of the state in the economy, a general code of economic conduct throughout the entire political and economic system characterizes developmental state capitalism. Lester Thurow's concepts of "consumer economics" and "producer economics" capture key differences in the guiding principles of laissez-faire and development capitalism, respectively.[7] Where principles of consumer economics reign, market participants are driven by the desire to maximize profits. In this case, the overall measure of economic performance for the society is consumer welfare.

In producer-oriented countries, on the other hand, profit maximization is certainly desirable for capitalists, but it is hardly an end in itself. In countries such as Japan, managers aim rather for market share as an avenue to "strategic conquest" for their firms. The measures of performance in a production-oriented system are high savings and high investment, not increased consumption and leisure.

A frequently noted feature of the Japanese economy is the substantial size of its national savings. Japan's gross national savings (as a percent of gross national product) at its zenith reached nearly 40 percent in the postwar period.[8] Japanese households account for a substantial share of the national savings. Between 1960 and 1980 the Japanese on average saved around 20 percent of their disposable personal income, which was at least three times the amount the average American saved during the same period.[9] Countries geared toward producer economics are organized to suppress consumption and encourage investment.

### Underlying Philosophical Assumptions

Finally, distinct assumptions about the essential nature of economic activity undergird both laissez-faire and developmental capitalism. From your knowledge of liberalism and mercantilism (see

Chapters 2 and 3), you have probably already been able to identify the intellectual forebears of each of these strands of capitalism. Whereas capitalism as we have come to know it in the West clearly has liberal roots, capitalism in Japan was built on mercantilist assumptions about the nature of economic production and exchange.

In an article in the *Atlantic Monthly*, James Fallows examined the different premises operating behind "Anglo-American" and Japanese thinking about economics.[10] He noted the great extent to which John Locke and Adam Smith influenced British and U.S. understanding of how society should function. From Locke we learned the supreme importance of individuals. From Smith we learned that free markets maximize prosperity. These beliefs, which are articles of faith in the West, are not universally accepted in other parts of the world. In Japan, the welfare of the group takes precedence over individual rights. And in Japan, the ideas of German philosopher Friedrich List carry much more weight than do those of Adam Smith. As Fallows noted: "In Japan economics has in effect been considered a branch of geopolitics—that is, as the key to the nation's strength or vulnerability in dealing with other powers."[11]

The two economic visions divide dramatically over their perception of the degree of harmony and conflict in the international political economy. In outlining the two clashing worldviews of Adam Smith and Friedrich List, Fallows commented on the tremendous optimism among Americans and British that everyone can prosper at once from international economic exchange. World trade is viewed as a *positive-sum* game. However, mercantilists in general, and the Japanese in particular, view business rather as war. Superior economic powers will inevitably vanquish those nations that fall behind. Trade is a *zero-sum* game. "Therefore nations must think about it strategically, not just as a matter of where they can buy the cheapest shirt this week."[12]

## HOW JAPAN WON THE COLD WAR

The cultural explanation, the "free markets" explanation, and the "developmental state capitalism" explanation of Japanese economic development all share one common feature: They focus on the domestic determinants of Japanese economic success. An argument that we have not yet considered draws attention to the importance of the international context in which Japan's phenomenal economic growth occurred. Arguably, Japan's economic success can be explained largely by the Cold War and the relationship between the United States and Japan that it produced.

Kenneth Pyle and Don Hellman are among those who have underscored the extent to which Japan benefited from the post–World War II international order. Pyle details the ways in which the Cold War rivalry between the United States and the Soviet Union led the United States to shelter Japan from the vagaries of international politics, permitting the Japanese to focus their attention and resources on achieving economic growth.[13] Similarly, Hellman refers to the "international greenhouse effect" of U.S. patronage, which permitted Japan to flourish "free from the costs and uncertainties of full participation in international political and security affairs."[14]

U.S. policy toward Japan in the post–World War II period logically followed from its preoccupation with the Soviet Union. In order to "contain" the spread of Soviet communism, the United States established alliances around the world. As noted earlier, the mission of the U.S. occupation of Japan thus shifted from promoting democratic reforms to rehabilitating Japan as the chief Asian ally of the United States against the Soviet foe at the outset of the Cold War.

Advocates of the "free rider" thesis have pointed to at least three specific ways in which the U.S.–Japanese relationship during the Cold War supported Japanese economic growth. First, the United States footed the bill for Japanese defense, thus freeing Japanese resources for industrial production. By the terms of the U.S.–Japanese security treaty signed in 1951, the United States guaranteed Japan's security in exchange for extensive military prerogatives in Japan. Japan had essentially allowed itself to become a military satellite of the United States in order to focus single-mindedly on a mercantilist program of catching up with the West economically.

Second, the United States provided cheap technology transfers to Japan following World War II. The importation of technology from the more industrially advanced United States allowed Japanese producers to accelerate the development process. Japan was especially dependent on technology imports in the high-growth industries that were targeted for development.

Finally, the United States promoted the Japanese economic buildup through its international trade policy. Following World War II, the United States worked to maintain a free trading order in the capitalist world. The United States opened wide its markets to Japanese exports and did not require the favor to be returned in kind during much of the Cold War period. However, the increasing global competitiveness of Japanese industry, and Japan's accompanying trade surplus with the United States, gave rise to expanding political friction between the trading partners. Since the late 1960s, trade tensions between the United States and Japan have gradually heightened in intensity and broadened in scope (see Chapter 6). However, as long as Cold War security concerns prevailed in U.S. policymaking circles, The United States did not require Japan to maintain reciprocity in bilateral relations. Over time, however, growing U.S. protectionist sentiment has increasingly impinged on Japan's ability to take a "free ride" in the international trading arena.

Whether the source of Japan's economic growth was mainly domestic, as the theory of the developmental state asserts, or due in greater measure to the particular international political and economic environment in which the developmental state operated remains an open question. There is no ambiguity, however, about the outcome. Japan won the Cold War in the sense that it emerged from the long years of the U.S.–Soviet conflict with substantial economic wealth and growing political influence. In the first edition of this textbook we concluded that the main problem facing Japan in the international political economy would be to decide what to do with its wealth and power. The events of the 1990s showed that this question was, at the very least, considerably premature.

## WINNING THE COLD WAR BUT LOSING THE PEACE

The first decade of the post–Cold War era was not kind to Japan. Its economy suffered several sharp reversals that shook the foundations of its unique economic institutions, such as lifetime employment. Japan's political system was also badly shaken by a series of corruption scandals and partisan realignments.

The contrast between recent economic conditions and the Cold War years can be seen by looking at Japan's real **gross domestic product (GDP)**, the most basic indicator of national economic conditions. Table 12–1 provides data from 1984 to 2002 for both Japan and the United

**TABLE 12–1    Japan's Economic Growth in Perspective**

| YEAR | ECONOMIC GROWTH (CHANGE IN REAL GROSS DOMESTIC PRODUCT) | |
|------|------|------|
| | JAPAN | UNITED STATES |
| 1984–1993 | 3.7 | 3.2 |
| 1994 | 0.9 | 4.0 |
| 1995 | 1.7 | 2.7 |
| 1996 | 3.6 | 3.6 |
| 1997 | 1.8 | 4.4 |
| 1998 | −1.2 | 4.3 |
| 1999 | 0.8 | 4.1 |
| 2000 | 2.4 | 3.8 |
| 2001 | −0.3 | 0.3 |
| 2002 | −0.5 | 2.2 |

*Source:* Data from *Economic Report of the President,* 2003.

States. Both countries experienced healthy economic growth during the decade 1984–1993, as the Cold War wound down and communist states collapsed. Japan's average annual growth rate of 3.7 percent per year was in fact half a percentage point higher than the U.S. growth rate. After 1993, however, the story was much different. Japan's growth rate was lower than the U.S. rate, apart from 1996 when they were equal, and Japan's real GDP actually fell during three years, 1998, 2001, and 2002. Each percentage change in real GDP represents billions of dollars of income and hundreds of thousands of jobs. When real GDP falls during a recession, the impact is widespread and significant in economic, social, and political terms—all the more so in a nation like Japan, which had come to count on the developmental state's ability to keep the economy moving steadily ahead. Japan's developmental state stagnated and fell dramatically behind the United States in these years.

The economic crises in Japan were accompanied by proliferating political scandals and rampant party realignments. Although campaign finance scandals are certainly not new to Japan's political scene (or those of other electoral democracies), the number and nature of these scandals during the past fifteen years have been particularly troubling (and scandalous).

Generous and occasionally illicit contributions from the private business sector to the coffers of political parties (particularly the ruling Liberal Democratic Party or LDP) and individual politicians have been a fundamental aspect of Japanese politics. In the past, however, these payments, and certainly these scandals, had involved (or at least embroiled) only politicians, not the highly respected bureaucratic policymakers. These bureaucrats or civil servants were seen by the public as being above the fray of backroom political deals, acting in the national interest as they guided the nation's finely tuned economic machine. The winding down of this economic juggernaut in the early 1990s coincided with a proliferation of both campaign and corporate finance scandals and the unprecedented revelation that bureaucrats from the respected ministries of finance, health, and trade were also participating (and profiting) from the arrangements. This unfortunate convergence of events called into question not only the wisdom of bureaucratic policies (which, it was argued, had led to the bubble and its collapse), but also the legitimacy of Japan's system of stable bureaucratic governance that had been its post–World War II hallmark.

These events (and the increasing unpopularity of government policies) in turn led in 1993 to the rapid and unprecedented fragmentation of the ruling LDP, which had dominated the Japanese political scene for nearly four decades. Sensing the declining popularity of the LDP and increasingly frustrated at the conservative intransigence of its party elders, a number of reformers within the party jumped ship with their supporters, launching a rush to the exits that swept the LDP from office and threw Japanese parliamentary politics into disarray. During the subsequent three years, eleven separate political parties shared power and four different individuals (tenuously) held the office of prime minister.

The LDP was able to reenter government, initially in an alliance with two other parties and then as the sole party of government by 1996. It adapted successfully to the electoral reforms that its opponents enacted. Every prime minister since 1996 has come from the LDP—a statistic that exaggerates somewhat the party's position of dominance. The legitimacy of the LDP however, remains in question, and its ability to enact policies decisively is always in doubt.

Japan experienced two bubbles in the 1990s: an economic bubble and a political bubble. When or how Japan will recover its economic growth and political efficacy remains unclear at this writing. The next two sections will look more deeply at the economic and political problems and speculate about how and when they might be resolved.

Japan's problems are striking. However, what is striking is not that Japan has suffered political and economic crises—it seems that no nation can avoid such problems indefinitely. What is striking is that these problems have persisted over more than a decade. Surprisingly perhaps, given our earlier characterization of its "well-drilled army corps," Japan has been unable thus far to reverse its direction and begin to move ahead again.

## THE BUBBLE ECONOMY

In retrospect, it is clear that the Japanese economy became dominated by a financial bubble in the 1980s and early 1990s. The bubble burst, although the pieces have stopped falling, and it may be some time before the full effect of the bubble's explosion has been felt. The problem that Japan faces today is how to reinvigorate its economy without reinflating the bubble.

"Bubbles" are a common problem in financial markets, as we saw when this concept was introduced in Chapter 8. A financial bubble takes shape when economic activities are driven more by expectations of growth than by the fundamental factors that produce growth. Japan's dramatic economic successes in the years after World War II set up expectations that high levels of growth would continue into the future. Slowly and subtly, investors began to act on this expectation instead of on a realistic assessment of current and future events.

It can be argued that the bubble economy was perhaps one of the first signs that the 1940 Plan, designed to mobilize resources for war and successful in building the nation during the Cold War, was breaking down. As Japan's economy prospered, increasingly gigantic sums were channeled to the state through the Postal Savings Bank and other parts of the financial system. Some of these funds were used to increase Japan's already strong infrastructure, and some went to support further expansion of the *keiretsu*. Infrastructure investment boomed, to the delight of Japanese construction firms that were strong supporters of the LDP officials who brought them contracts each year. With easy access to cheap credit, *keiretsu* were free to make risky investments, financing losses with additional loans from a seemingly inexhaustible pool of funds. Japan, the producer economy, surged ahead.

But who was going the buy the products that these investments would ultimately produce? The 1940 Plan encouraged production, not consumption. Productive capacity in Japan continued to rise, but not the desire to consume. During the Cold War, Japanese firms might have aggressively sought to market their products abroad. However, things were different after the collapse of communism, and Japan's mercantilism was no longer tolerated to the same degree. The bottom line is that large firms and the banks that supported them were not able to invest the funds as productively as in the past. So the money found its way into financial bubbles instead.

The first bubble occurred in the market for land and real estate and was called the "property bubble." Land has long been an expensive item in Japan. Land-intensive products, such as golf course memberships, are startlingly costly in Japan, relative to their price in more land-abundant countries such as the United States and Canada. As the economy grew and more funds were available to spend on luxuries, the price of land shot up. As price increases continued, a bubble was formed. Investors bought land not because they wanted to use it, but only because they were convinced that someone else would soon be willing to pay even more for it.[15]

As the property bubble inflated, real estate prices soared in Japan, creating a mountain of financial wealth. Soon a form of contagion occurred as investors used the inflated value of their property as collateral for loans, which were invested in Japan's stock market. The property bubble thus fueled a stock market bubble. Soon investors were buying stocks based only on the expectation of future price rises, not on the profitability of the underlying businesses. Table 12–2 shows how the bubble inflated. The Nikkei stock index doubled between 1983 and 1987 and then nearly doubled again between 1987 and 1989—a growth in stock prices that exceeded the growth of the Japanese economy by an astronomical amount.[16] Essentially, the money flows that once built up Japanese industrial productivity were now bidding up the prices of Japan's businesses instead.

Financial bubbles can only sustain themselves as long as expectations continue to rise. A sudden shift in expectations can lead to a sell-off, when prices collapse suddenly as the force driving the market switches. This happened in the property market first. Japanese investors became concerned that real estate prices would not continue to rise and tried to sell off their property holdings before the price fell. A panic ensued and the Japanese land market collapsed.

Falling real estate prices were an even bigger problem than you might expect, however, because the stock market bubble was supported in part by loans based on high property values. As

**TABLE 12–2   Japan's Stock Market Bubble**

| YEAR | NIKKEI 225 STOCK AVERAGE |
|------|--------------------------|
| 1983 | 9,893 |
| 1985 | 13,113 |
| 1987 | 21,564 |
| 1989 | 38,915 |
| 1991 | 22,983 |
| 1993 | 17,417 |
| 1995 | 19,868 |
| 1998 | 13,842 |
| 1999 | 18,934 |
| 2001 | 10,542 |
| 2002 | 8,578 |
| 2003 | 9,752 |

*Source:* Data from Bank of Japan and CNN. Data for 2003 is closing average on August 13, 2003. Data for all other years is the closing price on the last trading day of the year.

real estate prices fell, investors were forced to sell off their stock holdings, too. The result was the stock market crash seen in Table 12–2. Japanese stocks lost over 50 percent of their value between 1989 and 1993. To the extent that Japanese families and businesses had invested their wealth in property and stocks, they were now very much poorer. Stock prices fell even further in 2001 and 2002 as Japan experienced a national recession. Overall, the Nikkei stock index fell from 38,915 at the end of 1989 to just 9,752 in 2003.

Japan's banks were caught in the middle of the property and stock bubbles. They had accepted property as collateral and had lent money to customers who bought stocks. Many had actively encouraged prospective borrowers (some Japanese banks employ agents who call at customer homes every month to collect deposits, solicit loan opportunities, and sell financial products such as life insurance). As both real estate and stock bubbles burst, many banks were left with huge liabilities and few assets of real value. Japan began to experience a banking crisis that got less publicity than the property and stock bubbles but that has proved to be of even greater long-term economic significance.

Banks were in many ways the key economic institutions of the Japanese postwar miracle. The close ties that the developmental state forged between Japan's government (especially the powerful Ministry of Finance) and its financial community provided many benefits when the Japanese economy was growing rapidly, and later during the period when the property and stock bubbles were building. However, these relationships exacerbated problems during the collapse and its aftermath. Insolvent banks were propped up and kept going by sympathetic regulators, rather than being shut down or forced to merge with solvent banks. Some of these insolvent banks lent good money after bad, as they extended credit to insolvent customers, in the hope that things would turn around, so that their loans could be repaid and things would return to normal.

Viewers of old horror movies know that "zombies" (*zonbi* in Japanese) are the living dead. They can no longer live, but they can't die either. Many Japanese businesses became zombies in the aftermath of the bubble collapse. They were so indebted that there was no way that they could recover and operate independently again. However, their banks would not let them die, because the bad loans might drag the banks down as well. So the banks continually extended loans and injected new financing into the veins of failing bussinesses, keeping them alive just a little longer on the chance that conditions might change radically.

Where was the developmental state? "Teamwork" between Japan's bankers and their government regulators, a key aspect of the system, made the financial system's problems worse, not better. The last thing that government regulators wanted to do was to shut down the businesses they were charged with strengthening. The bank funds that once went to build these firms now functioned as life-support systems.

Critics of the Japanese economic system gave a new name to the developmental state in the wake of these economic woes. They began to call it **crony capitalism.** The Japanese political economy was not so much a "team" of able bureaucrats, loyal politicians, and efficient producers that sought the shared goals of national wealth and power, the critics said; rather, it was a set of tight personal and professional relationships that systematically exploited the public interest for the gain of a narrow group at the top.

If Japan's developmental state was slow to respond to the recession, the famous *keiretsu* form of business organization only compounded the problem. During the boom years, the *keiretsu* were seen as a key to Japan's growth. These complex "teams" of businesses could support each other and take organized actions that were in their long-term collective interests (as opposed to U.S. firms, which compete for short-term gain). At the heart of each of the *keiretsu* was a banking system that channeled funds to needy member businesses. As long as the economy was growing rapidly, there was plenty of money in the *keiretsu* to cover losses and to subsidize short-run problems with long-run investment strategies.

As Japan's economy slowed down and then eventually contracted, these banks found that their role within the *keiretsu* was in direct conflict with the fundamental principles of sound finance. During a recession, a bank should make loans only to the best-financed and most creditworthy customers. During a recession, however, a *keiretsu* bank is supposed to make loans to money-losing team members. As the economic slowdown persisted and intensified, the financial condition of *keiretsu* banks worsened dramatically until, finally, they represented a liability to the collective enterprise.

The *keiretsu*, the engines of Japan's economic miracle, gradually became more like black holes, the collapsed stars whose gravity is so dense that not even light can escape their hold. As the economic miracle unraveled, the *keiretsu* became monetary black holes. Deeply indebted, they immediately used any funds they received to pay down debt, not to create jobs. As much money as could be pumped their way was absorbed into the black holes, but made little dent in their indebtedness. This became a major problem. It is a serious mistake to systematically channel a nation's wealth into a black hole. This could not change, however, without breaking the iron triangle, which was ultimately a political arrangement.

## THE POLITICAL BUBBLE

According to many economic liberals, the bubble that formed in Japan's political system during its years of growth and prosperity was distinctly different from its economic bubble. The economic bubble was like a balloon that grew bigger and bigger until it finally burst. The political bubble was more like a soap bubble—bright, shining, but fragile on the outside and essentially empty on the inside. The political turmoil that Japan experienced in the 1990s popped this illusory shell and revealed the vacuous contents of Japan's politics. The Japanese political bubble was the illusion that the Liberal Democratic Party, Japan's "ruling" party for nearly four decades, genuinely governed Japan, when in reality Japan's elected politicians engaged in little more than soap-bubble politics. Some claim that the LDP is grossly misnamed: It has been neither liberal, democratic, nor even a party. As already discussed, the policies the LDP stood for have been neomercantilist, not liberal. Its politics have been decidedly elitist, not democratic. And organizationally, it has not been a party with shared policy goals and ideological values so much as a broad collection of factions or miniparties, divided by personal loyalties and favors. LDP politics in Japan was not so different from the picture of organized crime painted in the classic movie *The Godfather*—little more than contests between and among factions in the LDP for leadership and the spoils of political office.

Thus, a bubble facade of unity, democracy, and political effectiveness masked intramural divisions not over policy differences, but rather over the struggle for essential electoral resources—campaign funds and access to political pork barrels. This facade was perpetuated to please the U.S. Cold War patrons (who desired both liberal policies and democratic politics) and to mollify the Japanese electorate. The underlying inefficacy that such a system entailed persisted because the politicians were never intended, expected, nor allowed to rule; rather, they reigned. Rather than being governed by elected politicians, Japan has been ruled by the bureaucratic mandarins who make up the powerful ministries responsible for Japan's developmental state. In a frequently used Japanese metaphor, elected politicians have been *Kabuki* puppets, whose strings have been pulled not by voters (nor even by special-interest groups), but by the hidden bureaucratic puppet masters. These insulated architects of the developmental state were seldom questioned as long as the economy grew.

How could politicians *not* be in charge of the policies carried out in their name? The answer is that political institutions in every country evolve according to their own logic. In Japan, politicians are considered to be responsible for advancing the interests of their narrow body of constituents, not for looking out for the policies of the nation as a whole. (The bureaucrats have that role.) Politicians are valued and trusted middlemen who negotiate the bureaucratic maze in their constituents' behalf. In simple terms, much as is in the U.S. House of Representatives, it is the politician's job to bring home the bacon, not to look after the hog it comes from. With politicians thus focusing on voter relations, and the two-way exchange of money and favors that this entails, bureaucrats are free, more or less, to play an independent role in the political economy.

Elected politicians, sustained in office by generous financial support from the *keiretsu* businesses, dutifully "rubber-stamped" policies that were formulated and ultimately implemented by the bureaucracy. However, the implosion of the political bubble—which tore down the curtain and revealed the manipulators—coincided with the bursting of the economic bubble, casting a particularly unfavorable light on bureaucrats and politicians alike, as well as on the oftentimes unseemly strings that connected them to each other and to big business.

If the developmental state was a success, it was partly due to the skill, dedication, and influence of bureaucrats in agencies such as the *Ministry of International Trade and Industry* (MITI)—now called the *Ministry of Economy, Trade and Industry* (METI)—and the *Ministry of Finance*. The essence of this developmental state was administrative influence, not political control. While political factions plotted and warred over pork-barrel programs, bureaucrats in the ministries, undeterred by narrowly conceived special interests, implemented the long-term strategies that we associate with the developmental state. While the LDP factions frequently sought to further only their particular interests, the bureaucrats could look to larger concerns.[17] In short, Japan's bureaucracy was an island of stability in a stormy political sea.[18]

At the same time, the unwillingness or inability of Japan's government to take decisive action to reverse economic decline is more the result of decisions within the bureaucracy than of policies adopted by elected leaders. In Japan the LDP "reigns," but the bureaucracy truly rules.

The idea that the government is controlled by nonelected government employees may strike many readers as undemocratic and undesirable. However, American management guru Peter F. Drucker defended Japan's system, saying that it is both common and desirable.[19] Drucker asserts that elite bureaucracies are more the rule than the exception, even in market economies, and that Japan's system of bureaucratic rule is a good deal less authoritarian than that of some "liberal Western" nations, such as France. The key, Drucker says, is that a bureaucratic elite, elevated above political squabbles and insulated from economic pressures, is able to put society's interest above any narrow group's economic or political interest. This, according to Drucker, is one reason why the Japanese government was so slow and unwilling to act during the growing economic crisis.

Ultimately, Drucker argues, Japan's bureaucracy acted wisely in the face of economic crisis. Rather than caving in to demands for politically expedient policies that would have torn apart important elements of Japan's social structure (for example, forcing insolvent banks to close, thereby destroying some of the *keiretsu*), the bureaucrats confidently preserved Japanese society, sacrificing short-term wealth for long-run social stability.

In the end, the most important key to understanding how the Japanese bureaucracy thinks, works, and behaves is an understanding of Japan's priorities. Americans assume that the economy takes primacy in political decisions, unless national security is seriously threatened. The Japanese, on the other hand—and by no means the bureaucracy alone—accord primacy to society.[20]

Despite the benefits of the bureaucracy and the iron triangle to Japan, however, incomes continued to decline three of the five years between 1998 and 2003. By then, political and economic pressures on Japan to reform its institutions and change paths seemed overwhelming. If Drucker is right about the benefits of the iron triangle, these crises should have been viewed as bumps in the road, not a reversal of fortune. Not everyone agreed, however, with Drucker's optimistic analysis of the situation. It had become harder and harder for citizens to believe that the bureaucracy knew best.

In 2001 Junichiro Koizumi, an LDP member running as a reformist "outsider," won election on a pledge to dismantle the iron triangle and start Japan on the path to political and economic reform. He pledged to shake out the banking system and to privatize the Postal Savings Bank system. However, his repeated efforts have been only partly successful. In the fall of 2006, Prime Minister Koizumi stepped down after serving the maximum five years allowed by the ruling Liberal Democratic Party. Though his tenure did not bring the sweeping systemic overhaul originally promised, his final years in office witnessed what many consider the beginning of a turnaround in the Japanese economy after nearly two decades of economic stagnation. Real estate values are rising and Japanese consumers are beginning to spend more freely.[21] In April 2006, Japan's consumer confidence index peaked above 50 for the first time in sixteen years.[22] What are we to make of this development in light of Japan's long recession during the 1990s? Have reforms worked?

## JAPAN TURNS THE CORNER?

Understandably, until 2004, many economic liberals blamed Japan's iron triangle for the nation's long recession economy and thought it was the reason why the state could not jump start its economy again. Whereas the iron triangle had formerly been a symbol of strength and prosperity, it had become weak and ineffective. During the peak years of Japan's growth in the 1970s and 1980s, bureaucrats provided *keiretsu* with privileged access to scarce resources. In turn, the *keiretsu* made political contributions to LDP politicians, who fought among themselves for rewards but gave the bureaucrats a relatively free hand. At the end of their careers, senior bureaucrats could "descend from heaven" (*amakudari*) while still in their fifties into jobs with big business or pursue a political career and thus benefit personally from their successful strategies.

In the 1990s the bureaucracy's stature was diminished by the failures of its policies and the many scandals that undermined its credibility. Politicians were blamed for the failures of the system they were elected to govern, but which they could not or would not change. Business leaders were saddled with huge debts and a stagnant domestic market. LDP politicians and financial bureaucrats responsible for the Postal Savings Bank collaborated to shore up their position. The Postal Savings Bank extended more loans to medium-sized domestic businesses, rather than to just the large transnational *keiretsu* conglomerates, thus creating a stronger local business constituency for LDP candidates. Ironically, this change may have been a positive one from an economic standpoint, assuming local firms are better able to use Postal Bank funds than the huge, debt-laden enterprises.

Other scholars pointed to uniquely Japanese macro- and microeconomic trends and conditions for answers. Rising consumer expenditures often drive economic growth in the United States. This source of growth, however, seemed to be out of the question in Japan. One reason is Japan's traditionally high savings rates, which, though they were a distinct advantage during the boom years because they made possible investments in Japan's economy, also inflated property and stock bubbles.[23] Now Japan needed its consumers to spend more, but they were naturally hesitant to do so. The stability of the banking system was also very uncertain because of the extensive nonperforming loans extended to "zombie" companies that were unable to repay.

It also did not seem likely that investment spending could provide the boost that Japan needed. Financial investors, of course, lost enormous sums in the property and stock crashes. *Keiretsu* investment was discouraged both by the stagnant economy and by their internal financial problems. In an attempt to stimulate domestic investment, the Bank of Japan in 1998–1999 drove interest rates down to 1 percent, then to $\frac{1}{2}$ percent, and finally to 0 percent! But even at 0 percent interest, no strong demand for investment loans appeared!

Japan's recession and financial crisis also made it more difficult for its firms to export their products. As the financial system weakened, firms began to shift foreign investments back home to shore up their accounts in Japan. As they did this, however, they had to purchase yen on foreign exchange markets, and the rising demand for yen caused the currency to appreciate. As we saw in Chapter 7, a strong yen makes Japan's products more expensive to foreign buyers. The Japanese have given a name to the problem of an overvalued yen: they call it *endaka*. And *endaka* frustrated Japan's attempts to export its way out of recession at several points in the 1990s.

Ironically, as Japanese incomes fell, so did their demand for imported goods and services. Conversely, as economic growth increased in the United States in the 1990s, the demand for Japanese products rose. It appears possible, then, that the U.S. market economy might have done for Japan what it was unable to do for itself: revive the moribund economy. However, as is common in the interdependent global economy, a combination of lower exports to Japan and higher imports from that country also caused the U.S. trade deficit with Japan to soar. Once again, many U.S. political leaders put pressure on Japan to reduce its trade surplus with the United States. Thus, just at the point when Japan wanted to export more to create jobs, it faced stern international pressure to do just the opposite, or in some cases, face a trade war with the United States, which it did on several occasions.

This discussion leads to the suggestion that neither consumers, nor investors, nor exporters could alone answer Japan's economic problem. Since the time of John Maynard Keynes, even the liberal economic tradition has held that sometimes the government needs to do what the private sector, for whatever reason, cannot do. In Japan's case, this would mean a series of spending increases, tax cuts, and financial reforms to stimulate consumer and investment spending. Interestingly, in this case, even most economic liberals do not look to the market to solve Japan's problem—they believe that the market is unnaturally inhibited by the impositions of the iron triangle and must be freed to bring about effective change. To recover economically, then, Japan has been trying to figure out how to escape the quandary of a too strong an iron triangle with a weak political system and economy. Much has been written on how much and where to reform Japanese political institutions, the assumption being that different institutions will produce very different economic results.

## LIVING WITH SUCCESS: UNDOING THE KNOTS

Throughout his term, Prime Minister Koizumi made genuine efforts to reform. Ko Mishima points out two major successes of Koizumi's tenure. Koizumi was able to weaken the position of party powerbrokers, the cornerstones of the LDP who make up factions that are stronger than the party itself. Koizumi limited their ability to nominate candidates. He also weakened *zoku* tribal politicians—mid- and senior-level LDP members of the Diet (the Japanese parliament) who specialize in certain policy areas. In many cases these members block reform to the extent that they serve special interests. Koizumi's other reforms included the Central Government Reform of 2001, which increased the use of examinations for bureaucratic positions and adding more political appointees. The results of these efforts have been only meager so far. In many cases Koizumi proved not to be as assertive a reformer as he might have been and was reluctant to constrain the bureaucracy.[24]

An interesting question is how much reform of the iron triangle would have been possible given its continuing strength. *The Economist* writer John Grimond believes that the iron triangle has remained strong enough to resist reform. For Grimond, "it is hard to say that power resides any-where in particular: the iron triangle is really a Bermuda triangle, within which power—and cer-tainly responsibility—simply disappears."[25] Furthermore, Grimond suggests that because things could not get much worse than they were before 2004, at least in the short term, Japan would not be forced to change by a crisis.

Another important question, then, is this: Even if the iron triangle had been reformed, how much success would a different political institutional structure have had, given the variety of do-mestic and international issues Japan has faced since the 1990s? The implied assumption on the part of many economic liberals seems to be that Japanese institutions should be reformed along with lines of U.S. and British institutions, and that doing so would lead to higher levels of economic growth. Undoubtedly, some features of those bodies might have benefited the Japanese. However, as we have seen in many cases, these institutions are certainly no guarantee the economy will grow much faster than it has grown since the turn of the new century.

When it comes to reform, John Miller argues that the Japanese people have a strong attach-ment to the status quo. Although Japan is capable of abrupt change in the face of crisis, it also has a "striking tendency toward incremental 'change within continuity.'"[26] According to Miller's ob-servations, the Japanese prefer to modify their institutions only gradually. As is the case in the United States, policy change tends to be cautious and incremental. Part of the explanation for this behavior is structural—that slow change is built into Japanese institutions and political values. Miller goes on to characterize the role of society in this issue when he remarks that, in Japan, "con-servatism is not unusual, perhaps rooted in their insularity, respect for tradition, and preoccupation with consensus."[27] This does not preclude the Japanese from seeing themselves as progressive, however, even if they often postpone hard decisions.

## Losing the Past

Instead of institutional reform, what many economic liberal analyses of Japan's political economy fail to take sufficiently into account is a variety of systemic or international economic structural con-ditions that no longer favor Japan. Nor do they particularly favor the United States, the EU, or other industrialized nations to the extent that they did in some other periods. Instead of focusing so much on the issue of reform under the assumption that reform will help "grow" the Japanese economy and ensure that Japan remains democratic, more attention should be placed on what changes in Japan's economy mean in terms of its role in the international political economy and its relation-ships to other states. As we discussed earlier, it is quite difficult for Japan or any other nation to make an economic move without generating protectionist moves from others in reaction. For strong states these moves might include liberalization of one policy area as a means to achieve protec-tionist ends.

One of the biggest changes in the international economy is that, in relative terms, Japan is no longer the economic powerhouse it was twenty years ago. Koizumi's successor, Shinzo Abe, faces a global marketplace that is markedly different from the landscape in which Japan excelled through the 1970s and 1980s. The structure of the international economy is not as easy to benefit from as it was when Japan could employ neomercantilist trade policies at little political and economic cost to itself. Now wealth and power are more evenly distributed among states. Japan is no longer the leader in technology development, production, and foreign direct investment that it once was. As in the case of many of the other developed industrialized nations, Japan's success accounts for part of its downfall in a dynamic international economy in which being successful is sometimes a stroke of luck, but more often is something that has to be earned but that cannot easily be sustained. If any-thing, since the late 1980s, China has been replacing Japan as the major economic power in East Asia.

Japan's mercantilist state so far has kept itself and the nation together incrementally, weath-ering some big storms along the way. The Japanese state has proven to be adaptable. It often makes sacrifices in the short term in pursuit of long-term social objectives that protect and sustain society.

In contrast to those who argue that economic interdependence and globalization have weakened the state, these factors may have limited Japan's options, but they have not rendered it incapable of using different tools or shifting course slightly when it needed to.

## THE FUTURE: A NEW REALISM?

This is only part of the story, however. In terms of the external factors that shape both Japan's economy and its foreign policies, John Miller sees Japan as moving in four relatively distinct but also overlapping directions at the same time.[28] First is a popular movement toward political **reluctant realism** by virtue of its acceptance of collective security responsibilities in concert with a stronger alliance with the United States. Prime Minister Koizumi took significant steps throughout his tenure to expand the role of Japan's **Self-Defense Force (SDF)**, committing troops to participate in noncombat operations in Iraq, UN peacekeeping operations in Cambodia, and signing an agreement in July 2006 to co-develop a ballistic missile defense system with the United States.[29] Since the mid-1990s, military spending has increased in the face of increasing turmoil in Northeast Asia, especially because of North Korea's missile testing and its recent resistance to U.S. and UN efforts to stop the development of its nuclear arsenal. China is also a potential future threat to Japan on a variety of fronts, including missile testing, the increasing size of the Chinese navy and its projection capabilities (the ability to move its forces), and tension caused by skirmishes with the Chinese over the Spratly Island in the South China Sea. Japanese public opinion is divided over the use of the SDF as well as increasing taxes to pay for defense. However, it does support cooperation with the United States in the war on terrorism—a mandate that Abe likely intends to push further.[30]

A second direction is the revival of militarism and ultranationalism favored by a distinct but growing minority of Japanese citizens and officials. This movement has roots in the "Japan Can Say No to the U.S." movement of the 1980s. In the past, Japan was slow to react to issues such as support of the United States and other allies during the Persian Gulf War. The United States cajoled it into paying $13 billion to help cover the cost of that war. Some ultranationalists would like to see Japan once again have a strong military presence in both Asia and globally. One common theme through all of these circumstances is a marked move to the realist right in the LDP's top political leadership—arguably both a factor in and a result of Japan's current regional and global challenges.

Many analysts, particularly those in neighboring countries, see this as a returning theme of militarism and nationalism that recalls Japan's pre–World War II imperial mindset. Both Koizumi and Abe have paid frequent visits to the Yasukuni shrine, a memorial to Japan's World War II dead, that many feel is an inappropriate tribute to past war crimes. They have also implicitly supported local educational authorities in the approval of school textbooks that downplay those same crimes.[31] Actions such as these have sparked popular protests in China and South Korea, invited criticism from other neighbors, and drawn a skeptical international eye.

Shinzo Abe has already taken this remilitarization to a new level. He was overwhelmingly chosen by the LDP as prime minister on a platform dedicated to the reform of Japan's pacifist constitution to accommodate an increasingly proactive—indeed, possibly preemptive—military doctrine, strategy, and arsenal. On the eve of assuming office, he introduced legislation to upgrade the Self-Defense Force to a formal ministry and increase its funding by nearly 60 percent.[32]

A third direction is just the opposite: In many ways Japan is now a democracy built on a pacifism that reflects a change in the character of the Japanese since World War II. The measures introduced and supported by Koizumi and Abe to strengthen Japan are not popular with those who would like to see Japan sustain a more peaceful direction in the international political economy in the future.

Fourth, and finally, there are those who prefer to see Japan continue a mercantilist strategy that stresses accumulating national wealth and insulating itself from international conflicts. Japan's new right also retains values of unilateral mercantilist action—particularly when it comes to energy resources. Inpex, for example, an oil company in which the Japanese government is a major share-holder, is in the process of developing a $2 billion deal to develop an untapped oil field in Iran despite increasing U.S. pressure for sanctions against Iran.[33] This follows an incident in the fall of 2005, when Japan authorized private oil speculation in contested territorial waters of the East China Sea. When China boosted military activity in response, Japan pledged to defend the policy by force if necessary.[34] Ultimately, it is clear that Japan's mercantilist past will remain part of its future policy for some time.

## CONCLUSION

Japan's rise and fall in the past fifty years is a classic study in continuity and change. The Japanese are noted for their ability to transform their political economy and society in the face of external threats, including Great Power colonialism and imperialism in the 1870s, which required a concerted effort to Westernize their society and political economy, militarism, and ultranationalism in the 1930s, and the adoption of democracy and pacifism after World War II.

By 1980 the LDP had successfully sold society a political economic "new orthodoxy" that blended pacifism, consumerism, isolationism, and mercantilism, helping Japan achieve record levels of economic growth, trade surpluses, and the lead in development of new technologies and production techniques.[35] Japan's success was founded on two important factors. One was an iron triangle that linked politicians, bureaucrats, and big business, a system that is still in place today. The second factor was an international political economy that was receptive to the iron triangle's neomercantilist strategy of economic recovery and growth. Likewise, the Japanese benefited from U.S. free-trade policies, which generated markets for Japanese goods.

By the early 1990s, Japan's economic growth had slowed dramatically, leaving structural imbalances everywhere and production far outpacing consumption. Most economic liberals fault an entrenched iron triangle that could not and would not shift to economic liberal trade and development strategies more appropriate for a globalizing economic system. Japanese society has become far more complex, and younger generations of Japanese consumers are not as prepared to make the sacrifices their parents did in the name of national development. At the same time, the global economy is more competitive than ever, and mercantilist policies are not tolerated as they were during the Cold War as the acceptable price of maintaining a strong Japanese ally.

At the same time, Japanese officials continue to resist adopting liberal economic policies, both at home and abroad. Although some officials have promoted political and economic reform, most efforts to change the system have produced little real change. Most economic liberals would like to see Japan reform its political and economic institutions along the lines of the U.S. and British models. They also assume that reform alone will generate growth. However, Japan's iron triangle is still strong enough to resist real reform, leading some experts to wonder if Japan can ever reform its economy and political system. John H. Overholt argues that "postwar Japan was built on a series of institutions that functioned well both for war-fighting and postwar reconstruction, but its economic and political structures have proved too rigid for success in a fast-paced, postindustrial, and global age."[36] Overholt worries that the Japanese economy cannot be sustained, especially in the face of a coming debt crisis.

A mercantilist-realist perspective of the situation suggests that it might be a mistake to expect Japan's iron triangle to crumble, because all three sides of it have much to lose if it collapses. Likewise, intentionally breaking it up may not solve a variety of Japan's complicated and interrelated problems at home and abroad. Japanese history suggests that state officials need a new cause or challenge to fight for or against—a threat so serious that changes, no matter how painful, must be made. The recession of the 1990s in Japan was not serious enough to cause state officials to reverse course or change their policies dramatically. Likewise, globalization has not weakened the state nor prevented it from employing a range of tools to achieve many of its objectives.

Any assessment of Japan's political economy must take into account not only its domestic economy—including the extent to which it reflects a unique combination of political institutions and cultural values and beliefs—but also Japan's changing role in the international system. Although it has become increasingly harder for Japanese officials to separate Japan from international political and economic developments related to security, energy dependence, and relations with its neighbors in Asia, they continue to try to do so on their terms. The real dilemma for officials is not how to return to record levels of economic growth, which is an unrealistic objective given Japan's current place in the international economy. Instead, it is how to reconcile its values, institutions, preferences, and reliance on protectionist policies with the need to realize that many of Japan's interests today lie in cooperating with other states to generate an order that reflects the interests of all states. This lesson applies not only to Japan but to all states.

## DISCUSSION QUESTIONS

1. Are Japan's mercantilist proclivities a product of its culture (and thus unlikely to change), or are they more a result of the effect of external forces on Japan? Cite evidence from this chapter to support your view.
2. In what respects was the international environment different during the period of Japan's economic rise and during the period of its economic decline?
3. Discuss Peter Drucker's theory of bureaucracy. What role does the bureaucracy play that is different from the role of elected political leaders? What trade-offs are associated with placing decision-making authority in the hands of insulated and unelected bureaucrats versus elected politicians, who must be responsive to both voters and special-interest groups?
4. How were Japan's economic and political bubbles related? Use the problems of Japan's banking system as a lens through which to view both bubbles.
5. Explain the interrelationships encompassed by the iron triangle. How do these relationships reinforce one another when the economy is prosperous? How do they undermine each other when the economy is stagnant or in recession?

## INTERNET LINKS

Japan-American Society:
   www.us-japan.org/resources.html
Ministry of Finance:
   www.mof.go.jp/english/index.htm
Ministry of Economy, Trade and Industry:
   www.meti.go.jp/english/index.html
Japan Politics Central:
   http://jpcentral.virginia.edu
Japan Policy Research Institute:
   www.jpri.org

## SUGGESTED READINGS

Peter F. Drucker. "In Defense of Japanese Bureaucracy," *Foreign Affairs*, 77 (September/October 1998), pp. 53–67.
James Fallows. *Looking at the Sun*. New York: Pantheon, 1994.
Yoichi Funabashi. "Tokyo's Depression Diplomacy," *Foreign Affairs*, 77 (November/December 1998), pp. 26–36.
Frank Gibney. "Introduction," in Frank Gibney, ed., *Unlocking the Bureaucrat's Kingdom: Deregulation and the Japanese Economy*. Washington, DC: Brookings Institution Press, 1998, pp. 1–15.
John Grimond. "What Ails Japan?" *The Economist*, April 20, 2002, Special Section, pp. 3–16.
Chalmers Johnson. "The End of American Hegemony and the Future of US–Japan Relations," *Harvard International Review* (Anniversary Issue 1990), pp. 126–131.
Edward J. Lincoln. "Japan's Financial Mess," *Foreign Affairs*, 77 (May/June 1998), pp. 57–66.
William H. Overholt. "Japan's Economy at War with Itself," *Foreign Affairs*, 81 (January/February 2002), pp. 134–147.

Kenneth Pyle. *The Japanese Question: Power and Purpose in a New Era.* Washington, DC: American Enterprise Institute Press, 1992.

Lester Thurow. *Head to Head: The Coming Economic Battle Among Japan, Europe, and America.* New York: William Morrow, 1992.

Kozo Yamamura. "The Japanese Political Economy After the 'Bubble': Plus, a Change?" *Journal of Japanese Studies*, 23(2) (1997), pp. 291–331.

Kozo Yamamura and Daniel Okimoto, eds. *The Political Economy of Japan: The Changing International Context*, vol. 2. Stanford, CA: Stanford University Press, 1987.

## KEY TERMS

iron triangle
corporatism
Postal Savings Bank
1940 System

*keiretsu*
developmental capitalism
gross domestic product (GDP)
*endaka*

reluctant realism
Self-Defense Force (SDF)

## NOTES

1. Karl Fields and Elizabeth Norville were the authors of this chapter in the first edition of this book. Karl Fields and Michael Veseth collaborated on revisions for the second and third editions. Dave Balaam and Ryan Cunningham collaborated on the fourth edition.
2. As cited by Kenneth Pyle, *The Japanese Question: Power and Purpose in a New Era* (Washington, DC: AEI Press, 1992), p. 12.
3. See William H. Overholt, "Japan's Economy at War with Itself," *Foreign Affairs*, 81 (January/February 2002), pp. 134–147.
4. Some representative works include Gary Saxonhouse, "Industrial Restructuring in Japan," *Journal of Japanese Studies* (Summer 1979), pp. 273–320; Charles Schultze, "Industrial Policy: A Dissent," *Brookings Review*, 2 (Fall 1983), pp. 3–12; Philip H. Trezise, "Industrial Policy in Japan," in Margaret Dewar, ed., *Industrial Vitalization: Toward a National Industrial Policy* (New York: Pergamon Press, 1982), pp. 177–195; and Hugh Patrick, "The Future of the Japanese Economy," *Journal of Japanese Studies* (Summer 1977), pp. 219–249.
5. For an overview of alternative explanations of the Japanese miracle, see Chalmers Johnson, "The End of American Hegemony and the Future of U.S.–Japan Relations," *Harvard International Review* (Anniversary Issue 1990), pp. 126–131.
6. Adherents to this position have been labeled revisionists because they reject the orthodox view that capitalist democracies all look and act alike. Revisionists do not argue that Japan is evil or wrong, but rather that Japan is different from other advanced industrial democracies. See *Business Week*, August 7, 1989, pp. 444–451.
7. See Lester Thurow, *Head to Head: The Coming Economic Battle Among Japan, Europe, and America* (New York: William Morrow, 1992), pp. 113–151.
8. Kozo Yamamura and Yasukichi Yasuba, eds., *The Political Economy of Japan: The Domestic Transformation*, vol. 1 (Stanford, CA: Stanford University Press, 1987), p. 138.
9. Ibid., p. 100.
10. See James Fallows, "How the World Works," *Atlantic Monthly*, 272 (December 1993), pp. 61–87.
11. Ibid., p. 64.
12. Ibid., p. 71.
13. Pyle, *The Japanese Question*, p. 43.
14. Donald Hellman, "Japanese Politics and Foreign Policy: Elitist Democracy Within an American Greenhouse," in Kozo Yamamura and Daniel Okimoto, eds., *The Political Economy of Japan: The Changing International Context*, vol. 2. Stanford, CA: Stanford University Press, 1987, p. 345.
15. This is sometimes called the "greater fool theory." You buy land at foolishly high prices because you can be sure that an even greater fool will soon appear to buy it from you at an even higher price.
16. The Nikkei stock index is an indicator of stock prices in Japan, much like the Dow Jones index in the United States. The figures listed in the table are index numbers, not prices, designed to show relative changes in price, not any actual prices.
17. This is obviously a broad generalization offered as a stylized fact. Clearly, there were many individual political actors who sacrificed self-interest for Japan's national interest.

18. Fans of old British TV shows may remember a series called *Yes, Minister* (and later, *Yes, Prime Minister*) that told how wise career bureaucrats in British government were able to protect the true interests of the government from the politically driven short-term interests of apparently imbecilic elected officials. Each week's show would begin with some new moronic political policy and would end only when the bureaucracy had managed to stave it off and save the nation.

19. Peter F. Drucker, "In Defense of Japanese Bureaucracy," *Foreign Affairs*, 77 (September/October 1998), pp. 53-67.

20. Ibid., p. 79.

21. Beth Hutton, "Real Estate Rises Again in Tokyo and Beyond," *Financial Times*, March 13, 2006, p. 9. See also John M. Miller, "Will the Real Japan Please Stand Up," *World Policy Journal*, XXII (Winter 2005/2006), pp. 36–48.

22. Yoji Inata, "Reality Check: Japan Consumers Spending Despite Bad Weather," *Market News International*, July 26, 2006, p. 59.

23. Paul Krugman, *The Return of Depression Economics* (New York: W. W. Norton, 1999), pp. 60–82.

24. Ko Mishima, "The Failure of Japan's Political Reform," *World Policy Journal*, XXII (Winter 2005/2006), pp. 47–55.

25. John Grimond, "What Ails Japan?" *The Economist*, April 20, 2002, Special Section, p. 16.

26. Miller, "Will the Real Japan Please Stand Up," p. 44.

27. Ibid., p. 45.

28. Ibid., p. 36.

29. "Japan: Agency Seeks More Funds to Develop Missile Defense," *The Wall Street Journal: Asia*, September 1, 2006, p. 9.

30. Steven Vogel, "Japan After Koizumi: The Abe Opportunity," *Brookings Northeast Asia Commentary*, October 2006.

31. Norimitsu Onishi, "Japan's Likely Next Premier in Hawkish Stand," *The New York Times*, September 2, 2006, p. 6.

32. "Japan Premiership Contender Aims to Upgrade Defence Agency," *BBC Monitoring Asia Pacific*, September 3, 2006, p. 32.

33. "Iran and Japan Close to Oil Deal," *BBC News*, September 3, 2006, p. 57.

34. Kent E. Calder, "China and Japan's Simmering Rivalry," *Foreign Affairs*, 85 (March 1, 2006), p. 129.

35. Miller, "Will the Real Japan Please Stand Up," p. 38.

36. Overholt, "Japan's Economy at War with Itself," pp. 146–147.

*13*

# *States and Markets in Transition*

## *By Patrick H. O'Neil*

### OVERVIEW

One of the greatest challenges that a nation can face is to change the entire nature of its political and economic system. Making such a dramatic change essentially redefines the ways that individuals relate to each other and to the state. The fundamental tension between states and markets is magnified as social institutions and individual responsibilities are altered.

This chapter examines the problems of states and markets in transition from one system of national political economy to another. The goal of this chapter is to explore the nature of the transitions from communism to capitalism and the changing tensions these transitions produce.

The chapter begins with a general overview of the problems of states and markets in transition, and the global context within which their changes occur. We then focus first on what might be called the *classical socialist system,* commonly referred to as the *communist system,* and explore the economic, political, and social changes that formerly communist nations are experiencing. Russia, Eastern Europe, and China are singled out for special attention in this discussion because they represent three different approaches to the problems of economic and political transition.

Finally, we reflect on the problems and opportunities of the transition states and speculate about the future that awaits these nations. How to balance political and economic change is difficult, because change in one area is certain to affect the other.

*Accounting and Control—these are the chief things necessary for the organizing and correct functioning of the first phase of communist society. All citizens are here transformed into hired employees of the state, which is made up of the armed workers. All citizens become employees and workers of one national state "syndicate." All that is required is that they should work equally, should regularly do their share of work, and should receive equal pay. The accounting and control necessary for this have been simplified by capitalism to the utmost, till they have become the extraordinarily simple operation of watching, recording and issuing receipts, within the reach of anybody who can read and write and knows the first four rules of arithmetic.*[1]

V. I. Lenin (1918)

In Chapter 4 we read how Karl Marx envisioned the rise and fall of capitalism. Recall that, according to his logic, the material world is driven primarily by economic forces, such that all aspects of society—politics, culture, history—derive from the way in which the economy is structured. These structures inevitably generate hostility between those with economic power and those without, until violent revolution eventually destroys the existing order, creating in turn a new economic and social system that in time succumbs to its own internal flaws. History is thus not an incremental process, but one of sudden shifts and dramatic change resulting from underlying pressure—much like earthquakes. Although capitalism is a necessary historical phase of human development, it will eventually fall in the face of revolution, in which the oppressed working class will rise up and seize control of the wealth of society for the good of all.

The theories of Marx attracted many committed followers—not just those who found such arguments convincing, but also those who sought to realize these ideas in practice. V. I. Lenin in Tsarist Russia and Mao Zedong in China turned Marx's ideas from *theory* into *practice*, enabling them to carry out revolution in their own countries. Yet while communist theory became a powerful mobilizing force for revolution in many countries, upon seizing power the communist leaders found themselves confronted with a problem: Once the revolution had overthrown capitalism and gained control over private property, how was the economy to be structured? Marx, after all, had provided no blueprints for what was to be done next. Many believed that the economy could easily be run by the government in a rational manner that would serve the public's best interest. As we see above, Lenin believed that the actual work of managing an economy would be no great task; he likened it to running a post office.

As history showed, however, the challenge of replacing capitalism with a state-controlled system of economic production proved much more difficult than expected. By the early 1990s, Eastern Europe and the Soviet Union had rejected communism, while in China more evolutionary economic reforms had led to a unique fusion of state and market forces. This chapter focuses on the crucial issues of states and markets in transition from one system of state–market relations to another.

## STATES AND MARKETS IN TRANSITION

Change is stressful. Change in something as complex and important as a nation's system of political economy causes stresses and strains at all levels: individual, market, class, nation, region, globe. It is significant, therefore, that perhaps half of the world's population is experiencing the stress of a change in their system of political economy at the beginning of the new millennium. These are stressful times for the international political economy, with many states and markets in transition. The nature of the strain, however, is different in each case.

One group of nations is engulfed in the problems of the dramatic transition from communism, or classical socialism, to some form of democratic capitalism. These are the "formers," as Czech leader Václav Havel has called them: the former members of the Warsaw Pact, including Hungary and Poland, and the former states of the Soviet Union, such as Russia and Ukraine.[2] These nations are trying to develop liberal economic institutions and democratic political institutions at the same time—a daunting task that requires a wholesale shift from a focus on collective interests to an emphasis on individual rights. Other nations, such as China and Vietnam, are engaged in a somewhat less extreme but perhaps even more difficult transition, from communism (classical socialism) to **market socialism**, a hybrid system that retains central power in the state but encourages private economic activities.[3]

The many tensions that these nations experience and the problems they must solve derive fundamentally from the conflict between a political economy system based on individual economic and political choices (a "bottom-up" approach) and the desire to make choices collectively for the greater public good (a "top-down" approach). No system of political economy is totally "bottom up" or completely "top down"—the problem of balancing individual and collective choices is universal. The problem of transition is to change dramatically the general direction of the flow of social choice without destroying valuable social institutions or undermining social stability. This, as we will see, is not an easy task.

This chapter cannot predict what will happen to these states and markets in transition. We can, however, explore the nature of the changes under way and examine briefly the recent history of economic and political reform. This survey will help us better understand the problems and stresses of today's world and the prospects for tomorrow.

Every transition has three stages: the old order; the transition process itself, often characterized as *reform* of the old order or *revolt* against it; and the new order that finally emerges. We begin our discussion with an examination of the "old order" of communism. This is what Hungarian political economist János Kornai calls **classical socialism**, which is the set of fundamental political economy relationships implemented by Joseph Stalin (1879–1953) in the Soviet Union and Mao Zedong (1893–1976) in China. This is the system of political economy that we commonly call **communism**.[4]

## COMMUNISM AND THE CLASSICAL SOCIALIST SYSTEM

**Socialism** is a political economy system of communal ownership of production resources with a strong emphasis on economic equality. There are various degrees of socialism, ranging from limited public ownership of resources in the United States, for example, to the opposite extreme, the classical socialist system, that we associate with communism in the Soviet Union and elsewhere. It is common to call these nations "communist" because of the importance of the Communist Party in their political structures, and so it is tempting to label their form of political economy "communism." For Marx, however, and for the Communist parties in these countries, the term *communism* is reserved for the final stage in Marx's historical progression, when the state "withers away" and communal ownership becomes the natural order. Communism in this sense was never achieved, and the state was always a dominant force in the communist nations.

To preserve this distinction, we generally will use the term *classical socialism* to refer to the social and political economy structure and use *communism* the way Marx did, to refer to the social goal and final stage of the historical progression. We hope this will not be too confusing. Table 13–1 shows the fourteen countries that adopted "communist" or classical socialist systems,

**TABLE 13–1    The Classical Socialist Countries**

| COUNTRY | YEAR |
| --- | --- |
| Soviet Union | 1917 |
| Mongolia | 1921 |
| Albania | 1944 |
| Yugoslavia | 1945 |
| Bulgaria | 1947 |
| Czechoslovakia | 1948 |
| Hungary | 1948 |
| Poland | 1948 |
| Romania | 1948 |
| North Korea | 1948 |
| China | 1949 |
| East Germany | 1949 |
| Vietnam | 1954 |
| Cuba | 1959 |

with the dates of transition.[5] With the exception of North Korea and Cuba, each of these countries had begun the transition from the "old order" of classical socialism to some "new order" by the early 1990s.

It is instructive to consider the general characteristics of the classical socialist system. The sections that follow provide highly stylized and oversimplified descriptions of the principal political and economic aspects of classical socialism, which will be useful background for us in considering the problems of transition.

The politics and economics of the classical socialist system are completely intertwined—the state *is* the market, for all practical purposes. It is a mistake, therefore, to discuss political and economic aspects of the system separately. Having made this point, it is still true that we must begin somewhere, and so we start with a discussion of the fundamental nature of politics in classical socialism, so that we can see more clearly, in the next section, the strong effect of politics on the economy.

## THE POLITICS OF CLASSICAL SOCIALISM

It is convenient to break this analysis into three parts: power, ideology, and government. Together, these elements define the political and economic basis of classical socialism.

### Power

In the classical socialist states, power was rooted in one party, the Communist Party, whose "leading role" was usually written directly into the nation's constitution, meaning that there was in effect no constitutional way to remove the party from power. Democracy as we define it, with limits on governmental power, individual rights, and open competition among different political viewpoints and groups, did not exist. Membership in the Communist Party was generally limited to about 5 to 10 percent of the population, although a much larger percentage participated in party-led programs and movements. Power in this system was thus *political* power; moreover, because economic resources are held by the state, political power also translates into *economic* power. This system of political divisions was commonly referred to as the *nomenklatura*, which refers to those positions that require party approval. For example, those with higher political standing could count on preferential treatment in terms of better housing, or the ability to travel abroad, or access to scarce consumer goods. In the last case, the most evident example was the existence of special stores, often stocked with Western goods or basic necessities in short supply, which were open only to the *nomenklatura* or those who had hard currency—usually one and the same, because possession of hard currency was highly restricted. Although these stores were often explained as existing for tourists, anyone who wandered into one of these stores (as did the author) quickly noted that most of the goods offered were of little interest to a foreign tourist—unless one was looking for a Japanese television set as a souvenir. The resulting irony of class divisions within a theoretically classless society was the source of a well-known Soviet joke: "Under capitalism, man exploits man. Under communism, it is the other way around."

However, we should also keep in mind that although economic differences did exist in these states between ruler and ruled, by and large they were nothing like the economic divisions found in capitalist economies such as the United States. Communist Party leaders lived well, but few lived in the manner commonly seen in the West among the rich. This concentration of power in the Communist Party is perhaps the most important distinguishing characteristic of "communism." Under democratic capitalism, power is separated into its political and economic components, though clearly there is overlap between the two. Those with economic power often seek to influence politics, and vice versa. Yet one does not automatically convert into another: Just because Bill Gates is fabulously wealthy does not mean that he could necessarily become President of the United States. However, under the classical socialist system, the concentration of economic power into the hands of the state meant that economic and political power were one and the same.

This combination of economic and political power also meant that economic and political reform were tightly linked, because reform would change the distribution of power between the government and society, rulers and ruled. This made reform all the more difficult, and helps explain why most of these countries did not so much reform as collapse. *Reform* assumes that the basic structure can be preserved. However, attempts to reform these systems threatened the economic and political resources of those in power. As a result, rejection, rather than reform, of communism eventually became the dominant path.

## Ideology

The exercise of power in the classical socialist system was guided by a set of official beliefs, "the Party line," concerning social, economic, and political relationships. Based fundamentally on the work of Marx and Lenin, this ideology enshrined the achievements of communist revolution in terms of eliminating inequality and promoting economic development. Because the means of production are collectively owned, this argument holds, resources can be allocated to those industries that best serve the collective interest and achieve the highest levels of economic growth (compared with a capitalist system of private ownership, in which resources go where the private benefits are highest). Indeed, in many countries under socialist rule, the leadership could point to a rapid leap forward in economic development, typified by the growth of heavy industry, infrastructure, educational and health facilities, and urbanization. For many socialist countries, which had been in a stage of early capitalist or precapitalist development, these changes were indeed profound—though such progress eventually ground to a halt, for reasons we will explain later. "Personality cults," which use leaders and heroes to personify these official beliefs, were also often used to communicate ideology to the masses. Stalin and Mao were important both as real leaders and as ideological symbols, reminding citizens of the important beliefs that guided their country. Many observers have noted that classical socialist ideology, in keeping with Marx's view of communism as a utopia on earth, is in many ways a kind of secular religion, which asks for faith in a set of beliefs without question and for sacrifice for a future reward, and which boasts its own set of saints, martyrs, and devils.

## Government

One confusing element of politics in classical socialist systems is the distinction between the party and the state or government. In fact, when many referred to the "leader" of a socialist country they were usually referring to the General Secretary of the Communist Party. However, this was not a government office—rather, it was the top leadership position of the Communist Party. However, because of the dominance of the Communist Party over the state, the actual state positions were often viewed as of secondary importance at best. Thus, the term **party-state** is often used in place of the term *government*. Power flowed from the party, and the leadership rose and fell from power based not on public elections, but rather on power struggles within the party. This lack of a clear set of mechanisms to make leadership accountable proved to be dangerous. In the first decades of socialist rule in the Soviet Union, China, and Eastern Europe, terror was used as a means to eliminate opposition to the leadership or socialist rule. This in turn often set the economy back by eliminating people the leaders mistrusted (such as intellectuals or other professionals). Millions perished in such campaigns, especially in the Soviet Union and China.

As for the actual structure of the party-state, the government by and large resembled political systems we see elsewhere in the world, typically with a prime minister or president (again, often a person of secondary importance), a parliament, judiciary, and local government—all positions that fell within the auspices of the *nomenklatura*. The Communist Party mirrored the state to a large extent. The General Secretary and the Political Bureau (or *Politburo*) functioned as the party leader and his cabinet; a Central Committee acted as a kind of legislative body for the party; while below that, committees existed at the regional and local levels. These bodies extended all the way down to the place of work or residence, where party members were organized into basic party organizations or *cells.* These cells were ostensibly intended to represent the interests of the people by transmitting their concerns to those higher up, but they were also mechanisms by which the party could keep watch over the population. Traditionally, the party as a whole would hold a party congress every few years at which the party leadership would be elected, though these "elections" tended to be little more than confirmations of those already in power.

## THE ECONOMICS OF CLASSICAL SOCIALISM

The economy of a classical socialist state was heavily conditioned by politics and ideology. It is convenient to examine the economy in terms of the role of property, the nature of economic coordinating mechanisms, the role of prices, and the role of incentives.

### The Role of Property

Communal ownership of the means of production is the hallmark of any form of socialism, and this was especially true of classical socialism in its extreme form. This is not to say that there was no private property. Private ownership of personal possessions unrelated to economic production was allowed, and in some countries limited forms of private property continued to exist—for example, agriculture remained largely private in Poland, and small private shops thrived in Hungary. However, most of the means of production—factories, land, property—were owned by the state on behalf of the people as a whole. Given what we have read about Marxism, this makes sense: If private property is a means by which one person can exploit another (an owner of a factory exploiting a worker, for example), then public ownership should eliminate any means by which one individual can exploit another. With the means of production held by the state, many of the typical aspects of capitalism that we take for granted—individual profit, unemployment, competition between firms, even bankruptcy—were eliminated. Individuals lost their right to control property, with the party-state instead making decisions about how resources should be used. A classical socialist economy functions in essence as a single large firm, with the public as employees of that firm. How well that firm does will directly affect the public—if resources are squandered, it is the public that will suffer as a result.

### Economic Coordination Mechanisms

Along with the elimination of private property, socialist systems also eliminated the market mechanism. Like private property, markets were viewed in communist theory as an instrument of exploitation, leading to an ever-vicious cycle of competition that drove firms into bankruptcy, consolidated wealth among the successful few, and generated unemployment and misery for the working class. As a result, only in a few areas were free prices allowed, typically in small-scale agriculture, where people were allowed to freely sell the produce from their gardens. Given their hostility to markets, socialist systems needed a different way to allocate resources, one that would be more just. What resulted was the creation of a large state bureaucracy in charge of deciding what should be produced, in what amounts, how it should be priced, and where it should be delivered. This system of state control over the market has led to classical socialist economies sometimes being referred to as **centrally planned economies,** because fundamental economic decisions flowed not from the market, but from plans issued by the state.

As one might imagine, planning an entire economy was an extremely difficult task. A market economy is not centralized, and so it responds to demands spontaneously as they emerge; if there is a market for something, a producer will typically come along to fill it. In a centrally planned economy, however, planners must determine what needs to be produced. How much steel? How many women's size 8 shoes? How many apartments? As one can imagine, this is an overwhelming task, as the needs of the public are hard to determine and are always subject to change. Misjudgments in planning at this level led to many shortages in some areas and overproduction in others. A second problem involved the actual process of planning itself: determining what factories should be in charge of what production, where they should get their resources from, and how the final goods should be distributed. This is referred to as *material balancing*, because it requires that all of the inputs (what goes into production) and all of the outputs (what is being produced) match. If the inputs don't match the outputs, the plan will be thrown out of balance. And, as socialist planners found, perfect planning was impossible. There were simply too many things to plan—in the Soviet Union, some 40,000 to 50,000 items—and too many unforeseen outcomes, such as a factory failing to deliver its full output. Because most of these inputs and outputs were interdependent, small problems could have a huge effect on the entire plan.

For example, say a factory making steel failed to meet its quota or planned output. This would create a shortage of steel in the system for other factories that need the steel to produce their output. Let us speculate further that one of those factories that uses that steel makes turbines, which are necessary to the production of electricity. Now there will be a shortage of turbines for national electrical production, and so a shortage of electricity. Some factories will now get less electricity than they need for production (including the steel factory!), leading to further shortages. This is what is meant by the *interdependence* of many goods—one error in the plan or its execution can have a huge ripple effect on the plan as a whole. However, one place where the planners could shift resources without throwing the plan out of balance was the consumer sector, because consumer products are not "intermediate inputs" that go into the production of another good. Therefore, if there is not enough steel to make turbines, why not take it from the auto industry and simply produce fewer cars? The result is that consumer goods were often shortchanged.

Many believed that these problems were simply a result of processing large amounts of information, and that better computers or mathematical formulas would have solved these problems. Certainly, information overload was a problem, but a more critical issue was gathering the necessary information in the first place. Setting a fixed plan for the economy requires one to have perfect information about the present and the future—exactly what needs to be produced and what resources exist to produce it. Any mistakes or changes and the system begins to break down.

## The Role of Prices

Prices are key elements of any system based on market coordination. Prices are signals that tell individual consumers and producers about the costs and benefits of different actions and thus coordinate their independent actions in the market. Prices also serve to ration scarce items. Scarcity drives prices up, which limits the quantities purchased in the market. In a capitalist system, therefore, prices rise and fall all the time. Under socialist systems, however, given the lack of a market to send price signals, central planners set prices for goods themselves. Because there was no market, prices could not accurately reflect the true value of any good, because a value is established by the interaction of supply and demand. Many resources were wasted as a result, because questions of cost were of no real concern.

In addition, prices did not change to reflect shifts in supply or demand over time. This contributed to what has been called *repressed inflation*. As opposed to inflation in market economies, in which prices rise when demand outstrips supply, under repressed inflation, demand expresses itself in different ways. Let's take as an example, consumer goods and services. For many people living in socialist countries, prices for goods were relatively low in relation to their wages, but, as noted earlier, the supply of consumer goods and services was often limited and of poor quality. Consumers found themselves with more money than they could spend. What did they do with it? In many cases a *black*, or illegal, market emerged in imported goods, hard currency, or products and services in short supply. In addition, a complex system of bribery also developed in such areas as health care to ensure access to better treatment. Although the socialist system had outlawed the market, it continued to operate on the margins of the economy, allocating scarce resources and setting prices—albeit illegally.

## The Role of Incentives

Just as prices for goods were set in ways that did not reflect their true value, this was also true for labor. As one might expect, classical socialist systems were hostile to large differences in wages, viewing this as the source of class inequality and exploitation. Highly trained workers thus could not expect to receive substantially more pay for their work than, for example, manual laborers. This quest for equality in work also extended to the concept of unemployment, which was viewed as a core injustice of capitalism. Not only was unemployment ended, it was also made illegal—everyone who was able to work was required to do so.

Problems came to plague socialist economies as a result of this relationship between labor and the market. Because firms were evaluated largely on whether they had fulfilled their plan targets, and because workers realized that there was little relationship between their salaries and how hard they worked, factories concentrated on the *quantity*, not *quality*, of their products. Firms received a bonus if they met their target under the plan, but whether those goods were substandard was of no concern. In a market system, a producer of shoddy goods would be run out of business by a competitor, but in a socialist system there were no such alternatives.

This led to an economy in which many goods were of such low quality as to be virtually worthless, resulting in the waste of huge amounts of resources. This author recalls buying a new Soviet-made radio in Hungary in the late 1980s, where it took the store clerk four tries before he could actually find one that worked. A related problem could be found in the diversity of goods. Because planning targets were set using numerical indicators of some sort, firms concentrated primarily on meeting this figure, even if production were distorted as a result. For example, Robert Campbell notes that shortages in plumbing fixtures in the Soviet Union could be traced to the fact that the factories making pipe were evaluated on how many tons of pipe they produced—thus encouraging the production of large-scale and heavier-diameter pipes. This not only wasted metal, it led to shortages of the small-diameter pipes needed for apartment plumbing.[6]

Finally, the key element for economic development—innovation—was also undermined. Not only was there no reward for economic innovation (firms or their workers would see no profit from improved goods), most firms resisted change as a costly diversion from fulfilling the plan. The Soviet-made radio discussed above was not only of poor quality but was also very heavy and was decades out of date in comparison to Western models. Having been designed once, why improve it?

## THE PROBLEMS OF TRANSITION

Our discussion so far should give you some idea about why classical socialism eventually fell apart. Rather than being a system based on the allocation of resources by the market, socialist economies attempted to use the state to make these decisions for both goods and labor. In doing so, however, they eliminated the effect that the market has on economic performance. Under such conditions, economic production eroded as the quality of work declined, and resources were wasted by an inefficient planning system. It is important to keep in mind that socialism did not fail because the people in these societies were not "smart." On the contrary, in many of these countries the educational systems ranked among the best in the world in many fields. However, while socialist systems could generate ideas, they could not harness them and in fact often turned against them. Stagnation and resignation reigned; economic performance ground to a halt, and in some countries even life expectancy began to decline, while in the West technological change grew exponentially.

It was this deepening problem that led leaders such as Soviet General Secretary Mikhail Gorbachev to seek some reform of the system starting in the mid-1980s. Gorbachev's policy of *glasnost* (openness) and *perestroika* (restructuring) were meant to reform, not eliminate, socialism. Gorbachev, along with some leaders in Eastern Europe, hoped that a limited amount of political and economic liberalization would give the populace a greater stake in the system and help reinvigorate socialism. However, recall our earlier observation that reform is difficult under such conditions, because it may threaten those in power; indeed, by admitting to the flawed nature of the system, the leadership only exposed its weakness. Allowed to speak openly for the first time in decades, the public quickly raced ahead of the leaders, demanding not just reform but complete transformation of the system. The public did not know exactly what capitalism or democracy would look like, but many people were convinced that it had to be better than the system under which they currently lived. By 1989 Hungary and Poland had initiated a series of economic and political changes that paved the way toward democracy and capitalism, and many of their socialist neighbors soon followed.[7] Even the Soviet Union, more than seven decades after the Russian Revolution, saw not only socialism but the country itself collapse in 1991, as a failed coup against Gorbachev sparked its breakup into fifteen separate countries. Each country would have to contend with building a new political system, economy, and society out of the ruins of communism.

Communism did not collapse everywhere, of course. Most important whereas in Eastern Europe and the Soviet Union the year 1989 marked liberalization and the first moves toward democracy, in China similar protests in Tiananmen Square, led by students and encouraged by Gorbachev's example, were met by deadly force. Communist leaders in China did not back down in the face of public demands for reform and political liberalization, and they showed themselves both willing and able to use the army to quell peaceful protests by force. Why this difference? One reason may be that in China the Communist Party had already begun to carry out a set of wide-ranging economic reforms in the late 1970s. These, however, were *not* accompanied by simultaneous political reform. In fact, in China the Communist Party used economic reform as a way to stave off public discontent and increase its own legitimacy. Because these reforms focused on economics and not politics and were carried out over a much longer period of time, the Chinese Communist Party in 1989 did not confront the kind of rapid decompression and disarray that the Soviet Union or East Europe did. Furthermore, by initiating reforms primarily in the area of economics, Chinese leaders limited political mobilization and were able to crack down effectively against public protest. Change is under way in China, but the Communist Party intends to control and limit its course, as we will discuss.

## POLITICAL INSTITUTIONS IN TRANSITION

So far, we have discussed how communist theory saw the origins of, and solutions to, the problem of inequality; the difficulties in translating theory into reality; and how eventually these institutions unraveled across the communist world. Although the downfall of communism was dramatic, what followed was no less awesome. These countries faced, and continue to face, the challenge of building new political and economic institutions.

Perhaps the biggest challenge to postsocialist countries was the fact that there was no blueprint for what to do; many countries had moved to socialism over the past seventy years, but not one had moved from socialism to capitalism. A second problem involved the fact that many of these countries were attempting to carry out economic and political transformation at the same time. Could a country carry out economic and political change without one undermining the other? Let us begin with the reconfiguration of politics in postcommunist countries.

### Reorganizing the State

An underlying task in the transition from communism was to reorganize the state in terms of its autonomy and capacity. Under communism the party-state was able to dominate virtually all aspects of human relations without any effective check. State power was extremely high. With the collapse of communism, the party was ejected from its leading role in political life, and new leaders had to change the very role and scope of the state. No longer could it dominate all aspects of human relations. Reducing state power was not easily achieved, in part because new leaders saw state power as vital to carrying out painful reforms. This is a paradox of political transitions: Dramatic political change occurs alongside a substantial weakening of the state precisely when such power is most needed. Many postcommunist countries thus sought to narrow the state's capacity without making it ineffective—a difficult task.

Another important aspect of this reform is the establishment of the rule of law. Under communist systems the rule of law was weak. The Communist Party could make, break, or change laws as it saw fit, and as a result, people came to view laws rather cynically. Laws were not considered legitimate either by the public or by those in power. This encouraged evasion and corruption—problems that expanded dramatically once the repressive power of the state was retracted or weakened.

Postcommunist countries have thus been challenged by the task of building a rule of law. Those in power must adhere to regulations and legal structures, not act in a capricious manner or take advantage of their authority. In society, too, the rule of law must be instilled in such a way that people willingly obey the system even when it is not in their personal interest to do so. Unless rules can be institutionalized, postcommunist states will find it difficult to be effective and have their laws obeyed by citizens and leaders. Finally, alongside reconstructing state power and the rule of law, postcommunist countries have faced the prospect of building a democratic regime where authoritarianism has long been the norm. This requires numerous tasks: revising or rewriting the constitution to establish civil rights and freedoms, creating a separation of powers between branches of government, revamping judicial bodies and high courts, generating electoral laws, and regulating political parties—and doing all of this in such a way as to generate support on the part of the majority of actors in society. If a large portion of the public does not accept these structures as legitimate, political instability and violence can result.

Civil rights are a final area of concern. Under communism the constitution typically established an elaborate set of civil liberties, though in reality these were largely ignored by those in power. With the collapse of communism, leaders were faced with deciding how civil liberties should be constitutionally protected. This meant not only strengthening the rule of law so that those once hollow rights were now enforced, but also deciding what kinds of rights should be enshrined in the constitution. For example, in the case of freedom of speech and assembly, should the constitution ban the Communist Party? Do communists deserve the right to participate in a new democracy as well? To what extent should old communist-era rights, such as the right to health care or education, be retained? Who should be the final arbiter of disputes over these rights? The role of a constitutional court became a major issue in countries where traditionally the judiciary had been anything but independent.

## Evaluating Political Transitions

It has been over a decade since the fall of communism in Eastern Europe and the Soviet Union. How have their political transitions fared? In brief, the picture is mixed. A number of countries have in the past fifteen years made dramatic strides toward democracy and the rule of law, to such an extent that some experts now consider these countries to be consolidated democracies—meaning that their democratic regimes have been fully institutionalized. The majority of these consolidated democracies can be found in Central Europe (countries such as Hungary, Poland, and the Czech Republic) and the Baltics—areas that share in common a precommunist history of greater economic development, democratic institutions and the rule of law, more contact with Western Europe, and a shorter period of communist rule. All of these factors may help explain why democratic transition in these regions has been more successful, as well as explaining their imminent entry into the European Union.

However, this group makes up less than half of all the postcommunist countries in Eastern Europe and the former Soviet Union. In the majority of these states, democracy is either weakly institutionalized or completely absent. These countries tend to have little historical experience of democracy and a long period of Soviet control (this category includes most of the former republics of the Soviet Union). In many of these countries a new set of authoritarian leaders has consolidated power, many of them former members of the communist elite and *nomenklatura*. Democratic rights and freedoms are restricted, and those in power have frequently enriched themselves through corrupt practices. In many of these cases it is difficult to speak of the rule of law. Equally disturbing, many of these countries have become less democratic over the past decade. This includes Russia.

Outside Eastern Europe and the former Soviet Union the picture is even less clear, for not only has democracy been slow to spread, several communist regimes continue to hold on to power. China, Laos, Vietnam, North Korea, and Cuba remain steadfastly authoritarian, with only China initiating significant economic changes. Elsewhere in Asia and Africa, communist regimes have fallen, but in many cases this has resulted in state collapse and civil war, as in Afghanistan. There, upon the Soviet Union's withdrawal in 1989, civil war raged until 1996, when the Taliban gained power. Not everywhere has the end of communism been peaceful or democratic, or even taken place.

## ECONOMIC INSTITUTIONS IN TRANSITION

In addition to transforming the state and the regime, transitions from communism have also confronted the task of reestablishing some separation between the state and the economy. This involves two processes: **marketization**, or the re-creation of market forces of supply and demand; and **privatization**, the transfer of state-held property into private hands. In both cases, how to carry out these changes, and to what end, was influenced by different political-economic alternatives: Should social democracy, liberalism, or mercantilism be the country's new path? Let's consider the ways in which privatization and marketization can be approached before we investigate the different paths postcommunist countries have taken in each area.

### Privatization

The transition from communism to capitalism requires a redefinition of property. In order to generate economic growth and limit the power of the state, economic resources must be placed back into private hands. However, this task is neither easy nor straightforward. In fact, prior to 1989 no country had ever gone from a communist economy to a capitalist one, leading to many questions and concerns. First, what are the various elements of the economy—factories, shops, land, apartments—actually worth? In order to privatize these assets the state must first figure out their value, something that is difficult in a system in which previously there existed no market to value such things.

Second, who should get these assets? One option is to simply give the assets away—for example, transferring ownership of a factory to its workers or a house to its occupants. On the surface this might seem to preserve a certain degree of equality among the members of society. Inevitably, however, some workers would wind up owning a factory that turns out to be profitable while others would not be as fortunate. Is this just? Another option is to sell assets to the highest bidder. However, in a society in which wages and profits have been restricted under communism, who would have the money to buy something as large as a factory? Often only the old *nomenklatura* could be expected to have amassed any significant wealth, which would mean that the old party bosses would become the new capitalist bosses. An alternative is to allow foreigners to buy these assets. The benefit here would be the injection of foreign investment and Western managerial skills and technology. The downsides, however, might be expensive politically, because such sales could generate public anger that the results of the workers hard labor were sold to foreigners (a critique similar to mercantilist thought). With all of these options, old questions of inequality resurface.

In tackling these issues, privatization was eventually carried out in a number of different ways, depending on the country and the kind of economic assets concerned. In many cases small businesses were sold directly to the employees. In the case of large businesses, some countries did sell many off to the highest bidder; in Hungary and Estonia, foreign investors such as General Electric purchased many large businesses. Other countries, such as the Czech Republic, relied more on what is known as **voucher privatization**. Under voucher privatization, citizens were given vouchers that they could then use to purchase shares in firms. Imagine, if you will, a huge auction in which everyone has a number of vouchers, which can be used to bid for shares in a business. Although this method has the advantage of being more rapid and superficially more equitable, the trade-off is that a firm is not sold outright to a new investor, who could bring new capital and expertise. Whether direct sales or voucher privatization was chosen, both were fraught with the danger that those in power might use the process to enrich themselves or their political allies.[8]

No matter which privatization process was chosen, in the end many firms were overstaffed, outdated, and unable to turn a profit in a market economy. Most problematic were some very large industrial firms, such as coal mines and steel plants, that had been built in the early years of industrialization and were uncompetitive in the international market. Such firms could be sold or even given away, but rather had to be closed, leading to unemployment in a society in which previously a job had been guaranteed. In some cases, such firms employed thousands of people and represented the main source of work in a city or region. To close down such firms is not an easy task for any politician, especially in a newly democratic system in which people are likely to vote with their pocketbooks and turn such leaders out of office. As a result, in some countries privatization has been slow because of the fear of widespread unemployment and social unrest. Moreover, state-owned firms remain an important source of power in postcommunist countries, a way in which political and economic power can remain fused.

## Marketization

In addition to re-creating private property, states must re-create a market in which property, labor, goods, and services can all function in a competitive environment to determine their value. On the surface, doing this appears to be easier than privatizing, a matter of simply eliminating central planning and allowing the market to resurface naturally. However, creating a market is also a complicated process. One issue of debate concerns how rapidly marketization should take place. Some argue that, given the profound nature of economic transformation, changes should be gradual to minimize social disruptions than might undermine these fledgling economies and democracies. In particular, supporters of this *gradualism* fear that sudden marketization will lead to wild jumps in prices as sellers are able to freely charge whatever they want for their goods. Inflation and even hyperinflation might result, undermining confidence in the transition process and generating widespread poverty.

Others reject these arguments, favoring rapid market reforms that would free up prices and bring an end to central planning and state subsidies for businesses virtually overnight. Such a change would be painful, and might initially involve a high degree of inflation, but the result might be that the pain would be shorter in duration. This policy (one particularly favored by some liberal Western advisors), which came to be known as *shock therapy*, was pioneered in Poland and later attempted in Russia.

## Evaluating Economic Transitions

How successful have all of these reforms been? The answer depends on what country you look at.[9] Table 13–2 shows growth in gross domestic product (GDP) from 1990 to 2005, per-capita GDP at purchasing power parity (PPP, the equivalent in U.S. dollars in 2005), the percentage of the economy held in private hands (as opposed to being owned by the state), and unemployment. The

**TABLE 13–2    Economic Conditions in Selected Transition Countries**

| COUNTRY | PER-CAPITA GDP PPP,* 2004(a) | PERCENT OF GDP PRIVATELY OWNED(b) | GDP AVERAGE ANNUAL GROWTH RATE, 1990–2005(a) | PERCENT UNEMPLOYED, 2005(c) |
|---|---|---|---|---|
| Poland | $12,953 | 75 | 2.89 | 19.0 |
| Hungary | $15,838 | 80 | 1.65 | 6.1 |
| Estonia | $14,925 | 80 | 5.75 | 10 |
| Czech Republic | $17,220 | 80 | 1.26 | 8.3 |
| Latvia | $11,396 | 70 | 4.52 | 10.6 |
| Bulgaria | $ 8,464 | 75 | −1.4 | 13.7 |
| Moldova | $ 2,184 | 65 | −0.82 | 7.9 |
| Russia | $10,150 | 65 | 1.08 | 8.6 |
| Tajikistan | $ 1,261 | 55 | 1.26 | 40 (estimated) |
| Belarus | $ 6,987 | 25 | 2.97 | 10–30 (estimated) |
| China | $ 6,425 | 70 (estimate only) | 9.72 | 10 (estimate only) |

*PPP, purchasing power parity.

*Sources:*

a. International Monetary Fund, World Economic Outlook Database, September 2006, www.IMF.org.

b. European Bank of Reconstruction and Development, 2006, www.EBRD.com.

c. The World Bank, *World Development Indicators (2006)*, www.WTO.org.

results of the past fifteen years are very mixed. In some cases marketization and privatization have produced economies with a relatively high rate of growth, especially in Poland, which has outpaced Hungary and the Czech Republic. In 1990, for example, Poland's shock therapy had an initially dramatic and painful effect on the economy as prices rose and inflation soared. Standards of living and GDP declined. By the mid-1990s, however, the economy began to recover, and now Poland's GDP is higher than it was in 1989 even though its unemployment is much higher than in Hungary and the Czech Republic.

Marketization was much more gradual in the Czech Republic and Hungary, but privatization was carried out more rapidly than in Poland. The Czech Republic relied heavily on voucher privatization, while Hungary sold many firms to foreign investors. Many of the other countries still struggle with incomplete privatization and high unemployment, although Estonia appears to have made great strides in transforming its economy.

In spite of these differences, Poland, Hungary, and the Czech Republic are often cited as the most successful examples of economic transition among the postcommunist countries. All three countries also embraced aspects of economic liberalism and social democracy. Moreover, they and nine other Eastern European countries have since joined the European Union (see Chapter 11). For many observers, membership in the European Union (EU) has been a recognition of the progress these countries have made both toward developing markets economies and toward institutionalizing democratic reform. Most became full-fledged members of the North Atlantic Treaty Organization (NATO) before being accepted for EU membership. However, joining NATO and the EU has been no panacea. For example, EU membership has imposed its own set of financial burdens on most new Central European EU states, which must grapple with bringing their regulations and standards up to EU levels. In addition, the large financial subsidies (such as in agriculture) that older member states have traditionally enjoyed have been much more limited for the new members. Extending the old EU system of supports and subsidies to the new member states would have quickly bankrupted the organization, and thus the new wave of accession has necessarily been a much more financially modest affair.

Finally, some observers in the newer EU countries wonder whether the costs of membership have outweighed the benefits because, for some, a new set of "top-down" bureaucratic regulations look uncomfortably like the old socialist order. Other observers, however, raise questions of equity and fairness that reflect the views of those who have not enjoyed the benefits of transition as much as others. Although public opinion surveys in these countries suggest that the majority of people feel they are better off than they were under Communism, many have "soured on both the new politics and the new economy."[10] Many people complain of a growing gap between rich and poor and that corrupt former party elites and economic managers took advantage of newly unregulated industries to become wealthy. In many cases, women also complain that conditions for them have not improved substantially, as they must deal with lack of child and maternal care and antifeminist attitudes and cultural traditions. Interestingly, the result has been an *increase* in the strength of communist, socialist, and social democratic parties and of the governments in countries such as Poland, Hungary, the Czech Republic, Bulgaria, Romania, and Albania.

In contrast to the positive results of the last decade in much of Eastern and Central Europe, the transition has not gone as well in Russia and most of the republics that once made up the former Soviet Union. In Russia, the Communist Party has emerged as one of the strongest parties in the Duma. Economic reforms in Russia in the early 1990s were modeled after Poland's shock therapy, though with disastrous results. Freeing up markets did not lead to economic growth, but rather to uncontrollable inflation and a rapid decline in the standard of living as people found their savings wiped out and their salaries unable to keep up with rising prices. Hyperinflation was eventually brought under control, but by 1999 about a third or more of the Russian population lived in poverty.[11] These difficulties in marketization were compounded by similar problems in privatization. The Russian government initially used voucher privatization for many small and medium-sized businesses, but the most important sectors of the economy (such as natural resources including oil) were sold to a handful of local investors with ties to the government and the old *nomenklatura*. The result was the emergence of "oligarchs," a small number of individuals with huge influence in the economy, government, and the media.

The 1990s were a troubled time for the Russian economy, but in recent years the country has shown much greater growth in its GDP, leading some to conclude that the country has finally turned the corner in terms of reform. However, much of Russia's economic growth has been based on oil exports rather than the development of a diversified market economy. Indeed, though most Russian firms are now in private hands, many of them have suffered from insolvency and interference from the state bureaucracy. The result is an economy built on a handful of large firms that emerged out of insider privatization that can hold their weight against the Russian government, alongside numerous small firms that hide in order to avoid onerous regulations, high taxes, and bribery.[12] In recent years President Vladimir Putin has gone after many of the oligarchs who benefited from privatization, and he has called for a strengthening of the legal system. However, organized crime and corruption remain serious problems. According to Transparency International, an anticorruption watchdog group, Russia's level of corruption is among the worst in the world, on a par with that of many developing countries.[13] To varying degrees the same problem can be found across many postcommunist countries, creating a climate that is not conducive to business growth.

Finally, postcommunist countries still struggle to varying degrees to foster a culture of capitalism that reconciles individual responsibility, risk, and reward. For example, over a third of the Russian population still believes that privatized assets should be renationalized, and the Communist Party remains a powerful political force, especially among older voters.[14] However, a new generation is quickly growing up across the region who have no memory of life under communism, making any retreat to the past highly unlikely.

Overall, some postcommunist countries continue to progress in developing well-functioning markets and states, but most have been stunted by incomplete economic reforms, insider privatization, and continued government intervention and ownership of the economy. Among the countries of the former Soviet Union, the GDP on average is now only around 60 percent of what it was in 1989.[15] In these countries one sees a political-economic system that has strong elements of mercantilism in its desire for state influence over the economy and in its belief that markets must serve national goals. This mercantilism also carries an anti-Western current, rejecting liberalism in particular as a foreign ideology that helped bring down the Soviet Union.

In considering political and economic transitions, one theme that runs through all these cases is the correlation between economic growth and the rule of law. Where the rule of law is weak, economic transition is much less successful. Entrepreneurs (both domestic and international) lack a predictable environment in which to invest, while political leaders and state officials use their position to siphon off resources for themselves, often hiding the money overseas. Under these conditions the result has often been **crony capitalism**, in which some have become extremely rich, often through government connections, while many others have seen their standard of living decline as businesses close and inflation destroys their savings. Where economic change was introduced without similar moves toward the rule of law, results have been disastrous. Some observers expect greater growth across the region in the future as reforms slowly take hold. Even if this does occur, however, it will be years or even decades before the people in some countries regain even the standard of living they had in 1989.

## CHINA'S TRANSITION TO MARKET SOCIALISM

In contrast to the bumpy transition in the former Soviet Union and parts of Eastern Europe, many point to China's transition from a planned to a market economy as a great success. However, China's case is unique, and any attempt to distill lessons from China's experience must take into account its special features. We must also recognize the challenges that China still faces in its move to transform both the state and the market. Because of the Communist Party's ongoing centrality in facilitating China's development, China's transition is most accurately viewed as one from classical socialism to market socialism.[16]

The transition from classical socialism began in 1978 in response to the tumult and upheaval that had characterized Mao Zedong's leadership of the party-state. After the revolution of 1949, Mao instituted a socialist system based on the Stalinist model, with state ownership of the means of production, collective farms, central planning, and other features described earlier in this chapter. This top-down model relied on urban intelligentsia to make most economic decisions through highly bureaucratic procedures, resulting in an uneven distribution of income and prestige across economic sectors and geographic areas.[17] Ideologically, Mao, whose revolution had been primarily peasant-based, was hostile to these notions of bureaucracy and centralization, seeking instead a "continuous revolution" that would counter these tendencies. These ideological ambitions were emboldened by deteriorating relations with the Soviet Union and the success of several campaigns of mass political mobilization during the 1950s, which culminated in the **Great Leap Forward** (1958–1960). All rural inhabitants were organized into *people's communes,* which were intended to strengthen collective behavior and organize labor to maximize industrial productivity. Using "backyard steel furnaces" and other low-grade industrial techniques, communes so deemphasized agriculture that an acute famine developed, resulting in the death of tens of millions of people. A return to Soviet-type economic planning was disrupted by the **Cultural Revolution** (1966–1976), in which Mao encouraged the people to attack the party-state itself, which he saw as having grown too bureaucratic and resistant to revolutionary change. The resulting anarchy nearly led to civil war, dramatically weakening the internal organization of the party-state and upsetting the stability of the economy.

Mao's death in 1976 instigated a power struggle that was eventually won by Deng Xiaoping (1904–1997). The events of the Mao years seriously degraded party legitimacy, and ideology was no longer sufficient to command obedience from the population. Deng concluded that the party-state could not survive without major reforms aimed at raising the Chinese people's standard of living.[18] In 1978, Deng's plan for economic reform was adopted. Deng described his program as "socialism with Chinese characteristics," combining elements of socialism with a greater role for markets and private property.

Two of the most important reforms initiated by Deng were in agriculture and in increasing China's openness to international markets. In agriculture, communal farms were dissolved and farmers were granted increased autonomy to select which crops to plant, as well as the ability to sell excess crops in free markets.[19] Food production soared and farmers' incomes rose, stimulating the growth of private rural enterprise. At the same time, Deng's plan created what was termed "the open door." Barriers to international trade and finance were lowered, opening China to global markets and foreign investment.[20] International trade increased access to the resources, technology, and know-how that have fueled China's rapid assent. A necessary consequence of these reforms has been a greater recognition of private property rights: Farmers gained the right to sell their land (with restrictions) in the mid-1980s, and private businesses have been gradually legalized. The role of market forces has also increased dramatically, and today, aside from major state-initiated infrastructure projects, no part of the economy is centrally planned.[21]

The effects of the reforms begun by Deng can be felt throughout the world economy. China's economy is the fourth largest in the world measured by GDP, and it is the second largest after factoring in purchasing power parity.[22] Total imports and exports make up around 70 percent of China's GDP, and by 2007 China is predicted to account for 10 percent of world trade.[23] Because of China's voracious demand for resources, global prices for many commodities have reached all-time highs, providing a boon for countries that are rich in raw materials. At the same time, many economists credit China with keeping global inflation levels low by providing the world with so many inexpensive goods.[24]

Despite these encouraging developments, China's transition away from classical socialism is not yet complete, and a number of obstacles remain to be surmounted. The most serious involves the ongoing dominance of the Communist Party. Unlike the transitions in Eastern Europe and Russia, China has introduced market forces to stimulate the economy without giving up party power. Private enterprise and markets have flourished but still remain what the Chinese have called "the bird in the cage"—that is, held firmly within the cage of state control.[25] State-run companies suffer from the same problems as their Soviet and East European counterparts: They are inefficient and outdated, and they are kept afloat by government financial support that could be used elsewhere. The party-state has been forced to rely on tactics of repression to maintain control, as seen during the 1989 Tiananmen Square crackdown against pro-democracy activists and the suppression of the Falun Gong religious movement in 1999. Many economic liberals consider economic liberalization to be a sure path toward political liberalization, which raises the prospect of growing disorder as the country grows even richer and confronts the entrenched power of the party.

China's transition has also contributed to a sharp rural–urban divide. Development of the country has been very uneven, concentrating gains in the coastal regions to the neglect of the interior of the country. Compounding this lack of opportunity has been deliberate exploitation of the rural population to facilitate development: The state has pursued a highly regressive taxation system in the rural areas, and as many as 40 million peasants have lost their land to development since the early 1990s with little or no compensation.[26] At the same time, state-provided services to rural areas have declined dramatically. As a result, more than 100 million farmers have left the land to look for work in urban areas. However, the members of this "floating population" are in effect illegal immigrants in their own country; they are deprived of many of the social services available to urban dwellers and are often exploited by employers against whom they have no recourse.[27]

Chinese officials acknowledge the need to continue a breakneck rate of development in order to absorb as many displaced rural workers as possible. However, they also fear that the economy is on the verge of overheating. Investment accounted for about 60 percent of China's GDP growth in 2005, enabled in large part by bank lending.[28] A remnant of the central planning era, state-owned banks are put at the service of the state to meet growth goals, rather than being allowed to evaluate independently the potential risks and rewards of any particular investment opportunity. As a result, China's banking system is burdened with billions of dollars worth of underperforming or nonperforming loans, and officials fear that this practice is unsustainably eroding China's fiscal and financial health. Another concern is that too much investment has created industrial overcapacity. Supply gluts have already begun to appear, which risk pushing prices downward and cutting into profits.

In 2002, Hu Jintao became China's Paramount Leader when he assumed the top leadership positions in the Chinese government and the Communist Party. Hu was considered a reformist and pledged to address growing income inequality and party corruption. In September 2006, the central government began a widespread probe into corruption, which at the time of this writing had implicated several high-ranking party officials. The investigations seem intended to deter future corruption with a high-profile demonstration of the leadership's resolve to eliminate it, but also to give Hu a pretext for weakening the faction of the party that is loyal to his predecessor Jiang Zemin, which has resisted Hu's policy agenda.[29] In recognition of the danger that growing inequality and social unrest pose to party legitimacy, Hu has advanced a new set of policies under the slogan of "Harmonious Society." The objective is to balance the long-held imperative of rapid and uncompromised growth with the goal of reducing the wealth gap, improving public services for the poor, and protecting the environment.[30]

China has also made progress in protecting human rights. In late 2006 it passed legislation preventing death sentences from being imposed without the approval of the country's highest court. In 2005 China was estimated to carry out more than 80 percent of the world's executions, putting to death perhaps 10,000 people, many for nonviolent offenses.[31] In October 2006 it also drafted a law designed to crack down on sweatshops and grant legal protection to workers trying to organize unions.[32] Finally, direct democracy has expanded with the popular election of village committees: In 2005 the government claimed that 470 million people cast ballots in these elections.[33]

Whether these and further reforms will preserve China's political stability may have a considerable effect on its development as a regional power. China's role in Asian economic and security affairs has escalated in recent years: It has spearheaded regional economic integration through the East Asian Summit (which excludes the United States); led talks on transforming Central Asia's Shanghai Cooperation Organization into a NATO-like military alliance; and conducted massive joint military exercises with Russia. As the country with the most influence over the North Korean government, it has played the foremost role in the six-party talks aimed at convincing North Korea to abandon its nuclear weapons program. China's attempts to gain influence have also expanded beyond Asia, including political support for some of the world's worst human rights abusers in exchange for access to much-needed natural resources. At the UN Security Council, China has given diplomatic support to the government of Sudan, which is accused of contributing to genocide in Darfur, and also to Iran, which is accused of having a secret nuclear weapons program. Both countries are Chinese energy suppliers. In November 2006 China signed an expansive agreement with forty-eight African nations, promising them billions in aid and loans in exchange for access to oil resources and African markets.[34]

The emergence of China as a potential counterweight to U.S. power was a source of concern for many in the second Bush administration. For neoconservatives, who believe the United States should use its global primacy to spread the values of freedom and democracy, the prospect of a stronger China, with its repressive political system and human rights practices is considered unacceptable.[35] Under the belief that a state's internal political configuration predetermines its foreign policy behavior, a strong authoritarian China is by nature an aggressive China. Other fears are driven by the strategic landscape in Asia, which contains a number of dangerous flashpoints. The first involves Taiwan, an island nation that has enjoyed *de facto* independence from China since 1949, but which China still professes to rightfully own. Under the U.S. doctrine of "strategic ambiguity" toward Taiwan, the United States officially supports the vision of "One China" yet opposes any nonpeaceful means of reunifying Taiwan and China, and also refuses to indicate whether it would come to Taiwan's defense if it were attacked. Cato Institute analyst Ted Carpenter, in a recent book, argues that this incoherent strategy makes it exceedingly likely that a miscalculation will draw the United States into a war with China.[36] China is also involved in territorial disputes with numerous countries over several uninhabited islands and reefs in the Western Pacific, which are thought to contain vast undersea petroleum deposits. A stronger China would have greater capacity and self-confidence to resolve these disputes militarily, which stands to damage U.S. interests in Asia and could even precipitate war between the United States and China.

In contrast to these security concerns, economic liberals downplay the imminent threat posed by China and argue that economic interdependence between the United States and China will deter an aggressive reordering of the balance of power in Asia. China's leaders have shown themselves to be entirely pragmatic, subordinating all other concerns to the imperative of developing the economy. China's militarization appears to be designed to deter a Taiwanese declaration of independence rather than to provide the capacity to project power beyond China's immediate periphery.[37] Even if China's motivations for militarizing are not benign, the vitality of its economic ties with the United States, which is China's principal export market and one of its leading sources of foreign direct investment, will make China exceedingly careful to not upset its relations with the United States. Many also point out that the United States enjoys such a dramatic advantage in military technology that even a concerted effort by China to improve its military would give the United States plenty of time to react.

Ultimately, China's future role in the world will depend in large part on the trajectory of its internal development. If social unrest and massive inequality cannot be tamed, the party's legitimacy may erode unsustainably, allowing demands for greater political liberalization to gain traction. Clearly, continued growth and modernization are essential, but the current dynamic poses considerable risks and yet reform carries significant danger as well. If China continues to develop at its current rate, it risks a serious economic crisis in the long term; however, if it slows development now, it risks tremendous social upheaval in the short term. China's ability to navigate these contradictions will determine to a large degree whether it emerges as the dominant economic and political power of the twenty-first century.

## CONCLUSION

According to Marxist thought, capitalism inevitably leads to great industrialization but also great injustice, a contradiction that would prove to be its downfall. Communism would then build on the ruins of capitalism and create a society of total equality. However, constructing communism proved to be a daunting task. People in communist systems found little incentive for hard work and innovation, and they had little freedom to express themselves individually.

For the Soviet Union and Eastern Europe, eventual attempts to solve these problems led to outright collapse. One might use the analogy of renovating a dilapidated house only to find that the whole structure is unsound and the renovations are only making the situation worse. At that point, one has to either demolish the whole structure or have it come down on top of you. In 1989, people in a number of Eastern European countries chose to pull down the institutions of communism. In the Soviet Union, the structure collapsed on the Communist Party and the society in 1991.

China seems to be in a process of endless (and perhaps precarious) remodeling, while some countries, such as Cuba and North Korea, have yet to carry out any major changes.

In Eastern Europe the transition away from communism is nearing the end of its second decade, and the changes are unmistakable. State-owned enterprises have been privatized, economic liberalization has created incentives for entrepreneurialism and innovation, and foreign direct investment has accelerated. The result has been robust economic growth that is, in many cases, far more impressive than is being enjoyed in Western Europe. Many of these countries have joined the European Union and have functioning electoral democracy. For all this progress, however, many obstacles remain, and new ones have become apparent. Corruption and rent-seeking behavior (see Chapter 5) stymie confidence in the economic transition and the competence of the politicians tasked with overseeing it. For many, the economic reforms proved very upsetting to established expectations and ways of life, and inability to adapt to the changes meant unemployment and poverty. Voters in many countries rose up in a backlash against the reformist agendas, strengthening the power of xenophobic, populist, and authoritarian elements.

The transition process is extremely diverse, and the results have been dramatically different across the communist and postcommunist world. In some countries we see the institutionalization of democracy and capitalism; in others, authoritarianism and state-controlled economies remain in place. Moreover, it is apparent that over time these countries will grow increasingly dissimilar to one another. Democratic consolidation and economic growth in Eastern Europe appear to place many of these countries on a slow path toward becoming industrial democracies. Within much of the former Soviet Union, economic stagnation or decline, political instability, and authoritarianism are more common, more closely resembling the less developed world. China remains an enormous question mark. And whatever the path, all these countries will continue to struggle over the dilemma of freedom and equality, a concern as pressing now as it was on the eve of the Russian Revolution in 1917.

## DISCUSSION QUESTIONS

1. What is the classical socialist system, and how does it differ from communism? What nations adopted the classical socialist system at different times during the twentieth century? Which nations currently employ this system? Explain.
2. What are the essential characteristics of the classical socialist system? How does the system differ from market socialism and from capitalism? How do the roles of state and market differ among these three systems of political economy? Explain.
3. Compare and contrast the economic and political reforms in Russia and Eastern Europe. Suggest factors that have made Eastern Europe's reforms more successful, at this point, than those in Russia. Are there any general lessons to be derived from this experience? Explain.
4. How are China's reform experiences different from those of Russia and Eastern Europe? Focus on differences in both means and ends. China aims to reform its market without a radical alteration in its political system. Is it possible to change the market so dramatically without changing the state? Explain.

## INTERNET LINKS

Russian and East European Network Information Center:
    http://reenic.utexas.edu/reenic.html
Freedom House:
    www.freedomhouse.org
Carnegie Endowment for International Peace, Russian and Eurasian Program:
    www.ceip.org/files/programs/rea_home.ASP
European Bank for Reconstruction and Development:
    www.ebrd.com
Transitions Online:
    www.tol.cz

## SUGGESTED READINGS

Robert F. Ash and Y. Y. Kueh, eds. *The Chinese Economy Under Deng Xiaoping.* Oxford: Clarendon Press, 1996.

Joseph R. Blasi, Maya Kroumova, and Douglas Kruse. *Kremlin Capitalism: Privatizing the Russian Economy.* Ithaca, NY: Cornell University Press, 1997.

Maxim Boycko, Andrei Shleifer, and Robert Vishny. *Privatizing Russia.* Cambridge, MA: MIT Press, 1995.

Robert Campbell. *The Socialist Economies in Transition: A Primer on Semi-reformed Systems.* Bloomington, IN: Indiana University Press, 1991.

Feng Chen. *Economic Transition and Political Legitimacy in Post-Mao China: Ideology and Reform.* Albany, NY: State University of New York Press, 1995.

Maurice Ernst, Michael Alexeev, and Paul Marer. *Transforming the Core: Restructuring Industrial Enterprises in Russia and Central Europe.* Boulder, CO: Westview, 1996.

Ted C. Fishman. *China Inc.: How the Rise of the Next Superpower Challenges America and the World.* New York: Scribner, 2005.

Shangquan Gao. *China's Economic Reform.* New York: St. Martin's, 1996.

*The Gate of Heavenly Peace* (videorecording, PBS *Frontline* series). Boston: WGBH, 1995.

Marshall I. Goldman. *Lost Opportunity: Why Economic Reforms in Russia Have Not Worked.* New York: W. W. Norton, 1994.

János Kornai. *The Socialist System: The Political Economy of Communism.* Princeton, NJ: Princeton University Press, 1992.

V. I. Lenin. *The State and Revolution.* New York: International Publishers, 1932.

Roderick MacFarquhar, ed. *The Politics of China, 1949–1989.* Cambridge: Cambridge University Press, 1993.

Barry Naughton. *Growing Out of the Plan: Chinese Economic Reform, 1978–1993.* Cambridge: Cambridge University Press, 1996.

Adam Przeworski. *Democracy and the Market.* Cambridge: Cambridge University Press, 1991.

Carl Riskin. *China's Political Economy: The Quest for Development Since 1949.* Oxford: Oxford University Press, 1988.

Jeffrey Sachs. *Poland's Jump to the Market Economy.* Cambridge, MA: MIT Press, 1993.

The World Bank. *Transition—The First Ten Years: Analysis and Lessons for Eastern Europe and the Former Soviet Union.* Washington, DC: The World Bank, 2002.

Salvatore Zecchini, ed. *Lessons from the Economic Transition: Central and Eastern Europe in the 1990s.* Dordrecht, the Netherlands: Kluwer, 1997.

## KEY TERMS

| | | |
|---|---|---|
| market socialism | party-state | privatization |
| classical socialism | centrally planned economies | voucher privatization |
| communism | *glasnost* | crony capitalism |
| socialism | *perestroika* | Great Leap Forward |
| *nomenklatura* | marketization | Cultural Revolution |

## NOTES

1. V. I. Lenin, *The State and Revolution* (New York: International Publishers, 1932).
2. Václav Havel, "A Call for Sacrifice," *Foreign Affairs*, 73 (March/April 1994), pp. 2–7.
3. Classical socialism is sometimes called *state socialism* to make clear its difference from *market socialism.*
4. See János Kornai, *The Socialist System: The Political Economy of Communism* (Princeton, NJ: Princeton University Press, 1992).
5. Excerpted from Table 1–1 of Kornai, *The Socialist System,* pp. 6–7. The reference date for this list is 1987, before the collapse of the socialist governments in Eastern Europe.
6. Robert Campbell, *The Socialist Economies in Transition: A Primer on Semi-reformed Systems* (Bloomington, IN: Indiana University Press, 1991), p. 46.
7. For an excellent discussion of the collapse of communism in Central Europe, see Timothy Garton Ash, *The Magic Lantern: The Revolution of 1989 as Witnessed in Warsaw, Budapest, Berlin and Prague* (New York: Random House, 1990).
8. See Saul Estrin and Robert Stone, "A Taxonomy of Mass Privatization," www.worldbank.org/html/prddr/trans/novdec96/doc6.htm.

9. For an analysis, see The World Bank, *Transition—The First Ten Years: Analysis and Lessons for Eastern Europe and the Former Soviet Union* (Washington, DC: The World Bank, 2002).

10. "Westward, Look, the Land Is Bright," *The Economist,* October 26, 2002, p. 25. For a more detailed discussion of these more recent political economic developments in Eastern Europe, see David S. Mason, "Fairness Matters: Equity and the Transition to Democracy," *World Policy Journal, 20* (Winter 2003/2004), pp. 48–57. See also Rasma Karklins, "In Eastern Europe, Corruption in the Crosshairs," *Current History, 104* (November 2005, pp. 374–380).

11. See United Nations, *2000 Human Development Report for the Russian Federation* (Moscow: United Nations Development Programme, 2000).

12. John McMillian, Simon Johnson, Daniel Kaufmann, and Christopher Woodruff, "Why Do Firms Hide? Bribes and Unofficial Activity after Communism," *Journal of Public Economics, 76* (June 2000), pp. 495–520.

13. See Transparency International, Global Corruption Report 2003, www.globalcorruptionreport.org.

14. See How Russia Votes, www.russiavotes.org.

15. The World Bank, *Transition—The First Ten Years,* p. xiii.

16. See Shangquan Gao, *China's Economic Reform* (New York: St. Martin's, 1996).

17. Kenneth Lieberthal, *Governing China: From Revolution Through Reform* (New York: W. W. Norton, 2004), pp. 99–100.

18. Ibid., pp. 127–130.

19. Ibid., p. 250.

20. Feng Chen, *Economic Transition and Political Legitimacy in Post-Mao China: Ideology and Reform* (Albany, NY: State University of New York Press, 1995), pp. 130–136.

21. Lieberthal, *Governing China,* pp. 260–261.

22. International Monetary Fund, World Economic Outlook Database, April 2006, www.imf.org/external/pubs/ft/weo/2006/01/data/index.htm.

23. "A Survey of the World Economy," *The Economist,* September 16, 2006.

24. "From T-Shirts to T-Bonds," *The Economist,* July 30, 2005, p. 66.

25. Barry Naughton, *Growing Out of the Plan: Chinese Economic Reform, 1978–1993* (Cambridge: Cambridge University Press, 1996), p. 120.

26. *The Economist,* "How to Make China Even Richer," March 25, 2006, p. 9. David Balaam and Josh Anderson updated this part of the chapter.

27. Li Zhang, *Strangers in the City: Reconfigurations of Space, Power and Social Networks Within China's Floating Populations* (Stanford, CA: Stanford University Press, 2001).

28. Nerys Avery, "Hu Concerned as Chinese Economy Speeds up," *The Seattle Times,* April 17, 2006, p. A10.

29. Joseph Kahn, "Corruption Inquiry Grows, and China's Leader May Profit," *The New York Times,* October 27, 2006, p. A3.

30. Martin Fan, "China's Party Leadership Declares New Priority: 'Harmonious Society,'" *The Washington Post,* October 12, 2006, p. A18.

31. Audra Ang, "China Tightens Rules on Executions," *The Seattle Times,* November 1, 2006, p. F1.

32. David Barboza, "China Drafts Law to Empower Unions and End Labor Abuse," *The New York Times,* October 13, 2006, p. A1.

33. Xinhua News Agency, "470 Million Chinese Villagers Vote in Village Elections Last Year," May 18, 2006.

34. Charles Hutzler, "China, Africa End Summit with Pledge of Closer Ties, More Trade," The Associated Press, November 6, 2006.

35. The website www.newamericancentury.org has a collection of articles and reports that express the neoconservative point of view.

36. Ted Galen Carpenter, *America's Coming War with China: A Collision over Taiwan* (New York: Pelgrave Macmillan, 2006).

37. China's militarization is detailed and its implications discussed in the 2005 Annual Report to Congress on the Military Power of the People's Republic of China, available at www.defenselink.mil.

# The Middle East: The Pursuit of Development, Democracy, and Peace

## By Bradford Dillman

### OVERVIEW

In 1950, U.S. Secretary of State Dean Acheson forwarded to U.S. diplomats in the Arab world the following excerpt from a classified State Department newsletter:

> Anti-Americanism is resurging in the Arab world. . . . The bombings at our Legations in Beirut and Damascus; vitriolic public statements by Syria's Dawalibi, Iraq's Suwaidi and other high officials; diatribes and fantastic rumors in the vernacular press of Syria, Egypt, and Iraq; all testify to the rekindling of Arab animosity against the United States. Whether promoted by Communists or Moslem extremists, whether encouraged by irresponsible journalists or by weak government officials who seek to divert attention from their own inadequacies, or whether attributable to a sincere objection to America's part in Palestine developments, the current emotionalism bodes no good for the interests of the United States, nor for that matter for the best interests of the Arab states themselves.[1]

Fifty-five years later, the State Department sent its new Undersecretary of State for Public Affairs, Karen Hughes, on a public relations tour of the Middle East to counter another wave of anti-Americanism that had emerged from the U.S. invasion of Iraq, the Abu Ghraib scandal, U.S. backing of Israel, and perceived hypocrisy on democracy. Hughes emphasized in her speeches the importance of fighting against extremism and terrorism. Whether at the beginning of the Cold War or the start of the recent "war on terror," many in the Middle East have mistrusted the world's hegemon and condemned it for caring more about its own interests than about what is good for people in the region. Then, as now, Middle East residents are seen as reacting to the West on the basis of conspiracism, weakness, and poor leadership. The State Department seems to be telling Middle Easterners that their extremism diverts them from the task of solving their own problems of poor governance and slow growth.

This chapter assesses the efforts of the Middle East to adapt to the global economy, provide security for its citizens, and deal with growing pressures for democracy. How well the Middle East adapts to globalization depends partly on its relationship with the United States, but also on a much larger set of economic, political, and social factors. First, the chapter examines how the region was historically integrated into the international economy and security structure under European colonialism and during the Cold War. This is followed by a discussion of the causes of conflict and an examination of the beliefs and actions of Islamist political movements. We then assess competing claims about whether the region is "falling behind" in the global economy or successfully integrating itself into the global trade, finance, and knowledge structures. Finally, the chapter assesses why the region—with a few exceptions—has yet to succumb to the waves of democratization that have swept over other parts of the world.

The Middle East reveals important tensions among states, markets, and societies. Governments are clinging to authoritarianism while societies are demanding political rights. International markets are demanding openness and adaptiveness while states jealously guard sovereignty and individuals demand protection from some of the changes that globalization brings with it. With a few exceptions, the Middle East has responded to these contradictory pressures by muddling through—adopting some economic liberalism and political openness but resisting fundamental change. The weight of history is putting a damper on development. Lack of freedom is stifling innovation and accountability. Lack of economic diversification is making the region more vulnerable to economic pressures from overseas. The promises of liberalism have yet to trump the impulses of mercantilism. Outside powers, however, can probably do little to make the region change rapidly. A shift to a new model of governance and development will of necessity come from bold leaders within the region.

**W**hich countries constitute the Middle East? This chapter focuses on the region that U.S. social scientists commonly refer to as the Middle East and North Africa (MENA), an area that is tied together by history, self-identification, and economic–political interactions. It includes Israel, Iran, and Turkey (all non-Arab countries), and the numerous Arab states in the *Mashriq* (Syria, Lebanon, Jordan, Iraq, and the Palestinian Territories), in the Arabian Peninsula (Saudi Arabia, Yemen, Oman, Kuwait, Bahrain, Qatar, and the United Arab Emirates), and in North Africa (Egypt, Libya, Tunisia, Algeria, and Morocco). The distance from one end of the region to the other (Rabat, Morocco, to Tehran, Iran) is nearly 3700 miles.

In addition to official languages of Arabic, Farsi, Turkish, and Hebrew, there are also millions of Kurdish speakers (especially in Turkey and Iraq) and millions of Berber speakers (especially in Morocco and Algeria). Arabic is the most widely used language (even Iran, Israel, and Turkey have Arab-speaking minorities), and the majority of people are Muslims. Of a total regional population of approximately 400 million people, there are about 15 million Christians and 5 million Jews. Substantial minorities of Christians live in Egypt and Lebanon. Although most Israelis are Jewish, 15 percent of Israeli citizens are Muslims. Most Muslims in the MENA are Sunnis, but the majority of the population in Iran and Iraq is Shi'ite.

MENA countries share some common economic challenges but differ significantly in terms of level of development and relationship to the global economy. For example, Yemen, one of the poorest countries in the world, has a per-capita Gross National Product (GNP) of only $920, whereas Israel's per-capita GNP is $25,280—equal to that of Spain's and close to that of the most developed countries in the world.[2] Grouping countries on the basis of exports, GNP, and population yields four general categories of MENA countries (see Table 14–1). First are the big oil exporters of the Gulf Cooperation Council and Libya, with comparatively small populations and high per-capita incomes. A second group includes big oil exporters such as Iran, Iraq, and Algeria, with large populations and historically highly protectionist economies. Third are non–oil exporters such as Israel, Turkey, Jordan, Tunisia, and Lebanon, with significant agriculture, industrial exports, tourism, and openness to foreign direct investment. Fourth are the countries like Egypt, Morocco, Syria, Yemen, and the Palestinian Territories, with mostly large populations, low per-capita GDP, and high rates of rural poverty.

There is a great deal of variation in political regimes, but the Middle East as a whole lags behind every other major region of the world in terms of political freedom. Freedom House, an independent

**TABLE 14–1**

| COUNTRY | 2006 POPULATION (IN MILLIONS) | GNP PER CAPITA 2005 (PPP) |
|---|---|---|
| **High-Income Oil Exporters** | | |
| Saudi Arabia | 27.0 | 14,740 |
| Libya | 5.9 | 11,400 |
| Oman | 3.1 | 14,680 |
| United Arab Emirates | 2.6 | 24,090 |
| Kuwait | 2.4 | 24,010 |
| Bahrain | 0.7 | 21,290 |
| Qatar | 0.9 | 31,400 |
| **Middle- to Low-Income Oil Exporters** | | |
| Iran | 68.7 | 8,050 |
| Algeria | 32.9 | 6,770 |
| Iraq | 26.8 | 3,400 |
| **Diversified Exporters** | | |
| Turkey | 70.4 | 8,420 |
| Tunisia | 10.2 | 7,900 |
| Israel | 6.4 | 25,280 |
| Jordan | 5.9 | 5,280 |
| Lebanon | 3.9 | 5,740 |
| **Low-Income, Significantly Agricultural Countries** | | |
| Egypt | 78.9 | 4,440 |
| Morocco | 33.2 | 4,360 |
| Yemen | 21.5 | 920 |
| Syria | 18.9 | 3,740 |
| Palestinian Territories | 3.9 | 660 |

*Sources:* The World Bank, *World Development Indicators*; CIA, *World Factbook.*

organization that annually measures countries' political rights and civil liberties, ranks only Israel (in the Middle East) as being "free."[3] Seven countries—Turkey, Lebanon, Kuwait, Bahrain, Yemen, Jordan, and Morocco—are assessed as "partly free" because they have (unfair) competitive elections and fail to ensure individual and minority rights. All eleven other countries are considered "not free." There is not a strong correlation between level of freedom and level of development in the region. And surprisingly, four of the freest countries are monarchies (Kuwait, Bahrain, Jordan, and Morocco), and two of the freest make religious identity a fundamental criterion for political rights and privileges (Israel and Lebanon).

## THE MIDDLE EAST'S HISTORICAL LEGACY

History shapes the problems and opportunities in front of any country today. To help us understand the roots of current conflicts and the structure of current markets, we need to know something about the history of the Middle East's deep involvement in the global economy and contentious relations with the Western powers. Most of today's Middle East countries (except Iran and Morocco) were once part of the Ottoman Empire, which for hundreds of years was a commercial power in the Mediterranean and a military adversary of the European countries.

### The Ottoman Heritage

By the nineteenth century, the Ottoman Empire had turned into the "sick man of Europe." European imperial powers extended their military and economic influence, gaining commercial concessions throughout the empire. France colonized Algeria in 1832, and in the 1880s Britain and France took control of Egypt and Tunisia, respectively, on the pretext that they were no longer able to pay their debts to European creditors. The Ottomans and local rulers in the Middle East tried with very limited success to keep up with the Europeans through "**defensive modernization**"—reorganizing their governments, adopting European military technology and legal codes, and building state-owned factories.

Why was the Middle East unable to compete militarily and economically with Europe? A similar question is posed today by many in the Middle East who wonder why their countries have fallen so far behind the West in terms of technology and have been unable to challenge successfully the military "aggression" of the United States and Israel. In his influential book, *What Went Wrong?*, Princeton University historian Bernard Lewis points to a lack of separation of church and state, cultural immobilism, and lack of political freedom (especially for women) as factors that hindered modernization in the Muslim Middle East.[4] Some economic historians point out that Ottoman "**capitulations**"—special economic privileges and legal rights granted to Europeans over several centuries—prevented the region from imposing high tariffs to protect infant industries. Some Muslim reformist thinkers saw decline as tied to stagnation in Islamic thought. They believed that Muslim societies could keep up with Western societies by discarding historical accretions in Islam and engaging in *ijtihad* (reinterpretation of Islamic legal sources).[5]

Alternatively, political scientist L. Carl Brown argues that the Middle East got locked into a system of international diplomacy called the **Eastern Question Game**, in which outside countries continuously penetrated the region and jockeyed for power. The result of this mercantilist game was that Middle Eastern political leaders tended to favor "quick grabs," eschew bargaining, and treat politics as a zero-sum game.[6] As we will see later in the chapter, the kinds of explanations we have listed here are still in vogue today as interpretations of the roadblocks for Middle Eastern countries trying to adapt to globalization.

## Twentieth-Century Colonialism and Its Aftermath

By the end of World War I, the European powers had carved up the region—excluding Turkey, Iran, and Saudi Arabia—into colonies. They drew the (often artificial) boundaries of today's Arab states and often excercised strong influence over dependent monarchical regimes in "protectorates" and "mandates." The violence that colonial powers used against inhabitants seeking independence was ferocious, sometimes setting back industrialization and state formation for decades. For example, during the "pacification" of Libya from 1911 to 1933, the Italians killed most of the country's livestock and caused the displacement, imprisonment, or death of a majority of the inhabitants.[7] During the Palestinians' Great Revolt from 1936 to 1939, Britain's counterinsurgency caused 10 percent of the entire male population to suffer imprisonment, exile, injury, or death.[8]

Soon after World War II, nationalist movements blossomed across the MENA. The Zionist dream of a Jewish state in Palestine was fulfilled in 1948 when Israel declared its independence and rebuffed an invasion by its Arab neighbors. By the late 1950s, most of the countries in the region were independent. Algerians, however, fought a brutal guerrilla war for independence from the French from 1954 to 1962, during which more than 750,000 people were killed (and many tortured by the French).

Many independent states still had to deal with a colonial legacy of exploitation and the lingering presence of European powers. In the Suez Crisis of 1956, for example, Israel, France, and Britain briefly invaded Egypt after its President Gamal Abdel Nasser nationalized the Suez Canal. The oil industries were dominated by the West's "Seven Sisters," who for decades deprived Middle Eastern countries of a "fair share" of oil revenues. Colonial powers had deliberately hampered industrialization in most Arab countries.

Ordinary citizens had little role in governance, and there was a huge economic divide between urban and rural dwellers. Poor health care and poor education were the norm, not the exception. For example, a Rockefeller Foundation–sponsored study of Egypt in the early 1950s found that about half of children died before the age of 5. In a survey of five typical villages near Cairo, researchers found that nearly all inhabitants had dysentery, bilharzia, and trachoma, and two-thirds suffered from intestinal worms.[9] At the time of Algeria's independence from France in 1962, less than one-third of Muslim children were enrolled in elementary school. As late as 1970, Oman had only 10 miles of paved roads and one hospital.

Arab socialists and military officers who staged a series of *coup d'états* in the 1950s and 1960s sought to break the cycle of dependency and inequality they blamed on the West and its lackeys in the region. They implemented mercantilist-style modernization programs, complete with subsidies on basic goods, state-owned industries, and high tariffs. Their success, however, was tempered by the intrusion of the Cold War into the region.

### The Cold War to the Present in the MENA

Proxy regimes relied on the superpowers for weapons and economic aid. Washington was more than happy to support authoritarian leaders like Iran's Shah as a bulwark against communism and to secure oil supplies. Moscow was eager to detach Third World countries from the Western orbit.

The Cold War had at least two lasting effects on the region. First, it pushed the oil-producing states of the Organization of the Petroleum Exporting Countries (OPEC) to assert control over oil production and pricing. Responding to U.S. support for Israel in its 1973 struggle against Soviet allies Syria and Egypt, Arab members of OPEC nationalized oil companies and temporarily cut off oil exports to the United States. The net result in the 1970s and early 1980s was a massive transfer of wealth from industrialized nations to oil producers, whose leaders spent generously on infrastructure and education. Second, in their struggle against leftist political parties and Soviet proxies, the United States and its Middle East allies often accommodated conservative Islamist movements, even supplying massive amounts of weapons to the *mujahideen* (freedom fighters) in Afghanistan. The "blowback" from this marriage of convenience with Islamists would haunt the West in the 1990s.

At the end of the Cold War in 1990, points out British political scientist Fred Halliday, Russia virtually disappeared from the Middle East and the United States emerged as the unrivaled external hegemon.[10] Violent, nonstate organizations such as al-Qaeda and Hizballah became the West's new bogeymen. Neoliberal economic policies spread in the face of a deep slump in oil prices that began in 1985 and mounting inefficiencies in state-dominated economies. The 1993 Oslo Accords between Israel and the Palestinians lowered the level of violence, but the Gulf states and Iran, points out Halliday, started an arms race. And military spending in the Middle East in the 1990s still averaged about 7 percent of GDP, the highest rate of any region in the world.[11] Unfortunately, a 1990s "peace dividend" never materialized.

The contemporary history of the MENA states since September 11, 2001, has been shaped by the crackdown on radical Islamists. The United States has been preoccupied with the war on terror and the occupation of Iraq, suffering a sharp decline in its moral authority. A new regional dynamic is the flexing of political and military muscle by the Shi'ites in Iran, Iraq, and Lebanon. At the same time, dramatically higher oil prices have flooded the treasuries of oil exporters, allowing them to pay down foreign debt and boost government spending. The higher growth rates are welcome news for the region's people but will not necessarily end inequality. It remains to be seen if unaccountable elites will avoid the old temptation to waste new money on weapons and political patronage.

## THE ROOTS OF CONFLICT AND COOPERATION

This outline of Middle East history shows that there were many injustices in the past. Today there are many lingering grievances that contribute to conflict in the region. To understand why so much interstate and intrastate violence occurs, we will look primarily at political forces operating at the international and domestic levels. Of course, the MENA is not just one big zone of conflict or a vast "arc of crisis." Many forms of interstate cooperation can be identified, and with a few exceptions, countries are not on the verge of civil war. By analyzing patterns and causes of both conflict and cooperation, we can better understand the prospects for prosperity and modernization.

Tracing the roots of MENA conflict can be a difficult task, partly because the causes of violence are as much domestic as they are international and as much ideological as they are material. Conventional wisdom holds that ancient hatreds—traceable to Biblical times, the Crusades, or the Sunni–Shi'a split in early Islam—are at the heart of conflicts. This "clash of civilizations" explanation of global problems—popularized by political scientist Samuel Huntington—is tempting, especially when we look at the current war on terror. Although modern-day combatants frequently use imagery from history or holy texts to justify their struggle, we should be wary of accepting their worldviews as a basis for explaining conflict. It is more accurate to tie regional insecurity to four contemporary political factors: (1) the search by external powers for influence in the region; (2) adventurism by regional leaders; (3) oppressive regimes; and (4) the politicization of cultural and religious differences.

## Blaming the Outside World

As we have already seen, non–Middle Eastern powers have been searching for control of the MENA for centuries. Their "meddling" has often had terrible consequences. Slicing up territories or combining different ethnolinguistic and religious communities to create new states, the Great Powers often ensured future strife. During the Cold War, the Soviet Union and the United States struggled for dominance in the region by sponsoring different political forces. The superpowers' support for their proxies played a role in stoking the Arab–Israeli conflict. Staunchly anti-Israeli regimes in places such as Syria found the Soviet Union eager to sell them military equipment. On the other side, monarchs such as the King of Jordan and the Saudi royals looked to the United States for a security umbrella against pan-Arab socialist regimes seeking their overthrow. Turkey and Israel earned aid and weapons from Washington by touting their front-line role in the struggle against communism. Although Iran turned rabidly anti-American after the 1979 Islamic Revolution, Egypt under Anwar Sadat warmed up to the United States in the 1970s. Although some forms of anti-Americanism are prevalent, the majority of governments today have close military ties and/or friendly relations with the United States. Yet, Iran, Syria, Lebanon, the Palestinians, and some elements of the Iraqi government resist "**Pax Americana**"—a supposedly benevolent form of imperialism under which countries are expected to make peace with Israel, end terrorism, and host U.S. military bases (or at least cooperate with the United States on military and security issues).

Given the United States's deep military penetration of the MENA, countries trying to defy the hegemon face potentially heavy costs. For example, Arab states have squandered billions of dollars in their unsuccessful wars against Israel. U.S. weapons and economic assistance to Israel for nearly forty years have helped ensure that there is no fundamental change in the Arab–Israeli balance of power. In addition, the United States and its allies have imposed a variety of economic sanctions on MENA countries. These mercantilist penalties have included cutoffs of aid, denial of World Bank financing, freezing of assets in the United States, trade embargos, and prohibitions on Western investments.

Ostensibly designed to foster regime change or "better behavior," these sanctions have in some cases ravaged vulnerable populations without achieving their political objectives. For example, the UN's punitive (and corrupt) **Oil for Food Program** allowed Iraq to export only a certain amount of oil after 1992, and the profits were to be used to import food and medicine. Iraq's population suffered malnutrition, declining health standards, and sometimes death. Indications of this were found in a UN-sponsored survey of 21,000 Iraqi households soon after the U.S. occupation in 2003. The survey report registered dramatic signs of malnutrition in Iraqi children under the age of 5: 23 percent suffered chronic malnutrition (low height for their age), 13 percent suffered general malnutrition (low weight for their age), and 8 percent suffered acute malnutrition (low weight for their height).[12] In 2006 the Palestinian population, already reeling from years of Israeli closures and trade restrictions, suffered another setback when the United States and the European Union cut off aid to the elected, Hamas-led government. Only Libya caved in to international sanctions in 2003, owning up to its involvement in the 1988 airplane bombing over Lockerbie, Scotland, and agreeing to dismantle its incipient nuclear weapons program.

Three different measures provide a clear indication of how many people in the Middle East blame outsiders for regional violence. First, conservative analyst Daniel Pipes argues that for decades there has been a widespread political culture of **conspiracism** in Iran and the Arab countries, wherein the "hidden hand" of the West or Israel is seen lurking behind all the region's wars and other ills. This mindset, he asserts, encourages extremism and "engenders a suspiciousness and aggressiveness that spoil relations with the great powers."[13] Second, a discourse shared by some Muslim scholars chastises the West for its nefarious role in the region. For example, at a conference in Egypt in 2000, one prominent Muslim scholar characterized the West in these terms:

> Your globalization, oh you craven braggarts, is an arbitrary hegemony, a despotic authority, an oppressive injustice and a pitch-black darkness, because it is a globalization without religion and without conscience. It is a globalization of violent force, heedless partisanship, double standards, pervasive materialism, widespread racism, outrageous barbarism and arrogant egoism. It is a globalization that sells illusions, leading to perdition and to burying dreams in the depth of nowhere, spreading flowers over the corpses of the hungry.[14]

Finally, public opinion polls reveal a high level of fear of the United States, *even among its Middle East allies*. A Pew Research Center survey in 2003 conducted around the world found that more than 50 percent of all respondents in Turkey, Lebanon, and Jordan were somewhat or very worried that the United States might pose a military threat to their country.[15]

## Blaming "Aggressive" Regional Leaders

The use of terms such as "The Butcher of Baghdad" (Saddam Hussein), "The Mad Dog of the Middle East" (Muammar Qaddafi), and the "Mad Mullahs" (Iran's Shi'ite clerics) implies that these "brutal" or "irrational" leaders are responsible for sparking conflict. Although demonizing Middle East leaders is not good social science, it is clear that **adventurism** by regional leaders since 1980 has been as important a source of insecurity as superpower meddling or transnational terrorism. Adventurism takes many forms, including territorial aggression, punitive strikes, threats of invasion, and covert operations. These acts may be designed to destabilize political rivals, expand a country's territory, or solidify control over strategic natural resources.

For example, Saddam Hussein's 1980 invasion of Iran sparked a terrible eight-year war, and his 1990 occupation of Kuwait prompted a multinational counterattack led by 500,000 U.S. troops. His actions—perhaps rooted in megalomania—can better be explained by Iraq's longstanding desire to gain ports on the Persian Gulf and dominate oil production. Morocco's 1975 takeover of the large but sparsely populated Western Sahara stemmed in part from King Hassan II's desire to boost his domestic legitimacy and control the territory's valuable phosphates and Atlantic fisheries. And the post-1979 efforts of Iranian Mullahs to spread Islamic revolution throughout the Middle East contributed to instability in Lebanon.

Israeli leaders have sanctioned the long-term occupation and settlement of Arab territories seized during wars with Palestinians and Arab armies. In its War of Independence in 1948, Israel won control of 80 percent of Palestine, causing a mass exodus of 750,000 Palestinians, who abandoned land and property worth billions of dollars in today's terms. As a result of the 1967 Six-Day War, Israel took control of the West Bank, the Gaza Strip, the Golan Heights, and the Sinai Peninsula. Access to aquifers and rivers in the West Bank and the Golan Heights has been important for Israeli agriculture and water needs. A relentless program of settlement expansion has boosted the Jewish population in the Occupied West Bank and East Jerusalem to 400,000.

In 1982 Israel occupied southern Lebanon, and it did not fully withdraw until 2000. But in the summer of 2006 it extensively bombed Lebanese infrastructure in a month-long war during which Hizballah launched hundreds of missiles into Israel. Israeli leaders have consistently justified their military engagements on the basis of their inherent right of self-defense, and they often rationalize settlement expansion as a historical right. In 2005 Israel withdrew from the Gaza Strip. Whatever the justifications offered by Israel, Arabs view settlement expansion as a form of colonialism that violates international law. Large-scale human rights abuses have inflamed Palestinians, whose two violent *intifadas* (uprisings) in 1987 and 2000 were designed to force an Israeli withdrawal.

## The Oppression Factor

Regional conflicts also involve cycles of oppression–terrorism–counterinsurgency within states. Leading participants in these terrible cycles are often dominant ethnolinguistic and religious groups who subject minorities to discrimination and who try to "explain" their violence via "myths" that serve as little more than cover stories for the pursuit of self-interest. Moderate, secular Arabs claim that they are fighting retrograde Islamic fundamentalists. Islamists claim that they are fighting governing elites whose cultural beliefs reflect **"Westoxication"**—a seduction to poisonous, imported Western culture and institutions. Israel portrays its struggle as one against Palestinian terrorists. Kurds and Algerian Berbers fight perceived political and cultural oppression by Arabs. And Ahmed Hashim, a U.S. adviser to General John Abizaid in Iraq, in 2005 observed that ethnosectarian hatreds had grown in Iraq, with Sunnis viewing Shi'a as "primitive and childlike," Kurds holding contempt for non-Kurds, and Shi'a seeing Sunnis as oppressors and Kurds as "arrogant backstabbers."[16]

What these Manichean portrayals often do not explain are the politics of oppression and resistance at the heart of struggles and the multitude of local factors that affect political behavior. Although transnational terrorist groups such as Al-Qaeda have caused some havoc in the region, they are far from being the central actors in MENA countries. At its base, much of the violence is a political struggle over control of the state. Kurds, Sahrawis, and Palestinians are struggling for independence and sovereignty (or at least autonomy) over a given territory in which they are currently facing political oppression. They sometimes justify violence as a legitimate tool, noting international norms of self-determination and human rights protection.[17]

Many Islamists seek the right to implement conservative social policies they claim are based on Islamic law. Shi'ites in Iraq and Lebanon (and to some extent in the Arabian peninsula), seeking to reverse decades of Sunni (or Maronite Christian) discrimination, are claiming political power and voice commensurate with their size of the population. And the Shi'ite movements such as Muqtada al-Sadr's Mahdi Army in Iraq claim a legitimate right to resist an occupying military power. Whether governments and occupying powers call their opponents "terrorists," or whether nationalist insurgents and *mujahideen* call their opponents "state terrorists," the fact is that all these combatants mostly injure and kill innocent civilians, not other armed fighters.

An example of the role that oppression can play in sparking conflict is provided by Lisa Hajjar, who has studied the Israeli military court system in the Palestinian Occupied Territories.[18] She finds a system of military rule and military "justice" since 1967 that regulates the movements of Palestinians and subjects inhabitants to arrest, detention, humiliation, and sometimes torture. Since 1967 the military courts have prosecuted more than 500,000 of the 3.5 million Palestinians in the West Bank and Gaza. The reality of constant surveillance, lack of due process, and constant disruption of normal life has served to stiffen Palestinian resistance, some of which turns violent.

## Blaming the Islamists

Extremist Islamic movements and terrorist groups use religion as a political tool, even if reasonable people agree that these groups fundamentally misinterpret Islam. Much has been written about the motivations and actions of violent Islamists. From an IPE perspective, we are particularly interested in the relationship of these movements to global and system-level processes and how these groups affect the global security structure. Some of the roots of these movements can be found in economic troubles and political repression. Rising unemployment and inequality after the 1970s pushed many poor Muslims to become foot soldiers in extremist movements. In contrast, the leaders of these radical movements often are well educated (many have science and engineering backgrounds) and from the middle class, suggesting that they feel unfairly excluded from the ruling elite.

At another level of analysis, we can see these groups as reflecting a change of ideas within the Muslim world. In the last thirty years, militant Islamist movements have spread a puritanical interpretation of Islam with emphasis on the application of Islamic law and jihadist rhetoric. Why has radicalism spread and attracted adherents to groups like Al-Qaeda and Islamic Jihad in Palestine? One reason is that millions of Arabs who since the 1970s have migrated (often temporarily) to work in the conservative, oil-rich Gulf states have been exposed there to a more "fundamentalist" perspective on Islam. Second, Gulf regimes and wealthy Gulf citizens have funded *madrasas* (Muslim schools) and charities throughout the Muslim world that have sometimes taught a chauvinistic form of Islam. Iran has been a purveyor of the ideology of revolutionary Shi'ism.

Globalization empowers not just liberal, peaceful movements but their antithesis as well. Extremists are adept at using modern technology and financial internationalization for nefarious purposes. At another level, extremists are a reaction to the perceived humiliation of Middle Eastern countries by the Americans, Europeans, and Israelis. In their writings and propaganda, extremists repeatedly invoke the presence of U.S. troops in Saudi Arabia, the Israeli occupation of Palestinian land, and the U.S. repression in Iraq as justifications for *jihad*.

### Misconceptions About Insurgency, Instability, and WMD in the Middle East

Several common misconceptions about Middle East terrorism should be noted. First, "Islamic terrorists" are not necessarily the main groups using violence. In Iraq, for example, most of the insurgents are Sunnis and ex-Baathists who are not so much fighting for "Islam" as they are against the "injustices" of the occupying Americans and the Shi'ite-dominated government.[19] Al-Qaeda and foreign fighters have never made up a significant number of the insurgents in Iraq. Second, the MENA is hardly the only region in the world where groups instrumentalize religion in pursuit of violent political goals. The idea that the Middle East produces most—or at least a disproportionate number of—"fanatical" terrorists is simply incorrect. The Congo, Rwanda, Sudan, Colombia, and Chechnya, to name just a few places, have also suffered horrible conflict. According to the U.S. State Department's annual terrorism reports since 1996, there have been more terrorist incidents *outside* the Middle East—in places such as Russia, Kashmir, Sri Lanka, and Colombia—than *inside* the region. However, by 2005 Iraq alone accounted for more than half of all of the world's deaths from terrorist incidents, according to the State Department.[20]

Third, historically, violence has been used by movements seeking independence from colonial rule or liberation from oppression. For example, Hamas and Hizballah utilize violence in pursuit of explicit political goals. Interpreting them as simply using terrorism for terrorism's sake or attacking foreign occupiers because they "hate our freedoms" is a convenient way of ignoring or discounting their stated goals. As sociologist Charles Tilly has stated, "Properly understood, terror is a strategy, not a creed."[21]

Many analysts presume that the threat of weapons of mass destruction comes almost exclusively from "rogue" regimes intent on acquiring them and/or giving them to terrorists. Saddam Hussein is exhibit number one. He used chemical weapons extensively in the 1980s against Iranian soldiers and Kurdish civilians, and he launched a serious nuclear weapons program that was dismantled under UN monitoring after 1992. Iran's development of a civilian nuclear energy program, uranium enrichment capacity, and long-range missile capacity suggests that it is putting together the pieces of a nuclear weapons program. Nevertheless, these regimes are hardly alone: Western powers and their regional allies have also been eager to acquire and use weapons of mass destruction (WMD) or proscribed weapons.

Spain was the first country to use WMD in the region. Sebastian Balfour, a professor of contemporary Spanish studies, has carefully documented Spain's extensive use of chemical weapons—mostly mustard gas—on rebels in Morocco's northern Rif region in the 1920s.[22] Britain used incendiary devices and possibly mustard gas against Iraqi rebels in 1920. France in the late 1950s and early 1960s conducted seventeen nuclear tests in Algeria's Saharan desert during Paris's development of a nuclear weapons arsenal. France also used napalm extensively against Algeria's *mujahideen* during the 1954–1962 War of Independence. Morocco used napalm against Sahrawis in the 1980s, and Algeria is suspected of using napalm against Islamist guerrillas in the 1990s. Israel is the only country in the region that is known to possess nuclear weapons—perhaps 200 to 300—and a capacity to deliver them against regional enemies. The UN condemned Israel for dropping hundreds of cluster bombs over Lebanon near the end of its 2006 war with Hizballah. Even the United States has been criticized for using depleted uranium ammunition and white phosphorus incendiary devices in Iraq since 2003.

In light of Iraq's sectarian strife, battles between Israelis and Arabs, and frequent suicide bombings, many observers believe the MENA region is on the verge of political collapse. Civil wars in Lebanon (1975–1990), Algeria (1992–2000), and Iraq (since 2003) have also caused enormous damage, population displacement, and loss of life. Only a few small countries such as Tunisia and the United Arab Emirates have not participated directly in some sort of interstate conflict or been racked by domestic strife in the last thirty years.

Despite the persistence of insecurity in some parts of the region, most of the MENA's citizens do *not* face violence daily. In fact, most of the countries have low crime rates (although domestic violence against women and children remains a big problem). In the last ten years there has *not* been widespread political violence in the Gulf Cooperation Council, Turkey, Iran, Syria, and North Africa (except Algeria). Since 1970, only one dictator (Iran's Shah) has been overthrown by his own people, and only one regime (Iraq's Baathists) has been overthrown by an outside power.[23] Compared to many other governments in the developing countries, Middle Eastern regimes have usually survived in the face of mounting social pressures. In light of the absence of fundamental regime change in the last thirty-five years, it is perhaps more accurate to describe the MENA as "stable" rather than "unstable."

## Cooperation at the Interstate Level

Drowned out by media coverage of regional conflicts are the many enduring forms of state-to-state cooperation in the MENA and positive relations with Western powers. Almost all the countries in the Middle East have at some time benefited from their security relationship with the United States. In 1787 Morocco and the United States signed a Treaty of Friendship and Amity that is still in force today and that constitutes the longest unbroken treaty between the United States and another country. President Woodrow Wilson supported self-determination for states after World War I, and the United States helped liberate North Africa from fascism in World War II. The United States supported Algerian independence from France, helped Israel defend itself during wars, and liberated Kuwait (with EU support) from Saddam Hussein's occupation.

Europe and Uncle Sam have extended large amounts of aid to southern Mediterranean countries since the 1950s. NATO has undoubtedly secured Turkey, one of its founding members. Since the mid-1990s, the European Union has promoted formal security cooperation with southern Mediterranean countries. Spain, Italy, and Poland joined the U.S.–UK "Coalition of the Willing" in 2003 to oust Saddam Hussein and help secure Iraq. In the aftermath of the 2006 Israel–Hizballah war, France and Italy took the lead in contributing troops to a robust UN peacekeeping force in Lebanon.

Cooperation among Middle Eastern states is not yet well institutionalized, largely owing to historical rivalries. The Arab League, headquartered in Cairo, represents so many different countries with competing interests that it cannot easily act in concert on major issues. The Arab Maghreb Union in North Africa has essentially ceased to operate owing to Moroccan–Algerian tensions.

The Gulf Cooperation Council has probably been the most successful organization, coordinating trade and security policies. Bilateral military cooperation between Israel and Turkey and between Iran and Syria has been quite strong.

## Cooperation at the Human Level

Some of the most robust and sustained cooperation occurs within cross-national human networks. Scholars of IPE increasingly recognize that interactions between people and non-state organizations have profound effects on security and growth.

On an individual level, emigration and dual citizenship tie Europe and the United States more closely to the Middle East than many observers realize. According to Philippe Fargues, a leading French demographer, more than 8 million first-generation immigrants from the Arab countries and Turkey may be living in Europe, including 4 million North Africans and 3 million Turks.[24] Many came to Europe as temporary "guest workers" in the 1950s through the 1970s but stayed and raised families. For example, approximately 10 percent of the population of France is Muslim, the majority of whom are from the Maghreb. As is the case in the United States, many immigrants remain connected to their home countries through extended family ties and remittances (see the next section).

Many Middle Easterners who have become naturalized U.S. citizens retain citizenship in their country of birth. These dual citizens often vacation, work, or live in the Middle East. When war broke out between Israel and Hizballah in July 2006, there were more than 25,000 Americans living in Lebanon. American military forces evacuated 15,000 of these scared and displaced Americans, many of whom are dual citizens. European governments also rescued thousands of their own citizens from Lebanon in one of the largest international evacuations in decades. Approximately 200,000 American Jews live in Israel, most of whom have gained Israeli citizenship under the Law of Return (which grants citizenship to Jews from anywhere in the world who return to Israel). It should also be noted that tens of thousands of Americans are working and fighting "temporarily" in the region. As of July 2006, more than 130,000 U.S. troops, at least 11,000 U.S. citizens working for private contractors, and 1000 embassy personnel were present in Iraq. For an examination of how education ties together citizens of the West and the Middle East, see the box, "International Education and the Middle East."

---

### INTERNATIONAL EDUCATION AND THE MIDDLE EAST

Having citizens knowledgeable about other region's languages and cultures is what political scientist Joseph Nye considers a source of a hegemon's "soft" power (see Chapter 9). For a region as important to the United States as the Middle East, it is surprising that so few Americans learn the region's primary languages—Arabic, Farsi, and Turkish—or study abroad there. In 2002 approximately 10,000 U.S. college students were taking Arabic courses—double the pre-9/11 number—but they represented only 1 percent of all students taking foreign language classes.[a] The second Bush administration significantly increased funds for training intelligence agents and military personnel in "strategic" foreign languages, but only a small percentage of those government employees who study a critical Middle East language will gain fluency or working proficiency.

Studying abroad is another way to increase cultural understanding. Although the number of U.S. students studying in the Middle East steadily increased after 9/11, the overall number of Americans choosing to learn about the region first-hand is low. In the 2003–2004 school year, only about 2000 participated in a study-abroad program in the Middle East and North Africa—just 1 percent of the nearly 191,000 U.S. students who studied overseas that year, mostly in Europe and Latin America.[b]

The United States—like Europe—has for decades attracted many of the best-educated Middle Easterners to study in its universities. Many of these students stay in the United States after their undergraduate or graduate training, contributing to the U.S. economy. International political and economic trends dramatically affect which countries in the Middle East send how many students to the United States. Following the first oil boom, Iran—then a key secular ally of the United States—sent a slew of students to the United States (50,000 in 1979 alone). At the height of the second oil boom in the early 1980s, Middle East oil exporters flooded U.S. schools with students pursuing scientific and technical degrees (and English-language proficiency). By contrast, 9/11 accelerated the decline of Arabs studying in the United States, many of whom felt unwelcome or had trouble getting visas. Only 3000 Saudis now study in the United States, an example of how U.S. security policies conflict with other U.S. interests. Turkish students are filling the void left by Arabs: by 2005 there were 12,500 Turks studying in the United States, nearly equal to the number of Mexicans studying in U.S. universities.[c]

Many Middle Easterners return home with their U.S. or European degrees, taking up important positions in the government and the business community. Europe and the United States hope that these individuals will become surrogates for the West, spreading secular values. In addition, U.S.-style, English-language universities are popping up like mushrooms in the region. This new trend derives from the desire to modernize higher education and the need to have citizens master language and technical skills vital to participating in the global economy. In addition, dozens of U.S. universities in recent years have set up branch campuses in Arab countries or entered into cooperative agreements with Middle Eastern institutions of higher education. Even France now realizes it needs to compete better in the knowledge realm. In 2006 the Sorbonne opened the Paris-Sorbonne University Abu Dhabi campus in the United Arab Emirates, the first branch campus that the premier French university has ever set up outside France and the only French-language university in the Arab Gulf region. All of these educational ties have the potential to foster long-term cooperation and understanding between the West and the Middle East.

*References*

[a] Chuck McCutheon, "U.S. Confronts Complex Set of Obstacles in Fielding Spies Who Speak Arabic," Newhouse News Service (2005). Available at www.newhousenews.com/archive/mccutcheon092705.html.
[b] See Institute for International Education, *Open Doors 2005* (New York: Institute for International Education, 2005).
[c] For detailed data, see Institute for International Education, *Open Doors 2005*, at http://opendoors.iienetwork.org.

## FACING THE GLOBAL ECONOMY: INTEGRATION OR MARGINALIZATION?

There is a significant debate among scholars about whether the MENA is "keeping up" with globalization or "falling behind" the rest of the world. It is part of a long-running discussion about the nature of "modernization" and "development." As the global economy changes, development strategies that once worked well may be running out of steam. In this section we discuss two different hypotheses about economic processes in the region. The first suggests that the MENA is successfully integrating itself into the global economy and preparing for a sustainable future. The second asserts that the region is becoming increasingly unimportant and uncompetitive, failing to switch to high-growth economies that can resolve sociocultural problems. A number of indicators will help us assess which claims seem most valid. As will become evident, the MENA is a very diverse region with many kinds of ties to the global economy.

### Oil, Industry, and Growth

Growth in many parts of the MENA is tied to hydrocarbons. The years 1973 to 1984 were a golden age for oil exporters that raised incomes dramatically and expanded infrastructure. Adjusted for inflation, oil prices from 1985 to 1999 were in a slump, lowering growth rates throughout the region. But since 2000, oil prices have recovered nicely as a result of OPEC production cuts and rising demand from China. Growth rates are healthy again. According to the World Bank, growth in the MENA (not including Turkey and Israel) averaged 6.2 percent from 2003 to 2005, the best three-year spurt since the late 1970s.[25] The turnaround in energy prices—which could last for many years—allows Middle East oil exporters to rebuild infrastructure and boost employment. In addition, in the last decade, smaller states such as Yemen, Oman, and Syria have begun to exploit their small but valuable oil and gas reserves.

Saudi Arabia has taken advantage of its abundant hydrocarbons to expand into energy-intensive industries that benefit from subsidized domestic oil. The country has become an exporter of cement, steel, and especially petrochemicals that China is gobbling up. In the global petrochemicals market, Saudi Arabia is now a more important competitor with Germany, historically the world's largest petrochemical exporter. Moreover, the MENA as a whole in 2005 was the source of one-fourth of the oil and gas imported into the United States, 60 percent of China's, and three-fourths of Japan's imported energy.

Non–oil exporters seem to be finding their own successful growth models based on a variety of paths. For example, in the space of less than twenty years, Dubai has transformed itself from a desert backwater into a transportation, financial, and tourist hub (see the box, "Dubai: The Las Vegas of Arabia"). Tunisia has adopted an export-oriented strategy that looks as if it were borrowed from Asia. Like Egypt and Turkey, Tunisia has a world-class tourism sector.

Israel is a standout case, more developed and globalized than any other MENA country. It has transformed itself from a state-dominated economy in the 1950s that exported mostly agricultural goods and polished diamonds to a diversified industrial economy exporting mostly high-technology products. Since the U.S. technology boom in the 1990s, more than 100 Israeli companies have raised significant capital by listing on the New York Stock Exchange. Some Israel-based companies are global players, including pharmaceutical giant Teva. Israel has some of the highest numbers of engineers, scientists, and patent holders per capita of any country in the world. It has become an important exporter of information technology and advanced weaponry. In 2006 Israeli investors opened Jerusalem Animation Lab, a company that they predict will become the "largest animation and gaming studio outside Hollywood."[26]

How was the dramatic economic takeoff and transformation in Israel possible? Manuel Trajtenberg, an Israeli economist at Tel Aviv University, gives us a mercantilist answer: "Israel stands as one of the most prolific innovating economies, and as one of the few 'Silicon Valley' types of technology centers in the world. There is no doubt that Government policy was key to the emergence and early success of the [high-tech] sector, a policy embedded for the most part in the programs and budgetary resources of the Office of the Chief Scientist (OCS) at the Ministry of Industry and Trade."[27]

---

### DUBAI: THE LAS VEGAS OF ARABIA

Two generations ago, Damascus and Cairo were the "happening" places in the Middle East in terms of political ferment, economic dynamism, and cultural attraction. A generation ago, Beirut, the so-called "Paris of the Middle East," was the place to go for tourism and trade. Now the most dynamic city-state in the entire Middle East is Dubai, a small desert patch on the conservative Arabian peninsula. It is a wheeler-dealer's kind of place, open to big ambitions and grandiose schemes. How did this backwater become a fast-growing financial, trade, and tourism hub in just three decades?

Dubai is one of seven sheikdoms that make up the loosely federated United Arab Emirates (UAE). It has a coastline only 45 miles long. Before the UAE's independence in 1971, Dubai City was a sleepy town known for pearl diving that was connected to a surrounding Bedouin population. Oil was discovered in the 1960s, and the emir at the time—Sheikh Rashid bin Said al Maktoum—invested proceeds in an international airport and dredged the main harbor for international shipping.[a] He encouraged investment in high-rises and hotels and established a modern telephone system. His sons—part of the ruling Maktoum family—have invested government funds heavily in basic infrastructure. Realizing that limited oil supplies would soon diminish, they set up free-trade zones, established incentives for international container business, imported cheap labor from Asia, and made sure there were no income or corporate taxes. Theirs has been a vision of a global *entrepôt*, attracting business from any company in the world. The annual rate of growth of GDP in the last ten years has been estimated at 10 percent, one of the highest in the world.[b]

Openness to the world has been only part of the city-state's recipe for success. Equally important has been the Maktoum family's own private investments throughout the emirates and their strong reliance on state ownership. As in many parts of the Arabian Peninsula, the separation between state finances and family finances has never been absolute. As one author has noted, "Dubai is a leading case study in successful state capitalism. . . . [The Maktoum family's] city state has been aptly described as a family conglomerate run by Sheik Mohammed as ruler and CEO. He is the visionary behind the leading enterprises in Dubai, including investment, media and hotel companies, as well as Emirates Air."[c]

The results on the ground stagger the imagination. The sheikhdom headquarters Al Arabiyya, a satellite TV network that is a strong rival of Al-Jazeera for the Arab news market.[d] Soon to be completed are two of the largest shopping malls in the world. By 2008 Dubai's second indoor ski slope will be competed, along with Burj Dubai, the tallest building in the world (which will be twice as tall as the Empire State building). At least two huge real estate developments are being built on artificial islands off the coast. One under construction and due to be completed in 2008 consists of "several hundred man-made islands representing regions of the world in their respective continental groups. There are to be private-estate islands, resort islands, community islands, each ranging from 150,000 to 450,000 square feet in size. . . . Rod Stewart is said to have bought Britain for . . . more than $33 million."[e] Despite a population of only 1.2 million people (mostly expatriates), there were more than 5 million visitors in 2005. Also under construction is a $19 billion tourist complex called Dubailand, which, when completed, will be four times larger than Manhattan and, as its promoters claim, "the biggest, most varied leisure, entertainment and tourism attraction on the planet."[f]

In Dubai we see the conflation of mercantilist, liberalist, and structuralist forces. The state has made growth possible through its investments and policies. The international market has swarmed in to take advantage of the city-state's deregulated, Las Vegas-style economy. But the whole edifice, a structuralist would point out, rests on exploitation of hundreds of thousands of poor Asian workers with no unions and no political rights.

*References*
[a] Jeremy Smith, "Dubai Builds Big," *World Trade*, April 2005, p. 58.
[b] Nick Tosches, "Dubai's the Limit," *Vanity Fair*, June 2006.
[c] William Underhill, "The Wings of Dubai Inc.," *Newsweek*, April 17, 2006, p. 34.
[d] Lee Smith, "The Road to Tech Mecca," *Wired*, July 2004.
[e] Tosches, "Dubai's the Limit."
[f] Ibid.; Seth Sherwood, "The Oz of the Middle East," *The New York Times*, May 8, 2005.

## Trade and Investment with Europe and the United States

Southern Mediterranean countries are being integrated into the global economy through the World Trade Organization, free-trade agreements, and bilateral agreements with Europe and the United States. Since 1995 the European Union has been touting a comprehensive free-trade and cooperation agreement called the **Euro-Mediterranean Partnership (EMP)**. Littoral states such as Tunisia and Egypt are reducing tariffs and trade barriers over a 12-year period, after which most goods will move duty-free between them and the EU. (Turkey is an EMP member but something of an exception—it has a customs union with the EU and will begin accession talks soon. Israel is an EMP member, too, but already has a bilateral free-trade agreement with the EU). In exchange for lowering trade barriers and reforming their economies, Arab Mediterranean countries have been receiving from Europe more aid, loans, investment, and market access.

Since 1995 the EU has given the EMP members more than $5 billion in aid, and the European Investment Bank has loaned at least as much for projects to reform economies. The EMP also is designed to foster security cooperation and cultural understanding. Those countries that make demonstrable progress in neoliberal reforms will gain greater aid and market access from Europe. By flexing its "soft" power, the EU is trying to accelerate growth in this part of the Middle East.

Not to be outdone by Brussels, Washington is pushing for a Middle East Free-Trade Area by 2013. In pursuit of that goal, the United States has signed bilateral free-trade agreements with five close allies, including Jordan and Morocco. The hope is that more open economies will increase trade, investment, and democracy. Since 2001 the region has become a boom market for U.S. companies. Microsoft, Cisco, Bechtel, Boeing, and General Electric—to name just a few—have garnered contracts to supply, build, and operate many new infrastructure projects. The region is a major importer of machinery, aircraft, vehicles, grain, and engineering services from the United States (and it is an even more important trade partner with the EU and Japan).

It is also a major importer of weapons from the United States, Europe, and Russia. From 1996 to 2003, U.S. arms sales agreements with Middle Eastern countries totaled $35 billion. Marxist economists Jonathon Nitzan and Shimshon Bichler have argued that U.S. arms sellers (the "Arma-Core") have a common interest with U.S. oil companies (the "Petro-Core") in the periodic outbreak of wars in the Middle East, because the resulting hike in oil prices after conflicts boosts their profitability.[28] In other words, when conflicts cause oil prices to rise, Middle Eastern countries almost inevitably use the windfalls to buy more weapons. That is good for trade, but not necessarily for long-term MENA growth.

Middle East countries not only use oil revenues to import; they recycle profits back to oil-consuming countries in the form of investments in stock markets, purchases of real estate, and deposits in Western banks. This **petrodollar recycling**, first witnessed in the 1970s (see Chapter 7), jumped into high gear again after 2000, tying the economic fortunes of the MENA closely to the international financial system. Middle East companies and individuals have looked for profitable investment opportunities abroad, buying shares in Western companies and purchasing real estate in the countries of the Organization for Economic Cooperation and Development (OECD)—a group of democratic, market economies in North America, Europe, and Japan. For example, a Dubai company bought Madame Tussaud's wax museum in London for $1.5 billion, and an Egyptian company bought an Italian wireless phone network for $15 billion. As of 2006, Prince Alwaheed bin Talal, a Saudi royal family member, was the single largest foreign investor in the United States, owning significant shares in Citicorp, Apple, and Saks Fifth Avenue. Dubai Ports World, a Dubai-based company that manages port facilities around the world, is an example of the greater role of the Middle East in overseas services. The company's bid in 2006 to manage some ports in the United States provoked a mercantilist response from the U.S. Congress, whose protestations over security threats killed the deal.

**Remittances**—money transferred by foreign workers to their home countries—also strongly integrate people in Europe and the Middle East. IPE scholars increasingly recognize that remittances from migrants can have a very positive effect on economic development. Countries in North Africa rely on billions of dollars of annual remittances from workers in Europe to help with their balance of payments and to supplement the incomes of poor families. Since the 1960s, Turkish workers in Europe have remitted an estimated $75 billion back to Turkey, providing financial security to many families.

## Globalization in the Gulf Cooperation Council

The six countries in the **Gulf Cooperation Council (GCC)**—Saudi Arabia, the United Arab Emirates, Kuwait, Oman, Bahrain, and Qatar—are deeply integrated into the global economy via their labor markets. Alongside the often conservative indigenous population is a huge foreign workforce. Expatriate workers make up more than 70 percent of the entire workforce in these six countries and nearly 40 percent of all the people living there (in 2006 there were 12.5 million expatriates among 40 million people).[29]

Where do the expatriate workers come from? During the 1970s oil boom, three-fourths of immigrant workers came from fellow Arab countries. However, after the end of Operation Desert Storm in 1991, Kuwait and Saudi Arabia expelled more than 1.5 million Yemenis, Jordanians, and Palestinians as punishment for their leaders' support for Iraq's invasion of Kuwait. By 2004, only one-third of foreign workers were Arabs, many of whom had been supplanted by Indians, Pakistanis, Bangladeshis, Filipinos, and other Asians.

Although the GCC has benefited enormously from the skills and low labor costs of its internationalized workforce, the region's ruling families are increasingly worried about the political and cultural dangers from heavy reliance on foreigners. The noncitizen workers lack labor rights commonly available in other countries. Expatriate grievances have provoked some strikes and unrest. Asian women who work as nannies and domestic helpers often complain of physical and sexual abuse by employers. Gulf leaders worry that children raised by Asian nannies and taught by foreigners will lose their Arab and Islamic identity. They are also concerned about the large number of illegal aliens and "stateless" residents who are politically loyal to foreign countries.

Non–GCC countries are also turning to expatriate labor, which can usually be taken unfair advantage of more easily than domestic workers. According to an extensive investigation by the U.S.-based National Labor Committee (NLC), tens of thousands of guest workers from Bangladesh, China, and India are working in Jordanian textile factories that export garments duty-free to the United States.[30] Many of these (often Asian-owned) companies, in which workers are frequently abused or exploited in sweatshop conditions that the NLC asserts constitute forced labor, supply Wal-Mart, Target, L.L. Bean, and other U.S. retailers. Jordan, like its GCC neighbors, has found that importing Asian workers (especially Chinese) fuels export growth. Even Israel in the last fifteen years has replaced low-wage Palestinian workers with low-wage Asians—more out of security concerns than economic ones. The presence of so many non-national, nonunionized workers may be hampering the development of a powerful labor movement within civil society.

## The Falling-Behind Thesis

So far in this section, we have focused on evidence of the MENA's seemingly successful integration into the global economy through trade, finance, and migration. Nevertheless, there is a powerful counterargument that the Middle East is falling behind other modernizing countries and failing to move up in the global hierarchy. Many in the region itself recognize that there is little technological or industrial dynamism. Politically the region has largely been out of step with the rest of the world, ruled by monarchs and dictators that many other developing countries cast away years ago. Growth rates per capita have only recently begun to recover from stagnation in the 1980s and 1990s. Many countries' economies are still dominated by inefficient state-owned enterprises and unprofitable public banks. Periodic conflict and threats of violence have stunted foreign investment and tourism. In a powerful analysis of these problems, a team of Arab social scientists published the *Arab Human Development Report 2002,* which identified the Arab MENA as suffering a gap with the rest of the world in terms of knowledge, freedom, and women's empowerment.[31]

## The Challenge of the Historical Legacy

Some of the region's inheritance from the past seems to be hampering its adaptation to globalization. As mentioned earlier, colonial powers left many unfortunate legacies. Palestinian, Libyan, and Algerian peasants and tribesmen lost much of their land to settler colonialists. Overdependence on a single, exported commodity, such as oil, cotton, or phosphates, slowed economic diversification in some states. Colonial regulations stifled educational opportunities and growth of an indigenous private sector. Many countries did not gain full independence until the 1950s and 1960s. The loss of well-educated and entrepreneurial minorities—Greeks fleeing Turkey, Jews leaving Arab countries, French *pied noirs* abandoning Algeria—set some economies back for years. Postindependence Arab socialist regimes expropriated foreign property, nationalized private businesses, and squandered public resources on fighting Israel.

After independence, many countries adopted development policies that were popular and even beneficial in the short term but that eventually, by the 1980s, were burdening the economy. Agrarian reform and land redistribution lowered agricultural productivity. High tariff barriers protected inefficient domestic companies. Government subsidies, price controls, and overvalued currencies all contributed to a misallocation of resources. Nevertheless, Middle East growth rates in the 1950s and 1960s were quite remarkable in some countries such as Israel, Syria, and Iran, and most countries dramatically increased literacy, access to health care, and job opportunities. The 1970s witnessed another growth spurt fueled by oil revenues.

Development troubles came to a head in most of the region by the early 1980s, when neoliberalism and economic reform began sweeping through many parts of the world. From 1980 to 2000, per-capita GDP in the MENA (excluding Israel and Turkey) *failed to grow at all*, while in East Asia during the same period it expanded at an annual rate of 4.1 percent.[32] Unemployment and foreign debt grew sharply. Weak or nonexistent regional stock exchanges meant that a wave of Western private investment spreading to Latin America and Asian simply bypassed the region. When was the last time you read about a U.S. company outsourcing to the Middle East? There was significant public investment in infrastructure, but the efficiency and quality of those outlays were often poor. When oil prices (adjusted for inflation) began to tumble in 1983, countries began to have trouble servicing their debt. Not until 2002 did crude oil prices (adjusted for inflation) recover dramatically.

## Limits on Free Trade

Only a handful of countries in the world have yet to join the World Trade Organization, and a surprisingly large number are in the Middle East: Algeria, Iran, Iraq, Yemen, Sudan, Libya, and Lebanon (Saudi Arabia joined in December 2005). As a whole, the region also has high average tariff levels. This indicates that many regimes are reluctant to reduce protectionist barriers dramatically and adjust rapidly to international trade rules. The MENA has not significantly diversified its exports. Eighty percent of its exports to the United States consist of oil, gas, and minerals.

Although the long-term benefits of trade openness are higher growth and productivity, the short-term consequences are politically unpalatable. Many Arab businesses—especially in textiles and consumer goods—will not be able to compete with European or Asian imports, causing unemployment to rise. Lower tariffs will crimp government revenues that come from import duties, forcing regimes to find new tax sources.

Surprisingly little investment and trade occurs *between* MENA countries. Arab countries' main exports are to the industrialized countries, and the main imports they need are not produced regionally. The North African countries, despite U.S./EU urging, have made no progress toward economic integration in thirty years, mostly because of historical rivalries. For example, less than 4 percent of Algeria's total trade is with other Arab countries, whereas two-thirds of its trade is with the EU. Arab boycotts have for decades prevented any integration with the Israeli economy. Turkey and the GCC have had the most success in increasing trade with other MENA countries. Economic exchange between MENA countries will probably take off only if durable solutions to long-running conflicts are found. Until then, regional integration will remain a hostage to war and historical grievances, forcing countries to look for commercial opportunities with the West rather than in their own backyard.

Unfortunately, some MENA nations have growing *illicit* trade connections with the global economy. This often-overlooked form of integration has an important effect on security and society. If governments do not make more concerted efforts to control activities such as drug smuggling, money laundering, and corruption, social deviancy will rise and foreign investors will stay away. Morocco and Lebanon are important suppliers of marijuana to Europe, while Turkey and Iran are important countries in the transit of heroin from Afghanistan to Europe. Despite stronger border policing in Europe, illegal immigrants from North Africa and sub-Saharan Africa continue to flow across the Mediterranean to Italy and Spain. Turkey is a sender of illegal immigrants and a transit point for illegals from Iraq. Human trafficking and sex trafficking are big business in Turkey, Israel, and the GCC.

Illicit financial transactions continue in the GCC despite crackdowns on banks and unlicensed money traders since 9/11. Arms trafficking via the United Arab Emirates is extensive. Iran and Syria are major "covert" suppliers of weapons to Hizballah and Hamas. Corruption on international contracts—a widespread practice for decades—enriches the pockets of ruling elites. Arab officials often demand commissions and under-the-table payments from multinational corporations that are eager to win contracts to build power plants, supply weapons, and set up mobile phone networks.

## Societal Problems

It has become increasingly fashionable to blame sociocultural factors for the Middle East's catching-up problems. Women face significant restrictions in job opportunities and social freedoms. Few countries in the world have as dismal a record of female employment as the Arab Gulf countries, where women with citizenship constitute less than 10 percent of the total workforce. Even large countries such as Algeria and Iran have comparatively low female employment rates. Underutilization of female human capital, in other words, has been a substantial drag on MENA economies. Appropriate education for the needs of the global market is still lacking. For example, perhaps one-third of college graduates in Saudi Arabia major in Islamic studies. Some "information-shy" regimes such as that in Iran place restrictions on access to independent newspapers, the Internet, and/or satellite dishes.

Intrusive governments have hampered growth of dynamic private sectors in many places. Arab elites are reluctant to break up state enterprises and downsize the public administration for fear of provoking the wrath of public-sector workers and bureaucrats. Iran is unusual in having huge quasi-independent conglomerates called **bonyads**, which clerics and their private business allies use to dominate the economy and siphon off public resources. It is inaccurate, however, to say that the Middle East lacks a culture of entrepreneurship. Economic dynamism in the private sector is particularly strong in Israel, Lebanon, Turkey, and Morocco. This may be due in part to the fact that large emigrant communities from these countries are present in many parts of the world, forging strong trade and investment links with partners "back home."

## The Basket Cases

The worst performers in the region are Iraq, Yemen, and the Palestinian Territories. They will be hard-pressed to recover anytime soon from the tribulations of war and endemic poverty. International economic sanctions imposed on Iraq by the United Nations in 1992 and lasting for more than a decade devastated the economy and the health of the population. Poverty and malnutrition skyrocketed, while the middle class largely collapsed. Widespread insecurity after the U.S. invasion undermined the economy even more. Billions of dollars of international aid and U.S. spending have done almost nothing to improve living conditions, mostly because the aid has been devoted to basic security operations, invested in inappropriate projects, or squandered through massive corruption.

Yemen has struggled for different reasons. With a large, poor rural population, its government has never had strong control over its territory. Saudi Arabia's expulsion of nearly 1 million Yemeni workers after the 1991 Gulf War hurt households that relied on remittances. And a majority of Yemeni males habitually chew *qat*, a mild narcotic, thereby lowering worker productivity and depleting family finances.

The Palestinian Territories for over a decade have experienced one of the worst economic declines in the world, largely as a result of deliberate Israeli policies to isolate the territories from international trade and prevent Palestinians from working in Israel. Sara Roy has meticulously analyzed the horrendous economic and social conditions for Palestinians caused by Israel's policy of imposing curfews and travel bans, expropriating land, destroying civilian infrastructure, and uprooting tens of thousands of olive and citrus trees.[33] Israel insists that its punitive actions are triggered by Palestinian terrorism and rejection of compromise leading to a peace treaty. It is clear that Israel's collective punishment of Palestinians since 1996 is largely responsible for economic hardship.[34] Generous European aid to the Palestinian Authority has failed to make a dent in economic conditions. As in Iraq, massive aid from outside powers (Arabs and Europeans in this case) has not proven to be a panacea. Only a final peace settlement with Israel will lay the foundation for economic recovery.

# THE CHALLENGE OF DEMOCRACY

The Middle East stands out for its apparent resistance to democracy. While a "Third Wave" of democratization swept through much of the world from the 1970s to the 1990s, Arab countries remain mired in authoritarianism. Iran's clerics have manipulated elections, limited the scope of legislative powers, and violated human rights. By the beginning of the twenty-first century, only Israel and Turkey could be described as electoral democracies, but even their political systems are not models of Western "liberalness." Israel has discriminated against Israeli Arabs and deprived several million Palestinians in the West Bank and Gaza of basic political rights. Turkey has repressed minority Kurds, and the military has a significant role in politics. The rest of the region—despite extensive economic dependence on and pressure from the world's most powerful democracies—has yet to make a transition to constitutional, representative government.

How can we explain why most of the region's countries have not adopted democracy? Scholars have identified four main structural factors that may be to blame: the West, oil, weak civil society, and Islam. The debate over which of these factors is most important is still raging among theorists of the Middle East.[35] As we will see later, some optimistic scholars and policymakers dismiss the argument that these factors are unique to the Middle East and claim that there are signs that the region is ready for—and moving toward—political freedom.

## Potential Impediments to the Spread of Representative Government

Europe and the United States may bear much of the blame for lingering authoritarianism. After all, it was the European powers that colonized much of the region and created many "artificial states." Rashid Khalidi, a historian at Columbia University, argues that when European powers entered the region in the late nineteenth and early twentieth centuries, they actually halted an indigenous, incipient movement toward constitutional government and rule of law.[36] After World War II, the United States nurtured close relations with antidemocratic royal families in Iran and the Arabian Peninsula as a means of securing access to oil. In the context of the Cold War, the United States supported anticommunist leaders, going so far as to orchestrate a *coup d'etat* in Iran in 1953. Fear of Soviet expansionism led the United States to reward friendly authoritarian regimes and turn a blind eye to their human rights violations. Since the 1990s, the United States has largely tolerated regional allies' repression of Islamist parties. And following a free and fair Palestinian legislative election in 2005, the United States, the EU, and Israel starved the new Hamas government of revenue in an apparent attempt to disrupt its ability to rule effectively.

Oil is another seemingly important reason for resistance to political change. Scholars use the term **rentier state** to describe a country whose economy is heavily dependent on oil and gas income and whose government derives a large percentage of its revenues from the taxation of oil exports.[37] Iran, Iraq, Libya, Algeria, and the GCC countries meet the definition of a rentier state. Governments of non–OPEC countries such as Egypt and Syria have also developed their oil and gas production as a significant source of government revenue.

Because rentier states do not need to tax their citizens heavily, there are fewer demands for representation. Oil concentrates resources in the hands of a small elite, who buy political loyalty and foster political dependency. Because the state controls the most important resource in the economy, it can finance a strong coercive apparatus. Support for this explanation also comes from the fact that the countries in the region that have no significant oil—Israel, Turkey, Morocco, Jordan, and Lebanon—are democracies or have undertaken the most political liberalization.

Weak civil society may also explain why so many MENA countries rank low on Freedom House's annual ranking of political freedoms and civil liberties in the world. Civil society is made up of autonomous social groups such as private businesses, the press, labor, and voluntary associations that historically have been forces for liberalization. These groups face significant legal restrictions in the MENA and often do not have the finances to sustain a long confrontation with the government. Historically weak property rights have made it difficult for a thriving private sector to resist state interference. It could also be argued that powerful barriers to the entry of women into the workforce and lack of leadership roles for women in religious institutions have prevented a strong, representative civil society from emerging.

## Blaming Islam and Islamists

Religious and cultural explanations of democratic weakness in the MENA are quite prevalent, but should be viewed with much caution. Political culture in predominantly Muslim countries, to the extent that it reaffirms patriarchy, delegitimizes minority rights, and devalues secular thought, may create an inhospitable environment for freedom. Daniel Pipes, as we learned earlier, blames a culture of "conspiracism" in Iran and the Arab countries for fueling extremism, undermining political accountability, and encouraging political fatalism.[38] Governments in the region often claim that Islamists are undemocratic forces that believe in "one man, one vote, one time." In other words, the Islamists support the idea of free elections if it will help them, but once in power they will presumably impose harsh Islamic law. Thus, authoritarian regimes argue that these allegedly undemocratic movements cannot be allowed to come to power through democratic means.

Many casual observers of the Middle East tend to believe that Islamic political parties are prone to violence and anti-Westernism. In reality, most of the large, "mainstream" Islamist movements, such as Egypt's Muslim Brotherhood, Jordan's Islamic Action Front, and Morocco's Justice and Charity Group, behave like opposition political parties everywhere in the world, seeking to build large coalitions to come to power through elections and improve their societies. Although their leaders draw upon the language of Islam, they are modern political entrepreneurs. Many of the parties are very conservative on gender issues and frustrated with U.S. and European policies, but they frequently espouse a commitment to free elections, rule of law, and social equity. Their leaders usually have the technical, organizational, and rhetorical skills required to govern modern states. Their private welfare programs fill a large gap left by the state's breaking of its social contract since the 1980s.

Many charismatic Islamist leaders have been threatened, imprisoned, and sometimes tortured by allies of the United States. They are deeply frustrated by Israel's and the West's humiliation of their countries and the inequalities in their societies. They do not preside over monolithic movements; they are all wracked by internal disagreements. Some are eager to reduce government economic regulation and wipe out corruption—which makes them much more neoliberal than revolutionary! For example, Turkey's democratically elected, Islamist-leaning governing party has worked to prepare the country for eventual membership in the European Union by passing legislation to strengthen minority rights, religious freedom, and economic reform. Although some large movements (for example, Hamas and Hizballah) still justify violence against enemies, and others, such as the Muslim Brotherhood, are not keen about women's rights, most are committed to political reform.

Radical Islamists tend to garner a lot of attention in the Western press, but there are a number of reformist Islamic intellectuals from the Middle East whose influence on public opinion has been underestimated. These intellectuals are part of a long line of Islamic reformers who emerged in the first decades of the twentieth century to challenge traditional interpretations of Islam and adapt religious practices to the demands of modernity. Most readers of this textbook have probably never heard of Iranian philosopher Abdelkarim Soroush, exiled Tunisian Islamist Rashid Ghannouchi, or Swiss scholar Tariq Ramadan (the grandson of Hassan al-Banna, founder of Egypt's Muslim Brotherhood). These influential thinkers stress the importance of embracing modernity, challenging clerical government, expanding universal human rights standards, interacting peacefully with Western countries, and adopting democracy.[39]

## Some Optimism About Democracy

Optimists dispute the assertion that nondemocratic values are pervasive in the region. Public opinion polls, including the rigorous Pew Global Attitudes surveys, indicate that people in the MENA support the idea of democracy in large numbers. For example, more than three-fourths of Lebanese, Moroccans, and Jordanians surveyed believe democracy can work well in their country. Fundamental democratic values (with the exception of equal rights for women) are supported by large majorities in the Middle East, even if there are disagreements about the most appropriate democratic institutions. Economic development and social mobility may increase democratic pressures. Globalization and technological change are undermining information monopolies that governments held until quite recently.

Islam is hardly the impediment many believe it to be. Many Muslim leaders and scholars emphasize the compatibility of their religion with freedom. They repeatedly call for a withdrawal of the military from politics and protection of civilians from arbitrary arrest and torture. Women have been very active in Islamist movements. Even radical Islamist parties such as Hizballah in Lebanon and Hamas in the Palestinian Territories have participated in elections. These trends are strengthening civil society, at a minimum, whether or not the leaders of Islamist parties are "true democrats" at heart.

The countries that have made the most democratic progress have for the most part not done so because of Western political or military pressure. Foreign "carrots" have induced more lasting political change than the blunt foreign "sticks" of aid cutoffs and covert action. In Turkey, for example, the European Union's offer of potential EU membership has created powerful incentives for Turkey's military and Islamist parties to adopt more democratic institutions. Royal families in Kuwait, Jordan, Bahrain, and Morocco seem to have calculated that moves toward constitutional monarchy, competitive elections, and women's rights will increase political stability and please foreign investors.

## CONCLUSION

There are many contradictory trends in the MENA's political economy. Each country has its own unique set of state–society–market tensions. Some countries are faring much better than the others, open to modern ideas and global interchanges. Some are locked in the jaws of war or unable to free themselves from the specter of the past. All face some structural pressures from the international community over which they have very little control. Individual leaders have decisive choices to make, but they alone cannot transform their countries. Forces from within society are clamoring for a role in reshaping governance, even if they disagree strongly over what an ideal nation should look like.

Each of the main IPE perspectives interprets developments in the Middle East differently, based on different assumptions about history and what motivates actors. A mercantilist might see hints of power politics and old colonial wars in Spain's decision in 2002 to militarily evict a handful of Moroccan soldiers from Parsley Island, a tiny bit of rock just several hundred meters from the coast of Morocco that Spain claims as its own. A scholar of this type would probably attribute many of the conflicts and development outcomes discussed in this chapter to the struggle by states for power and protection of national interests.

A liberal theorist might stress the inevitability of MENA change as a result of global market forces. The dynamism of Dubai and Israel, as well as the democratic advances in MENA monarchies, could be proof that free people open to the world's ideas and goods are most likely to thrive.

A structuralist might see in Abu Ghraib or in the actions of so-called security forces in the MENA parallels with France's widespread torture of Algerians during the 1950s—evoked in Gillo Ponecorvo's powerful film, *The Battle of Algiers* (1965). Structuralists could point to the MENA's weak industrialization and great disparities of wealth as evidence of the exploitation inherent in global capitalism.

All of the IPE perspectives give us insights on the Middle East, but none alone can tell us how soon and how far democracy, peace, and development will spread. Our analysis of the region, nevertheless, does allow us to have some optimism. History does not have to repeat itself; the new generation in many countries is forgetting old grievances. Fears of a civilizational clash are overblown: many Islamists are reconciled to modernity, and the ties with the West are deep. The Middle East's future will mostly depend not on the actions of foreigners but on what Middle Easterners do to, and for, themselves.

## DISCUSSION QUESTIONS

1. Compare and contrast the economic conditions and development strategies of several MENA countries. Which countries are most prepared to face the challenges of globalization? Explain.
2. Are most of the MENA's security problems due to foreign meddling or to the bad decisions of domestic political leaders? How much should we blame "history" for today's woes?
3. What are the main impediments to democracy in the region? Will economic growth and diversification likely lead to more representative government? What are the most appropriate ways in which the Western countries could encourage democracy?
4. Is there a "clash of civilizations" between the Middle East and the West? What evidence suggests the divide is growing? What are the roots of anti-Americanism? What evidence suggests that cooperation between the MENA and the Western powers is still strong?
5. What are the most important "human connections" between the Middle East and the rest of the world? Are individuals and nongovernmental organizations able to influence changes in the region? How do you think that past and present human tragedies will shape the perceptions of the next generation in the MENA?
6. Which IPE theoretical perspective—mercantilism, liberalism, or structuralism—helps us the most in understanding changes in the Middle East? Explain.

## INTERNET LINKS

International Crisis Group, Middle East and North Africa Program:
    www.crisisgroup.org
The Middle East Institute:
    www.mideasti.org
The Middle East Research and Information Project (MERIP):
    www.merip.org
The Middle East Review of International Affairs:
    http://meria.idc.ac.il
Qantara.de—Dialogue with the Islamic World:
    www.qantara.de
United Nations Development Programme, Human Development Reports:
    http://hdr.undp.org/reports
The Washington Institute for Near East Policy:
    www.washingtoninstitute.org
The World Bank—Middle East and North Africa
    www.worldbank.org/mena.nsf

## SUGGESTED READINGS

Galal Amin. *Illusion of Progress in the Arab World: A Critique of Western Misconstructions*. New York: The American University in Cairo Press, 2006.
François Burgat. *Face to Face with Political Islam*. London: I. B. Taurus, 2003.
James Gelvin. *The Israel–Palestine Conflict: One Hundred Years of War*. New York: Cambridge University Press, 2005.
Clement Henry and Robert Springborg. *Globalization and the Politics of Development in the Middle East*. Cambridge: Cambridge University Press, 2001.
Fred Halliday. *The Middle East in International Relations: Power, Politics and Ideology*. New York: Cambridge University Press, 2005.
Rashid Khalidi. *Resurrecting Empire: Western Footprints and America's Perilous Path in the Middle East*. Boston: Beacon, 2004.

Bernard Lewis. *What Went Wrong? The Clash Between Islam and Modernity in the Middle East.* Oxford: Oxford University Press, 2002.

Daniel Pipes. *The Hidden Hand: Middle East Fears of Conspiracy.* New York: St. Martin's, 1996.

Alan Richards and John Waterbury. *A Political Economy of the Middle East,* 2nd ed. Boulder, CO: Westview, 1996.

Dan Smith. *The State of the Middle East: An Atlas of Conflict and Resolution.* Berkeley: University of California Press, 2006.

## KEY TERMS

| | | |
|---|---|---|
| *Mashriq* | Oil for Food Program | petrodollar recycling |
| defensive modernization | conspiracism | remittances |
| capitulations | adventurism | Gulf Cooperation Council |
| *ijtihad* | *intifadas* | (GCC) |
| Eastern Question Game | Westoxication | *bonyads* |
| *mujahideen* | Euro-Mediterranean Partnership | rentier state |
| Pax Americana | (EMP) | |

## NOTES

1. U.S. Department of State, "Circular Airgram to American Diplomatic and Consular Offices," May 1, 1950. Available at www.gwu.edu/~nsarchiv/NSAEBB/NSAEBB78/propaganda%20003.pdf.
2. The GNP figures are calculated on the basis of purchasing power parity (PPP).
3. See Freedom House, *Freedom in the World 2006* (Lanham, MD: Rowman & Littlefield, 2006).
4. Bernard Lewis, *What Went Wrong? The Clash Between Islam and Modernity in the Middle East* (Oxford: Oxford University Press, 2002).
5. See Suha Taji-Farouki and Basheer M. Nafi, eds., *Islamic Thought in the Twentieth Century* (London: I. B. Taurus, 2004).
6. L. Carl Brown, *International Politics and the Middle East: Old Rules, Dangerous Game* (Princeton, NJ: Princeton University Press, 1984), pp. 16–18.
7. For a detailed examination of Libya under the Italians, see Lisa Anderson, *The State and Social Transformation in Tunisia and Libya, 1830–1980* (Princeton, NJ: Princeton University Press, 1986).
8. James Gelvin, *The Israel–Palestine Conflict: One Hundred Years of War* (New York: Cambridge University Press, 2005).
9. Cited in Manfred Halpern, *The Politics of Social Change in the Middle East and North Africa* (Princeton, NJ: Princeton University Press, 1963), p. 85.
10. Fred Halliday, *The Middle East in International Relations: Power, Politics and Ideology* (New York: Cambridge University Press, 2005).
11. Ibid., p. 153.
12. *Iraq Living Conditions Survey 2004, Volume II: Analytical Report* (Baghdad: Ministry of Planning and Development Cooperation, 2005), p. 57. Available at www.iq.undp.org/ILCS/PDF/Analytical%20Report%20-%20English.pdf.
13. Daniel Pipes, *The Hidden Hand: Middle East Fears of Conspiracy* (New York: St. Martin's, 1996), p. 27.
14. Quoted in Fauzi Najjar, "The Arabs, Islam and Globalization," *Middle East Policy, 12* (Fall 2005), p. 95.
15. *Views of a Changing World* (Washington, DC: The Pew Research Center, June 2003), p. 2.
16. Ahmed S. Hashim, *Insurgency and Counter-Insurgency in Iraq* (Ithaca, NY: Cornell University Press, 2006), pp. 72–73.
17. The Sahrawi leaders of the Western Sahara, however, have never justified attacks against civilians and have not attacked the Moroccan military since 1990.
18. Lisa Hajjar, *Courting Conflict: The Israeli Military Court System in the West Bank and Gaza* (Berkeley: University of California Press, 2005).
19. Hashim, *Insurgency and Counter-Insurgency in Iraq.*
20. National Counterterrorism Center, *Report on Incidents of Terrorism 2005* (April 2006), p. ix. Available at http://wits.nctc.gov/reports/crot2005nctcannexfinal.pdf.
21. Charles Tilly, "Terror, Terrorism, Terrorists," *Sociological Theory, 22* (March 2004), p. 11.
22. Sebastian Balfour, *Deadly Embrace: Morocco and the Road to the Spanish Civil War* (Oxford: Oxford University Press, 2002).
23. Although Kuwait's rulers fled their country in the wake of Saddam's invasion in 1990, the United States reinstated their government at the end of the Gulf War.

24. Philippe Fargues, "How Many Migrants from, and to, Mediterranean Countries of the Middle East and North Africa?" Euro-Mediterranean Consortium for Applied Research on International Migration (2005), p. 17. Available at www.carim.org/publications/CARIM-AS05_16-Fargues.pdf.

25. The World Bank, *2006 Economic Developments and Prospects: Financial Markets in a New Age of Oil* (Washington, DC: The World Bank, 2006), p. xv.

26. Matthew Kalman, "New Town for Toons: Animation Exec Hopes Jerusalem a Big Draw," *San Francisco Chronicle*, June 15, 2006, p. C1.

27. Manuel Trajtenberg, "R&D Policy in Israel: An Overview and Reassessment," in Maryann P. Feldman and Albert N. Link, eds., *Innovation Policy in the Knowledge-Based Economy* (Boston: Kluwer, 2001), p. 409.

28. Jonathon Nitzan and Shimshon Bichler, *The Global Political Economy of Israel* (London: Pluto, 2002).

29. Andrzej Kapiszewski, "Arab Versus Asian Migrant Workers in the GCC Countries," United Nations Expert Group Meeting on International Migration and Development in the Arab Region, 2006. Available at www.un.org/esa/population/publications/EGM_Ittmig_Arab/P02_Kapiszewski.pdf. See also Andrzej Kapiszewski, *Nationals and Expatriates: Population and Labour Dilemmas of the Gulf Cooperation Council States* (Reading, UK: Ithaca, 2001).

30. Charles Kernaghan, *U.S. Jordan Free Trade Agreement Descends into Human Trafficking and Involuntary Servitude* (New York: National Labor Committee, 2006). Available at www.nlcnet.org/live/admin/media/document/jordan.pdf.

31. *The Arab Human Development Report 2002: Creating Opportunities for Future Generations* (New York: United Nations Development Programme, Regional Bureau for Arab States, 2002).

32. Dalia S. Hakura, "Growth in the Middle East and North Africa," IMF Working Papers 04/56 (2004), p. 3. Available at www.imf.org/external/pubs/ft/wp/2004/wp0456.pdf.

33. Sara Roy, *The Gaza Strip: The Political Economy of De-development*, 2nd ed. (Washington, DC: Institute for Palestine Studies, 2001).

34. Israel's bombing of basic infrastructure in Lebanon in the summer of 2006 also caused billions of dollars of damage, potentially undermining a fifteen-year economic recovery there.

35. For a useful overview of the different theories used to explain the lack of democratization in the Middle East, see Raymond Hinnebusch, "Authoritarian Persistence, Democratization Theory and the Middle East: An Overview and Critique," *Democratization, 13* (2006), pp. 373–395.

36. Rashid Khalidi, *Resurrecting Empire: Western Footprints and America's Perilous Path in the Middle East* (Boston: Beacon, 2004).

37. For an overview of the "rentier state" concept, see Michael Ross, "Does Oil Hinder Democracy?" *World Politics, 53* (April 2001), pp. 325–361.

38. Daniel Pipes, *The Hidden Hand: Middle East Fears of Conspiracy* (New York: St. Martin's, 1996).

39. Soroush's website has many of his works translated into English. See www.drsoroush.com/English.htm. For more background on Ghannouchi's ideas, see Azzam Tamimi, *Rachid Ghannouchi: A Democrat Within Islamism* (New York: Oxford University Press, 2001). See Ramadan's website at www.tariqramadan.com. In 2004, the U.S. government denied Ramadan a visa to come to the United States to start a tenured position at the University of Notre Dame.

# PART IV

# IPE North and South

❀❀❀❀❀❀❀

**M**any of the most interesting and important IPE problems revolve around what are termed "*North–South*" relations. The *North* is made up of the industrialized nations that were the first to develop and have grown to be relatively rich. The *South* consists of the poorer, less industrialized nations of the world, many of which are former colonies of North states. North–South is therefore international political economy (IPE) shorthand for rich–poor, with differences in wealth creating further differences in power, status, and influence.

The three chapters in Part IV look at different aspects of North–South IPE that are especially relevant today. Chapter 15 examines the "two faces" of development—the elements of economic development that simultaneously attract and repel less developed countries (LDCs)—and examines how this dilemma has evolved in the past half-century.

IPE is about states and markets, but it is fundamentally about people, as Chapter 16 makes clear. This chapter analyzes migration, tourism, and human networks from an IPE perspective.

Chapter 17 tackles a particularly controversial aspect of North–South IPE—that of transnational corporations (TNCs). TNCs are seen by some as engines of growth for LDCs, and by others as tools of exploitation. Chapter 17 looks at how TNCs have in the past helped define the North–South debate and then goes beyond this framework to consider the key issues surrounding TNCs today.

# 15

# The Two Faces of Development

## By Sunil Kukreja

### OVERVIEW[1]

For much of the twentieth century, the overwhelming majority of the world's population did not experience the economic prosperity and affluence that the vast majority of people in developed countries did. An obvious question is this: Given the great amount of wealth produced in the world each year and within the developing nations, why have so many less developed countries (LDCs) remained impoverished, "underdeveloped," or "undeveloped"? The issue of development has confronted most of the LDCs at least since the middle of the twentieth century, when many of them formally became independent nations. For the most part, economic development is a goal that LDCs will continue to struggle to achieve.

This chapter looks at the development dilemma through the metaphor of the "two faces" of development. Development has an attractive face, one that appeals to the citizens and leaders of LDCs with the promise of less poverty, improved standard of living, longer life, and greater status. However, development also has an objectionable face—one that raises concerns for many citizens and leaders of LDCs because the cost of development, sometimes conceived in terms of lost local culture or independence, can seem too high.

We analyze the two faces of development through three phases. The period that we call "Independence?" spans the 1950s and 1960s: the time when many LDCs emerged from colonial status into a world of growing international markets, multinational corporations, and the Cold War. The question mark in the title of the section suggests that LDCs might have wondered if they had achieved true independence. Three options seemed to present themselves: Accept the situation, try to change the international system, or drop out of it.

The period of problematic independence gave way to an era during which discussions of LDC development strategy often boiled down to a choice between two powerful theories of development: inward-looking development, as then practiced in India and much of Latin America, based in part on experience with strong state mercantilist or structuralist influences, such as France and the Soviet Union; and outward-looking development, as practiced by the East Asian "Tiger" economies, based in part on the successful postwar development experience of Japan. Each of these strategies represented a particular approach to the two faces of development. Neither proved flawless. We label this discussion with the heading "Which Way?"

We call the current era, which began in the 1990s, "Confronting Globalization." The development dilemma today is perhaps less about grand theories of national strategy than it is about dealing with a myriad of issues that present both opportunities and obstacles. The two faces have changed a bit, and perhaps multiplied, but the dilemma they represent remains.

*What the countries of the South have in common transcends their differences; it gives them a shared iden-tity and a reason to work together for common objectives. . . . The primary bond that links the countries and peoples of the South is their desire to escape from poverty and underdevelopment.*[2]

The South Commission (1990)

There is very little that the nations and peoples of the South have in common, but the few character-istics they do share are critically important. When we talk about the South, or the Global South, or less developed countries, or developing countries, we are talking about societies with very diverse histo-ries, cultures, religions, economies, and political systems. What they have in common are two things: devastating and persistent economic poverty, and hence the imperative to confront what we call the two faces of economic development.

Whereas incomes have risen and material living standards have improved in the North over the past 500 years, living standards have changed very little for a large cross section of people in the South in all this time. Many in the South live perilously close to the edge and are constantly at the mercy of natural and man-made threats. One measure of the material living standards of a country is the amount of income available per person per day to spend on food, shelter, health care, education, and so forth. In advanced industrial countries, this figure is relatively high. Per-capita income in the United States, for example, is about $100 per person per day on average, although a few people have much more than this and many people have much less. An income of $100 per day is enough to purchase a comfortable and healthy lifestyle by global standards. By comparison, many people in the South have a per-capita in-come of $2 per day or less, and millions live on less than $1 per day. They are the focus of this chapter.

Table 15–1 shows the incidence of very severe poverty in the global South. The first three columns shows the proportion of population in different regions that lived on less than one U.S. dollar's worth

**TABLE 15–1    The Incidence of Extreme Poverty, 1990, 2001, and Predicted 2015**

| REGION | POPULATION (%) LIVING ON $1 PER DAY OR LESS | | | POPULATION (%) LIVING ON $2 PER DAY OR LESS | | |
|---|---|---|---|---|---|---|
| | 1990 | 2001 | 2015 | 1990 | 2001 | 2015 |
| East Asia and Pacific | 29.6 | 14.9 | 0.9 | 69.9 | 47.4 | 11.3 |
| China only | 33.0 | 16.6 | 1.2 | 72.6 | 46.7 | 9.7 |
| Excluding China | 21.2 | 10.8 | 0.4 | 63.2 | 49.2 | 14.7 |
| Europe and Central Asia | 0.5 | 3.6 | 0.4 | 4.9 | 19.7 | 5.2 |
| Latin America and the Caribbean | 11.3 | 9.5 | 6.9 | 28.4 | 24.5 | 19.6 |
| Middle East and North Africa | 2.3 | 2.4 | 0.9 | 21.4 | 23.2 | 11.9 |
| South Asia | 41.3 | 31.3 | 12.8 | 85.5 | 77.2 | 54.2 |
| Sub-Saharan Africa | 44.6 | 46.4 | 38.4 | 75.0 | 76.6 | 69.2 |
| **Total** | 27.9 | 21.1 | 10.2 | 60.8 | 52.9 | 32.0 |
| (excluding China) | 26.1 | 22.5 | 12.9 | 56.6 | 54.9 | 38.6 |

*Note:* Figures are based on purchasing power parity exchange rates.

*Source:* The World Bank, *Global Economic Prospects,* 2005.

of income per day in 1990 and in 2001 (with a predicted proportion in 2015). A dollar a day is a critical point in discussing real poverty. Less than a dollar a day means inadequate diet, shortened life span, poor health, and high infant mortality. About a quarter of the people living in the South experienced material living standards equivalent to having less than $1 per day, with deep poverty especially concentrated in South Asia and sub-Saharan Africa. The good news in this table is that deep poverty declined somewhat in several regions. The bad news is that the overall figures were and are so high. Many readers of this book are able to feed their pet dogs and cats better than many LDC parents are able to feed their sons and daughters.

The second group of three columns in Table 15–1 shows the population percentage with income less than the equivalent of $2 per day in 1990 and 2001 (with a predicted proportion in 2015). The difference between existing on $1 per day and $2 per day is significant. With $1 or less, a person struggles simply to survive. Two dollars, considering the conditions of poverty we are discussing here, buys a little more than bare subsistence and offers, therefore, some possibility of better health and human dignity. Of course, $2 a day is so small an amount to many citizens of advanced industrial countries that it may seem an inadequately modest goal, yet it is not realized for millions of people around the world. Note especially that the incidence of poverty according to this indicator is much more geographically widespread, with high poverty rates not just in South Asia and sub-Saharan Africa, but in East Asia, Latin America, and even Eastern Europe.

Much is made of the gap between North and South and whether global inequality has increased, decreased, or remained about the same over the last twenty-five years. Inequality is important, both between nations and within nations, and concern over inequality drives much of the North–South debate. There are endless debates over how the global pie ought to be divided and why the division is so uneven today, but there is no debate about poverty. Poverty pervades in the South, and improving the material and human living standards of much of the world's population is perhaps the most serious task we face as global citizens.

Being trapped in a world that is unequal and unfair, whether you are poor or not, is the repulsive and objectionable face. Escaping poverty is the attractive face of economic development. Yet it is not easy or cheap to gain economic development. Many costs must be borne in economic, social, political, cultural, and environmental terms. These costs, and the fears and anxieties that they produce, repel many in the South even as the promise of development attracts them. This chapter traces how LDCs have perceived the two faces of development from the 1950s until today and then attempts to draw some conclusions from their experiences.

## INDEPENDENCE? THE TWO FACES OF ECONOMIC DEVELOPMENT

As the former European colonial empires began to disintegrate by the 1950s, new nation-states emerged in their place. The dismantling of the empires unfolded differently in Asia, Africa, and Latin America. By the end of the 1950s, many of the former colonies had become independent, and others were on the threshold of a new international order shaped by the Cold War between the United States and its industrial democracy allies (the so-called First World) and the Soviet Union and its allies (the Second World in Cold War terminology).

As these new nation-states began to shape their respective national identities, it appeared that the long-standing colonial domination of the West had come to a close. Politically, the **Third World** had been born, yet these new nations of Asia, Latin America, and Africa confronted pressing and complex economic, political, and social problems that made it difficult to create truly sovereign national institutional structures.

For the LDCs, economic development is crucial not just as an end in itself, but also as a means for ensuring sustained political development, independence, and a cultural identity. Much of the success of the newly independent states in the postwar international climate as well as in domestic politics has depended on the ability of leaders to deliver on the promises that helped propel nationalist and independence movements. As such, economic development—characterized by a growing and prosperous economy—has been crucial to establish a national identity and to ensure political stability domestically.

The LDCs, however, approached economic development with mixed emotions. One face of development promised an end to poverty and the start of true independence and was powerfully attractive to LDCs; but the other face of development was the face of exploitation, manipulation, and continued subjugation. This face repelled LDCs as much as the other face attracted them. We can see both faces of economic development by looking at the four major forces that shaped the development dilemma for LDCs in the early postwar period, with decolonization under way.

First, colonial wounds were in many ways still fresh and deep. In this regard, political leaders often viewed former colonial powers with some suspicion. The social and economic exploitation they had endured under colonialism and capitalism were surely responsible for the economic "backwardness" of their new nation-states.

Second, the way many LDCs dealt with their development problem was not merely a response to the exploitative colonial conditions but a resistance to cultural domination by the West as well.[3] In some parts of the developing world, these sentiments helped shape a cautious approach to adopting Western influence and methods of economic development. As we shall see, this view of the developed countries by Third World leaders remained quite strong and influential, and became a central notion behind the solidarity of developing countries in the 1970s.

The third force to shape the economic development dilemma for many LDCs was the Cold War. Proximity to the United States or its allies, or historical connections to former mother countries, often shaped the kind of political and economic strategies the LDCs chose when it came to economic development. Likewise, support for the Eastern bloc of nations by some LDCs blended with a preference for non-Western development strategies.

Finally, and paradoxically, the economic success of the developed countries also provided a strong rationale for some LDCs to follow in their footsteps, or at least adopt market-oriented prescriptions for economic development. The emergence of new international institutions such as the International Monetary Fund (IMF), the World Bank, and the General Agreement on Tariffs and Trade (GATT), whose role was to coordinate international trade, symbolized the expanding significance of the market in the world economy. To many in LDCs, these institutions were controlled largely by the developed countries. The political significance of pursuing a Western economic development strategy would also signal a tacit association with the West in the Cold War. In many cases, however, association with Western institutions offered real opportunities that LDCs had to consider in pursuing a partnership with the industrialized nations and economic development. Hence, engagement of the LDCs in the postwar international economy with the developed countries remained a debatable option.

## THE FACE OF NEOCOLONIALISM

Recognizing that, individually, LDCs were unable to exert significant influence on the international system and its institutions, a number of these countries attempted to promote a collective identity. The 1955 Afro-Asian Bandung Conference in Indonesia is widely regarded as the first major step to forging that identity and is the genesis of what came to be viewed as a Southern perspective. Led by Jawaharlal Nehru of India, Marshal Tito of Yugoslavia, Achmed Sukarno of Indonesia, and Gamal Abdel Nasser of Egypt, heads of state from the developing countries initiated an effort that subsequently led to the formation of the Non-Aligned Movement in 1961. As a political banner of many newly independent LDCs, the Non-Aligned Movement expanded to include a number of countries in Latin America. This movement served three purposes. First, it was to be the LDCs' political arm for addressing initiatives against the remaining remnants of colonialism (especially in Africa). Second, it was to be their vehicle for positioning themselves outside the sphere of the Cold War scenario; and lastly, it was to promote the interests of the LDCs.

One of the main priorities of what came to be referred to as the nations of the South was the issue of **neocolonialism,** or the continued economic domination of LDCs by the industrialized countries. A number of political leaders and intellectuals argued that although the era of colonialism was largely over, former colonies were basically trapped in a capitalist international economic system dominated by institutions and mechanisms tilted in favor of the developed countries.[4] In a neocolonial environment, multinational corporations and their subsidiaries, for instance, owned and controlled a substantial part of LDC economic resources. The wealth and political influence of multinationals, often backed by their home-based governments, gave them and the industrialized nations the ability to control international markets of commodities from LDCs.

One such scenario frequently noted involved oil companies. For much of the twentieth century, seven major (Western) oil companies controlled the exploration, processing, and supply of oil in a number of oil-rich regions. These "Seven Sisters," as they were known, often worked to divide the market share, regulate supply, and preserve their control over resources in developing countries. In varying degrees, these companies were seen to be supported by their respective home governments. With such political support, the major oil companies negotiated terms (involving some royalties for the host country) that ensured the companies' control of oil exploration and distribution in the international market.[5]

Advocates of the neocolonial argument claimed that complementing the domination of multinational corporations was a restrictive system of trade, financial, and technological transfer that compounded the economic vulnerability of LDCs and weakened development prospects. In Chapter 6 we discussed the LDC claim that the international terms of trade committed them to be producers of raw materials and primary goods. LDCs were disadvantaged by the head start the industrialized nations had in the production of value-added products and their extensive use of protectionist trade measures. Technological innovations and gains in productivity largely occurred in the developed countries, and LDCs found themselves lagging and unable to compete in the areas of new product development and production. Tight legal controls, copyrights, and licensing often curbed LDCs' access to such technology. The financial power of large transnational corporations (TNCs), coupled with the developed countries' influence on the international financial system, also meant that developed countries and TNCs could influence the LDCs' access to funds for economic development.

## CHANGING THE SYSTEM: UNCTAD AND THE NIEO

Frustrated by their meager success, increasing numbers of LDCs turned to their membership in international organizations to foster Third World solidarity and momentum for change in the international political economy. In 1964 the United Nations Conference on Trade and Development (**UNCTAD**) was established, spearheaded by seventy-seven LDCs that became known as the **Group of 77 (G-77).** UNCTAD meets roughly every four years in the capital city of an LDC. Although its membership has increased over the years, the G-77 has been the LDCs' representative organization at UNCTAD sessions. The G-77 sought to make UNCTAD a mechanism for dialogue and negotiation between the LDCs and the developed countries on trade, finance, and other development issues. At UNCTAD I, the G-77 proposed a new international trade organization to replace GATT. For the most part, the developed countries resisted UNCTAD initiatives. Nevertheless, through UNCTAD, LDCs were gradually able to secure some concessions and preferential treatment—a Generalized System of Preferences (GSP)—on tariffs for their exports to developed nations.

The Organization of Petroleum Exporting Countries (OPEC) helped generate attention for Southern concerns in 1973 when this **cartel**, made up of oil-producing LDCs, embargoed oil shipments to some of the industrialized nations and significantly raised the price of oil.[6] A 400 percent increase in the price of oil jolted the developed economies and temporarily altered the global balance of political and economic power. By extension, it also complicated the development dilemma.

Following World War II, the industrialized countries (in spite of the postwar reconstruction, or perhaps largely fueled by it) had experienced considerable economic growth. Western oil companies dominated the petroleum industry, from exploration to marketing, and had historically provided cheap and abundant access to the energy needs of the industrialized world. However, OPEC's pricing actions helped dampen economic growth and spurred an inflationary trend in the developed countries. From the standpoint of relations between the developed and many LDCs, the latter were to gain considerable leverage for the time being. The developed countries—being highly dependent on oil-exporting countries for their energy—could no longer ignore the considerable effect that oil-producing countries from the South had on the economic well-being of the industrialized world.

OPEC political and economic leverage resulted in the sixth special session of the UN General Assembly in 1974, which called for the establishment of a **New International Economic Order (NIEO)**. This program for action was designed largely to facilitate the pace of development among LDCs and to change the unequal economic balance between the LDCs and the industrialized nations. The development prospects of the LDCs were believed to be intimately tied to the larger functioning of the world economic order. Unlike previous efforts, the NIEO was seen by LDCs not so much as an attempt to fine-tune the existing international economic order as an effort to elevate the issue of economic development to the top of the international agenda, changing respective institutional structures and making them more conducive to LDC development concerns. The NIEO included calls for

1. Creation of an Integrated Program for Commodities (IPC) to stockpile and control the price of commodities during periods of oversupply and scarcity.
2. Extension and liberalization of the GSP.
3. Development of a debt-relief program.
4. Increasing official development assistance from the rich, developed nations of the North to the less developed South.
5. Changing the decision-making process in major international institutions such as the United Nations, the IMF, and the World Bank to give more voice to Southern nations and reduce developed nations' control of these institutions.
6. Increasing the economic sovereignty of LDCs. Several initiatives were stipulated under this umbrella. Key among them were ensuring the LDCs greater control over their natural resources; increased access to Western technology; the ability to regulate multinationals; and preferential trade policies that would stabilize prices for commodities from LDCs and ensure these countries greater access to developed countries' markets.

Despite the UN's adoption of these objectives, implementation in the ensuing years remained problematic. A number of factors coalesced to render the NIEO ineffective. Foremost among these was the general opposition of the industrialized countries to the NIEO initiatives, making implementation difficult. These countries, led by the United States, did not consider the initiatives central to the development concerns of LDCs. Furthermore, many critics argued that the initiatives promoted an atmosphere of "micromanaging" the global economy, a task that, on the one hand, would be impractical, and on the other, restrictive of the free market. Many officials of the industrialized nations also saw demands for a NIEO as a political threat prompted by some radical LDCs to redistribute global wealth and power.

## IS DEVELOPMENT POSSIBLE?

Having failed to reform the international system, LDCs began to ask whether development was even possible within the existing international structure. An important voice in this discussion was provided by Raul Prebisch.[7] An early proponent of UNCTAD, Prebisch argued that the development dilemma in Latin America was inextricably linked to factors *outside* the region. Prebisch was especially critical of the existing international division of labor and the free-trade system. He and others argued that the international trade system reinforced the LDCs' role as producers of primary products and raw materials, while the developed countries continued to prosper as producers of industrial products. This international division of labor reinforced the dependence of the LDCs on the developed nations as outlets for LDC primary products. Further, production specialization perpetuated LDC dependence on the developed countries for capital and technology, which were essential for LDCs' economic development.

Dependence was considered significant because it contributed to the underdevelopment of the LDCs.[8] Early dependency theorists made a distinction between *under*development and *un*development. The latter was characterized by lack of development, the former by the outcome of a process that further undermined LDC economies while simultaneously contributing to the development of their counterparts in the industrial world. Thus, underdevelopment in LDCs was viewed as a product of the development process in industrialized regions. Underdevelopment and development were two facets of a singular global structure, much like the two sides of a coin.[9] Osvaldo Sunkel and Pedro Paz have noted that "both underdevelopment and development are aspects of the same phenomenon, both are historically simultaneous, both are linked functionally and, therefore, interact and condition each other mutually."[10]

This basic thesis represented the embryo of much of the analysis of dependency theorists during the 1960s and 1970s and was most forcefully articulated by Andre Gunder Frank in *Capitalism and Underdevelopment in Latin America*. For Frank, underdevelopment has its origins in the colonial order and European expansion prior to the twentieth century. Through political domination, the colonial powers successfully extracted raw materials and resources necessary for their development while impoverishing their colonies. Although decolonization removed the political dominance of the European powers, the basic economic linkage and division of labor between the two remained largely intact, resulting in neocolonialism. Frank argued that the international capitalist economic order was organized along the lines of a metropolis–satellite system (regions), under which the metropolis state exploited and controlled the satellite by extracting economic surplus and wealth from the latter.

A number of mechanisms reproduce this relationship and deepen the underdevelopment process in LDCs. Through transnational corporations, profits generated in LDCs are transferred out of LDCs. Investments in technology and other innovations are often dated or inappropriate and do not enhance the competitive edge of LDCs. The extensive resources of the TNCs also enable them to circumvent restrictive and regulatory measures in LDCs. Another widely cited mechanism is the unequal exchange relationship. The LDCs' "comparative advantage" in primary products and raw material is highly vulnerable to international market prices, which are generally well below those of manufactured goods that LDCs have to import from the developed countries. Over time, this creates a massive net outflow of revenue.

Some dependency theorists also find the international financial and foreign aid system to be exploitative. Foreign banks of the wealthier nations gain a stronghold on private lending. Critics charge that these banks are less interested in the development of a country than they are in acquiring lucrative terms for loans to LDCs. This results in a form of extended financial dependence for the indebted country and generous interest receipts for foreign banks. These theorists are also skeptical about foreign aid, arguing that the political and economic strings attached to such assistance reinforce a dominant–subordinate relationship between the developed and less developed nations.[11]

Hence the two faces of development presented early postcolonial LDC leaders with a dilemma. The global economic system seemed biased against their interests and structured to keep them in a snare of dependency. Efforts to change the system came to naught. To exit the system and attempt autonomous development meant turning their backs on all that global markets had to offer. But was accepting the global markets—and the possibility of dependent underdevelopment—a better choice? Thus LDCs approached development cautiously. These early experiences gradually evolved into a great experiment concerning two contrasting ideas of how best to approach the two faces of economic development.

## WHICH WAY? TWO STRATEGIES OF ECONOMIC DEVELOPMENT

How can LDCs achieve self-sustaining growth and enter the ranks of the **newly industrialized countries (NICs)**? The debate, rooted in policies and experiences of the 1950s and 1960s, became very clearly defined in the 1970s and 1980s as many LDCs in East Asia adopted strategies that, though quite diverse, are generally termed **export-oriented growth**. Meanwhile, several countries in Latin America opted for different, more inward-looking strategies generally termed **import-substituting industrialization (ISI)**. Each represents a particular approach to the two-faces dilemma.

Export-oriented growth attempts to maximize the benefits of modernization and industrialization by taking advantage of opportunities presented by international markets, relying on strong state policies to limit domestic disruption. Export-oriented growth is willing to risk dependency to gain the benefits of development. Import-substituting industrialization, on the other hand, views international market forces as a threat and attempts to achieve development with less risk of dependency. The lessons of this grand experiment in economic development are still somewhat controversial, as we shall see.

### Export-Oriented Growth

Export-oriented growth is a strategy that essentially resolves to embrace the attractive face of economic development and the global economy, but relies on strong state policies to mediate the fears of dependency and exploitation. The export-oriented approach is thus based on a combination of mercantilist and liberal prescriptions for economic growth and development. For one, it calls for the state to strongly emphasize a country's *comparative advantage* in selected sectors of the economy and to promote exports from these sectors. However, instead of depending on a noninterventionist state and free-trade policies, the East Asian NICs aggressively pursued specific national and international policies that changed the basic structure and functioning of their economies. Although there are specific differences among the East Asian NICs, certain common trends can be identified.

First, the export-oriented policies of East Asian NICs involved changing the fundamental composition of their production. Before the 1960s, like other developing countries, South Korea and Taiwan began promoting manufacturing with a particular emphasis on labor-intensive consumer goods. To accomplish this, the respective governments set up mercantilist-style restrictions to protect "infant" consumer manufacturing industries from foreign competition. This initial strategy had the added benefit of raising the level of employment, which also helped stabilize the political situation. The governments provided strong financial backing and incentives to promote manufacturing, which we will discuss later. The strategy used in this initial push to generate a viable manufacturing sector was not unlike the one pursued by Japan earlier in the twentieth century and later after World War II (see Chapter 13).

By the late 1960s, South Korea and Taiwan began to ease into the next phase of restructuring. These countries increased their international market share by promoting the export of domestically manufactured durable goods. State intervention again played a strategic role in launching this initial export promotion effort. Selective barriers on imported goods remained in place, although raw material imports necessary for manufacturing were not suppressed, and selected domestic manufacturing industries were targeted with fiscal incentives to stimulate the level of exports. Another policy was to devalue the national currency, making exports from these East Asian countries more competitive in the international marketplace and imports less attractive to domestic consumers.[12] In a sense, the NICs *created* comparative advantages for their manufactured products through these measures.

During the 1970s, South Korea's manufacturing sector expanded into heavy (technologically intensive) industries including steel, petrochemicals, and automobiles. By 1980 these efforts in restructuring the economy were bearing fruit. Manufacturing's share of gross domestic product (GDP) in South Korea climbed from 14 percent in 1960 to 30 percent by 1980 and has remained stable since. Agriculture's share decreased from 37 percent to 15 percent over the same period, and in 1995 it dropped to 7 percent of GDP. In Taiwan, manufacturing's share of GDP increased from 26 percent (1960) to 40 percent (1993) after hovering at a high of about 47 percent in the mid-1980s. Correspondingly, agriculture's share of GDP declined from 29 percent to only 3.5 percent by 1993.[13]

A second major component of this export-led growth strategy involved promoting a high level of savings and investment (including intense efforts in research and development). A combination of factors (in varying degrees) contributed to this process. In South Korea, for example, an increase in personal household savings was a major source of savings, largely stimulated by raising interest rates on bank deposits. The government also helped establish private banks and financial institutions, which began to overshadow traditional and informal money markets widely used by small private customers. This financial policy allowed the government to increase its oversight of financial stability and savings in the economy.[14] The growth of financial institutions in Singapore and Hong Kong was also crucial to the capital-formation process in these countries. Interestingly, the former developed an approach in which government maintained tight control and oversight over financial institutions, while the latter leaned in the opposite direction of minimal regulation of the financial sector.[15]

The influx of foreign capital and aid in East Asia was another crucial aspect of the capital-formation process there. Cold War tensions and the Korean War both had a strong influence on the flow of Western aid into South Korea and Taiwan. South Korea's dependence on foreign aid was especially crucial after the Korean War in the 1950s. According to one estimate, approximately 70 percent of South Korea's domestic capital formation came from foreign aid during much of the 1950s.[16] Taiwan's domestic capital formation also depended heavily on foreign capital during the same period—about 40 percent was externally financed. Recall that this was also the period when South Korea and Taiwan underwent structural transformation in production, using protective measures to insulate their newly emerging light manufacturing industries from foreign competition.

Throughout the literature on economic development, education and human resource development are recurrent features. It is no surprise that the successes of the East Asian NICs have put even more attention to these issues. The combined effect of investment strategies in education and job training in the NICs resulted in a quality labor force, creating increased economic efficiency, industrial flexibility, and greater economic equality. Government initiatives to reduce illiteracy and provide adequate access to job training are evident in comparatively high enrollment rates and government investment in creating an educated and skilled workforce. The important point here is not that government expenditures on education resulted in economic development. Rather, the emphasis on education led to the growth of a literate and skilled workforce, which was essential to the success of the industrial and investment policies and thereby promoted growth in productivity.

Finally, as we have seen, the state in these countries was instrumental in setting and shaping development policies. South Korea presents a typical case in point. Following a coup in 1961, the military established the Economic Planning Board, which, among other things, acquired powers to control the nation's investment strategy. With the guidance of the military government, which dictated economic policy, the board became a coordinating body among the various governmental agencies. This centralization of power corresponded with the weakening of political parties and electoral politics in South Korea. Another significant development was the systematic weakening of labor unions, which allowed the government greater control over enforcing its economic agenda. Hence, it should be noted that the East Asian "Tigers" didn't simply "roll back the state" and let free competition reign, as had been advocated by some neoliberals since the early 1980s.

## Import-Substituting Industrialization

The experience among the major Latin American economies was quite different. Recall that during the 1950s, Latin American scholars were increasingly skeptical of the "comparative advantage" road to development, and the dependency critique became an influential framework for development in that region. This critique fostered opposition to dependence on foreign capital and trade to promote development, resulting in restrictive trade policies and stringent regulation and control of foreign investment. Hence, an inward-looking and nationalistic *import substitution* approach was implemented, which was expected to reduce dependence on foreign capital, technology, and markets by promoting "home-grown" industries.

Government leaders and scholars alike were convinced that specializing in primary commodity products was an inherent disadvantage for developing countries in the region. The adverse terms of trade made manufactured imports a major foreign exchange drain that did not add to any tangible development. For this to change, countries such as Brazil and Mexico, which had a relatively fragile industrial base, had to undertake significant steps to build a viable and sustaining manufacturing sector. After all, given the large internal consumer market in Brazil and Mexico, a shift in emphasis from importing manufactured consumer products to producing them locally would translate into new jobs across the economy, improve the adverse balance of payment situation, and promote economic development.

The import-substitution path taken by countries such as Brazil and Mexico can best be described as a series of stages during which these countries moved from being exporters of primary commodities to developing an indigenous industrial base. The first stage of the import-substitution strategy was not unlike that followed by the East Asian NICs. By the 1950s, Brazil and Mexico were well into the process of promoting local manufacture of consumer goods (such as processed foods, textiles, and footwear) and curtailing foreign imports with protectionist measures. However, there were significant differences between the import-substitution strategies in East Asia and Latin America. Historically, the resource- and agriculture-rich Latin American economies have been more dependent on primary exports than their East Asian counterparts such as Taiwan and South Korea.[17] Diversifying from this deeply entrenched primary-product economy was easier said than done.

Furthermore, protectionist policies were used more heavily in countries such as Brazil to displace the foreign share of its consumer market, whereas in East Asia the focus of these measures was to enhance the international competitiveness of locally produced goods. Hence, by the late 1960s, as South Korea was moving into promoting its exports while maintaining some barriers, Brazil and Mexico were moving into the next stage of intensifying their import-substitution strategy. Ironically, instead of reducing their dependence on foreign capital, borrowing from abroad to finance the deepening of their import substitution was necessary. This second stage of import substitution involved expanding the manufacture of labor-intensive consumer goods along with diversifying into capital-intensive goods as well.[18] In this stage, the role of the government and state-owned enterprises expanded. This increasing presence of the state was associated with increased concentration of production in the hands of a few firms (often state-owned) that were not as productive as privately owned enterprises.[19]

However, the performance of these economies was not as strong as that of the export-oriented East Asian NICs. Brazil and Mexico had largely managed this growth by depending heavily on the domestic consumer market, not the international market. In order to sustain growth, production reflected the consumption patterns of those with purchasing power. Ironically, this further aggravated income inequality, as the gap between the "haves" and "have-nots" increased. By contrast, the income-inequality gap among the East Asian NICs narrowed.[20]

What lessons were learned from the debate between import-substituting industrialization and export-oriented growth? The answer to this question depends on whom you ask and when. By the early 1990s, for example, the evidence seemed clearly to favor the export-oriented strategy, based on the dynamic growth experience of the East Asian "Tigers" (South Korea, Taiwan, Hong Kong, and Singapore) and the "Little Dragons" (Thailand, Indonesia, the Philippines, and Malaysia). James Fallows best-selling book, *Looking at the Sun* (see Suggested Readings), argued that the East Asian system of state-led export-oriented economic growth had proved itself superior to both the ISI strategy and liberal laissez-faire policies. The East Asian results were very strong in terms of success in creating income and growth.

The results in Latin America were not as good. It had proved impossible, as discussed earlier, to avoid entanglement in international trade and finance. The strategy of borrowing abroad to build domestic industry created huge foreign debt and devastating debt crises in Latin America (see Chapter 8). The heavy controls adopted to avoid dependency created opportunities for corruption and special-interest manipulation. Latin America experienced less growth and less stability and possibly greater inequality, too. The scorecard seemed clearly to favor East Asia and export-oriented growth over import-substituting industrialization.

## LESSONS OF THE EAST ASIAN MIRACLE AND CRISIS

In 1993 the World Bank released a study titled *The East Asian Miracle: Economic Growth and Public Policy*,[21] which sought to assess the lessons learned from the debate between import-substituting industrialization and export-oriented growth. The report argued that the "East Asian Miracle"—high growth without great inequality—was due to two basic factors.

The first factor was that the East Asian countries were successful at "getting the fundamentals right." This is development jargon for avoiding the tremendous economic distortions that the Latin American countries had been forced to introduce as they sought inward development. Compared with the Latin American countries, the East Asian countries had avoided inefficient wage, price, and exchange rate distortions that favored key sectors of the economy at the cost of reduced economic efficiency and flexibility overall. The East Asian countries, as noted above, also promoted and experienced high rates of saving (so that investment was possible without large foreign debts), high levels of education and training, and stable macroeconomic policies. In short, their economic strategies avoided certain fatal policy mistakes.

Second, some of the state policies were effective in increasing growth, especially "export-push" policies. Ironically, the great contest between state-led import-substituting industrialization and state-led export-oriented growth showed, according to the World Bank, that the key to success was not so much what the government did but what it *avoided* doing. If the state avoids making a number of critical mistakes, the report seemed to say, development has a pretty good chance.

Many people who read the report concluded that its recommendation was that LDCs avoid *both* types of state-led growth strategies and adopt instead the neoliberal "Washington consensus" of free trade, free capital markets, and limited government intervention. This conclusion was highly contested, especially by East Asian leaders and scholars who believed that their sound state leadership policies were the key to their success. It seemed to many observers that the World Bank report blamed all failures on the state and credited all successes to natural market forces. These observers pointed out that many of the positive factors in Asian economic development, such as high savings rates, strong education systems, and relative income inequality, were *dictated by state actions*, not due to the absence of them. In the end, this World Bank report did not settle the question, but it perhaps served further to divide scholars into contending camps: those who believed in the Washington consensus and those who remained skeptical for one reason or another.

The Asian financial crisis that began in 1997 called the World Bank's judgment into question and reopened the question of development strategy. Although some analysts argued that the crisis was caused by (or exacerbated by) unwise state involvement in the economy (often called *crony capitalism*), others argued that the rapid adoption of Washington consensus policies, especially free capital markets, was more to blame. The Washington consensus advocated opening developing economies to global financial markets as soon as possible, which was often before necessary domestic institutions and regulations were in place. This "premature globalization" made the Asian economies unusually susceptible to financial crises.

This was an important issue to resolve. Do laissez-faire policies produce rapid growth, as the 1993 report suggested? Or do they open up an economy to instability and crises, as the 1997 Asian financial crisis seemed to indicate?

In 2001 the World Bank released another study, called *Rethinking the East Asian Miracle,*[22] that addressed these critical questions. Reading this report, one appreciates that both miracles and crises are complicated phenomena that cannot and should not be oversimplified. The Asian financial crisis, for example, was due in part to market imperfections and to what states did (business–government relations that sometimes encouraged financial abuse) and in part to what they did not do (the lack of effective financial and business regulation and more comprehensive social safety nets). Thus the "Asian miracle" might have been the result of a propitious combination of market failures and governmental action/inaction.

The key is not that LDCs need more open markets, less government, or more government, but that they need good government, which is a more complicated thing. Smaller government (and supposedly a more unregulated market) is not necessarily better government if it sacrifices necessary societal goals and institutions and does not advance development objectives. Similarly, grand state strategies alone will not ensure successful development: The devil is in the details.

## CONFRONTING GLOBALIZATION

As LDCs entered the twenty-first century, the world was changing in many important ways that made economic development seemingly more attainable but riskier and more complex. We often sum up these changes in a single word, **globalization**. This section streses that globalization is not one thing, it is many things; and thus for LDCs, confronting globalization has meant confronting a complicated array of problems and opportunities.

The development dilemma is no longer a simple matter of choosing a grand development strategy such as import-substituting industrialization (if it ever was that simple). The dilemma now is how to deal with both the big policy choices and the myriad of critical details that together form the two faces of development today. Following is a brief discussion of some of the most important issues that LDCs must confront.

### Global Competition

The 1990s began the era of truly global economic competition and global interdependency. Much of the world's population had for the previous forty years been walled out of global markets (or had walled those markets out). Then the walls came down in three huge stages.

- First, the government of China began a system of regional economic liberalization in the 1980s that accelerated as Hong Kong was returned from British rule in 1997 and China was granted membership in the World Trade Organization (WTO) in 2001.
- Second, the collapse of the communist governments of the former Soviet Union and its Eastern European satellite nations turned them all into "emerging market" economies.
- Third, a series of government reforms in India turned its strategy from inward-looking state development to outward-looking market development.

These three big changes, and numerous smaller ones, meant that more than half of the world's population was suddenly, at least theoretically, part of a global market as never before. Such global competition for products, resources, investment, and markets created problems and opportunities both for LDCs and for the advanced industrial countries.

### Trade Policy and the WTO

As the option of completely autonomous development gradually faded from the scene, it was replaced by the notion that development needed to take advantage of global resources and global market opportunities. The Washington consensus that influenced policies of the World Bank and the IMF was part of the story, but the other part was simple pragmatism: More and more of the resources for development came from financial markets, not from transfers of aid. Borrowed funds needed to be repaid, with interest, so LDCs needed to earn money through exports to pay the bills that inevitably came with economic development and urbanization. So LDCs needed to export to grow—but on what terms?

A growing consensus emerged among LDCs that the "rules of the game" of international trade—the rules of the WTO—were unfavorable to the interests of LDCs. So long as LDCs remained buyers of manufactured goods, for example, richer countries favored liberalization of trade in manufactured goods. However, things changed, LDC leaders noted, once countries such as China and Mexico became major *exporters* of manufactured goods. LDCs began to demand more open access to rich-country markets, both for manufactured goods and for their agricultural exports. LDCs were also frustrated that their attempts to develop critical agricultural resources were often undermined by, ironically enough, the existence of heavily *state-subsidized* agriculture policies in the United States and the European Union.

The LDC demands were placed on the table forcefully at the Seattle WTO meetings of 1999 and then again, with even more force, at the Doha meetings of 2001. LDCs confronted the fact that they needed the global markets, so they could not just walk away, but they also needed rules more favorable to their development interests, which were not necessarily compatible with the protectionism practiced by the United States via its own subsidized agriculture policies.

## The IMF and Financial Policy

The Washington consensus formula for the economic development of LDCs included both free trade and free capital mobility. The case for free trade is a strong one, according to economists, even though it is politically very controversial. The case for free capital mobility is less strong from an economic theory standpoint, but paradoxically it received great political support. This created a dilemma for LDCs.

To promote free capital mobility means, essentially, to allow virtually free movement of investment funds into and out of a country. These investment funds may come in many forms; some are long-term and stable, others are short-term and volatile. Some go to purchase productive assets, some to make portfolio investments in company stocks; others are speculative, pure and simple. Free capital mobility means allowing potentially dangerous forms of investment along with relatively safe forms, because it is hard to control one without potentially discouraging the other. The risk, and it is a big one, is that short-term speculative funds—what Keynes called "hot money"—rushes in and rushes out, creating a boom, a crisis, and the need for IMF assistance, as discussed in Chapter 8.

Global capital markets created freer access to the funds, and the lure of capital was almost irresistible. In truth, it *was* irresistible. However, with capital came financial instability, speculation, and the possibility of a devastating collapse. For LDCs, the returns increased, but so did the risk.

## New Donors, New Priorities

The nature of North–South aid flows changed dramatically. Nation-to-nation (bilateral) aid fell as the Cold War came to a close. Less aid was given based on security concerns (with noteworthy exceptions in the war against terrorism) and more aid was given for other purposes—humanitarian, economic, or both.

Multilateral aid, channeled through institutions such as the World Bank, changed, too. For example, whereas the World Bank saw itself as a main conduit for development finance, in the 1990s it realized that some of the projects it had once supported could reasonably be funded through private capital markets. The World Bank's priorities changed to a "fill in the gaps" strategy, focusing on projects that private markets could not finance, and priorities, such as environmental sustainability, that have values beyond market value. This shift in the World Bank's focus, although widely praised, did have the effect of making LDCs even more reliant on other sources of funding. For a discussion of reforms at the World Bank, see the box, "Reforming the World Bank."

Nongovernmental organizations (NGOs) such as CARE, the Red Cross, World Vision, and the Gates Foundation filled part of this gap. It is worth noting that literally thousands of nongovernmental organizations develop or fund projects in LDCs. They make up a critical third source of development resources, alongside state and market sources.

The NGO sector is complex, however. There is probably no "typical" NGO. They come in all sizes; some are funded by churches, others by foundations or through state-based aid. Some aim at economic development, others focus on issues relating to the environment, women's issues, reproductive issues, health care, agriculture, infrastructure, technology education, and much, much more. Some provide emergency humanitarian aid—during famines, for example—and leave when the crisis has passed. Others make a long-term commitment and attempt to develop local roots. Some try to be sensitive to indigenous cultures and beliefs, whereas others openly confront them, as, for example, women's rights organizations operating in countries with strong male-dominance traditions. Some NGOs work *with* the governments of the LDCs where they operate, but others avoid the governments because of concerns about corruption, or they even work against the governments by supporting politically unpopular causes or groups.

LDC relations with NGOs, therefore, also fit the two-faces theme. It is easy to see why LDCs might both desire the help that NGOs can offer yet remain wary of the strings attached or that the aid will reflect donor preferences as much as local priorities.

### REFORMING THE WORLD BANK

The International Bank for Reconstruction and Development, generally known as the World Bank, was created at the Bretton Woods conference on postwar economic planning in 1944. The purpose of the World Bank, as its original name suggests, was first to foster the reconstruction of countries after World War II and then to aid in the process of economic development generally.

John Maynard Keynes was the chairman of the Bretton Woods committee that drafted the plan for the World Bank. Keynes was determined to avoid the mistakes that had been made at the end of World War I, when the victors imposed harsh conditions on the vanquished, which caused them to suffer poverty and deprivation.

Keynes's best-selling book, *The Economic Consequences of the Peace,* predicted that these policies would produce resentment and further conflict, and time proved him correct. The job of the World Bank, in Keynes's vision, was to make sure that *all* the countries, winners and losers alike, would experience recovery and growth so that old wounds would heal, not fester. This, he thought, was the path to a lasting peace.[a]

Ironically, the World Bank is not a bank. It was impossible at the time to get countries to commit enough government resources to provide adequate loans for recovery and development. Instead, the Bank is a fund, which means that it borrows on international capital markets and then lends those funds to member nations. Because the Bank is such a good credit risk, it can borrow funds at much lower cost than can LDC borrowers. Of course, the loans must be repaid so that this process can be continued. For the poorest nations, a World Bank agency called the International Development Association provides very-long-term interest-free loans.

The World Bank has long been criticized for the fact that it makes loans, and not outright grants, and that it has generally supported projects that promise to create economic growth (to repay the loans) rather than social development growth or environmental progress. Part of the problem, of course, derives from the basic structure of the Bank, which needs to collect interest because it must itself pay interest. Some critics, however, argue that the Bank's real problem is that it reflects the capitalist bias of its largest member, the United States. Proposals have been circulated for many years to reform the Bank or to terminate it and replace it with an aid-based agency that would put social development ahead of economic development.

As the development environment changed in the 1990s and LDCs began to confront globalization, the World Bank reassessed its role and, to the amazement of many, began—albeit slowly—to change. Former World Bank chief economist (and globalization critic) Joseph Stiglitz wrote:

Part of the reason I remain hopeful about the possibility of reforming the international economic institutions is that I have seen change occur at the World Bank. It has not been easy, nor has it gone as far as I would have liked. But the changes have been significant. . . . Reforms involved changes in philosophy in three areas: development; aid in general and the Bank's aid in particular; and relationships between the Bank and the developing countries.[b]

Now, Stiglitz argues, the Bank views development as a more holistic process of social and economic transformation. It takes issues such as environmental sustainability and social equality more seriously in working with LDCs on development packages.

Discussions continue about how the World Bank should be changed to better address the problems of a world that is far different from the one that Keynes imagined in 1944. In particular, some ask whether the World Bank should get out of the loan business entirely and become a conduit for direct aid to less developed countries.

*References*

[a]  John Maynard Keynes, *The Economic Consequences of the Peace* (New York: Harcourt, Brace and Howe, 1920).
[b]  Joseph E. Stiglitz, *Globalization and Its Discontents* (New York: W. W. Norton, 2002), p. 241.

## Beyond Sweatshops

The transnational corporations are a major source of capital, jobs, export revenues, and technology in LDCs. However, there is global competition for TNC investments, and governments around the world are constantly trying to attract foreign investment funds.

Many are concerned that TNC investments create sweatshop factories, with low wages, poor working conditions, and no future for the workers. At the same time, others propose that the sweatshop syndrome is also contagious and that working conditions in richer nations are driven down—a "race to the bottom"—by competition with LDC sweatshops. If the increasing importance of TNCs does correspond with these negative sweatshop conditions, then it is obviously a very bad thing for workers everywhere. Karl Marx, who wrote about sweatshop abuses in Great Britain in the 1850s, might well not be surprised to know that they still exist in the twenty-first century.

For many LDCs, sweatshop industries are the most difficult aspect of the two faces of development. These LDCs need the jobs, technology, and export earnings. However, the dangerous and abusive working conditions that the worst sweatshops create seem to follow much TNC investment in LDCs. Still, the race-to-the-bottom scenario is not the whole story of TNC investment, as Theodore H. Moran has explained (see Suggested Readings). Most TNC investment, Moran points out, is North–North in direction, going from one advanced industrialized country to another, not North–South as is commonly assumed. And most of that investment is targeted at industries that pay much more than sweatshop-level wages. Even so, it must be said that TNC investments do go into industries such as textiles, clothing, leathers, and footwear that are low-wage and low-skill and therefore susceptible to sweatshop organization. Frequently the foreign TNCs do not so much operate sweatshops—and may therefore absolve themselves of responsibility for sweatshop conditions—as they are likely to contract with local suppliers who do.

It is often proposed that sweatshops should be eliminated around the world, and Moran discusses various strategies for trying to do this, such as adopting global labor standards or trying to integrate sweatshop concerns into WTO agreements. One interesting part of his book is his discussion of what LDC governments can do to move "beyond sweatshops." Moran argues that a passive strategy that counts on sweatshop earnings to "trickle down" and eventually create more growth is wrong-headed. It usually doesn't happen and, in any case, trying to compete on the basis of cheap labor is a fool's game, because there is always even cheaper labor somewhere else—jobs that come today are gone tomorrow.

Rather, Moran proposes a "build-up" strategy that uses resources created in part by today's TNC activities to improve worker skills and attract progressively higher-skill industries and jobs.

Interestingly, the build-up strategy must be broad-based, not just aimed at attracting TNC funds. Moran cites experiences in the Philippines, Costa Rica, and the Dominican Republic as evidence that build-up government programs can help LDCs to move beyond sweatshops.

Foreign investment will always have two faces, especially for LDCs that still struggle with memories of colonial control. Moran's studies indicate that how LDCs experience the two faces depends in part on the policies—trickle down or build up—with which they approach them.

## The Informal Economy and the Mystery of Capital

"Microcredit" gives many households a chance to participate in the market economy, often through what has been termed the **informal economy**. The informal economy is the part of the economic system that operates outside of direct government control or regulation. It is often a very important part of the economy of LDCs and an important source of opportunity for grass-roots entrepreneurship.

In many countries, however, government regulations and legal issues make it difficult for ordinary people to get started in the informal economy, to take full advantage of the opportunities it presents, and to leverage their success. This point has been made most powerfully by Peruvian economist Hernando de Soto. De Soto's books, *The Mystery of Capital* (2000) (see Suggested Readings) and *The Other Path* (1989, 2001), have been best-sellers in rich and poor countries alike. De Soto argues that capital is the key to unlocking grass-roots economic growth potential—an idea that the supporters of microcredit would agree with. De Soto goes further, however. He argues that poor people in many LDCs often have access to a good deal of capital, in the form of land or property that they use but do not own. A small farmer, for example, might live on and till some land on an absentee landlord's vast estate. Or a city street vendor might slowly build up a structure on a public sidewalk.

The problem, de Soto says, is that because these uses are informal and sometimes illegal, the people do not have any *property rights* in their capital. They cannot make full use of it because it can be easily taken away, and it may be costly and difficult to gain formal legal title. And, of course, it is impossible to use this capital to secure credit to expand a business or to build a permanent house. The poor have lots of capital, de Soto says, perhaps as much as $9.3 *trillion* worth, but they cannot make use of it in the same way that people in more developed nations can. If capitalism is to work for the poor, he argues, then the poor need to become capitalists, and that requires, obviously, that they have real rights to the capital that they already use.

*The Mystery of Capital* provides a number of case studies that illustrate this problem. In Lima, Peru, for example, the owner of a small business had to spend six hours a day for 289 days to work his way through the government bureaucracy and legally register his business. In Egypt, acquiring legal ownership of excess government land was found to take seventy-seven steps involving thirty-one public agencies over a period estimated at five to fourteen years. It takes even longer if you want to build a house on the land.

These regulations are roadblocks to grass-roots development, de Soto argues persuasively. Property-rights reform would not by itself eliminate LDC poverty, but such reform seems to be a necessary step toward that goal. In many LDCs, however, there are strong economic or political interests that are against such reforms. De Soto narrowly avoided an assassination attempt by a terrorist group that opposed his pro-capital and pro-capitalist agenda, for example.

## Microcredit Versus Macrocredit

One of the most interesting features of the globalization era has been the realization that economic development, if it is to succeed, must proceed at all levels at once. That is, LDCs cannot hope to grow if the focus is *only* on policies of the World Bank and IMF, or *only* on state development strategies. Both types of initiatives must move forward, and even more must happen: development must get down to the grass roots.

One of the great errors of the grand development strategies, perhaps, was the notion that development financed by what we might call **macrocredit** would trickle down from the big international capitalist institutions or the state planning agency to the villages and city streets. Globalization renewed interest in the possibility that development could grow from the grass roots up.

**Microcredit** is one of the beneficiaries of this "trickle-up" approach. The idea of microfinance is to provide credit to people at the grass-roots level so that they can start their own small businesses and both lift themselves up from poverty through their own initiative and also repay the loans, so that others can have a chance, too. The most famous example of microcredit is **Grameen Bank**, which was founded in Bangladesh in 1976 by Professor Muhammad Yunus, who was awarded the Nobel Peace Prize in 2006. By August 2002, the bank had made loans involving over a half-million households and had received cumulative loan repayments of more than $3 billion. The loans are very small, often just $20 or $50 to begin with, but the potential effect is large.

The reason that microcredit institutions are successful in some LDCs has to do with an economic problem called **asymmetric information**. The problem is, who can be trusted to repay a loan, even a very small one? If you know whom to trust, you can lend them money at low interest rates. But if you cannot tell who is trustworthy (or creditworthy), then you have to charge everyone a high interest rate to cover your expected losses. High interest rates, however, discourage trustworthy borrowers from getting loans and so also discourage them from starting new businesses or expanding old ones. The problem of finding out who is trustworthy, and the cost of monitoring borrowers to be sure they act responsibly, limits grass-roots development.

In advanced industrial countries, borrowers and lenders have found many ways around the problem of asymmetric information; there are even firms that specialize in providing credit ratings of individuals and businesses. However, the costs are too high to provide the same services in LDCs, especially when the loan amounts may be tiny. So credit, a key to economic development, is unavailable or too expensive to the poor, who need it most.

How do microcredit institutions solve this problem? Typically, they lend money to small groups of people, usually women. Each member of the group is individually responsible for repaying the group's loan. This fact makes participants very careful about who they let into their group. It is in each member's interest to work only with very productive and trustworthy colleagues—ones who can be relied on to work hard and pay their share of the loan. The information problem—Whom can you trust?—is thus shifted from the lender to the members of each group. Loans can be made at low interest rates to these groups, who qualify for larger loans based on their repayment record. By moving the burden of knowing who is creditworthy from the bank to the borrowing group, microcredit institutions unlock the possibility of credit-financed grass-roots economic development.

How can such very small loans create much economic development? People who are used to living in societies where credit is readily available may find it difficult to appreciate how even a little bit of credit can benefit people in very poor, credit-scarce parts of the world. A small group of women can use a loan to purchase fabric or other raw materials that are then processed and sold in local or regional markets. Without the funds for the raw materials, the market value of their labor cannot be exploited. The small incomes that are thus generated can change both the economic status of the households involved and the social status of the women who earn them.

Microcredit institutions such as the Grameen Bank have become an important conduit of economic development. The United Nations proclaimed 2005 as the International Year of Microcredit, to draw attention to its significance, and microcredit institutions have been developed both in LDCs and in low-income regions of rich countries, including even the United States.[23]

Microcredit is a great opportunity for LDCs to cultivate grass-roots economic development, but there are also concerns associated with it. Although microcredit institutions often begin with an agenda for socioeconomic change, some critics have argued that the need to be financially sustainable—to earn higher interest rates and achieve higher loan repayment rates—sometimes alters these priorities. The concern is that the pressure to be economically sustainable may ultimately cause them to avoid loans to the poorest of the poor, who are often exactly the people who most need access to credit. There is also a concern that microcredit institutions, if successful, may introduce capitalist practices and values into indigenous societies.

## Development in the New Millennium

Despite all the years of debates about competing development models, and investment strategies, the fact remains that in many parts of the world, the persistence of poverty (and lack of economic development) remains critical and endemic. This reality has been brought to bear on governments and international organizations by social activists and numerous NGOs. Rock stars such as Bono have campaigned aggressively about the need for the international community to make a deeper and more meaningful commitment to address the dire conditions of many of the poorest nations in the world. The growing spotlight on the extent of poverty, child malnourishment, and disease, especially in sub-Saharan Africa, serves as a glaring reminder that while much about the global development landscape has changed over the last half-century, the poor in many parts of the world are still far from being able to meet most basic needs, let alone experience tangible improvements in their quality of life.

Consider, for example, the problem of access to health care. The majority of us in advanced industrial countries take it for granted that we are not likely to be exposed to a variety of public health hazards such as malaria, smallpox, and tuberculosis. These contagious diseases have been virtually eliminated in most areas because of strong action by scientists and public health officials. Vast numbers of people in LDCs are not so lucky. Some diseases of the tropics get less medical research attention, and so remain a serious problem, because of the high cost of research and testing of drugs and the low incomes of potential buyers. Even where drugs are available and medical treatments well known, the costs of mounting a public health program are very high. Even governments that are not corrupt may struggle to make public health a high priority.

However, the costs of ignoring public health issues are high, too, as the AIDS epidemic in sub-Saharan Africa is teaching us. The UNAIDS/WHO task force on AIDS/HIV estimated that at the end of 2001 there were 28.5 million people living with AIDS in sub-Saharan Africa, but that fewer than 30,000 of these were receiving adequate drug treatment.[24] Over 11 million children had been orphaned by AIDS. About 9 percent of the adult population was infected. And the problem was getting worse. The reasons that AIDS or other health care issues remain such a severe problem in sub-Saharan Africa are many and complex. Lack of money for prevention, treatment, and education is part of the problem. However, other parts of the problem are beyond the immediate reach of money, such as the attitudes of some government officials, who deny the existence of the problem, and cultural, social, and sexual practices that permit the disease to spread. Solving such devastating problems therefore requires citizens to look abroad for help, but also to look in the mirror. Much rides on how the two faces respond.

It has become increasingly clear that some concerted effort to address the desperate condition of many poorer countries is needed. In 2005, through the leadership of then UN Secretary General Kofi Annan, the United Nations ushered in the **Millennium Development Goals** to reinvigorate and refocus the international community's commitment to addressing some dire economic and human conditions, especially among the world's poorest nations (see Chapter 8). The Millennium Development Goals project is built around pursuing the following eight broadly defined goals[25]:

1. To cut poverty and extreme hunger by half
2. To achieve universal primary education
3. To advance gender equality and empower women
4. To reduce child mortality by two-thirds by 2015
5. To reduce by two-thirds the mortality rate of women during pregnancy and childbirth
6. To reduce the spread of HIV/AIDS and malaria by half by 2015
7. To secure environmental sustainability
8. To develop a partnership for development that includes an open, rule-based, predictable, and nondiscriminatory trading and financial system.

To this end, former Secretary General Annan recruited the renowned development economist Jeffrey Sachs to advise the United Nations. Sachs, who is widely respected and has a record of having advised numerous governments coping with economic reforms in Eastern Europe, Asia, Latin America, and Africa, has been a strong advocate for a greater commitment from the advanced industrial nations toward achieving the aforementioned goals. Sachs has especially advocated for greater investment and financial assistance in critical rural sectors of the poorer regions and in sub-Saharan countries. Sachs argues that the wealthier nations and leading international institutions such as the World Bank and the IMF have been ideologically partial toward privatization while underestimating the importance of poverty reduction and financial assistance in their policies toward the poorer countries. He writes:

> Increased foreign financial assistance was deemed not to be needed. Indeed, foreign aid per person in the poor countries plummeted during the 1980s and 1990s. Aid per person in sub-Saharan Africa, for example, expressed in constant 2002 dollars, fell from $32 per African in 1980 to just $22 per African in 2001, during a period in which Africa's pandemic diseases ran rampant, and needs for increased public spending were stark. . . . Many African countries have heard an earful from the World Bank . . . about privatizing their health services, or at least charging user fees for health and education. Yet most of the high-income-country shareholders of the World Bank have health systems that guarantee universal access, and all have education systems that ensure access to public education.[26]

As a neoliberal but also a critic of the market model of development, Sachs and a multitude of NGOs argue that the industrialized states can afford and should provide more aid to the poorest developing nations. Table 15–2 indicates that net official development assistance (ODA) by major donors has begun to increase again, but at least one motive for the increase has to be the war on terrorism. To those concerned that this aid would go to corrupt officials or only make matters worse for LDCs,[27] Sachs and the UN both agree and argue that the developing nations themselves ought to be working toward making government more effective and responsive to the needs of the poorest people. However, both Sachs and the UN are not depending on good government alone to solve development problems when issues such as fighting disease, promoting agricultural production, and building up the infrastructure in poor countries are also just as important.

Sachs has also become a vocal proponent for the cancellation of the foreign debts of many of these desperately poor countries (see Chapter 8). Indeed, he has gone so far as to suggest that if the wealthier nations opt not to cancel these debts, the highly indebted poor nations should refuse to service the exorbitant payment burdens they now carry—estimated to be over $200 billion.[28]

A critical part to understanding Sachs's advocacy of the Millennium Development Goals is to appreciate his critique of past strategies—such as the conditional structural adjustment programs—pursued by the IMF. His critique is especially noteworthy because it is accompanied by his prescription

**TABLE 15–2   Net Official Development Assistance Disbursements (billions of dollars)**

| DONOR | 1988–1989 AVERAGE | 1993–1994 AVERAGE | 2000 | 2002 | 2004 |
|---|---|---|---|---|---|
| United States | 8.9 | 10.0 | 10.0 | 13.3 | 19.7 |
| Japan | 9.0 | 12.2 | 13.5 | 9.3 | 8.9 |
| United Kingdom | 2.6 | 3.0 | 4.5 | 4.9 | 7.9 |
| France | 5.6 | 8.2 | 4.1 | 5.5 | 8.5 |
| Germany | 4.8 | 6.9 | 5.0 | 5.3 | 7.5 |
| Canada | 2.3 | 2.3 | 1.7 | 2.0 | 2.6 |
| Italy | 3.4 | 2.9 | 1.4 | 2.3 | 2.5 |

*Source:* Organisation for Economic Co-operation and Development, *Statistical Annex of the 2005 Development Co-operation Report.*

for what he calls "clinical economics." In his new book, *The End of Poverty* (see Suggested Readings), Sachs takes issue with the conventional economic logic that had long dominated the Washington consensus, asserting that the "main IMF prescription has been budgetary belt tightening for patients much too poor to own belts. IMF-led austerity has frequently let to riots, coups, and the collapse of public services."[29] For Sachs, in lieu of the failed "one size fits all" approach typical of the Washington consensus and reflected in the actions of the IMF and other such bodies, experts need to emulate the "clinical" approach to development as practiced in medicine. Not unlike individuals, economies are "complex systems," and hence "differential diagnosis" is essential to differentiate ailments or illnesses even when some common symptoms may be present among two or more cases. Carrying out "differential diagnosis" is critical to being able to precisely diagnose economic problems—and hence the appropriate case-specific treatment that may be necessary. For Sachs, then, "clinical economics"[30] can be the method to pursuing the broader eight-point goals articulated in the Millennium Development Goals project.

Many of Sachs's views about development are currently being supported by both the IMF and the World Bank.[31] As we have noted, the latter has always been more focused on development issues than the former. The World Bank has also gradually over the years shifted its focus to targeting poor people directly with its programs as opposed to banking on "top-down" industrial development and market-oriented programs. In the conclusion of this book we discuss in more detail a recent study by the World Bank that has shifted even more away from the market-oriented development outlook to a "catch-all" approach that suggests that what works best for each country will be a unique set of policies.[32] This and other studies represent a continuing pattern of experts rejecting neoliberal development ideas that aren't nation specific.

## CONCLUSION

This chapter has demonstrated that, since World War II, economic development has remained an objective of many different states, international organizations, and recently, nongovernmental organizations. A variety of different strategies have resulted in some successes, especially for the NICs of East and Southeast Asia, modeled on Western ideas about development goals and methods. However, the search for a single solution—a silver bullet—to the problems of many developing countries has given way to a growing realization that currently there is not one foolproof strategy that works for all developing nations, nor might there ever be one. Just some of the factors that have helped some nations develop successfully are, among other things, their geopolitical position, their colonial past or other history, their position in the international economy (what each produces and trades), and a myriad of domestic factors that have either fostered or acted as barriers to development.

More studies seem to be accepting the idea that no one factor can explain the success or failure of any developing nation. Rather, for most nations it has been a rather specific mix of factors that favor their achievement or success or setbacks.

In the case of the world's poorest nations, especially those in sub-Saharan Africa, nothing seems to have worked or is now working when it comes to development. In many cases these nations have encountered numerous problems associated with inappropriate demands made on them by the major powers, the WTO, the IMF, the World Bank, and even the UN. On top of that is a myriad of factors within their own societies that act as major barriers to change, such as geographic location, access to water, government corruption, and ethnic and religious differences among different social groups.

The AIDS epidemic and acute poverty in Africa, for instance, remind us that the goal of development is not just having a better income; it is also about having a better life. It is about rights and opportunities. People in LDCs certainly want better lives. And they would grasp opportunities now and hold on tight, for themselves and their families, if it were an easy thing to do. The Millennium Development Goals project also reminds us that there is obviously much to be done. As a reflection of different objectives and goals, many states, international organizations, and NGOs especially are heavily invested in trying to promote reform, if not meaningful change, in many developing countries, employing a wide variety of techniques and methods (see the box, "The Globalization of Sport and Development").

Perhaps we should remain optimistic after all. Indeed, some progress has been made on the economic front for a number of states, and certainly lessons have been learned. However, development remains a complicated and frustrating problem that includes many opportunities and dilemmas. The metaphor of the two faces of development still holds, in the sense that the fruits of development attract but the methods of development continue to pose serious challenges and problems that are exceedingly difficult to deal with.

---

### THE GLOBALIZATION OF SPORT AND DEVELOPMENT[a]

Given its popularity everywhere in the world, it is not surprising to find that some scholars have proposed the emergence of a "transnational culture" or "global culture," of which sport is a part.[b] Its popularity has even led one commentator to remark, "God apart, only sports teams inspire such devotion."[c]

As an autonomous force, sport is also beginning to be seen as means rather than only an end. Rather than the development *of* sport, we now see development *through* sport, or, more specifically, "sport for development and peace." The UN's constructivist role in the process of globalizing human rights, in particular, has provided the catalyst for sport to serve the purpose of development. Former Secretary General Kofi Annan, a one-time U.S. collegiate athlete, has taken leadership in promoting a sport-based world order. This system is embedded in ideas about globalization combined with political liberal values that are at the heart of sport-based development initiatives.

In the past, sports initiatives had been *ad hoc*, informal, and isolated. However, sport represents an integrated industry that already contains an extensive system of transnational and grass-roots actors. Research shows that sport can contribute to economic and social growth, which in turn can have positive and enduring effects on development, public health, peace, and the environment.[d] In addition, effectively designed sports programs strengthen basic human capabilities, create connections between individuals, and teach core values and life skills.

No single policy sector possesses the full range of competencies and capabilities to combat the world's growing inequalities. With each partnership, the UN and sport-minded individuals and agencies are promoting a holistic approach to raising the number of stakeholders in the welfare of the world. They are essentially saying, "the more the merrier"—thumbing their collective noses at the unilateral realists of the world.

## Think Globally, Recruit Locally: Right to Play

Right to Play is an athlete-based international humanitarian organization that uses sport to aid the healthy development of children and youth in the most underprivileged areas of the world. Its programs are intended to empower communities and foster the physical, social, and emotional development of children. According to the organization, children represent a "very high percentage of the victims of war, poverty and preventable diseases."[e] Thus, in order to rebuild a civil society, Right to Play focuses on sports programs at the local level.

According to its 2004 Annual Report, thirty-six Right to Play sports projects were active in nineteen countries, reaching approximately 500,000 children. During the year, eighty international volunteers were sent into the field to train over 6000 local coaches. Indicative of Right to Play's field work is the SportWorks program in the city of Juba, Sudan. More than two decades of civil war has left the children there malnourished, orphaned, and traumatized. In a partnership with UNICEF, Right to Play has trained eighty-seven teachers working in fifty schools with 15,000 children to incorporate sport and play into the curriculum.[f]

Founded in 1992 by the Lillehammer Olympic Organizing Committee, Right to Play was spear-headed by Norwegian speed skater and five-time Olympic medalist Johann Koss. Now president and CEO, Koss has been integral in developing the NGO as a notable humanitarian cause. His inspiration came after delivering used sporting equipment from Norway to Eritrea, which was at the brink of famine in 1994.[g] Though he was at first wary of the benefits that sport equipment could provide to a nation in need of food, Eritrean President Isaias Afewerki praised Koss and the Norwegians for believing in the children and treating them as human beings. As Koss remembers, it was the first time the Eritrean children had been considered more than just mouths to feed under the current development policy. This perspective became the basis of Right to Play.

Instead of having international volunteers conduct the programs, Right to Play favors a successful "train the trainer" model. Volunteers train local coaches and teachers to develop the capacity for community ownership. Members of the community are fully involved in project implementation. Such capacity building increases the diversity of relevant stakeholders in the community and ultimately ensures the sustainability of projects. The model demonstrates that development initiatives should think globally but recruit locally.

## Ownership as Participants: MYSA

The Mathare Valley lies on the northeast side of Nairobi, the capital of Kenya. Made up of dilapidated shacks and hovels, Mathare is one of Africa's poorest and most notorious slums. There is no sewage system, electricity, or garbage pickup, and the strict austerity measures imposed by international lending agencies have left few resources for social services, education, and health care. One day in 1987, while waiting for his daughter to finish volunteering there, a Canadian expatriate named Bob Munro came across a group of barefooted boys playing soccer with a ball made of plastic grocery bags and twine.[h] Munro had been working in Nairobi as a UN consultant on water use and sustainable development. After watching the game for some time, Munro finally asked if the boys would like a better ball; the response was unanimous excitement.[i] From such modest beginnings, the largest youth sports program in Africa took hold.

Munro's initial aim was to help establish a small organization that would provide opportunities for the youth of Mathare to participate in sport. Rather than imposing a structure of perceived needs, it was an attempt to address unmet needs as determined by the participants themselves. Responsibility for the initiative was to be shared with the youth. Munro insisted that they make efforts to clean up the epidemic levels of garbage in Mathare before starting their weekend games. In 1987, the crew of soccer players and garbage collectors became officially recognized as the Mathare Youth Sports Association (MYSA). Their initial office, all 9 square meters, was located above a derelict bar in Mathare. One year after it was founded, though, MYSA had 120 soccer teams in its youth league.[j]

Today, MYSA includes over 14,000 soccer players on roughly 1000 teams, with hundreds of volunteers facilitating their matches. Because of the high demand, the organization has also had to expand beyond its epicenter in Mathare. MYSA is now composed of sixteen zones covering an area of 80 square kilometers of the city. In addition, a full- and part-time staff of seventy-three oversees an annual budget of US$500,000.[k] Most of the MYSA staff, including league officials, coaches, referees, and linesmen, are local teenagers.[l]

For their efforts, Bob Munro and all of the MYSA soccer players and staff were nominated for a Nobel Peace Prize in 2004. A major factor in their success has been the degree to which organizers have fostered youth ownership and self-empowerment. From the onset, MYSA has adopted a functional approach to sport. The program takes the most marginalized members of society and uses sport to facilitate integration and maintain order. With few alternatives, sport is one of the most effective means for attracting public participation and the mobilization of youth in Africa who have a stake in their community. The case of MYSA provides an alternative to development strategy and demonstrates that Africans, not to mention youth, can own their development.

Bob Munro, a Canadian, Johann Koss, a Norwegian, and Kofi Annan, a Ghanaian, have all contributed to the emerging field of development through sport. The nature of the emerging partnerships in sport lends credence to individuals and civil society driven to achieve change. By combing the resources and expertise of the private sector with the grass-roots links and staff of nongovernmental organizations, the operational infrastructure of sports associations, and the ideas of individuals, development projects spearheaded by sport are end-running the state and circumnavigating the globe.

*References*

[a] This topic was researched and drafted by Greg Groggel, who, as part of a Watson Fellowship, is currently conducting a study of cities that have hosted Olympic games.

[b] J. A. Maguire, *Global Sport Identities, Societies, Civilizations* (Malden, MA: Blackwell, 1999).

[c] "Golden Goals," *The Economist*, May 31, 1997, pp. 57–59.

[d] The UN has compiled a great deal of the available research into a single report. For more information, see Inter-Agency Task Force on Sport for Development and Peace, *Sport for Development and Peace: Towards Achieving the Millennium Development Goals* (New York: United Nations, 2003).

[e] Right To Play, *Annual Report, 2004,* p. 6.

[f] UNICEF, *Sport, Recreation and Play* (New York: United Nations, 2004), p. 20.

[g] Swiss Foundation for World Affairs, "More than Just a Game: The Role of Sports in International Relations," *For the Record,* November, 2004, p. 4.

[h] J. Warick, "Kenya's Game of Life," *Saskatchewan News Network,* April 17, 2004, p. E1.

[i] O. Willis, "Sport and Development: The Significance of Mathare Youth Sports Association," *Canadian Journal of Development Studies, 21* (2000), p. 831.

[j] E. Kameo, "From Battlefield to Playing Field," *Supporter,* November, 2005, pp. 14–15.

[k] Willis, "Sport and Development," p. 831.

[l] "The Slums Wallop the Toffs," *The Economist,* October 31, 1998, p. 49.

## DISCUSSION QUESTIONS

1. How serious is the problem of global poverty today? Explain, citing data from this chapter.
2. What four forces have shaped the development process for LDCs? How do these forces create tensions within LDCs and between LDCs and industrial nations? Explain.
3. Briefly trace how issues of economic development have changed since the early postcolonial days of the 1950s and 1960s. In particular, discuss the tensions between the UNCTAD and the NIEO, between import-substitution industrialization and export-oriented growth, and between the advocates of the "Asian miracle" and those who favor the Washington consensus.
4. The chapter's author argues that developing countries need good government more than they need less government or more government. What are the characteristics of good government with respect to economic development? Explain. (Hint: Consider some of the factors discussed in the last section of this chapter.)
5. Microfinance is a very promising development tool. Explain briefly how microcredit programs such as the Grameen Bank works. Why are microcredit banks more successful in stimulating development in some cases than regular banks? Explain, citing specific aspects of the microcredit system.
6. How hopeful are you that the Millenium Development Goals project will work? Explain. Do you think funding such a project is worthwhile, or is it a waste of time and energy? Explain.

## INTERNET LINKS

The World Bank:
www.worldbank.org

UNCTAD:
www.unctad.org

World Bank quarterly magazine, *Finance & Development:*
www.imf.org/external/pubs/ft/fandd

The World Bank Poverty Map:
www.povertymap.net

The United Nations Development Programme:
www.undp.org

The United Nations Millennium Development Goals:
www.un.org/millenniumgoals

Third World Network:
www.twnside.org.sg

Grameen Bank website:
www.grameen-info.org

Transparency International Global Corruption Report:
www.transparency.org/publications/gcr

## SUGGESTED READINGS

Kevin Danaher. *50 Years Is Enough.* Boston: South End Press, 1994.

Hernando de Soto. *The Mystery of Capital: Why Capitalism Triumphs in the West and Fails Everywhere Else.* New York: Basic Books, 2000.

James Fallows. *Looking at the Sun: The Rise of the New East Asian Economic and Political System.* New York: Pantheon Books, 1994.

Stephen A. Marglin. "Development as Poison: Rethinking the Western Model of Unity," *Harvard International Review,* 25 (Spring 2003), pp. 70–75.

Theodore H. Moran. *Beyond Sweatshops: Foreign Direct Investment and Globalization in Developing Countries.* Washington, DC: Brookings, 2002.

Oxfam International. *Paying the Price: Why Rich Countries Must Invest Now in a War on Poverty.* Oxford: Oxfam International, 2005.

"Recasting the Case for Aid." *The Economist,* January 22, 2005, p. 79.

Tina Rosenberg. "That Taint of the Greased Palm," *The New York Times Magazine,* August 10, 2003, pp. 28–33.

Jeffrey D. Sachs. *The End of Poverty: Economic Possibilities for Our Time.* New York: Penguin, 2005.

Joseph E. Stiglitz. *Making Globalization Work.* New York: W. W. Norton, 2006.

Muhammad Yunus. *Banker to the Poor: Micro-lending and the Battle Against World Poverty.* New York: Public Affairs, 1999.

## KEY TERMS

Third World

neocolonialism

UNCTAD

Group of 77 (G-77)

cartel

New International Economic Order (NIEO)

newly industrialized countries (NICs)

export-oriented growth

import-substituting industrialization (ISI)

globalization

informal economy

macrocredit

microcredit

Grameen Bank

asymmetric information

Millenium Development Goals

## NOTES

1. Michael Veseth contributed to a previous version of this chapter for the third edition of this book.
2. The South Commission, *The Challenge to the South* (New York: Oxford University Press, 1990), p. 1.
3. See Daniel Chirot, *Social Change in the Twentieth Century* (New York: Harcourt Brace, 1977), p. 173.
4. One of the leading voices of the antineocolonial movement was the former president of Ghana, K. Nkrumah, who articulated this thesis in his book, *Neo-colonialism: The Last Stage of Imperialism* (London: Nelson, 1965).
5. Joan Edelman Spero, *The Politics of International Economic Relations* (New York: St. Martin', 1981), pp. 246–247.
6. OPEC was formed in 1960, and its membership includes Iran, Iraq, Algeria, Nigeria, Libya, Kuwait, Qatar, Saudi Arabia, the United Arab Emirates, Venezuela, Indonesia, and Angola.
7. Raul Prebisch, *The Economic Development of Latin America and Its Principal Problems* (New York: United Nations, 1950).
8. It is worth noting that many analyses of these early dependency theorists were based on the experiences of countries in Latin America.
9. Andre Gunder Frank, *Capitalism and Underdevelopment in Latin America* (New York: Monthly Review Press, 1967).
10. Osvaldo Sunkel and Pedro Paz, *El subdesarrollo latinoamericano y la teoría del desarrollo* (Mexico: Siglo Veintiuno de Espana 1970), p. 6, as quoted in J. Samuel Valenzuela and Arturo Valenzuela, "Modernization and Dependency," *Comparative Politics, 10* (1978), pp. 543–557.
11. For a good discussion of this position, see Teresa Hayter, *Aid as Imperialism* (Middlesex, England: Penguin, 1971).
12. For example, see Wontack Hong, *Trade, Distortions, and Employment Growth in Korea* (Seoul: Korea Development Institute, 1979).
13. Seiji Naya, Miguel Urrutia, Shelley Mark, and Alfredo Fuentes, eds., *Lessons in Development* (San Francisco: International Center for International Growth, 1989), p. 287; The World Bank, *World Development Report 1997* (New York: Oxford University Press, 1997); C. J. Dahlman and O. Sananikone, "Taiwan, China: Policies and Institutions for Rapid Growth," in Danny M. Leipziger, ed., *Lessons from East Asia* (Ann Arbor: University of Michigan Press, 1997), p. 85.

14. William E. James, Seiji Naya, and Gerald M. Meier, *Asian Development: Economic Success and Policy Lessons* (Madison: University of Wisconsin Press, 1989), pp. 69–74.
15. Ibid., p. 81.
16. Stephan Haggard, *Pathways from the Periphery: The Politics of Growth in the Newly Industrializing Countries* (Ithaca, NY: Cornell University Press, 1990), p. 196.
17. Jorge Ospina Sardi, "Trade Policy in Latin America," in Naya et al., eds., *Lessons in Development*, p. 81.
18. Haggard, *Pathways from the Periphery*, p. 26.
19. Youngil Lim, "Comparing Brazil and Korea," in Naya et al., eds., *Lessons in Development*, pp. 102–103.
20. Nigel Harris, *The End of the Third World* (New York: Meredith, 1986), pp. 90–91.
21. The World Bank, *The East Asian Miracle: Economic Growth and Public Policy* (New York: Oxford University Press, 1993).
22. Joseph Stiglitz and Shahid Yusuf, eds., *Rethinking the Asian Miracle* (New York: Oxford University Press, 2001).
23. Muhammad Yunus, *Banker to the Poor: Micro-lending and the Battle Against World Poverty* (New York: Public Affairs, 1999).
24. United Nations, www.un.org/millenniumgoals.
25. Jeffrey D. Sachs, *The End of Poverty: Economic Possibilities for Our Time* (New York: Penguin, 2005), p. 82.
26. Oxfam International, *Paying the Price: Why Rich Countries Must Invest Now in a War on Poverty* (Oxford: Oxfam International, 2005).
27. See Jeffrey D. Sachs, "Institutions Matter, but Not for Everything," *Finance and Development*, 40 (June 2003), pp. 38–41.
28. Sachs, *The End of Poverty: Economic Possibilities for Our Time*, p. 74.
29. Ibid., pp. 74–89.
30. See Rina Bhattacharya and Benedict Clements, "Calculating the Benefits of Debt Relief" *Finance and Development*, 41 (December 2004), pp. 48–50.
31. See The World Bank, *Economic Growth in the 1990s: Learning from a Decade of Reform* (Washington, DC: The World Bank, 2005).
32. See Dani Rodrik, "Goodbye Washington Consensus, Hello Washington Confusion," *Journal of Economic Literature*, 44 (December 2006), pp. 973–987.

# The Human Connection

## By Monica DeHart and Nick Kontogeorgopoulos

### OVERVIEW[1]

Movements of people are every bit as controversial and important as flows of corporate bonds, auto parts, prescription medications, or arms negotiators. Indeed, some of the most contentious political battles of the last few years have been about how to deal with various kinds of human movement. In 2005, youth from immigrant families rioted in the suburbs of Paris to challenge their long-standing social and political exclusion. Millions of Latino immigrants marched through U.S. cities in 2006 to demand a path toward citizenship for the estimated 12 million irregular immigrants in the United States. Meanwhile, Ukraine put in place new laws to curb an alarming trend of human trafficking of its women. Germany debated the failure of a guest worker program designed to bring in highly skilled labor to support its growing information technology sector.

Whether we are talking about the global circulation of unskilled migrant laborers, technology industry professionals, political refugees, tourists, terrorists, or nongovernmental organization activists, new patterns of human flows have been both a central feature and an important effect of globalization. These changing forms of human movement can have important consequences for how states, international organizations, nongovernmental organizations, and local communities perceive and negotiate their relationship to people inside and beyond national borders.

Consequently, new and different forms of human connection challenge and raise questions about some of the basic precepts of international political economy. For example, why do people increasingly define their identities, communities, livelihoods, politics, and leisure activities in terms other than those related to the nation-state? And what effects do these movements have on the four structures of IPE (security, production and trade, knowledge and technology, and money and finance)? Through a focus on two particularly salient forms of human movement—migration and tourism—this chapter explores the changing nature of local and global connections and their implications for IPE.

International political economy (IPE) is not just about state and markets. If anything, issues that focus specifically on various societies and their cultures and values have not received the attention they deserve in the IPE literature, which is dominated by issues surrounding the relationship of states to markets. As noted in Chapter 1, society is one of the basic elements of IPE. States represent one type of social group—the national society—whereas markets reflect and influence what various societies need and produce. This chapter focuses more directly on people and their connections to one another, which result in what some experts refer to as a social network, system, or structure. Regardless of the label, each of these sets of human connections shapes the behavior of international and national actors, IPE structures, and the outcome of a variety of policy issues and problems.

The analysis of human connections is one of the important new directions of IPE as it broadens its scope to account for global change. In this chapter we cover two important networks of human connection: migration and tourism. One theme of the chapter is that IPE theories can help explain a variety of developments in these networks. The United Nations estimates that about 191 million people, or almost 3 percent of the world's population, are migrants living away from their native country.[2] The United States is home to the largest number of those migrants, who make up 12 percent of the U.S. population. In many cases, migrant flows are related to the collapse of governments; efforts to gain "guest worker" privileges in another country; efforts to escape war, poverty, or natural disaster; or simply the search for freedom and prosperity.

Tourism accounts for the movement of individuals from one location to another. Unlike migrants, tourists travel for reasons related to leisure and recreation.[3] To many people, travel is an escape from the routines of everyday life, but tourism should receive serious academic and policy consideration. Patterns and trends in the global travel and tourism industry closely mirror several features of the world system.

In this chapter we will also consider the major roles played by many different international organizations (IOs) and nongovernmental organizations (NGOs) alongside nation-states in managing migration and tourism issues. As noted in previous chapters, not only have the numbers of IOs and NGOs proliferated greatly since World War II, so have their efforts intensified to solve a variety of international and global problems. This has been especially true in the case of human connections: In many cases, civil society or nonstate actors are challenging nation-states in dealing effectively with interdependencies or new issues generated by globalization.[4]

## THE IPE OF MIGRATION

### Redefining Migration

In its simplest sense, **migration** refers to movement from one place to another—to a nearby city, another region, or another country entirely. Migration may be temporary or permanent; there is nothing about the notion of migration itself that guarantees either the length of residence or the strength of the commitment to the migratory destination. The reasons for migration are diverse: People may not have permanent work or sufficient resources to sustain themselves in their home environment. They may wish to pursue advanced educational or professional opportunities. They may not be able to express their ideas or practice their religion in the way that they choose. They may face environmental devastation or political turmoil. They may be separated from family members.

Migration has long been an integral force in shaping both individual nation-states and their relationships to one another within the global landscape. Nonetheless, over the last few decades we have seen human movement occur on a scale and intensity that was unheard of in the past. Breakthroughs in technology and travel have allowed a broad array of people to move across borders and time zones as part of (or to ensure) their daily lives. Both men and women have blazed new migration trails and contributed to the construction of vibrant multicultural communities that extend across the globe. By 2005, the UN estimated that more than 191 million people were residing in a country other than where they were born. In forty-one countries, migrants constituted as much as 20 percent of the total population![5]

The increased frequency of migration in the world has also been accompanied by new patterns of movement. Whereas previous travel routes were characterized by journeys east and west, or colonial forays south, current migration is characterized by more south–north or even south–south migration. This pattern is reflected in the fact that one-third of international migrants moved from developing to developed countries (often from former colonies), while another third moved from developing to other developing countries. Nearly six of every ten international migrants now live in high-income countries that include developing countries such as Bahrain, Brunei, Kuwait, Qatar, the Republic of Korea, and Saudi Arabia.[6] Furthermore, whereas people were once presumed to migrate in order to take up permanent residence in their destinations, their movement is now often temporary and circular.

Despite the diverse reasons why people move, when we talk about migration we tend to focus mostly on the temporary movement of labor. In general, labor migrants relocate on a short-term basis to take advantage of employment opportunities. This kind of movement can take the form of **internal migration**—for example, movement from the country to the city, or from one area of the country to another. Internal migration, and rural–urban migration in particular, has been a central feature of IPE theories of development (see Chapter 15). In these theories, migration within the nation has often been seen as a crucial component of national efforts toward urbanization, industrialization, and modernization. As the case of China illustrates, however, internal migration can also have complex unintended consequences for state development efforts. See the box, "Mapping Modernization: China's Internal Migration."

---

### MAPPING MODERNIZATION: CHINA'S INTERNAL MIGRATION

The relationship between internal migration and national development is the subject of much debate in contemporary China. Over the past two decades, massive national economic growth has caused a steady flow of rural peasants to China's booming cities. The rural–urban flow was estimated to have reached 140 million in 2003, representing a doubling in volume since 1993.[a] This migration reflects China's explosive modernization, but contemporary rural–urban migration has also caused some serious social and political dilemmas.

In China, all people must register in their place of birth in order to receive citizenship and government services there. In the past, the Chinese state relied on this system of registration (*hukou*) to separate urban and rural populations and thus ensure a sufficient rural population to provide agricultural production for the nation. However, just as in the Western industrialized countries, the introduction of the market economy, the modernization and mechanization of rural agriculture, and the shift from collective to household production systems in China have made many rural farmers "surplus" labor. In an effort to take advantage of growing economic opportunities in the cities, many have taken part in a large-scale exodus from agriculture toward urban economic enterprises. These mobile peasants are known as a "floating population" because they have become part of a nonregistered community without permission to reside permanently in the cities.

Some of these migrants work in seasonal occupations, sending money back to their rural communities until they return at harvest time to complete the agricultural cycle.[b] Other migrants set up informal businesses—as reflected in the growing garment industry in Beijing. In both cases, however, migrants face serious discrimination from urban natives, who often see them as dirty, crafty delinquents who are responsible for urban disorder and crime.[c] Furthermore, they must confront discriminatory labor and business licensing practices put in place by the state to dissuade them from settling permanently in the cities. China argues that it must control migration to avoid producing urban slums in and around its large cities, as we see in India or

São Paolo. Nonetheless, the Chinese state has also resorted to issuing new identification cards that travel with the individual, rather than being tied to place (as *hukou* is), as a means of regulating this increasingly mobile population. Ironically, then, part of China's development strategy involves looking for new incentives to keep people in the rural areas.

*References*

[a] See China News, "China's Floating Population Exceeded 10% of Total," January 16, 2005, www. chinanews.cn, accessed June 16, 2006; and Li Zhang, *Strangers in the City: Reconfigurations of Space, Power and Social Networks Within China's Floating Population* (Stanford, CA: Stanford University Press, 2001).

[b] See "The Floating People," *U.S. News & World Report*, June 20, 2005, www.usnews.com, accessed August 7, 2006.

[c] Dorothy Solinger, *Contesting Citizenship in Urban China* (Berkeley: University of California Press, 1999).

## Transnational Migration

An important trend in today's migration is the increasing tendency of people to move not simply to nearby cities, but to different countries altogether. Whether we are talking about unskilled labor or highly educated professionals, **transnational migration** describes the now-frequent process by which people cross state borders in search of temporary work or for other reasons. This more global migration trajectory is compounded by a tendency toward **circular migration**, by which migrants follow a shifting pattern of movement back and forth between home and work communities in response to different economic opportunities, employment conditions, and family needs or responsibilities.

For example, every September, thousands of young men from Mali and Niger travel to the Cote D'Ivoire and other West African countries to seek wage-labor opportunities along the coast. They remain in these jobs until the spring, when they return home to attend to their crops.[7] This migration pattern, and the income it provides, is essential to sustaining a rural agricultural lifestyle, even though it requires the men to spend half of each year abroad. As another example, women from the Philippines and mainland China migrate to Hong Kong to labor as domestic workers for middle- and upper-class professional families. The Filipina maids' residence in Hong Kong is limited by the term of their employment contract, such that many return home after completing a few years of service.[8] Once home, however, they often solicit a new employment contract and return to Hong Kong for another cycle of labor.

Circular transnational migration is an essential part of changing economic conditions and political relations associated with globalization. As global capitalist production becomes more mobile, migrant workers tend to move to labor markets where there is high demand and low domestic supply. For this reason, migrants often fill jobs at both ends of the labor market. Engineers and scientists take highly specialized professional positions within the technology or aerospace industries. Unskilled workers fill labor and service jobs that few native workers will do—for example, in the food service and garment industries, meat packing, domestic labor, or agriculture. Furthermore, declining population growth in countries such as Germany and Japan has increased the need for workers in general, thus making them a prime destination for foreign labor migrants.[9] From Saudi Arabia to Spain to the United States, changing economic and demographic conditions have required most developed countries to make some accommodations for migrant labor within their borders.

States with high demand for foreign workers, such as Singapore, Kuwait, or Germany, have developed temporary foreign worker, or **guest worker**, programs that regulate the provisional admission, residence, and employment of a specific class of migrant labor. These migration policies usually do not allow whole families to enter the country or provide for the possibility of long-term residence or eventual citizenship. Instead, guest worker programs are aimed at utilizing cheap labor and then keeping migrants moving.

A prime example of this kind of program was the U.S. Bracero Program. Between 1942 and 1964, the initiative permitted the entry of temporary workers from Mexico to fill U.S. wartime labor shortages in the agricultural sector. By the 1950s, however, the United States sought to deter the permanent settling of Bracero workers and the entry of new Mexican migrants, to prevent the expansion of immigrant labor into nonagricultural sectors and to curb the rising levels of unemployment among domestic laborers. The United States thus launched the unfortunately named initiative, Operation Wetback, to locate and deport "illegal" migrants.[10]

The circumscribed residency status of temporary workers is exacerbated by their limited labor rights and potential subjection to discrimination and abuse. In a recent study of Jordanian garment factories, Bangladeshi workers who were interviewed reported that their employers had confiscated their passports, forced them to work 48-hour periods, provided insufficient sleeping accommodations, and refused to pay mandated overtime pay.[11] The situation for undocumented workers can be just as bad or worse, as these workers often have no recourse in filing complaints against employers who abuse or fail to pay them.

National programs are therefore complemented by international treaties such as the UN's 1990 International Convention on the Protection of Rights of All Migrant Workers, which clarified migrant worker categories and reiterated the receiving states' responsibility to protect migrants' rights. These treaties acknowledge the need for global standards to regulate human flows and protect individual rights as people increasingly live their lives in places outside their place of birth.

One reason that temporary labor migration is attractive to both migrants and sending states is because of the possibility for **remittances**—income earned abroad that is sent back to the home country. Global remittances have doubled over the last decade, reaching $232 billion by 2005.[12] To give a sense of the relative effect of these payments, the more than 1 million Guatemalans estimated to be living in the United States in 2005 remitted over $3 billion to families and communities in Guatemala; this amount exceeded the income from exports and tourism for the country as a whole![13] Most remittances are used to supplement individual household incomes, but they are also important for offsetting the cost of education and health care. Furthermore, in some cases, home-town associations—formed by migrants from a single community—have consolidated their remittances to finance infrastructure and development projects in their home communities.[14] Migrants are thus a vital element in the development of their home countries.

Migrant trajectories are shaped not only by economic incentives but also by political and social factors. As an example, Thai migrants have a long history of moving back and forth across the Malaysian border to perform temporary work; however, because of the ease of movement, they tend not to settle permanently in Malaysia. Indonesian migrants, on the other hand, encounter much stricter controls on their entry into Malaysia, and therefore tend to stay once they arrive.[15] Circular migration to and from the United States has declined over the last few decades as border security has increased. Ironically, then, because undocumented migrants from Mexico have found it more and more difficult to return home, border security has actually accelerated the rate of growth of the undocumented population.[16] As these cases demonstrate, factors such as official entry requirements often influence the type and permanence of migration.

The degree and frequency of temporary labor migration is also encouraged by the growing presence of transnational social networks of kin and neighbors on whom migrants can depend to find a place of residence and work. This pattern of **chain migration** promotes the concentration of migrant communities in enclaves or gateway cities, which are oriented around immigrant culture and practical needs. In these enclaves, it is possible for a migrant to speak his or her native language, buy "home-style" food, make quick wire transfers to people back home, and practice local customs.

For example, Roger Rouse studied the large numbers of Mexicans who moved between Aguililla, Michoacan, and Redwood City, California.[17] The concentration of migrants moving between one small town in Michoacan and Redwood City had become so marked by the mid-1990s that many people began referring to parts of Redwood City itself as Aguililla. Indeed, most men in the community spent a portion of their lives moving back and forth across the border between what were, in essence, the two communities of Aguililla. Consequently, community members were able to draw on a deeply embedded transnational network to facilitate ongoing transfers of people, money, and resources.

Though it is widespread, the current global pattern of transnational migration has created some serious problems for both sending and receiving states. At the most basic level, temporary migration patterns have complicated efforts to determine national populations. After all, states govern according to the size and characteristics of their national population. So how do we count population when a significant segment of that population may be working or residing abroad? Although this may not seem like a big problem for some states, you can get a sense of the problem when you look at countries such as the Philippines, which has an estimated 8.1 million residents (that is, 10 percent of the population) living and working abroad.[18]

In receiving states, new migration patterns have created another kind of demographic predicament, one with similarly important political implications. In the United States and Great Britain, the combination of increasing immigration rates and higher population growth rates among immigrant families has meant that the immigrant population is growing faster than the native-born population. This has led some nativist constituencies to worry about becoming a minority in their own country.[19] It has also fueled concerns about the potential effect that the growing immigrant population will have on electoral politics—a point to which we will return later.

## Irregular Migrants

Many states are also struggling with a high incidence of **irregular migrants**—undocumented or illegal migrants—flowing into their countries. Rather than getting the necessary work permits before entering the country, these migrants are entering the country without visas or staying on after their work visas have expired. In Spain, North African migrants from Senegal have been streaming into the country in large numbers over the past few years by using the Canary Islands (a Spanish territory just off West Africa) or Malta as the first step on their route. In 2006, their large numbers caused a humanitarian crisis in the Canary Islands and also protest from native Spanish residents, who saw them as a threat to economic stability and national security.[20] In Brunei, because of the high level of temporary migrant labor from India and the Philippines, a special task force was set up to "apprehend" workers who had stayed in the country beyond the stipulated term of their work visa.[21] These cases raise the question of how to regulate temporary labor flows so as to complement domestic needs while also maintaining control over one's borders.

The European Union (EU) has grappled with this issue as it has extended membership to post-Soviet states and now contemplates Turkey's admission. Many of the original EU members imposed migration limits to mitigate the prospective flood of migrants that they feared would emerge with the inclusion of poorer Eastern European members in 2004. Even though this flood never occurred, and studies show that states that maintained labor limits suffered "undesirable economic side effects" compared to countries that maintained open borders, one of the main points of opposition to Turkey's inclusion has been the ongoing fear of waves of cheap labor from Asia and the Middle East.[22] These fears grow out of the fact that Turkey, like Spain, is no longer defined by out-migration of its citizens but rather by inmigration—in this case, of migrants from Afghanistan, Bangladesh, Iraq, and Iran, as well as former Soviet states. These irregular migrants often move to **transit states** such as Turkey, as a first step toward greater economic opportunities in more affluent countries of the EU. In the context of increasing regional migration, the migration policies of individual EU member states thus come to matter greatly.

## Brain Drain

Temporary labor migration includes not only flows of unskilled labor but also the movement of highly educated professionals. Thus, increasing levels of global migration also pose another kind of problem for developing states. These nations often lament the **brain drain** that occurs as the most educated members of their societies migrate to more developed nations where there are higher salaries and more employment opportunities. Through brain drain, developing states not only lose important human resources necessary for their own development, they also complain that they are essentially subsidizing the development of human capital for the richer nations. For this reason, developing countries often create incentives and/or sanctions to either keep their professionals at home or to ensure their return from education abroad as a crucial means of repatriating knowledge and technology.

A contentious example of this phenomenon can be seen today in the U.S. nursing industry. In the context of negotiating immigration reform, U.S. lawmakers decided *not* to place limits on the number of visas allotted for foreign nurses. This move was in response to a grave shortage of domestic nurses. The move, however, has caused great controversy in developing nations such as the Philippines and Fiji, which anticipate grave consequences as the United States woos some of their most valuable health care resources, leaving them without the personnel to deal with serious public health issues.[23] Meanwhile, U.S. nurses are frustrated at the thought of solving the shortage by importing foreign labor rather than promoting more training programs and incentives in the United States.

## Citizenship

The complex economic, political, and social implications of new forms of human movement are intensified when we consider what happens when immigrants stop moving. Whereas migration simply signals movement from one place to another, **immigration** refers to migration to a new country for the purpose of settling and becoming a resident of the destination country. In many ways, we might think of the distinction between a migrant and an immigrant as the difference between a round-trip traveler whose affiliations remain rooted in his home community and a traveler with a one-way ticket who has an interest in making a new life in his destination community. However, though these differences appear clear on paper, their distinction in real life is much fuzzier. Indeed, the saying, "Nothing is as permanent as a temporary migrant" rings all too true for many a state. So, why is the distinction between migrant and immigrant important? In many ways, this question reaches to the heart of current immigration debates, highlighting the importance of changing formulations of national identity, political security, and global economics.

One of the chief functions of the modern state is to control its borders and protect its citizens' rights. *Citizenship* is a legal category that entitles a person to full and equal rights within a given state, perhaps most importantly including the right to vote. However, states have various means of assigning that status. Citizenship may be granted based on birth, ethnicity, or naturalization. Anyone born on U.S. soil is eligible to apply for citizenship. Furthermore, once immigrants to the United States obtain a "green card," they can eventually earn the chance to be naturalized as citizens. Because they provide immigrants the opportunity to become permanent residents, countries such as the United States or Australia are known as **settler states**. By contrast, people born on German soil do not necessarily receive citizenship. Instead, German citizenship is granted through one's parents: One must have a German mother or father, or a parent with established permanent residence, to become a German national. Restrictive migration policies in countries such as Japan and Saudi Arabia make it even harder for migrants to become citizens of those countries.

Another way that people can make a claim for permanent residence in a country that is not their own is through refugee status or asylum. Indeed, refugees currently account for 23 percent of all international migrants in the least developed countries.[24] **Refugees** are displaced people who are unable or unwilling to return to their country of origin because of fear of persecution on account of race, religion, nationality, membership in a particular social group, or political opinion. A Sudanese victim of factional violence who has moved to a temporary camp in Chad could be considered a refugee. Often the UN High Commission on Refugees may be responsible for negotiating a permanent resettlement destination—either in Chad or in another country—for this Sudanese refugee.

People who seek **asylum** are also permanently displaced people who face persecution in their home countries. These immigrants, however, often make their claims for protection to a court within the nation in which they hope to reside, usually from within that nation's territory. Between 1994 and 2004, 6.1 million asylum applications were filed globally, 79 percent in Europe, 20 percent in North America, and the rest in Australia, Japan, and New Zealand.[25] A Bosnian Muslim suffering from political persecution in the former Yugoslavia might petition the Canadian government for asylum once she was on Canadian soil or in a Canadian port of entry. If her asylum claim were granted, she would be given refugee status and permitted to stay in Canada with social and economic rights.

Currently, the countries responsible for generating the most asylum seekers worldwide are China, Russia, and Serbia. In 2004, over 20,000 people from China applied for asylum in other countries. The top countries for receiving asylum claims are Germany, the United States, and the United Kingdom.

Citizenship and asylum are much more than just legal categories, however. In practice, these two terms are highly contested designations with important political and cultural significance for society, states, and the international system in general. The rules for defining refugee status can often be a highly politicized matter of geopolitics, such as the U.S.'s opposition to communism. For example, a recent study shows that the U.S. government has granted political asylum to 80 percent of Cuban asylum applicants. This high rate might be read as a reflection of the assumption that all Cubans are political refugees fleeing an authoritarian, communist regime. In contrast, the same study showed that the United States granted asylum to only 10 percent of Haitian applicants. Even though these immigrants come from a neighboring island wracked by violence and political instability, Haitians tend to be seen as economic migrants rather than refugees.[26]

Even when foreigners acquire legal residence or citizenship in their adopted countries, another problem remains: how to integrate them into the social fabric of their new homes. Despite their legal status, immigrants may still feel like second-class citizens in their day-to-day encounters with community members and local institutions, being denied everyday privileges afforded to native residents. Often this marginalization coincides with perceived differences in language, customs, and cultural values. Instead of following a process of **assimilation**—whereby an immigrant takes on the values and customs of the new prevailing culture—immigrant communities are frequently marked by their difference. However, immigrant disenfranchisement also correlates with structural inequalities such as differences in education, class, and race. In other words, even when immigrants assume local language, values, and orientations, they sometimes remain subject to discrimination. Consequently, immigrant struggles for social recognition and political inclusion have fueled some of the major social and political conflicts in recent years. The term **cultural citizenship** effectively describes immigrants' demands within these conflicts—that is, they seek a sense of social belonging that is not contingent on assimilation, but rather is built on a respect for diversity.[27]

Two weeks of rioting by youth in Paris suburbs during 2005 represent a case in point. The clashes between youth and the French police were attributed largely to the extreme social marginalization and impoverishment experienced by North African immigrants and their descendants, despite their official French citizenship. This contradiction prompted a *New York Times* article to raise the important question, "What makes someone French?"[28] Because the French have always insisted on a secular national identity, they have glossed over racial and cultural distinctions rather than try and address their social and political effects. The French government's 2004 ban on the wearing of head scarves or other religious paraphernalia in public schools illustrates just such an attempt to suppress the visibility of cultural differences.[29] Now, however, the French and many of their European counterparts are trying to find a way to recognize diversity, both to create a more multicultural society and also to defuse the move by disenfranchised immigrant youth toward radical or fundamentalist organizations.[30]

As the French case makes clear, the increasingly multicultural societies created by immigration require new ways of thinking about what makes someone an authentic citizen of the nation and thus brings into focus contradictions in the definition of the nation itself. Porous state borders and fluid patterns of human movement challenge the assumption that the modern nation is defined not only by a sovereign state but also by a singular, common history and culture. This challenge is true in the United States, as well, despite the fact that immigration is a central feature of U.S. national identity. For example, in 2006 a musical collaboration produced the first Spanish-language version of the U.S. national anthem ("The Star Spangled Banner"). "Nuestro Himno," as the track is called, emerged at a moment of intense national debate over the immigration question. It called attention to what many view as the increasingly diverse and politicized reality of U.S. national culture. However, it also perturbed many pundits who saw the song as an attack not only on the United States's primary language—English—but also on the Anglo values and identity that they claimed defined U.S. history.[31]

Both the French and the U.S. immigration debates highlight the importance not simply of cultural values, but also of race, in defining the terms of national identity and citizenship. To explain the marginalization of immigrant groups, many scholars of U.S. immigration history have compared the experience of early twentieth-century immigrants from Europe with the experience of post-1965 immigrants from Asia and Latin America. Although earlier immigrants were originally identified as distinct races—Irish, Italian, Jewish—a sense of their racial difference largely disappeared as they assimilated to Anglo values and became upwardly mobile. Consequently, these European immigrants have increasingly been seen as "white." In contrast, later immigrants who are marked by darker skin or other phenotypical differences have been unable to shed their racial identities even when they assume "American" values, speak English, and acquire middle-class status.[32] In these cases, it is the perceived racial difference, as much as or more than cultural difference, that explains specific groups' lack of cultural citizenship.

The continued importance of race in conversations about citizenship indicates some of the contradictions inherent in the new forms of human movement and connections emerging through globalization. We frequently hear stories about how our new globalized world has allowed mobile, enterprising migrants to access resources and opportunities unimaginable in their home country. This perspective chalks up immigrant success or failure, belonging or marginalization, to individual actions and values that are sometimes extended to an entire ethnic or national group. A closer look, however, demonstrates how racial, gender, class, and national differences (among others) continue to exert a strong influence over individual and group mobility and the outcome of that movement. For example, what forces govern who migrates, how, and to where? How is the immigration experience shaped by whether one is white or black, male or female, urban and educated or a rural peasant? Furthermore, how do certain patterns of migration reproduce inequalities between regions and groups rather than transcend them? In other words, does the fact that Dominicans emigrate in high numbers and remit large amounts of money to the Dominican Republic evidence growing individual freedom and a globalized form of national development or ongoing dependency and underdevelopment? Although increased global migration seems to point to expanding opportunities for individual autonomy and mobility, immigrants' experiences also ask us to reconsider the ongoing structural inequalities that condition their movement and ultimate migration outcomes.

## Political and Economic Effects

Clearly, then, new global migration patterns present many complex trade-offs. Politicians, policy analysts, academics, and community members often debate these trade-offs in terms that invoke IPE theories. For example, those adhering to an economic liberal perspective argue that migrant labor is a natural part of the free-market system and therefore should be allowed to flow freely. From this view, foreign labor supports economic growth in industries in which domestic labor is too expensive or unavailable. Therefore, even if immigrant labor displaces small numbers of native labor, depresses wages, or requires benefits, neoliberal perspectives highlight these facts as economic trade-offs that are outweighed by the lower prices enjoyed by consumers, the higher profits enjoyed by employers, and the generalized levels of economic growth that result from immigrant labor. Supporting this view, a recent study estimated that legalizing the more than 12 million irregular migrants in the United States would cost approximately $54 billion in benefits between 2007 and 2016; however, those costs would be offset by $66 billion of new revenue that immigrant workers would add to the Treasury through income and payroll taxes, Social Security withholding, and fines and fees required by law.[33]

Political liberals also tend to support migration on the basis of their belief in the individual's right to freedom of movement as part of a bundle of basic human rights. This view is especially prevalent in cases of migrants fleeing repression or violence in their home country because, according to liberal political philosophy, our obligations as humans extend beyond national borders. What many political liberals call for, then, is simply more effective ways of regulating the flow of immigrants across borders.

Some of the most strident opposition to migration these days comes from those who claim that migrants pose a threat to domestic labor markets, stealing jobs and lowering wages, especially for low-skilled native workers. Many of these critics claim that immigrants place a heavy toll on health care, schools, and other state services.[34] An extreme manifestation of this ideology in 1994 prompted California's Proposition 187, which attempted to deny social services to immigrants who could not prove legal residency. This perspective has also fueled vigilante groups such as the Minutemen, who claim that their efforts to patrol and actively deter immigration along the U.S.–Mexico border are born of a sense of patriotism and defense of U.S. sovereignty.[35] Similarly in Europe, conservative politicians in Italy, France, the Netherlands, and Britain have made nativist politics and opposition to immigration a central feature of recent elections.[36] We might identify this perspective as mercantilist because of its economic nationalist sentiment and use of comparative advantage to justify limits on the mobility of labor. In its current ideological manifestation, mercantilist positions also tend to equate domestic political security with economic security, worrying that migrants represent serious breaches to both.

Those adhering to a structuralist view may also oppose some dimensions of migration, but for radically different reasons than their mercantilist counterparts. Structuralists see increasing migration is a result of the underdevelopment produced by global inequality. From this standpoint, the global division of labor is responsible for creating impoverished nations whose citizens have no choice but to migrate in order to support their families. Free-trade zones flood local markets with foreign goods, destroying local production and local enterprises so that workers must migrate to find new labor opportunities. Furthermore, structuralists often criticize the exploitation of these unskilled migrants within the richer countries as further evidence of the need to restructure the terms of global capitalist production and trade.

Multiculturalism and citizenship also figure into the political and economic debates on immigration. North American society has struggled to assimilate its large numbers of Latino and Asian immigrants—a task that some claim has been made easier by the shared faith between immigrants and natives, as well as the active role that churches play in integrating new arrivals.[37] However, many conservative politicians worry about the growing ranks of what they see as historically liberal constituencies. In Europe, large numbers of Muslim immigrants from Northern Africa and the Middle East have made cultural assimilation more difficult and, in a post-9/11 world, the stakes higher. In both places, states and citizens are grappling with how to reconcile democracy's values with changing demographics and cultural politics.[38] Some argue that the prospect of achieving social and political integration is further complicated by efforts to restrict migration though "temporary worker" programs. For example, critics have slammed efforts to create a contract labor program in the United States on the basis that it would institutionalize an already disenfranchised workforce with no voting rights, weakening U.S. democracy.[39]

From these examples, we can see that moral and ideological considerations are just as important as economic calculations in deciding what is at stake in new patterns of global migration. The complex human dimensions of globalization force us to question the role of the nation-state in defining identity and political action in the world today. If people increasingly live their lives across borders, what new kinds of communities are important for defining identities and politics?

## Diaspora

**Diaspora** is a term that has historically been used to describe communities that were displaced and dispersed across a number of communities worldwide. The Jews' expulsion from Babylon in the fifth century B.C. produced one of the first examples of diaspora, with subsequent generations proliferating Jewish communities across the globe. The trade of African slaves throughout South and North America, as well as the United Kingdom, created what is now known as the African diaspora. In both of these cases, the forcible displacement of people from their homeland resulted in transnational communities that identify with a common history and ethnic identity even though they might speak different languages and be citizens of other states.

Today, the concept of diaspora has expanded to refer to a much broader array of transnational communities. We can talk of the Indian, Iranian, Filipino, Chinese, or Haitian diasporas as communities created through an intense process of migration and global dispersion. Diasporic communities may be linked to a specific nation-state—such as the case of the Irish diaspora—or may be a stateless nation—such as the Kurds. Regardless of type, diasporas are increasingly significant both for the new kinds of social, political, and economic organizations they represent and also for the effects they have had on political and economic processes in their home countries.

New information technology has played an important role in consolidating and supporting diasporic communities. Now, even when immigrants cannot easily or frequently travel between origin and adoptive countries, they can keep abreast of local news through online media, participate in virtual chatroom conversations with other diaspora members, and manage individual and group finances through Internet banking. Many local communities have begun creating Web pages to keep residents living abroad informed about local needs and goings-on, as well as to stimulate outside investment and participation in local events.[40] The global expansion of cellular phone service to rural areas, as well as Internet conferencing services, have facilitated real-time communication between immigrants and their kin in historically remote areas. All of these technologies allow people to maintain social connections across borders, preserving community language, identity, and politics at any distance.

In some cases, the formation of a diasporic or transnational community is self-consciously cultivated as a means of promoting national development in a home country. In these cases, rather than emigration and permanent residence in a foreign country signifying a shift in one's national identity, migration simply signals a shift in the place from which this happens. For instance, Haitian refugees in New York see their long-term residence and labors abroad as part of a concerted campaign to improve and support their homeland. Glick-Schiller and Fouron have called this phenomenon "long-distance nationalism" because of the way that residence abroad becomes simply another way of practicing a deeply felt nationalist identification with one's home country. In this formulation, the Haitian community is defined not by its residence on Haitian soil but rather by its common Haitian blood and obligation to the homeland.[41] Migrant circuits, such as the Mexican Aguilillan community discussed earlier, represent another case in point, using transnational community to promote development at home in Michoacan.

The connection between diaspora and development is also evident in the wake of the destruction wrought by the 2005 tsunami in Indonesia. Following the disaster, victims called on Indian, Sri Lankan, Indonesian, and Thai diasporic groups to aid their fellow countrymen in the recovery effort. Vishwa Hindu Parishad, an Indian organization in the United States, raised $40,000 to help tsunami victims in India. A Tamil federation in South Africa launched a special fund to help Sri Lankans left homeless by the disaster. The Sri Lankan president demonstrated the Sri Lankan state's reliance on these important foreign resources by asking Sri Lankan doctors to bring their professional skills home to help.[42]

However, diaspora's influence goes far beyond the power of remittances and emergency organizing; diasporic communities have also demonstrated themselves to be powerful political agents and advocates. For example, in 2005, Somalis living in Canada successfully lobbied the Canadian government to increase its aid to Somalia when international funding for the country waned.[43] Jewish and Cuban diaspora members have been a powerful constituency in U.S. national politics, intensely lobbying and effectively shaping U.S. foreign policy on issues pertaining to the Middle East and Cuba. As the examples in the following box illustrate, these transnational communities both reflect and reproduce the blurred boundaries between "local" and "global" political and cultural processes.

---

### GLOBAL FOLKS: ANGELINA JOLIE AND BLUEGRASS MUSIC

What do Angelina Jolie and banjos have in common? On the one hand, the frantic Hollywood hype about Angelina and the rural folk traditions that define the banjo might seem to reflect opposite poles of a uniquely U.S. popular culture. On the other hand, celebrity activists and bluegrass music also exemplify the complex, fluid relationship between what we often distinguish as either local or global forces. A quick look at popular trends highlights this changing face of culture within the international political economy.

In 2002, UN Secretary General Kofi Annan approached the podium at UN Headquarters and admitted to the assembled, "When I walked into this room, I wasn't sure I was in the right place. I wondered whether it was a combination of the Oscars, the Olympics, the Grammies or the Pulitzers."[a] The reason for Annan's feigned confusion? Rather than the diplomats and heads of state that frequent the corridors of the UN Headquarters, Annan was instead standing before some of the world's most famous athletes, entertainers, and artists. These notables were the UN's Messengers of Peace and Goodwill Ambassadors, volunteer celebrity advocates promoting the UN's mission around the world. "Seriously," he continued, "it fills me with bewilderment and awe to enter a room filled with such talent and fame—and what is more, talent and fame that is being used for the betterment of mankind."[b] With those flattering words, Kofi Annan opened the UN's second-ever conference and workshop on celebrity advocacy.

Increasingly, mass media outlets and national and international leaders are trumpeting the work and effects of celebrity activists on the international political economy. Supermarket glossies such as *Us Weekly*, television shows such as *Entertainment Tonight*, even major national newspapers such as *USA Today* highlight the philanthropy of stars from Angelina Jolie to Bono. What does celebrities' increased presence in politics tell us about the changing nature of our globalized world?

Although globalization is certainly nothing new, one of the characteristics of the current moment is a heightened appreciation for "global" issues. Poverty and disease, the environment, arms proliferation, human rights, energy crises—these are all areas in which we recognize how our own lives are intricately interlinked with people and events across the globe. Consequently, rather than acting as citizens of a particular nation-state, politics increasingly involves mobilizing people as citizens of a global community or *global civil society* (GCS).

New kinds of political actors, aided by new technologies, must work across borders to achieve this task. As a case in point, in 1997 a broad-based coalition of 350 humanitarian NGOs in twenty-three countries was able to coordinate efforts to ban the use of landmines, culminating in the ratification of an international treaty to that effect.[c] Significantly, these groups were awarded a Nobel Prize for their efforts, but couldn't receive the honor on time because they were so dispersed that they did not have a physical address. Thus, in this context, global celebrities clearly have an important role to play.

Bono lobbied heads of state leading up to and during the Gleneagles G8 summit, where a substantive debt-relief package was signed. Jolie, through her extensive travels throughout Africa, has brought much attention to the plight of that continent's refugees. Although the overall effect of celebrity activism is debated, the lasting effect of these efforts might be better understood in terms of the visibility that celebrities bring to global issues and their ability to recruit the global community to act. When it comes to achieving global results, activism in our current context often means mobilizing a dispersed transnational constituency, one fan at a time.

## Localization

Global fan clubs are not only evident in the changing dynamics of the international political activism; a look at the music scene might compel us to switch the activist adage "Think globally, act locally" to "Think locally, act globally." The appropriation of bluegrass music—a folk style native to Appalachia—by countries as geographically distant and culturally different as Japan, the Czech Republic, and Scotland provides a powerful example of how current international music trends often recombine local and global traditions.

Despite its humble rural origins, the international popularity of bluegrass music has been propagated through a burgeoning bluegrass music industry. Publications such as *Bluegrass Unlimited* and organizations such as the International Bluegrass Music Association have promoted the popularity of bluegrass festivals and local jam sessions worldwide. Despite this global marketing, in each of its new venues, bluegrass music is played as a way of expressing uniquely "local" feelings, experiences, and identities. Consequently, bluegrass represents not so much an example of Americanization of the world, but rather of the increasing tendency of people to use global forms to express and redefine local traditions.

In Japan, a small community of musicians has embraced bluegrass as a way to escape pop music and homogenized national culture. Although they perform their songs in English, these Japanese musicians regard bluegrass as their own form of musical expression. One musician states, "It was certainly an American tradition when it was born. However . . . it's not an American music anymore but an international music. I love bluegrass more than anybody but it's only a word. I have my own bluegrass inside me, and you have yours."[d] Groups such as the Japanese Bluegrass Band promote Japanese culture through artwork on CD covers, but the majority of tradition is implemented in community jam sessions. In jam sessions in Tokyo, "Amazing Grace" transforms into a Japanese version based on improvisation. Thus, monthly "pickings" allow the bluegrass community to build a collective identity in which Japanese tradition and bluegrass rhythms converge into a new sound.

The band Druhá Tráva is just one of the 167 bluegrass groups in the Czech Republic's thriving club scene, and it has played an influential role in cultivating the unique sound of "Czechgrass." Although critics recognize that "Many Czech musicians so exalt the American identity of bluegrass that they meticulously attempt to recreate the exact sound of American Appalachia, Druhá Tráva rejects this approach."[e] In 1999, Druhá Tráva and American musician Peter Rowan collaborated efforts on the album *New Freedom Bell* to create a "powerful meld of American and Czech sensibilities."[f] The strength of this union is evidenced by the existence of the Bluegrass Association of the Czech Republic, which supports *Bluegrassove Listy* (a bi-monthly newsletter), gives annual awards, and organizes the oldest bluegrass festival in Europe—known as the Banjo Jamboree in Caslav—along with bluegrass workshops and CD releases of nonprofessional bluegrass bands.[g] These outlets for Czechgrass prove the international role of bluegrass as an innovative form for articulating and expressing dynamic cultural traditions.

Scotland's current bluegrass scene is kept in rhythm by bands such as Goldrush and Redwing. These bands combine many interests including Scottish tradition and jazz with bluegrass, but the music remains traditional through the use of Scottish ballads. Banjo player Josh Sheldon organized the first Guildtown Bluegrass Festival in 1987, leading to the inauguration of this now-annual event and the creation of the Scottish Bluegrass Association. The festival is held "in the rural heartland of Scotland in a traditional farming community steeped in history and traditional music. People can see the connection with bluegrass and appreciate the enthusiasm it generates."[h] The Scottish Bluegrass Association establishes the country's mission to recognize and celebrate its Celtic connection, thus promoting Scottish tradition within bluegrass music.

On the global music scene, Japan, the Czech Republic, and Scotland take part in the global exchange of banjo licks and fiddle tunes, appropriating this "American" art as a way to invent and express *local* musical traditions. On the global political scene, celebrity activists use their fame to mobilize people and institutions *across* borders to confront issues that affect us all as members of a global community. Clearly, in these cases, culture plays a powerful role in defining and transcending the borders of our international political economy.

*References*

[a] Kofi Annan, "Secretary-General Urges Goodwill Ambassadors 'to Help Us Make the World a Better Place,'" United Nations, UN Conference on Celebrity Advocacy, United Nations Headquarters, New York City, June 18, 2002, www.unis.unvienna.org/unis/pressrels/2002/sgsm8277.html, accessed April 23, 2006.

[b] Ibid.

[c] P. J. Simmons, "Learning to Live with NGOs," *Foreign Policy* (Fall 1998), p. 84.

[d] Caroline Wright, "OffStage with Saburo Watanabe," www.wrightforyou.com/offstage29.html, July 2004.

[e] Ruth Ellen Gruber, "Tramping to Czechgrass," *The New Leader, 88* (September–October 2005), p. 19.

[f] Ruth Ellen Gruber, "Czechs Take Bluegrass and Make It Their Own," *The New York Times*, Online ProQuest, July 4, 2005.

[g] "Bluegrass Association of the Czech Republic," www.bacr.czechweb.cz/english.php

[h] Joe Ross, "Scotland: A Bonny Place for Bluegrass," *Bluegrass Unlimited*, April 1992, Scottish Bluegrass Association, www.scottishbluegrass.com.

The political power of diaspora is a force with which European states have increasingly had to contend. In February 2006, when a Danish newspaper published a cartoon satirizing the Prophet Muhammad, a group of Denmark's fundamentalist Muslim clerics lobbied the embassies of eleven "mostly Muslim" countries to demand a meeting with Denmark's prime minister.[44] The Danish prime minister's refusal provoked a boycott of Danish goods across the Middle East, as well as violent protests against European offices, media, and tourists throughout the region. This example demonstrates how a transnational community can be mobilized not simply on the basis of a common national identity but also on the basis of a common religious identity. With Islam as Europe's fastest-growing religion,[45] the social and political implications of an increasingly active Muslim diaspora have become the source of much debate across the continent.

Diasporas, therefore, force us to question the assumption that national identity, politics, or even development is something that is rooted within the boundaries of the nation-state. With the help of new information technologies and a highly mobile population, national identity and politics may be practiced and coordinated across the globe. Furthermore, transnational communities formed around beliefs, identities, or politics that are not tied to a particular state reflect new kinds of human connections that thus raise new challenges for both the states that contain them and the international system in general.

## INTERNATIONAL TRAVEL AND TOURISM

Like migration, tourism refers to the movement of individuals from one location to another. However, unlike temporary and permanent migrants, who move to another location to find employment or escape persecution at home, tourists—with the possible exception of business travelers—travel for reasons related to leisure and recreation.[46]

Voluntary travel across international borders produces the single largest transnational flow of human beings in the world. The World Tourism Organization (UNWTO), a specialized agency of the UN that focuses on travel and tourism, estimates that in 2004 alone, 764 million tourists traveled from one country to another, spending at least one night in the destination country. This temporary movement of people across international borders is in addition to the enormous number of domestic tourists traveling within their national borders; domestic tourists are estimated to be four to ten times the number of international tourists.[47]

Travel and tourism is the world's largest industry.[48] According to the World Travel and Tourism Council (WTTC), a privately funded global organization that brings together representatives of 100 of the world's leading travel companies, international tourists spent over $6 trillion in 2005, an increase of 5.7 percent over the previous year. The WTTC estimates that the strong growth of international travel and tourism will continue into the near future, forecasting an average annual growth rate of 4.2 percent from 2007 to 2016.[49]

Because of its mental and physical association with pleasure, tourism is often considered a light-hearted subject. To many people, travel is indeed an escape from the routines of everyday life, but tourism should, in addition to providing pleasure, receive serious academic and policy consideration because of its widespread and growing global significance. Tourism is fundamentally an IPE issue, with political, economic, social, cultural, and environmental implications. Patterns and trends in the global travel and tourism industry closely mirror, and in some cases magnify, such features of the world system as global integration, inequality, and the clash between traditional and modern cultures.

### Tourism and Economic Development

In the decades following World War II, the reconstruction of wartorn Europe, the growing prosperity of the U.S. middle class, and the implementation (especially among newly independent post-colonial states) of policies aimed at encouraging economic growth led to the rapid expansion of international tourism. Reflecting a liberal perspective, tourism advocates argued that countries should use their comparative advantage in cultural traditions, historical sites, or attractive natural landscapes in order to attract tourists and the money that they bring. In these early days of the modern tourism boom, few questions were asked about the potential harmful consequences of tourism, particularly because the economic benefits of tourism promotion seemed so significant and lasting.

There is no doubt that tourism produces tangible economic benefits. The most obvious, and attractive to governments around the world, is the creation of direct revenues that flow from tourist spending both before and during the trip, as well as from tourist payments of taxes while traveling in the host country. International tourism receipts, defined by the World Trade Organization as all payments made by international tourists for goods and services (such as food, drink, accommodation, airfare, souvenirs, and entertainment), stood at $623 billion worldwide in 2004.[50] As direct revenues circulate and are respent in the local and national economy, backward linkages to other sectors of the economy, such as transportation, construction, and agriculture, also take place as tourists stimulate demand for certain goods and services. The direct revenue created by the initial spending of tourists therefore multiplies as it percolates throughout the economy and creates linkages to industries that are not directly related to travel and tourism.

It is obvious that tourism is an important source, in absolute terms, of revenue for governments of tourist-receiving countries. Its importance is further illustrated when examining tourism's relative contribution to the Gross Domestic Product (GDP) of popular tourist destinations. It is commonly accepted in the field of tourism studies that when tourism contributes 5 percent or more to a national economy, it is considered a highly significant component of the economy.[51] Of 172 countries or dependencies for which such statistics are available, over one-third (sixty-one) feature economies in which tourism contributes 5 percent or more of the total value of the economy.[52] For the following countries and dependencies in the Caribbean, the travel and tourism industry alone produces a large percentage of the economy's total value: Anguilla (25 percent of total GDP), Antigua and Barbuda (24 percent), Aruba (23 percent), British Virgin Islands (23 percent), Saint Lucia (19 percent), and Bahamas (17 percent).[53] For the world economy as a whole, the travel and tourism industry generates roughly 4 percent of total GDP.[54] When tourism's indirect effects on economic activities are included, this figure rises to 10 percent.

Many less developed countries (LDCs) that depend on just one or two primary commodities for the bulk of their export earnings turn to tourism as another source of national income, thereby diversifying the economy. Moreover, for economies heavily burdened by external debt, tourism provides a valuable source of foreign exchange by producing direct revenues for businesses and various levels of government. The United Nations Conference on Trade and Development (UNCTAD) points out that tourism ranks as a top-three export for nineteen LDCs and is the single largest source of foreign exchange earnings in seven LDCs.[55] Further, the combined tourism export earnings of all LDCs account for over 15 percent of all nonoil export receipts. Overall, tourism accounts for over one-third of all export earnings in twenty-eight countries or dependencies, most (but not all) of which are LDCs.[56]

The creation of employment is another economic benefit of tourism that attracts the attention of governments hoping to create sources of income for its citizens. It is estimated that roughly 77 million people work in the travel and tourism industry around the world and that 2.5 million new jobs would be created in 2006.[57] The travel and tourism industry accounts for roughly 3 percent of total world employment. Although most employment in the travel and tourism industry is concentrated in hotels, tour operators, airlines, and travel agencies, tourists also stimulate indirect employment in other sectors that meet the needs of tourists but that are not dependent on tourism alone. For instance, hotels require many goods and services, including marketing, security, and catering, so companies that offer these services are induced to hire workers, thereby creating more employment. The International Labor Organization (ILO) estimates that every job in the tourism industry induces roughly one-and-a-half additional jobs in the economy as a whole.[58] Even in highly diversified economies such as Spain's, direct employment in the tourism industry accounts for 8 percent of total employment.[59]

As a result of both its association with fun and pleasure, and its association with the benefits discussed above, tourism is seen by the vast majority of governments, organizations, and tourists themselves as an economic panacea and "smokeless industry," providing income and employment without requiring the construction of polluting factories. This liberal view of tourism as a progressive force—in which communities and countries take advantage of their natural or cultural comparative advantage and contribute to a positive-sum game whereby tourism provides benefits for tourists and hosts alike—reflects what is known in the tourism literature as the **advocacy platform**.[60] The advocacy platform, or perspective, asserts that states should take a laissez-faire approach to tourism and allow the travel and tourism industry to develop naturally, because doing so will most likely maximize the inevitable economic benefits produced by participation in international tourism.

Though it was especially popular in the 1950s and 1960s, the advocacy platform is today still common in the marketing activities of travel and tourism businesses and government tourist boards, as well as in promotional organizations such at the World Tourism Organization and the World Travel and Tourism Council. Those who espouse a liberal advocacy perspective also support the General Agreement of Trade in Services (GATS), a World Trade Organization (WTO) agreement that establishes rules governing trade in services, including the "Tourism and Travel-Related Services" cluster. GATS requires that members of the WTO grant foreign-owned companies free access to domestic markets in services and avoid giving preferential treatment to domestic companies over foreign-owned services firms.[61]

In the late 1960s and early 1970s, the advocacy platform faced serious questioning from some who took a critical perspective, known as the **cautionary platform**. This perspective on tourism questions the wisdom of unfettered markets and views tourism as a destructive force that promises many benefits but in practice creates more problems than it solves. Although some proponents of the cautionary platform are modern liberals (see Chapter 3) who wish to use government intervention to minimize some of the costs created by natural market activities in tourism, others are structuralists who believe that the exploitation and inequality inherent in capitalism and global economic relations poison tourism, particularly for developing countries.

Structuralists point out that the direct revenue so touted by boosters of tourism growth is offset not only by direct expenditures such as advertising but also by **revenue leakages**, which result in tourism receipts "leaking" out of an economy as repatriated profits to foreign-owned tourism multinational corporations, or in order to pay for imported goods and services required by the tourism industry (such as bathroom fixtures in hotels) or tourists themselves (such as luxury food items that are not grown locally). Most estimates of revenue leakages suggest that over half of all tourist-related spending leaks out of, or never even makes it to, destinations in the developing world.[62] Further, the majority of economic benefits associated with tourism are concentrated in the hands of the economic and political elites who have the capital and political connections to utilize the opportunities afforded by investment by tourism multinational corporations.

It is true that tourism creates employment, structuralists argue, but the jobs made available by tourism are low-skilled, often dangerous, and carry little room for advancement because of poor pay and few benefits. Tourism is also a notoriously fickle industry. Small changes in tourist tastes, or more significant events within the destination itself such as political instability or natural disasters, can severely damage a country's tourism industry. Coupled with the seasonal, casual, and part-time nature of much tourism in most destinations, the vulnerability of tourism to changes in demand weakens the potential of tourism as a development strategy.

Structuralists, and many of those adhering to the cautionary platform, liken modern international tourism to neocolonialism, whereby formally independent states still suffer from unfair relationships associated with colonialism. Dependency theory links the development of the industrial, wealthy core countries of the world to the exploitation and underdevelopment of the poor, weak, and dependent former colonies in the periphery of the world system (see Chapter 4). Taking a dependency approach, structuralists point out that tourism destinations in the developing world serve as the **pleasure periphery** for core countries.[63] For North American tourists looking for a cheap sunshine holiday, the islands of the Caribbean region serve the role of pleasure periphery. Similarly, Southeast Asia and the Mediterranean Basin (southern Europe and North Africa) provide pleasure peripheries for Japan/Australia and Northern Europe, respectively.

Statistical data on international tourism lend support to the structuralist view that tourism reflects the inequality in wealth and power between the core and periphery. Developing countries collectively accounted for 35 percent of all international tourist arrivals in 2004.[64] Though this is much higher than the 8 percent share of arrivals claimed by developing countries in 1960, it still remains small compared to the 66 percent share of arrivals held in 2004 by Europe and North America.[65] Similarly, receipts from international tourism remain concentrated in the wealthy countries of the world, with Europe and North America together receiving 68 percent of the $623 billion in international tourism receipts in 2004.[66] Residents of just five wealthy, industrialized countries—Germany, the United States, the United Kingdom, Japan, and France—accounted for 42 percent of all international tourist spending in 2004.[67]

Travel is linked directly to economic prosperity. In particular, affluence leads to higher levels of discretionary household income (money that is not spent on basic needs such as food, housing, and clothing). As the number of individuals with discretionary income grows, demand for travel services also grows. Thus, individuals in societies that are affluent, urban, economically productive, and industrial tend to participate much more in tourism activities—at first domestically and eventually internationally—than individuals in poor societies. It is no surprise then that the majority of international tourists are nationals of wealthy countries and regions: 55 percent of all international tourists in 2004 were European, while another 11 percent were North American.[68] Aside from technological innovations such as wide-bodied long-haul jet aircraft, computerized booking systems, and Internet access to information about destinations, the principal reason that there are thirty times more international tourist arrivals currently than there were in 1950 is rising material prosperity, particularly in industrialized countries.

A clear indication of the connection between economic prosperity and travel is the recent explosion in domestic and international tourism in and from China. China's rapid economic growth since the 1980s has resulted in a dramatic growth in domestic tourism as well as a surge in outbound tourism. By 2020, China is projected to be the fourth-largest source of international tourists in the world.[69] Improved infrastructure, government policies that encourage openness to the outside world, and economic growth in neighboring countries have also made China a major tourism destination. By 2004, China had surpassed Italy as the fourth most popular tourism destination in the world (42 million international arrivals), surpassed only by France (75 million), Spain (54 million), and the United States (46 million).[70] China is set to become the world's number-one tourism destination in terms of arrivals by 2020.[71] As other countries, such as India, continue to become more economically productive and prosperous, domestic and international travel will boom, thereby continuing the long-term postwar trend of virtually uninterrupted growth in travel and tourism.

### The Politics of Tourism

Just as the uneven global distribution of wealth influences patterns of international tourism, differences in political systems and individual governments also play a key role in determining the shape of tourism in specific locations. At a fundamental level, domestic and international travel is premised on freedom of movement, which itself stems from broader political rights and freedoms. Because political freedom is a prerequisite for travel to occur in the first place, the global trend toward democracy and openness will, along with growing economic prosperity, contribute to a burgeoning global tourism industry.[72]

States figure prominently in the supply of tourism. The supply side of tourism includes factors that "pull," or attract, tourists to a destination. By contrast to destination-based circumstances that shape supply, the demand side of tourism relates to forces generated within tourist-producing countries that "push" tourists to take vacations. States in destination countries certainly strive to influence tourist demand, but they are usually powerless to affect "push" factors in tourist-generating countries, such as technological innovation, rising life expectancy, urbanization, and rising discretionary income.[73] For this reason, virtually all states, regardless of their level of wealth or dominant political system, attempt to influence the supply-side factors that drive tourism. Public administration becomes crucial in this regard, because the drafting and implementation of government policies regarding tourism greatly affects the ability of a country to attract and service international tourists, as well as to curtail the negative consequences of tourism.

Though popular tourist destinations are usually positioned naturally to attract visitors because of unusual geographic landscapes or "exotic" cultural attributes, tourism destinations are in fact created, not born. In other words, it takes both states and markets—and specifically states acting to influence market forces—in order for a location to become attractive and accessible, let alone even known in the first place, to international tourists. In some cases, eager governments identify suitable locations for tourism and then proceed to create destinations from scratch by encouraging public and private investment in the form of subsidized infrastructure and facilities. One such case is Cancun, the famous sunspot destination located on the northeast coast of the Yucatan Peninsula in Mexico. In 1967 the Mexican government identified Cancun as a **growth pole**, a deliberately chosen location meant to serve as an engine of economic growth in the surrounding region. This growth-pole strategy quickly transformed Cancun from a sparsely populated coconut plantation and site of small Mayan ruins into a globally renowned beach resort destination with almost half a million permanent residents, hundreds of hotels, and 4 million international tourist arrivals per year. As a result of Cancun's rapid growth as a tourist destination, Quintana Roo, the state in which Cancun is located, is now among the wealthiest states in Mexico and receives one-third of all foreign tourist expenditures in Mexico.[74]

With few exceptions, governments around the world prefer policies that promote tourism growth, placing top priority on maximizing tourist arrivals and expenditures, despite the negative costs associated with hasty tourism development. States therefore either intervene directly in the economy to create financial, regulatory, and social environments conducive to tourism growth or, alternatively, take a laissez-faire approach to tourism, whereby a largely unfettered market determines the nature and direction of tourism. The exception to this pattern is the Himalayan mountain kingdom of Bhutan, which, unlike the overwhelming majority of other states, particularly those in the developing world, heavily restricts the growth of tourism through policies that exclude all but the wealthiest tourists. The Bhutanese government demands that every tourist pay daily tariffs, surcharges, and expenditures totaling a minimum of $200 per night, and issues visas only to those on expensive organized group tours. By tailoring tourism toward a wealthier clientele, Bhutanese tourism authorities are able to generate greater per-tourist revenues while at the same time limiting the social, cultural, and environmental effects of tourism in Bhutan.

Aside from identifying strategic locations for deliberate tourism development, as in the case of Cancun, governments also use the power of incentives in the form of subsidies and tax breaks, and constraints in the form of regulations and prohibitions, to concentrate tourist activities in spatially circumscribed enclaves. For example, the Maldives, an island nation in the Indian Ocean, concentrates tourism development on a handful of uninhabited atolls. Similarly, the government of Indonesia in 1971 drew up a master plan for tourism on the island of Bali, a long-established international tourism destination. The master plan called for the construction of a new luxury resort enclave on the Bukit Peninsula on the southern tip of the island, and in general for the confinement of tourism development to the area surrounding the airport on or near the Bukit Peninsula.[75] As a result of the efforts of the Indonesian government, the southern tip of Bali absorbed the benefits, and costs, of international tourist arrivals, leaving the rest of the island sheltered from what was perceived to be the corrupting cultural influences of foreign tourists. State planning and marketing also led to an explosion of international tourist arrivals, which grew from 6000 in 1960 to almost 1.5 million in 2004.[76]

There is of course a risk in becoming too popular as a destination, and without state management and regulation of tourism growth, destinations tend to become "loved to death" by eager tourists. The very things that attract tourists in the first place, be it mountains, beaches, or rainforests, often become threatened as visitors quickly exceed the destination's carrying capacity. During the 1980s, governments, tourists, and tourism businesses responded to concerns about the negative effects of tourism by shifting toward forms of tourism that could provide alternatives to tourism experiences based on the standard "sun, sea, and sand" formula. The view, promoted by the advocacy platform, that mass tourism provides the best policy choice for host communities was thus challenged (but ultimately not displaced) by the **adaptancy platform** which called for small-scale, ecologically sustainable, and community-based tourism. The most popular example of this approach is **ecotourism**, defined by the International Ecotourism Society as "responsible travel to natural areas that conserves the environment and improves the well-being of local people."[77] In addition to drafting appropriate laws, and enforcing existing ones, to minimize the environment effects of tourism, states can promote ecotourism by restricting the number of tourists in sensitive areas. States can also create national parks and wildlife reserves that provide the locations for many ecotourism activities. Unfortunately, with rare exceptions, governments that have to choose between rising tourist arrivals, and therefore profits, and environmental protection almost always pick the former.

The liberal perspective on tourism is well represented by the travel industry and the governments of most tourist-receiving states. The structuralist perspective pervades criticisms of tourism. Though it is not as common, the mercantilist approach to tourism is nevertheless important when one considers the ways in which states limit access to travel within their borders. States determine which nationals are allowed entry and under which conditions (permissible length of stay, for example). Countries that enjoy a close relationship, usually reflected in high cross-border traffic among its citizens, allow each others' visitors to enter easily. Until recently, Canadians wishing to visit the United States required only a valid driver's license. On the other hand, some states forbid or heavily restrict the entry of the nationals of particular countries. Several countries—including Afghanistan, Algeria, Comoros, Indonesia, Iran, Libya, Pakistan, Somalia, Saudi Arabia, and Tunisia, among others—refuse to recognize passports from Israel, thereby precluding travel to those countries by Israeli citizens. On the whole, tourist access to other countries varies widely. Citizens of Finland, Denmark, and the United States can enter 130 countries and territories without needing a visa, but tourists from Iraq, Iran, and Afghanistan enjoy this privilege in only fifteen or so countries.[78]

Perhaps the most important role played by states insofar as tourism is concerned is the management of a country's international image. Changing tastes and preferences among international tourists makes it difficult for tourism planners to predict whether a destination will remain popular in the future. Tourist demand depends heavily on prevailing perceptions of a destination, however incorrect they may be. Thus, anything that alters perceptions in a negative manner carries enormous implications for the travel and tourism industry in host societies. Natural disasters, political stability, and terrorism are all examples of forces that can dramatically shift demand away from a destination. States therefore need to focus a great deal of energy and resources on countering the negative effects of such events.

Natural disasters make popular headlines in newspapers and television news reports. Despite how limited the effects may be, especially geographically, the average person with no detailed knowledge of (or specialized interest in) the affected country naturally forms a negative mental association of that country and becomes much less inclined to travel there. The damage unleashed by the natural disaster is then compounded by the loss of income created by a drop in tourist demand. The Indian Ocean tsunami in December 2004, which killed over 200,000 people, resulted in extensive damage to the infrastructure of several tourist-dependent economies, including the Maldives, Sri Lanka, southern Thailand, and India's Andaman and Nicobar Islands. Further, much of the tsunami footage aired nonstop on television stations around the world featured shots of floating tourist corpses and waves crashing into tourist hotels. The immediate drop in tourism to these regions only made things worse, as tourism revenues rendered even more necessary by the tsunami dried up overnight.[79]

States must address the challenges posed by damaging media coverage of natural disasters, but reports of political instability also strike fear in the hearts of potential tourists. Of course, states that foster political stability assist their tourism promotion efforts, but creating stability at the expense of human rights can also backfire, as the example of Burma (Myanmar) illustrates.

---

### BURMA TOURISM BOYCOTT: SHOULD YOU STAY OR SHOULD YOU GO?

To most people, travel and tourism are innocent affairs, devoid of any political significance. However, a vacation—which to most tourists is merely an escape from the rigors and routines and everyday life—can be a matter of life or death to others. A prime example of the political significance of tourism, and the high personal stakes involved in a person's decision to travel, is provided by the case of international travel to Burma.[a] In 1988, demonstrations against the military regime of Burma ended with the massacre of thousands of students, monks, workers, and farmers. In 1990, Burma's ruling council, known as the State Law and Order Restoration Council (SLORC),[b] allowed elections in which the National League for Democracy (NLD), led by Aung San Suu Kyi, won over 80 percent of the parliamentary seats. However, the military rulers of Burma prevented the NLD from assuming power. Despite being given the opportunity to leave the country at any time, Aung San Suu Kyi has instead chosen to stay in Burma and fight for democracy. As a result, the military rulers of Burma have kept Aung San Suu Kyi under house arrest for all but six years in the seventeen-year period between 1989 and 2006.

In 1995, the military rulers of Burma announced plans to promote tourism heavily beginning in the following year, designated by the regime as "Visit Myanmar Year 1996." Soon after the regime announced these plans, several British NGOs, most notably The Burma Campaign UK and Tourism Concern, launched a campaign against tourism to Burma, arguing that guidebook publishers, tour operators, and tourists should avoid promoting tourism to, operating in, or traveling to Burma because of the ongoing human rights abuses there. Reports from human rights organizations confirm Burma's terrible human rights record. Amnesty International and Human Rights Watch, for example, report the use of forced labor, torture, extrajudicial execution, child labor, child soldiers, forced relocation of villages, and rape against dissidents, particularly non-Burman ethnic minorities such as the Karen. In 2006, Freedom House, an independent NGO that monitors political rights and civil liberties around the world, gave Burma its lowest possible rating (along with seven other countries) in its annual survey, *Freedom in the World*.[c]

Supporters of the Burma tourism boycott campaign give many reasons to avoid travel to Burma. First, both Aung San Suu Kyi and Burma's government in exile—the National Coalition Government of the Union of Burma (NCGUB)—support the boycott and have since 1995 repeatedly asked tourists not to visit Burma until its political situation has improved. Second, even for those using privately owned accommodation and transportation, it is difficult to travel to Burma without providing income for the military regime. Though Burma receives only approximately 240,000 tourists per year, the bulk of the tourism revenues that Burma receives ($84 million in 2004) remains concentrated in the hands of its military rulers. Tourist spending and investment related to tourism infrastructure, such as roads, railways, airports, and hotels, contribute directly to sustaining a military junta that threatens and uses force to suppress its own people. Third, undemocratic governments facing a question of legitimacy at home can turn to participation in the international tourism industry as a means of bolstering their legitimacy and credibility. A visit to Burma, according to critics, serves as a stamp of approval of the political status quo. Third, evidence from several sources, including NGOs, journalists, and the U.S. State Department, indicates that human rights abuses in Burma are related directly to official efforts to attract or service international tourists. Whether forcing residents from their homes in order to build golf courses and hotels, or using forced labor to prepare ancient temple ruins for tourist arrivals, the Burmese government frequently violates human rights in the name of tourism development. Fourth, the number of ordinary Burmese who benefit from tourism, and are potentially harmed by a tourism boycott, is small compared to the number of people who suffer because of the continuing rule of military elites, most of whom are sustained partly by tourism revenues. It is hoped that by cutting the economic lifeline of the regime through a tourism boycott, the campaign will foster political, economic, and social changes that will benefit the vast majority of Burmese.

Several travel companies and guidebook publishers, including Austrian Airlines, Carnival Corporation/ P&O, Frommer's Guides, Intrepid Travel, Kuoni, and Rough Guides, have decided in recent years to support the boycott; the European Union and the United Kingdom have also both taken official stands in support of the boycott. Among the thirty-seven travel companies still on The Burma Campaign UK's "Dirty List" (as of mid-2006), the one most targeted by the campaign is Lonely Planet, the largest independent guidebook publisher in the world. In 2000, The Burma Campaign UK and Tourism Concern called for a boycott of all Lonely Planet guidebooks because of the company's promotion of tourism to Burma and its continued publication of a Burma guidebook. In spite of the bad publicity generated by the boycott of its products, Lonely Planet continues to publish its Burma guidebook, arguing that by providing a detailed discussion of both reasons to go *and* reasons to stay, the company "aims to provide independent travellers with balanced information so that they are able reach their own informed conclusions."[d] Lonely Planet points out that tourism is among the few economic opportunities available to poor Burmese. Further, a careful traveler is able to divert spending into privately owned businesses that are not connected to the government. Most important, Lonely Planet believes that economic and political isolation serves only to bolster, rather than diminish, the power and authority of autocratic regimes.

Whether the choice is made to stay or to go, one cannot escape the political implications of the seemingly innocent act of choosing a holiday destination.

*References*

[a] Burma was renamed Myanmar by the country's military rulers in 1989. Several countries, including Australia, Canada, the United Kingdom, and the United States, continue to use the name Burma in defiance of the current military regime.

[b] SLORC was renamed the State Peace and Development Council (SPDC) in 1997.

[c] See www.freedomhouse.org.

[d] See www.lonelyplanet.com/help/faq_myanmar.htm.

Countries that experience civil war or internal political upheaval have a difficult time luring back international tourists when the violence subsides. In 1987, a series of military coups in Fiji, located in the South Pacific Ocean, led to a 72 percent drop in tourist arrivals between June 1986 and June 1987.[80] Elsewhere, the civil war in the Former Yugoslavia in the 1990s resulted in overnight visits to Croatia plummeting from 5 million in 1990 to 1.3 million in 1995.[81] It is indeed telling that immediately following the September 2006 military coup in Thailand, one of the first actions taken by the leaders of the coup was to reassure tourists that they were still welcome and safe in Thailand.

The means by which tourists are able to travel from one country to another are also employed by individuals intending to commit acts of terrorism. In addition to combating terrorist organizations that target their citizens, states must also counter the damage done by terrorism to their tourism industries. Terrorists favor tourists as targets for several reasons: Some tourists travel to remote, dangerous locations that serve as the base for terrorist groups; tourists are much "softer" targets than heavily defended military or political sites; the killing of tourists generates extensive international media coverage; and terrorism disrupts economies that depend on tourism revenues, thereby helping to cripple unpopular regimes.[82] Since the late 1990s, tourists have become especially popular targets for terrorist organizations. In 1997, terrorists killed fifty-eight foreign tourists at Luxor in Egypt. In 1999, seventeen tourists visiting Uganda's Bwindi's National Park were kidnapped (and eight later killed) by Hutu extremists from Rwanda. In 2001, Abu Sayyaf, a militant Islamic group, took twenty local and foreign tourists hostage on the island of Palawan in the Philippines.

It is significant that the first people to die in the September 11, 2001, attacks on the World Trade Centers in New York and the Pentagon in Washington, D.C., were travelers aboard aircraft, and that jet airplanes, the most important technological innovation in the growth of travel and tourism, were used by the hijackers as weapons. Most acts of terrorism are local or national in consequence, in that the resulting drop in tourist demand is usually confined to that destination alone, or at most to the broader region. By contrast, the 9/11 attacks had global effects. A study by the International Labor Organization (ILO) found that the 9/11 attacks spurred a prolonged downturn in global travel and the tourism industry that cost 6.7 million tourism workers their jobs and led to a 4 percent decline in international tourist demand.[83] By September 2006, a full five years after the attacks, the number of internal flights in the United States remained 8 percent lower than in September 2001.[84]

States that experience terrorism within their borders usually react immediately to restore their international image and lure back tourists. The United States after 9/11 stands as an exception. Because the majority of the nineteen hijackers who carried out the attacks entered the United States on tourist visas, concerns were raised that freedoms given to tourists to visit the country were being abused by individuals who intended to participate in terrorist acts against Americans. As a result of domestic political pressure, the U.S. government implemented several measures aimed at better screening and monitoring of visitors to the United States. These measures include, since 2004, the requirement that all visitors with a visa entering the United States at air and sea ports have fingerprints and photographs taken. As a result of deteriorating global perceptions of the United States, and the more stringent entry requirements imposed by the U.S. government on visitors, 4.3 million fewer overseas tourists visited the United States in 2005 than in 2000; this represents a 16.5 percent decline.[85]

Since September 11, 2001, terrorists have continued to carry out attacks against tourists. The deadliest of these attacks occurred in Bali in October 2002, when members of Jemaah Islamiyah, a Southeast Asian militant Islamic organization, detonated bombs outside two nightclubs popular with Western tourists. The explosions and resulting fires killed 202 tourists, eighty-nine of them Australians. The perpetrators of the attack targeted Bali specifically because of its association with tourist hedonism, and also because of Bali's economic importance to the Indonesian government, which Jemaah Islamiyah considers corrupt. Almost exactly three years later, another series of terrorist bombings in popular tourist spots in Bali killed five foreign tourists and injured another sixty-one.

Structuralists argue that tourism is a risky economic strategy because of the fickle nature of tourist demand. Tsunamis, outbreaks of "bird flu," and acts of terrorism can quickly wipe out a destination's tourism industry. Liberals are quick to point out, however, that fast action by businesses and government can reverse the initial losses associated with tragic events. The evidence seems to confirm this liberal view. Despite suffering a 23 percent drop in arrivals in the year following the 2002 bombings, Bali quickly returned to prebombing tourism levels; in 2004 it exceeded the number of international tourists in 2002 by 13 percent.[86] The persistent growth in global tourism praised by liberals is so assured, it seems, that even fears of death at the hands of terrorists is not enough to thwart our desire to travel.

## Tourism as an Agent of Social and Cultural Change

The critical cautionary platform in tourism that emerged in the 1960s and 1970s called attention to the harmful consequences of tourism. Though many of these criticisms challenged the existing euphoria prevalent in studies of the economic effects of tourism, it was the social, cultural, and environmental side effects of rapid incorporation into global tourism networks that generated the most concern. Social status has long underpinned motivations for travel, from the 1840s, when Thomas Cook first took English industrial workers to seaside resort towns, to contemporary travelers, who seek out locations off the beaten track as markers of superior taste and style. Social class also determines who can afford to travel in the first place.

Culture is also a crucial component of travel to many destinations for two reasons. First, throughout history, tourists have been motivated to visit cultures perceived to be exotic and unfamiliar. A desire for cultural authenticity has long characterized tourism, and some scholars have even argued that modern tourism is premised on the search for authenticity. As the global proliferation of

Western material goods seemingly erases cultural differences, tourists strive to experience a level of cultural authenticity that lies beyond the superficial, and supposedly inauthentic, "front stage," where hosts perform mostly for tourist consumption. Second, despite the role played by cultural "otherness" in luring foreign tourists, the majority of international tourists visit countries with similar cultural traits, particularly in language or religion. Cultural affinity is the reason that the British are the second largest inbound tourist market in Australia, and why U.S. residents made over 15 million trips to Canada in 2004.[87] Every year, millions of people travel on religious pilgrimages, the most sizable consisting of Muslims fulfilling their obligation to make the *hajj*, the pilgrimage to Mecca in Saudi Arabia.

Tourist demand stimulates both the rejuvenation of cultural traditions and the rehabilitation of historical architectural monuments. Funds that are collected as entry fees and donations at historical sites can be put to use on the site itself, but more important, the interest shown in historical sites by tourists motivates governments to allocate resources to the rehabilitation and maintenance of such sites. Without the incentives created by tourism revenues, historical sites such as Angkor Wat in Cambodia, Macchu Pichu in Peru, and the ancient city of Timbuktu in Mali would likely have remained crumbling ruins, or at least would have received far less attention and funding. In many cases, governments that wish to restore a historical site for tourism or other purposes succeed in acquiring funds from the United Nations Educational, Scientific, and Cultural Organization (UNESCO), which maintains a World Heritage list of cultural and natural properties deemed essential components of global heritage.

On the other side of the debate about the social and cultural effects of tourism are supporters of the cautionary platform, who believe that the unregulated nature of global tourism, particularly in developing countries with weak or uninvolved governments, makes harmful change inevitable. The presence of highly conspicuous tourists in local communities has two negative social and cultural effects. First, tourism is accused by critics of increasing criminal activity, especially in destinations whose residents are much poorer than the tourists visiting them. Several factors make tourists good targets for criminal activity: Tourists are likely to mistakenly stray into unsafe areas or become lost; tourists are more likely than locals to be taken advantage of because of their lack of familiarity with local norms or procedures; a holiday mentality makes tourists more trustful and less alert; and tourists are apt to display objects of value such as money, jewelry, and cameras openly and without caution.[88]

The second cost associated with the interaction of rich tourists and poor locals is the way in which tourism tends to have a demonstration effect, whereby some locals, especially youth, come to desire the material objects—and emulate the values, lifestyles, and behavior—of wealthier foreign tourists. As youth who interact with tourists adopt foreign, usually more modern, cultural values, social tension can occur between older members of the community who worry about the loss of traditional values and those who interact directly with tourists and wish to reject or modify traditional cultural practices. Aside from possibly fostering a sense of inferiority by creating a desire for, but inability to purchase, expensive material objects possessed by tourists, the demonstration effect is especially a concern when locals interact with tourists who exhibit sexual promiscuity or the open use of drugs and alcohol.

Tourist demand for cultural artifacts and traditions perceived to be exotic transforms certain aspects of host cultures into commodities to be bought and sold. The **commodification** of culture initiated by tourism ultimately strips the original meaning and purpose from cultural objects, customs, and festivals as locals respond to commercial pressures and incentives. Critics of tourism-induced cultural commodification decry the production of "airport art," bastardized versions of traditional arts and crafts sold as cheap tourist trinkets in airports and shopping malls. Rather than being allowed to evolve naturally, according to indigenous needs, cultural performances change in substance, timing, or length in response to the entertainment demands and short attention spans of most package tourists.

At a broader level, involvement in the tourism industry, and an overreliance on tourists as a source of economic livelihood, has the effect over time of encouraging locals to see themselves and their culture in terms dictated by the fantasy factory that tourism marketing represents. In Hawaii, for example, critics of tourism argue that decades of tourism marketing centered on Western notions of paradise has stripped Hawaiians of their cultural autonomy and has indoctrinated locals into internalizing notions of the friendly, exotic Hawaiian into their self-identity.[89] Similarly, Bali's long experience with receiving foreign tourists—dating back a century, to the implementation of Dutch colonial rule in Indonesia—and efforts to preserve Bali as a "living museum" have shaped how the Balinese see themselves. As one author puts it, "the Balinese, enjoined to preserve and promote their cultural identity in reference to the outside world's view of them, have come to search for confirmation of their 'Balinese-ness' in the mirror held to them by the tourists."[90]

Structuralists disagree with the rosy view that tourism promotes peace, security, and tolerance. The reason is not that tourism is inherently unable to promote cross-cultural understanding, but that the vast majority of tourists receive information from enormous multinational tourism companies that are concerned more with profit than accurate or balanced representations of host cultures. Though states can change perceptions abroad through their actions, governments are limited in their ability to change tourists' deep-seated cultural stereotypes, because these stereotypes are created or at least maintained by tour operators and travel agents who reduce complex cultures to a few recognizable, palatable nuggets for tourist consumption.

Liberals argue that, yes, tourists may have inaccurate or simplistic ideas about the cultures of their hosts, but don't the interactions between tourist and host that travel permits help to foster better cross-cultural understanding? Again, this may be possible under the right circumstances, but in practice, tourists and hosts are positioned unequally in wealth and power, especially when tourists from wealthy countries visit destinations in developing countries. Tourism is a service industry and thus demands a certain level of servility. Because tourism centers on pleasure and recreation, there is even greater pressure for tourism workers to ensure that the customer is satisfied. Moreover, tourists tend to travel in an "environmental bubble" in which encounters with locals outside the tourism industry are rare, fleeting, and predictable. Instead of challenging servile and demeaning views of their people, states and local tour operators often perpetuate the problem by reassuring tourists in brochures and other advertisements that locals will cater to their every whim.

Pictures of smiling, subservient locals serving tourists are ubiquitous in tourism marketing. At its extreme, the servility of tourism can lead to situations in which tourists swarm around indigenous people with unusual (to tourists) or colorful appearance and treat them as exhibits in a human zoo. For the Padaung, an ethnic group from Burma whose women are famous for wearing rows of brass rings on their seemingly elongated necks, political repression by the Burmese military and their status as refugees in Thailand has left them with few choices other than posing for ogling tourists in prefabricated villages run by Thai businessmen, and from which the Padaung are forbidden from leaving.

The most visible social cost of tourism in any destination is prostitution. Several factors make tourism both a target and a stimulant of prostitution. People on vacation tend to spend money much less cautiously than when at home, and they spend money on unusual items. A holiday frame of mind, characterized by inversions of normal routines and patterns of behavior, also makes tourists more inclined to engage in activities, including sexual, that are normally avoided at home.

These irregular patterns of spending and behavior, combined with their spatial concentration in conspicuous locations of consumption and hedonism, make tourists an easy and popular target for the local sex trade. It is therefore no surprise that in virtually all popular destinations, especially in poor countries, sexual services are easily available to tourists. Even in strictly controlled societies such as Cuba, the sex trade is supported partly by certain segments of tourists.

The most insidious side of the tourism–prostitution relationship is the sexual exploitation of children by tourists. Though some tourists who purchase the sexual services of locals may be unaware of the young age of the sex worker, most tourists who engage in such activities with minors are fully aware of what they are doing. Desperation, a lack of alternative means of survival, sexual abuse, and the collusion of corrupt government officials and police officers helps to sustain this trade. One study conducted in 2001 by World Vision in Cambodia discovered that 70 percent of children surveyed around the Angkor Wat archeological site had been solicited for sex by tourists; the same study reported that almost half of all Cambodian travel agents had witnessed local tour guides providing tourists with children for sexual purposes.[91] In response to the moral condemnation generated by images of tall male Western foreigners walking hand in hand with young Cambodian, Costa Rican, or South African girls (or boys), countries such as the United States, Australia, and New Zealand have passed laws that allow them to prosecute citizens who travel abroad to purchase sex from minors. Though progress is slow, governments of sex tourism destinations are also starting to take greater action, the most notable example being the 2005 arrest and imprisonment in Vietnam of British rock star Gary Glitter on charges of committing obscene acts with children.

The political, economic, and social consequences of tourism are impossible to analyze in isolation, as discussions of tourism's benefits and costs necessarily lead one to consider all three areas of analysis. The growing transnational flow of people, embodied by the international travel and tourism industry, stems from the same technologies and institutional arrangements that have intensified the global flow of goods, ideas, and money. To a large degree, discrepancies in wealth and power between individuals and countries, and interactions between states and markets, determine the distribution of benefits and costs of tourism, not to mention the distribution of actual tourists. Liberals portray tourism as a path to development, political legitimacy, and peace, whereas structuralists see tourism as a bringer of all things evil. Mercantilists, meanwhile, eschew the moral debate and focus instead on how to promote national security while at the same time attracting more tourists and tourism revenues than other states. The truth, as economists like to point out, is that tourism involves unavoidable trade-offs. Tourism generates revenues, but it comes with a price. When faced with the choice of whether to participate in tourism, the majority of individuals, and all but the most isolationist states, in the world accept the trade-offs as a worthwhile price to pay. The flow of tourists crisscrossing the globe is therefore unlikely to subside any time soon.

## CONCLUSION

Migration and tourism are two good examples of human connections in IPE. Each involves a pattern of human relations and flows of people who cross national borders for different reasons. In each network, people share many ideas, values, and beliefs, even if, as in tourism, they may be bound together for only a short time. One reason that economic liberals give in support of globalization is the benefit that many tourists have of more income to "enjoy life." Many structuralists, however, complain that globalization has forced migrants to seek a better life in another country where the economy is stronger than their own. In each case, we can appreciate the extent to which local economies are part of a global economy that benefits some more than others. These studies also allow us to appreciate that different cultural groups are part of a much bigger international society.

Focusing on these two areas also helps us to appreciate the interconnections among various IPE structures. Both migration and tourism involve finance or money, currency, and quite often the exchange of goods and services. For tourists, those goods may be simple mementos, whereas migrants are often the "goods" who provide others a service. Both cases involve a certain amount of technology and information. And both share concerns about security. Depending on the location, some tourists may fear for their personal safety in an environment that most people take for granted will be safe. On the other hand, in many places migrants themselves might be viewed as a security threat.

Finally, in studying both issues in some detail, we come to appreciate that much of the connection between these structures is human. Ultimately, IPE is about people who are rooted in different cultures and places, but who in today's globalizing society have also become quite mobile and routinely interact with one another. Broadening the focus of IPE to account for human relations, then, helps us appreciate that, when all is said and done, IPE is ultimately about human relationships.

## DISCUSSION QUESTIONS

1. Compare the situation of a female Cambodian refugee living in Wisconsin with that of a male irregular migrant from the Dominican Republic living in New York City. What similarities and differences might characterize their (a) reasons for coming to the United States, (b) their economic opportunities within the United States, and (c) their experience of cultural citizenship within the United States?
2. Draw a historical timeline on the blackboard. Each student should take a turn noting on the timeline the name and date of her first family member to migrate to this country. When all students' information is listed, each student should describe why her family member originally migrated and how (by boat, plane, land, etc.). Use this information to compile an analysis of historical patterns in migration flows, countries of origin, and reasons for migration. How does this information compare with representations about current immigration patterns and populations?
3. What makes tourism an attractive option for the state? How does tourism create risks for the state?
4. Why is it necessary to be concerned about "sustainable" tourism? Explain.
5. What are the rewards and risks of tourism according to liberals, mercantilists, and structuralists?
6. What are the trade-offs associated with tourism?

## INTERNET LINKS

### Migration

United Nations, Secretary General's International Migration and Development Report (2006):
   www.un.org/esa/population/hldmigration/Text/Report%20of%20the%20SG(June%2006)_English.pdf

Migration Information Source:
   www.migrationinformation.org/index.cfm

Center for Research on Immigration, Population, and Public Policy (University of California, Irvine):
   www.cri.uci.edu/papers.htm

Center on Migration, Policy and Society (Oxford University):
   www.compas.ox.ac.uk

Transnational Communities Programme (Economic and Social Research Council, Oxford University):
   www.transcomm.ox.ac.uk

### International Tourism

Ecotourism Society:
   www.ecotourism.org

World Tourism Organization:
   www.world-tourism.org

World Travel and Tourism Council:
   www.wttc.org

UNESCO World Heritage Centre:
   http://whc.unesco.org

## SUGGESTED READINGS

### Migration

Caroline Brettell and James Hollifield, eds. *Migration Theory: Talking Across the Disciplines.* New York: Routledge, 2000.
Stephen Castles and Alistair Davidson. *Citizenship and Migration: Globalization and the Politics of Belonging.* New York: Routledge, 2000.
Nina Glick-Schiller and Georges Eugene Fouron. *Georges Woke Up Laughing: Long Distance Nationalism and the Search for Home.* Durham, NC: Duke University Press, 2001.

Sarah Mahler. *American Dreaming: Immigrant Life on the Margins*. Princeton, NJ: Princeton University Press, 1995.

Aihwa Ong. *Buddha Is Hiding: Refugees, Citizenship, and the New America*. Berkeley: University of California Press, 2003.

Joshua Hotaka Roth. *Brokered Homeland: Japanese Brazilian Migrants in Japan*. Ithaca, NY: Cornell University Press, 2002.

**Tourism**

Jim Butcher. *The Moralisation of Tourism: Sun, Sand—and Saving the World?* London: Routledge, 2003.

Jafar Jafari. "The Scientification of Tourism." In V. L. Smith, ed., *Hosts and Guests Revisited: Tourism Issues of the 21st Century*. New York: Cognizant, 2001, pp. 28–41.

Alister Mathieson and Geoffrey Wall. *Tourism: Economic, Physical, and Social Impacts*. New York: Longman, 1982.

Martin Mowforth and Ian Munt. *Tourism and Sustainability: Development and New Tourism in the Third World*, 2nd ed. London: Routledge, 2003.

Richard Sharpley. *Tourism, Tourists and Society*. Huntingdon, UK: ELM, 1994.

David Weaver and Laura Lawton. *Tourism Management*, 2nd ed. Milton, Australia: John Wiley, 2002.

## KEY TERMS

**Migration**

migration
internal migration
transnational migration
circular migration
guest worker
remittances
chain migration
irregular migrants

transit states
brain drain
immigration
settler states
refugee
asylum
assimilation
cultural citizenship
diaspora

**Tourism**

advocacy platform
cautionary platform
revenue leakages
pleasure periphery
growth pole
adaptancy platform
ecotourism
commodification

## NOTES

1. Michael Veseth was the author of this chapter in the third edition of this textbook.
2. See the UN website, www.un.org/esa/population/publications/ittmig2002/press-release-eng.htm.
3. David Weaver and Laura Lawton, *Tourism Management*, 2nd ed. (Milton, Australia: John Wiley, 2002), p. 283.
4. A good overview of the role of IOs and NGOs is Margaret P. Karns and Karen A. Mingst, *International Organizations: The Politics and Processes of Global Governance* (Boulder, CO: Lynne Rienner, 2004).
5. United Nations, *International Migration and Development: Report by the Secretary General*. (New York: United Nations, 2006), p. 12.
6. Ibid.
7. T. Painter, S. Dusseini, S. Kaapo, and C. McKaig, "Seasonal Migration and the Spread of AIDS in Mali and Niger," International AIDS Conference, Amsterdam, 1992, 8:D425, www.aegis.com/conferences/iac/1992/PoD5228.html, accessed July 31, 2006.
8. Nicole Constable, *Maid in Hong Kong*. Ithaca, NY: Cornell University Press, 1997. Also see Sze Lai-Shan, "New Immigrant Labor from Mainland China in Hong Kong," *Asian Labor Update*, no. 53 (October–December 2004), www.amrc.org.hk, accessed February 9, 2006.
9. Jeffrey Fleischman, "Europe in Immigration Quandry," *The Seattle Times*, June 7, 2006, p. A3. Also see Edward Alden, Daniel Dombey, Chris Giles, and Sarah Laitner, "The Price of Prosperity: Why Fortress Europe Needs to Lower the Drawbridge," *Financial Times*, May 18, 2006, p. 13.
10. Kitty Calavita, *Inside the State: The Bracero Program, Immigration and the INS* (New York: Routledge, 1992). See also Jonathan Inda, *Targeting Immigrants* (Malden, MA: Blackwell, 2006).
11. Steven Greenhouse and Michael Barbaro, "The Ugly Side of Free Trade," *The New York Times*, May 3, 2006, p. C1.
12. United Nations, *International Migration and Development: Report by the Secretary General*, p. 54.
13. James Smith, "Guatemala: Economic Migrants Replace Political Refugees," Migration Policy Institute, www.migrationinformation.org, April 2006, accessed June 19, 2006.
14. Manuel Orozco, "Mexican Hometown Associations and Development Opportunities," *Journal of International Affairs*, 57 (Spring 2004), pp. 33–34.
15. Graeme Hugo, "Circular Migration: Keeping Development Rolling?," Migration Policy Institute, www.migrationinformation.org/Feature/print.cfm?ID=129, June 1, 2003, accessed June 9, 2006.
16. Carolyn Lochhead, "A Legacy of the Unforeseen," *San Francisco Chronicle*, May 7, 2006, p. A1.
17. Roger Rouse, "Mexican Migration and the Space of Postmodernism," *Diaspora, 1* (1991), pp. 8–23.

18. Migration Policy Institute, "Country Profile: The Philippines," www.migrationinformation.org/Resources/philippines.cfm, accessed June 10, 2006.
19. Alden et al., "The Price of Prosperity."
20. International Herald Tribune, "Europe Fails to Agree on 'Safe' Destination for African Migrants," *The New York Times*, May 25, 2006, www.nytimes.com, accessed May 31, 2006.
21. M. K. Anwar, "Brunei Immigration Enforcers Launch 'Ops Berkas,'" *Borneo Bulletin, Financial Times* Information Limited—Asia Intelligence Wire, January 6, 2006, www.lexis-nexis.com, accessed June 7, 2006.
22. Nicolas Brussells, "Migrant Workers from East Helping to Boost EU's Fortunes, Says Report," *The Guardian* (London), *Guardian International*, February 9, 2006, p. 22.
23. Celia Dugger, "U.S. Plan to Lure Nurses May Hurt Poor Nations," *The New York Times*, May 24, 2006, www.nytimes.com, accessed May 31, 2006.
24. United Nations, *International Migration and Development*, p. 42.
25. Ibid., p. 43.
26. Rachel Swarns, "Study Finds Disparities in Judges' Asylum Rulings," *The New York Times*, July 31, 2006, www.nytimes.com, accessed August 4, 2006.
27. Renato Rosaldo, "Cultural Citizenship and Educational Democracy," *Cultural Anthropology, 9* (August 1994), pp. 402–411.
28. Craig Smith, "France Faces a Colonial Legacy: What Makes Someone French," *The New York Times*, November 11, 2005, p. A1.
29. Elaine Sciolino, "Ban on Head Scarves Takes Effect in a United France," *The New York Times*, March 9, 2004, www.nytimes.com, accessed August 9, 2006.
30. Victor Simpson, "Wary Europeans Watch as France's Riots Spread," *The Seattle Times*, November 8, 2005, p. A1.
31. See, for example, Samuel Huntington, *Who Are We? The Challenges to America's National Identity*, reprint ed. (New York: Simon & Schuster, 2005).
32. See Aihwa Ong, *Buddha is Hiding: Refugees, Citizenship, and the New America* (Berkeley: University of California Press, 2003). Also see Karen Sacks, "How Did Jews Become White Folks?," in Steven Gregory and Roger Sanjek, eds., *Race* (New Brunsick, NJ: Rutgers University Press, 1994), pp.78–102.
33. Thomas Friedman, *The World Is Flat: A Brief History of the 21st Century*, expanded and updated ed. (New York: Farrar, Straus & Giroux, 2006).
34. June Kronholtz, "Politics & Economics: Immigration Costs Move to the Fore; Differing Estimates Open New Battleground Over Senate Bill," *The Wall Street Journal*, May 24, 2006, p. A4. See also Edurdo Porter, "Illegal Immigrants Are Bolstering Social Security with Billions," *The New York Times*, April 5, 2005, www.nytimes.com, accessed April 11, 2005.
35. Ibid.
36. Diego Cevallos, "U.S.-Mexico: 'We'll Do it Ourselves' say Immigration Vigilantes," Global Information Network, June 14, 2006, www.proquest.umi.com, accessed August 7, 2006.
37. See, for example, Mark Rice-Oxley and James Brandon, in "Britain, Far-Right Push Threatens Tony Blair," *The Christian Science Monitor*, May 6, 2004, p. 1; "World Briefing Europe: The Netherlands: Government Resigns," *The New York Times*, July 1, 2006, www.nytimes.com, March 28, 2005, accessed August 7, 2006; Peter Keifer and Elisabetta Povoledo, "Illegal Immigrants Become the Focus of Election Campaign in Italy," *The New York Times*, March 28, 2005, www.nytimes.com, accessed August 7, 2006.
38. Alden et al., "The Price of Prosperity."
39. Ibid.
40. Paul Krugman, "The Road to Dubai," *The New York Times*, March 31, 2006, p. A9.
41. See, for example, municipal webpages for Todos Santos Cuchumatan in the Western Highlands of Guatemala at www.inforpressca.com/municipal/siam.htm or www.stetson.edu/~rsitler/TodosSantos.
42. Nina Glick-Schiller and Georges Fouron, *Georges Woke Up Laughing*: *Long Distance Nationalism and the Search for Home* (Durham, NC: Duke University Press, 2001).
43. Frank Laczo and Elizabeth Collett, "Assessing the Tsunami's Effects on Migration," Migration Policy Institute, April 1, 2005, www.migrationinformation.org/Feature/print.cfm?ID=299, accessed June 9, 2006.
44. Ibid.
45. Craig Smith, "Temperatures Rise over Cartoons Mocking Mohammed," *The New York Times*, February 3, 2006, p. A3.
46. The World Tourism Organization (UNWTO) defines internationalist tourists as visitors who stay at least one night in a collective or private accommodation in a destination outside their normal country of residence. In 2004, according to the UNWTO (*Tourism Highlights 2005*), 52 percent of international tourists traveled for "leisure,

recreation and holidays," 24 percent for "VFR [visiting friends and relatives], health, religion, other," and 16 percent for "business and professional" reasons; 8 percent traveled for no specified reason (see www.unwto. org/facts/menu.html).

47. Lisa Mastny, *Traveling Light: New Paths for International Tourism* (Washington, DC: Worldwatch Institute, 2001), p. 11.

48. Though organizations such as the World Travel and Tourism Council (WTTC) consider tourism the largest industry in the world, this really depends on how tourism is measured. Because tourism encompasses many sectors of the economy, it is difficult to measure the size and economic value of tourism in isolation. Thus, estimates regarding tourism tend to be less reliable than for other, more clearly bounded industries.

49. World Travel and Tourism Council (WTTC), *Executive Summary: Climbing to New Heights—The 2006 Travel & Tourism Economic Research* (London: WTTC, 2006), p. 6, www.wttc.org/2006TSA/pdf/Executive%20Summary% 202006.pdf, accessed September 30, 2006.

50. UNWTO, *Tourism Highlights 2005*, p. 4.

51. David Weaver and Laura Lawton, *Tourism Management*, 2nd ed. (Milton, Australia: John Wiley, 2002), p. 245.

52. Ibid., pp. 417–425. Dependencies are territories that lack formal independence but that in some cases enjoy limited sovereignty (for example, the British "overseas territories" of Bermuda and the British Virgin Islands, or the French "overseas departments" of Martinique and Réunion).

53. WTTC, *Executive Summary*, p. 23.

54. Ibid.

55. United Nations Conference of Trade and Development (UNCTAD), *Information Economy Report 2005* (Geneva: United Nations, 2005), pp. 161 and 182. The seven LDCs in which tourism is the largest source of foreign exchange earnings are Comoros, Gambia, Maldives, Samoa, Tuvalu, Tanzania, and Vanuatu.

56. WTTC, *Executive Summary*, pp. 23–25.

57. WTTC, *Executive Summary*, p. 23.

58. International Labor Organization (ILO), *Output and Employment: "Hotels; Catering; Tourism" Sector* (Geneva: ILO, 2002), www.ilo.org/public/english/dialogue/sector/sectors/tourism/emp.htm, accessed September 30, 2006.

59. WTTC, *Executive Summary*, p. 23.

60. Jafar Jafari, "The Scientification of Tourism," in V. L. Smith, ed., *Hosts and Guests Revisited: Tourism Issues of the 21st Century* (New York: Cognizant, 2001), pp. 28–41. In this chapter, Jafari, the founder and editor-in-chief of the *Annals of Tourism Research* since 1973, discusses the various platforms, or perspectives, that have characterized the field of tourism studies since the 1950s.

61. GATS is being renegotiated as part of the Doha round of WTO negotiations, launched in November 2001.

62. Martin Mowforth and Ian Munt, *Tourism and Sustainability: Development and New Tourism in the Third World*, 2nd ed. (London: Routledge, 2003), p. 174.

63. For the structuralist perspective on tourism, see Louis Turner and John Ash, *The Golden Hordes: International Tourism and the Pleasure Periphery* (New York: St. Martin's, 1976); Stephen Britton, "The Political Economy of Tourism in the Third World," *Annals of Tourism Research, 9* (1982), pp. 331–358; Jamaica Kincaid, *A Small Place* (New York: Farrar, Straus & Giroux, 1988); Mowforth and Munt, *Tourism and Sustainability*.

64. UNCTAD, *Information Economy Report 2005*, p. 150.

65. UNWTO, *Tourism Highlights 2005*, p. 3.

66. Ibid.

67. UNWTO, *Tourism Highlights 2005*, p. 10.

68. UNWTO, *Tourism Highlights 2005*, p. 2.

69. Weaver and Lawton, *Tourism Management*, p. 90.

70. UNWTO, *Tourism Highlights 2005*, p. 4.

71. UNCTAD, *Information Economy Report 2005*, p. 150.

72. Freedom House, an NGO that ranks countries and territories as free, partly free, or not free according to their political rights and civil liberties, reported in its *2004 Annual Report* that the number of countries classified as free increased from seventy-two in 1993 to eighty-eight in 2003. This is just the latest evidence of a long-term global trend toward democracy. See www.freedomhouse.org/uploads/special_report/23.pdf.

73. See Weaver and Lawton, *Tourism Management*, pp. 70–82.

74. Ana Juarez, "Ecological Degradation, Global Tourism, and Inequality: Maya Interpretations of the Changing Environment in Quintana Roo, Mexico," *Human Organization, 61*(2) (2002), p. 117. Juarez notes that despite the wealth generated by tourism in the state of Quintana Roo, the benefits are poorly distributed and the state has the fourth highest rate of malnutrition among Mexico's thirty-two states.

75. Michel Picard, *Bali: Cultural Tourism and Touristic Culture* (Singapore: Archipelago, 1996).

76. Bali Tourism Authority, *Direct Foreign Tourist Arrivals to Bali by Nationality by Month in 2005,* available at www.balitourismauthority.net/news/Statistic_Nationality.xls, accessed September 30, 2006.

77. See www.ecotourism.org.

78. Henley and Partners (an international consulting firm) has compiled a Visa Restriction Index, which ranks countries according to the freedom of international travel that their citizens enjoy. See www.henleyglobal.com/visa_restrictions.htm.

79. A similar reversal in tourism occurred in El Salvador, Honduras, and Nicaragua after Hurricane Mitch in 1998.

80. John Lea, *Tourism and Development in the Third World* (London: Routledge, 1988), p. 33.

81. P. Needham, "War is Over . . . Peace Gives Tourism a Chance," *Travelweek,* no. 897, July 16, 1997, p. 10.

82. Weaver and Lawton, *Tourism Management,* p. 104.

83. Dirk Belau, *The Impact of the 2001–2002 Crisis on the Hotel and Tourism Industry* (Geneva: ILO, 2003), p. 8. Belau estimates that the 9/11 attacks alone account for 85 percent of the drop in global tourist demand (p. 7).

84. OAG Data, "Media Fact Sheet—9.11 Five Years On," www.oag.com/oag/website/com/OAG+Data/News/Press+Room/Press+Releases+2006/Media+Fact+Sheet+-+9.11+Five+Years+On+060906, accessed September 28, 2006.

85. Office of Travel and Tourism Industries (OTTI), "International Travelers to (Inbound) and from the U.S. International Visitors (Inbound) and U.S. Residents (Outbound) 1995–2005," http://tinet.ita.doc.gov/outreachpages/inbound.total_intl_travel_volume_1995-2005.html, accessed October 2, 2006.

86. Bali Tourism Authority, *Direct Foreign Tourist Arrivals to Bali by Nationality by Month in 2005.*

87. Canadian Tourism Commission, "Canadian Tourism Facts and Figures 2004," www.canadatourism.com/ctx/app/en/ca/statsfigures.do?path=templatedata\ctx\statsAndFigures\data\en_ca\Tourism_Fact_Figures\Year_2004&hasChildren=false, accessed September 28, 2006.

88. Weaver and Lawton, *Tourism Management,* p. 283.

89. Haunani-Kay Trask, "Lovely Hula Hands: Corporate Tourism and the Prostitution of Hawaiian Culture," in Margaret Andersen and Patricia Hill Collins, eds., *Race, Class, and Gender: An Anthology* (Belmont, CA: Wadsworth, 1998), pp. 90–98.

90. Picard, *Bali: Cultural Tourism and Touristic Culture,* p. 197.

91. Imtiaz Muqbil, "The War on Paedophiles in Tourism," *Travel Impact Newswire,* New Edition 28 (June 27, 2001).

# 17

# Transnational Corporations: In the Hurricane's Eye

## OVERVIEW[1]

Transnational corporations (TNCs) are a distinctive feature of international political economy (IPE) today. TNCs compete in regional and global markets and engage in foreign direct investment that is much sought after by national governments seeking jobs, technology, and the resources for economic growth. TNCs have always been controversial because of the power they seem to possess and because their "global reach" makes them difficult for nation-states to regulate or control.

This chapter looks at the contemporary pattern of TNC investment and answers a number of important questions: Who are the TNCs? Where do they operate and why? How much power do they have?

Perceptions of TNCs have evolved as IPE has changed over the past half-century. TNCs have been perceived as agents of capitalist imperialism, tools of U.S. hegemony, and state-level actors engaged in "triangular diplomacy."

Many scholars have called for a formal international regime to govern state–TNC interaction, much as the World Trade Organization (WTO) provides a system of governance for international trade flows. However, recent attempts to negotiate such a regime have been unable to overcome the self-interest and fears of TNCs and of states. TNC investment flows have fallen recently, and competition for transnational markets and investment has intensified, putting more pressure on states and TNCs. Although the importance of TNCs to IPE analysis remains clear, their future is still uncertain.

One of the distinctive features of the twenty-first century is the central role played by transnational corporations in IPE. International trade, global finance, national security, and knowledge and technology are all affected by transnational corporations and the competition among them in regional and global markets. This chapter examines the issues raised by a world in which territorial states confront transnational markets and the business enterprises that have evolved to compete in them.

Before we begin, however, we must deal briefly with terminology. Businesses that compete in global markets have been given different names at different times and in different fields of study. Once they were called simply *international businesses,* to distinguish them from firms that operated in local

**TABLE 17–1    Twenty Largest Nonfinancial Transnational Corporations in 2004, Ranked by Foreign Assets**

| RANK | TNC | HEADQUARTERS COUNTRY | MARKET |
|------|-----|----------------------|--------|
| 1. | General Electric | United States | Electrical and electronic equipment |
| 2. | Vodafone | United Kingdom | Telecommunications |
| 3. | Ford Motor Company | United States | Motor vehicles |
| 4. | General Motors | United States | Motor vehicles |
| 5. | BP | United Kingdom | Petroleum |
| 6. | ExxonMobil | United States | Petroleum |
| 7. | Royal Dutch/Shell | Netherlands | Petroleum |
| 8. | Toyota Motor | Japan | Motor vehicles |
| 9. | Total | France | Petroleum |
| 10. | France Telecom | France | Telecommunications |
| 11. | Suez | France | Electricity, gas, water |
| 12. | Electricite De France | France | Electricity, gas, water |
| 13. | E.On | Germany | Electricity, gas, water |
| 14. | Deutsche Telekom A.G. | Germany | Telecommunications |
| 15. | RWE Group | Germany | Electricity, gas, water |
| 16. | Hutchison Whampoa | Hong Kong | Diversified |
| 17. | Siemens A.G. | Germany | Electrical and electronic equipment |
| 18. | Volkswagen | Germany | Motor vehicles |
| 19. | Honda | Japan | Motor vehicles |
| 20. | Vivendi Universal | France | Diversified |

*Source:* United National Conference on Trade and Development (UNCTAD), *World Investment Report 2005.*

or national markets. For many years the term **multinational corporation (MNC)** was applied to indicate that the firm operated in several different national markets. As global markets and production structures have emerged, the accepted term has become **transnational corporation (TNC)**. The prefix *trans-* means "to go beyond," and the markets where these businesses compete are regional (such as NAFTA or the European Union) or global and clearly go beyond or transcend national markets.

You might not have encountered the term *transnational corporation* before, but you certainly are familiar with businesses that wear that label, the items they produce and sell, and the markets in which they operate. It is estimated that there are about 70,000 TNCs in the world today, with 690,000 foreign affiliates. Together they employ about 54 million workers. Table 17–1 lists the twenty largest nonfinancial TNCs in 2003, as compiled by the United Nations Conference on Trade and Development (UNCTAD), ranked according to foreign assets owned. (Rankings of TNCs vary according to year and whether the list is based on assets, revenues, or profits. The seating order varies, but the names for the most part remain the same.)

## TRANSNATIONAL CORPORATIONS IN PERSPECTIVE

Transnational corporations are constantly in the news, but they are anything but new themselves. TNCs have existed for hundreds of years; some of the earliest TNCs were state-chartered organizations such as the East India Company, which was granted a monopoly on trade with the East Indies by Queen Elizabeth I in 1600. These firms neatly combined visions of a business empire with the imperial territorial ambitions of the home states.

TNCs today are private business firms that compete in transnational, regional, and global markets. They are distinguished by the **foreign direct investment (FDI)** that they undertake as part and parcel of their operations. TNCs operate in markets that span national borders and so necessarily make investments in production, research, distribution, and marketing facilities abroad, often transferring technology abroad in the process. FDI is extremely important to countries seeking resources for economic growth, which amounts basically to all countries. The fact that TNCs are the institutions that allocate FDI resources makes them critical actors in IPE.

It is tempting but dangerous to generalize about what the 70,000 TNCs are and how they behave, beyond saying, as we have here, that they are creatures of transnational markets that have command of valuable FDI resources. A certain stereotypical image of transnational corporations has been formed in the press and elsewhere, however, and it is important to take a close look at it. Stereotypes are usually distortions based on a few exceptional cases, and this is true of TNCs as well. Here are some "facts" commonly associated with TNCs.

- TNCs are gigantic business organizations that dominate production, investment, and employment worldwide. They control global markets.
- TNCs invest in less developed countries (LDCs) to exploit their cheap labor and natural resources. TNCs gain and the countries of the South lose as natural resources and cheap labor-intensive commodities are traded for manufactured goods produced in the North.
- TNCs are so large that they dwarf all but a few states. They are the most powerful actors in the world today.

Let us look at these stereotypes to see how well they explain the actual pattern of TNC activities today.

## How Large Are TNCs?

Some transnational corporations are *very* large, but in general, TNCs come in different sizes and compete in markets of different scales. For example, the U.S.-based company, General Electric, the largest TNC in the UNCTAD ratings for 2003, owned $258 billion in foreign assets. By comparison, the firm ranked twenty-fifth, BMW of Germany, had foreign assets of just $44 billion. The Swiss pharmaceutical firm Novartis, the fiftieth-ranked TNC, had foreign assets of about $26 billion, and International Paper Company, the 100th-ranked TNC, had foreign assets of $12 billion. If we were to continue down the list through the nearly 70,000 other TNCs, we would come to some very small firms indeed. These businesses might be TNCs, and they might even be quite large compared to the typical firm competing in a local market, but they are of an altogether different scale from the "giants."

When we talk about giant TNCs, then, we are really talking about the largest 100 or 200 firms, not about TNCs generally. These business organizations are very large, as has been said before, because the markets in which they compete are very large and often require huge investments—markets such as electronics and electrical equipment (including computers), oil and gas, telecommunications, motor vehicles and parts, food and beverages, and pharmaceuticals.

There are several ways to measure the relative size of TNCs, and it is useful to look at several of them to get a better perspective on the competitive landscape. UNCTAD lists TNCs according to the value of their foreign assets, a good approach because it stresses the effect of FDI. Large firms that do not invest abroad and therefore do not own foreign assets would not appear on this list at all. The *Financial Times*, the distinctive conservative British newspaper, publishes a Global 500 listing based on the total value of company shares on world stock markets. Firms need not be TNCs to appear on this list, because rankings are based on share value, not FDI, but in practice most of them are. Table 17–2 lists the top fifteen firms from the *Financial Times* list.

Microsoft, the most valuable firm in the *Financial Times* Global 500, competes in a global market and is a technology leader, but it does not in fact engage in a great deal of foreign investment, so it does not even appear among the top 100 firms in the UNCTAD rankings. Microsoft does not invest abroad so much as it forms partnerships and alliances with foreign firms. This is a fundamentally different strategy from foreign direct investment.

Wal-Mart Stores is a big firm (by market value) and also a major foreign investor (number 35 on the UNCTAD list), but it is perhaps most noteworthy because of its large global workforce,

**TABLE 17–2     Largest Global Companies by Market Value, 2003** *Financial Times* **Global 500**

| COMPANY/MARKET | COUNTRY | MARKET VALUE ($ BILLION) | EMPLOYMENT TOTAL |
|---|---|---|---|
| 1. Microsoft/software and computer services | United States | 264 | 50,500 |
| 2. General Electric/diversified industrial group | United States | 259 | 315,000 |
| 3. ExxonMobil/oil and gas | United States | 241 | 92,500 |
| 4. Wal-Mart Stores/general retailers | United States | 234 | 1,400,000 |
| 5. Pfizer/pharmaceuticals and biotechnology | United States | 195 | 98,000 |
| 6. Citigroup/financial services | United States | 183 | 250,000 |
| 7. Johnson & Johnson/pharmaceuticals and biotechnology | United States | 170 | 108,300 |
| 8. Royal Dutch/Shell/oil and gas | Netherlands/United Kingdom | 149 | 115,000 |
| 9. BP/oil and gas | United Kingdom | 144 | 115,250 |
| 10. IBM/computer and services | United States | 139 | 325,889 |
| 11. American International Group (AIG)/insurance | United States | 130 | 80,000 |
| 12. Merck/pharmaceuticals and biotechnology | United States | 124 | 62,000 |
| 13. Vodafone/telecommunications | United Kingdom | 122 | 66,667 |
| 14. Procter & Gamble/personal goods | United States | 114 | 106,000 |
| 15. Intel/information technology hardware | United States | 112 | 78,700 |

*Source: Financial Times,* May 28, 2003, Smith Barney web database.

estimated at about 1.4 million workers in 2002. Many TNCs, however, do not employ as many workers as one might suppose given their economic scale. They are more important for the technology they can supply (Microsoft) or the FDI they can provide (General Electric) than for the absolute number of jobs they can create.

In conclusion, the largest TNCs are very large indeed, but not all TNCs are huge business operations. Many of the world's largest businesses do not engage in substantial amounts of FDI and therefore do not rank among the leading TNCs. The key aspect of transnational corporations to keep in mind is not their size, which varies, but their ability to provide foreign direct investment.

## The Rise of TNCs in the 1990s

If you imagine that TNCs have become more pervasive in recent years, you are correct. According to UNCTAD, the total amount of inward FDI flows increased dramatically from an average of about $225 billion worldwide in the period 1990–1995 to nearly $1.5 trillion in 2000 (FDI decreased after 2000, however, falling to $648 billion in 2003, as a result of a number of factors including economic recession and falling stock markets). The rise in TNC investment in the 1990s reflects the growth of transnational markets, both regional as in the European Union (EU) and global as in the North American Free Trade Area (NAFTA). UNCTAD identifies three forces driving this transnational market growth: policy liberalization, technological change, and increasing competition.

More and more countries have sought to attract FDI inflows to create jobs and encourage economic development. Many LDC governments have adopted the "Washington consensus" policies, for example, that facilitate open trade and free capital mobility. These policies create an environment more conducive to TNC investment. Countries that enter the main regional economic groups—NAFTA and the EU—adopt especially liberal trade and investment rules. China's entry into the WTO accelerated inward FDI flow. Countries such as India and Japan that have been slow to abandon mercantilist policies are disadvantaged in the competition for FDI resources. FDI is still controversial, but virtually all nations now actively seek FDI resources to advance their economic agendas.

Technological change has also encouraged FDI by reducing transportation and communication costs. Taken together, technological change and policy liberalization have expanded the domain of transnational markets relative to markets that are mainly domestic. This means that firms in these markets face greater competition than ever before. This competition for new markets, to gain technological advantages, or to find cheaper production processes, further accelerates the FDI process. Unlike the first TNCs, which benefited from monopoly power, most TNCs today are driven to invest abroad by the competitive environment found in transnational markets, the policy liberalization that encourages that competition, and the technological changes that make foreign investment more efficient.

### The Pattern of TNC Operations

Many people imagine that most TNCs are North-based businesses that have shifted production to the less developed South to take advantage of cheap labor or natural resources, but the facts do not support this conclusion. Most TNC investment is in fact North–North rather than North–South, and there is even an emerging pattern of some South–North TNC activity as firms in newly industrialized countries enter global markets and acquire foreign business assets. Four TNCs on UNCTAD's top 100 list are headquartered in newly industrialized countries: Hutchinson Whampoa (diversified businesses, Hong Kong), Petronas (oil and gas, Malaysia), Singtel Ltd. (telecommunications, Singapore), and Samsung Electronics (electronics, South Korea).

If we look at where FDI originates (by headquarters countries of TNCs), we find that the industrialized North dominates, as expected. Over 93 percent of global FDI flowed out of the developed countries, according to UNCTAD, with the member states of the EU (combined total of nearly 59 percent), the United States (18 percent), Japan (6 percent), and Switzerland (2.5 percent) at the head of the table. No surprises here.

But whereas many people imagine that TNCs invest mainly in low-wage developing countries, in fact the majority of FDI flows go into the high-wage North, because this is where the transnational markets are and because North countries have advanced technology and skilled workers whose high wages are matched by their high productivity. Of a total of $648 billion of FDI inflows in 2004, for example, $380 billion (about 59 percent) went to countries of the industrial North, led by the member states of the EU ($216 billion or 33 percent of total FDI inflows). Of the remainder, $96 billion (almost 15 percent) was invested in the United States by non–U.S. TNCs.

A great deal of FDI is regionally based, flowing out of countries in the EU into other EU countries and out of countries in NAFTA and into other NAFTA countries. This makes sense because TNCs tend to evolve and expand to compete in particular markets. Although markets for some commodities are truly global, especially petroleum and some primary products, much recent market growth has been regional, driven by EU and NAFTA expansion. The EU and NAFTA combined accounted for over 60 percent of all inward FDI in 2001.

Only $233 billion (about 36 percent) of FDI went to a group of countries that UNCTAD calls "developing countries," which excludes oil-exporting countries and the "least developed countries." Asian countries received $147 billion of FDI in 2004, with China ($60 billion) and Hong Kong ($34 billion) getting the lion's share. Two giant Asian economies, India ($5 billion) and Japan ($7.8 billion), received relatively little FDI. Both countries have domestic regulatory regimes that are perceived to be biased against foreign investment.

Latin America and the Caribbean received $67 billion of FDI in 2004, with Brazil ($18 billion) and Mexico ($16 billion) at the head of the pack. African nations tend to attract very little FDI, a total of just $18 billion in 2004, few nations attracting FDI of more than a few hundred million dollars. For the most part Africa is essentially ignored by TNCs because these countries do not have large markets, because they lack skilled labor, or because political or social instability makes them undesirable investment targets. Most "global" businesses are not really global at all, it seems, but instead channel investment to particular regional markets, leaving out large parts of the world's population, especially in Africa and South Asia.

## What Determines Where TNCs Invest?

The stereotype that TNCs invest only where labor and natural resources are cheap is clearly not a good general explanation of TNC behavior, although it does apply to some specific situations. A great deal of FDI goes from rich, high-wage countries such as Germany to other rich, high-wage countries such as the United States. And, in any case, the theory that TNCs go where labor is cheap is at best an incomplete theory because labor is cheap in many parts of the world—so why do TNCs invest here (China) instead of there (India), if wages are low in both places? The question of why TNCs invest where they do is thus a very interesting one. Because there are thousands of TNCs in the world, it is unlikely that a single theory can explain all of their behavior. Here are several explanations that attempt to account for different aspects of TNC behavior.

Why do TNCs invest abroad, especially in other high-wage countries, when they face so many obvious disadvantages in doing so? A U.S. company setting up operations in France, for example, must deal with different laws and regulations, different labor practices and union restrictions, a different language and culture, and a variety of other difficulties. It would seem that a French firm that is already equipped with this "local knowledge" would have a distinct competitive advantage. Why not simply reach an agreement to have the French firm produce and sell the product under license?

TNCs do not make much sense in highly competitive markets with standardized products and technology, where everyone has equal access to resources and decisions are made on the basis of cost or price alone. In markets like these, the disadvantages of operating abroad would doom any foreign firm. TNCs make sense, however, if there is some particular knowledge or advantage that compensates for other disadvantages. Raymond Vernon's **product cycle theory** provides one explanation for TNC investment behavior.

Vernon was particularly interested in TNCs that produced technologically sophisticated products, whereby a firm might possess a technological advantage over competitors, and by the surprisingly common phenomenon of trade reversals, whereby the country that invents a product sometimes finds itself a few years later importing that same item from abroad. His three-stage product cycle theory explains how this can happen and how TNCs are created in the process.[2]

In the first stage of the product cycle, a firm in a high-income country identifies a need that can be satisfied with a technologically sophisticated product. For example, the modern mobile (cellular) phone satisfies the needs of people who want to remain in communication in many locations. Countries such as the United States, Japan, and those in the European Union have the technology resources to address this sort of need and the income to pay for the products, which are often very expensive in the early stages. In the first stage, therefore, companies such as Motorola (United States) or Nokia (Finland) invest millions of dollars in product development and production to develop products to satisfy a home-country need.

Once the product has been developed and a market created at home, it is possible to export to other countries where consumers or businesses may have similar incomes and living standards. In the second stage, therefore, mobile phones may be exported to other high-income areas of Asia, Europe, and North America. The firms become multinational or transnational in this stage, according to Vernon's theory, as they establish sales offices and some production or distribution facilities abroad. Some of the North–North FDI that was discussed earlier occurs in stage 2.

Finally, the technology has become standardized to the point at which the product may be produced more efficiently in a newly industrialized country such as Mexico or Malaysia. At this point production moves abroad and the TNC makes another foreign investment.

Note that technology and market factors are important elements of the product cycle explanation of TNC behavior. Products are invented and developed where technology is abundant and incomes are high. The market expands to other high-income countries once the product has been developed, and FDI follows as firms rush to compete in the bigger market. Finally, when the technology matures, production becomes transnational via FDI flows.

**Appropriability Theory.**    Developed by Richard Caves and others, **appropriability theory**, helps explain why Vernon's product cycle firms invest abroad rather than licensing production to a local firm or taking on a local partner. The appropriability theory argues that some firms become TNCs because they have too much to lose if they enter into partnerships or licensing agreements with foreign firms, which might in fact appear more profitable in terms of a simple dollars-and-cents calculation. This is especially true if the firm has some specific "intangible asset" such as a valuable trademark or copyright, or has invested in new technology, a proprietary process (such as Coca-Cola's secret formula for its products), or efficient management techniques found in some Japanese firms.

The fear is that these advantages or technological innovations will be stolen, copied, or otherwise "appropriated" by the competition if the firm does not retain full control over them. If the firm gives up control of foreign production, distribution, or sales, it risks losing control of its key competitive advantage. The foreign partner or licensee might copy the product and sell pirated versions, for example, or learn how to manufacture the product itself and go into competition with the originating firm.

The only way to be sure that the key competitive factors are protected (and not appropriated by foreign firms) is to keep full control of the process. This means foreign direct investment when entering foreign markets, creating wholly-owned subsidiaries. Rather than licensing agreements, TNCs engage in foreign direct investment, according to this theory, as a defensive measure.

**TNCs and Underdevelopment.**    Stephen Hymer, a path-breaking radical political economist, was among the first to see that TNCs sometimes exist to protect and exploit unique advantages—factors such as those just discussed that might give them monopoly power and the ability to earn excess profits. Hymer argued that the desire to retain monopoly power and also to exploit foreign markets caused TNCs to engage in patterns of FDI that do not foster economic development, but rather lead to the "development of underdevelopment."[3]

If corporate headquarters executives fear that their competitive assets will be appropriated or diluted, they will tend to keep control of them at home and be sure that strategic decisions are made by home-country, not host-country, executives. This creates what is called the **branch factory syndrome**, in that critical technology and the most productive assets remain securely at headquarters, while inferior technology and less productive assets are transferred abroad to the branch factory. FDI that builds branch factories may transfer technology and create jobs, in this theory, but the technology will always be inferior and the jobs will never be as good as in the headquarters firm.

Hymer's theory, like the appropriability theory, views FDI as essentially a defensive mechanism. Hymer goes further, however, in linking TNC strategy to an international division of labor that privileges the industrial core and systematically prevents periphery countries from catching up.

**Politics and Protectionist Barriers.**    Political factors can also be important in TNC strategy. Transnational corporations depend on open international markets. They need to be able to invest abroad, of course, but they also depend on the ability to import and export. Trade barriers make their internal operations less efficient and disadvantage them compared with the domestic protected firm. This explains in part why so much FDI is regionally based, such as FDI within the EU or within NAFTA. The lower trade and investment barriers within the regional blocs encourage intrabloc FDI compared with other patterns of FDI.

Interestingly, however, trade barriers can also encourage certain types of TNC behavior. Some FDI is an unintentional result of mercantilist policies designed to keep out foreign products. A foreign firm can get around a tariff barrier by establishing a domestic factory and, in a sense, becoming a domestic firm. In the early 1980s, for example, the United States negotiated a voluntary export agreement with Japan that was intended to protect U.S. auto firms while they developed more fuel-efficient models. The agreement put numerical limits on car exports from Japan to the United States. The limits did not apply, however, to autos produced in the United States and sold by Japanese firms, so long as most of the parts and assembly took place in the United States or Canada. Honda, Toyota, and Nissan all began to invest in production facilities in North America so that they could retain or even expand their market despite the trade barriers.

In the U.S.–Japan auto agreement case, a policy that was intended to keep out foreign cars instead attracted foreign FDI and probably strengthened the Japanese firms. Such "defensive" FDI is not always possible or profitable, of course, but when it is, it helps us understand why firms invest abroad.

Politics can affect FDI patterns in other ways as well. The Boeing Company, for example, markets its commercial aircraft to many airlines that are owned by governments or whose decisions are strongly influenced by government policymakers. Boeing often finds that, to get a large order for its aircraft, it must accept "offsets," which are agreements that certain components will be produced in the country buying the airplanes. Investment resources and technological know-how are sometimes exchanged for purchase orders. In situations like these, as Stopford and Strange pointed out, TNCs may become so involved in international politics that their negotiations, with host states and home states as well as with other TNCs, are more like diplomacy than simply business.[4]

**Currency Instability.**     Transnational corporations are especially susceptible to the effects of unstable foreign exchange rates because they often have costs that are denominated in one group of currencies and earn revenues in other currencies. An unexpected shift in exchange rates can raise effective costs and reduce the value of revenues. Some international businesses have seen profits collapse into loss and foreign markets disappear as a result of exchange-rate swings. In 2003 Nestlé, the world's largest food company, announced that profits had fallen by half despite a higher quantity of goods sold, because of the unexpected appreciation of the Swiss franc. What Nestlé gained in consumer purchases it lost—and then some—in the foreign exchange markets.

There are many ways to reduce this exchange-rate risk, including the use of complex financial instruments. One very direct way is to establish production facilities in each major market so that costs and revenues accrue largely in the same currency. The problem of currency instability is a factor that drives TNCs to behave more like national firms than like global giants.

The combination of trade barriers and exchange-rate factors encourages firms to produce goods in the countries where they are sold rather than simply exporting from a central location. The globalization of markets, therefore, is sometimes associated with what might be called "multilocal" production and a corresponding pattern of TNC investment. That is, the corporation is regional or global, but each country's operations are configured along more national or local lines in order to minimize or avoid trade barriers and currency problems.

Another pattern of FDI occurs when foreign exchange rates are misaligned, either undervalued or overvalued, as explained in Chapter 7. When a currency is overvalued, for example, imported products are systematically less expensive than domestic goods. This can be a strong incentive for firms to invest in foreign production facilities. The foreign factories may be more or less efficient, but they benefit from advantageous foreign exchange rates.

The U.S. dollar was considerably overvalued during the early 1980s, for example—a fact that encouraged U.S. firms to set up offshore production facilities. The effect of the overvalued Japanese yen was so significant in the late 1980s that a Japanese term, *endaka*, was coined to describe its effect. The *endaka* effect was to force Japanese firms to set up production networks throughout East Asia and Southeast Asia and to ruthlessly cut costs at factories in Japan. *Endaka* was very stressful to Japanese businesses, but it forced them to evolve into superefficient TNCs.

**Location-Specific Advantages.**    Some FDI, as we have seen, is driven by the desire to protect firm-specific advantages, such as proprietary processes or trademarks. At other times, however, FDI may be influenced by location-specific advantages. Some of these advantages are obvious, such as access to natural resources that are available only in specific locations. At other times the advantages are more complicated. For example, if you want to compete in the computer software market, you'd need to set up shop where the best people are. This means that you would invest where many other firms have also located, so that you can benefit from the pool of highly trained individuals in that area and the intense competition and constant innovation that is built into this environment. You would channel FDI to Redmond, Washington (Microsoft's home), the Silicon Valley of California, and probably to Bangalore, India. These and just a few other places in the world have the right technological and human environment to make your firm very competitive.

    In the same way, if you wanted to compete in the world market for eyeware, such as designer sunglasses, you would probably open a facility near Belluno, Italy. As Michael Porter explains in his book, *The Competitive Advantage of Nations*, this region of northern Italy is where the world's top eyeglass design and manufacturing facilities are found and where the world's pickiest eyeglass customers live, too.[5] It is impossible to compete successfully in the global market without being exposed to the intense and innovative competition in this local market. Most of the quality eyeware in the world is manufactured by companies that have at least some of their facilities in Belluno.

**Competition.**    Finally, it is important to remember that TNCs are transnational because the markets in which they compete are transnational. In some cases, a firm may be driven to invest abroad because of simple competitive pressures: If our firm does not contest this market, other firms will, and they may gain an advantage from doing so. In this regard, firms may act a bit less like coolly rational profit-maximizing enterprises and a bit more like mercantilist states, which see an opponent's gain as their own potential loss.

    To summarize, some TNC investments are driven by the desire to exploit low wages or cheap natural resources, but, given the types of products that TNCs produce and their actual pattern of FDI, other factors are much more important. TNCs invest abroad to protect a competitive advantage, to exploit a monopoly position, to get around trade barriers, to avoid currency problems, to take advantage of special production environments . . . and because they are driven to do so by their competition with other TNCs.

### How Powerful Are TNCs?

Many people assume that TNCs are very powerful because they are such large organizations and because, through their FDI flows, they influence the global distribution of investment and technology. Some people go so far as to assert that TNCs are as powerful as states—or more powerful than states.

    One commonly cited "fact" is that 51 of the top 100 "economic entities" are corporations—and the other 49 are countries. This statistic is based on tables that compare the gross domestic products of countries with the total revenues of corporations. The sales of the top 200 corporations are calculated to have combined sales that are greater than those of all of the countries of the world combined, minus the ten largest countries. The message of such data is obvious: TNCs are bigger than all but the biggest nation-states and must, therefore, have tremendous power. This message is also, of course, nonsense. To make this comparison is to misunderstand what a TNC is and also to misunderstand what a state is.

    From a technical standpoint, comparing countries and TNCs this way is comparing apples with oranges. The gross domestic product of a country is not equivalent to the total revenues of a corporation. Wal-Mart has high revenues, to be sure, but why are its revenues the correct measure of Wal-Mart's power and not its wage bill, its net profit, its employment total, its FDI resources, or the technology that it can potentially offer a host country? One suspects that total revenues are selected simply because they are large and therefore make Wal-Mart appear large relative to states.

Transnational corporations do have tremendous influence over economic resources (see the box, "Are TNCs Really Bigger Than States?"), but not so much as this biased methodology suggests.

The second problem is that this analysis compares TNCs and nation-states in strictly monetary terms, ignoring many factors that really matter a great deal more. This focus on one factor, money, is ironic, because many critics of TNCs criticize corporations for ignoring important non-monetary factors, such as security or the environment. States possess territory and make laws; they have sovereignty, citizens, and they have armies and navies. They have legitimacy, too, which means that the international community accepts their right to make important social decisions. TNCs have none of these things, unless you think that employees or customers are the same as national citizens. Even the giant Wal-Mart Stores, which have 1.4 million employees, have fewer workers than most countries have citizens, if we want to use this as our measure. States are fundamentally different from TNCs, and attempts to compare their power and influence based on simple numerical indicators must inevitably distort reality. Both states and TNCs have power, and so sometimes they must negotiate and engage in diplomacy; but their powers differ and so their relationship is complex and evolving.

---

### ARE TNCs REALLY BIGGER THAN STATES?

The question of whether some TNCs are really bigger or more powerful than some states begs for a clear answer. It is probably impossible to develop a simple quantitative measure to perfectly compare companies and countries, their differences being so many and so diverse. Clearly, comparing TNC revenues with state gross domestic products is misleading, but is it possible to come up with a better measure of their relative economic influence?

Paul De Grauwe and Filip Camerman set out to answer this question in a paper that was released in January 2002 (see Suggested Readings at the end of this chapter). De Grauwe is a noted professor of international economics and is also, along with Camerman, a member of the Belgian Senate. Their study was not entirely an academic exercise, as you may imagine. Belgium is a relatively small state (population of about 10 million, with the nineteenth highest gross domestic product in the world). Belgium's leaders might really be concerned about their power relative to corporations. Here is what De Grauwe and Camerman found out.

First, if you are going to try to compare states and corporations in terms of dollars and cents, the least distorting approach is to compare how much value they add per year to the resources they command. For a company, this means, approximately, subtracting the value of the resources that the firm uses (labor, raw materials, and so on) from the value of the products it sells. For a state, the value added is calculated in approximately the same way and is equal to the nation's gross domestic product.

Ranking corporations and states together, sixty-three of the top 100 entities were countries. The United States was at the top of the list, of course, followed by Japan, Germany, the UK, France, China, Italy, Canada, Brazil, and Mexico. These were the ten largest economic entities in the world in 2002 according to this measure. The first TNC to appear on the list is Wal-Mart Stores at number 44, just behind Chile but ahead of Pakistan. Exxon was number 48 (just ahead of the Czech Republic and New Zealand), and General Motors was number 58 (just ahead of Hungary, Ford Motor, and Mitsubishi).

There is a considerable difference in scale reported between the biggest states and the biggest corporations. The United States, for example, had total value-added of $9,882.8 billion, whereas the biggest corporation, Wal-Mart, had total value-added of $67.7 billion. Corporations are powerful, to be sure, but in simple economic terms the biggest corporations are no match for the biggest states. The distinction becomes greater, of course, when other factors are taken into account.

Looking at longer-term trends, De Grauwe and Camerman concluded that the relative size of corporations compared with states had actually declined somewhat over the previous twenty years. This creates a paradox. Corporations are smaller than many people believe relative to states and have grown more slowly than states. Why, then, is the public perception just the opposite? The authors did not offer an explanation.

One possible answer to the riddle is that although states have actually grown faster than TNCs, perhaps the nature of the competition among states is different now, more intense, giving corporations an advantage.

Perhaps, too, the investment resources and technology that TNCs have to offer are seen as more critical to economic development than they were a few years ago.

For his part, *Financial Times* columnist Martin Wolf, reporting the study's findings, concluded that the answer lies more in changing political conditions than economic ones. He writes that

> The change we have seen over the past 20 years should not be called "corporate globalization." It is market-driven globalization unleashed, consciously and voluntarily, by governments. Corporations are neither as big nor as powerful as critics claim. The firmly held belief in the opposite position is another urban myth.[a]

*Reference*
[a] Martin Wolf, "Countries Still Rule the World," *Financial Times,* February 6, 2002, available at www.globalpolicy. org/socecon/tncs/2002/countriesrule.htm.

## CHANGING REACTIONS TO TRANSNATIONAL CORPORATIONS

Apart from business leaders and economists, who tend to view the growth of TNCs as the natural consequence of emerging regional and global market structures, most authors interpret the expansion of TNCs as a decisive shift in the balance of power in IPE. They speculate about who will benefit from this shift and argue about how. Several quite distinctive viewpoints have emerged that we will discuss in this section: TNCs as a form of capitalist imperialism, TNCs as a tool of U.S. hegemony, and TNCs as state-level actors in IPE.

### TNCs and Capitalist Imperialism

Transnational corporations and foreign direct investment were distinctive elements of the first modern era of globalization, which reached its zenith about 100 years ago and ended with the opening shots of World War I. V. I. Lenin famously characterized this era in a book called *Imperialism: The Highest Stage of Capitalism.*[6] Lenin focused on "finance capitalism," not transnational corporations per se, but his approach and many of his conclusions are easily applied to TNCs. Lenin argued that colonial imperialism had been replaced by economic imperialism. Foreign armies and occupying forces were no longer necessary because the same result (exploitation by and dependency on the capitalist core) could now be accomplished by foreign investors and business corporations.

If you read Lenin's famous little book on imperialism, you will quickly appreciate that it is very much a creature of a particular time and place, full of references to long-forgotten people and events. It was not a book written for the ages but rather an argument written in the present tense. His indictment of international investment as a form of imperialism, however, does live on through books such as William Greider's *One World, Ready or Not: The Manic Logic of Global Capitalism* (see Suggested Readings).

Stephen Hymer is responsible for the direct link between TNCs and imperialism today, as was discussed earlier in this chapter. Hymer's path-breaking theory of TNC behavior suggested that many TNCs engage in FDI because they wish to exploit a monopoly position while protecting a key asset, such as a trademark or a patented process. Their profit-maximizing strategy is to exploit the foreign market in favor of higher profits at home. In terms of financial strategy, terms of trade, and technology transfer, Hymer's analysis predicts that TNCs will engage in a pattern of behavior that is imperialism in everything but name.[7]

### TNCs as Tools of U.S. Hegemony

Transnational corporations came to be viewed by many as tools of U.S. hegemony during the Cold War era. There were several reasons for this association. First, U.S. TNCs were especially active and focused on foreign expansion in the immediate post–World War II years. U.S. foreign policy seemed to be directed in part to creating opportunities for U.S. firms to expand abroad. And once FDI had taken place, U.S. investments abroad created economic interests favorable to U.S. policies. So it seemed as though the United States promoted its TNCs and they in turn supported U.S. policies.

IPE scholar Robert Gilpin, writing in his 1975 book, *U.S. Power and the Multinational Corporation* (see Suggested Readings), argued that U.S.-based TNCs were a tool of U.S. hegemony. Citing a famous international economist, he asserted that

> As Jacob Viner has pointed out, from the initial movement of American capital and corporations abroad the State Department and the White House have sought to channel American investment in a direction that would enhance the foreign policy objectives of the United States. With respect to the foreign expansion of the multinational corporation, these objectives have been seen as maintaining America's share of world markets, securing a strong position in foreign economies, spreading American economic and political values, and controlling access to vital raw materials, especially petroleum.[8]

One example of Gilpin's thesis is found in the role that the Boeing Company played in U.S. relations with China over the last forty years. Table 17–3 provides snapshots of a few of the notable events in this relationship.

President Richard Nixon went to China in 1972 in a move to solidify U.S. hegemony relative to the Soviet Union. He also went to sell airplanes, specifically Boeing 707s like Air Force One, his official airplane. Although U.S. and Chinese officials exchanged endless toasts, it was the aircraft sale that sealed the deal by providing meaningful economic benefits to both countries.

Chinese purchases of Boeing aircraft later in the 1970s were symbolic of Chinese commitment to modernization and U.S. government commitment to closer diplomatic relations with China. Chairman Deng Xiaoping's tour of Boeing assembly facilities near Seattle to mark U.S. diplomatic recognition is but one example.

By the mid-1970s, when Gilpin's book appeared, U.S. hegemony was apparently in decline. U.S. wealth and power had not declined in *absolute* terms, but Europe and Japan had closed the gap, resulting in a *relative* decline in U.S. influence. Ironically, Gilpin viewed this as a consequence of the strategic use of U.S. FDI.

> From a political perspective, the inherent contradiction of capitalism is that it develops rather than that it exploits the world. A capitalist international economy plants the seeds of its own destruction in that it diffuses economic growth, industry, and technology and thereby undermines the distribution of power upon which that liberal interdependent economy was rested.[9]

Gilpin was concerned that the relative decline of U.S. hegemony would bring an end to the international political environment that had made the expansion of U.S. TNCs and the development

**TABLE 17–3   China, Boeing, and U.S. Policy**

| YEAR | EVENT |
|---|---|
| 1972 | Nixon flies to China in Air Force One, a modified Boeing 707 airliner. He meets Mao Tse-tung in Beijing. China purchases ten Boeing 707s. |
| 1978 | Deng Xiaoping launches "Four Modernizations" program. China orders three Boeing 747s. |
| 1979 | Washington and Beijing establish formal diplomatic relations. Deng visits the United States and tours Boeing assembly plants in Renton and Everett, Washington. |
| 1980–1989 | China orders thirty-four Boeing 737s, thirty-three 757s, and ten 767s. |
| 1990 | China places one of the largest commercial aircraft orders in Boeing history, thirty-six airplanes and thirty-six options, for a total value of $9 billion. |
| 1994 | Clinton "delinks" human rights from debate over granting most-favored-nation trading status to China. Xian Aircraft Co. wins contract to produce 100 tail sections for Boeing 737-300/500. China takes delivery of its 200th Boeing airplane. |

*Source:* "China and Boeing Chronology," *The Seattle Times*, May 26, 1996, p. A1.

of Europe and Japan possible. He feared a return of protectionism as had occurred when British hegemony declined at the end of the nineteenth century.

Thirty years after Gilpin's book appeared, the viewpoint that U.S. TNCs are tools of U.S. hegemonic strategy no longer dominates the debate, but it has not entirely disappeared. The global influence of U.S. media TNCs has been frequently cited in this regard. U.S. films and television broadcasts are seen around the world, and the Internet is dominated by U.S.–based content providers. To the extent that these media outlets present world events and daily life in ways that emphasize U.S. values and interests or that view U.S. policies favorably, these TNCs are a source of what Joseph Nye calls "soft power." Some have argued that this soft power advantage is even more important to U.S. foreign policy in the long run than is its clear military dominance.

## TNCs as State-Level Actors

The decline of U.S. hegemony did not end the era of TNC expansion, as Robert Gilpin feared, but it did change its pattern. Protectionism did increase, both in the United States and elsewhere, but trade barriers can actually encourage FDI, as was noted earlier in this chapter. The most important change, however, was probably the rise of non–U.S. TNCs, especially firms based in Japan. TNCs based in the "triad" of Japan, the European Union, and the United States intensified their foreign investment activities. The United States, which had become accustomed to its position as a "home country" for U.S.–based TNCs, found itself also a "host country" to major TNCs based in Japan and Europe. The previously accepted distinction between home and host countries was starting to disappear, replaced with the realization that we are all host countries now.

The list of potential host countries expanded dramatically with the collapse of communism in 1989. Many countries, including even Russia, now opened their doors to foreign direct investment and the resources and technology that it promised. Other events brought even more countries into the world economy. The end of apartheid in South Africa, for example, opened that market to inward FDI and also allowed South African firms an opportunity to expand abroad (SABMiller, formerly South African Breweries, is the world's second-largest beer producer today, for example, with production facilities in more than forty countries). Economic policy liberalization in Latin America increased FDI flows to countries in this region, too.

In their 1991 book, *Rival States, Rival Firms* (see Suggested Readings), John Stopford and Susan Strange coined the term *triangular diplomacy* to describe the pattern of state–TNC relations that they saw emerging. In the past, they wrote, firms had competed with firms and states had engaged in diplomacy with other states. Now, they said, the largest TNCs had more power relative to states and relative to competitive markets, too. Diplomacy, in which actors bargain with each other, was a more accurate description of where the world was heading. States still bargained with states, they said. And, although businesses were still in competition with each other, the largest TNCs often bargained with each other much as states did. More and more often, TNCs would form alliances or other working arrangements to help them develop technologies and spread the risk of new investments.

An example of firm-to-firm diplomacy is New United Motor Manufacturing, Inc. (NUMMI), a joint venture between fierce competitors Toyota and General Motors (GM). NUMMI was established in 1984 when Toyota agreed to take over operations in GM's least efficient factory, located in Fremont, California. Using Japanese management techniques, Toyota soon had the NUMMI factory running at world-class quality and efficiency, churning out cars for both Toyota and GM. Today NUMMI makes three left-hand-drive models for sale in the United States (Toyota Corolla, Toyota Tacoma, and the Pontiac Vibe) and also a right-hand-drive Toyota Voltz, which is exported to Japan.

The NUMMI alliance, just one of many among automotive companies, allowed GM and Toyota to share risk, share markets, and combine strengths even as they competed for the same customers. Such joint ventures and working agreements among firms that compete in the same transnational markets are the result of the TNC-to-TNC diplomacy that Stopford and Strange pointed out.

State–TNC bargaining is the third side of the diplomacy triangle. Both states and transnational corporations control valuable resources, and they need each other. States would like access to the investment resources and technology that TNCs can offer. TNCs, for their part, desire access to the natural resources and skilled labor that states control and, of course, they also seek access to national markets for the goods and services that they produce. (A state that ignores education and training for much of its population and thus offers mainly unskilled labor has little to bargain with and can expect to attract low-productivity sweatshop-type FDI.) Because each side has much to offer and much to gain, it would seem that mutually advantageous agreements should be easy to achieve. However, it is not as simple as that, because both states and TNCs face competition.

Because TNCs are generally in competition with other big businesses for transnational markets, they have a strong incentive to attempt to negotiate the most favorable terms possible for their FDI projects. TNCs typically seek favorable tax treatment, state-funded infrastructure, and perhaps even weakened enforcement of some government regulations. A weak state, or one with few productive resources and a weak market system, may be at a fundamental disadvantage in such negotiations. Competition from other states may force it to grant many concessions to attract FDI. This is true both in less developed countries and in advanced industrial economies.

In the early 1990s, for example, the German automaker Mercedes Benz (MB), now DaimlerChrysler, announced that it would build a factory in the United States to produce a Mercedes sport-utility vehicle (SUV). MB had much to offer in this FDI project, although perhaps its most valuable bargaining chip was its reputation for quality. If a state or locality could satisfy MB, it would be a sign that it could meet high quality standards. More FDI would be likely to follow. The stakes, therefore, were very high in bargaining over this investment.

MB increased its bargaining power by creating competition for its FDI. MB published its requirements for the FDI project and invited a large number of state and local governments to submit bids for the factory. By 1993 the list was narrowed to three options: potential factory sites in South Carolina, North Carolina, and Alabama. All three states had right-to-work laws that limited union power. North Carolina offered $108 million worth of investment incentives. South Carolina offered a package similar to the one that had previously attracted a BMW factory; the total value was about $130 million. Alabama won the bidding, however, with a package worth $253 million. The value of Mercedes' end of the FDI package itself was $300 million. As Leon Grunberg wrote in the second edition of this textbook,

> Alabama, a state with a reputation as a backward place holding few attractions for MNCs, went all out to win the investment. The incentive package included $92 million to purchase and develop the site; $77 million for improvements to highways, utilities, and other infrastructure; tax abatement on machinery and equipment; and $60 million on education and training. The University of Alabama even agreed to run a special "Saturday School" to help the children of German Mercedes managers keep up with the higher standards in science and math back home in Germany. All this would be paid for by the taxpayers of Alabama. The governor of North Carolina was particularly upset by a tax break the Alabama legislature passed (labeled by some the "Benz Bill"), which allowed Mercedes to withhold 5 percent of employees' wages to pay off Mercedes debts.
>
> The wooing of Mercedes went beyond financial incentives. It included an offer to name a section of an interstate highway "the Mercedes-Benz autobahn," airplane and helicopter tours, visits by the governor of Alabama and other state officials to Mercedes headquarters in Germany, a billboard in German near the site welcoming Mercedes, and the governor driving a Mercedes as the official state car. It is not surprising to read that a Mercedes executive claimed it was "Alabama's zeal" that was the deciding factor.
>
> In return, 1,500 workers would get good-paying jobs, and several more thousand jobs would be created in supplier firms, restaurants, and the like.[10]

The lesson seems clear: When a TNC has unique resources to offer while the state has few and faces stiff competition from other states, the TNC has a tremendous advantage and the diplomacy can be very one-sided. This need not always be the case, however; if states make their own investments in education, resources, infrastructure, and so forth, then they can have the upper hand. The competition that TNCs face from each other can press them to make concessions, too.

It is controversial to say so, but the conventional wisdom until just a few years ago was that TNCs generally come out ahead in TNC–state negotiations. Not in every case, of course, because TNCs are so many and so diverse and states are a mixed bag as well, but perhaps more often than not. TNCs are "footloose" and have many possible investment options, whereas states are rooted, like trees, in the territory they control. TNCs ought to be able to play one state against another to get the best terms, as in the case of the MB factory in Alabama. A shadow of doubt has fallen over this viewpoint in recent years, however, as the level of competition among TNCs has heated up.

Several European countries held auctions for third-generation (3G) wireless telecommunications rights beginning in 2000, for example. At stake were a limited number of slots in the part of the electromagnetic spectrum reserved for cutting-edge wireless communications networks. The bidding among telecom TNCs for these licenses was intense, and the sums that were paid to the European governments were astronomical—about $108 billion just for the right to set up the networks. Vodafone, a British mobile phone company, ranked high on the FDI list shown in Table 17–1 because of its huge investment in these networks in Europe.

It is clear today that the telecom TNCs overbid for the 3G rights; the payments are much higher than can be justified by potential revenues. Did the states "win" the diplomacy? In a dollars-and-cents view, yes. They received very large payments that allowed them to balance shaky budgets. In the long run, however, the outcome is less clear, because the states need the TNCs (and their resources) as much as the TNCs need the states (and their resources). When competition drives a bargain too far on either side, it puts the other party at risk and suddenly the whole enterprise is in jeopardy.

This is what bothered Raymond Vernon when he wrote his 1998 book, *In the Hurricane's Eye: The Troubled Prospects of Multinational Enterprises* (see Suggested Readings). Vernon was very concerned that competition among TNCs was forcing them to squeeze states for more and more concessions. Although we say that the states are squeezed, it is of course the citizens of the states who feel the pressure. They are squeezed in terms of higher taxes or reduced government services, lower labor standards, lax environmental enforcement, and in other ways. How would they react? One possibility is that they would react politically, putting pressure on their governments to protect them and to adopt protectionist measures generally. This was Vernon's fear. Although Vernon wrote prior to the protests at the 1999 World Trade Organization meetings in Seattle, the chaos of those protests is very much the eye of the hurricane he was describing.

TNCs thrive in a liberal political and economic climate. A new wave of protectionism—a return to the beggar-thy-neighbor policies of the 1930s—would severely jeopardize the future of TNCs and of the states as well. Ironically, just as many observers were predicting the endless expansion of TNCs, creating *The Borderless World* (the title of a book by Kenichi Ohmae) and *When Corporations Rule the World* (a book by David C. Korten—see Suggested Readings), Vernon saw the potential for a great collapse. *The Hurricane's Eye* concludes with this warning:

> The great sweep of technological change continues to link nations and their economies in a process that seems inexorable and irreversible. . . . Yet the basic adjustments demanded by the globalization trend cannot take place without political struggle. Too many interests in the nation states see the economic risks and costs of the adjustments involved, even if justified in the longer terms, as unfairly distributed and deeply threatening. . . . But a prolonged struggle between nations and enterprises runs the risk of reducing the effectiveness of both, leaving them distracted and bruised as they grope towards a new equilibrium. To shorten that struggle and reduce its costs will demand an extraordinary measure of imagination and restraint from leaders on both sides of the business-government divide.[11]

## A GLOBAL FDI REGIME?

The logical place for leaders of "imagination and restraint" from both business and government to negotiate would have been the Multilateral Agreement on Investment (MAI) talks, which were sponsored by the Organization for Economic Cooperation and Development (OECD) with the intent of creating a regime to provide governance for FDI in the same way that the WTO provides governance for international trade. What kind of governance? The goal of the MAI talks was to set norms and standards for states–TNCs negotiations.

Both sides of the table have something to gain from an international investment agreement. TNCs for example, would like to be assured of "national treatment." Under the WTO, nations can impose certain trade restrictions at the border, but once a product is inside the border it cannot be discriminated against in favor of domestic products. National treatment of international trade prevents domestic discrimination against foreign products.

National treatment for FDI would mean that, while a state has the right to regulate inward investment at the border, once that investment has been made it must treat the local subsidiary of the foreign TNC the same as it treats similar domestic firms. There must be no domestic discrimination against TNC affiliates, even if this means giving them tax preferences or subsidies intended for domestic firms only. This is one of several items on the TNC agenda that would make FDI more efficient and less vulnerable to political forces.

Although it might be too much to expect from an international agreement, TNCs would benefit if the nation-states were to coordinate or harmonize their regulation of big businesses. Increasingly, as we have noted, TNCs are driven to form alliances and to merge operations in order to be competitive with other TNCs. Because of their broad reach, however, TNCs often find themselves subject to antitrust or competition regulation in several different jurisdictions. If these regulatory regimes had similar policies and standards this would cause little bother, but this is seldom the case.

The United States and the European Union in particular have adopted different norms for business mergers, and when TNCs wish to join operations, they frequently confront the need to gain approval in both places. This problem appeared dramatically in 1996, when the EU competition regulators initially opposed approval of a merger between two U.S.–based aircraft firms, Boeing and McDonnell Douglas, which had been given a green light by U.S. authorities. It was suddenly very clear that an agreement between two U.S.–based firms could be vetoed by another government if both firms had important operations there. Subsequently the EU did veto a merger between General Electric and Westinghouse, both U.S.–based TNCs, despite prior U.S. government approval. Both firms suffered significant reversals when their merger plans were canceled.

Although TNCs cannot escape government controls such as antitrust approval for mergers and acquisitions, it would clearly be in their benefit if they were subject to one set of rules, not many contradictory ones.

For their part, states have a number of important interests that could be served by a multilateral agreement. These might include a set of standards for TNC behavior (to prevent labor rights abuses, for example) and rules on transfer pricing. When a TNC transfers resources (say, auto parts) from one subsidiary to another, it has to set an internal price, called the **transfer price**, which is used to calculate the profits and therefore establish the tax liability of operations in each country. It is well known that transfer prices can be manipulated to create artificially low taxable profits in jurisdictions where tax rates are high and artificially high taxable income for operations located in countries where tax rates are low. Transfer-price manipulation is essentially a way for TNCs to escape taxation to a certain degree, making it difficult for a state to enforce its own tax law. An investment agreement could prevent this.

A multilateral agreement would also be useful if it set rules to prevent states from getting caught up in bidding wars for TNC projects such as the MB factory in Alabama. If states would agree to abide by rules about what incentives they could provide, all might benefit in the long run. Some studies suggest that state incentives and giveaways are ultimately not very important in the pattern of FDI location, except perhaps on the margin. Except in exceptional cases, market factors may be more important in the decision to invest abroad at a particular location than all the goodies that states put in the packages they use to entice foreign firms. In the end, FDI largely goes where it would have gone, but with the bonus payments thrown in. The only way to stop this, however, is for all the states involved to agree to tie their own hands, and that is what international treaties and agreements are supposed to do.

The OECD's attempt to negotiate a multilateral agreement on investment failed, perhaps predictably. Instead of binding rules, all that could be agreed on was a set of voluntary guidelines, which hint at what might have been accomplished but was not. Why did the MAI negotiations fail? The short answer is that states were unwilling to give up the right to pursue their national self-interest. States were unwilling to sign away the right to discriminate in favor of domestic firms when this seemed prudent and to bid lavishly for foreign factories when the opportunity was presented.

Other factors also prevented agreement. LDCs, most of which are not members of the OECD, feared that the rules would be biased against them and would only serve to encourage FDI–based imperialism. Some richer countries, including Canada and France, were unwilling to give up the right to discriminate against foreign media firms. They feared that their distinctive national cultures would be washed away in a flood of U.S. music, film, and television programming. The United States, for its part, wanted to preserve the right of its states to regulate such factors as foreign ownership of farmland.

Finally, it must be said that the OECD was probably the wrong organization to negotiate an international agreement of this importance. Often called "the rich man's club" of nations, the Paris-based OECD evolved out of an international organization originally set up to administer postwar Marshall Plan funds. Its thirty members are advanced industrial countries. Although OECD nations account for the bulk of FDI, and so have a strong interest in an FDI agreement, both outflows and inflows, it is difficult to conceive how nonmember states such as India and China could ever accept a set of rules they had no direct voice in writing. Recently a movement has appeared to resume talks on a global FDI agreement within the broader framework offered by the World Trade Organization. The WTO membership includes many more countries that would like to have a voice in this debate.

The WTO may be a better forum in which to discuss FDI issues, but agreement may not be any easier to reach. Although all nations have an interest in reaching an agreement regulating TNC and state policies regarding FDI, their interests are not all the same, and conflict is inevitable on almost every issue. It is ironic that negotiations to regulate foreign investment are as much about tensions between states with different interests as they are about tensions between states and market forces.

## TRANSNATIONAL CORPORATIONS TODAY

Since the collapse of the MAI talks in 1998, foreign direct investment at first surged in 1999 and 2000, and then collapsed. Figures released by the OECD indicate that FDI outflows from its member nations rose from $1009 billion in 1999 to $1276 billion in 2000, only to plunge to $690 billion in 2001 and $606 billion in 2002. Data for FDI inflows to OECD countries are equally grim. From a base of $893 billion in 1999, inward FDI surged to $1272 billion in 2000 only to fall back to $614 billion in 2001 and $490 billion in 2002. The inward FDI figure for 2002 is less than 40 percent of the peak in 2000. FDI inflow and outflow data for the United States, United Kingdom, Japan, Germany, and France are presented in Table 17–4, along with a list of the OECD member nations.

The drop in foreign investment was so sharp and so sudden that it called into question many of the assumptions that had been made about TNCs and globalization. Maybe the world was not borderless after all? Maybe corporations would not eventually rule the world? Maybe TNCs were not more powerful than states? The December 16, 2002, issue of *Newsweek* magazine questioned whether all of the talk about globalization, borderless businesses, and transnational markets was not really just a bunch of "globaloney."

There are several reasons for the sudden slowdown in FDI flows. The terrorist attacks of September 11, 2001, and their aftermath caused many people to reevaluate the risk of foreign operations and international travel. Terrorist threats also had a severe negative effect on travel and

**TABLE 17–4   Recent Trends in FDI with OECD Countries**

| COUNTRY | 1999 | 2000 | 2001 | 2002 | 2005 |
|---|---|---|---|---|---|
| | | FDI OUTFLOWS ($ BILLION) | | | |
| **Total OECD** | 1009.7 | 1276.5 | 690.4 | 606.4 | 695.8 |
| United States | 189.9 | 178.3 | 127.8 | 123.5 | 21.5 |
| United Kingdom | 202.3 | 255.2 | 68.1 | 39.7 | 101.1 |
| Japan | 22.8 | 31.5 | 38.4 | 32.3 | 45.5 |
| Germany | 109.6 | 56.9 | 42.1 | 24.6 | 45.6 |
| France | 126.9 | 177.5 | 93.0 | 62.6 | 99.2 |
| | | FDI INFLOWS ($ BILLION) | | | |
| **Total OECD** | 893.0 | 1272.6 | 614.5 | 490.6 | 583.5 |
| United States | 289.5 | 307.7 | 130.8 | 30.1 | 128.6 |
| United Kingdom | 89.3 | 119.7 | 62.0 | 25.0 | 164.5 |
| Japan | 12.7 | 8.3 | 6.2 | 9.3 | 2.7 |
| Germany | 55.8 | 203.1 | 33.9 | 38.1 | 32.6 |
| France | 46.5 | 43.3 | 52.6 | 48.2 | 49.8 |

*Note:* The member states of the OECD are Australia, Austria, Belgium, Canada, the Czech Republic, Denmark, Finland, France, Germany, Greece, Hungary, Iceland, Ireland, Italy, Japan, Korea, Luxembourg, Mexico, the Netherlands, New Zealand, Norway, Poland, Portugal, the Slovak Republic, Spain, Sweden, Switzerland, Turkey, the United Kingdom, and the United States.
*Source:* OECD, April 2006. Data for 2005 are provisional.

tourism and related industries such as commercial aircraft. FDI in all these areas fell dramatically. The severe acute respiratory syndrome (SARS) epidemics in China, Hong Kong, Taiwan, and some other areas also discouraged foreign travel and business.

Economic recessions in Japan, parts of the European Union, and the United States further reduced FDI outflows and inflows. TNCs are creatures of transnational markets and they naturally tend to expand when these markets expand and contract during recessions. Thus the modest recent economic recovery in all three of the "triad" regions, seems to be encouraging a slight rebound in FDI flows, though the 2005 figure for inward FDI is still less than 46 percent of the peak in 2000.

Finally, corporate governance scandals in several countries have undermined the legitimacy that TNCs must have if they are to engage in serious triangular diplomacy. In the United States, for example, Enron Corporation was found to have made complex business deals in order to fraudulently overstate its profits and generate personal wealth for some employees and shareholders. Both Enron and its auditor, Arthur Andersen, collapsed when the fraud was exposed. Business and government leaders wonder who else is "cooking the books"—who can be trusted in this fiercely competitive environment. Businesses gain legitimacy in part through honest dealings and their determination to respect the rule of law. Until confidence in corporations is fully restored, the legitimacy and trust on which triangular diplomacy depends will be lacking.

Ironically, although FDI flows have slowed dramatically, they are perhaps now more important than ever. Competition among TNCs was fierce in the late 1990s, when global markets were expanding. As markets have contracted, TNCs have had to fight even harder to hold onto market share. One casualty of this battle has been what we might call the home-country preference. In the past, many TNCs did treat home-country operations differently from foreign ones, sacrificing some profit if necessary to maintain ties with home-based stakeholders. Many TNCs find that they can no longer afford to give home-country preference in an environment of contracting markets and increasing competition. TNCs look to their own interests now, not the interests of the home country or any other country. As far as states are concerned, the uncertain recent economic climate makes attracting FDI even more important. FDI means jobs, technology, and economic growth, which is what everyone wants in a stagnant or slow-growing economy.

Just as TNCs have evolved into the kind of organizations we have examined in this chapter in response to domestic and international forces, they most likely will continue to change and adapt in response to new political, economic and technological realities. Several of them are now doing business in a way that may finally herald the arrival of the truly global corporation—what Samuel Palmisano, the CEO of IBM calls the "globally integrated enterprise."[12] Such corporations become adept at integration—at linking together multiple partners and suppliers from around the world to collaborate and share in the finance, design, and production of new products. The production of Boeing's new plane, the 787, provides a striking example of this. Most of the design and production, along with 40 percent of the $8 billion development costs, are being outsourced to subcontractors and suppliers around the world (among the countries involved are Japan, China, South Korea, Australia, Russia, Canada, England, France, Sweden, and Italy). According to Leslie Wayne, "the outsourcing is so extensive that Boeing . . . has no idea how many people around the world are working on the 787 project."[13] Not to be outdone, Boeing's rival, Airbus, itself the creation of four European countries, plans to outsource 60 to 70 percent of the value of the new planes it produces, much of this work going outside Europe. The emergence of such global corporations raises several questions for students of IPE. Will the interests of TNCs and home countries become even more complex and decoupled than they already are? Will such cross-national business partnerships and collaboration in production and finance help form a fledgling "global governing class" that shares interests and power but is increasingly deaf to the needs of the citizens of the putative home countries, as Jeff Faux argues in *The Global Class War*?[14] Will the fact that offshore outsourcing increasingly threatens the jobs of service workers and skilled professionals, such as accountants, computer programmers, and engineers, and not just blue-collar workers and the unskilled, create sufficient political heat that politicians will respond with measures to slow the process or assist the vulnerable? And finally, will the spread or export of "good" jobs across the world by these global corporations help raise the living standards of developing countries, or will they exacerbate class inequalities? (See the box, "TNCs, Global Commodity Chains, and the Issue of Accountability.")

To summarize, TNCs today both face more competition than ever from other TNCs and yet increasingly find ways to diffuse risk by creating global financial and business networks. States face more competition with states for the pool of FDI flows. Attempts to reach agreement on a set of "rules of the game" to govern state–TNC relations have failed at exactly the time when it would be most useful to have them. Lacking such an agreement, the triangular pressures on state–state, TNC–TNC, and state–TNC negotiation will increase and the political and economic struggles that Raymond Vernon observed will grow more desperate. TNCs will remain the critical and controversial "eye of the hurricane."

---

### TNCs, GLOBAL COMMODITY CHAINS, AND THE ISSUE OF ACCOUNTABILITY

Most transnational corporations fall into one of two types of organizational structure. They are either vertically integrated firms or horizontally integrated firms. In the past ten years, however, a new TNC structure has appeared: the global commodity chain.

A vertically integrated TNC is one that creates a regional or global production line all under the ownership of one firm. An auto company, for example, might own an engine factory in Japan, a transmission factory in Canada, a body-parts factory in Mexico, and a final assembly line in the United States. The company might choose to produce all these parts at its own subsidiaries (rather than buy them from other manufacturers) to maintain quality or to keep design details secret.

A horizontally integrated TNC is more or less "multilocal": Its subsidiaries in different countries all produce more or less the same goods. McDonald's has restaurants around the world, for example, although it seldom owns the local suppliers of beef, buns, or secret sauce. It owns most of these restaurants so that it can control quality and therefore its valuable reputation and brand name. McDonald's is a horizontal TNC.

A global commodity chain TNC is interesting, by comparison, because the TNC does not in fact own most of the elements of its foreign operations. With improved information technology, some TNCs find that they can "outsource" vital functions to foreign-owned firms. The TNC builds a transnational network of contacts and contracts that it coordinates to create a regional or global business presence.

Nike, for example, is a high-profile transnational corporation, but you will not find it ranked near the top of the FDI rankings of firms. Nike owns very few production assets either outside or inside the United States. Most Nike products (its line of baseball caps is a notable exception) are manufactured and distributed by foreign-owned firms under contract to Nike. Both the vertical elements of Nike's production (from design to raw materials to finished shoes and apparel) and the horizontal elements of its distribution are chains of contracts and business relations that are coordinated (or "linked," because this is a chain) by Nike but owned by other firms. The one asset that Nike absolutely controls and guards jealously is its brand name, its image, and the famous trademark "swoosh."

Global commodity chains raise all sorts of interesting questions in IPE. One question concerns power. We say that TNCs have power, and it is easy to see why, if they own global production lines or multinational distribution systems. TNCs that are organized around global commodity chains do not own many assets, yet it is clear that they have power. Where does that power come from? And how is it different, if it is, from the power that other TNCs wield?

A second and more controversial question concerns accountability. TNCs are often called to account for the activities of their foreign subsidiaries. But is a global commodity chain accountable for what is done in its name by contracting firms? When Nike was criticized for labor conditions in factories in its chain, it did eventually respond to change them. A TNC might not be legally accountable, but in competitive market environments it sometimes must establish accountability for actions of other firms in order to have credibility in the marketplace and legitimacy in its negotiations with states, other TNCs, and nongovernmental organizations that are concerned about corporate social conduct.

The issue of sweatshop conditions in some apparel global commodity chains illustrates this point. Although they do not directly own the factories where their products are made, apparel TNCs are increasingly being pressed to take responsibility for the working conditions in these factories. Some of the nongovernmental organizations that have targeted sweatshops and focused on improving working conditions in them are Global Exchange, Clean Clothes Campaign of Europe, Co-op America, Sweatshop Watch, and the United Students Against Sweatshops, which was set up in 1998 at Duke University. Other university groups are part of a large network of more than 110 academic institutions focused on generating a code that permits only "sweat-free" clothes. In September 2002, some twenty-six apparel companies signed an agreement to establish a monitoring system that would oversee working conditions in their subsidiaries in developing countries. Some 250 U.S. companies have created codes of conduct for their subcontractors.[a]

Many TNCs, especially those concerned about their reputation and the image of their brands, have taken the issue of accountability very seriously. The nongovernmental organization Business for Social Responsibility (BSR) defines its goal as "achieving commercial success in ways that honor ethical values and respect people, communities, and the natural environment." BSR argues that corporate social responsibility (CSR) can have a positive effect on business performance. Among other things, it can improve finance performance, reduce operating costs, enhance brand image and reputation, increase sales and company loyalty, increase productivity and quality, and help retain employees. BSR also claims that "mainstream investors increasingly view CSR as a strategic business issue."[b] Companies that have been recognized for their commitment to CSR are The Co-operative Bank, Starbucks Corporation, B&Q, and Novo Nordisk.

It remains to be seen, however, whether the corporate social responsibility movement will be limited to a few high-profile TNCs or whether it will become a part of the general pattern of business conduct.[c] As global commodity chains become more important in transnational production, the question of their power and the issue of accountability are likely to rise toward the top of the public policy agenda.

*References*

[a] See Robert Collier, "For Anti-Sweatshop Activists, Recent Settlement Is Only Tip of Iceberg," *San Francisco Chronicle*, September 29, 2002.

[b] See Business for Social Responsibility, "Overview of Corporate Social Responsibility," www.bsr.org/BSResources/IssueBriefDetail.cfm, 2003.

[c] See David Vogel, *The Market for Virtue: The Potential and Limits of Corporate Social Responsibility* (Washington, DC: Brookings Institutions Press, 2005).

## DISCUSSION QUESTIONS

1. What are transnational corporations, and how are they different from other business firms?
2. Why do TNCs engage in foreign direct investment when there are good reasons why they might be less efficient than foreign firms? Explain several factors that contribute to the decision by TNCs to establish operations abroad.
3. What is right and what is wrong with the following statement: "Most TNCs invest in less developed countries because of the low wages that they can pay there."
4. How have reactions to TNCs changed in the last half-century? Why? Explain briefly.
5. How would an international agreement on governance of foreign direct investment benefit TNCs? How would such an agreement benefit states? What prevents such an agreement from being realized? Explain.

## INTERNET LINKS

UNCTAD *World Investment Report*:
www.unctad.org/Templates/Page.asp?intItemID=1465

UNCTAD *Transnational Corporations Journal*:
www.unctad.org/Templates/Page.asp?intItemID=2926&lang=1

Dictionary of International Trade and Business:
http://pacific.commerce.ubc.ca/ditb

Directory of Transnational Corporations:
www.endgame.org/dtc/directory.html

OECD website on FDI:
www.oecd.org/topic/0,2686,en_2649_34529562_1_1_1_1_34529562,00.html

## SUGGESTED READINGS

Paul De Grauwe and Filip Camerman. "How Big are the Big Multinational Companies?" www.econ.kuleuven. ac.be/ew/academic/intecon/Degrauwe/PDG-papers/Recently_published_articles/How%20big%20are% 20the%20big%20multinational%20companies.pdf.

Robert Gilpin. *The Challenge of Global Capitalism: The World Economy in the 21st Century*. Princeton, NJ: Princeton University Press, 2000.

Robert Gilpin. *U.S. Power and the Multinational Corporation: The Political Economy of Foreign Direct Investment*. New York: Basic Books, 1975.

William Greider. *One World, Ready or Not: The Manic Logic of Global Capitalism*. New York: Simon & Schuster, 1997.

Stephen H. Hymer. *The International Operations of National Firms: A Study of Direct Foreign Investment*. Cambridge, MA: MIT Press, 1976.

David C. Korten. *When Corporations Rule the World*. West Hartford, CT: Kumarian, 1996.

John Stopford and Susan Strange. *Rival States, Rival Firms: Competition for World Market Shares*. Cambridge: Cambridge University Press, 1991.

Raymond Vernon. *In the Hurricane's Eye: The Troubled Prospects of Multinational Enterprises*. Cambridge, MA: Harvard University Press, 1998.

UNCTAD (United Nations Conference on Trade and Development). *World Investment Report*. United Nations, annual publication. www.unctad.org/en/docs/wir2005_en.pdf.

## KEY TERMS

| | | |
|---|---|---|
| multinational corporation (MNC) | product cycle theory | branch factory syndrome |
| transnational corporation (TNC) | appropriability theory | transfer price |
| foreign direct investment (FDI) | | |

## NOTES

1. Michael Veseth was the principal author of this chapter in the third edition of this text. Our thanks to Leon Grunberg, who revised it for this edition.
2. Raymond Vernon, "International Investment and International Trade in the Product Cycle," *Quarterly Journal of Economics, 80* (1966), pp. 190–207.

3. Stephen H. Hymer, *The International Operations of National Firms: A Study of Direct Foreign Investment* (Cambridge, MA: MIT Press, 1976).
4. John Stopford and Susan Strange, *Rival States, Rival Firms: Competition for World Market Shares* (Cambridge: Cambridge University Press, 1991).
5. Michael Porter, *The Competitive Advantage of Nations* (New York: The Free Press, 1998).
6. V. I. Lenin, *Imperialism: The Highest Stage of Capitalism* (New York: International Publishers, 1939).
7. Hymer, *The International Operations of National Firms.*
8. Robert Gilpin, *U.S. Power and the Multinational Corporation: The Political Economy of Foreign Direct Investment* (New York: Basic Books, 1975), p. 147.
9. Ibid., p. 260.
10. David N. Balaam and Michael Veseth, *Introduction to International Political Economy,* 2nd ed. (Upper Saddle River, NJ: Prentice Hall, 2001), p. 361.
11. Raymond Vernon, *In the Hurricane's Eye: The Troubled Prospects of Multinational Enterprises* (Cambridge, MA: Harvard University Press, 1998), p. 219.
12. Samuel Palmisano, "The Globally Integrated Enterprise," *Foreign Affairs, 85* (May–June 2006), pp. 127–136.
13. Leslie Wayne, "Boeing Bets the House" *The New York Times,* May 7, 2006, p. BU7.
14. Jeff Faux, *The Global Class War* (Hoeboken, NJ: John Wiley, 2006).

# PART V

# *Global Problems*

❊❊❊❊❊❊❊

It is increasingly clear that many problems in international political economy (IPE) are more than international: they are global in nature. That is, these problems are not just conflicts or tensions between and among nation-states. They transcend the boundaries of nation-states and have become truly global in their effects. The final part of this book looks at four aspects of these global problems. Chapter 18 surveys illicit transactions in the global economy, emphasizing that illegal flows of goods, services, and people across borders pose important challenges to governments. Chapter 19 examines the IPE of food and hunger, with special emphasis on the roles of states and markets as sources of the food and hunger problem. Chapter 20 presents an analysis of the IPE of the global environment, perhaps today's most serious global issue. Three case studies explore the IPE of the greenhouse effect, deforestation, and ocean nuclear waste dumping. Finally, in Chapter 21, we summarize and explore a number of issues related to the use of the IPE method, the three major IPE approaches, and the four IPE structures. Drawing on concepts and ideas covered throughout the book, we also discuss five dominant sources of tension in the international political economy and some possible future scenarios for the international political economy. A glossary of IPE terms follows Chapter 21.

# 18

# The Illicit Global Economy

## By Bradford Dillman

### OVERVIEW

In early 2006, U.S. immigration agents discovered a half-mile-long underground tunnel linking warehouses in Tijuana, Mexico, and Otay Mesa, California. Equipped with electricity, ventilation, a concrete floor, and water pumps, the tunnel—dubbed *El Grande*—probably took two years to build.[1] Agents suspected that it was used for drug smuggling: they found 2 tons of marijuana inside. They also worried that illegal aliens, terrorists, and weapons of mass destruction could have transited into the United States through this 80-foot-deep corridor. Since September 11, 2001, agents have discovered more than forty tunnels along the U.S.–Mexican border.

*El Grande* is just one link in an illicit global economy that clandestinely moves goods, services, and people across borders every day. Law enforcement officials occasionally give the public a glimpse of the world of illicit actors and the threats they pose. Nevertheless, illicit international exchanges usually occur in a shadowy world that most consumers never see directly.

This chapter analyzes a broad range of illicit actors and activities such as smuggling, drug trafficking, and human trafficking that pose significant challenges to governments and legitimate businesses throughout the world. In this chapter we make several arguments. Far from reducing black market activity, globalization gives criminals new ways to profit from their cross-border business. Well-intentioned attempts by governments to stop the supply of illicit products sometimes cause more harm than good. International cooperation against transnational crime is hard to sustain and often ineffective. Consumers bear as much responsibility as international suppliers for nurturing illegal commerce. The threats to national security, social well-being, and legal commerce seem to keep growing.

*Behaving as if only the licit side of IPE exists because it is the easiest to measure and quantify is the equivalent of the drunkard saying that the reason he is stumbling around looking for his keys under the streetlight is because it is the only place where he can see. What we need are better flashlights so that we can also look for our keys down the dark alleys of the global economy.[2]*

Peter Andreas

*Dirty money kills people. How many? Since the 1950s and 1960s . . . how many people have died as a result of our failure to deal with dirty money flowing out of developing and transitional economies and into western coffers? Or, to put the question differently, how many lives could have been saved if we had put the issue on the table 40, 30, 20, or even 10 years ago?*[3]

Raymond Baker

The illicit global economy is a network of international trade relationships that brings goods, services, and people across borders in defiance of the laws of at least one state. It is cross-border transactions that are technically illegal. It consists of markets that states cannot easily regulate or tax. A variety of adjectives are commonly used to describe these global markets: illicit, illegal, informal, black, gray, shadow, extrastate, underground, and offshore. The processes going on in these markets generally fall into categories such as smuggling, trafficking, money laundering, tax evasion, and counterfeiting. The actors conducting these transactions make profits by breaking laws, defying authority, ignoring borders, and often exploiting other people.

Until recently, scholars of international political economy (IPE) left the study of the illicit global economy to other social scientists. Criminologists have for years studied transnational organized crime groups. Sociologists have looked at the social effects of criminal activities such as drug trafficking and prostitution. International relations experts have been examining closely the connection between money laundering and terrorism since 9/11. Comparative politics specialists have studied the effects of corruption and clientelism on political development. Anthropologists have conducted research on informal markets in developing countries. And law professors have produced a burgeoning literature on efforts to protect intellectual rights from patent thieves and copyright infringers.

IPE scholars have increasingly recognized the theoretical and practical implications of the illicit realm. They have begun to synthesize the work of the other disciplines and branch out beyond the study of what is legal and measurable in the global economy. They realize that a close look at the illicit global economy helps us garner new insights about the relationships among states, markets, and societies.

Political scientist Peter Andreas notes that existing IPE perspectives help us understand some—but not all—of what we witness in the shadows.[4] Realists help us understand why security-obsessed states invest so much money and resources in international law enforcement. Liberal theorists help us understand under what conditions multilateral cooperation against crime will occur. Constructivists highlight the role that transnational nongovernmental groups play in changing the public's perception of illicit transactions. And structuralists point out that countries that rely on exports of illegal drugs and blood diamonds are stuck in a dependent, exploitative relationship with the "core" countries.

However, the illegal economy also provides a challenge to the three main IPE perspectives. Although mercantilists stress the primacy of the nation-state, the illicit global economy is full of nonstate actors that sometimes thwart the best intentions and institutions of even powerful countries. Whereas liberals focus on the market's invisible hand and individual freedom, the illicit global economy is full of powerful, manipulative criminal hands. The open commercial interchange and deregulation that liberalism promotes is supposed to lead to peace and prosperity, but in the illicit realm unfettered trade can spread horrible conflict, pervasive coercion, and social decay. Structuralists tend to portray capitalist, developed countries as exploiters of the developing countries, but in the illicit global economy, developing countries can sometimes take revenge on the rich North, as when China steals intellectual property or when **secrecy jurisdictions** (places with strong bank privacy laws) in the Caribbean attract billions of dollars from wealthy tax evaders.

In this chapter we apply tools from different IPE perspectives to understand the growing problems of illegal cross-border transactions. By so doing we help identify and explain changes in the global economy and encourage readers to check and refine theories in light of empirical observations from the "real" world.

## THE ILLICT ECONOMY IN HISTORICAL PERSPECTIVE

Illicit transactions did not suddenly appear a decade or so ago; there have been many illicit activities in history that have fundamentally shaped relations among states. Centuries ago European rulers and Barbary Coast potentates authorized pirates to seize other countries' ships and split the booty with them. European countries colonized many parts of the world, seizing their territory and the property of their inhabitants. Although at the time the colonial powers tried to justify colonialism as a kind of civilizing mission, their activities amounted to little more than theft.

Historians Kenneth Pomeranz and Steven Topik argue that violence used to be an important way to gain "comparative advantage" and important commercial benefits in the world. Great Britain, the United States, Spain, and other European countries moved up the rungs of the ladder of development by engaging in land grabbing, slavery, looting, and dope peddling in what we now call the less developed countries (LDCs). As both authors argue, "The bloody hands and the invisible hand often worked in concert: in fact, they were often attached to the same body."[5] They recount how Britain once forced China to buy opium; Belgium brutalized millions of Congo inhabitants and slaughtered elephants for ivory; Spain and Portugal literally plundered the Aztec and Inca civilizations; and U.S. entrepreneurs trafficked in slaves for decades.

Marxists, too, have long recognized that the development of capitalism is rooted in processes of **primitive accumulation**, whereby classes coercively or violently seize assets (such as land) from other actors. Sociologist Charles Tilly famously asserted that state-making is quite similar to organized crime.[6] Just like crime bosses, would-be leaders centuries ago used violence against their rivals and extracted "protection money" that they used to expand their territory and make war. Eventually these state-makers gained legitimacy as kings and turned extortion into legal taxation, masking their sometimes violent and thuggish beginnings.

History shows us that leaders of states have often participated in or sanctioned violent illicit activities. At the same time, these leaders have the power to define *what* is legal or illegal and *who* is a legitimate entrepreneur or an illegitimate one. We see that illicit activities can be very beneficial to some states while being simultaneously disastrous for others. Capitalism in its early stages was more like the Wild West than a contemporary, well-planned industrial park.

Illicit transactions today often mirror, replicate, or repeat these historical processes, even though we often tend to give new names to modern processes. For example, human trafficking is a modern-day form of slavery practiced around the world. Today's drug lords expropriate from peasants and addicts alike, expanding their turf and productive apparatus as would-be kings once did. Corrupt leaders in places such as Nigeria and Iraq have stolen massive amounts of public resources, just as European powers stole from the colonies that they were supposed to be helping. Some leaders in recent decades, such as Slobodan Milosevic in Serbia and Charles Taylor in Liberia, ran their states like criminal enterprises, working in cahoots with *mafiosos* to keep their kleptocracies running before they were ultimately ousted by foreign countries. Israel's seizure for decades of Palestinian real estate and farmland is little different from state-sanctioned theft by pirates and imperialists hundreds of years ago. States and entrepreneurs today still sometimes use violence and coercion to harm their competitors. Although we like to think that the excesses of the past are limited today by international law, good government, and even globalization itself, the reality is that illicit history repeats itself (albeit with new names, new faces, and new *modus operandi*).

## THE STAKES AND THE ACTORS

How big and how important is the illicit global economy? There are many disagreements about the answers to these questions, partly because extralegal transactions are so difficult to measure. Governments and multilateral institutions often engage in hyperbole, sometimes either to tout their supposed achievements against the "bad guys" or to heighten threats for political reasons. Canadian economist R. T. Naylor warns us against having too much faith in estimates of the illicit economy's size, which often are based on bad information and false assumptions. For example, he notes that a widely cited estimate of annual global sales of illegal drugs at $500 billion was concocted by a UN official giving a speech in 1989 to grab public attention.[7]

In 1996 the International Monetary Fund (IMF) estimated that criminal money laundering was worth from 2 to 5 percent of global gross domestic product (GDP). This suggests that the annual proceeds of illicit transactions may be between $600 billion and $1.5 trillion. Even this estimate is probably inflated, because it includes the amount of taxes that multinational corporations and investors evaded by shifting their money around different jurisdictions. Raymond Baker, a fellow at the Center for International Policy in Washington, D.C., gives us a more reasonable calculation of "dirty money" that results from public corruption and criminal activities (other than tax evasion).[8] He estimates that annual cross-border sales of illegal drugs and counterfeit goods may amount to a minimum of $120 billion. Revenues from human trafficking could amount to $10 billion annually. International smuggling of arms, cigarettes, cars, oil, timber, and art may be worth at least $35 billion annually.

"Guesstimates" though these figures may be, they indicate that the scale of the illicit problem has important implications for development, democracy, and security. The stakes are high. Baker believes that growing illegality is a major contributor to inequality and poverty in the world: "With common techniques and use of the same structures, drug dealers, other criminals, terrorists, corrupt government officials, and corporate CEOs and managers are united in abuse of capitalism, to the detriment of the rich in western societies and billions of poor around the world."[9] Likewise, Moisés Naím, the editor of *Foreign Policy* magazine, does not believe that democracy can emerge in countries dominated by powerful criminal networks.[10] The illegal economy can also undermine fragile new democracies by putting money into the hands of rivals of the central government, corrupting institutions such as the judiciary, and decreasing government efficacy. In all democracies, it lowers social trust and the perception of shared values with fellow citizens.

Who are the central actors in the high-stakes illegal networks? We all have a tendency to believe that the main actors are *mafia* dons, drug lords, and other organized crime figures. The ruthless criminals of Hollywood movies do exist, but full-time gangsters are only one part of a much wider puzzle. Many participants have one foot in the legal world and one in the illegal world, making it difficult to create a profile of the typical illicit actor. Participants include soldiers who loot, government officials who extort, CEOs who engage in transfer pricing, bankers who loan to Third World dictators, and consumers who buy fake Louis Vuitton handbags on eBay. Even humanitarian workers in war-torn African countries have been known to participate in diamond trafficking.

Just as law-abiding citizens sometimes dabble in the black market, well-trained, "normal" economic actors such as accountants and computer programmers sometimes lend their skills to unethical or criminal operators. For example, anthropologist Carolyn Nordstrom has pointed out that "smugglers today are more likely to be armed with a degree from a leading ICT/computer technology course than an assault rifle."[11] The work skills that the world of international trade demands are also needed in the shadow economies.

There is often no clear wall between the licit and the illicit global economy.[12] Buyers may not know (or not care to know) where their suppliers get their products. A consumer may burn CDs of illegally downloaded music at night and pay for licensed software the next day. A multinational corporation paying almost no taxes in the high-tax country where it is headquartered could be scrupulously paying corporate taxes in low-tax countries where its affiliates operate. Products that start out in some kind of shady operation often enter the "regular" market at a later point. Items produced in the legal market (such as cigarettes) may end up being smuggled across borders. Machine guns sold legally to an army in one country may end up in the arms of insurgents in a neighboring country.

## STUDYING THE ILLICIT ECONOMY: KEY FINDINGS

Studying cross-border illegal activities helps provide deeper insights into problems we see in the global economy. Consider the following questions: Why is it so hard to prevent nuclear proliferation? Why don't economic sanctions work well in changing the behavior of rogue regimes? Why aren't governments winning the war against drugs? Why did millions die from war in resource-rich Congo after 1998? In this section we examine six important analytical findings about the illicit global economy that help us answer important questions like these. These findings demonstrate the role that consumers, law enforcement, and globalization play in the growth of black markets. They also explain how illicit transactions affect war, development, and cooperation among states.

## Six Degrees of Separation

"I am bound to everyone on this planet by a trail of six people" says one of the characters in John Guare's play, *Six Degrees of Separation*.[13] In illicit markets, producers and consumers are also related to one another through a small number of people living in many parts of the world. Between a procurer and consumer are other actors, including financers, processors, shippers, importers, distributors, and retailers. If we look at international transactions involving the movement of goods and services, we see a global chain along whose links many points of illegality can occur.

If we look at the human connection in the chain, it becomes clear that none of us is completely divorced from the illegal world. Whether at the beginning, middle, or end of a chain of market interactions, we wittingly or unwittingly are involved in a process that may have been part of the extralegal world. Sometimes we can see our part in the chain, as when, for example, American parents hire illegal aliens from Mexico to care for their children but do not pay social security tax on behalf of their employees. At other times, our part in the chain is largely invisible, as when someone buys an engagement ring for his fiancée that contains a diamond dug from a mine run by a warlord in Sierra Leone. The greater our degree of separation from the illicit part of a global commodity chain, the less we feel responsible for it.

Carolyn Nordstrom points out that ordinary consumers around the world are deeply complicit in smuggling. She found that in the African war zones where she did research, everyday, mundane commodities such as rice, cigarettes, vegetables, and antibiotics constitute a big chunk of unofficial trade.[14] One can hardly survive in some of these areas without buying smuggled, untaxed items in the informal economy. In developed countries, consumers of software, downloaded music, drugs, vehicles, art, and jeans, to name just a few products, often know that the products they are buying are knock-offs, pirated copies, untaxed items, or stolen property.

Even government officials sometimes join the illegal market, much to their embarrassment when their hypocrisy is publicly revealed. In 1998, U.S. Trade Representative Charlene Barleshefsky accompanied President Bill Clinton on a trip to China, where she urged Chinese authorities to crack down on the country's counterfeit manufacturers. While she was there, she bought some thirty fake Beanie Babies in Silk Alley, a notorious counterfeit market, and brought them back to the United States, despite a U.S. law limiting each returning family to only one Beanie Baby import (and an agreement between Ty, Inc., and China that the toys would not be sold in China).

However, a countertrend is emerging. Multinational corporations and retailers are taking into consideration that increasing numbers of consumers want to widen the degree of separation between themselves and any potential unethical or illegal practices. The fair-trade coffee movement and the antisweatshop movement have conditioned consumers to think about the ultimate effects of their domestic purchases on overseas workers. Similarly, businesses are keen not to be tainted by ties to illegal activities overseas that transnational advocacy groups are publicizing. Lowe's was one of the first home improvement retail chains to introduce a wood procurement program to help ensure that the company bought timber only from sustainable forests and not from forests that were being harvested illegally in the Third World. In the face of criticism that diamonds from some African countries were fueling wars, the De Beers company participated in a global scheme to track the origins of diamond purchases so as to weed out those coming from conflict zones.

## DE BEERS AND "BLOOD DIAMONDS"

Thanks to years of advertising by De Beers Consolidated Mines, the world's largest diamond multinational company, most consumers are familiar with the phrases, "A diamond is forever" and "Diamonds are a girl's best friend." In the last decade, nongovernmental organizations (NGOs) that are critical of the connection between the diamond trade and African civil wars have spread two alternative slogans: "An amputation is forever" and "Diamonds are a guerrilla's best friend." They argue that the diamond industry has helped to finance rebel groups in places such as Sierra Leone, the Congo, and Angola, where millions of people have been killed, mutilated, raped, or displaced during civil war. The recent attention to "blood diamonds" (also called "conflict diamonds") has forced the diamond industry, as well as governments of diamond-producing and -receiving nations and multilateral institutions, to better regulate the international trade.

It is estimated that 500 tons of diamonds have been mined in the last 100 years, with one-third of them mined in the 1990s alone.[a] The company responsible for a large portion of diamond mining and wholesaling is De Beers, co-founded in 1880 by Cecil Rhodes, who formed a syndicate with the ten largest diamond merchants in South Africa by guaranteeing them a certain percentage of the diamonds from the De Beers–controlled mines in return for the provision of key information about the diamond market so that Rhodes could maintain and control supply.[b] Since the 1920s the company has managed to support a stable price by controlling supply and creating demand through expensive advertising campaigns.

De Beers established the London-based Diamond Trading Company (DTC), which sells diamond parcels at ten annual "sights" to approximately 125 "sightholders." The parcels, which contain stones that vary in size and originate from several different countries, are prepriced by De Beers and purchased in whole by the sightholders. These sightholders then take the diamonds to other cities, where they are repackaged for further sale to companies that then cut, polish, and resell the diamonds to independent retailers. The diamond industry operates in relative secrecy. As of 2002, De Beers reportedly controlled two-thirds of the world's annual supply of rough diamonds.[c] With De Beers' level of control of the market, close to 60 percent of the world's diamonds will go through the DTC in a given year.[d] De Beers' share in the market has declined over the decades, but the rest of the industry still relies heavily on the marketing scheme that continues to convince international consumers that diamonds are as rare as the love that inspires them to buy one. Ultimately, De Beers' contribution to diamond prices is not just the maintenance of high price levels and demand; it is the maintenance of high price levels and demand over time.[e]

Diamonds are perhaps the most highly concentrated form of wealth in the world. Because of the difficulty of tracing the origin of any particular diamond and the ease with which diamonds can be moved, these gems have become a key form of currency among illegitimate actors in the international market. Until the 1980s De Beers was involved directly in Sierra Leone and maintained an office in Freetown. In the 1990s it purchased diamonds in neighboring Liberia, Guinea, and Cote D'Ivoire—countries that were transit points for diamonds smuggled from war-torn Sierra Leone. Rebels in Sierra Leone also smuggled gems through Lebanese, West African, and Eastern European intermediaries. Sometimes raw diamonds were smuggled directly to the main international market in Antwerp, Belgium.

How did diamonds contribute to Sierra Leone's bloodshed? In 1991 a group of Libyan-trained rebels in Sierra Leone formed the Revolutionary United Front (RUF) and began attacking government forces. They seized some government-run diamond mines and over the next decade ran an illicit economy, smuggling diamonds to neighboring nations and trading them for weapons and drugs. The RUF also cut off the limbs of thousands of civilians. In 1999 the international community could no longer ignore the tiny West African country that was becoming one of the most dangerous locations on the globe. The RUF had killed 75,000, turned over 500,000 into refugees, and displaced over 4.5 million people. In January of that year the RUF attacked Freetown, Sierra Leone's capital, and conducted Operation No Living Thing—murdering, raping, and mutilating hundreds of civilians.

The United Nations helped broker a weak peace accord between the RUF and the government of Sierra Leone. The UN Security Council adopted a diamond embargo that banned the direct or indirect import of rough diamonds not controlled by the government of Sierra Leone through a certificate-of-origin regime. From July to October 2000 the government of Sierra Leone and the Belgium Diamond High Council created a system under which each diamond required a certificate of origin printed on security paper, registration through an electronic database, electronic confirmation upon arrival, and transmission of digital photographs of the diamond packages being exported. The RUF was quick to find a way around the new requirements, using Liberia and Guinea as cover for the export of their diamonds into the legitimate market. This prompted the Security Council to impose sanctions against Liberia in May 2001, which included a harsh ban against the export of rough diamonds.

In the face of the blood diamond problem, civil society groups such as Britain's Global Witness and Canada's Partnership Africa Canada joined diamond companies such as De Beers, the World Diamond Council, and dozens of governments to establish the Kimberly Process Certification Scheme (KPCS) in January 2003. KPCS members voluntarily cooperate and collaborate to prevent illegal diamonds from entering international trade networks and to shun countries and companies that cannot ensure that their diamonds are conflict-free. The Kimberly process is a significant example of a global public–private partnership to combat an illicit activity. Although it is not a panacea, KPCS has helped to foster peace in Sierra Leone and Angola, boost government revenues from legitimate exports, and make consumers more knowledgeable about where their products come from.

*References*

[a] Ingrid J. Tamm, "Diamonds in Peace and War: Severing the Conflict-Diamond Connection," World Peace Foundation Report (Cambridge: World Peace Foundation, 2002), p. 5.
[b] Ibid., p. 3.
[c] Ibid.
[d] Ibid., p. 4.
[e] Ian Smillie, "Dirty Diamonds: Armed Conflict and the Trade in Rough Diamonds," Programme for International Cooperation and Conflict Resolution Fafo-report 377 (Oslo, Norway: Fafo Institute for Applied Social Science, 2002), p. 22.

A fascinating new global trend is the rise of **socially responsible investing**. This is an effort to allow ordinary citizens to put their money in investment funds that avoid certain types of companies or countries that are perceived as being socially or environmentally unethical. Financial markets are offering new instruments for ethical investors. Related to this are a host of divestment-type movements led by some local governments, pension funds, and boardrooms to avoid investing in regimes where the capital will benefit dictators or criminals. These types of divestment strategies often indirectly target companies and countries linked to illicit activities such as land expropriation, oil corruption, and terrorist financing. Sometimes they go beyond divestment to turn into bans on doing any business or trade with certain companies and countries. Divestment strategies are basically a form of boycott that challenges economic liberal principles governing trade and capital flows.

## The Unintended Consequences of Supply-Side Policies

Another pattern is a strong tendency of governments to adopt policies designed to cut off or interdict the source of illicit products. These policies can be described as interdiction, repression, and eradication. Political leaders like to target suppliers in foreign countries rather than demanders in their own country, even though this focus has been shown in many cases to be more expensive and less effective. For example, the United States spends enormous funds trying to stop illegal aliens from crossing the border with Mexico but significantly less money or effort punishing U.S. businesses that hire undocumented workers. Similarly, money and labor-hours expended trying to stop drug production and smuggling from Latin America far exceeds federal spending on the treatment of drug users. In the global sex industry, law enforcement has a long history of cracking down on prostitutes rather than on the "johns" who pay for their services.

The reasons states mostly go after the supply side of the problem have a lot to do with the powerful political, economic, and cultural interests in a society. Governments often feel obliged to balance entrenched special interests with the public interest. There is often a sacrifice of efficiency and social goals when powerful actors force governments to attack illicit problems in "someone else's backyard." When law enforcement tries to stop or interfere with the supply side of robust global markets, it often does not achieve the intended results. In fact, there are often perverse consequences. An illicit activity can simply be displaced from one place to another, as when a ratcheting up of policing on one part of a border causes smugglers to move to a less secure part of the border. A supply-side crackdown might drive an illegal activity further underground, making it even harder to control. And a campaign against suppliers can often increase violence and "turf wars" in a society.

Phil Williams points out that efforts to restrict activities create a **restriction-opportunity dilemma**: the more that countries try to impose arms embargoes or ban substances such as drugs or Freon, the more they "provide inroads for the creation of new criminal markets or the enlargement of existing markets."[15] Eva Bertram and her colleagues illustrate a similar unintended outcome they call the **profit paradox**.[16] When states use law enforcement to try to prohibit drugs, the reduction of supply tends to drive up prices. This bolsters the profits of those entrepreneurs willing to take the risk to keep on supplying the black market. And the higher price encourages other would-be criminals to get into the business. One result is that, after a temporary lull, supply climbs up again as criminals find more ingenious ways of getting around prohibitions—and the price goes back down. Another possible result is that the most ruthless and violent criminals gain even more dominance of the illicit market. This dilemma is evident in many areas, leading some to argue in favor of decriminalization of certain types of illicit activity.

## Globalization: The Double-Edged Sword

Liberal theory touts the positive aspects of freer international markets. In his most recent book, columnist Thomas Friedman portrays a heady new stage of globalization in which changes in technology empower individuals and companies that collaborate and compete peacefully across increasingly invisible borders.[17] Like other liberal theorists, Freidman views global integration as a mostly desirable trend.

However, from studying illicit markets we learn that globalization is a double-edged sword: open markets may increase global efficiency, but they also empower the bad guys. Although we still do not know if the ratio of illegal to legal business in the world is increasing, we can be sure that in some countries the ratio has risen. Technological change, which has become something of an object of devotion in Western societies, can also be a false idol. For each potentially desirable trend in neoliberal globalization, there is a criminal downside. This does not mean that the bad outweighs the good, rather that any compelling analysis of global change must account for negative externalities.

Naím points to the dark side of the end of the Cold War: the breakdown of the Soviet Union and the proliferation of weak, postcommunist states created new homes for illegal operations.[18] The transition to market economies gave rise to powerful *mafias*, influence peddling, and old-fashioned gangsterism. And some of the weak states that emerged from the collapse of the Soviet Union became smugglers' lairs. A case in point is **Transdniestra**, a sliver of Moldova that claimed independence in 1992 (even though no country has recognized its claim). It became a hub of weapons trafficking, contraband, and stolen cars. And at the end of the Cold War, ex–Warsaw Pact countries off-loaded many small arms into Third World markets.

Naím also identifies globalization, including deregulation and privatization, as the culprit in the rise of the illicit.[19] Deregulation of airlines and shipping industries since the 1980s has fueled arms trafficking. The rapid-fire sale of state enterprises has contributed to widescale corruption. Regional integration based on free-trade agreements weakens border control. And the opening of capital markets has facilitated the flow of "hot" money around the world (see Chapter 7). New technologies of globalization are used by shadow actors just as they are used by governments to police the bad guys. For example, Global Positioning System (GPS) technology helps governments track criminal activities such as illegal timber harvesting and illegal waste disposal, but it also helps drug cartels manage international logistical operations. Businesses looking for technical solutions to smuggling, such as by embedding radio frequency emitters in products, often find themselves out-smarted by criminals.

## The Problem with Coordination Between States

One of the important questions that IPE examines is why states succeed or fail in cooperating with one another. As we learned in earlier chapters, realists view states as constantly competing with one another, whereas liberals stress the ability of governments to coordinate their interactions peacefully. Another of the major findings from the study of illicit markets is that state sovereignty makes coordinated policies by states against the shadows very difficult. Why is this so?

One major reason is that states are jealous of their sovereignty. They do not like interference in their domestic affairs, and they do not want to be responsible for enforcing the laws of other states. In fact, they will sometimes take advantage of illicit activities outside their borders. Although illicit markets can threaten sovereignty, sovereignty can also shield black markets. For example, some states—such as Liberia under former President Charles Taylor—can be said to have become criminal operations. They charge criminals a fee for protection behind their sovereign cocoon. In this kind of failed state, leaders can issue diplomatic passports to dubious businessmen, offer **flags of convenience** (places to register ships and airlines that actually conduct all their international business somewhere else), and allow the establishment of servers to conduct Internet gambling or pornography distribution. In exchange for a payoff, they may look the other way as criminals use their territory to smuggle goods.

These activities are part of a wider phenomenon that Ronen Palan calls the **commercialization of sovereignty**—the renting out of commercial privileges and protections to citizens and companies from other countries.[20] A state can market itself as a place to disguise the origin of dirty money. For example, dozens of mostly small countries and territories are **tax havens** (also referred to as off-shore financial centers or secrecy jurisdictions), where foreigners can park their money and conduct international financial transactions with very little regulation by local officials. These places—such as the Cayman Islands—attract money launderers and tax evaders who want to stay entirely out of the reach of their home governments. These sovereign jurisdictions benefit both indirectly and directly from global crime (as well as from legitimate international business).

It is often not easy for powerful states to force these sovereign havens to "shape up" and stop "prostituting" themselves to the criminals of the world. For example, the British Virgin Islands is, on paper, the second largest investor in China, but the vast majority of that money has moved from another country, where a company or individual is trying to avoid taxes or investment restrictions.[21] China cannot force the British Virgin Islands to reveal who the true investors are behind shell companies.

Pressure on pariah states is one way of trying to shut down illicit networks, but it is not necessarily the most effective. The technique often backfires. Leaders of pariah states do not always want to get rid of illicit transactions (especially if these leaders themselves are participating in illegal activities). Even if these leaders really do want to reduce corruption or shadow activities, they might not have the capacity to do so; or if they try to, they may end up being overthrown. In this latter case, punishing a government for not cooperating may have the unintended effect of weakening institution-building in poorer countries. The World Bank under Paul Wolfowitz seems to be headed toward a punitive model of anticorruption: cutting off aid to countries that fail to stop criminal activities that siphon off (sometimes indirectly) foreign loans and development aid. This may deprive weak but well-intentioned leaders of the very resources and assistance they need to fight the "bad guys" in their economy.

This raises the bigger question of under what conditions one country has the "right" to use force against another country in which illicit activities are occurring. If a government allows terrorists to launder money through its nation's banking system, does an offended country have the natural right to use force against that government? Can one country use force to prevent massive counterfeiting of its currency in another country? North Korea, for example, is a sophisticated counterfeiter of U.S. currency. If intellectual property is property, and if another country allows massive piracy and counterfeiting of that property to occur, is it stealing property? Is this tantamount to grabbing another country's territory?

There are many other reasons why states do not cooperate against crime. For one thing, illicit cross-border activities often occur precisely because laws differ from one state to another. Combating this would require states to better harmonize their legal systems, which is politically unpopular. Second is a problem of defection: how to guarantee that a state will actually carry out its commitments to another. Third is a question of privacy. Effective international cooperation requires sharing information about one's citizens and companies, something states have always been reluctant to do. This is a classic mercantilist impulse. States are worried about how rival states will use this information, however well intentioned the initial cooperation.

Fourth, rival states sometimes encourage black market activities to undermine their enemies. For example, the Reagan administration sought to undermine the Soviets and leftist regimes by pouring weapons into places such as Afghanistan, Angola, and Latin America, fueling arms bazaars that remained long after covert programs ended. And R. T. Naylor reminds us that, as part of their mercantilist economic warfare hundreds of years ago, European powers tried to undermine rival states by encouraging counterfeiting, pirating, embargo busting, and the development of smuggling centers.[22]

Fifth, it is hard to obtain serious cooperation with police forces and governments that are sometimes themselves complicit in illicit activities. In many weak states, officials may protect crime syndicates, be on the payroll of syndicates, or simply look the other way in exchange for payoffs. And sometimes they are simply too afraid to take on powerful criminal organizations and drug cartels. Former Colombian drug kingpin Pablo Escobar, for example, conducted a violent campaign against the government when it came after his cocaine empire in the 1980s and early 1990s, ordering dozens of assassinations of judges, police, and reporters and bombings of public facilities.

In the absence of effective state cooperation, private companies and international civil society are stepping up to the plate to change norms and practices related to illicit activities. These voluntary efforts are not always successful, but they do put pressure on governments to do more, and they are influencing public opinion. The private sector—worried about bad press and potential legal liability—has taken the lead in establishing codes of conduct and standards of behavior for big players. For example, some of the world's largest private banks have voluntarily adopted regulations to minimize money laundering and other financial crimes. This is part of a broader, post-9/11 shift by multinational corporations to **know-thy-customer** principles, whereby multinational corporations more carefully screen their depositors, suppliers, and contractors.

**Name-and-shame campaigns** bring international attention to illegal and unethical practices. Transparency International is a prominent example of a group whose annual index of corruption—derived from surveys of businesspersons who conduct business in other countries—can pressure governments into trying to get out of the bottom of the list. Multilateral institutions can also blacklist countries that fail to adopt international financial standards. Whitelisting is another inexpensive way for civic groups and governments simply to publicize companies with clean records in hopes that the market will shift toward their products and practices.

## War and Natural Resources

It has become increasingly clear since the 1980s that black market influences on natural resources have important effects on the global security structure. Weak governments and rebel groups in developing countries need money to buy weapons, pay off supporters, and finance activities within their borders. Controlling the extraction and export of natural resources is an important way to guarantee a revenue flow. Insurgents also know that if they deprive the government of control over natural resources, they can achieve important political goals. International commodities dealers generally do not have any compunction about buying from criminal insurgents or corrupt governments.

In Sierra Leone, several factions in the civil war that devastated the country in the 1990s financed their fighting in part by illegally controlling diamond mining. (See the box, "De Beers and 'Blood Diamonds'" earlier in the chapter.) Cambodia's Khmer Rouge relied on illegal timber and gem exports from the territory they controlled to fight the government in Phnom Penh in the 1980s and 1990s. Colombia's FARC rebels tax the drug trade to finance their rebellion. Rachel Stohl points out that the same networks that smuggle timber, gems, and drugs out of troubled countries also bring illicit small arms back in.[23]

In a particularly tragic case beginning in 1998, the Democratic Republic of the Congo was torn apart by militias and neighboring armies that jockeyed for control of rich mineral deposits. Armed groups with no legitimate claims to sovereignty engaged in the illegal extraction and export of minerals such as coltan, which is refined into tantalum, a high-value, strategic metal used in cell phones, computer chips, and aircraft engines. Vodafone and Motorola, manufacturers of cell phones, have pressured their suppliers to avoid purchasing coltan/tantalum from the Congo, afraid that they will be accused of being responsible for some of the slaughter.

## Corruption Is Hampering Development

Political economists have spent decades trying to explain why some countries develop and others fall behind. They have correlated many factors with development, including the degree of trade openness, levels of political stability, and even the "squiggliness" of borders. As pointed out in Chapter 15, corruption is another key factor that is hampering poor countries. For example, former leaders of Indonesia, the Philippines, and Nigeria skimmed billions of dollars from government coffers, leaving their countries indebted and unable to attract foreign investment. Corruption in China has become an increasingly important political problem, leading to social unrest and inequality. The World Bank under Paul Wolfowitz has launched an international campaign to promote good governance and reduce corruption.

Analysts of the illicit global economy agree that corruption is a big problem, but they argue that the cause of corruption is not simply bad leaders in developing countries. In other words, they find that corruption is a transnational process in which many legal and illegal actors are complicit. Therefore, the fight against it must focus on global actors. Economist William Easterly argues in his book, *The White Man's Burden,* that foreign aid is frequently eaten up by corrupt governments, and he calls on "utopian social planners" in wealthy countries to adopt much more humble programs to help developing countries.[24] Raymond Baker and R. T. Naylor criticize Western governments, bankers, and businesses for encouraging corruption.

In his book, *The Blood Bankers,* James Henry goes even further in blaming the illicit realm for Third World problems. Why, he asks, despite several trillion dollars of loans to developing countries since 1970, have so few countries closed the development gap with the West? The answer, he claims, is corruption, bad loans, and a global banking system that soaks up dirty money from around the world. According to Henry, "The conventional portrait of the global development crisis is an economist's fairy tale. It leaves out all the blood and guts of what really happened—all the payoffs, corrupt privatizations, fraudulent loans, intentionally wasteful projects, black market 'round trip' transfers, arms deals, insider information, and the behind-the-scenes operation of the global haven banking network that facilitated this behavior."[25] If skeptical liberals like Easterly and structuralists like Henry are correct, the roots of development crises are as much in the North as they are in the South.

## CASE STUDIES IN THE ILLICIT GLOBAL ECONOMY

Thus far we have looked at six significant analytical findings in studies of the illicit international economy. We have also estimated the stakes involved and identified some of the key players. Now we turn to some case studies—smuggling, drug trafficking, and human trafficking—to illustrate some of the general themes and to specify how and why illicit activities occur and with what consequences for societies.

## Smuggling

Smuggling is one of the oldest professions in the world. Enterprising individuals seek to profit from transporting goods across borders in defiance of the rules that political leaders have imposed on exchanges. The objects of smuggling are as numerous as the techniques to avoid getting caught. Some of the most important smuggled items are oil, tobacco, counterfeits, antiquities, animal parts, and military technology.

Cross-border transactions are illegal only if states say they are illegal. In other words, it is states that define what is smuggling and what is not, and these definitions often change over time. A product may be legal in the source country and illegal in the receiving country. Or it might be illegal in the source country and legal in the receiving country. Or it might be illegal in both countries. Which of the three cases holds will affect the scale of smuggling and the likelihood that states will cooperate to fight it.

What are the motives of those who engage in smuggling? Greed is an obvious reason. Smugglers are willing to take risks because they want to make higher profits than they could achieve through legal trade. However, keep in mind that mercantilist states also engage in smuggling for purposes of security. For example, an aspiring nuclear power such as Iran may look to the international black market to obtain uranium and nuclear technology that existing nuclear powers try to deny it. When the United States tries to restrict the sale of high technology to China, Chinese officials have an incentive to steal the technology and transfer it. Governments also feel that they have a right to defy sanctions and embargoes imposed on them by hostile powers. Despite facing the most sophisticated, UN-run sanctions regime the world has ever deployed, Saddam Hussein smuggled oil out of Iraq and garnered billions of dollars to keep his regime afloat in the 1990s.

How do smugglers justify their actions? Many have self-serving rationales that mask greedy impulses. Nevertheless, there are other justifications. Often smugglers simply do not recognize the legitimacy of the political authority that is regulating trade or the legitimacy of a law that makes a particular type of trade illegal. For example, importers fed up with paying bribes to customs officials may see smuggling as legitimate avoidance of a predatory government. Similarly, some smugglers feel that import taxes are too high. Some smugglers simply do not recognize borders drawn by colonial powers. Others believe that they are supplying poor people with a product at a lower price, thus offering a sort of social service. In failed states or war zones, smuggling is sometimes the only way people can get access to food, medicines, and other necessities.

Smugglers take advantage of differing laws and regulations in neighboring countries to engage in **arbitrage**—buying a product in a lower-price market and selling it in a higher-price market. This opportunity for smuggling arises from price differentials that sometimes result from cross-border variations in taxes, regulations, and availability. When governments restrict the supply of goods and services in the name of morality, public health, environmental protection, and workplace standards, they unintentionally encourage smuggling. For example, the U.S. government bans the individual reimportation of prescription drugs from Canada and Mexico, partly out of a concern for the safety of U.S. consumers and partly to protect the profits of U.S. drug companies. However, the lower prices of prescription drugs in Canada and Mexico have enticed many elderly Americans to look north and south for technically illegal sources. In a classic case, U.S. Prohibition in the 1920s spurred smuggling of alcohol from Canada. Borders in North America have always been quite porous.

Tobacco is one of the most important smuggled products in the world. The World Health Organization (WHO) estimates that about 25 percent of all exported cigarettes will enter smuggling networks, depriving governments of some $25 billion in taxes they are owed.[26] Once cigarettes are "in transit" in the global trade system, smuggling allows distributors to avoid all taxes, thus enhancing profitability. Cigarettes are often exported legally to duty-free zones outside the United States and then diverted to other countries.

The WHO has found that major U.S. and European tobacco companies are actually complicit in the smuggling, because it is a way of opening up new markets.[27] In developing countries such as Iran, cigarette manufacturing, importing, and distribution are often a state monopoly. Thus, competition from contraband cigarettes cuts into an important source of government revenue. (Developed countries often forget how much their treasuries relied on "sin" taxes on alcohol and tobacco before World War I, and do so again today, as many U.S. states, for instance, continue to raise their taxes on cigarettes).

In her study of cigarette smuggling between the United States and Canada, Margaret Beare found that traffickers included Indian tribes, diplomats, soldiers, and tourists, who took advantage of special privileges they had under the law to move tobacco products across the border.[28] Canadian consumers have been very willing participants, partly because they view high taxes on cigarettes as unfair. Since 2003, the Canadian government and the European Union have sued major U.S. and Japanese cigarette manufacturers to force them to take steps to prevent smuggling of their products. This is a move to force manufacturers to take more responsibility for knowing what wholesalers do with tobacco products and what the chain of trade is from factory to the consumer. The WHO has even proposed that every pack of cigarettes have an electronic mark on its packaging.

Another major impetus to smuggling is **differential taxation**—when taxes on the same product differ significantly from country to country. Even tax differences between states within the United States are an important cause of domestic black market operations. After 9/11, officials broke up several rings of people who were buying low-taxed cigarettes in North Carolina and Virginia, transporting the cigarettes to high-tax states such as Michigan and New York, where they were sold at a markup in the black market. U.S. federal law enforcement officials estimate that some traffickers made millions of dollars and transferred proceeds to Hezbollah.[29] By 2004, U.S. authorities were investigating more than 300 cases of cigarette bootlegging.

Antiquities are also big business for smugglers. Countries as widespread as Greece, Italy, Bolivia, and Thailand have laws that severely restrict the export or sale of antiquities, which are considered part of the national patrimony. Nevertheless, the huge demand for art and antiquities in wealthy countries supports a thriving transnational trade in stolen cultural property. Simon Mackenzie points out that art dealers and collectors have a strong sense of entitlement to enjoy and preserve cultural items, and they take insufficient steps to verify the legal provenance of objects they purchase.[30]

Illegal timber trade is causing massive deforestation in places such as Indonesia, Malaysia, Burma, and South America. Timber harvested illegally on state-owned land or in defiance of national regulations finds a hungry market in Japan, China, and the United States. There is also a thriving international trade in toxic wastes. In this case, however, the smuggling route starts in developed countries and ends in poor developing countries.

Smuggling of animals and animal parts is having a devastating effect on many species around the world. One of the difficulties in stopping wildlife trade is that the more endangered the animal, the higher the price for it and the greater the incentive to poach it, which accelerates its move toward extinction. The illegal ivory trade is responsible for drastic reductions of the stock of elephants and rhinoceroses in Africa and Asia. After a multinational treaty to ban the trade of ivory came into effect in 1989, the unintended effect was an assault on hippopotamuses and walruses, whose tusks became a substitute for ivory.[31] R. T. Naylor argues that all those who consume animal products are part of the chain of responsibility for poaching and illegal trade. Blame must be pointed in the direction of the fashion and cosmetics industry, tourists who buy trinkets made from animal parts, pet owners, and zoos.[32] There are only a few degrees of separation between us and those who are destroying some animal species.

## Drug Trafficking

Drug trafficking is one of the most entrenched and lucrative illicit activities in the world. Although many drug plants, such as coca, marijuana, and poppies, are grown in developing countries and the refined drug products are mostly consumed in rich Northern countries, marijuana is one of Canada's largest cash crops, and in some states in the United States it is also a key cash crop. The United Nations Office of Drugs and Crime estimates that at least 5 percent of the world's adult population used illegal drugs at least once in 2005 (compared to 30 percent using tobacco, which helps explain why cigarette smuggling supplies a much larger market).[33] Most of the profits from the drug trade are at the retail end (in the West), where the markup on the product is the greatest.

The global fight against drugs illustrates the enormous costs and limited success of supply-side policies. Between 2000 and 2006, the United States spent $4.7 on **Plan Colombia**, an elaborate program to drastically reduce coca production in Colombia. Despite massive aerial spraying and assistance to Colombia's military, the amount of coca cultivation did not drop, and there was no effect on supply or prices in the United States.[34]

Bertram et al. have attributed these disappointing outcomes to the **hydra effect**, whereby an effort to stop drug production or trade in one area simply causes it to sprout up somewhere else.[35] Mexico and Puerto Rico have become drug transit centers as a result of crackdowns in South America. And whatever success there has been in breaking up big cartels in Latin America has been offset by the spawning of a larger number of smaller trafficking groups.

Former U.S. Ambassador to Peru David Jordan offers some provocative arguments about the war on drugs that may explain why it is so hard to win.[36] He argues that neoliberalism and deregulation have facilitated criminal activity in developing countries. Banks are active participants in the drug business, usually as a repository of laundered criminal proceeds. Governments in developed and developing nations alike often have political or economic reasons for protecting the drug business. And many aspects of popular Western culture—music, movies, and art—promote drug consumption.

Drug production and trafficking have had very negative effects on society, security, and government in developing countries (and in developed countries as well). Colombian economist Francisco Thoumi has documented the pervasive effects of drugs on the economies of the Andean countries (Colombia, Bolivia, and Peru).[37] Drug revenues have funded unsustainable real estate booms and other speculative investments. There has been a sharp decline in social trust, which makes it more costly for everyone to conduct normal business. Traffickers use drug export networks simultaneously to import contraband and weapons.

Thoumi argues that programs to encourage farmers to switch to alternative, legal crops have largely failed. Returns to farmers from illegal crops usually surpass potential revenues from food crops. The United States has seen a similar problem in Afghanistan, where poppy production since the 2002 invasion has skyrocketed. The illicit industry also has profound environmental consequences. Drug production has spurred the destruction of rain forests as growers move into new territory. And in Yemen, the poorest Arab country, widespread cultivation of *qat*—a tree whose leaves are chewed for their narcotic effect—has put a strain on water resources and reduced the amount of acreage devoted to food crops.

In many parts of the world, guerrilla groups and paramilitaries have turned to drugs as an important source of revenue. Rebels in Colombia, Cambodia, and Afghanistan have all used drug revenue to buy weapons and finance their insurgencies. In Latin America as a whole, gun crime and violence tied to the drug trade have ravished major cities. Homicide rates have increased in Mexico in the last decade, sparked by drug rivalries. A significant proportion of those who end up in prison in developed countries have some connection to drug offenses.

Can drug trafficking be stopped? Probably not. David Mares points out that Northern countries have not had much success with unilateral threats to withhold aid from countries that fail to fight drugs seriously.[38] The United States sometimes threatens to "decertify" countries that do not adhere to U.S. priorities and to cut off aid and trade privileges. Multilateral police cooperation, border controls, spraying, and anticorruption programs probably have some marginal benefits, but they rarely make a dent in overall drug flows. The European Union has focused many of its policies on the demand side, decriminalizing sales and use of marijuana. Many public policy specialists believe that demand reduction or harm reduction in consuming countries through public spending on health and education can be least costly and most effective in the long run.

---

## THE DEVELOPMENT OF COLOMBIA'S SUPPLY CHAIN

The history of the illicit drug economy in Colombia sheds light on how this complex web of incentives and interrelationships has developed. Francisco Thoumi, a Colombian economist, argues that his country's current role as the leading world producer of hard drugs began with a small, disorganized network of local marijuana farms in the 1960s.[a] Unlike early producers in Mexico and Jamaica, who supplied the initial adoption of the drug in the developed world, Colombia's marijuana growers did most of their business domestically. It was not until the early 1970s that U.S. eradication efforts in the former two countries drove an incentive for entrepreneurial growers to look farther south.

Initially, it was these American illicit entrepreneurs who supplied everything from seeds to distribution channels to poor Colombian peasant farmers. As news of the profits spread, however, Colombians quickly took more control over the supply chain and began expanding into new, higher-margin products such as cocaine. As the 1970s progressed and the drug industry boomed, the United States and other developed nations suffering from the effects of drug consumption pressured the Colombian government to take action against the rapidly expanding domestic production networks.

Thoumi argues that these efforts were, from the start, more or less doomed to exacerbate the problem rather than mitigate it. Colombia has never been a strong or cohesive nation-state, and government drug-eradication efforts have solidified that situation over the past three decades. The government programs, based largely on aerial spraying of crops with herbicides and extradition programs to send wanted criminals to the United States, have never created a sufficient cost incentive to decrease production of highly lucrative drugs. Rather, these programs have had a number of unintended direct consequences, including:

1. *The displacement of drug production* to more remote and dangerous areas of the country, where the state has little or no real influence
2. *The involvement of guerilla and paramilitary groups,* such as the Communist-influenced Revolutionary Armed Forces of Colombia (FARC), who control those regions and have become increasingly dependent on illicit drugs for revenue as other funding sources (such as from the former Soviet Union) have waned
3. *The organization of cartels,* large and small import/export networks that bring raw and chemical materials into the country for the processing of hard drugs and then traffic finished products to markets in North America, Europe, and beyond, and have expanded their work into other illicit industries such as arms trading
4. *The corruption of government and financial institutions* as increasingly wealthy cartels have taken steps to influence political regulations, avoid extradition, and launder large sums of illicitly obtained cash—resulting in a long history of violence, bribes, and high-profile political assassination.

These primary factors have led to a cyclical situation in which multiple actors profit directly from the illicit drug industry and thus have an incentive to see it persist. Poor peasant farmers depend on illicit drug crops for subsistence and support the guerilla leaders who allow them to maintain these crops. Guerilla rebel organizations depend on revenues from the crops for income as well as the support they bring from peasants, to whom the guerillas often provide basic services in the absence of the state. Many politicians and bureaucrats depend heavily on contributions and bribes from the very cartels that they are pressured to combat while in office. Banks, real estate, and financial markets have willingly flourished with an infusion of laundered cash and capital generated by illicit actors. The extended network of organizations and individuals profiting from the trafficking of illicit drugs reaches far beyond Colombia itself—including private and governmental actors throughout the Andean region, central America, the United States, Europe, and beyond.

Thoumi challenges popular assumptions about the effects of this paradigm on Colombia. Though the initial boom of the industry did bring an influx of cash and capital into the country, the growth of the illicit drug trade does not represent the only significant piece of the Colombian economy, nor has it been a cause for exceptional economic growth over the long term. Indeed, Thoumi argues that the condition is quite the opposite—the

Colombian economy is growing at a slower rate than before the drug boom (and in some recent years has even declined), largely because of the increasing transaction costs and decreasing levels of trust that the illicit economy has promoted in legal industries. As the government continues to combat drug production and demand in international markets grows at unstable rates, mounting pressure on the industry has led to increasing levels of volatility and violence. Thoumi refers to this trend as an "institutional crisis" marked by eroding levels of social capital.

Is there a viable solution for countries such as Colombia and Afghanistan that suffer from endemic illicit drug activity? It seems that most of the strategies attempted thus far have proven ultimately ineffective. Unilateral action by governments such as the United States has consistently pressured the governments of producing nations to attempt to eradicate crops and incarcerate illegal actors. Weak nations have rarely been able to implement these efforts effectively, however, because they battle with rebel groups for control of significant portions of territory. Even when crops are successfully sprayed and criminals jailed, corruption impedes criminal justice systems, a lack of resources results in poorly run prisons, and the profit motive to continue production leads to rapid relocation of destroyed crops and facilities.

Ultimately, any supply-side effort to combat elements of the drug production cycle faces these two core challenges: weak governments that struggle to implement and fulfill policies, and an end-user demand that has maintained tremendous fiscal incentives to continue producing at every level of the illicit supply chain. Billions of dollars have been invested by developed and developing nations in such supply-side reduction tactics, most of which have consistently failed to reduce the volume or value of illicit drugs on the market. Demand-reduction programs in consuming nations have also experienced significant challenges and had dubious results.

These observations lead to the inference that effective eradication programs must be truly multifaceted and multilateral. The extensive and fluid global network of producers, refiners, traffickers, money launderers, suppliers, and users ensures that the illicit drug industry does not have an Achilles' heel or a single solution. The core challenge to governments and institutions confronting the future of the global illicit drug trade is to form a genuinely united, integrated approach to the problem. Anything less will merely become yet another line item on an inherently stacked balance sheet.

*Reference*

[a] Francisco Thoumi, "Illegal Drugs in Colombia: From Illegal Economic Boom to Social Crisis," *Annals of the American Academy of Political and Social Science, 582* (July 2002), Cross-National Drug Policy, p. 103.

## Human Trafficking

At least a half-million people are trafficked each year, mostly women and children who are forced into prostitution. According to the U.S. State Department, an estimated 20,000 people are trafficked to the United States annually. As many as 150,000 non-Japanese work in Japan's sex industry. Organized crime groups play an important role in this business. They include the Russian Mafia, the Chinese Triads, and the Japanese Yakuza. The former Soviet Union has been an important source of trafficked women since the collapse of communism sent economies in Russia, Ukraine, Moldova, and Belarus into a tailspin. Burma, Nepal, India, and Thailand are also important suppliers to the world's brothels. The trade is usually from poor countries to wealthier countries.

The roots of sex trafficking are in patriarchy and poverty. Where women and minors lack political rights, education, and legal protections, they tend to be victims of organized criminal networks. Global and national economic crises tend to disproportionately affect women and children, who are pushed into the international sex industry against their will. Child trafficking is practiced in many countries, in which poor families place children into debt bondage or indentured servitude to an employer in another country. Even governments have become direct and indirect supporters of the exploitation of women and children by sex predators. Cuba and Burma, for example, have promoted international tourism and concomitantly acquiesced in the growth of a private sex industry in order to attract foreign currency.

Illegal migration is another large and growing part of the human trafficking problem. David Kyle and John Dale point out a paradox: the more tightly a country controls its borders, the more would-be illegal aliens have to turn to traffickers to get across the border, and the higher the profits of professional smugglers.[39] It is employers of illegal aliens in Europe and the United States that share much of the blame for human trafficking. Powerful businesses need low-cost labor and are willing to break the law, absent credible threats of punishment. The United States and Europe are caught in a contradiction: mercantilists and zenophobes want to restrict the flow of migrants, but liberals who want flexible labor markets and low wages favor more migrants—legal or illegal.

How can human trafficking be diminished? One way is to build fences on borders and beef up interdiction at sea. An amnesty for illegal aliens and a expansive "guest worker" program is another possibility. Advocates for prostitutes argue that if trafficked women in the sex industry were provided immunity from prosecution and protection from deportation, they would provide extensive evidence and testimony against organized crime figures. Some believe that consensual, commercial sex between adults should be decriminalized. R. T. Naylor, for example, believes that personal vice done voluntarily by adults should not be criminalized because there is no clear victim. A structuralist would argue, however, that personal choice is not really voluntary, especially in the case of poor people who are compelled to participate in illicit acts in order to obtain an income. Liberal theorists increasingly argue that labor migration is an inherent part of globalization, and states can reduce illicit flow by simply allowing more legal flows. Labor-importing countries would gain valuable, young, low-cost workers, and labor exporters would boost remittance flows to their economies.

International organizations, governments, and nongovernmental organizations (NGOs) have taken significant, albeit insufficient, steps in the last decade to tackle trafficking in persons. In 2000 the United Nations adopted the Convention on Transnational Crime and a related Protocol to Prevent, Suppress, and Punish Trafficking in Persons, Especially Women and Children. The United States ratified the Convention and Protocol in October 2005, joining more than 150 countries that are party to the Convention. Other organizations that cooperate to combat the scourge of trafficking include the International Labor Organization and the Organization for Security and Cooperation in Europe.

Individual states have also taken unilateral action to address the problem. In October 2000, the United States passed into law the Victims of Trafficking and Violence Protection Act, which, among other things, allows the President to impose sanctions on countries that do not meet minimum standards in fighting human trafficking. In 2005 the U.S. State Department determined that fourteen countries had serious human trafficking problems and were not making significant efforts to meet minimal standards for eliminating it. Of those fourteen countries, President Bush imposed full sanctions on Burma, Cuba, and North Korea, but he waived sanctions on Saudi Arabia, Kuwait, and Ecuador on national security grounds.[40] More than thirty countries—including the United States and many European countries—have extraterritorial laws that make it a crime for their citizens to engage in sex with children overseas.

NGOs have been very active against the sex trade and sex tourism industries. They publicize the poor records of governments, help women and children in danger, and lobby for better national and international legislation. The Coalition against Trafficking in Women, founded in 1988, Amnesty International, and Anti-Slavery International are important organizations with antitrafficking networks around the world. Many international charitable organizations also have programs to help the victims of trafficking.

## CHILD PROSTITUTION IN THE INTERNATIONAL POLITICAL ECONOMY: WHO'S PROTECTING THE WORLD'S CHILDREN?

Child prostitutes are perhaps the most tragic victims of the international illicit economy. The United Nations International Children Fund (UNICEF) estimates that 2 million children, girls and boys alike, are sexually exploited worldwide each year, particularly as part of the growing child sex tourism industry that has accompanied development. The child sex trade is part of a greater problem of indentured servitude, though prostitution is its most visible element. Children labor as indentured servants in mines and markets, in factories and fisheries worldwide. The life of a child prostitute is one of varying horrors. Some live in concrete cells or cages. Many are gang-raped or see tens of clients a night. The International Labour Organization (ILO) estimates that 1.2 million children are trafficked each year and that 1.8 million children labor in prostitution and pornography industries.[a] These numbers are difficult to estimate because of the clandestine nature of the trade. According to the International Bureau for Children's Rights, child trafficking generates $12 billion annually.[b]

Liberals argue that the root of the problem is economic underdevelopment. Poor families that can scarcely afford life's necessities sometimes see selling one or more of their children as the best available option, because it earns money for the rest of the family. When the United States banned imports produced using child labor in 1993, 50,000 children were dismissed from the garment industry in Bangladesh. Though 10,000 of those children went back to school, the remaining 40,000 took inferior jobs, including prostitution.[c] A widespread lack of education about the futures of indentured servants exacerbates the problem, as families are misled by the people who recruit children. Often, children are sold to traffickers by impoverished families, who believe their children will become employed in respectable jobs where they can learn skills and earn a salary. The child then becomes indebted to the trafficker and is forced to pay back the sum for which she was purchased.

Structuralists agree that underdevelopment contributes to child prostitution but argue that the development mechanisms proposed by liberals worsen the problem. To structuralists, economic liberal policies that emphasize growth, such as the export-oriented development strategies of the International Monetary Fund and the World Bank, demonstrate a preference for wealth over the safety of individuals and thereby encourage child prostitution. According to Aaron Sachs, social support services that were previously provided by the Thai government were cut when Thailand invested in logging and large-scale export agriculture as a means to development, leading to an increase in child prostitution.[d]

Furthermore, as a corollary to export-oriented growth, developing countries are encouraged to attract rich foreigners by strengthening their service industries, amounting to direct encouragement to the sex tourism industry. Tourist agencies in developed countries sometimes advertise the services of women and children in developing nations; in February 2004, the owners of Big Apple Oriental Tours in New York were indicted for promotion of prostitution after the nonprofit organization Equality Now pursued legal action against the company.[e] Brochures from Big Apple Oriental advertised "plenty of young women to keep you occupied for the whole trip." To Sachs, sex tourists like the clients of Big Apple Oriental exploit the income gap between rich and poor countries. Sachs attributes child prostitution to the "fundamental injustice in the current materialist world order—a global willingness to sacrifice society's most vulnerable members for the sake of others' economic and sexual gratification."[f]

For instance, the "rest and relaxation" needs of U.S. soldiers during the Vietnam War were a major stimulus to sex tourism in Thailand, now one of the most notorious sites of child prostitution. In 1967, the U.S. government signed a treaty with Thailand permitting U.S. soldiers to enter Thailand for "rest and relaxation." Buttressed by Thailand's 1966 Entertainment Places Act, which legalized brothels disguised as massage parlors and other service locations, the international sex tourism industry took flight. Policies of individual nations are thus a source of the sex tourism problem.

Child prostitution also has roots in cultural tradition. Some Hindus in southern India practice *devadasi*, a system in which a prepubescent girl is dedicated to a deity or temple and becomes a prostitute for upper-caste men, believing sex with men a spiritual act akin to sex with a deity. According to the nongovernmental organization Human Rights Watch, many *devadasis* come from the *Dalit* (or "untouchable") caste, so they are often disempowered on three fronts, as children, women, and *Dalits*. Several Indian states have illegalized the *devadasi* system, such as in the Prohibition of Dedication Act of Karnataka in 1992. These laws are scarcely enforced, however, and the *devadasis* (rather than their clients) are criminalized.[g] Use patterns of prostitution vary from culture to culture as well. In these cases, questions arise as to whether it is just for outsiders to impose restrictions on prostitution; the implication is that it is cultural imperialism when Westerners restrict other traditions based on their own cultural prejudices. Cultural differences also make it difficult for multi-lateral, consensus-seeking bodies such as the United Nations to intervene.

The global AIDS pandemic is both a fueling factor and a consequence of the child prostitution industry. Many perceive children as virginal and think they are less likely to contract HIV from children. In fact, young people are more prone to contracting HIV and then spread the disease to other clients. Child prostitutes who have contracted AIDS may return to their rural homes if they are found to be infected, spreading the disease from urban centers to rural villages.

In 2000, the UN General Assembly adopted the Optional Protocols to the Convention on the Rights of the Child on the Sale of Children, Child Prostitution, and Child Pornography. The resolution calls for a "holistic approach, addressing the contributing factors," as well as the improvement of national policies to deal with the sexual exploitation of children.[h] Many nations have taken steps to punish offenders and reduce the sex trade in recent years. According to the *Seattle (Wash.) Times*, village surveillance committees in Africa have led to the freedom of hundreds of children from prostitution; in Ghana, the government now provides loans to mothers and has eliminated school fees, in order to provide families with alternatives to selling their children.[i]

Thirty-two countries, including the United States, have enacted laws that allow citizens to be prosecuted for engaging in child sex acts abroad. Michael Clark became the first person to be charged for such activities under the U.S. Protect Act, enacted in 2003. Clark was arrested in Seattle, Washington, for having sex with two boys in Cambodia. He was sentenced to 97 months in jail; under the Protect Act, the maximum sentence is 30 years. The U.S. State Department also established the Office to Monitor and Combat Trafficking in Persons, an office that monitors countries' efforts and produces an annual report. Playing the role of global police, the United States may impose sanctions and the suspension of assistance to countries that allow the problem to persist.[j]

Ultimately, children must be provided with better alternatives, such as improved access to education, and families must be lifted out of poverty. It is also necessary to reduce the corruption of governments and law enforcement officers, who often allow the problem to persist and even are clients of child prostitutes. The onus of eliminating the child prostitution industry falls largely on individual nations, though nongovernmental organizations such as Equality Now play a large role in bringing offenses to the attention of the public and government agencies.

*References*

[a] International Programme on the Elimination of Child Labour, "Every Child Counts: New Global Estimates on Child Labour" (Geneva: International Labour Organization, 2002).

[b] "Child Trafficking," International Bureau for Children's Rights, www.ibcr.org/PAGE_EN/E_FOCUS_3.htm.

[c] Pranab Bardhan, "Does Globalization Help or Hurt the World's Poor?" *Scientific American*, April 2006, pp. 84–91.

[d] Aaron Sachs, "The Last Commodity: Child Prostitution in the Developing World," *World Watch*, July 1994, p. 24.

[e] "Sex Tourism: Big Apple Oriental Tour Operators Indicted for Promoting Prostitution," *Equality Now*, www.equalitynow.org/english/actions/action_1202_en.html.

[f] Sachs, "The Last Commodity."

[g] "Discrimination and Exploitative Forms of Labor," Human Rights Watch, www.hrw.org/reports/1999/india/India994-09.htm.

[h] "Optional Protocols to the Convention on the Rights of the Child on the Sale of Children, Child Prostitution and Child Pornography," United Nations General Assembly, May 16, 2000. Available at www.unhchr.ch/html/menu2/6/crc/treaties/opsc.htm.

[i] Sharon LaFraniere, "Already Vast, Child Servitude Grows in Africa," *The Seattle Times*, October 29, 2006, p. A20.

[j] Murray Hiebert, "Red Light for Sex Tourists," *Far Eastern Economic Review*, 22 (April 2004), p. 18.

## CONCLUSION

This chapter has examined illicit international transactions that are sometimes overlooked by IPE scholars, who have only recently begun to draw on the work of criminologists, anthropologists, and legal scholars. It has shown that many illicit activities shaped the history of the global economy. The chapter also stresses that illicit activities are sometimes an unanticipated result of global free trade, and that the well-intentioned efforts of governments to halt black markets sometimes have unintended negative consequences.

The illicit global economy has important effects on the world's security, trade, and growth. It challenges the power of sovereign states and makes global governance more difficult. It is a structure through which the world trades a wide array of products that threaten corporate bottom lines and public health. It often fuels conflict and violence, hinders development, and threatens the environment. It has the power to make the world both more equal and less fair. It shows us that globalization and technological innovation are not necessarily forces for the global good.

The illicit global economy blurs the line between the legal and illegal worlds of production, trade, and distribution. It makes it necessary for international organizations to establish and enforce new regulations and codes of conduct. It forces businesses to ask: Do I know my customers? How can I protect my property and my reputation? It forces consumers to ask: Am I responsible for knowing where the products I buy come from? What degree of separation is there between me and others I am tied to in global commodity chains? Do I have the right to defy some state laws and social prohibitions in the name of individual freedom and economic necessity? Increasingly, international civil society is mobilizing to tackle illicit activities. NGOs realize that, with pressure (and support) from the grass roots and from consumers, states and businesses can make more progress against illegal actors.

States still tend to rely on supply-side approaches to illicit problems. Their mercantilist reflex to repress and interdict clashes with the hidden hand of the market and the not-so-hidden power of transnational criminals. However, this hardly means that political authorities are helpless. Governments in Europe and North America are increasingly receptive to newer strategies such as decriminalization, harm reduction, and partnerships with civil society groups. As developing countries institutionalize democracy, increase transparency, and strengthen market regulation, they should be better able to keep illicit transactions in check.

Without studying the shadows, our understanding of international trends will be incomplete. Without factoring in flows in informal markets, we cannot be sure the data we use to test theories and hypotheses reflect the real world accurately. And unless we recognize the terrible human exploitation that often takes place in the shadows, we cannot adequately assess the moral and ethical consequences of neoliberal globalization.

## DISCUSSION QUESTIONS

1. List some of the reasons why people participate in illicit markets.
2. How does a focus on illicit transactions help us explain development problems in the Third World? Is illicit activity an inherent aspect of global capitalism?
3. How are licit and illicit markets tied to each other? Are all those actors who benefit directly or indirectly from illicit transactions—even if they themselves don't engage in illegal acts—to be considered "guilty?" What responsibility do consumers and legitimate businesses have for illegal transactions and illicit networks?
4. On balance, does technological progress make illicit activities easier or harder? How can governments and corporations use technology to protect themselves from shadow actors?
5. How do the major findings about the illicit global economy confirm or challenge the key tenets of mercantilism, liberalism, and structuralism?
6. What are some of the unintended consequences of efforts to regulate the illicit global economy? How can states more effectively reduce the negative consequences of black markets?

## INTERNET LINKS

United Nations Office on Drugs and Crime:
    www.unodc.org/unodc/index.html

Radio Free Europe/Radio Liberty (Organized Crime and Terrorism Watch):
    www.rferl.org/reports

Transparency International:
    www.transparency.org

Global Witness:
> www.globalwitness.org

Saving Antiquities for Everyone (SAFE):
> www.savingantiquities.org

Corporate Watch:
> www.corporatewatch.org

CorpWatch:
> www.corpwatch.org

Transnational Crime and Corruption Center at American University:
> www.american.edu/traccc

## SUGGESTED READINGS

Peter Andreas and Ethan Nadelmann. *Policing the Globe: Criminalization and Crime Control in International Relations.* New York: Oxford University Press, 2006.

Raymond Baker. *Capitalism's Achilles Heel.* Hoboken, NJ: John Wiley, 2005.

Kevin Bales. *Understanding Global Slavery.* Berkeley: University of California Press, 2005.

Greg Campbell. *Blood Diamonds: Tracing the Deadly Path of the World's Most Precious Stones.* Boulder, CO: Westview, 2002.

Douglas Farah and Stephen Braun. "The Merchant of Death," *Foreign Policy,* November–December 2006, pp. 52-61.

Moisés Naím. *Illicit: How Smugglers, Traffickers, and Copycats Are Hijacking the Global Economy.* New York: Doubleday, 2005.

R. T. Naylor. *Wages of Crime: Black Markets, Illegal Finance, and the Underworld Economy.* Ithaca, NY: Cornell University Press, 2002.

Carolyn Nordstrom. *Shadows of War: Violence, Power, and Profiteering in the Twenty-First Century.* Berkeley: University of California Press, 2004.

U.S. Department of State. *Trafficking in Persons Report.* Washington, DC, June 2006. www.state.gov/documents/organization/66086.pdf.

## KEY TERMS

| | | |
|---|---|---|
| secrecy jurisdiction | Transdniestra | name-and-shame campaigns |
| primitive accumulation | flags of convenience | arbitrage |
| socially responsible investing | commercialization of sovereignty | differential taxation |
| restriction-opportunity dilemma | tax havens | Plan Colombia |
| profit paradox | know-thy-customer | hydra effect |

## NOTES

1. "Trafficking: 24 Hours on the Border" (Anderson Cooper 360 Degrees), May 19, 2006, *cnn.com.* Available at http://transcripts.cnn.com/TRANSCRIPTS/0605/19/acd.01.html.
2. Peter Andreas, "Illicit International Political Economy: The Clandestine Side of Globalization," *Review of International Political Economy,* 11 (August 2004), pp. 651–652.
3. Raymond Baker, *Capitalism's Achilles Heel* (Hoboken, NJ: John Wiley, 2005), p. 275.
4. Andreas, "Illicit International Political Economy," p. 645.
5. Kenneth Pomeranz and Steven Topik, *The World That Trade Created,* 2nd ed. (Armonk, NY: M. E. Sharpe, 2006), p. 149.
6. Charles Tilly, "War Making and State Making as Organized Crime," in Peter B. Evans, Dietrich Rueschemeyer, and Theda Skocpol, eds, *Bringing the State Back In* (Cambridge: Cambridge University Press, 1985).
7. R. T. Naylor, *Wages of Crime: Black Markets, Illegal Finance, and the Underworld Economy* (Ithaca, NY: Cornell University Press, 2002), p. 33.
8. Baker, *Capitalism's Achilles Heel,* pp. 166–168.
9. Ibid., p. 206.
10. Moisés Naím, *Illicit: How Smugglers, Traffickers, and Copycats Are Hijacking the Global Economy* (New York: Doubleday, 2005).

11. Carolyn Nordstrom, "ICT and the World of Smuggling," in Robert Latham, ed., *Bombs and Bandwidth: The Emerging Relationship Between Information Technology and Security* (New York: The New Press, 2003).
12. Naím, *Illicit,* pp. 6–8.
13. John Guare, *Six Degrees of Separation: A Play* (New York: Vintage, 1994).
14. Carolyn Nordstrom, *Shadows of War: Violence, Power, and Profiteering in the Twenty-First Century* (Berkeley: University of California Press, 2004).
15. Phil Williams, "Crime, Illicit Markets, and Money Laundering," p. 143. Available at www.ceip.org/files/pdf/mgi-ch3.pdf.
16. Eva Bertram, Morris Blachman, Kenneth Sharpe, and Peter Andreas, *Drug War Politics: The Price of Denial* (Berkeley: University of California Press, 1996).
17. Thomas Friedman, *The World Is Flat: A Brief History of the Twenty-First Century* (New York: Farrar, Straus & Giroux, 2005).
18. Naím, *Illicit,* pp. 24–30.
19. Naím, *Illicit,* pp. 17–18.
20. Ronen Palan, "Tax Havens and the Commercialization of State Sovereignty," *International Organization, 56* (Winter 2002), pp. 151–176.
21. Shaun Breslin, "Power and Production: Rethinking China's Global Economic Role," *Review of International Studies, 31* (October 2005), p. 744.
22. R. T. Naylor, *Economic Warfare: Sanctions, Embargo Busting, and Their Human Cost* (Boston: Northeastern University Press, 2001).
23. Rachel Stohl, "Fighting the Illicit Trafficking of Small Arms," *SAIS Review, 25* (Winter–Spring 2005), pp. 63–64.
24. William Easterly, *The White Man's Burden: Why the West's Efforts to Aid the Rest Have Done So Much Ill and So Little Good* (New York: Penguin, 2006).
25. James S. Henry, *The Blood Bankers: Tales from the Global Underground Economy* (New York: Four Walls Eight Windows, 2003), p. xxiv.
26. World Health Organization, *The Cigarette "Transit" Road to the Islamic Republic of Iran and Iraq: Illicit Tobacco Trade in the Middle East* (WHO), 2003. Available at http://repositories.cdlib.org/context/tc/article/1137/type/pdf/viewcontent.
27. Ibid.
28. Margaret Beare, "Organized Corporate Criminality—Corporate Complicity in Tobacco Smuggling," in Margaret E. Beare, ed., *Critical Reflections on Transnational Organized Crime, Money Laundering and Corruption* (Toronto: University of Toronto Press, 2003).
29. Sari Horowitz, "Cigarette Smuggling Linked to Terrorism," *The Washington Post,* June 8, 2004, p. A1.
30. Simon Mackenzie, "Dig a Bit Deeper: Law, Regulation and the Illicit Antiquities Market," *British Journal of Criminology, 45* (May 2005), pp. 249–268.
31. R. T. Naylor, "The Underworld of Ivory," *Crime, Law, and Social Change, 42* (4–5) (2004), pp. 261–295.
32. Ibid.
33. United Nations Office of Drugs and Crime, *2006 World Drug Report. Volume 1: Analysis,* 2006, p. 8. www.unodc.org/pdf/WDR_2006/wdr2006_volume1.pdf.
34. Juan Forero, "Colombia's Coca Survives U.S. Plan to Uproot It," *The New York Times,* August 19, 2006.
35. Bertram et al., *Drug War Politics.*
36. David Jordan, *Drug Politics: Dirty Money and Democracies* (Norman, OK: University of Oklahoma Press, 1999).
37. Francisco Thoumi, *Illegal Drugs, Economy, and Society in the Andes* (Baltimore: The Johns Hopkins University Press, 2003).
38. David Mares, *Drug Wars and Coffeehouses: The Political Economy of the International Drug Trade* (Washington, DC: CQ Press, 2006).
39. David Kyle and John Dale, "Smuggling the State Back In: Agents of Human Smuggling Reconsidered," in Rey Koslowski and David Kyle, eds., *Global Human Smuggling: Comparative Perspectives* (Baltimore: The Johns Hopkins University Press, 2001).
40. Congressional Research Service, "Trafficking in Persons: The U.S. and International Response," July 7, 2006. Available at http://fpc.state.gov/documents/organization/70330.pdf.

# 19

# The IPE of Food and Hunger

## OVERVIEW[1]

The title of this chapter is purposely missing the word *world* because, technically speaking, the whole world is not hungry. Paradoxically, some countries are awash in a "sea of grain" and other commodities such as meat, vegetables, and fruits, while people in other parts of the world do not receive the daily required amounts of protein and calories necessary to fight off diseases usually associated with malnutrition and hunger, such as kwashiorkor and marasmus. The United Nations estimates that as a result of natural disasters, war, and poverty, among other conditions, hunger afflicts 800 million people.

Since World War II, media coverage and public attention to hunger in various places in the world have seemed greatest during or shortly after episodes of localized mass starvation brought on by drought or war. Yet malnutrition and even starvation remain permanent features of many countries. Why is this so? What can international political economy (IPE) teach us about the causes of hunger and about how the problem might be overcome? This chapter makes two arguments. First, an IPE of hunger incorporating the three traditional political economic perspectives of mercantilism, liberalism, and structuralism better explains hunger than the accepted dictum that hunger is chiefly the result of overpopulation and/or a lack of food production. Second, an IPE of hunger points to many of the conflicting interests and values of some of the many food actors who do not share a consensus about the causes or solutions to hunger. These analytical and practical issues will make it difficult to solve in the near future what have become hunger problems of global proportions.

*It is observed by Dr. [Benjamin] Franklin, that there is no bound to the prolific nature of plants or animals but what is made of their crowding and interfering with each other's means of subsistence. . . . Necessity, that imperious, all-pervading law of nature, restrains them within the prescribed bounds. The race of plants and the race of animals shrink under this great restrictive law; and man cannot by any efforts of reason escape from it. . . . When population has increased nearly to the utmost limits of the food . . . [v]icious habits with respect to the sex will be more general . . . [and] the probability and fatality of wars and epidemics will be considerably greater; and these causes will probably continue their operation till the population is sunk below the level of the food; and then the return to comparative plenty will again produce an increase, and, after a certain period, its further progress will again be checked by the same causes.[2]*

Thomas Malthus (1798)

Until the 1970s, the dominant approach many scientists (especially biologists), commentators, and popular journalists used to explain *world hunger* was in terms of an imbalance in the amount of food produced in a particular geographic area in relation to the people who consumed it. In the eighteenth century, Thomas Malthus popularized the idea that food production increased arithmetically while human population grew exponentially, and so "man cannot by any efforts of reason escape" from hunger and famine. Malthus argued that because labor-intensive food production techniques did not lend themselves to producing surplus quantities of agricultural commodities, war, famine, and disease were left to check population growth rates.

In the 1930s and 1940s, the application of new technology such as tractors and other labor-saving devices, along with chemical fertilizers, eventually helped spur agricultural production to the point of huge surplus capacity in the United States, Canada, Western Europe, and Australia. Farm policies in these countries after World War II subsidized crop production, which led to huge surpluses of wheat, corn, pork, dairy products, and beef. In an effort to increase farm prices and income, periodically many farmers in the United States were even paid not to grow certain commodities.[3]

Before World War II was over, hunger became of major concern to the United States and its European allies, who had incurred a good deal of damage to their economies during the war. President Franklin Roosevelt called a meeting in Hot Springs, Virginia, in 1943 to discuss hunger and the possibility of increasing world food supplies. This meeting produced the United Nations' first specialized agency, the Food and Agriculture Organization (FAO). The FAO studied the food situation in Europe and in the rest of the world, including the newly independent nations and colonies of the Western European nations—countries that collectively came to be known as the Third World.

Many experts questioned whether food production in the developing areas of the world would be able to keep up with expected global population growth rates. The solution to the problem looked fairly simple: Help less developed countries (LDCs) produce more food while encouraging them to lower their population growth rates. The tendency to view hunger as a lack of adequate food production coupled with an overpopulation problem endemic to developing nations continued in the 1950s and 1960s. Some experts believed that assistance from an assortment of international organizations and individual countries, in particular the United States, was necessary if LDCs were eventually to overcome their hunger problems. During the 1950s and 1960s, food shortages in some developing nations were temporarily overcome when surpluses of U.S. commodities were distributed or "dumped" overseas in trade and aid channels. **Public Law 480 (PL 480)** and the U.S. "Food for Peace" program made food aid easily available to nations whose governments were also anticommunist and whose economies looked to be good markets for future sales of U.S. commodities and commercial products.

Many government officials and academics felt that hunger was likely to prevail in developing nations as long as "traditional" societies remained underdeveloped or "backward." LDCs were expected to eventually overcome their hunger problems as their economies developed and their governments and societies modernized. During the Cold War the World Bank and other financial institutions funded development projects that promoted the industrialization of underdeveloped economies along the lines of Western nations (see Chapter 15).

None of these measures overcame the malnutrition and starvation that occurred routinely in India, parts of Southeast and East Asia, and Africa. In many Third World Asian and African nations, hunger continued to be attributed to either poor growing conditions, traditional farming techniques, and/or a lack of capital and economic infrastructure. Once again, overpopulation and rising birth rates were expected to wreak havoc on countries such as India and China. Assistance from international relief agencies and financial institutions seemed to be too little, too late.

In the 1960s, a number of well-intentioned private foundations and nations financially supported the research and development of new varieties of wheat in Mexico and rice in the Philippines. The so-called **green revolution** produced grains that supposedly could be adapted and grown in

LDCs that faced adverse growing conditions. Another technological solution to the hunger problem that gained popularity about the same time was the proposal to educate people in the Third World about birth control. Stanford University Professor Paul Erhlich argued persuasively that the world's growing population was a time bomb waiting to explode.[4]

## LIFEBOAT ETHICS

Other food and population experts were not so optimistic. Many of them painted a picture of a world fated to experience global starvation and wars if more commodities were not produced in time to feed growing numbers of hungry people in developing regions of the world. In the late 1960s, this view was made popular by biology professor Dr. Garrett Hardin. Hardin's views were well received in some official circles and by many food experts, religious groups, and well-intentioned concerned citizens.

Hardin used the analogy of overgrazing a commons to explain the relationship of population to the availability of food.[5] He argued that the world was much like a commons, whereon only so many animals could graze without eventually destroying it. The **tragedy of the commons** was that people acted in their short-term, rational interests by continually producing more livestock, which eventually used up the commons (an unfenced, communal grazing area), dooming both them and society. For Hardin, freedoms and liberties must be restricted or people would have too many children and destroy the global commons.

Based on this analogy, Hardin developed a proposal to deal with overpopulation and the shortage of food in Third World nations. Given that the industrialized nations were not likely to transfer a sufficient amount of food and other resources to Third World countries to stave off their hunger (because it was not in their political or economic interest to do so), it would be merciful if the donors instead practiced triage or "lifeboat ethics."[6] **Triage** is the medical practice of separating patients into three groups in an emergency situation when resources are limited. Some injured need only minimal assistance, some require attention and even surgery to survive, and some will die anyway, in which case it will be wasteful to use precious resources on them.

For Hardin, the world was like a lifeboat overcrowded with people and about to be pulled under as more and more survivors clung to the lifeboat. If the industrialized nations did not want to be swamped by the growing masses of people in the Third World, they should cut them off and let those who were not going to make it on their own simply perish. Furthermore, Hardin argued that food aid was an unethical disservice to those whose lives would end anyway after aid was discontinued.

In the early 1970s this argument was well received by many U.S. aid administrators and other government officials who felt that assistance to Third World countries was equivalent to pouring money down a rat hole.[7] These officials were already under attack from critics of U.S. aid programs and those who wanted to limit food aid because of the political strings attached to it. Coinciding with this development, in the late 1960s U.S. foreign aid laws were changed as part of an effort to market grain to industrialized nations, or to at least earn some income from developing nations for the commodities they received.

### Lifeboat Ethics Critiqued

Some critics charge that Hardin's analogies of the world as either a commons or a lifeboat with limited resources are flawed. Even if the world does have a finite amount of resources, they say, he is wrong to suggest that the earth has reached the point where there are just enough resources available for a certain number of people to live comfortably while others should perish. A question some critics often ask is: Must those in the industrialized nations live as lavishly as they do compared with people in developing nations? Might the rich still live relatively comfortably at a lower level of existence if it meant that more people could survive by consuming what the "haves" do not want to share with the "have-nots"? Is it fair, for instance, that the United States, with 6 percent of the world's population, consumes 35 percent of the world's resources? How can the United States and other major commodity producers such as Canada and the European Union (EU), for instance, justify "mountains" of surplus wheat, butter, and cheese stored in the major food-producing nations, while so many people in the developing regions of the world are malnourished, hungry, and starving?

Critics such as Colin Tudge argue that the poor do need the world's rich, given the wealth the rich produce, and that the rich cannot be expected to change their political and economic interests or their consumption habits enough to solve hunger problems.[8] More important, Tudge and many others challenge Hardin's assumption that overpopulation is the root of the hunger problem and that LDCs are overpopulating the earth. Many demographers point out that Hardin's assumptions about population growth rates do not adequately reflect the history of population growth in the industrialized countries. Population growth rates went up in the Western developed nations when their economies were transformed from primarily an agricultural to an industrial base. Death rates gradually decreased as a result of improved hygiene and life-saving medical care. However, as people lived longer and per-capita incomes increased, population growth rates naturally slowed. There is evidence that the newly industrialized countries (NICs) are in or have already passed through the **demographic transition**—the point at which income growth exceeds population growth. Family financial security takes away the incentive to have more children to serve as laborers or secondary sources of income.

The debate about how fast developing nations are overpopulating themselves has been hotly contested for years. In 1997 the United Nations Population Division used a new formula to estimate population growth rates and reported that instead of LDCs contributing to an estimated 11 billion people by 2050, world population will reach about 7.7 billion in 2040, and then decrease. According to this study, fertility replacement rates are dropping faster than expected in developing regions. Some twenty-seven LDCs have already reached the below-replacement population level.[9] Tudge and others point out that people in LDCs often adopt a variety of positive measures to control their population during times of drought or severe food shortage. Furthermore, with the possible exception of China, massive social intervention programs to control population growth have not worked. In places such as India and elsewhere, these programs are often viewed as another example of Western imperialism toward the developing nations—blaming the LDCs instead of focusing on Western (over)consumption habits.

The point here is not to claim that (over)population is not a serious problem—of even global proportions—given the stresses put on the earth's carrying capacity. In many societies, especially in developing regions, the amount of food and other resources is often inadequate to meet the needs and demands of the local population. And, of course, it may be that at some point in the future, food production may not be able to keep up with demand, given the earth's population and its income levels. However, as so many now recognize, overpopulation is not a problem for all societies. Rather, in some of the developed industrialized nations such as Austria, for example, sustaining the current population is a problem and a worry for many people.

Although it *is* important to look at demand and production levels, Hardin was also criticized for overlooking the distribution of the world's resources, including food. By some estimates, enough food is produced in the world to feed each person more than 2700 calories a day. However, developing societies that need it the most lack the financial resources to purchase what they need in terms of calories and nutritional needs. Many of them also lack the mechanisms and distribution channels necessary to ensure that individuals receive the daily minimum requirements of nutrients and calories (1800 for women and 2100 for men). Hardin also overlooks the "pockets of hunger" in developed regions of the world. Many of his critics complain that even if population growth rates were to come under control, more food would *not* necessarily be available to poorer members of society. Society's elites or the rich quite often control a nation's food distribution channels.

Furthermore, living in an industrialized nation does not guarantee one an adequate diet; the "diseases of affluence" include several chronic diseases associated with diet. With a plentiful food supply rich in calories and fat, increasingly sedentary lifestyles, and other factors such as alchohol and tobacco use, affluent regions of the world are marked by the widespread occurrence of diseases such as Type 2 diabetes and hypertension, as well as an alarming number of obese people. In 2000, more than 20 percent of the population in thirty-three states were obese, a condition that leads to tremendous social, psychological, and economic (medical) costs.

Thus, some critics of lifeboat ethics raise the question of how much the relationship of the rich Northern industrialized nations to the poor Southern developing nations is responsible for poverty and, ultimately, hunger. The developing nations were relatively food self-sufficient before they were colonized by the West. A number of structuralists (see Chapter 4 and later in this chapter) point out that colonization or interaction with the industrialized nations via trade, aid, and investment in LDCs by Western banks and industries "immiserized" local economies. Those developing nations that overcame poverty and hunger, such as South Korea and Taiwan after World War II, were given huge amounts of aid because of their strategic (military) interest to the Western powers.

In the 1970s a number of critical works appeared with the theme that overpopulation alone was not responsible for hunger. Lappé and Collins, George, and Tudge, among others,[10] popularized the **"food first" thesis**—that hunger is more a matter of income and land distribution than of food production and distribution. In direct contrast to Hardin's views, these authors argue that hunger is a product of inadequate distribution mechanisms, but, more important, hunger is a direct consequence of poverty. Poorer people anywhere in the world are likely to be malnourished or face starvation. Only a small sector of a poorer economy profited from political and economic relations with industrialized nations. The great masses of people in large "underdeveloped" sectors of these economies become less capable of either producing the food they need themselves or purchasing it through trade channels. The relationship between the North and the South is defined by international *interdependence,* albeit one that is asymmetrical (unequal).

Hunger, then, is *not endemic* to LDCs but is a *by-product* of their political and economic relationship to the industrialized nations. In many cases, traditional farming knowledge was lost during the social and environmental restructuring of colonization and the chaos of the ensuing wars. Many poorer nations were left with no choice but to become dependent on food and financial aid handouts to sustain their already low food-per-capita consumption levels. According to Lappé and others, what officials and international organizations should aim for in developing nations is producing food first for themselves before growing it for export markets or becoming dependent on food aid. "Food first" also challenged conventional methods of agriculture and promoted small farms, claiming that they are actually more productive than large farms. Not only does this improve food security, it also provides for a more varied diet and preservation of traditional cultures. Finally, "food first" drew attention to the role of women in sustaining these smaller farm enterprises.

Together Hardin and the "food first" people drew necessary attention to the hunger issue from a global perspective. Together they outlined some of the multidimensional political, economic, and social factors and conditions that have made it difficult if not impossible to solve this problem. In the early 1970s a "world food crisis" drew even more attention to the multidimensional IPE character of hunger, when people in developing nations and all over the world were faced with the prospect of the declining availability of food supplies related to poor growing conditions and other factors that disrupted food trade and aid channels.

## THE WORLD FOOD CRISIS

In 1972 the FAO proclaimed a world food crisis[11] because the supply of world grain reserves had reached record low levels and commodities of grain and feed grains usually available to food-import-dependent nations in the Third World were no longer available to them. During this crisis, several events occurred almost simultaneously that resulted in a good deal of hunger and starvation in some of the poorer regions of the world.

The crisis began when the United States and the Soviet Union experienced two consecutive years of drought in the major grain-producing regions of their countries. Before the Soviet shortfall became public information, the U.S. government purchased huge quantities of wheat from its producers and subsidized wheat and other grain sales to the Soviet Union. U.S. foreign policy officials used these grain sales, among other things, to promote détente (relaxation of tension) with the Soviet Union after the two countries signed the Strategic Arms Limitations Talks (SALT I) agreement in 1972. At first, U.S. farmers praised the deal because it would clear away surpluses that were holding down commodity prices. Soon, however, they felt cheated when the Soviet shortfall was made public and the price of grain shot up.

One consequence of the U.S. and Soviet shortfalls and their grain deal was to reinforce the shift that had been occurring in the pattern of international grain trade since the late 1960s. Changes in the international production and finance structures, especially after the United States devalued its dollar in 1971 (see Chapter 7), made U.S. grain exports more attractive to nations such as Japan and EU countries that wanted to "upgrade" their diets to include more wheat and meat products. Poorer nations that had relied on food imports to meet basic needs could no longer afford higher-priced commodities of the major food exporters. Thus, many LDCs became even more dependent on food aid at a time when aid channels were drying up or grain corporations were more interested in selling grain than in getting rid of it through aid channels.

As grain stocks in the United States declined to record low levels, commodity prices shot up, resulting in food price inflation, which generated more demand by U.S. consumers to limit commodity exports and food aid. Commodities such as wheat and feed grains were rerouted away from LDCs to the industrialized nations that could more easily afford them at a time when poorer countries found themselves in great need of them.

Many developing nations also found themselves hostage to another political-economic development that drained them of resources and limited their ability to pay for food imports. In 1973 the OPEC oil cartel embargoed shipments of oil to the United States and then dramatically raised the price of oil (see Chapter 18). Many LDCs found it necessary to limit imports of food commodities and food products in order to pay their higher oil bills. Rather than remain dependent on food exporters for needed supplies, many LDCs reluctantly adopted food self-sufficiency policies.

On top of these political and economic conditions during the world food crisis, many LDCs were crippled by other routinely occurring natural events such as monsoons in Asia and drought in the Sahel desert region of Africa. Across the Sahel, almost a million people starved to death when food relief efforts were intentionally blocked.[12] Fertilizer production for many Third World countries was also hurt by an unexpected shortfall in the anchovy catch off the coast of Peru. After the world food crisis ended, hunger conditions did not improve that much for many people living in the poorer areas of many Third World countries. Later in the 1970s, instances of mass starvation mounted because of civil war in Bangladesh and in many African nations; a drought in the Sahel region of Africa only served to make matters worse. Food was also intentionally used as a weapon in many wars, including Ethiopia and the "killing fields" of Cambodia.

The events of the world food crisis, along with numerous events and conditions that came after it, highlight the extent to which factors that routinely contribute to hunger and starvation in some of the poorest countries of the world do include an immediate supply-and-demand problem. At the same time, however, they are also part of a much broader set of political-economic issues.

## HUNGER AMIDST PLENTY

Throughout most of the 1980s, the entire Sahel region of Africa experienced several more rounds of mass starvation and hunger. Ethiopia and Sudan, in particular, seemed beyond help. Efforts by international food relief organizations such as the FAO[13] and the Office of the UN High Commissioner for Refugees (UNHCR), for instance, resulted in few victories when it came to dealing with hunger in these and other countries. At the same time, the major grain producers were cutting back on and shifting much of what had been food aid into concessional (trade) channels. Similarly, many of a growing number of private organizations and agencies such as World Vision, *Médecins Sans Frontières* (Doctors Without Borders), and Oxfam, to name only a few, were unable to do much more to halt the spread of hunger and starvation that seemed to be occurring more often on the African continent.

Interestingly, in the 1970s and 1980s hunger gained some attention as a public policy issue in some of the industrialized nations that experienced two economic recessions.[14] Even as they took as much as 20 percent of their land out of production, most major food-producing countries—especially the United States and EU nations—continued to accumulate surpluses of agricultural commodities after farmers put pressure on their national legislatures for export subsidies and other income-support measures.

In the 1980s the World Bank and the International Monetary Fund (IMF) also became more attuned to hunger problems in connection with efforts to promote economic development (see Chapter 15) and deal with debt issues (see Chapter 8) in many of the poorer LDCs. As noted in earlier chapters, these institutions in particular employed many neoliberal ideas and strategies to "grow" developing economies in ways that often emphasized the application of large machinery, pesticides, fertilizers, and capital to larger tracts of land. The surplus commodities that resulted from these "agribusinesses" would earn foreign exchange in trade markets that in turn would go to pay off national debts. As we noted in Chapter 6, in many cases the agricultural commodities of many developing countries encountered protectionist import barriers in many of the developed nations in support of their own farmers.

Meanwhile, the Persian Gulf War in 1991 once again demonstrated the connection between war and hunger, when millions of Kurds were left stranded in a desolate region between Iran, Turkey, and the Soviet Union. The United States set a new precedent in 1992 by sending its forces (backed by a UN resolution) into Somalia to feed millions of starving people besieged by civil war and political strife.

---

### THE IPE OF FAMINE IN SOMALIA

Hunger, in its deadliest form, is often the result of political strife and war. Market forces in Somalia were disrupted by civil war and efforts to gain political control of the country. Nations that try to use food as a military weapon usually withhold food from enemies in order to extract concessions from them. In Somalia, however, food was used as a peacekeeping tool to overcome famine and starvation brought on by war as much as anything else.

In 1992 the United Nations peacekeeping operation in Somalia marked the first time that UN or U.S. forces intervened in a nation for the express purpose of humanitarian relief. The United States headed a UN multinational military contingency and rescue operation, using 12,000 of its own troops and 13,000 troops from twenty other nations to distribute 100,000 tons of food supplies to millions of starving Somalis. The operation was also intended to settle political conflicts among a variety of clan leaders who controlled food supplies and distribution networks in Somalia.

Another objective of these combined forces was to reestablish some kind of national government in Somalia. Located on the "horn" of Africa's East Coast, Somalia had been besieged by famine and civil war. Intense rivalry among six major clan families and, to a lesser extent, drought resulted in 300,000 people dead and another estimated 2 million facing starvation. In 1992 the government of President Mohammed Siad Barre quit and went into exile, leaving local clan leaders to fight it out for control of the country. Refugees streamed into cities in search of aid and medical assistance. Clan members ambushed truck convoys and confiscated food supplies. Clans blocked and disrupted food distribution efforts in the parts of the country they controlled and in many cities. They also blocked port facilities from receiving Red Cross and World Food Program food relief supplies. Many of the clans attacked officials and workers of the international food relief agencies who were conducting relief operations in cities and in rural areas.

Ironically, the roots of this internal strife and starvation can be traced to the geopolitics of the Cold War international security structure, namely, the superpower conflict between the United States and the Soviet

Union. Many of the clans acquired their weapons from both the Soviet Union and the United States and its allies in the 1970s and 1980s, when the two superpowers competed for political influence in Somalia. The Soviets supplied the Somalis with AK-47 assault rifles and small weapons in the 1970s as part of a program to expand Soviet influence within Africa. After Somalia invaded Ethiopia, a Soviet ally, in 1977, the Soviet Union withdrew support. Iran, along with Egypt and other Arab nations, then supplied Somalia with weapons. From 1981 to 1989 the United States supplied the government of President Barre with $35 million worth of "lethal assistance" that included TOW antitank missiles and armored personnel carriers.

During the famine rescue operation, the United States and allied military forces tried to stay neutral among local clan leaders. Contrary to accepted military practice, the weapons of these groups were not quickly confiscated. After an ambush resulted in twenty-two dead Pakistani soldiers and then nineteen U.S. Rangers were killed, the United States and its peacekeeping partners withdrew from Somalia. The operation itself became stigmatized as one of the biggest peacekeeping failures in history, leading the major states on the UN Security Council to resist sending UN peacekeepers into Rwanda, where some 200,000 people would be slaughtered.[a]

Many situations such as these have occurred since the Somalia debacle. Since 2000, almost 2 million Africans in the Darfur region of Sudan have been driven from their homes and wantonly murdered by the *Jangaweed*, a state-backed militia that many accuse of genocide.[b] Many of these people are now in exile in Chad and other neighboring states, putting pressure on the food and other resources of these countries. Despite the claim that the numbers of hungry people in developing nations have declined as those countries have experienced more economic growth, widespread violence in Africa and many other developing nations renders hunger and starvation both a tool and a product of war.

*References*

[a]   See, for example, Fergal Keane, *Season of Blood* (New York: Viking Press, 1998).
[b]   See Nelson Kasfir, "Sudan's Darfur: Is It Genocide?" *Current History*, 104 (May 2005), pp. 195–202.

During the rest of the 1990s and into the early 2000s, war, especially civil war, contributed to the deaths of millions as a result of hunger and even starvation in Rwanda,[15] Sudan, the Central African Republic, Angola, Ethiopia, Sierra Leone, and Liberia, among a large number of African countries. Much of the time, aid agencies and nongovernmental organizations (NGOs) have been at a loss to make a significant impact on hunger in Tanzania, Namibia, Botswana, Malawi, Mozambique, Lesetho, Swaziland, Zambia, and Zimbabwe, all of which have been stricken by drought at one time or another. Many of these states have also had to overcome high incidences of HIV/AIDs infection, which has contributed to and worsened their hunger problems.[16]

Against a backdrop of these dramatic conditions, production conditions in the 1990s went on a roller-coaster ride from worry in the mid-1990s about depleted food reserves and predictions of an outbreak of global famine[17] to concerns that oversupply conditions in the late 1990s were clogging trade markets and lowering farm incomes to the point where legislatures had to find new measures to deal with these surpluses.[18] Oversupply conditions made it still more difficult for the World Trade Organization (WTO) to negotiate away export subsidies and other assistance measures that national governments use to assist their farmers financially (see Chapter 6).

Despite increased production in some areas of the world, in 1996 the FAO sponsored a world food conference in Rome. The 187 states represented at the meeting produced a World Food Summit Plan of Action that pledged to halve the number of hungry people in the world (about 800 million) within twenty years. Its Plan of Action also included a Declaration on World Food Security, in which food was recognized as a human right. Despite pledges to increase food reserves and to use stocks for more humanitarian assistance, little was accomplished toward these objectives. If anything, the conference returned to emphasizing population control as a means of dealing with hunger in Third World countries. These efforts met with opposition from the Vatican as well as from states that view population arguments as distracting from bigger issues of poverty and inequality.[19]

One factor that more than likely played a role in states not meeting their pledges to the World Summit was that since 2000 world grain production has shifted from surpluses to shortfalls. Lester Brown reports that the world has fifty-seven days of consumption left in its stock, or what is the lowest level in thirty-four years.[20] Absorbing these stocks is grain used to produce "gasohol" in the United States, which for example has tripled its use of ethanol as an additive to gasoline since 2001. Meanwhile, food continues to be channeled into trade markets and away from international and bilateral food aid programs. The United States in particular linked food aid to its strategic security interests in, among other states, Russia, Indonesia, and North Korea.[21] Recently an estimated 2 million people died of starvation in North Korea, while the United States linked food assistance to North Korea's cooperation over development of its nuclear weapons system, among other things.[22]

Even though the major grain-producing nations did not meet their World Food Summit Plan of Action, they and other industrialized nations have signed on to the UN-sponsored Millennium Project, which includes as one of its eight major objectives the halving of world hunger by 2025, nearly the same objective agreed to under the Summit Plan some thirty years earlier. Although some might argue that this does not bode well for seriously decreasing world hunger, Professor Jeffrey Sachs, UN Special Advisor to the Secretary-General, argues that the Millennium Development Goals (MDGs) are directed toward solving a combination of poverty and development issues, only one of which is hunger. Sachs and celebrities such as Bono have initiated a global campaign to overcome poverty and debt (see Chapters 8 and 15) through not only official donor assistance but also through a wide network of NGO help and private money.[23] This time, hunger is to be addressed not directly so much as a consequence of alleviating poverty in LDCs in general.

## AN IPE OF FOOD AND HUNGER

What specifically does IPE teach us about world hunger? Broadly speaking, an IPE of hunger accounts for the ways in which a combination of political and economic forces and factors generate hunger in different geographic areas of the world. Two important questions are: What is the connection between the acquisition of power and wealth and poverty and hunger? What role does the international political economy play in preventing people from acquiring the food necessary to sustain themselves?

We can begin to answer these questions by outlining some basic features of the international political economy, especially the relationship of states to markets. The state (a collective set of each nation-state's governing institutions; see Chapter 1) plays an important, if not the central, role in the international system today. International organizations such as the FAO exist at the behest of nation-states that regulate both public and private international affairs. International organizations do not, as yet, have the authority to unilaterally impose solutions to hunger on states or subnational actors. Officials of both nation-states and private nongovernmental organizations usually identify themselves as nationals from one country or another. Transnational corporations (TNCs) are not sovereign political entities either. That status still belongs to the nation-state, which regulates the money supply and establishes the political conditions in which international corporate agribusinesses must operate.

Subnational groups may contend with the state for authority to govern a distinct territory or nation of people. These groups also play key roles when it comes to producing commodities or making any national or local food distribution system work. However, as many realists note, in most cases national governments adopt policies that, for good or bad, influence hunger and/or provide the resources necessary to overcome a myriad of hunger-related problems.[24]

Interacting with states are markets (or exchanges), which also take place within and among all nation-states at various levels of analysis. Markets, together with developments in the international production and finance structures, influence hunger directly in a number of important ways. First, some agricultural commodities are routinely sold by the United States and other major commodity exporters to earn foreign exchange. Commodities are also purchased by nations that are unable to produce them for themselves or whose consumers desire to purchase items that cannot be grown locally. Actually, only about 10 percent of all agricultural commodities are exchanged via international commercial transactions. The rest are produced for domestic consumption and exchanged in local markets. However, for some groups and even entire nations, accessibility to that 10 percent of exchanged commodities can mean the difference between maintaining a healthy diet and slipping into a state of malnutrition and hunger.

Second, markets play a role in establishing agricultural commodity prices. In most societies, prices reflect the demand for goods related to their supply or availability. In cases of communist, socialist, or otherwise highly regulated societies, prices may be fixed according to some ideological principle. Prices can either deter or act as an incentive for farmers to produce and market their commodities. Furthermore, the price of commodities makes them relatively more or less available to certain individuals or income groups, thus influencing the amount of hunger present in a society.

The third way that markets influence hunger is more generally in the way they condition the economic vitality of a particular nation-state or group of its people. Tension often occurs between states and markets when states attempt to regulate markets in order to accomplish a variety of national, political, social, and economic objectives. Both domestic and international markets—the latter more often—are looked to by groups and nation-states as sources of economic growth. The extent to which goods are successfully produced and marketed, either at home or in trade channels, can significantly influence the hunger problem. Those who profit from market transactions are less likely to go hungry, while those who do not are more likely to feel the effects of poverty, malnourishment, and even starvation.

Aside from international trade, agricultural commodities and food products are affected by at least two other types of international economic transactions characteristic of the international finance structure. A good deal of controversy surrounds the issue of food aid or money that is donated or loaned to a group of people on a short- or long-term basis. Finally, international food production and distribution are affected by the international investment practices of various nations and TNCs. These businesses provide jobs for people, and in the case of agribusinesses, produce crops that are often sold abroad to earn foreign exchange. In many cases, crops grown specifically for export substitute for commodities that would be grown and consumed locally.

Each of the three traditional IPE perspectives—mercantilism, liberalism, and structuralism—locates the causes of hunger and solutions to the problem in a variety of relationships of states and other actors to the market. What follows is a brief discussion of how each ideological school of thought looks at agricultural trade, food aid, and agribusiness activity as specific causes and/or solutions to the hunger problem.

## The Mercantilist Perspective

For mercantilists, food and hunger issues are tied up in considerations of national wealth and power. Mercantilists, or economic nationalists, view the world in ways similar to political realists (see Chapters 2 and 9). Nation-states compete with each other for power and wealth in order to improve their relative position in a self-help international system in which there is no sovereign political authority above the nation-state. Mercantilists emphasize how a nation's wealth and money ultimately contribute to its security.

For mercantilists, hunger is a regularly occurring condition related to a combination of physical and political-economic situations. Some countries are simply better endowed with a variety of natural resources, raw materials, and growing conditions that enhance food production. Mercantilists and realists consider food to be one of the most important ingredients of power. Those states that are relatively food self-sufficient or that have the capacity to feed their population are less likely to be dependent on other states for food. Thus, they are less vulnerable to those that during a time of crisis or war would be likely to cut off their food supply. Many nations will go out of their way to enhance their food security. Japan, for instance, has always been very self-conscious about its dependency on other nations for raw materials and food supplies. Its desire to achieve food security in part explains its willingness, up until recently, to assist rice farmers with price and income support measures that at one time pushed the price of rice in Japan as much as ten times higher than world market rice prices. Japan still resists efforts to decrease support for its farmers, adding to the protectionist voices in the Doha round of the WTO (see Chapter 6).

Nations with the capacity to produce large surpluses of commodities, such as the United States, Canada, EU members, Australia, and a few others, quite often benefit from the dependency of other nations on their agricultural commodities and food products. Agricultural commodities sold abroad earned the United States a good deal of foreign currency after World War II. Agricultural trade accounted for as much as 26 percent of all U.S. exports in the 1980s and still did in the 1990s. Many governments have also resorted to neomercantilist protectionist trade policies to insulate their farm support programs from international market forces and the protectionist policies of other countries. The major grain-trading countries also use export subsidies and a variety of other measures to compete with one another for what have been declining shares of commodity export markets.

In the 1990s the U.S. Department of Agriculture set its sights on markets in East and Southeast Asia as a chance to help U.S. firms and farms boost sales in the region. According to a recent report, the region has 1.9 billion people and a rapidly growing population.[25] However, Australia and some Third World countries have adopted a variety of economic liberal measures to make their commodities more competitive with U.S. commodities. China now competes with the United States as the world's biggest grain producer.

The existence of large stockpiles of agricultural commodities has put pressure on major producers to clear markets of surplus commodities and also to attract new buyers and markets. Nor are states eager to pay the costs of domestic economic and social adjustments after reducing protection for their farmers and making them more internationally competitive.

Agricultural trade enhanced U.S. power and its positions in the international security structure after World War II in other ways. A case in point are the power and influence the United States derived from supplying many of its allies with commodities through trade and aid channels. Along with loans and technical assistance, PL 480 food aid helped shore up pro–democratic-capitalist economies in the Third World and helped the United States contain Soviet influence in those regions. Many recipients of U.S. food aid, such as South Korea, Taiwan, and Egypt, later "graduated" from U.S. assistance and became major purchasers of U.S. commodities and food products.

At times, the United States has intentionally tried to use "food as a weapon." One case in point was in 1972, when the United States used a grain deal with the Soviet Union as a "carrot" to reward its arch-rival for entering into an arms control agreement (SALT I) and pursuing détente with the United States. In 1980, the United States embargoed shipments of grain to the Soviet Union because it had invaded Afghanistan. In this case, the United States used its commodities as a "stick," not so much to change Soviet behavior as to embarrass it and force the Soviet people to reduce their consumption of meat—an unpopular policy, given that the government had recently promised Soviet citizens more meat.

Robert Paarlberg argued quite convincingly that food does not have a lot of political utility unless the supplier has a monopoly over food supplies.[26] In this case, the Soviet Union sought out other suppliers—and Argentina responded to the call. Argentina became a major grain producer and exporter and also an export competitor of the United States. To some extent the use of food as a weapon backfired on the United States. U.S. farmers complained that the government played politics with U.S. trade policy. President Jimmy Carter responded by raising government deficiency payments to farmers. President Ronald Reagan later rescinded the embargo, in part because U.S. officials feared that other importers of U.S. grains and foodstuffs would consider the United States an "unreliable supplier" in international grain markets. Many LDCs that formerly were willing to purchase agricultural commodities from abroad were no longer willing to do so and turned to self-sufficiency policies, encouraging local farmers to meet consumer demand.

If anything, the case of the Soviet grain embargo demonstrates that the United States was discomforted as much as the Soviet Union: U.S. officials realized the extent of U.S. dependency on agricultural exports. More important, however, the embargo demonstrated that regardless of who was most inconvenienced, nations are always *tempted* to use food as a weapon, even if only symbolically, if their political and military arsenals lack appropriate instruments. Foreign aid is merely another tool of foreign policy. The United States employed PL 480 food aid quite effectively in its effort to contain the Soviet Union. Grain shipments benefited U.S. farmers and shippers and helped hold down costs of government price and income support programs. Few experts would disagree with the argument that food aid provided to countries to deal with short-term emergencies benefited the donor as much as it aided the recipient.

For mercantilists, *agribusinesses* (large corporate farming businesses) operate at the behest of nation-states, which benefit from their investment and production of commodities. Most of the Western industrialized countries, along with some international organizations, have chosen not to seriously restrict agribusiness practices in other countries (see Chapter 17). What formal regulations of agribusinesses and other transnational corporations there are as yet originate with host governments. Agribusinesses and other TNCs add to the wealth and power of both the host and country of origin. Aside from providing investment opportunities, from a mercantilist perspective they help transform the traditional agriculture sector of the economy from primarily labor to modern capital-intensive production techniques. They provide employment opportunities and infrastructure for people. They also benefit many of the LDCs in which they are located by transferring to them technology, managerial skills, and marketing and production techniques. TNCs also help LDCs earn foreign exchange, which, in turn, the LDCs can use to purchase needed commodities or consumer items.

According to mercantilists, agribusinesses and other types of TNCs earn income for the country in which they originate and help eradicate poverty in host nations. Higher income levels mean that locals generally eat more nutritious and larger quantities of food. Development also means that revolution is less likely and that governments that support TNC investment efforts in their country are likely to support the political and economic policies of the countries in which the enterprise originated.

In sum, to mercantilists, states regulate markets—employ trade, aid, and investment policies—in such a way as to attain state goals and objectives, which ultimately affect the state's ability to secure itself. As has recently been the case in the African states of Sierra Leone, Ethiopia,[27] and Liberia, hunger is not likely to be overcome in any great measure unless it is in the national interest of states or warring parties to overcome the problem, and even then more on a local or national as opposed to global basis. In the 1970s it became clearer all the time that the distribution of financial resources and food was as much the result of how much power a nation had as it was of a nation's ability to produce needed commodities. People in the industrialized-developed Western nations have been less likely to go hungry than their counterparts in developing nations. Mass starvation has been much more likely to occur in the politically weaker nations than in the more powerful countries.

In the past, the rule of thumb has been that, more often than not, food insecurity weakens some states and works to the advantage of food suppliers. And yet economic interdependence among nations has made suppliers quite dependent on foreign markets to absorb excess commodity surpluses and food products. Thus, as long as nation-states compete with one another for limited resources, food is likely to remain a symbolic, if not real, weapon in national arsenals.

## The Liberal Perspective

Liberals look on the food problem in ways that mercantilists find politically naive, if not wishful thinking. For liberals, hunger is a problem that could easily be overcome if nation-states followed some basic economic principles and, for the most part, kept politics out of the hunger issue. For liberals, individuals or households *should* be the major actors who make economic and political decisions. Liberals prize efficiency, economic growth, and productivity beyond other values. When it comes to the relationship of food production to hunger, their outlook is simple: Market forces should be allowed to set food prices, which—if governments did not interfere in markets—would result in enough food produced to meet even the tremendous demand in developing regions of the world.

States that cannot produce enough food locally usually import needed commodities from abroad. Liberals do not view imports as inherently bad, in and of themselves. If nations specialize in producing items for which they have a comparative advantage and trade with other nations for what they need, both countries gain and increase the wealth of both nations. Imports, then, are justified if they comprise products that cannot be efficiently grown domestically. What bothers liberals more than anything else are trade problems that originate in national farm-income and price-support programs. When large surpluses develop, governments in the major grain-producing regions of the world have distorted market forces by paying farmers not to grow food. Governments may also pay farmers a "deficiency" payment to bring farm prices or farm income up to the level of nonfarm workers. Inflated or artificial prices merely generate more production, compelling governments to adopt an array of agricultural export enhancement and/or food aid measures to get rid of these surpluses. States also often employ a variety of measures to limit agricultural imports to protect their farmers.[28]

Implied in a liberal argument about food and hunger is the assumption that many grain-exporting countries support their farmers because farm organizations are still quite politically influential despite the declining numbers of farms and farmers. In effect, state agencies are "captured" by farm groups and organizations when it comes to designing and implementing government farm policies and programs—extending the life of the farming vocation beyond its economic worth.

Because of their effects on food trade conditions, liberals ultimately place a lot of faith in WTO trade negotiations to help solve hunger problems. Agricultural import barriers and export subsidies were a major stumbling block to liberalizing the international trade system in the Uruguay round and once again have helped block progress in the Doha round (see Chapter 6). Liberal trade experts blame national government farm support, self-sufficiency, and food security policies for failure to significantly reduce the level of trade protection for agricultural products and for failure to realize the goal of making the food production process more efficient.

Liberals also have strong feelings about both trade and aid policies when it comes to LDCs and their efforts to overcome hunger. Hunger is a result not only of government intervention in markets in industrialized regions of the world, but also LDC mismanagement of their own economies. In the past, liberals have generally believed that the Western development model, and the neoliberal IMF and World Bank policies that emphasized industrial productivity and economic growth, were applicable to developing nations. LDCs would eventually grow out of and overcome their poverty and hunger problems if they imitated the West's approach to development. Trade was viewed as an "engine to growth." LDCs were to specialize in producing a few commodities, such as bananas, coffee, sugar, or tea, that could be exported abroad to earn foreign exchange. Food deficits would be made up by imports. This strategy required government at first to play a relatively strong role in the economy to ensure that market forces determined prices and that the growth of industry would be carefully coordinated and balanced with the extraction of resources from the agricultural sector of the economy.

Food aid was to help a government overcome the lack of infrastructure or a short-term capital deficit. Aid of all types would allow the government the opportunity to invest in industry and manufacturing. Food aid was supposed to give LDC governments some breathing room. Food aid would make up for agricultural production deficits and help governments overcome immediate hunger problems.

Liberals view dependency on long-term aid, and food aid in particular, as likely to distort local food production and distribution. Corrupt officials can always be counted on to misuse funds or sell food aid on the black market. Liberals continue to fault many governments for keeping food prices artificially low for financially better-off consumers in urban areas; this acts as a disincentive for farmers to produce more commodities. Food aid is to be used only in short-term emergency situations and/or in consideration of efforts to correct market deficiencies.

Liberals generally view TNCs and agribusinesses as an asset to LDCs because of their economic effect on local economies. The positive economic effects of agribusinesses "spill over" and "trickle down" from the top to lower levels of the economy. What bothers liberals is when, for largely political reasons, agribusinesses do not realize their full potential because local officials are either suspicious of them or tax them to the point of discouraging them from investing further in the local economy.

Liberals also seem to have an implicit faith in the ability of technology to help solve the hunger problem. In the 1960s and 1970s a good deal of attention was given to the green revolution, the effort to produce new varieties of rice and wheat appropriate for soil and climate conditions in developing nations. One of the most important figures associated with the green revolution was plant pathologist Dr. Norman Borlaug, who started the revolution in Mexico and the Philippines in 1944 with his work for the Rockefeller Foundation. Fifty years later, he was still working to apply the practical and scientific principles of the green revolution to 150,000 farms in Ghana, Sudan, Tanzania, Togo, Nigeria, and Ethiopia. Dr. Borlaug cites China and other Asian nations as major success stories in the green revolution.[29]

More recently, another revolution in plant production is linked to the information and knowledge structure and centers around the use of newer varieties of bioengineered plants and animals, or **genetically modified organisms (GMOs)**. Once again, new crops and virus- and insect-resistant plants are expected to revolutionize and increase crop production.

---

### THE IPE OF GENETICALLY MODIFIED ORGANISMS[a]

#### Who Owns What: Intellectual Property Rights

Genetically modified organisms (GMOs) are organisms containing genes that have been put in them by processes that do not occur in nature. A recent innovation in the scientific community, GMOs hold the potential to create profitable new markets. For this reason, investors in companies that make GMOs are watching closely the ongoing World Trade Organization (WTO) debates concerning intellectual property rights (IPRs) (see Chapter 6). IPRs, among other things, are crucial to support of the research and development of GMOs. In the WTO debates, many Western powers employ neoliberal reasoning that IPRs are essential for a properly functioning international economy. Their argument has been challenged by critics who point out the practical realities of IPRs. Such realities include the facts that inventing new GMOs without violating IPRs is practically impossible, biopiracy is threatening the economic heritage of Third World countries, and farmers are being sued for the accidents of genetic drift.

These problems exist because in 1980 the U.S. Supreme Court ruled that living cells are patentable.[b] The case was a major shift in the treatment of agricultural patents and led to the national and international liberalization of patent law. That same year, the U.S. Congress passed the Bayah-Dole Act, which allowed universities to file patents on biological innovations resulting from federally funded research. In 1985 the Hibberd patent was awarded in the United States, as a result of which plant breeders were allowed to patent the genome of a plant and farmers were denied the traditional right to save and replant seeds without paying patent owners. In 1993 the WTO TRIPS agreement liberalized international patent law by declaring that IPRs could also be assigned to biological resources.[c]

Since the liberation of patent law there has been a frenzy among corporations and universities to file patents. As part of this effort, many corporations have sent delegates around the globe to retrieve genetic resources and patent them. In many cases the collectors have not had the permission of local governments and have effectively stolen national heritage. For instance, India found that U.S. and European firms had filed patents for the native herbs turmeric and neem and were claiming that they had exclusive rights to market the herbs and their genetic properties.[d] Proponents for the rights of Third World countries call this biopiracy and advocate for protecting states' rights to their genetic heritage. There has been some progress in this area; for instance, Article 15 of the Convention on Biological Diversity asserts that states have sovereignty over their natural resources,[e] but biopiracy continues to be a problem.

Another expression of patent frenzy is that biotech corporations are constantly warring with each other over who owns biological innovations. Many corporations and universities claim to own the same scientific processes and genomes. Golden Rice is an example of this overlap; it is covered by seventy patents held by thirty-two different entities.[f] Fiercely protective of their biological resources, companies not only sue each other over patent violations, they also sue farmers. Monsanto funded a toll-free "rat line" in Canada to allow farmers to report neighbors who were using GMO seeds without paying for them.[g] Unfortunately for both Monsanto and the farmers, farmers can do little to prevent GMO plants from growing in their fields.

## Mercantilism Versus Neoliberalism: The EU Ban on GMOs

IPR complications are not the only reason that GMOs have been questioned; there is also a concern with health and safety, particularly in the European Union (EU). In 1999 the EU announced that it would no longer accept imports of genetically modified organisms.[h] The loss to the world's major GMO exporters—the United States, Canada, and Argentina—was substantial: U.S. soy exports alone dropped by $5 million.[i]

Angry at being shut out of the European market, these countries brought their case to the WTO, arguing that the EU was practicing illegal protectionist policies and impeding free trade. The EU countered that the ban was legal under the Agreement on Agriculture that was reached during the Uruguay Round (see Chapter 6), which states that a nation has the right to impose trade barriers in order to protect public health. Thus far, the WTO's Dispute Settlement Understanding (DSU) has ruled against the EU.[j] The EU has largely ignored the DSU decisions.[k] By doing so the EU has exposed itself to retaliatory measures from GMO-exporting states as well as undermined the authority of the international trade regime on which a large part of its economy depends.

## Validating GMOs: World Hunger

To combat criticism of GMOs, many proponents have highlighted their potential to solve world hunger. Former U.S. President Jimmy Carter, for instance, once argued that "responsible GMOs are not the enemy, starvation is."[l] Today, roughly 20 percent of the world's population is hungry, and the number is expected to grow as population increases to a projected 9 to 12 billion people by 2050.[m] Compounding the world's food supply deficient is the fact that many subsistence farmers are quitting their land and moving to cities; they can no longer make a living selling their wares in a market saturated with subsidized agricultural products. How will world leaders provide the food that is needed today and the increasing amounts that will be needed in the future? Scientists (and some policymakers) such as Potrykus, Wambugu, and Conway have argued that GMO research could provide the answer by creating plants that are more nutrient-dense, grow in arid climates, and produce higher yields.[n]

Although GMOs have the potential to reduce world hunger, very little research aims toward reaching this goal. Corporations, which do the majority of GMO research, are interested in inventing plant species they can market to affluent farmers, not in making social progress. Two exceptions are the Bill Gates Foundation and the Rockefeller Foundation,[o] but otherwise there is very little money available. Even if scientists do obtain the necessary funding to invent beneficial GMOs, they must overcome the tangle of patent claims before their inventions can be put to good use.

Some structuralists draw attention to such obstacles and use them to strengthen their argument that humans should not play God with nature. They assert that GMOs should not be considered the "silver bullet" against hunger and point out that enough food is already produced in the world today to feed the global citizenry. Furthermore, structuralists tend to stress that the solution to hunger lies not in science but in altering food distribution channels and addressing social inequalities.[p]

*References*

[a] Casey Dillon did background research for this box and wrote the first draft of it. Our thanks to her.

[b] Peter Pringle, *Food, Inc.: Mendel to Monsanto—The Promises and Perils of the Biotech Harvest*. (New York: Simon & Schuster, 2003).

[c] Ibid.

[d] Ibid.

[e] Convention on Biological Diversity, art. 15, sec. 1, www.biodiv.org/convention/articles.asp?lg=0&a=cbd-15.

[f] Pringle, *Food, Inc.*

g   *The Global Banquet.* Maryknoll World Productions. Houston, Texas: Orbis Books, 2001.
h   United Kingdom Department of Trade and Industry, *WTO Dispute Settlement*, www.dti.gov.uk/ewt/wtorules.htm, accessed October 28, 2006.
i   Tim Josling, Donna Roberts, and David Orden, *Food Regulation and Trade* (Washington, DC: Institute for International Economics, 2004).
j   Andrew Pollack, "World Trade Agency Rules for US in BioTech Dispute," *The New York Times,* February 8, 2006.
k   See Josling et al., *Food Regulation and Trade.*
l   Gordon Conway, *The Doubly Green Revolution* (Ithaca, NY: Cornell University Press, 1997).
m   William H. Bender, "How Much Food Will We Need in the 21st Century?" *Environment,* March 1997, pp. 7–14.
n   See, for instance, Conway, *The Doubly Green Revolution.*
o   Donald McNeil, "Better Bananas, Nicer Mosquitoes," *The New York Times,* December 6, 2005.
p   See, for example, Miguel Altieri, *Genetic Engineering in Agriculture,* 2nd ed. (Oakland, CA: Food First, 2004).

Ironically, one of the biggest critics of GMOs, Jeremy Rifkin of The Foundation on Economic Trends, maintains that the new frontier of **genomics**[30] is a cutting-edge technology that will render gene splicing and transgenic crops obsolete. This new technology greatly accelerates classical breeding. Interestingly, Rifkin posits that many groups that have opposed GMOs are guardedly supportive of genomics, or the manipulation of an organism's genetic code. Many liberals argue that many of these technologies will be developed through commercial markets and trade and their benefits diffused throughout the world via TNCs. Furthermore, TNCs are expected to work closely with national and local governments to implement the technology and spread its benefits.

In sum, liberals emphasize that hunger results when governments intervene in markets and distort the food production and distribution processes. The result is a glut of food in the major grain-producing countries of the world, most of whom are Western industrialized nations. Meanwhile, demand for food in much of the developing and overpopulated regions of the world goes unmet. Abundance coexists with hunger and starvation. Economic growth achieved through trade investment in production promises to help nations move through the demographic transition, bringing down birth rates but also helping these countries and their farmers produce more commodities and trade for what they need with their surpluses.

## The Structuralist Perspective

For structuralists, the dominant actors are classes within a nation-state and classes of rich and poor whose interests cut across national boundaries. The nature of the relationship of rich classes and nations to poor ones is one of exploitation (see Chapter 4). Exploitation is a feature of the international production and finance structures that link rich with poor nations. Formal colonialism is supposedly a thing of the past, but rich nations continue to subjugate dependent countries by practicing **neoimperialism**, that is, penetrating Southern economies via trade, aid, and investment policies and practices.

In agreement with liberals, structuralists argue that markets fail because of government intervention in the economy. However, the two perspectives differ in their rationale for that interference. For structuralists, state policies reflect not so much protection of private (group) interests but the interests of a wealthy class of financiers, manufacturers, and businessmen. The rich become wealthy at the expense of the poor, both nationally and internationally. Rich nations continue to dominate poor ones, intentionally making them dependent on the rich for a variety of goods and services to develop their economies.

Hunger is the result of this exploitative relationship. Structuralists criticize mercantilists and liberals for not giving enough attention to factors and conditions that prevent food from being distributed more equitably in local, national, and international distribution systems.[31] Rich nations usually produce more food than their consumers can eat, yet millions of people in poor countries go hungry simply because surplus food is not redistributed to those who need it most. Dependency theorists emphasize the negative consequences of the transfer of wealth and resources from Southern LDCs to Northern industrialized nations. Linkages between rich and poor nations impoverish the poor, who become worse off as a result of various transactions with the North. Most LDCs were relatively self-sufficient food producers until they were colonized by imperial powers. Exposure to the West brought about development of only a small sector of the economy, while in the larger poor enclaves of the economy, the masses became impoverished and were more likely to be malnourished or even starve to death.

From the perspective of dependency theorists, trade is a weapon used by the rich to penetrate and make poor countries dependent. The **terms of trade** (value of trade exchanges) favor rich nations. Free-trade policies benefit advanced industrial economies at the expense of the development of poorer economies. In the past, LDCs have produced mainly primary commodities that earned less income than the value-added products of rich nations. Elites within developing nations joined with their counterparts in rich nations to establish and benefit from a local power structure that exploited the masses.

Instead of focusing on meeting the needs of its people, these governments adopted an array of policies that continued to benefit rich nations. Many LDCs specialized in producing one or two major export crops to earn foreign exchange. Quite often these crops are still financed and grown by large agribusinesses that were encouraged to invest in the country by the national power structure. These enterprises grow soya beans (Brazil), vegetables (Mexico), beef (Costa Rica), or peanuts (Senegal), while the masses of people subsist on substandard diets and local staple crops.

In cases where states belong to regional trade associations, as Mexico does to NAFTA, imports of U.S. corn have "ravaged the countryside."[32] There are two consequences of playing the development game. First, most of the masses never share in the income earned from trade. "Trickle down" does not work. Instead, the rich get richer and the poor get poorer. Second, governments of these countries are forced to import food they need to make up for food deficits created by an inappropriate development strategy that relies on trade.

In many cases, people and governments are simply too poor to purchase the commodities grown in their own country and instead become even more dependent on donations of food aid to make up the difference. Foreign aid usually has strings attached to it, such as requiring that payment be made in certain currencies. Governments are also known to resell aid to earn foreign exchange, or to distribute aid to the middle class or to those groups, such as the police, they feel are likely to make a significant contribution to the economic development of society. Foreign aid, then, merely further entrenches poor countries in a vicious cycle of dependency, poverty, and hunger.

Agribusinesses and other TNCs also affect LDCs negatively in many ways. Their high-tech production methods displace local labor and small farmers, destroying the traditional agriculture or farm sector of local economies.[33] Masses of people leave agriculture to find work in cities, putting pressure on urban centers for social services. Aside from producing inappropriate crops for export, agribusinesses use pesticides and insecticides that are outlawed in their home country. Many of them bribe local or national officials, complicate land ownership and reform programs, and disturb local food distribution programs.

Structuralists are just as pessimistic about the benefits of biotechnology today as they were about the first green revolution. They worry that attempts to diffuse biotechnology throughout the Third World will contribute to environmental damage and widen the income gap between rich and poor within developing nations as well as between the North and South. Critics charge that the use of genetically modified foods will result in a monoculture crop production system, with fewer plant and animal varieties, more reliance on herbicides, and, because of its close relationship to business, lack of state regulation of the technology itself.[34] Structuralists also worry that those who support the green revolution or biotechnology in the Third World overlook the food distribution system, the land tenure system, and the fact that many LDCs continue to grow cash crops for export instead of producing food for domestic needs.

Many dependency theorists would have LDCs cut themselves off from the industrialized nations and adopt either self-sufficiency or import-substitution policies.[35] The development strategy China practiced before 1978 was often recommended by these theorists as a way for LDCs to eradicate poverty and hunger before exposing the economy to outside political and economic influences. Poverty and hunger are wasteful and inefficient. Development experts should find ways to build an economy from the inside out rather than from the outside in. Other critics of industrial-nation practices believe that the North and South can accommodate each other provided a "new international economic order" (NIEO) is worked out between them. So far, however, the NIEO movement that began in the 1970s has ground to a halt. The South simply does not have the political clout to demand and bring about major reform of the entire international political economy.

The "Modern World System" approach (see Chapter 4) focuses more directly on international structures of wealth and power that cause hunger in LDCs. Rich core states have dominated world trade networks since the sixteenth century. Peripheral regions were first colonized and then exploited for their resources and labor. Only semiperipheral countries like the NICs have been able to develop successfully to any great extent. However, they did so because it was in the strategic and foreign economic interests of the United States to flood them with technical assistance, loans, food aid, and military security. As clients of the United States that bordered the Soviet Union, many of the NICs played a major role in helping the United States contain the Soviet Union. From the perspective of modern world system scholars, conditions for the poorest countries are not likely to improve until or unless the international division of labor changes.

Finally, a number of antiglobalization scholars focus on the effects of globalization on agriculture and food production and distribution systems.[36] Structuralist in tone because they focus on how the underlying economy shapes political and economic behavior, some antiglobalists have examined the connection between trade and aid policy and the role of agribusiness and international conglomerates. Much of the antiglobalist campaign is directed at international organizations, especially the IMF and the World Bank, for the way their policies perpetuate poverty, hunger, and malnutrition in poorer nations by supporting local tenure systems and encouraging these nations to be dependent on foreign aid and investment.

A number of NGOs have worked to promote alternative production and marketing strategies for family farmers and growers in developing nations. As part of the "fair trade" campaign, their efforts are directed at trying to ensure that growers get their fair share of the profit from sales of coffee, bananas, and other food commodities. These measures can help overcome hunger to the extent that poorer farmers in LDCs realize more income from their production.

## CONCLUSION

Currently, record numbers of people are malnourished and starving in various parts of the world, while obesity is an issue of increasing significance in many industrialized nations as well as in some developing nations. Since the early 1970s, studies of hunger have moved decidedly away from an almost exclusive focus on the lack of food accompanied by overpopulation in developing areas of the world, to placing more attention to international political-economic explanations of the issue. Now hunger is more often seen as a multidimensional problem that affects different locales, nations, and regions of the world differently. An IPE of food and hunger accounts for how both food production and distribution are influenced specifically by international trade, aid, and investment practices, and how they interact with the international production, finance, knowledge, and national security structures. Each traditional IPE perspective accounts for a piece of the hunger puzzle.

An IPE of hunger also teaches us that solving the problem is nothing short of a Herculean task. This chapter has outlined just some of the conflicting interests of the many actors—nation-states, international organizations, international businesses, and NGOs among others—as well as their different values and what they see as causes and possible solutions to the hunger problem. However, reconciling the conflicting political and economic interests of these actors seems unlikely given their lack of consensus about the causes of hunger, let alone what to do about it. For instance, many people find Hardin's suggestions about triage and lifeboat ethics unethical; similarly, they view Hardin's suggestions about population control as either politically unacceptable or unnecessary at this time.

In the meantime, however, what to do about immediate hunger problems in some of the poorer regions of the world? The "food first" people would have national and international leaders and officials develop economic growth and food production strategies that promote self-sufficiency, or that at least attempt to limit the exploitative connections between rich and poor nations. Others believe that permanently solving the hunger problem requires attention to promoting **food security**[37] for each and every individual and a focus on how that security is linked to national and international political and economic structures of wealth and power. Still others argue that there is no truly global solution to hunger because these problems vary so much from place to place or region to region of the world. They want to solve hunger problems by promoting food security on both a national and regional basis.[38]

Although these recommendations are all worthy of consideration, they cannot overcome the fact that local and national elites profit a great deal from trade and foreign investment, from local land tenure systems, and from domestic public policies that often favor the rich over the poor. In essence, significantly improving hunger conditions in many poorer countries requires nothing short of a complete political and economic transformation of both the international and domestic political economic orders.

At the level of international organizations, food and hunger issues have become more difficult to separate from other issues such as economic growth and development strategies, the environment, and human political and economic rights. Once again we regret to report that an IPE of hunger compels us to expect continued incidences of malnutrition and even starvation given the relationship of states and other actors to market conditions and the distribution of wealth and power in the world. For the moment, however, at least we have a better understanding of why this is the case.

## DISCUSSION QUESTIONS

1. Outline the overpopulation/lack of production thesis about world hunger and discuss some of the consequences of this argument for dealing with the hunger problem. Whose problem is it? What is being done about it? What should be done about it?
2. Do the same as in Question 1 for the political-economic "food first" thesis about hunger.
3. Outline the dominant themes and concepts applied to the hunger problem from the perspective of each of the major approaches to IPE: mercantilism, liberalism, and structuralism.
4. Discuss the extent to which you feel the hunger problem can be overcome. What are the major political-economic fault lines or dilemmas one has to consider if the problem is to be solved?
5. Discuss some of the proposed solutions to the hunger problem. Which do you favor, or not favor? Explain.
6. Pick a single country or several countries in a region of the world and study the nature of their hunger problems. Are they more political, economic, or social in nature? Explain.

## INTERNET LINKS

FAO:
> www.fao.org

World Food Program:
> www.wfp.org

Bread for the World:
> www.bread.org

The Hunger Program:
> www.thp.org

Gender and Food Security:
   www.fao.org/Gender/gender.htm
CGIAR (Consultative Group on International Agricultural Research):
   www.cgiar.org
Lutheran Church:
   www.ecla.org/hunger
World Hunger:
   www.worldhunger.org
Common Dreams:
   http://Commondreams.org

## SUGGESTED READINGS

J. I. Hans Bakker, ed. *The World Food Crisis: Food Security in Comparative Perspective.* Toronto: Canadian Scholars' Press, 1990.
Alessandro Bonanno, Lawrence Busch, William Friedland, Lourdes Gouveia, and Enzo Mingione, eds. *From Columbus to Conagra: The Globalization of Agriculture and Food.* Lawrence: University of Kansas Press, 1994.
Douglas Boucher. *The Paradox of Plenty: Hunger in a Bountiful World.* San Francisco: Institute for Food and Development Policy, 1999.
Bread for the World. *The Changing Politics of Hunger: Hunger 1999.* Washington, DC: Bread for the World Institute, 1999.
Joseph Collins. *What Difference Could a Revolution Make?* San Francisco: Institute for Food and Development Policy, 1982.
David Grigg. *The World Food Problem: 1950–1980.* New York: Basil Blackwell, 1985.
Betsy Hartman and James Boyce. *Needless Hunger.* San Francisco: Institute for Food and Development Policy, 1979.
Marc Lappé and Britt Bailey. *Against the Grain.* Monroe, ME: Common Courage Press, 1998.
Frances Moore Lappé, Joseph Collins, and Peter Rosset. *World Hunger: Twelve Myths.* New York: Grove Press, 1998.
Philip McMichael. "Rethinking Globalization: The Agrarian Question Revisited," *Review of International Political Economy,* 4 (Winter 1997).
Eric Schlosser. *Fast Food Nation: What the All-American Meal Is Doing to the World.* New York: Houghton Mifflin, 2001.
Ross Talbot. *The Four World Food Agencies in Rome.* Ames: Iowa State University Press, 1990.
Joachim von Braun, Tesfeye Teklu, and Patricia Webb. *Famine in Africa.* Washington, DC: International Food Policy Research Institute, 1998.
Mitchell B. Wallerstein. *Food for War—Food for Peace.* Cambridge, MA: MIT Press, 1980.
E. M. Young. *World Hunger.* London: Routledge, 1997.

## KEY TERMS

Public Law 480 (PL 480)
green revolution
tragedy of the commons
triage

demographic transition
"food first" thesis
genetically modified organisms
   (GMOs)

genomics
neoimperialism
terms of trade
food security

## NOTES

1. Our thanks to Casey Dillon for comments and research assistance on this chapter.
2. Thomas Malthus, *An Essay on the Principle of Population,* excerpted in Charles W. Needy, ed., *Classics of Economics* (Oak Park, IL: Moore, 1980), pp. 48, 55.
3. See, for example, Joseph Belden, ed., *Dirt Rich, Dirt Poor: America's Food and Farm Crisis* (Washington, DC: Institute for Policy Studies, 1986).
4. Paul Ehrlich, *The Population Bomb* (New York: Ballantine Books, 1971).
5. Garrett Hardin, "The Tragedy of the Commons," *Science,* 162 (December 1968), pp. 1243–1248.
6. Garrett Hardin, "Lifeboat Ethics: The Case Against Helping the Poor," *Psychology Today,* September 1974, pp. 38–43 and 124–126.
7. See, for example, William and Paul Paddock, *Famine—1975* (Boston: Little, Brown, 1967).
8. See, for example, Colin Tudge, *The Famine Business* (New York: St. Martin's Press, 1977), p. 9.
9. See "Diminishing Population Takes Wind out of Alarmist Sails," *The* (Tacoma, Wash.) *News Tribune,* January 24, 1997, p. A13.

10. See, for example, Tudge, *The Famine Business;* Susan George, *How the Other Half Dies: The Real Reasons for World Hunger* (Montclair, NJ: Allanheld, Osmun, 1977); and especially Frances Moore Lappé and Joseph Collins, *Food First: Beyond the Myth of Scarcity* (Boston: Houghton Mifflin, 1977).

11. For a more detailed discussion of the world food crisis, see Sartaj Aziz, ed., *Hunger, Politics and Markets: The Real Issues in the Food Crisis* (New York: New York University Press, 1975).

12. For a classic study, see Jack Shepherd, *The Politics of Starvation* (New York: The Carnegie Endowment for International Peace, 1975).

13. For an interesting and yet devastating critique of the four major world food agencies, see Ross Talbot, *The Four World Food Agencies in Rome* (Ames: Iowa State University Press, 1990).

14. See, for example, the Physicians' Task Force on Hunger in America, *Hunger in America* (New York: Harper & Row, 1985).

15. See, for example, the excellent account of the Rwandan civil war in 1994 in Fergal Keane, *Season of Blood* (New York: Viking, 1998).

16. See, for example, "A Holocaust of Hunger," *The* (Tacoma, Wash.) *News Tribune,* January 10, 1999, p. C6.

17. Some of the most pessimistic outlooks about hunger come out annually from Lester Brown, head of the Worldwatch Institute in Washington, D.C. See Lester Brown, Christopher Flavin, Hilary French, and Linda Starke, *State of the World 1999: The Millenium Edition* (New York: W. W. Norton, 1999).

18. See, for example, "The New Economics of Food," *Business Week,* May 20, 1996, pp. 78–87.

19. John Tessitore and Susan Woolfson, eds., *A Global Agenda: Issues Before the 52nd General Assembly of the United Nations* (New York: Rowman and Littlefield, 1997), p. 165.

20. See Lester Brown, "Exploding U.S. Grain Demand for Automotive Fuel," www.earth-policy.org/Updates/2006/Update60_printable.htm, accessed November 21, 2006.

21. See "Latest US Diplomatic Tool: Corn and Grain," *The Christian Science Monitor,* February 9, 1999, p. 15.

22. See "North Koreans Flee a 'Creeping Famine,'" *The* (Tacoma, Wash.) *News Tribune,* March 31, 1999, p. A9.

23. See Jeffrey Sachs, "Africa Can Escape Poverty, Says Economist," www.developments.org.uk/Search?Searchabletext=Jeffrey+Sachs, accessed March 15, 2007.

24. The classic statement to this effect is by the realist Hans Morgenthau, *Politics Among Nations* (New York: Knopf, 1948).

25. See Steven A. Breth, James A. Auerbach, and Martha Lee Benz, *The Future Stakes for U.S. Food and Agriculture in East and Southeast Asia,* NPA Report No. 291 (Washington, DC: National Policy Association, 1999).

26. Robert Paarlberg, "Lessons of the Grain Embargo," *Foreign Affairs,* 59 (Fall 1980), pp. 144–162.

27. See "Famine vs. War in Ethiopia," *The* (Tacoma, Wash.) *News Tribune,* April 23, 2000, p. A3.

28. See David N. Balaam, "Agricultural Trade Policy," in Brian Hocking and Steven McGuire, eds., *Trade Politics: International, Domestic, and Regional Perspectives* (London: Routledge, 1999), pp. 52–66.

29. See "Bringing the Green Revolution to Africa," *The New York Times,* September 14, 1992, p. A13.

30. See Jeremy Rifkin, "Beyond GM Food: New Cutting Edge MAS Technology Makes GM Food Obsolete," at http://CommonDreams.org, accessed October 20, 2006.

31. For a classic example of this argument, see Betsy Hartman and James Boyce, *Needless Hunger: Voices from a Bangladesh Village* (San Francisco: Institute for Food and Development Policy, 1979).

32. Tim Weiner, "In Corn's Cradle, U.S. Imports Bury Family Farms," *The New York Times,* February 26, 2002, p. A4.

33. See Brian Halweil, "Where Have All the Farmers Gone?" *World Watch,* September/October 2000, pp. 12–28.

34. See, for example, Marc Lappé and Britt Bailey, *Against the Grain* (Monroe, ME: Common Courage Press, 1998).

35. Andre Gunder Frank, *Latin America: Underdevelopment or Revolution* (New York: Monthly Review Press, 1970).

36. The literature on the effects of globalization on agriculture has proliferated recently. See, for example, Karen Lehman and Al Krebs, "Control over the World's Food Supply," in Jerry Mander and Edward Goldsmith, eds., *The Case Against the Global Economy and for a Turn Toward the Local* (San Francisco: Sierra Club Book, 1996), pp. 122–130; Philip McMichael, "Rethinking Globalization: The Agrarian Question Revisited," in *Review of International Political Economy,* 4 (Winter 1997); and Alessandro Bonanno, Lawrence Busch, William Friedland, Lourdes Gouveia, and Enzo Mingione, eds., *From Columbus to Conagra: The Globalization of Agriculture and Food* (Lawrence: University of Kansas Press, 1994).

37. The issue of food security is discussed and applied in J. I. Hans Bakker, ed., *The World Food Crisis: Food Security in Comparative Perspective* (Toronto: Canadian Scholars' Press, 1990).

38. This is the central thesis of David N. Balaam and Michael J. Carey, *Food Politics: The Regional Conflict* (Totowa, NJ: Allenheld, Osmun, 1981).

# The Environment:
# The Green Side of IPE

## OVERVIEW[1]

In December 2005, more than a million people marched in over 100 cities in thirty countries to demand greater action on the issue of global warming. Concurrently, at a United Nations meeting in Montreal, 180 state representatives worked to establish new targets for the reduction of greenhouse emissions when the Kyoto Protocol expires in 2012, while trying to coax the United States, the world's biggest producer of greenhouse gases, into ratifying the Kyoto Protocol. By the summer of 2006, reports that the glaciers in Greenland, near the North and South Poles, and elsewhere are breaking up at record rates made headlines in many press reports. Former U.S. Vice President Al Gore, in the documentary, *An Inconvenient Truth*, presents evidence that global warming is real and therefore that solutions to the problem must be found now at the risk of serious catastrophes of global proportions. By November of that same year, climate negotiators met for the twelfth time since 1992 in Nairobi, Kenya, to discuss the problem of global warming. Meanwhile, another controversial report, sponsored by the British government and written by the World Bank's former chief economist, Nicolas Stern, once again warned that global warming could have a disasterous effect on the world's economy.

Apart from recent events, many other environmental issues have grown in importance (sometimes to crisis proportions) and in the past few years have moved near the top of both domestic and international agendas. More than ever, newspapers report that people the world over are concerned about a variety of environmental issues related to the physical limits of the earth's resources and raw materials, poverty and the resulting tension and conflict in developing nations, and the viability of industrialization as a development goal everywhere in the world.

Environmental problems have always existed in many nations and regions of the world. However, today's ecological and environmental problems are increasingly *global* in nature. Because interdependence and globalization connect people and issues in new and different ways, the nature and effects of most environmental issues are broader in scope and more difficult to deal with than any single nation's ability to solve them. Managing these issues involves states, international organizations and, increasingly, nongovernmental organizations (NGOs), local governments and cities, **epistemic communities** (groups of scientific experts), and even the influence of individual politicians or otherwise distinguished people who have made "environmentalism" their cause.

This chapter probes the frontiers of the **green** side (pertaining to the environment and the earth's ecology) of international political economy (IPE). A major question for students of IPE has become: How do nations and other political actors create or sustain wealth for today's generations without leaving a despoiled and depleted environment for future generations? There are many indications of agreement that this *is*, in fact, the most important question to ask about the relationship of the new global economy growth to the environment. As yet, however, the international system has not seen much progress in reconciling these two goals.

### Pavement

Dinosaurs, antique oak tree forests,
palm tree jungles gave their all for oil.
Petroleum goo drawn up,
refined, cooked into paving
laid on the land so cyclists could
smoothly pedal on miniature roadways
and leave their autos at home.

Michael Carey[2]

The relationship between the environment and the international political economy is a two-way street with many twists and turns. Tensions among markets and among political and economic actors affect the environment locally and, increasingly, on a global basis. Likewise, environmental problems routinely influence the international political economy. For instance, in Chapter 6 we discussed the connection between the international political economy and the environment in the World Trade Organization's efforts to arrive at multilateral agreements that cover a host of rules concerning tuna, dolphins, and other plants and animals. Environmental issues are also increasingly more difficult to separate from trade policies that emphasize mass production of goods in less developed countries (LDCs) that also severely affect food-growing conditions in many developing economies. Likewise, Chapter 17 touched on some of the major criticisms of transnational corporations and their investment practices, which in some cases seek to escape local environmental regulations and standards.

This chapter focuses on the IPE of the global environment. In it we discuss a number of political, social, and economic aspects of global environmental problems, including a brief history of environmental issues in the international political economy that documents the broadening scope of those problems, the proliferation of actors involved in these issues, and the role they play in different facets of managing what has become a truly global issue. Applying some of the concepts used to explore various environmental issues, we examine in some detail three interrelated cases of air, land, and sea problems: global warming, deforestation, and ocean disposal of nuclear waste. Finally, we explore a variety of proposed global solutions to environmental problems, focusing on the roles that states and other actors, markets, technology, and even social and ethical values play in these solutions.

## A BRIEF HISTORY OF ENVIRONMENTAL ISSUES: THE WIDENING SCOPE OF ENVIRONMENTAL PROBLEMS

Environmental and ecological problems have been around for centuries. Beginning in the eighteenth century during the Industrial Revolution, science and technology were harnessed to produce new labor-saving devices, industrial machines, and goods for mass consumption. Karl Marx and many of his contemporaries in the mid-nineteenth century complained of the damaging effects that "satanic mills" had on labor but also on the physical presence of England's bigger cities. Manufacturing industries in Europe were fueled by great quantities of inexpensive natural resources and raw materials, some of which were located nearby but the preponderance of which were located in colonial regions of the world. During the period of classic imperialism, Europeans conquered and colonized "underdeveloped" territories, exploiting them for, among other things, their resources and raw materials. Meanwhile, on the European continent, air, water, and soil pollution spread beyond local areas. The development of the gasoline-powered engine at the end of the nineteenth century shifted demand away from coal and steam to oil and petroleum-based energy resources. Resources remained plentiful in supply and relatively inexpensive in cost—transportation being the biggest expense.

As industrialization spread throughout Western Europe and the United States, industrial pollution gradually became a bigger problem there, too. Local authorities were primarily responsible for clean-up efforts. Many problems became more international in scope—that is, they covered several or more nation-states. For instance, in the 1920s, the United States and Canada argued about the residue of lead and zinc smelting in British Columbia that was carried down the Columbia River into the United States. For the most part, however, environmental issues, at least in the industrialized parts of the world, were state-based problems. As realist ideas (see Chapter 9) dominated the outlook of most officials during the Great Depression of the 1930s, so states dealt with environmental problems only when it was in their interest to do so.

The global magnitude of environmental problems today was not fully realized until the 1960s. In the United States, global resource depletion became one of the issues of the student movement and the environmental movement that developed at the same time. As the absolute amount of pollution discharged worldwide grew, so did scientific knowledge and public awareness.[3] In 1972 a Conference on the Human Environment was held in Stockholm, Sweden, at which the UN instituted its Environment Program (UNEP). The conference also produced an Action Plan for the Human Environment, which included 109 recommendations for governmental and international action on a wide variety of environmental issues.

The OPEC oil embargo of 1973 and resulting high oil prices pushed the issue of energy resource scarcity onto the agenda of many nation-states and further up the global agenda. Many developed nations became aware of their dependence on oil and other energy resources to sustain economic growth. Likewise, developing countries grew ever more aware of their dependence on these resources for industrial and economic development. This fundamental difference between the way developed and developing states viewed their relationship to economic growth framed the ways in which both viewed environmental problems. As in the case of trade, finance, and many other issues, these differences are often referred to in the context of North–South relations.

### The Limits to Growth and the Tragedy of the Commons

The critical importance of the environment was further stressed in a shocking study by the Club of Rome and released to worldwide attention in 1972. *The Limits to Growth*[4] provided a set of projections for the world based on economic and environmental trends since World War II. The study argued that if previous patterns of economic activity and environmental abuse continued, it would be the *environment,* not land, food, or other factors, that would limit global progress. A rich financial future on an uninhabitable planet was the report's shocking prediction. In 1980 U.S. President Jimmy Carter commissioned *The Global 2000 Report to the President,*[5] which predicted continued population growth, depletion of natural resources, deforestation, air and water pollution, and species extinction. A less pessimistic outlook, however, was issued two years later by Julian Simon and Herman Kahn in their *The Resourceful Earth: A Response to Global 2000.*[6] Kahn went on to refer to the fatalistic outlook of the ecopessimists as "globaloney."

Another concept applied to most environmental problems was the **tragedy of the commons**[7] (introduced in a different context in Chapter 19). Biology Professor Garrett Hardin argued that the earth's stock of resources are limited—finite resources such as oil can be used up, living resources such as forests and fish runs can be overused and depleted. For the most part, the environment is a **collective good**, shared by everyone but owned by no one. (Another term used to communicate this idea with regard to resources is "the common heritage of mankind" (belonging to no one or not to any state[s]), which is often applied to the **Law of the Sea Treaty** that covers the world's oceans.) As the tragedy of the commons explains, such goods are prone to abuse because political and economic systems rationally compel us to (over)produce as much as we can, without thinking of the effects on the earth's resources. In many cases we have the freedom (which takes the form of political rights) to be self-interested.

Nearly all economic systems are based on the production of manufactured goods and services that, while benefiting the individual, abuse the environment to some extent. This tragedy can easily be seen in the current concern over global warming and toxic waste dumping in the oceans. Harm to the environment is shared by all the inhabitants of earth and may not become apparent for years to come. In weighing costs and benefits, the benefits are clear and immediate, whereas the indirect costs (to the person making the choice) are negligible, diffused, and hard to evaluate. In effect, consumers, businesses, and states get a "free ride" to the extent that there is no incentive for them to pay the costs associated with helping overcome the problem. Hardin and others argued that the state therefore *should* play a role in preventing or correcting the (environmental) tragedy of the commons. If society values the environment but individuals abuse it, it must be up to the state to take corrective action.

In the 1980s oil supplies gradually increased and oil prices declined or held steady, weakening interest in resource scarcity and environmental problems. Yet national and international attention to environmental issues reached new heights of intensity and worry in response to a number of problems related to pollution and broader issues of ecological (mis)management. Just some of these events included a major chemical spill at a Union Carbide plant in Bhopal, India; the acid rain debate between the United States and Canada; the Chernobyl nuclear reactor incident in the Soviet Union; discovery of a hole in the ozone layer over Antarctica; major drought and famine in Africa accompanied by drought in the United States; a chemical spill in the Rhine River; accelerated rates of deforestation in Brazil, the Ivory Coast, Haiti, Thailand, and other nations; the closing of many U.S. beaches because of toxic waste or spills; the Exxon tanker *Valdez* oil spill in Alaska; and the effects of greenhouse warming on the earth.

## The Global Management Issue

In 1987, UNEP published a report entitled *Our Common Future* that shifted more attention to the connection between the environment and the survival of developing nations.[8] Sometimes referred to as the Bruntland Report because the chair of the UN commission was Gro Harlem Bruntland (who later became the prime minister of Norway), the report linked hunger, debt, economic growth, and other issues to environmental problems. The environment was also gradually becoming an issue often linked to national security. In 1988 British Prime Minister Margaret Thatcher and Soviet Foreign Minister Eduard Shevardnadze gave speeches that connected the environment to concerns about global security. According to Shevardnadze, the environment is a "second front" that is "gaining an urgency equal to that of the nuclear-and-space threat."[9]

Not all leaders and nations felt the way these leaders did. For instance, the Reagan and first Bush administrations aligned themselves with many optimists who downplayed threats to the environment and argued that more studies needed to be done. Furthermore, they claimed, many of the measures proposed to protect the environment were too costly and unfairly penalized businesses. Western Europeans generally tended to be willing to adopt new environmental policies, but U.S. government officials adopted a neoliberal position that technology and markets could better solve these problems than coordinated efforts by nation-states in international forums.[10]

In 1975, scientists discovered a hole in the stratospheric ozone layer over Antarctica, and for a good part of the year over nations in the region such as Australia, New Zealand, and southern Chile. In the past twenty-five years, 2 to 10 percent of the stratospheric ozone layer over the Northern Hemisphere has disappeared. Chlorofluorocarbons (CFCs), which are chemicals used in many industrial products and processes, contributed the most to the ozone layer problem. CFCs were long used in refrigerants, aerosol propellants, cleaning solvents, and blowing agents for foam production, but the chlorine atoms in these compounds destroy ozone. The effects of a depleted ozone layer around the earth are global in scope, including a dramatic increase in the incidence of skin cancer, particularly melanoma, one of the most deadly varieties; more cataracts; damage to the body's immune system; and damage to crops and ocean phytoplankton. Scientists estimate that even if CFCs were completely banned, the ozone-layer problem would last at least another 100 years given the present level of atmospheric CFC concentration.

Because the effects of the deterioration in the ozone layer were so measurable and substitutes for CFCs were readily available, in 1987 diplomats signed the UN-sponsored Montreal Protocol to Control Substances that deplete the ozone layer, which required states to reduce CFC production by one-half by the year 2000. After discovery of more serious damage to the earth's ozone layer, the treaty was amended to call a complete halt to CFC production by the same year.

Multilateral efforts to deal with the environment occurred once again at the 1992 "Earth Summit" in Rio de Janeiro. Officially titled the UN Conference on the Environment and Development (UNCED), 178 national delegates, 115 heads of state, and more than 15,000 environmental NGO representatives focused their attention primarily on **sustainable development**, or ways to accomplish what seems like contradictory objectives—generating wealth and development while preserving the environment. **Agenda 21** laid out plans for states, international organizations (IOs), NGOs, and private-sector groups to achieve new goals in a variety of different issue areas connected to the environment. The Rio summit also produced a treaty on climate that sought to reduce greenhouse emissions (discussed in more detail later) and a treaty on biological diversity. After the conference, the UN General Assembly created a fifty-three-nation Commission on Sustainable Development (CSD) to translate the Rio accords into action.

Shortly before and at Rio, many nations became upset that the United States wanted to play only a minor role in managing the planet's environment and ecological system. The first Bush administration argued that emission cuts and timetables threatened economic growth, and it called for voluntary cuts in emissions. By signing the Biological Diversity Treaty in 1993, the Clinton administration tried to once again make the United States a major player in international negotiations to design and implement global environmental rules and regulations. In 1994 it also reversed the course of the Reagan and first Bush administrations and signed the Law of the Sea Treaty.

In December 1997, two thousand representatives from 159 countries met in Kyoto, Japan, to establish the **Kyoto Protocol**, to strengthen the treaty on global warming negotiated in Rio five years earlier.[11] The Kyoto Protocol requires industrialized countries to reduce their greenhouse gas emissions by more than a third by 2012, or 5.2 percent below the 1990 level of emissions. Carbon dioxide, nitrous oxide, methane, chlorofluorocarbons, ozone, and other infrared-absorbing gases are released by industrial, agricultural, and forestry activities. These greenhouse gases trap the sun's rays, contributing to a gradual warming of the earth's lower atmosphere, the process called **global warming**. Many scientists believe that the heavy concentration of industrial gases released into the atmosphere, especially since the mid-1970s, has rapidly accelerated the rate of the earth's warming. Carbon dioxide produced by the burning of fossil fuels (such as coal, oil, and natural gas), cement manufacturing, and the burning and clearing of land for agricultural purposes makes up the largest concentration of the greenhouse gases.

A unique feature of the Kyoto Protocol is **emission credits**, whereby countries can buy and sell or swap emission production quotas with one another. With 4 percent of the world's population at that time, the United States accounted for roughly 25 percent of the world's carbon emissions. By 2050 the LDCs are expected to account for most of the long-term buildup of gases, yet the Kyoto Protocol exempts them from cuts required by the treaty. China and India are expected to catch up to the United States in greenhouse gas production by 2020, but both have resisted calls for cuts in emissions of pollutants. African and Latin American countries are more supportive of the treaty but want guarantees they will get their share of aid from the developed nations to help them cut emissions.

The United States, represented by the Clinton administration, signed the Kyoto Protocol in November 1998. Many countries looked to the United States to ratify the treaty. However, the U.S. Senate passed a resolution 95–0 informing President Clinton that it would *not* ratify the treaty unless the same limitations put on the United States and other industrialized nations applied to the developing countries, or else the LDCs committed themselves to a complex scheme for trading emission permits and credits. In the spring of 2001 the new George W. Bush administration rather suddenly withdrew the United States from the Kyoto Treaty. U.S. officials cited natural gas and fossil fuel shortages as reasons to *expand* U.S. energy supplies. The new Bush administration claimed that the new treaty would cost the U.S. $400 billion and 4.9 million jobs. The administration also joined with skeptics who claimed that there was not enough evidence that power plant emissions contributed to global warming or that global warming itself was a serious problem.[12]

Focus on global climate and many other issues fizzled a bit in the early 2000s. After another series of meetings in The Hague, Netherlands, in 2000, and in Bonn, Germany, the United States, the European Union (EU), Canada, Russia, and Australia, among others, wrangled over such issues as the use of "carbon sinks" (forests or areas that naturally absorb carbon dioxide from the air) that allowed countries such as the United States and others to escape real reductions in the use of fossil fuels. The United States would also be able to buy its way into compliance with the Kyoto Protocol by paying Russia and other countries to cut their emissions more than the treaty required. And in its turn, the United States feared the effects that these proposals would have on U.S. industries. No significant new agreements were reached at these meetings.

To the dismay of the Bush administration, Russia finally ratified the Kyoto Protocol in November 2005, allowing the protocol to go into effect. In late November 2005, 180 countries met in Montreal to discuss how to implement the goals that had been established in Kyoto eight years previously. Some progress was made toward meeting various objectives, but some nations appeared to be "backsliding" on their willingness or ability to comply with the protocol. For example, Canada rejected its Kyoto emission targets. Meanwhile China, South Africa, Brazil, and Mexico were encouraged to take leading roles in planning for emission reductions after the Kyoto period ends in 2012.[13]

Since then, Al Gore's documentary seemed to personalize the issues of global warming, given its focus on rising water levels along various coastlines and other effects of global warming, including melting glaciers and destruction to coral reefs and other forms of sealife. Nicolas Stern's report accepts the conclusion that global warming is a problem of crisis proportions and estimates that it could cost the world 5 to 20 percent of its economic output "forever," but that trying to forestall the crisis would cost only 1 percent of the world's gross domestic product.[14] Furthermore, many officials and NGOs argued that the world cannot be held hostage by the United States and Australia—neither of which ratified the treaty—and, in fact, must move "beyond Kyoto" and cut emission levels drastically, by as much as half again. At present, the states bound by the Kyoto Protocol account for only 30 percent of greenhouse gases.

As we write in late November 2006, ministers at the latest climate talks in Nairobi have agreed to review the protocol in 2008 and to consider a Russian proposal to create a new mechanism that would let new countries sign up to cut emissions.[15] Even though many NGOs were hopeful that delegates would go further toward establishing Kyoto II (the next level), most officials noted an environment that was more positive about the need to cut back emissions.

## THE PROLIFERATION OF ACTORS AND THEIR ROLES

### States

In the last 300 years, as environmental problems have gone from being local and often temporary to being global and possibly permanent, the actors associated with managing them have also increased in number along with, in some cases, the scope of their interests, jurisdiction, and constituencies. This development reflects and at the same time has led to more awareness about environmental issues. However, more actors and more interconnections among them has also complicated both the analysis and management of many environmental problems.

Many nation-states deal with environmental problems in various ways reflecting different political, social, and economic systems. State environmental regulations are, in fact, prevalent in many Western European nations. In some EU nations, "green" and other political parties influence state environmental policy in this direction. However, in many LDCs in particular, environmental issues often produce tension between supporters of economic development and industrialization and supporters of income redistribution, conservation, and sustainable development. One group of experts reports that by the mid-1980s, 110 LDCs and thirty developed nations had created environmental ministries or agencies to deal with an array of problems.[16] However, there is much evidence that these agencies often do not comply with regulations or are simply ineffective.

In most cases, state officials still view environmental problems in the context of national interests and objectives, which often explains their reluctance to cooperate with other states and agencies in solving those issues. Rationally (at least in terms of short-term interests), they put achieving national objectives ahead of compromising or finding solutions that could cost them more than they expect to gain by working with other states and agencies. When it comes to managing global environmental problems, governments often fall victim to the Prisoner's Dilemma (see Chapter 8). As we will see in the case of ocean dumping, not only do security interests shape nuclear waste disposal policy, but if one state went to the expense of trying to solve a problem that affected others, one or more of the others could easily "defect" (or free-ride off other states) so as to gain the benefits of corrective measures without helping the first state pay. This is essentially what the Soviet Union and other states did until recently with regard to ocean dumping.

---

### OCEAN NUCLEAR WASTE DUMPING

Chemicals, solids, and nutrients from agricultural runoff, oil and gas development, and logging, dredging, filling, and mining are routinely dumped directly into the ocean or otherwise end up in rivers and streams and make their way to the world's oceans. Some of the effects of ocean pollution include destruction of the world's fisheries, climate and sea-level change brought about by changes in ocean temperature, and the destruction of salt marshes, mangrove swamps, coral reefs, and beaches, which means the loss of habitat and biological diversity.

The dumping of radioactive waste in the oceans is possibly an even greater threat to these ecosystems. Many assume that because oceans are so vast, they can absorb any amount of pollution. However, radioactive waste tends to be absorbed by clay on the ocean floor and spreads easily through ocean storms. The problem of ocean waste dumping is something that until recently, many of the major powers have been hesitant to admit to, let alone cooperate with one another to solve. Aside from accidental oil spills, which have become quite common, the United States, Great Britain, France, and the former Soviet Union have dumped large amounts of nuclear waste into various areas of the ocean since the mid-1940s. The International Atomic Energy Agency (IAEA) banned the dumping of high-level radioactive waste in the late 1950s. Over the next twenty years, Belgium, France, Germany, Italy, Japan, South Korea, the Netherlands, New Zealand, Sweden, Switzerland, and Great Britain admitted to having dumped nuclear waste into the ocean. The Soviet Union claimed never to have dumped radioactive waste at sea, but after the country broke up, Russian officials admitted having dumped waste into the Sea of Japan, the Arctic Ocean, and into ground wells. By some estimates, the Soviet Union dumped more nuclear waste into the ocean than the total of all other nations combined.[a] In the early 1990s, nuclear waste from fifty decommissioned missile submarine reactor cores, fuel rods, and other fission products was piling up on docks and in shipyards near Vladivostok.

The London Dumping Convention, with a membership of seventy-one nations, was formed in 1972. It permitted dumping at sea, except for materials on an approved list. In 1983, its members agreed to stop putting even low-level radioactive waste into the world's oceans. In November 1996, a new international convention was agreed to in London that permanently banned dumping of a variety of materials including radioactive waste, except for materials on a list. Since 1996, Greenpeace and other environmental groups have supported a major campaign to support the ban. Japan and the United States originally opposed the ban because they wanted to leave open the possibility of dumping low-level nuclear waste. Britain, France, and Belgium reserved the right to opt out of the new convention after fifteen years. Ninety percent of spent fuel originates in the United States, which has been forced to bury its contaminated submarine reactors in the sand at a site in Hanford, Washington, after moving the reactors up the Columbia River by barge.

Some ten years later now, the London Convention is finally going into effect, as Mexico became the twenty-sixth country to ratify the treaty, in February 2006.[b] The United States remains a party to the treaty but has not ratified it. The UK, New Zealand, Australia, Canada, Egypt, France, Germany, Norway, Spain, and South Africa, among others, are parties to the agreement. The protocol supposedly works on the basis of a "precautionary approach" that requires appropriate measures be taken where there is reason to suspect that wastes or other matters "are likely to cause harm even when there is no conclusive evidence to prove a causal relation between inputs and their effects."[c] Materials that can still be dumped include sewage sludge and items such as iron, steel, and concrete, but only in places such as on islands where there is no practicable access to other disposal options.

Ocean dumping continues to be a major problem. Pakistan has been accused of dumping (or allowing to be dumped) radioactive waste into the ocean off its largest province, Balochistan. About 150 drums of radioactive waste were dumped into the sea near Gadani, about 30 miles northwest of Karachi.[d] Radioactive lobsters have been found in the Irish Sea near an English plutonium plant at Sellafield. Greenpeace accuses the plant of releasing over 2 million gallons of radioactive material into the ocean each day. The UK environmental minister reported that after 2006, storage tanks on land might become unsafe and the government would have to consider dumping waste into the sea. Motivated by terrorist threats, the U.S. Department of Energy plans over the next decade to transport more shipments of waste from Asia to storage facilities in Idaho via San Francisco.

Many suspect that China dumps its waste down wells and mines or buries it in Tibet. Russia has asked the international community for aid in disposing of its nuclear waste, threatening to continue dumping in the ocean if aid is not forthcoming. The Russians continue to press the United States to help them deactivate their nuclear weapons as part of the Strategic Arms Reduction Treaty but are not as interested in dealing with the problem of naval waste. In 2001 President Vladimir Putin signed a new law whereby the Russians would earn $20 billion for storing 20,000 tons of nuclear waste. Some of this waste has gone to Zheleznogorsk in Siberia or Mayak in the Chelyabinsk region of the Urals, where a waste tank exploded in 1957, contaminating some 92,000 sqare miles. Some experts feel strongly that Russia cannot be trusted to manage this waste safely, given its track record of hiding problems about defects and accidents in Soviet submarines, low morale and wages in many of its plants, and efforts to punish whistleblowers.

*References*

[a] See "Extensive Dumping of Nuclear Waste," *The New York Times,* April 27, 1993, p. A1. See also "Ban on Dumping Nuclear Waste at Sea," *The Christian Science Monitor,* November 15, 1993, p. 15.
[b] See "Oil Pollution," http://seawifs.gsfc.nasa.gov/OCEAN_PLANET/HTML/peril-oilpollution.htm.
[c] See "Stronger Rules to Govern Dumping of Wastes at Sea," Environment News Service, http://ens-newswire.com/ens/mar2006-03-10-02.asp.
[d] See "Nuclear Wastes: The Threat to Our Oceans," EcoBridge, http://ecobridge.org/contents/n_wst.htm.

Some theorists and experts argue that international organizations help states overcome the free-rider problem to the extent that, by promoting cooperation and assigning costs to organization members, problems can be worked on in a collective fashion, if not solved, which might be the case with new regulations for ocean dumping.

Hegemonic stability theorists, however (see Chapter 5), argue that it is sometimes necessary or simply a reflection of the distribution of power in the international system that one state *imposes* a solution to a problem on other states. At times the hegemon's ideas or policies become "embedded" in international organizations and may remain the accepted norm of other states' practices even as the hegemon's power declines.[17] One could argue that, in effect, that is what the United States has been doing in promoting "Washington consensus"-style development since the 1980s, which emphasizes increased economic growth to solve environmental problems (see Chapter 15). However, because of some of the damaging effects of development policies on the environments of many developing countries, these countries are not always prepared to make the economic and social cost adjustments required to solve environmental problems. One could also argue that if this theory was true, then the United States *should have* supported India's and China's exemptions from the Kyoto Protocol so these countries could grow economically and become able to deal better with their environmental problems.

## International Organizations

Given that one of its objectives is development, the UN has been more active than any other international organization in dealing with environmental problems and policies. Within the UN, the issue of the environment cuts across many different agencies and commissions that have increased in number and function commensurate with increased numbers of issues. A few of these bodies are the Food and Agriculture Organization (FAO) and its subsidiary agencies, which monitor global hunger but also poverty and resource levels, especially in LDCs; the UN Population Fund, which supports population-control programs in South Korea, China, Sri Lanka, and Cuba; and UN regional and global population conferences, which have been held in Rome, Belgrade, Bucharest, Mexico City, and in Cairo in 1994.

The **United Nations Environment Program (UNEP)** has focused on environmental problems since it was created in 1972.[18] The first UN agency to be headquartered in a Third World country—Nairobi, Kenya—the UNEP has over the years built a rather extensive network of smaller organizations around itself while attempting to coordinate action within the UN on environmental problems. The UNEP's functions include drafting treaties, providing forums for cooperation, and creating databases and references for scientific assessments of the environment. The UNEP has also focused a great deal on the issue of global warming. Working with the World Meteorological Organization, the UNEP Earthwatch network monitors atmospheric and marine pollution conditions all over the world. An International Referral System connects national information centers to a central data bank in Geneva.

The UNEP plans conferences and conventions organized to produce studies, resulting in a number of treaties and protocols applicable to nation-states and businesses. It routinely spends millions of dollars a year on clean-up and management projects. Quite often, the UNEP brokers agreements and pulls together drafts of treaties by other agencies to make sure the environment is considered in them.

The UNEP has always had a funding problem, receiving significantly less than other UN agencies. It usually works on joint ventures with other agencies and organizations, including NGOs, often providing them with administrative assistance. Despite some success promoting environmental treaties, the UNEP is often accused of not doing enough to coordinate environmentally sensitive resolutions through the UN. With a staff of only 300, it cannot seem to muster the authority to coordinate agencies that are larger than itself. Finally, like other agencies, the UNEP has to rely on national and regional governments to implement its policies—actors that may see the UNEP as merely another voice for frustrated ex-colonial states. These and other problems were some of the reasons the UN bypassed the UNEP in 1992 in Rio and created the Commission on Sustainable Development to implement Agenda 21.

The environment, and its connection to investment and trade policies in particular, has been a topic of negotiations in the General Agreement on Tariffs and Trade (GATT) and World Trade Organization (WTO) rounds[19] (see Chapter 6). The WTO set about implementing a series of provisions referred to as Multilateral Environmental Agreements (MEAs) that were to accommodate the use of trade-related measures and the environment. In some cases LDCs were exempted from GATT articles and WTO agreements so they could place national environmental goals ahead of their obligation not to raise trade restrictions or use other protective measures. Many LDCs see these exceptions as necessary to overcome other advantages the developed countries have over them. Trade officials in developed nations often see them as LDC excuses for continued trade protection.

After the Rio Summit in 1992 the World Bank established a General Environment Fund (GEF) to help developing nations bring proposed projects into line with international environmental standards and goals. Although some experts view this as a positive step, others claim that it is largely "window dressing" and has not achieved its goal. The GEF often lacks funds, and its executives claim that despite their efforts to account for the environment, projects must still focus on growth or ways to enhance production efficiency.

The WTO and World Bank have been criticized most in terms of the environment as a result of their promotion of structural adjustments policies (SAPs) that LDCs must adopt to qualify for loans or other forms of assistance. Critics often charge that these policies (see Chapters 8 and 15) stress economic growth over the environment.

In nearly all cases, neoliberal precepts are reflected in the economic growth, industrialization, trade, and investment policies of the developed nations, many of which have proved to be very costly to the environment (see the box, "Deforestation"), given that they require vast amounts of energy resources. On the other hand, it has to be said that most trade protection policies that lead to the overproduction of agricultural and industrial goods have been just as damaging to the environment as free trade.

---

### DEFORESTATION

Deforestation threatens the earth's land, water, and air, making it truly a global problem. In many cases, forest material is burned, releasing greenhouse gases that contribute to global warming. Rain forests are also the home of thousands of species of mammals, birds, fishes, snakes, lizards, frogs, and insects as well as plant varieties. The financial loss attributed to deforestation is incalculable because prices cannot be fixed for the loss of the many genetic codes in plants and insects, the diversity that comes with organism mutation, and the 99 percent of naturally occurring species that are not exploited by humans for food and medicines. Many tropical rain forests also contain plants that have proven to be effective in the fight against some forms of cancer and other diseases.

Until recently, LDCs have resisted the arguments of environmental groups, international organizations, NGOs, and others who campaign for slowing down or even halting deforestation. From the perspective of the LDCs, deforestation is not a cardinal sin; rather, in many cases it has been a political and economic necessity. The forest helps pay off national debt and provides badly needed jobs. Many LDCs have complained that the industrialized nations and international organizations are practicing "ecocolonialism" or "ecoimperialism" to the extent that they demand that LDCs shift their development objectives and strategies away from an emphasis on the extensive use of tropical rain forests and industrial activities.

In places such as Haiti, Brazil, and the Ivory Coast, deforestation creates as many refugees as it resettles on land that has been stripped. Ecologically, deforestation often leads to increased watershed runoff, which can result in either desertifying countries such as Sudan or worsening flood conditions downstream in countries such as Bangladesh, India, and Thailand. Tropical rain forests now represent roughly 5 percent of the land surface of the earth, half of what they did fifty years ago. Since preagricultural times, they have shrunk by more than one-third. Some 30 million acres of forest are cut down each year. Large tracts in the Ivory Coast, the Philippines, Thailand, and more than thirty other developing and industrialized nations have been cleared for farmland, grazing, mining, and fuel. Only 7 percent of the Mata Atlantica rain forest remains on Brazil's south coast. One of the fastest rates of deforestation has occurred in Amazonia—the biggest rain forest in the world—at 12 percent per year.

On the other hand, nations such as Costa Rica have adopted forest conservation programs of their own. In an effort to pay off their bank loans, some LDCs have been willing to swap part of their debt for preserving a part of the rain forest. Some countries have also established parks in rain forests to protect their timber resources. Still, many LDCs want more aid from the industrialized nations to replace what they could earn from the forests. Many LDCs also complain that the industrialized nations have not done their fair share in reducing timber cutting in their own countries.

A number of multilateral lending institutions such as the World Bank and other international organizations have assisted in making agreements between a number of actors. The U.S. Agency for International Development

(USAID) joined with a number of NGOs and public-interest groups to sponsor a reforestation project in Haiti. In Brazil, indigenous protest groups have been active in defending large tracts of the rain forests from loggers. The UN reports that tropical timber "is worth $7.5 billion a year in an $85 billion-a-year global industry."[a] Finally, the Global Forest Watch campaign of the World Resources Institute is an effort to connect public and private groups that seek to deal with political, social, and economic changes in forests and rain forests alike (see the Internet Links at the end of this chapter).

Scientists, national and international officials, and environmentalists seemed to realize the severity of the problem almost overnight. Many feel that it may even be too late to overcome the damage done to the earth by logging and cutting down tropical rain forests. Compared with other environmental issues such as global warming, less controversy surrounds the causes of deforestation. Where most of the tension remains is between international organizations, national governments and business practices, and proposed political and economic solutions to the problem. In nations such as Brazil, deforestation results, in part, from a government effort to resettle people away from urban areas into undeveloped jungle areas. Quite often, huge quantities of wood are shipped overseas to earn foreign exchange. As many as thirty-three LDCs have been net exporters of wood, yet the 1990s saw many of them actually become net importers of wood. At one time Japan used much of this wood to make cement foundation forms for its office buildings. After several uses, the wood was usually discarded, ending up in landfills. The United States also supplied Japan and a number of other Pacific Rim nations with logs and lumber from its ancient forests in the Pacific Northwest and Alaska. Another cause of deforestation in countries such as Brazil is to clear large tracts of land for agribusiness such as Cargill to produce high-protein soya, which is used as animal feed. These feeds help grow chickens in the United States and as much as 50 percent of all chickens served in Britain and Europe. Greenpeace estimates that as much as 69,000 acres a year have been cleared for soya farmers. Greenpeace also accuses the World Bank of helping fund many of these production ventures.[b]

One estimate is that it would take 320 million acres (roughly twice the size of Texas) to begin to replace the rain forests that play such an important role in absorbing carbon dioxide[c] and perpetuating biodiversity. In many industrialized nations, conservation has a history of political support backed by national legislation. Even so, economic pressure to log timber continues in many regions in these nations. In some cases, environmentalists have successfully used legal tactics to slow down or even halt timber cutting and logging. Timber cutting remains a major public policy issue in the United States and Canada, where the economics of forestry come face to face with conservation and environmental values and ethics. Increasingly, in many places the timber industry has found it economically and also politically profitable to invest in tree replacement and to employ a variety of new technologies and management techniques to "sustainably manage" the rain forest and stabilize the relationship between economic and ecological forces.[d] The Brazilian government has cut back on tax breaks that promoted deforestation and has imposed stiff penalties on the illegal cutting of trees. By one estimate, forested land is worth 40 percent more than cleared land.[e]

Since the Earth Summit in 1992 there also have been a number of UN but also NGO-sponsored campaigns to protect the rain forests. These campaigns have included boycotts of imports from certain countries along with demands that wood imports come from sustainably managed forests. In 1995 the Commission on Sustainable Development (CSD) established an Intergovernmental Panel on Forests to promote forest sustainability. However, since 1997 the panel's recommendations about sustainability have encountered stiff opposition from those concerned about sovereignty and trade.

*References*

[a] "Rich and Poor Nations Close to Agreement on Forest-Preservation Pact," *The Seattle Times,* January 23, 1994, p. A19.

[b] See John Vidal, "The 7,000km Journey That Links Amazon Destruction to Fast Food," Guardian Unlimited, www.guardian.co.uk/globalisation/story/0,,1747904,00.html, April 6, 2006.

[c] Some Harvard University researchers have found that "temperate-zone forests may play a more important role in absorbing atmospheric carbon dioxide . . . than was previously believed." For a more detailed discussion of this finding, see "A Forest Absorbs More Carbon Dioxide Than Was Predicted," *The New York Times,* June 8, 1993.

[d] See "Managing the Rainforests," *The Economist,* May 15, 2001, pp. 83–86.

[e] Ibid.

## International Businesses

The chief executives of fifty of the world's largest corporations were active in the meetings preceding the Earth Summit. Although the Business Council for Sustainable Development opposed some language in Agenda 21, it advocated its own new standards to regulate international business and encourage the view that business practices should go hand in hand with environmental policies. Some lumber companies have made an effort to include environmental considerations and even the objective of sustainable development in their criteria for logging and other potentially damaging activities.[20]

These actions are part of a trend whereby many international businesses have become increasingly more concerned about the environment. Until recently, their attitude has been that environmental rules and regulations are annoying and lead to inefficiencies, to say the least. However, as environmental problems have become more pronounced, the definition of efficiency has come under attack for not including the cost of environmental damage. Ocean dumping, deforestation, and global warming are all examples. More businesses are taking into account objectives other than purely economic ones, such as the "public interest" in supporting the environment. Many have changed the ingredients of some of their products, or in some cases eliminated the product altogether. "Green products" such as "fair trade" items have in fact become big business. Likewise, enterprises that specialize in the production of environmentally friendly items have become big investment opportunities.

## Nongovernmental Organizations

Membership in various national environmental groups increased dramatically in the 1980s. Groups in the United States include the National Wildlife Federation, the Environmental Defense Fund, the Sierra Club, Friends of the Earth, the Public Interest Research Group, the Rainforest Action Network, and Public Citizen. The number of environmental NGOs with cross-national connections was estimated to be well over 23,000 at the time of the Rio Conference in 1992. The World Wildlife Fund (WWF), for instance, was established in 1961 to protect endangered species and habitats. It is the largest private NGO devoted to conservation, with a $40 million annual budget and over 5 million members in twenty-eight different countries. The WWF has over 800 projects under way and works with 7000 NGOs in developing countries to help preserve wildlife and educate people.

Similarly, Friends of the Earth has political or other connections with public-interest and pressure groups in other nations. And Greenpeace is well known for generating public awareness and promoting environmental campaigns. Greenpeace's goal is to influence national and international environmental legislation the world over, even if this means practicing civil disobedience on the high seas, for instance. Also known as transnational environmental advocacy groups (TEAGs),[21] these groups are increasingly known for their ability to shape environmental issues while also playing a role in helping enforce national compliance with international treaties (see the box, "Managing Global Warming").

---

### MANAGING GLOBAL WARMING

The problem of global warming has generated a great deal of controversy and even angst among state, IO, and NGO officials. Since the early 1990s, the publics of many nations have also become much more involved in the issue. First, there is now near-unanimity that the problem is real. The increased number and intensity of effects of the earth's warming has made it somewhat easier to convince people and officials that the problem is perhaps approaching crisis proportions or at least should be taken seriously. Second, the difficulty of reconciling economic development and sustainability with the earth's ecology and environment have politicized these issues, generating the attention of a wide variety of public and private actors, including the media. Third, much of that attention is the result of massive NGO efforts and campaigns to help publicize the issue.

Most scientists in this epistemic community with an interest in the issue have become convinced that there is a "compelling basis for legitimate public concern" about human-induced climate change.[a]

For many politicians and scientists alike, global warming is real and has dire consequences for the earth. In 1990 a UN-sponsored international committee of scientists who make up the Intergovernmental Panel on Climate Change (IPCC) predicted that global warming would continue through the twenty-first century because of the widespread release of carbon dioxide into the atmosphere. The atmospheric concentration of gases was expected to double from the 1900 level between the years 2030 and 2080, increasing the earth's temperature anywhere from 3.5 to 5 degrees Fahrenheit. The latest report by the IPCC concludes that over the last fifty years, greenhouse gases are likely to have contributed to a significant increase in the earth's temperatures.[b] Decreased rainfall and droughts threaten U.S. agricultural production in the Western states and Great Plains region, as well as growing conditions in Southern and Central Europe and many developing nations, all the while impinging on international food security. Many scientists expect global warming to produce a rise in sea level of 6 to 8 inches on all coasts, damaging groundwater supplies, covering many island nations, and producing large numbers of refugees, especially from coastal regions in Bangladesh, China, and Egypt. Global warming is also expected to increase the incidence of mosquito-borne diseases such as malaria.

A few scientists remain skeptical of the extent of global warming and of the methods used to test the earth's temperature. For example, Professor of Atmospheric Science Richard Lindzen of MIT claims that although levels of carbon dioxide in the atmosphere have increased by 30 percent since the turn of the last century, these "claims neither constitute support for alarm nor establish man's responsibility for the small amount of warming that has occurred."[c] Other skeptics argue that carbon dioxide is 15 percent less potent than other greenhouse gases because half of it is absorbed by oceans and green plants (so-called "sinks"). Unusually high volcanic activity between 1940 and 1975 may also help explain the release of abnormal amounts of sulfate particles. Even computer models cannot accurately account for complex interactions of oceans with atmosphere, cloud behavior, and the role of water vapor. According to the skeptics, recent weather patterns reflect natural variability and are not a cause for great concern.

Because efforts to solve the many problems associated with global warming conflict and even at times contradict the economic policies of most of the industrialized nations, a wide variety of approaches and policies have been adopted to dance around these issues. After withdrawing from Kyoto, the Bush administration announced its own plan for an 18 percent cut in greenhouse gases by providing businesses with incentives to invest in cleaner technology. In their view, market forces should be used to solve environmental problems whenever possible. The administration also promoted voluntary compliance with a variety of efficiency-enhancing measures that it claimed would eventually take 70 million cars off the road or remove 500 million metric tons of greenhouse gases from the atmosphere.

Critics of the administration charge that its withdrawal from the Kyoto Protocol reflected the President's support for large corporate oil interests, which sponsored a campaign to support "a sort of alternative intellectual universe of global warming skeptics."[d] Another argument, forwarded by Detlef Sprintz and Tapani Vaahtoranta is that when it comes to environmental policies, states can be "pushers" of those policies or "draggers" to the extent that they outright oppose them or fail to implement them fully.[e] In the case of the hole in the ozone layer, the United States acted as a pusher for the Montreal treaty because the effects of ozone depletion were measurable and sufficiently damaging to a large enough group of people that states felt compelled to cooperate with other states and agencies to try to solve it. Substitutes were also available to replace the banned substances that attack ozone.

Such has not been the case for global warming. Instead, the United States has consistently dragged its feet in addressing global warming in ways that require a bigger role for the state or more cooperation with other nations. Its response mirrors its reaction to many security issues, which has been to "go it alone" mixed with suspicion of international organizations and charges that IOs limit state sovereignty. Instead, the Bush administration (along with officials in other countries) have promoted a mix of policies that have been preventive in nature, such as efforts to cut auto and industrial plant emissions. Shifting from one type of fuel to another has been tried in some cases. Preferring to let the market work first, in the United States the development of hybrid cars, biodiesel fuel, and alternative energy sources has quietly and quickly emerged in reaction to demand from consumers for cleaner and more sustainable sources of energy.[f] In most countries, taxes on gasoline and oil-based products are much higher than in the United States, generating income for a variety of state programs but also helping to inhibit consumption. In countries that can afford them, new technologies have also helped local governments better monitor pollution levels and pinpoint those who can be held responsible for damages.

In the United States until recently, low oil prices have stifled research and the development of alternative energy resources. U.S. officials have traded off dealing with the negative effects of pollution for the benefits of the activities associated with it. For example, a large percentage of global warming is caused by forestry and agricultural practices. Cutting back on the production of greenhouse gases would mean major political and economic adjustments along with lifestyle changes in the industrialized nations. Given these conflicting interests, it is easy to see why the policy approach to solving atmospheric problems at the level of the U.S. national government has been incremental, if not meant to slow the process of change.

This situation may be changing, however, as in the past fifteen years the effects of global warming have increasingly become understood as real and serious threats at all levels of the international political economy, from nation-states all the way down to each citizen of the planet. When combined with the efforts of NGOs to increase awareness of climate change but also to pressure states and IOs to solve the problem, one consequence has been to shift attention *away* from states as the actor most capable of dealing with the problem. A case in point is the recent effort by twenty-two U.S. states to push utility companies to generate energy from renewable resources by 2020.[g] Eleven states have set goals to reduce greenhouse emissions by as much as 33 percent below 1990 levels by 2050. California passed legislation mandating a 30 percent reduction in emissions by automakers by 2016. Some U.S. cities have adopted measures to cut their use of greenhouse emissions far below the standards of the Kyoto Protocol. In essence, elements of civil society are going around the U.S. government to deal more assertively with the problem of global warming. Because states and cities are also much closer to the interests of their constituents than is the federal government, these efforts reflect an increasing amount of citizen support for policy change.

In July 2005 the EU Commission proposed a new plan to cut energy use by 20 percent by 2020 and increase renewable energy sources by 12 percent over the next five years. The Europeans have adopted a wide variety of practical measures to reduce energy consumption, such as replacing old refrigerators and inefficient lightbulbs, and insulating roofs. Japan has also made energy reduction a patriotic effort in what many believe is already a very efficient economy. Canada and other countries have plans to phase out some large coal-fired plants by 2009.[h]

Bjørn Lomborg agrees that global warming is real and that it should be dealt with quite assertively. However, he takes serious issue with those who argue that it should be the number-one or even one of the highest priorities of especially the industrialized states. His view is that the money that would be required to solve this problem might be better spent on a series of other problems in developing nations, such as access to safe drinking water, assistance in overcoming HIV/AIDS, and efforts to continue economic development. Therefore the industrialized states should prioritize their goals and spend more wisely for those things that will reduce emissions, but not to the point of overlooking measures that will help developing countries tackle their problems.[i]

Lomborg's arguments correspond to those of other development experts who suggest that, when it comes to global warming, the situation for most LDCs is similar yet quite different from that of the industrialized nations. Most LDCs have not realized their development objectives and in many cases have substantial debt to erase. Countries such as Brazil, Mexico, the Philippines, and others must, and are encouraged to by international finance and trade agencies, generate growth via trade or provide TNCs with more foreign direct investment opportunities to international businesses (see Chapter 8). Many of the newly industrialized countries, such as China, Taiwan, Indonesia, Thailand, and India, have also been criticized for their failure to take the environment into account. These criticisms apply equally if not more so to countries such as Poland and other Eastern European countries whose socialist development models were as industrial-oriented as the Western liberal industrial-based growth model.

For the time being, many LDC officials continue to argue that solving environmental problems must be subordinated to more immediate development objectives. It is not in the immediate interest of these nations to pay the cost of trying to limit damage to the atmosphere when those who do not pay are just as likely to enjoy the benefits of conservation and clean-up efforts as those who do pay. Furthermore, it was and still is the industrialized states that have generated the most pollution and caused the most damage to the earth's resources.

For many LDCs, then, dealing with global warming has meant conserving energy resources, which translates into slowing down economic development and industrial activity. In some cases, LDCs have begun to rethink their deforestation policies as well as some of their agricultural practices. An interesting situation has been developing in China for the past decade, in which smoggy skies in some major cities and toxic spills in rivers have generated public pressure to do something about these problems. A recent cabinet paper suggested that "relative shortage of resources, fragile ecology and insufficient environmental capacity are becoming critical problems hindering China's development."[j]

An example of the role of NGOs in shaping policies on global warming is their participation in the making and implementing of rules for compliance with the Kyoto Protocol. Some have been active in negotiations at several meetings since Kyoto at which the goals have been to amend and move the agreement past 2012. Finally, another area where NGOs have played a role is in establishing carbon sinks and the flexibility mechanisms of the agreement whereby states can sell or trade emission credits. Lars Gulbrandsen and Steinar Andresen outline in much detail many of the roles of green NGOs in this part of the protocol, including advising states, seeking funds through membership and popular support, and putting pressure on negotiators through letters, rallies, boycotts, direct actions, and even civil disobedience—all in an effort to influence public opinion.[k]

Because the issue of climate change affects so many societies and people in so many different ways, management of the global warming problem both requires and reflects the influence of states, IOs, NGOs, scientists, businesses, and many other political actors. Some NGOs, for example, have gradually pushed open political space so as to give a bigger voice for civil society and in decision making. This may politicize the issue even more, however, and may also make policymaking much harder.

*References*

[a] See William J. Broad "To Gore, a Call to Cool the Alarm on Warming," *International Herald Tribune*, March 14, 2007, p. 2.

[b] See The Intergovernmental Panel on Climate Change (IPCC) Report, Climate Change 2007: The Physical Science Basis: Summary for Policymakers, Paris, February 2007, at www.ipcc.ch/5PM. 2Feb.07.pdf, accessed March 15, 2007.

[c] See Richard Lindzen, "Climate of Fear," *The Wall Street Journal*, April 12, 2006, p. 1.

[d] See Paul Krugman, "Enemy of the Planet," *The New York Times*, April 17, 2006.

[e] See Detlef Sprinz and Tapani Vaahtoranta, "International Environmental Policy," *International Organizations*, 48 (Winter 1994), pp. 77–106.

[f] See Daniel Gross, "The Alternative-Energy Industry Is Sizzling," *The Oregonian*, July 31, 2006.

[g] See Juliet Eilperin, "Cities, States Aren't Waiting for US Action on Climate," *The Washington Post*, November 8, 2006.

[h] See Lester R. Brown, *Plan 2.0: Rescuing a Planet Under Stress and a Civilization in Trouble* (New York: W. W. Norton, 2006), especially chap. 10.

[i] See Carl Pope and Bjørn Lomborg, "The State of Nature," *Foreign Policy*, 149 (July/August 2005), pp. 66–74.

[j] See Lindsay Beck, "China Says Pollution Will Worsen with Economic Boom," Reuters, June 5, 2006.

[k] See Lars H. Gulbrandsen and Steinar Andresen, "NGO Influence in the Implementation of the Kyoto Protocol: Compliance, Flexibility Mechanisms, and Sinks," *Global Environmental Politics*, 4 (November 2004), pp. 54–75.

The size, cohesiveness, and effectiveness of all these groups vary in different nations, depending on the extent to which environmental causes permeate not only politics but also popular culture, music, and even esthetics and religion. For many environmentalists, especially in developed regions of the world, their cause has become another basis on which to attack the alienated individualism of a consumption-oriented capitalist society.

## SOLUTIONS: A GREEN IPE?

In considering solutions to these and other related issues, experts, officials, and activists must consider a number of questions: Who is most likely to pay the political and economic costs associated with solving these problems? And what about markets? What role should they play in solving environmental problems? Will new technologies help solve environmental problems or simply make them worse? As the box on global warming demonstrates, issues are becoming more global in scope all the time. Do international organizations have enough political authority and clout to design and implement solutions that work on the most appropriate level—in the local community, the region, the nation, and globally? Is attention to international organizations misplaced; would it be better directed at nation-states?

In a political-economic environment in which pressure on the earth's resources is likely to continue to grow, will nation-states and international businesses be willing to commit themselves to pursuing objectives that do not require excessive amounts of natural resource consumption? This raises an even more fundamental question: How does one reconcile social values that emphasize economic growth and the consumption of industrially manufactured goods and services with values that are more environmentally friendly? We will try to answer some of these questions briefly, focusing on the most often proposed solutions to environmental problems and on the role the international political economy plays in them.

## Limit Population Growth

Many studies demonstrate that (over)population can play a role in damaging a local environment.[22] However, there is still no conclusive evidence that overpopulation itself is a problem of *global* proportions at this point[23] (see Chapter 19). What worries some is that, as in China today, growing numbers of people in the future will have more income to make demands on their economy for more energy and food resources. As yet most of the world's poor live in developing regions of the world and do not have that much influence on their economies (see Chapter 15). Studies that purport to show that income levels for all people in LDCs have risen since the early 1990s include India and China in their calculations.[24] Robert Hunter Wade claims that when these two countries are left out of the equation the world as a whole exhibits even more inequality.[25]

The **demographic transition**, which accounts for population growth rates, will probably slow down naturally as people's income and standard of living increase (see Chapter 19). Assuming this is true, the global population problem is actually a political-economic problem of unequal distribution of wealth and power between the have and have-not nations of the world, accompanied by an unequal distribution of income within many developing societies. The states of many developing nations are quite authoritarian in nature and pursue development strategies that emphasize economic growth and the postponement of meeting people's basic needs (see Chapters 15 and 18).

In most cases, increased industrial activity is a result of growing demand and consumption by a relatively wealthy minority. As a result of increased income and living standards, people in the newly industrialized countries have been able to demand more of the industrial goods and products associated with the developed countries. At the same time, people in Thailand, Indonesia, Brazil, China, Mexico, and many other countries have also experienced higher rates of pollution and environmental degradation.

Does that mean that nothing should be done about current overpopulation problems in some nations? In the short term, many nations *should* make efforts and receive help to slow their population growth rate because of the economic burden more mouths place on their societies. Most have done this through education and by providing people with means of birth control. For many humanists and culture experts, the empowerment of women and society's guarantee of political rights based on democratic principles are the best solution to poverty and overpopulation problems. In all cases, better distribution of income is likely to slow population growth rates naturally. However, the point is that slowing population growth rates alone will not solve most environmental problems. For most experts, other policies and measures are needed to promote environmental sustainability.

## New Technology

A nation's access to modern technology affects its environment in many ways. Technology is not politically or socially neutral. It often involves the use of dangerous chemicals and potentially damaging processes, but it has also helped cut down on pollution and aided in solving a number of other, related problems. Neoliberals like to focus on technology as a factor that can do more good than harm when it comes to the environment. However, as we have seen in many of the NICs as well as poorer developing countries, technology has not been that easy to acquire, nor has it always been that helpful. Much of it is affordable only to more wealthy people.

Appropriateness is also an issue. Many of the poorer countries do not need or want more sophisticated technologies until they are better equipped to use them. New technologies related to wind and solar power may be well suited for some but not for others. In many cases, what markets produce in new technologies are not yet appropriate for many of the poorer LDCs.[26]

In many cases, NGOs focus on the kinds of technology that are most appropriate for developing nations, especially in terms of sustainable development. World Vision and many other civil groups usually make appropriate technology a primary objective of their development strategies. Their people are "in the field" and can assess and do what works best for people in a wide variety of cultural and political settings.[27]

## Beyond the Nation-State: International Organizations and Regimes

A popular recommendation is to shift political authority to bigger and more comprehensive units such as international organizations. The presumption is that these agencies will put cooperation and the interests of the globe ahead of national interests. The cases we have discussed demonstrate that a number of international organizations have indeed been quite busy when it comes to the environment. As yet, however, there is little evidence that they have been effective beyond the desire of their members to solve environmental problems. This is not to say that international organizations are not important or cannot be effective in some cases. Rather, they are as yet at the mercy of their nation-state creators.[28] Recent developments with regard to global warming suggest that this situation may change as problems become more severe and states are unable to solve them by themselves. Necessity being the mother of invention, international organizations are likely to continue to be looked to as cooperative ventures in the solution to many environmental issues. Whether states will endow them with more authority to act over the heads of nation-states, however, is another matter.

There are variations on this theme. One is that the agents most likely to help solve environmental problems are **regimes**—the norms, principles, values, and decision-making procedures that surround a particular issue. Some believe that a number of regimes have already formed around several different environmental issues.[29] What is not clear, though, is how much regimes matter apart from the activity of nation-states that comprise them. Some believe that hegemons (see Chapters 6, 7, 8, and 9) are necessary to promote cooperation and maintain regime institutions and procedures.

Another problem is the extent to which linkages between issue areas make it difficult to separate one regime from another. For instance, should deforestation be considered its own regime or part of a broader regime that deals with the bigger issue of development? It is likely that the term *regime* will continue to be used in recognition of the many principles, norms, values, and political institutions that already deal with such problems as global warming or deforestation, but not in the strict sense for which the word is intended.

Most feasible future solutions to environmental issues must account for political and economic structures of the international system as conditioned largely by the distribution of wealth and power in the world or by a hegemon. At present, the international system continues to shift away from a Cold War structure toward some type of, for lack of a better term, "new world order" that manifests a variety of North–South tensions and conflicts. As with the case of so many environmental issues and the behavior of the United States at the Rio Conference in 1992, and again when the Bush administration rejected the Kyoto Protocol and other international treaties, even if it stated that it wanted to "do it alone," it appears that the United States did not mean that it wanted to be a hegemon in the sense of accepting the political and economic costs that go along with that responsibility.

## Markets for the Environment

Another solution to environmental problems is the market. Its supposed benefits are its flexibility over more rigid command and control policies of states. Many economists argue that some environmental problems should be "privatized" or assigned "property rights," which would help overcome the free-rider problem. Some have argued that government regulations do not work and that the market could be used as a mechanism to curb pollution by assigning permits to polluters. The Kyoto Protocol includes the use of such permits, allowing states to sell or exchange with one another certain allowable amounts of pollution, hopefully lowering the overall level of pollution.

The market is usually not viewed as the best solution to environmental problems because the economic costs of pollution are hard to calculate. Someone has to impose sanctions on violators or assign property rights, and that is usually the state. Once again, the economy does not operate in a political vacuum. Governments often attempt to balance the costs with the benefits of any environmental problem. Despite the limits of the market, any realistic solution to the problem must include considerations about who pays and how far the money is likely to go to do what. Most experts want to use the market to stimulate people and nations to conserve resources or cut down on pollution. At the same time, it must be noted that market behavior can have exactly the opposite effect. This realization forces us to consider what purpose markets serve and whose interests they benefit.

## A New Vision

A number of critics have always been cynical about capitalism and its effects on the environment. Yet no comprehensive political economic system has been developed so far as an alternative to what remains the most popular economic system in the world. It is not clear yet that the idea of sustainable development can be squared with the drive for consumption and its effects on the earth's resources and societies. Agenda 21 sought to reconcile the interests of many cultural and political groups caught between the drive to generate economic growth while dealing with its consequences on society. These objectives were to be achieved by combinations of government-designed and -implemented programs that in some cases involved states, IOs, and NGOs, complemented by market activities.

Despite broad agreement as to the worthiness of what is routinely referred to as sustainable development, actually achieving the objective is another matter. Most states and individuals do not want to be forced to limit their consumption, nor to change their behavior in ways that would mean achieving sustainable development. Thus, some believe that the Earth Summit has already ended up on the rocks of history because the political and economic relationship of the North to the South has not been fundamentally transformed into a more cooperative and less polarized, confrontational relationship.[30] The rich seek to maintain or add to their wealth, while the poor find it hard to develop on the terms established for them by the rich.

Meanwhile, some scientists and politicians, including the George W. Bush administration, remain skeptical, believing that not enough is currently known about the normal fluctuations in nature to specify what a sustainable condition looks like. They suggest that science is probably incapable of predicting safe levels of resource exploitation. And even if accurate predictions were possible, history shows that human shortsightedness and greed almost always lead to overexploitation, often to the point of collapse of the resource.[31]

Finally, some experts have come to believe that many environmental problems are best solved at the level of governance that is best suited to the task. The intention is to involve as many people and grass-roots groups as possible in solving environmental problems. Many international businesses have also made some commitment to sustainable development. Others go further, beyond discussions of the immediate political economy, into the realm of religion and philosophy. A growing number of Christian communities and others, for example, emphasize the value of stewardship and trusteeship over the earth and its resources (see, for example, the box, "Royalty Leads the Way"). Increasingly, more emphasis is put on sustaining quality of life and replacing consumerism with an appreciation for respect and community with nature, instead of control over it.

### ROYALTY LEADS THE WAY: PRINCE CHARLES AND ENVIRONMENTAL SUSTAINABILITY[a]

Charles, the 21st Prince of Wales, has developed many roles for himself over the years, one of which is to use lands that he holds in trust to demonstrate responsible stewardship of the natural and built environment, proving in the process that environmental preservation is compatible with economic viability. The Prince insists that he has no political agenda, but he has nevertheless become enormously influential in promoting the principles of long-term environmental sustainability over short-term output. Indeed, many EU farm subsidies, following the Prince's example, are based on this rationale.

The Prince owns a group of land holdings, the Duchy of Cornwall, comprising about 135,000 acres of mainly rural land and located mostly in southwest England in such counties as Devon, Cornwall, and Somerset. The Duchy provides Prince Charles's entire annual income.[b] The Prince works with tenants, communities, and environmental organizations such as Britain's Soil Association to help him translate his ideas into the realities of environmental preservation and economic sustainability. The Duchy invests in such projects as tree planting, stone walling, lake and pond restoration, and repairs to buildings using local traditional materials.[c]

The Duchy also includes 1700 hectares of woodland. From 1997 on, Prince Charles has instituted forestry principles such as "close to nature" or "continuous cover" to promote reliance on the natural environment for sustainable, diverse woodlands.[d] Timber is harvested so as to preserve the surrounding environment, using native draft horses to drag it from the steep hillsides and not damage them with the wheels of heavy commercial vehicles.[e] Some timber is kept to make tools and furniture, repair houses, or smoke food products.[f]

Highgrove House in Gloucestershire is the family residence of the Duke and Duchess of Cornwall, the Prince's other title. Here Prince Charles first started gardening and developing his ideas about sustainable living and environmental stewardship. At Highgrove, for example, solar lights are used in the parking lots, everything possible is recycled, and kitchen waste is composted. A reed bed filters sewage from the main house, and all gardening is done organically. Heritage seeds are planted to preserve a diverse gene pool of species, and rare trees and plants are established on the property for all to enjoy.

Home Farm, where the Prince tries out his ideas for sustainable agriculture, is a working farm located near Highgrove in Gloucestershire.[g] Comprising 2352 hectares, the Home Farm began the process of becoming an entirely organic endeavor in 1986 and the conversion was completed nearly 10 years later.[h] The Prince insists on traditional practices such as hedge-laying. Hedges are living fences used in many areas of Britain to contain livestock naturally and to provide natural windbreaks and homes for many species of animals. The Farm supplies organic produce to local families and supports efforts to keep the gene pool viable by growing plants from heritage seeds.

In 1991 the Duchy launched a quality food and drink products company called Duchy Originals, which uses the best ingredients, tested recipes, and sustainable production practices for its food product lines. The enterprise has expanded over the years to include quality natural hair care products among its nearly 130 other items. Recently, the Prince also created a line of premium outdoor furniture using sustainable sweet chestnut from Duchy of Cornwall woodlands in Herefordshire. All profits from the sale of Duchy Originals products are donated to The Prince's Charitable Trust.[i]

One of Prince Charles's most innovative projects has been the creation of the village of Poundbury. Located on 400 acres in the county of Dorset, the town is a sustainable, mixed-use development in which neighborhoods feature houses, shops, restaurants, facilities, and some factories. Smaller, winding roads are not conducive to traffic, and the relatively high density, similar to traditional British villages and towns, encourages people to walk or cycle about town. Approximately one-third of the houses are designated for lower-income residents, again preserving the socioeconomic character of other villages. Many residents can easily live and work in the same community. All of the buildings, for example, are faced with hamstone, a proven local material, resulting in many beautiful homes. As the Prince explained, "What I was trying to do was remind people about the pointlessness of throwing away all of the knowledge and experience and wisdom—*wisdom*—of what had gone before."[j]

Over the objections of urban planners, architects, and economists, Charles has stood by his design principles. He believes strongly that investment and slightly higher-cost items up front result in greater value in the long run. Drawn by Poundbury's fame, city planners and government officials from around Britain, and from other countries including the United States, have visited and studied the village in person. And in response to a public resistant to the Prince's ideas about farming and land management, Patrick Holden, the director of the Soil Association, says, "I don't think it [the Prince's influence] can be overestimated. He has emerged as the clear global leader of the sustainable agriculture movement, and rightly so."[k]

*References*

[a] This topic was suggested, researched, and drafted by Deborah Hill, one of whose passions is sustainable development in gardening and horticulture. Deborah, a former librarian at the University of Puget Sound, has visited and lived in Great Britain on several occasions.

[b] See Sandy Mitchell, "Duchy of Cornwall," *National Geographic, 209* (May 2006), pp. 96–115.

[c] www.duchyofcornwall.org/accessible/naturalenvironment_a.asp, accessed October 20, 2006.

[d] www.duchyofcornwall/accessible/aroundtheduchy_woodlands_a.asp, accessed October 19, 2006.

[e] See Mitchell, "Duchy of Cornwall," p. 103.

[f] www.duchyofcornwall/accessible/aroundtheduchy_woodlands_a.asp, accessed October 19, 2006.

[g] See Mitchell, "Duchy of Cornwall," p. 101.

[h] www.duchyoriginals.com/duchy_story.htm, accessed October 21, 2006.

[i] Ibid.

[j] See Mitchell, "Duchy of Cornwall," p. 101.

[k] Ibid., p. 103.

## CONCLUSION

The international political economy is a source of many global environmental problems. IPE theories and concepts are an integral part of understanding and solving many of these issues. Many environmental problems are rooted in damage to the earth's oceans, lands, and air commensurate with industrialization and policies that promote globalization. In most instances, efforts to slow the emission of greenhouse gases, contain deforestation, and prevent the dumping of nuclear and other materials in the ocean run up against the policies and specific measures that promote industrialization and economic growth but that are also partially responsible for these problems.

On the other hand, these policies are part of some solutions to a number of environmental issues that are becoming more global and more severe all the time. Under these conditions, nations, IOs, businesses, and NGOs have found it necessary to adopt a wide variety of strategies to manage and in some cases overcome some of the many tensions between the drive for economic growth and sustainability. Something that resembles a constructivist paradigm shift in thinking about the relationship of people to nature has been going on at the international level since the early 1990s. Even though many political and economic actors have accepted the idea of sustainable development including measures to preserve the environment, the international system remains in the middle of fundamental changes that require actors to broaden their interests to include issues related to the limits of the earth's capabilities and our connection to that issue.

There has yet to emerge an alternative set of ideas that comfortably weds modern industrial society with the idea of preserving the environment and various national and subnational cultures. Market or one-size-fits-all solutions to most environmental issues will not satisfy everyone's interests. And yet political actors have to keep the question of *Cui bono?* in mind. This assumes, of course, that these actors still have choices to make. As we mentioned earlier, Pope and Lomborg and others would rather spend money on a variety of other serious problems such as poverty rather than on the environment, for which the chances of achieving real success are not that great.[32] Why spend billions on curbing greenhouse gases when it might be more efficient to purchase tropical forest reserves? Even if we do not agree with Pope and Lomborg's priorities, they have done us a favor by once again shining attention on the issue of priorities and the choices we have about them.

## DISCUSSION QUESTIONS

1. Outline and discuss the tragedy of the commons and the Prisoner's Dilemma. In what ways do these concepts contribute to our understanding of environmental problems?
2. The authors assert that environmental problems have become increasingly global in scope. What factors—political, economic, and social—contributed most to this trend? Explain. (*Note:* The category *economic* includes such items as trade and finance and also the role of knowledge and technology.)
3. Examine each of the three case studies (global warming, deforestation, and ocean dumping) in terms of:
    a. The source of the problem—political, economic, social?
    b. The major actors and their interests in the problem.
    c. Potential solutions to the problem, noting the tension between issues related to economic growth and the goal of sustainable development.
4. Do you think nation-states are capable of solving global environmental problems? Why or why not? Should we look to international organizations such as the UN to play a larger role in dealing with environmental problems? What conditions and factors limit the effectiveness of these IOs?
5. Discuss the assertion that we need to continue searching for a new vision or paradigm that will allow us to reconcile growth with sustainability. Do you agree or disagree? Explain. What other things would you say we lack or need in order to solve environmental problems?

## INTERNET LINKS

United Nations Environment Program (UNEP):
   www.unep.org

Worldwatch Institute:
   www.worldwatch.org

Center for Sustainable Development in the Americas:
   www.csdanet.org/home.html

Worldwide Web Virtual Library Sustainable Development Index:
   www.ulb.ac.be/ceese/meta/sustvl.html

The Community Learning Network:
   www.cln.org/subject_index.html

Earth Policy News:
   www.earthpolicy.org

EPA Global Warming:
   http://yosemite.epa.gov/oar/globalwarming.nsf/content/index.html

World Resources Institute:
   www.wri.org

Oxfam:
   www.oxfam.org.uk

European Union Forest Watch:
   www.fern.org

Friends of the Earth:
   www.foe.co.uk/campaigns/biodiversity/links.html

Nature Conservancy:
   www.nature.org

Ocean Conservancy:
   www.oceanconservancy.org

Greenpeace:
   www.greenpeace.org

IMF website:
   www.IMF.org

World Bank website:
   www.WorldBank.org

## SUGGESTED READINGS

Lester R. Brown. *Plan B 2.0: Rescuing a Planet Under Stress and a Civilization in Trouble.* New York: W. W. Norton, 2006.

Jeffrey A. Frankel. "The Environment and Economic Globalization," in Michael M. Weinstein, ed., *Globalization: What's New?* New York: Columbia University Press, 2005.

Thomas Homer-Dixon. "On the Threshold: Environmental Changes as Causes of Acute Conflict," *International Security,* 16 (Fall 1991), pp. 76–116.

Bjørn Lomborg. *The Skeptical Environmentalist: Measuring the Real State of the World.* New York: Cambridge University Press, 2001.

Mirian A. L. Miller. *The Third World in Global Environmental Politics.* Boulder, CO: Lynne Rienner, 1995.

Carl Pope and Paul Rauber. *Strategic Ignorance: Why the Bush Administration Is Recklessly Destroying a Century of Environmental Progress.* San Francisco: Sierra Club Books, 2004.

Gareth Porter and Janet Welsh Brown. *Global Environmental Politics,* 2nd ed. Boulder, CO: Westview Press, 1996.

Detlef Sprinz and Tapani Vaahtoranta. "International Environmental Policy," *International Organizations,* 48 (Winter 1994), pp. 77–106.

Marc Williams. "International Political Economy and Global Environmental Change," in John Vogler and Mark F. Imber, eds., *The Environment of International Relations.* London: Routledge, 1996, pp. 41–58.

## KEY TERMS

epistemic communities
green
tragedy of the commons
collective good
Law of the Sea Treaty

sustainable development
Agenda 21
Kyoto Protocol
global warming
emission credits

United Nations Environment
  Program (UNEP)
demographic transition
regimes

## NOTES

1. David Balaam is the author of this chapter. Kristine Kalanges and Sarah Garfunkel provided research assistance for it in the third edition of this book.
2. Michael Carey, "Pavement," *Commotion* (Portland: indie poetry, 2006).
3. See, for example, Rachael Carson, *Silent Spring* (Boston: Houghton Mifflin, 1962).
4. Donella H. Meadows, Dennis L. Meadows, Jorgen Randers, and William W. Brehens III, *The Limits to Growth: A Report for the Club of Rome Project on the Predicament of Mankind* (New York: Universe Books, 1974).
5. See the Council on Environment Quality and Department of State, *The Global 2000 Report to the President: Entering the Twenty-First Century* (New York: Penguin Books, 1982).
6. Julian Simon and Herman Kahn, eds., *The Resourceful Earth: A Response to Global 2000* (Oxford: Basic Blackwell, 1982).
7. See Garrett Hardin, "The Tragedy of the Commons," *Science,* 162 (December 1968), pp. 1243–1248.
8. For more discussion of this report, see Jim MacNeill, "Strategies for Sustainable Economic Development," in *Scientific American, Managing the Planet Earth* (New York: W. H. Freeman, 1990), pp. 109–124.
9. Cited in Jessica Tuchman Mathews, "Environmental Policy," in Robert J. Art and Seyom Brown, eds., *U.S. Foreign Policy: The Search for a New Role* (New York: Macmillan, 1993), p. 234.
10. See World Resources Institute, "Climate Change: A Global Concern," *World Resources 1990–91* (Washington, DC: World Resources Institute, 1990) p. 15, Table 2.2. According to this report, the biggest contributors to the global greenhouse effect in 1987 were the United States, the former Soviet Union, Brazil, China, India, Japan, West Germany, and the United Kingdom.
11. For a detailed description of the Kyoto Protocol, see Kyoto Protocol to the United Nations Convention on Climate Change, http://unfcc.int/resource/docs/convkp/kpeng.html, accessed March 14, 2007.
12. See Paul Krugman, "Enemy of the Planet" *The New York Times,* April 17, 2006.
13. See Stephen Leahy, "The Post-Kyoto Era Up for Debate," Inter Press Service New Agency, http://ipnews.net/news.asp?idnews=31224, accessed November 24, 2006.
14. See "U.N. Climate Talks Make Progress on Kyoto Overhaul," Reuters, http://today.reuters.co.uk/misc, accessed November 24, 2006.
15. Andrew Revlin, "Talks to Start on Climate Amid Split on Warming," *The New York Times,* November 5, 2006.
16. See Jessica Tuchman Matthews, "Environmental Policy," p. 239.

17. See, for example, Oran Young, *International Cooperation: Building Regimes for Natural Resources and the Environment* (Ithaca, NY: Cornell University Press, 1989).

18. Our thanks to Erin Speck for research assistance on this issue. See also Peter M. Haas, "United Nations Environment Programme," *Environment*, 36 (September 1994), pp. 43–46.

19. See the World Trade Organization website at www.wto.org for a detailed description of WTO activities that deal with the environment.

20. See "Rio Condor, An Experiment in Ecology," *The Seattle Times*, April 10, 1994, p. B5.

21. See Paul Wapner, "Politics Beyond the State: Environmental Activism and World Civil Politics," *World Politics*, 47 (April 1995), p. 311.

22. See, for example, Thomas Homer-Dixon, "On the Threshold: Environmental Changes as Causes of Acute Conflict," *International Security*, 16 (Fall 1991), pp. 76–116.

23. See Phillip Longman, "The Global Baby Bust," *Foreign Affairs*, 83 (May/June 2004), pp. 64–72.

24. See, for example, David Dollar, "Globalization, Poverty, and Inequality," in Michael Weinstein, ed., *Globalization: What's New?* (New York: Columbia University Press, 2005), pp. 96–128.

25. See, for example, Robert Hunter Wade, "The Rising Inequality of World Income Distribution," *Finance and Development*, 38 (December 2001), pp. 37–40.

26. Ibid.

27. Interview with Laura Grosso of World Vision, November 6, 2006.

28. See Jeffrey A. Frankel, "The Environment and Economic Globalization," in Michael M. Weinstein, ed., *Globalization: What's New?*, pp. 129–169.

29. See Young, *International Cooperation*.

30. Robin Broad and John Cavanagh, "Beyond the Myths of Rio: A New American Agenda for the Environment," *World Policy Journal*, 10 (Spring 1993), pp. 65–72.

31. William K. Stevens, "Biologists Fear Sustainable Yield Is Unsustainable Idea," *The New York Times*, April 20, 1993, p. B10.

32. See Carl Pope and Bjørn Lomborg, "The State of Nature," *Foreign Policy*, 149 (July/August 2005), pp. 66–74.

# Conclusion: Where Do We Go from Here?

## OVERVIEW

This chapter looks back on some of the most important concepts and ideas we have studied in this text and discusses how understanding of theories and issues of international political economy (IPE) can help you make sense of many issues you will encounter in the future. The first section of the chapter reviews briefly the IPE approach and especially the mercantilist, economic liberal, and structuralist analytical perspectives. We then review and comment on the increasing connections among the four structures of IPE, namely, the production, finance, knowledge and technology, and security structures that were developed in the first ten chapters of this text.

The second section of the chapter considers five important IPE issues or problems that are likely to shape and influence developments early in the twenty-first century. Finally, drawing on this discussion, in the last section of the chapter we examine four possible scenarios for how the international political economy may develop early in this new century.

> [IPE is] . . . a vast, wide open range where anyone interested in the behavior of men and women in society [can] roam just as freely as the deer and the antelope. There [are] no fences or boundary-posts to confine the historians to history, the economists to economics. Political scientists [have] no exclusive rights to write about politics, nor sociologists to write about social relations.
>
> Susan Strange[1]

## THE IPE APPROACH: SOME CONCLUDING THOUGHTS

IPE gives the student freedom to select an analytical approach or combination of approaches that best suits a particular issue or answers a specific question about an actor or set of beliefs and values. It is useful to examine an issue from several different angles or perspectives, consider how it is connected to other issues, how other matters are connected to it, determine the nature of the power relationships at play, and, finally, ask who benefits from these relations. IPE methods stimulate analysis and allow us to move our work beyond description and analysis to explanation and understanding of a problem or the role of a particular actor.

## IPE's Dominant Theoretical Perspectives

The IPE approach looks at problems and issues from several different points of view, trying to take into account all three levels of analysis (the individual, state, and international system—see Chapter 1). The three main theoretical perspectives discussed in this text were economic liberalism, mercantilism (and political realism), and structuralism. Each perspective focuses on different political actors and their unique relationship to the market, on different economic activities, and to different types of societies. Each emphasizes different values and usually a preference of the political over the economic or society, or some combination thereof. Each also has a unique outlook about how to solve problems today and what the future holds for individuals and society. On the other hand, each also obscures some important elements.

## Structures and Arrangements

As we noted in Chapter 1 and elsewhere in the text, the world of IPE reflects a tight interconnection among different actors and issues. States, markets, and society are tied together through multiple overlapping sets of arrangements and relationships. The United States and China, for example, are connected simultaneously by a variety of elements in the production, finance, security, and knowledge structures. Some of these relationships reflect bargains and agreements between only these two nations, whereas others are bargains that affect or are affected by some of the many other actors in the international political economy (such as transnational corporations, international banks, or any number of international organizations such as the United Nations). To truly understand any single aspect of U.S.–China relations it is necessary to gain an appreciation of how these bargains and institutions are connected and the nature of their interaction.

The fundamental contribution of IPE to the study of the modern world has been its success in tearing down the artificial boundaries that keep us from looking at the interconnectedness of the multiple overlapping structures that connect states, markets, and people. This helps us understand more clearly how an event that happens to someone or in some place that is seemingly unconnected to us can have a profound effect on us and on the world.

## Types of Power

Once we understand that individuals, states, and other actors are connected through structural systems, we can appreciate that two types of power are exercised by these actors. The first is called **relational power**, which is more or less what people think of as power in daily life: the ability to get someone to do something that you want them to do. Relational power is one-to-one power: your ability (or inability, as the case may be) to get your boss to give you a raise, for example. **Structural power** is the ability of actors to cause something to happen because their position within the structure allows them either control or the ability to effectively condition the behavior of states, markets, and society. The bourgeoisie are assumed to have power over the proletariat in (Marxian) structural analysis, for example, but it is not because they have guns and soldiers but because of their position within the structure of capitalist production, on which the proletariat depend for wages.

*Cui Bono?*    Finally, after examining an issue from the three perspectives, understanding the interconnectedness of the four structures, and determining the nature of the power systems at work, we are ready for the 64-million-dollar question: Who benefits? *Cui bono?*—Who ends up better or worse off in a particular situation because things are arranged in a particular way? *Cui bono?* is a question with an edge. It forces us out of a descriptive mode and into an analytical one. We are forced to make judgments and to have some opinions. In short, we are forced to think critically. For example, in the case of transnational corporations, it is often assumed that they benefit less developed countries (LDCs) and can help them develop.

In many cases, however, the *cui bono* questions help us understand some of the complex issues surrounding the issue of relations between LDCs and transnational corporations. In some cases TNCs do benefit some LDCs, but not in all cases. Yet our analysis also reveals that it would be too simple to say that LDCs do not benefit from their relationships to TNCs. Furthermore, the answer we eventually arrive at might or might not be an intellectually satisfying one, depending on which perspective or combination of perspectives we employ to analyze the issue. For reasons related to their values, liberals, for instance, are more prone to accept TNCs as beneficial to LDCs, whereas structuralists are not. Liberals, of course, focus on the economic gains to all the actors in the relationship, whereas structuralists focus on the resulting inequalities—who gained more at whose expense. To make the outcome work for them, mercantilists might focus on the strategies and tools that were employed.

## Strengths and Weaknesses of the IPE Approach

Let us consider briefly the strengths and weaknesses of the overall IPE approach we just outlined. The strengths of IPE are that it encourages us to consider different points of view, to draw on the tools and methods of different academic disciplines, to seek out the complex interconnections that characterize modern life and define today's most interesting problems. Essentially, in our quest for understanding, our motto should be "Don't fence me in."

However, we should also be aware of the weaknesses of the IPE approach. There are more than just three valid perspectives to consider, and we should avoid limiting ourselves in this regard. Mercantilism, liberalism, and structuralism have been very important theoretical perspectives in the past—their interactions have shaped the international political economy and human history as well, particularly in the twentieth century. However, there is no guarantee that these three perspectives will shape the future as much as they have the past. Thus, we especially draw your attention to the four other IPE perspectives presented in Chapter 5: the rational choice, constructivist, feminist, and hegemonic stability critiques of mainstream IPE thought. These and other perspectives should help us all open our minds to different views of the world around us.

Another issue that some IPE theorists deal with but that we have mentioned only in passing is the relationship of IPE to different political economic ideologies. Some comparative IPE researchers study the many connections among the state, society, and markets in different nations, especially the formerly communist states, but we have not specifically addressed the connection between IPE and democracy. Francis Fukuyama, in *The End of History* and *The Last Man,* and *New York Times* columnist Thomas L. Friedman, in *The Lexus and the Olive Tree* (see Suggested Readings), argue that economic liberalism's (and by implication, democracy's) triumph is based on the failure of all other political economic ideologies, especially since communism in the Soviet Union has collapsed and Japanese-style mercantilism no longer seems workable. Friedman is known for espousing the democratic peace argument when he suggested that two states that had a McDonald's (implying they were economic liberal minded when it came to investment policies) would not go to war with each other. However, Friedman does admit that in the case of NATO's attack on Serbia, the analogy did not hold so well, to which he retorts that the Serbs quickly rebuilt the McDonald's.[2]

In his book, *The Ideas That Conquered the World* (see Suggested Readings), in which he sounds much like a neoliberal, Michael Mandelbaum makes the case that the ideas of international peace, free trade, and democracy are mutually reinforcing. Democracy gives a voice to the people, and particularly to the middle class that has much to lose from war. Democracy promotes peace. Peace promotes free trade (or at least war makes free trade difficult or impossible). Free trade breaks down economic hierarchies within nations and helps strengthen the middle class, which is the key to democracy.

In a thoughtful book, author and editor of *Newsweek* magazine Fareed Zakaria (see Suggested Readings) suggests that we need to qualify the application of democracy to many countries that are essentially "illiberal." That is, although these countries may have elections, they do not have the liberal institutions such as a legal system with the authority to enforce the law and other processes that make democracy work throughout society. For Zakaria, democracy is not something that sprouted up overnight but rather emerged over centuries in Europe and the United States despite many political, economic, and social barriers facing it. Likewise, Benjamin Barber gives some attention to this issue in his classic book on globalization, *Jihad vs. McWorld* (see Suggested Readings). For Barber, *both* McWorld and *jihad* are fundamentally antidemocratic. In many developing nations, *jihad* would privilege traditional culture and hierarchies over political consensus that might favor some aspects of McWorld.

Others have been outright critical of the supposition that neoliberal ideals and democracy complement one another. For instance, writing in a similar vain, George Soros, who made his fortune as an investor in hedge funds in the 1990s, became a detractor of many of the features of globalization. In his article, "The Capitalist Threat," he draws attention to some of the fallacies of economic liberalism, especially to the idea that free markets lead to open and democratic societies.[3] In the late 1990s, Soros's investment firm Tiger played a major role in initiating the Asian crisis (see Chapter 8) that literally devastated many of those societies—politically, economically, and socially. Soros came to believe that the laissez-faire ideology behind economic liberalism is based on fundamental flaws of the theories of perfect competition and supply–demand equilibrium, which have become methodological requirements rather than assumptions. People's expectations about markets may also shape market behavior more than supply–demand conditions alone. Soros views Friedman's golden straightjacket not as one that frees the individual or that complements an **open society**, but rather as one that enslaves us as laissez faire has become another totalitarian ideology, much like communism was and still is in some places. For Soros, the open society we all want will not result from economic liberalism, but from institutions to protect it so that it benefits society.

Certainly, not enough experts have studied in depth the question of the relationship of democracy to globalization per se. Certainly there needs to be more research on the subject of the extent to which capitalism is conducive to democracy and vice versa.

Finally, one weakness that international political economists must take seriously is that the flip side of breadth is depth. In IPE we are let loose on a fenceless prairie, where we can take the long and broad view of world events. In doing so, however, we risk the natural tendency to sacrifice depth and rigor of analysis—and this we must avoid. This is the responsibility that comes with the freedom of IPE. Some details and descriptions of intricacies are needed if we are to explain, understand, and appreciate the relationships of different actors to one another and the effects the economy, society, and politics have on their behavior.

## IPE TODAY: FIVE FUNDAMENTAL TENSIONS

For this concluding chapter, we have selected five fundamental and interrelated tensions that appear in nearly every chapter of the book in one form or another. The issues that we highlight are the following:

1. Globalization and its effects on various actors, issues, and political-economic perspectives and outlooks
2. Production versus distribution
3. The fundamental tension between a state's domestic needs and its international obligations
4. The tension between security and freedom
5. Hegemony or leadership over the international political economy

### Tensions Related to Globalization

As we said earlier in the book, a century ago liberalism and globalization were the dominant forces in the IPE, but the forces of nationalism (before and during the two world wars) and the conflict between liberalism and structuralism (during the Cold War) drove many of the nations of the world apart. For economic liberals in particular, it took almost a hundred years to learn that benign nationalistic mercantilism is destructive and that socialism, however useful as a philosophy or method of analysis, is not a practical system of political economy. In the 1980s, many touted economic liberalism, globalization, and democracy as the keys to freedom, development, and economic prosperity. In the 1990s after the end of the Cold War, the U.S. economy came "roaring back," and many of the developed and newly industrialized states experienced steady if not high growth rates. TNCs' investments extended farther afield into developing nations, and profits soared for major industries and investors. In the 1990s in the industrialized nations especially, neoliberal ideas and globalization became quite popular.

## Neoliberals

Over the last decade many neoliberals, led by Friedman, became enthusiatic supporters of globalization and its emphasis on increased production, efficiency, the free flow of currency and capital, free trade, markets, positive-sum outcomes for actors, and individual empowerment. One of Friedman's themes in all of his publications is that globalization interconnects people by reaching around the world farther, faster, deeper, and more cheaply through an array of new communication and information technologies that include computers, the Internet, fiber optics, and a host of other new developments just over the horizon. *Speed* is a new and necessary major feature of twenty-first-century communication, commerce, travel, and innovation. Globalization is much like a siren song that officials will not be able to reject because the power of integrated markets trumps politics and greatly benefits society in more ways than any other ideological outlook. However, in his popular book, *The Lexus and the Olive Tree* (see Suggested Readings), Friedman also asserts that globalization requires a "golden straightjacket" or set of political restrictions on undesirable state policies that must be adopted and implemented if states want their benefits.

Friedman and others recognize the extent to which globalization has a homogenizing effect on cultures the world over, spreading what he labels Americanization—from Big Macs and iMacs to Mickey Mouse. However, Friedman also recognizes that empowered individuals may include terrorists who use the tools of globalization to communictate, organize themselves over the Internet, and even take down skyscrapers. These terrorist groups Friedman calls "super-empowered angry men." Likewise, Friedman has often said that globalization alone does not automatically achieve success for everyone. In fact, he suggests that if globalization occurs too quickly and leaves too many feeling left behind, or if it increases the rich–poor gap, it is likely to generate opposition and be viewed as a destructive force in the world. For many neoliberals like Frideman, globalization can certainly help transform most of the world into pacifist merchant nations, happy to grow rich and old, especially if renewed U.S. hegemony makes globalization an attractive option for the poor and threatened of the world, who might otherwise support rogue states and terrorists. With growing interdependence comes expectations that a mix of nation-states and international organizations (IOs) will have to deal with an array of development, debt, and environment issues to achieve the maximum benefit from globalization.

As the 1990s went on, however, many structuralists and detractors of globalization became quite critical of World Trade Organization (WTO), International Monetary Fund (IMF), and World Bank policies that from their perspective exploited labor and the environment and produced a host of other negative effects on all states and societies. Street protests against globalization and the policies of the IMF and World Bank in particular occurred regularly in major cities all around the world.

## Structuralists

Structuralist criticism of globalization are best exemplified in works by the Frenchman Ignatio Ramonet, who, for example, disagrees passionately with Friedman that globalization represents a new world structure that integrates states and people.[4] From a structuralist perspective, globalization divides and fragments different societies and reinforces a North–South division of the world between the rich and poor. Many structuralists point to figures that poverty, illiteracy, violence, and illness are all on the rise in the developing world; globalization benefits the well off more than the poor. If anything, it contributes to the continuation of class struggle between the world's richest fifth and nearly everyone else (discussed later).

Likewise, many structuralists are critical of a new brand or phase of capitalism associated with globalization that drives individuals, states, and TNCs to continually produce new and better products in a hypercompetitive global atmosphere in which individuals and their societies are made to feel better off. For example, many structuralists cringe at some of Friedman's ideas in his latest book, *The World Is Flat* (see Suggest Readings), in which he asserts that new technological developments are in the process of *leveling* the relationship of individuals to one another, to their states, and to those in other countries. Friedman argues that the continued diffusion of technology throughout the global market makes it easier for countries such as China, India, and others to move into a strategic position that could undermine the older U.S. and European economies. Sounding a familiar theme of the 1980s, he believes that a competitive international environment, globalization, and hypercapitalism necessitate that children everywhere learn how to use new technologies, lest they be unprepared for a world that is already upon them.

Once again, Friedman acknowledges that not everyone is excited by the possibilities the flat world offers them, nor comforted by the proposal that anyone can benefit from it. He recognizes that developing nations as yet account for only a fifth of the world's trade in manufactured goods (see Chapter 6) and that the income gap between rich and poor has continued to rise, despite the claim that globalization would have a leveling effect on nations.

Most structuralists (and some with other views) take issue with Friedman that the global playing field is really leveling people, in any sense of the word. For example, whereas outsourcing jobs from the West allows Indians to stay in India, to make decent salaries, and to be near family and friends, critics point out that most of these people work 24/7 in outsource centers answering calls from the United States and Europe. In many cases they learn to disguise their voices and usually acquire the most expendable skills related to anwering phones, accounting, and reading CT scans. These sorts of jobs provide little advantage to the vast majority of people in India.

Moreover, structuralists maintain that Friedman's golden straitjacket of neoliberal policies does not free and empower people. Instead, these policies are totalitarian in nature, as communist dogma was in the Soviet Union. Globalization is merely part of a new religious-like canon[5] that asserts capitalism cannot collapse and that globalization has also replaced democracy as the natural order of society. For Ramonet and others, society is becoming a slave to the market, which operates like clockwork, driven by economic and **social Darwinism** and leading to excessive competition and consumption, natural selection, and the necessity of individual adaptation to market conditions, at the risk of becoming a social misfit and slowing the global economy.

## Mercantilists

As noted earlier, most mercantilists view globalization as another tool to increase national wealth and power. For many realists, however, a important issue is separating national interests that support liberalizing (opening up) the international economy in the areas of trade, monetary relations, and foreign investment while at the same time adopting protectionist policies in reaction to a variety of political-security interests. For example, since September 11, 2001, and the invasion of Iraq (see Chapter 9), the Bush administration has adopted a variety of measures both at home and abroad, such as economic sanctions, the reading of Internet mail, freezing of other nations' assets, and other activites that both *contradict and undermine* the long-term economic liberal objectives of the United States, including globalization. This makes states like the United States and Great Britain often look hypocritical or willing to sell out globalization for more important (to them) objectives. If anything, it also demonstrates that globalization is not automatic but something that results from political choices and moves in fits and starts.

There are at least two good examples of the tension between globalization and security interests. Moisés Naím points out that the lack of state regulation of the international economy makes it easy for illigitmate sectors of the economy (see Chapter 18) to thrive. Examples include drugs, arms trafficking, alien smuggling, money laudering, and intellectual property pirating.[6] In her book,

*World on Fire* (see Suggested Readings), Yale Law School Professor Amy Chua documents cases in which neoliberal-oriented state officials in the Philippines, Indonesia, Sierra Leone, Cameroon, and Russia have also helped foster high levels of corruption, ethnic conflict, antidemocratic values and policies, and in some cases genocide or campaigns that violated basic human rights.

Friedman and other economic liberals have a difficult time separating the economic interests of the United States from an effort to improve the situation in the Middle East, the supposed hotbed of terrorism in the world today. In his *Longitudes and Attitudes*, Friedman argues that closing the gap between rich and poor or between the lexus and the olive tree in the Middle East and elsewhere *requires* that globalization, modernization, and democratization take root in Arab and Muslim societies and thereby help to produce more jobs, freedom of expression, and public goods—things that are certain to threaten the power structure of the local communities, as they most assuredly have done.[7] Is it any wonder that Friedman regularly visits the Middle East, where he feels obligated to help officials make good choices that will lead to peace!

Paradoxically, for many liberals, sounding more like supporters of Keynes than Hayek, the triumph of economic liberalism has been linked to the need for political reform and an active role for the state in many countries. However, in these and other examples, many economic liberals have a hard time reconciling a *limited* role for the state in the national economy with at times encouraging a *larger* role for it in the international economy when it comes to security interests, helping to open up markets, and encouraging reform in other countries. Contrary to the neoliberal idea that economics should be separate from politics, it is very difficult to disconnect the two in a state-dominated global system.

## Production Versus Distribution

For nearly every issue explored in this book, the problem of production comes up time and time again. Trade, finance, currency exchange rates, debt, development, and hunger are a few that come to mind. What and how much is produced has become one of the major bright spots associated with globalization and capitalism in the twentieth and twenty-first centuries. In many cases, however, the problems associated with distribution of goods and services are not dealt with as consciously or purposefully as other issues. For many neoliberals, the assumption is that growth will eventually reach ("trickle down") into society, eventually helping those in need. Most mercantilist-realists do not avoid the issue so much as view it as a consequence of state choices and strategies to help or hinder some members of society or an enemy in conjunction with national interests. More so than the other two perspectives, structuralists have focused on this problem.

China in particular is known for its heavy focus on distribution against monumental production difficulties. For many experts and state officials, China also demonstrates that distribution *without* production means little in that there is little to distribute. On the other hand, more than a few China experts suggest that by making efforts to carefully balance the two, Chinese officials built a firm floor under China's economy so it could pursue modernization efforts that included a place for markets and production without imposing too many hardships on the greatest number of people in China. An extension of this concern today is that China has shifted its focus dramatically toward production and has not done enough for its poorer and "floating" members of society, especially in rural and outlying urban areas.[8] Countries such as the Republic of China (Taiwan) have adopted a number of distribution policies that have not deterred economic growth but in fact may have contributed to it. Cases like these remind us that distribution need not be a drag on an economy and, to the extent that it is, may manifest political or other motives that prevent greater numbers of society from enjoying the fruits of production and wealth.

## Domestic Needs Versus International Responsibilities

One of the most difficult problems in IPE is how states are to reconcile domestic needs with their international obligations. States are pressured to address both the needs of their citizens for political and economic security and, at that same time, live up to their responsibilities as participants in international agreements and organizations and as members of the world community of nations. This tension that twists and pulls the nation-state mirrors the fundamental tension that all of us experience as we try to satisfy both our own needs and those of our families and friends, as well as our responsibilities as members of a larger society.

This dilemma was one of the main sources of tension in each of the four structures we discussed. In terms of the example of the production and trade structure, Keynes argued that states had to reach a compromise between domestic protectionist and international market-oriented trade policies (see Chapter 6). There have been many reactions as nations have tried to balance an international commitment to free trade with the need to protect domestic jobs and industries. Regional trade groups such as the European Union and the North American Free Trade Area (NAFTA), for example, can be seen as attempts to expand free trade on a regional basis without throwing open markets to the threat of global competition. Some nations—the United States and Japan are the most noteworthy examples—have supplemented the multilateral negotiations of the World Trade Organization with bilateral trade discussions.

Lately, we have also seen the expansion of restrictive trade policies and neomercantilism that reflect, in part, strong domestic pressures to protect certain industries from the effects of globalization on their economies. This development in particular has made it difficult for states to sign on to new WTO measures that would free up trade and open new markets for a variety of products and services. There are many views about how the tension between trade and jobs should be resolved. One view holds that this dilemma is irreconcilable: that the tradition of advocating free trade must be abandoned in the interests of domestic prosperity. A constructivist shift on trade is building, however, to pressure the state to step in and "manage trade" to keep jobs secure while also structuring international political economic conditions in ways that are favorable to the largest number of nations. No longer does this number include the developed nations only; it must account for the interests for the developing states as well.

Another measure that complements this suggestion also involves the states. It holds that free trade and jobs *can* be reconciled, especially on the state level, but only if nations are willing to make the many changes and investments necessary to make their economies more productive. The United States, for instance, would need to reduce its debts (especially the government budget deficit) and cut consumer spending to provide resources to invest in workers, factories, and technology. Proponents of this view call for an emphasis on "productivity" through investment rather than "competitiveness" through trade barriers.[9] Many economic liberals and some mercantilists, however, continue to promote trade competitiveness through such efforts as breaking down regional trade barriers and extending free trade to the entire globe in multilateral forums like the WTO.[10]

Ironically, this example demonstrates that globalization or the integration of markets has *not* erased the need or desire of states to serve the interests of its members. Despite Keynes's hope that domestic and international interests could be reconciled in the case of trade (see Chapters 3 and 6), neoliberal policies continue to generate reactions from domestic groups that oppose those policies. As far back as 1944, Karl Polanyi (an Austrian political economic historian and Hungarian communist) pointed out that neoliberal policies tend to undermine themselves and that their negative effects tend to produce a **countermovement** against policies that benefit some more than others—contrary to the precepts of neoliberal thought.[11]

Until the tension between free trade and domestic jobs is resolved one way or another, then, many nations face a difficult dilemma. Both domestic *and* international policies are bound to lack unassailable credibility when their foundations are weakened by such fundamental fissures as these. How can the deadlock be broken?

## Freedom Versus Security

The tension between freedom and security is a fundamental issue in IPE that has become even more important in the wake of the 9/11 terrorist attacks. This tension appears everywhere in IPE in various forms. As individuals, we wait in long security lines at airports to have our bags and clothes prodded, searched, and X-rayed. In the name of freedom, a number of new measures in the U.S. Patriot Act restrict people's rights and freedoms. Phone calls, email messages, library and bank records, and numerous other databases are routinely monitored in many countries for suspicious activity that could be connected to terrorist plots. Although many of these measures remain acceptable to the majority of Americans, the Bush administration's effort to limit the right of *habeus corpus* (the right to a speedy trial) has pushed the issues of citizen freedoms front and center and leaves some wondering what and whose freedom we are fighting for.

Businesses are also affected, because even routine business transactions can affect national security. Firms that deal in national defense goods, such as parts for submarine and missile guidance systems, have long understood that some foreign sales that might be good for their business would be bad for national security and are therefore subject to strict regulation. The war on terrorism makes this problem more severe because the list of potential weapons is so long. The tension between shareholder returns and national security becomes more severe, especially for financial firms, because access to money is critical to large-scale terrorist plans.

The roles of nongovernmental organizations (NGOs) and international organizations (IOs) are also affected in many ways. These organizations want the freedom to pursue their agendas (in the case of NGOs such as Greenpeace) and freedom to undertake their missions (in the case of IOs such as UN agencies). Both of these freedoms have been limited at times in the name of national security. After 9/11, for example, many NGOs in the antiglobalization movement found the political climate had changed drastically. Protests against WTO meetings were no longer welcomed by some groups, especially if they risked violence, because of their possible association with terrorism.

The tension between security and freedom also affects diplomatic relations between states. As issues of security increase in importance, they affect many other issues as well. One might wish that international agreements could be reached on one issue at a time, such that the diverging security policies of France and the United States, for example, would not limit their ability to agree on other issues such as agricultural policy. Agreement and disagreement in one area, however, inevitably constrain negotiations in other areas. Many countries find that the need to gain allies on one issue, such as security, limits their ability to set their own national policies elsewhere.

The tension between freedom and personal security is a fundamental IPE dilemma and not a phase that will soon fade away. We examined a classic debate on this topic in Chapter 3, when we looked at the evolution of liberalism in the twentieth century. Keynes, writing during the Great Depression of the 1930s, argued that the lack of security caused rational people to make irrational collective decisions. When people are afraid, Keynes argued, they often make rational personal decisions that result in unwise social policy, such as saving their money when it would benefit all of society if they spent their money. Yet Keynes also worried about speculation in the international economy and the damage it could do if it was not regulated in some fashion. Keynes therefore argued that a liberal system—one that respects individual freedom—must first see that the environment in which free actions take place is secure. Security permits freedom, if you will.

Keynes's arch rival, Hayek, saw the tension in the exact opposite way. Security destroys freedom! Hayek believed that an obsessive search for security was *The Road to Serfdom* (see Suggested Readings). People want security, of course, and are willing to have their behavior restricted to a certain extent—to sacrifice their freedom—to get it. However, security is like quicksand, Hayek argued. When you are secure from one threat—say, a terrorist threat—you don't *feel* secure. Rather, your attention turns to another threat—say, an economic threat in the form of China's vast labor force—and you sacrifice more of your freedom (in the form of trade restrictions, for example) to gain a bit more security—until you become a slave to security in one way or another. When Hayek was writing his book, he could see such slaves clearly, in Hitler's Germany and in Stalin's Russia. Today we might look at a sweatshop factory, where unskilled workers are imprisoned by their need to grasp a bit of economic security.

Since the Bretton Woods meetings in 1944, the international system has attempted to convince nations to set aside their obsession with the need for domestic security, at least in part, in order to achieve a liberal world order. On the other hand, at times we have also witnessed many situations in developing countries where efforts to promote economic growth (and financial security) lead to restrictions on people's personal freedoms and liberties. Thus, as individuals we might be richer but unable to enjoy our wealth fully because of personal and economic security concerns—crime and depression would haunt us. Call it the Age of Anxiety.

### The Leadership Problem: What About Hegemony?

As we saw in Chapters 3 and 5, a **hegemon** is a rich and powerful state that undertakes to organize the international political economy by setting and enforcing the "rules of the game" under which states and markets interact. In effect, the job of the hegemon is to help break the tension between freedom and security so that states can meet their international obligations without necessarily sacrificing their domestic needs. In other words, the hegemon is supposed to make it possible to have both freedom and security while benefiting people at home and abroad.

As the world's richest and most powerful nation, the United States has been and remains in the running for what amounts to a cherished but also undesirable position. The United States has had and still has enormous hard power, as it has tried to demonstrate in Iraq. It also has considerable soft power in terms of its political and social influence in the world. The question remains, however: Is the United States able and willing to provide the necessary collective goods, such as security or economic compensation, to the groups that lose out in the open trade of the international political economy in order to maintain a stable and efficient world order?

The issue of U.S. hegemony or global power is important given the 9/11 terrorist attacks. Some view 9/11 as an attack on the United States, the mighty nation-state. Others see it as an attack on U.S. culture, which some argue is slowly destroying other cultures around the world.[12] Finally, some view 9/11 as an attack on global capitalism, which the United States has promoted around the world. These views share the notion that U.S. hegemony can be malevolent and destructive—of other states' and peoples' national, cultural, and economic security.

With regard to global security, the question remains whether other states will go along with the hegemon to sustain a particular order. In Gramscian terms, what is the nature of that order—does the liberal one still exist? Would others share those goals and strategies?

Ironically, as we saw in several chapters, that is what precisely many structuralists claim the United States and some of its allies are trying to do via the promotion of neoliberal ideas in the globalization campaign. The WTO, IMF, and World Bank "Washington consensus" ideas merely "front" underlying hegemonic goals for fear that developing nations will recognize them as the latest U.S. efforts at neoimperialism, neocolonialism, or empire building. What most structuralists argue is that this latest effort since the 1980s has not resulted in an equitable distribution of collective goods but instead has increased inequality and underdevelopment.[13] Hegemony is yet another tool of the global bourgeoisie in the capitalist struggle against the proletariat.

Some economic liberals avoid the issue of empire or modern forms of imperialism. Because globalization automatically integrates the world's economies and people of different cultures into a global culture, hegemony should not be required or even encouraged. A few economic liberals feel otherwise, however. For example, former British diplomat Robert Cooper *supports* the idea of proactively promoting **liberal imperialism**, to cultivate peace, prosperity, and democracy where they do not exist and to protect other states from the security threats of premodern or failed states (see Chapter 9). Cooper would like the United States or the European Union to intervene more often in states near total collapse, such as Afghanistan, Somalia, Sierra Leone, upcountry Burma, parts of the former Soviet Union, and much of Africa. Unlike classical imperialism, which sought to conquer territory and population, Cooper's vision of liberal imperialism includes the *imposition* of liberal values and institutions, which perhaps not by coincidence were mentioned many times as motives for U.S. intervention in Afghanistan and Iraq.

Another economic liberal, David Rothkopf, a former Clinton administration official, seems to view the integration process as an automatic one, not one that results from conscious manipulation of the international economy. In an aptly titled article, "In Praise of Cultural Imperialism," Rothkopf *praises* globalization for passively stripping away identity that leads to cultural conflicts while providing "a home to diverse peoples [that] requires certain social structures, laws, and institutions that transcend culture."[14] He maintains that "Americans should not deny the fact that of all the nations in the history of the world, theirs is the most just, the most tolerant, the most willing to constantly reassess and improve itself, and the best model for the future." Finally, he acknowledges that globalization is most definitely both an instrument and strategy to shape the development of a global information infrastructure along the lines of the U.S. model.

For many mercantilists and realists, globalization is merely another hegemonic tool used to serve state interests.[15] Hegemons act in their enlightened self-interest—helping other countries because by doing so they can manipulate the international political economy to increase their own wealth and power. At the same time, they seek consciously to make other countries dependent on them, the hegemon. For most realists, hegemony is not exactly the same as either empire building or imperialism. The United States does not maintain an empire in the same manner that Rome did, nor does it have colonies.[16]

On the issue of global leadership, then, there is much to ponder. Whether there will be a global hegemon in the future and the issues with which it might deal will depend on the kinds of problems it is likely to face. Let's look at some of the possibilities and, in so doing, apply some of the three IPE perspectives to some of the problems we have encountered in the text.

## THE FUTURE? FOUR SCENARIOS

Concerning some of these tensions, there are four possible scenarios of the future to ponder and critique. Most of them reflect different views about globalization and security in particular, the two fundamental issues that have shaped most of the issues in the international political economy for the past thirty years or so.

### Scenario 1: Once Again, Globalization and Neoliberal Ideas Recede into History

The current round of globalization has generated a series of criticisms and issues, some of which have undermined what many neoliberals suggest are the economic gains that have been made in the international political economy. Since the late 1990s there has emerged evidence that the popularity of both globalization and globalism (its underlying neoliberal principles) have gradually come under attack, not only by structuralist-oriented protestors but also by a number of serious academic officials and policy officials. Many of these newer critics are professed neoliberals, who still believe in the instrinsic value of globalization but would like to see it *managed* to serve people better.

For example, Professor Joseph Stiglitz of Columbia University (who in the 1990s was chief economist at the World Bank) wrote the controversial book, *Globalization and Its Discontents* (see Suggested Readings). Stiglitz maintains that in many cases in the 1990s the IMF and World Bank helped to *preseve* the status quo in many developing countries instead of promoting genuine social and political reform aimed at distributive and moral justice, let alone democracy. The noted economist Robert Hunter Wade carefully analyzed the issue of income distribution and its connection to poverty and globalization. Whereas some economic liberals argue that globalization has increased the income of the world's poor, thereby decreasing their numbers, Wade argues that income increases in China and India are mainly responsible for closing the income gap with some middle-income countries, whereas income gaps within those nations continue to increase.[17] Wade is adamant that roughly 85 percent of world income goes to 20 percent of the world's population and 6 percent to 60 percent of the world's population, concluding that this level of inequality is morally unacceptable.

Finally, as we noted in Chapter 8, Jeffrey Sachs, a Harvard economist and advisor to many nations making the transition to democracy and market economies in Eastern Europe and elsewhere in the 1990s, has swung around to become quite critical of IMF and World Bank policies that have not especially helped the world's poorest countries get out of debt and develop. According to Sachs, currently the Special UN Representative on the Millenium Development Goals project (see Chapter 8) these goals are achievable everywhere and in particular, in some of the poorest states in Africa.[18]

It is interesting to note that Stiglitz and more than a few IPE enthusiasts of late have discovered the work of Karl Polanyi (see Suggested Readings). What makes Polanyi's work so interesting and different from that of other economic historians is that in the mid-1940s he went to great lengths to challenge the basic assumptions and rhetoric about self-regulating markets, laissez faire, and what today we view as economic liberalism. Polanyi, in *The Great Transformation*, focuses on events and conditions surrounding the birth of the modern market in England and the development of economic liberal ideology from approximately 1600 until the Great Depression of the 1930s. Polanyi argues that despite the development of a "creed" surrounding liberalism's self-regulating qualities, the market is *not* self-regulating. Instead, the market is an artificial construction employed by politicians at the time in England in reaction to many of the changes in society associated with the Industrial Revolution. As a market mentality arose, the utilitarian saying of the greatest good for the greatest number gained in popularity. By the mid-nineteenth century the idea of a self-regulated market had blossomed and was being promoted throughout the world by England, in particular, while its wealth and power helped institute and maintain a stable international economic order that took the form of the (self-regulating) gold standard and political balance of power, both of which allowed Britain to dominate and influence other political and economically competitive states. After declining in popularity at the end of the nineteenth century, neoliberalism remerged in the 1980s to once again lead all contending political-economic perspectives.

Polanyi points out that because of its negative effects, mainly on the masses, large-scale markets often resulted in a countermovement whereby many working-class groups attacked economic liberal policies for their severe negative effects on society. Because self-regulation did not protect workers from unfair management practices, as suffrage spread, social legislation helped soften the effects of the market. At the same time, grave doubts about economic liberalism were raised by *economic liberals themselves,* who often sought protection and gained it in the form of trade protection and other policies designed to reduce the effect of the market on their interests. Polanyi claims that this renewed protection resulted in a breakdown of the gold standard and gradual replacement of the European balance of power with one that lead to World War I in 1914.

For Polanyi, economic liberal ideas do not work, not because markets fail as Keynes would have said, but because the fundamental tenets and assumptions of economic liberalism and market behavior are inherently flawed. Furthermore, Polanyi challenged the neoliberal assumption that markets can be separated from society. For Stiglitz and others, markets, society, and politics must be reconciled with one another.

One could argue that, because globalization has not effectively managed many of its negative effects, it continues to undermine itself. As states employ neoliberal policies to open up the international economy, more losers are created than winners. A recent IMF study concludes that financial globalization has *not* generally increased economic growth in LDCs and, although there are some notable exceptions, *has* caused greater instability through the financial crises that it invites.[19] In Chapter 8 we examined some of the opposition to other ways of dealing with the issues of debt and capital market instability.

Many of the managers of globalization contend that if neoliberalism is to prove workable, states are needed and cannot be rendered too weak. They, along with IOs, regional organizations, TNCs, and NGOs, must help solve common problems. It is therefore not surprising that many trade and finance experts are advising LDCs, despite strong pressures, to be very careful in opening their economies to global financial markets and in some cases to adopt protectionist policies. In this era of intensive globalization, one has to conclude that domestic financial controls are necessary for some states because global governance of international trade and finance is still relatively weak. Each case is different and requires careful study.

Can globalization continue to steer the global economy? Economic liberalism does not guarantee success in making everyone happy. In fact, the finance and monetary structure's rules provide for no global lender or lender of last resort to prevent another series of financial crisis. Nor do the rules outlaw speculation. In Chapters 7 and 8 we learned that the more global the financial structure has become, the more prone to crises it has also become. If anything, the rules of the international finance and monetary structure today allow for and even encourage currency and other forms of speculation that could easily lead not only to several financial and currency crises but also to another major recession or even depression of global proportions.

Today capitalism has taken on what Keynes labeled **casino capitalism**. No nation-state can hope to even out the ups and downs in the global economy as Keynes proposed states do with their own national economies. One must ask, then, if globalization's negatives can really be "managed" in such as way that it benefits society—down to the level of individuals—and in ways that they all benefit from the production of more consumer goods, not just wealthier people, states, and corporations? An ardent supporter of globalization, Columbia University Professor Jagdish Bhagwati writes in his book *In Defense of Globalization* that such issues as the poor in developing nations, women, labor (including child labor), the environment, and the issue of promoting democracy through globalization would benefit from "institutional changes and support mechanisms to smooth out its occasional rough edges."[20]

Like those of Friedman, Bhagwati's views are consistent with those of many other economic liberals, who have a hard time reconciling their views that as a process globalization *should separate* the economy from politics and society with the realization that globalization *requires* some, if not a good deal of, state intervention to manage its sticky bits. For some economic liberals and most mercantilists, the answer is negotiations between different actors for the benefits states and their societies continue to derive from globalization. We can no longer assume that, like the trickle-down concept of the economy, globalization will inevitably make consumers better off. As yet, though, there are no clear social and political criteria as to what constitutes progress or the social betterment of people everywhere. In this sense, it is easy to see why antiglobalization activists view globalization as inhuman and amoral and encourage people to battle it at the local level in order to achieve social justice.

Today, a paradox exists whereby globalism and globalization work to limit the power and authority of states, yet at the same time produce conditions to which states feel compelled to respond with protection of some sort. This reflects the intersection of states, markets, and society, or at least the recognition that they cannot be separated from one another. Globalization may not have brought down many national walls (especially on the border between the United States and Mexico, and in Palestine!) so much as punched holes in them that, for the sake of society, are then patched up by state protectionist policies of some sort or the other. Instead nationalism, ethnic, and religious identities remain as strong as ever.

As discussed earlier in this chapter, it remains to be seen if economic liberal objectives and globalization can succeed to any degree separate from the interests of the states that sponsor them. Would they even exist in a system other than the state system in which we live now—with its laws, courts, methods of adjudication, constitutions, and the like? Hegemonic theorists argue that without state sponsorship and authority, the current economic liberal international political economy would not be as as open as it is. Examples of liberal regimes sustaining themselves over a long period of time are few.

Finally, at least three other problems exist for globalization and its relation to the nation-state. First, as mercantilists so often point out (and we noted above), at times globalization generates threats to national security and to the security of various groups and individuals in society. A good example is the illicit activity that states cannot manage due to globalization (see Chapter 18). A second point is that globalization alone cannot guarantee peace and security and in some cases may generate more conflict than it resolves. In many cases economic liberalism reflects Western values, ideas, and assumptions that are hard to transplant into other societies. Most markets today remain embedded in national political systems that reflect unique cultures and social orders.

Finally, as explained in Chapter 20, neoliberal policies that support globalization are viewed by many as the root of most environmental problems today. Some would like to reform capitalism and people's behavior to curtail the use of the earth's resources, but it is resasonable to assume that these strategies will not achieve the levels of sustainability necessary to account for the effects that China, India, and many other developing nations will soon have on "Spaceship Earth's" resources. For many, this is one of the big surprises that awaits everyone on earth—that the short-term rational economic choices we have made have led to a series of problems that cannot be reversed. This compels those who contemplate such matters to develop an alternative to capitalism that not only distributes income and services more fairly but does so in a way that does not completely destroy the earth's resources.

The late, distinguished economic historian Robert Heilbroner reminded us that capitalism as we now know it is relatively new. Before 1600, empires exhibited command economies in which goods were produced by slaves or serfs. In this and earlier societies, resources were distributed according to social needs, local markets were not connected, nor was there time and energy to produce for beyond the local market. Capitalism and economic liberalism as we know them today reflect many of the values that accompanied the Enlightenment and the gradual entrenchment of the nation-state system in Europe. Should not rational people be interested in the long-term consequences of consumer behavior? If resources are in short supply, as economists often deem they are, should not efforts to develop and design a new economic system and order be extremely politically, socially, and economically rewarding? Perhaps we need another Age of Enlightenment.

### Scenario 2: Global Class Conflict

A second scenario to consider is a global class conflict that could play out in at least two different ways. The first possibility is a classic Marxist capital-versus-labor conflict on a global scale. William Greider described this scenario in his 1997 book, *One World, Ready or Not: The Manic Logic of Global Capitalism* (see Suggested Readings). Like many other structuralists, Greider contends that capitalism makes the rich richer and the poor poorer. Footloose capital has the advantage over place-bound labor. Multinational firms set nations against one another in a bid for capital, technology, and jobs that global firms can provide. In a "race to the bottom," states feel compelled more than ever to offer foreign investors lower taxes, lower wages, lower benefits, lower labor standards, and lower environmental regulations in a world in which the lowest bidder gets the investment—jobs.

This example of global income inequality leads us to consider the connection of the new global economy to imperialism, which is often asserted to be one of the major causes of poverty and lack of development in many developing nations. Most structuralists are not so sanguine about the benefits of globalization, which they view as nothing but another name for U.S. imperialism related to either its control over oil in the Middle East along with new markets and resources in developing nations, or maintaining control over a new global capitalist structure that benefits chiefly U.S. and European corporate interests.

Professor of Geography and Anthropology Neil Smith traces the development of recent economic liberal ideas throughout U.S. history up to recent efforts to pacify Iraq and the Middle East. According to Smith, "couched in language of freedom, equality and rights, these [earlier] measures and agreements . . . were aimed, bluntly, at opening up the world economy for exploitation while maintaining the privileged position of the world's largest economy."[21] For the neocons of the Bush administration (see Chapter 9), the war in Iraq was a conscious quest for empire, albeit not labeled as such. In many ways, globalization and U.S. political and economic interests complement one another. Smith argues that the conflict in Iraq and the Middle East "is not simply a war for oil but a larger war to control the global economic infrastructure, practices and relations that orchestrate the global economy. . . . In short, it is about the endgame of globalization."[22]

Welcome once again to the world of Karl Marx! In these circumstances, would the workers of the world finally unite? Is a global revolution inevitable? Possible? Imminent? Reading Greider and Smith's books in particular, it is easy to arrive at the conclusion that conditions for revolution are riper today than they were when Marx and Engels wrote the *Communist Manifesto*. Certainly, capitalism has become a more potent global force today than it was in Marx's day, with all the costs and benefits that go along with it. Greider seems to advocate the rise of global labor unions as a countervailing force to the global corporations. Global power against global power—a whole new framework on which to negotiate the arrangements of production, finance, knowledge, and security. Even if Greider does not condone revolution and the overthrow of capitalism, he does envision a revolutionary change in the fundamental fabric of the international political economy. It is dialectical materialism on a global scale. Call this the Age of Discontinuity.

A second global class conflict scenario to consider is probably more realistic and perhaps more frightening than this one. Greider imagines a capital-versus-labor conflict, but others see globalization pitting North against South. Everyone wants to use global markets to get rich, this argument goes—labor as well as capital. However, globalization pits the interests of rich capital and labor in the North against the interests of poor capital and labor in the South.

For fifty years the nations of the South have tried but failed to gain open access to global markets. Now they are pressing their case more forcefully. The agricultural trade negotiations of the WTO Doha round are an example of the potential for this sort of conflict. For once, many of the nations of the South have set aside their national differences to present a united front in opposition to agricultural subsidies in the North, mainly in the United States and the European Union (see Chapter 6). Their argument is that the generous agricultural subsidies to farmers in the North create huge food surpluses that are dumped on the markets of the South, hurting farmers and food security there. As if this were not enough, the countries of the North also maintain high trade barriers on food and other imports from many southern nations.

In his book, *Dark Ages: The Final Phase of Empire* (see Suggested Readings), cultural historian and social critic Morris Berman argues that globalization is helping to foster a return to the period of medieval history. Aside from its negative effects on developing nations, rather than producing educated people who are much better off in the more developed states, money and globalization are leading to a downward spiral in Western culture. Berman deplores the loss of community values and acceptance of those closely associated with the economic drive for productivity, an increased pace of life, mass consumption of goods and services, and less concern about globalization's effects on family life, the environment, the widening rich–poor gap, and labor. Americans in particular increasingly care less about political and human rights, necessary for a working democracy. Consumerism is celebrated as self-expression while, as in the Middle Ages, most people relate to the rest of the world as a battleground between the forces of good and evil. In short, "liquid modernity" has made the United States a society without an orientation and quite rigid: "the ultimate anticommunity."[23] As Berman sees it, globalization has helped foster particular cultural structural problems that are difficult to change, in part because they are so entrenched in our society and culture, where few recognize them as problems.

## Scenario 3: The Resurgence of Nationalism

Although it is convenient to think of global tensions in terms of North versus South, to whom do farmers, workers, and business owners in both North and South turn with their fears of global competition? They turn to the state, because economic security is one of the state's principal functions. Fear of foreign competition therefore could create a rebirth of the sort of nationalism and beggar-thy-neighbor policies that the world has not seen since the 1930s. Of course, these fears were magnified in the 1930s by a global recession. That couldn't happen here, could it?

Princeton University Professor Paul Krugman raised this question in his provocative 1999 book, *The Return of Depression Economics* (see Suggested Readings). Much of the world's population, in fact, experienced economic collapse or stagnation during the "boom" years of the 1990s. How can we continue to believe in unending prosperity when we consider the harsh economic results of the Asian crisis on Japan and the Asian Tigers, for example, or if we ponder the continuing economic meltdown in Russia? In Chapter 7 we noted how this issue concerns not only people in the newly industrialized nations but people in the wealthy countries as well.

What do people do when a severe recession hits—when they are forced to tighten their belts because of market forces beyond their control? What do they do when they are asked to sacrifice their children's futures to pay yesterday's bad debts? The answer in the 1930s was that they turned inward and became isolationist. Nationalism, either benign or corrosive, was the flavor of the decade, and zero-sum mercantilism dominated every IPE structure. Nations sacrificed their international responsibilities so they could attend to the needs of domestic citizens and interests. The return of nationalistic mercantilism would not be an unexpected outcome of a global recession. It would change everything, however. It could mean the death of liberal globalization and the beginning of an even more divided, even more conflict-prone, international political economy.

Another example of potential nationalist-oriented conflict is the transformation of China from a closed communist state to a social market economy (see Chapter 14's discussion of economic transition). Already workers in the North are becoming nervous and fearful. The surge of investment into and products out of China has been dramatic since that nation entered the WTO, assuring it of equal access to foreign markets. As China's economy develops (and as India becomes more integrated into global markets), the center of balance of the world economy will shift and increase North–South tensions. India and China, taken together, have about a third of the world's population. Optimists in the North see this as a huge potential market, but pessimists see enormous (often labeled unfair) competition. China's economic potential raises the stakes in any North–South negotiation and raises many fears, too. The result might be a clash between North and South (call this the Age of the New Great Wall).

These scenarios are not very comforting. In fact, given the wide proliferation of nuclear weapons today, this vision is positively scary. Add to it the fact that many U.S. officials fear that Communist China is bent on confronting the United States on the battlefield at some time in the near future. Reports are common about China's buildup of nuclear weapons and efforts to become a regional hegemon (see Chapter 9). Security concerns for many states regarding China run just behind those related to North Korea and Iran. Other U.S. officials have stayed faithful to the argument that continued development of trade and other forms of economic relations with the Chinese will continue to diffuse Chinese efforts to increase their military power, leading to more emphasis on ways to strengthen common economic interests. In this case, globalization could very well serve those who support this argument. However, failure to deal with the negative effects of globalization, which China is bound to experience, could very well result in an intensity of national friction between the two major powers. The Age of Anxiety becomes the Era of Paranoia!

### Scenario 4: The Unexpected Surprise!

Any number of unexpected events such as 9/11 could have changed the course of history and turned the first three scenarios discussed here into merely recyclable paper. Briefly, let us consider the possibility of a Surprise Scenario. One surprise, for example, would be the reemergence of a bipolar security structure such as the one that characterized the Cold War years. The Soviet Union is gone, but Russia remains a potent force, with a large population, vast geography, and huge quantities of natural and human resources. It also still has a large stock of nuclear weapons. If not the Russian surprise, then perhaps a Chinese surprise awaits us. If China's political and economic relations with the West deteriorate, then another Cold War standoff could result.

A more likely scenario is increased and intense violent conflict in the Middle East. At this writing, the Bush administration's efforts to pacify Iraqi insurgents appear to have failed, and civil war seems likely. Because of conflicting political and social interests of other nations in the region, the entire region could easily devolve into a major conflagration of regional, if not global, proportions. To prevent or deal with such a possibility will require serious efforts to solve a myriad of problems through negotiations and diplomacy. This effort will surely test the hegemonic resolve of the United States and other actors to reestablish and maintain some sort of order in the region, if not globally.

In another surprise scenario, there is still an outside chance that OPEC or the rise of another resource-based cartel may emerge. OPEC's power has waned since the 1970s, but strong dependence on oil imports means that just a few unexpected economic or political events could once again put OPEC in the driver's seat of the international political economy. Who knows what group might set OPEC policy, and to what end? Related to this could be the discovery and development of an alternative energy resource. Although such a development might solve some problems, it is not likely to be widely available.

Robert Kaplan and Amy Chua, among others (see Suggested Readings), argue that the world is likely to continue to see even more conflict and bloodshed in the developing regions. Interestingly, Kaplan and Chua feel almost the opposite about the value of neoliberal policies. And Samuel P. Huntington has made popular the ideas that the clash of different views about political economy will eventually be replaced by *The Clash of Civilizations* (see Suggested Readings). The Western values of liberalism, Huntington argues, are not universal. Political and economic pressure to adopt these values and to organize society along these lines risks a dangerous backlash from social systems with different norms and values. And once again, with the spread of nuclear and other weapons of mass destruction, a war of any size could break out between the West and East, this time the East being represented by Islamic nations and their supporters.

Finally, as noted earlier, many experts and officials expect the continued accummulaton of problems and events that point to a possible catastrophe of global proportions. The growing number of hurricanes, increasing hydrocarbon emissions, and conflict related to environmental damage foretell of a situation that many fear will be irreversible. Such an event(s) could render moot the concept of sustainable development and lead to a drastic reordering of national priorities and the world order.

## CONCLUSION: DAYS OF FUTURES PAST

At the Great Depression's darkest hour, Keynes penned an essay called "Economic Possibilities for Our Grandchildren," in which he speculated about the future of you who now read this book. Keynes wrote that the problem that preoccupied his times—the *economic* problem of unemployment—was temporary. Looking a hundred years ahead, he saw economic growth sufficient to meet the material needs of all humans. With material want cured, he believed, we could turn our attention to other concerns about human existence. For Keynes, the *pace* at which we can reach our destination of economic bliss will be governed by four things: our power to control population, our determination to avoid wars and civil dissensions, our willingness to entrust to science the direction of those things that are properly the concern of science, and the rate of accumulation (saving). "Meanwhile, there will be no harm in making mild preparations for our destiny, in encouraging and experimenting in the arts of life as well as the activities of purpose."[24]

Notice that the liberal Keynes did not believe that this would all happen automatically. He emphasized that we *could* achieve many of these objectives if we (of the proverbial sort) set our minds to it. Ironically, in the newest age of globalization this effort has not come forward. The world on the outside remains coated with the by-products of capitalism and globalization everywhere: rising incomes, new technologies, high consumption levels, vacations in Spain, France, Italy, Mexico, or Hawaii. Inside and behind that structure there remains plenty to be gravely concerned about: terrorism, volatile economies in both the North and South, the continued existence of poverty, inequalilty, famine, HIV/AIDs and other diseases, along with increased levels of environmental degradation.

At the same time, more actors play a bigger role in the international political economy all the time, making it harder to agree about goals, strategies, and institutions. Markets alone cannot solve most of these problems. Meanwhile, society itself has become more global in nature. Hopefully, there is enough time to choose collectively what kinds of institutions and processes will best be able to manage the global commons in the next century. These choices will necessarily be quite political and ethical in nature, as Smith, Keynes, Polanyi, and so many others were so keenly aware.

The future *is* uncertain. Fear and doubt are justified. The best way to prepare for an un-knowable fate is with knowledge, and that has been the goal of this chapter and this text. The twentieth century was a century of great change. One thing we are sure of is that change will continue, even at accelerated rates. It is critical to appreciate change and to be able to interpret its effects. We hope that this book has given you tools you can use to grasp and understand some of the most important and vital issues of the international political economy. You have a personal stake in what happens in the future. It is important that we all continue to study the events, issues, and forces that shape the environment of our daily lives. It is also important that we have opinions—informed opinions—about these things. Armed with understanding, the future is yours—go for it!

## WHAT CAN *I* DO?

Many of our students ask us, "What can *I* do about the problems that we study in IPE?" Typically, we tend to give different answers. Be involved, Professor Balaam says. There are many routes to constructive activism. One mechanism introduced throughout this book is the increasing role of NGOs in the international political economy. More students than ever are trying to help solve problems they care about by becoming active in a local, regional, national, or international NGOs. Idealist.Org (www.idealist.org) is an excellent website for students who want to find out how they can become active or even have a career in this line of work.

Be informed, Professor Veseth advises: You are what you read. He stresses the need for informed global citizens, who can evaluate arguments on complex issues and detect bogus syllogisms (B.S. for short). Veseth believes in the power of ideas to change the world and encourages his students to read, think, and write. Both he and Professor Balaam strongly recommend Pietra Rivoli's book, *The Travels of a T-Shirt in the Global Economy* (see Suggested Readings), for an exciting and provocative account of the many different theories and issues that dominate IPE studies today. For a more theoretical tone, Professor Balaam suggests Karl Polanyi's *The Great Transformation* for its perspective and for the questions it raises about economic liberal values and ideas. Whatever you decide to read, may you benefit from many of the ideas and issues we have examined in this book.

Finally, if you really want to set the world on fire, try something like rowing across the Atlantic some summer, as four of our students at the University of Puget Sound did in the summer of 2006. As part of an international competition, Captain Jordan Hanssen, with Brad Vickers, Dylan LeValley, and Gregg Spooner, rowed from New York City to Falmouth, England, in just under 70 days on a small four-man "craft." Together they *did* IPE! They competed against three British teams, in a boat made in Germany, equipped with sophisticated navigational technology from all over the world, financed by private donations. As Brad Vickers recently said, after winning the race, "Like IPE, despite all the gear and technology, it all came down to relationships with other people and the human spirit."

## DISCUSSION QUESTIONS

1. Review the basic elements and features of the IPE approach: the three main theoretical perspectives, four structures, and types of power. Which ones do you feel most comfortable and most uncomfortable with? Discuss the connection between how comfortable you are and your own values related to IPE.

2. Briefly outline the five fundamental tensions states are likely to encounter in the near future. Which do you feel is most important? Explain. Discuss the connections among all five of these tensions.
3. Is globalization a positive or a negative force in the world today? Explain, citing both theoretical arguments and personal observations.
4. This chapter ends with four scenarios for the future. Compare and contrast these different visions of the future. Which do you think is the most likely? Explain. Why does it matter which of these scenarios (or other set of conditions) actually occurs? How does what happens in the IPE affect you? Explain. Can you think of a scenario the authors might have overlooked?

## INTERNET LINKS

The Center for the Study of Alternative Futures:
   www.csaf.org
SPACECAST 2020 Alternative Futures:
   www.au.af.mil/Spacecast/alt-futr/alt-futr.html
Idealist.Org:
   www.idealist.org
The Commanding Heights:
   www.pbs.org/wgbh/commandingheights

## SUGGESTED READINGS

Benjamin Barber. *Jihad vs. McWorld*. New York: Ballantine Books, 1995.
Morris Berman. *Dark Ages America: The Final Phase of Empire*. New York: W. W. Norton, 2006.
Amy Chua. *The World on Fire: How Exporting Free Market Democracy Breeds Ethnic Hatred and Global Instability*. New York: Anchor, 2003.
Bill Emmott. *20:21 Vision: Twentieth Century Lessons for the Twenty-First Century*. New York: Farrar, Straus & Giroux, 2003.
Duncan K. Foley. *Adam's Fallacy: A Guide to Economic Theology*. Cambridge, MA: Harvard University Press, 2006.
Thomas L. Friedman. *The Lexus and the Olive Tree: Understanding Globalization*. New York: Farrar, Straus & Giroux, 1999.
Thomas L. Friedman. *The World Is Flat: A Brief History of the Twenty-First Century*. New York: Farrar, Straus & Giroux, 2005.
Francis Fukuyama. *The End of History and the Last Man*. New York: Avon, 1992.
William Greider. *One World, Ready or Not: The Manic Logic of Global Capitalism*. New York: Simon & Schuster, 1997.
Friedrich A. Hayek. *The Road to Serfdom*. Chicago: University of Chicago Press, 1944.
Samuel Huntington. *The Clash of Civilizations and the Remaking of World Order*. New York: Touchstone, 1996.
Robert D. Kaplan. "The Coming Anarchy," *Atlantic Monthly*, 273 (February 1994), pp. 44–65.
Paul Krugman. *The Return of Depression Economics*. Cambridge, MA: MIT Press, 1999.
Richard C. Longworth. *Global Squeeze: The Coming Crisis for First-World Nations*. Chicago: Contemporary Books, 1998.
Michael Mandelbaum. *The Ideas That Conquered the World*. New York: PublicAffairs, 2003.
Karl Polanyi. *The Great Transformation: The Political and Economic Origins of Our Time*. Boston: Beacon, 1944.
Pietra Rivoli. *The Travels of a T-Shirt in the Global Economy: An Economist Examines the Markets, Power, and Politics of World Trade*. Hoboken, NJ: John Wiley, 2005.
Jeffrey Sachs. *The End of Poverty: Economic Possibilities for Our Time*. New York: The Penguin Press, 2005.
Joseph Stiglitz. *Globalization and Its Discontents*. New York: W. W. Norton, 2004.
Joseph E. Stiglitz. *Making Globalization Work*. New York: W. W. Norton, 2006.
Fareed Zakaria. *The Future of Freedom: Illiberal Democracy at Home and Abroad*. New York: W. W. Norton, 2005.

## KEY TERMS

| | | |
|---|---|---|
| relational power | social Darwinism | liberal imperialism |
| structural power | countermovement | casino capitalism |
| open society | hegemon | |

## *NOTES*

1. Susan Strange, ed., *Paths to International Political Economy* (London: George Allen & Unwin, 1984), p. ix.
2. Thomas Friedman and Ignacio Ramonet, "Dueling Globalization: A Debate Between Thomas L. Friedman and Ignacio Ramonet," *Foreign Policy, 116* (Fall 1999), pp. 110–127.
3. George Soros, "The Capitalist Threat," *The Atlantic Monthly, 279* (February 1997), pp. 45–58.
4. See Friedman and Ramonet, "Dueling Globalization."
5. This is one of the themes of Duncan K. Foley, *Adam's Fallacy: A Guide to Economic Theology* (Cambridge, MA: Harvard University Press, 2006).
6. Moisés Naím, *Illicit: How Smugglers, Traffickers, and Copycats Are Hijacking the Global Economy* (New York: Doubleday, 2005).
7. Thomas L. Friedman, *Longitudes and Latitudes* (New York: Farrar, Straus & Giroux, 2002).
8. See, for example, Mei Zhang, *China's Poor Regions: Rural-Urban Migration, Poverty, Economic Reform and Urbanisation* (London: Routledgecurzon, 2003).
9. Paul Krugman is a leading advocate of this viewpoint. In his *Peddling Prosperity* (New York: W. W. Norton, 1994), he criticizes political entrepreneurs who "sell" trade policy as a "patent medicine" cure for economic woes.
10. See, for example, C. Fred Bergsten, "Globalizing Free Trade," *Foreign Affairs, 75* (May/June 1996), pp. 16–37.
11. Karl Polanyi, *The Great Transformation: The Political and Economic Origins of Our Time* (Boston: Beacon, 1944).
12. See, for example, Neil Smith, *The Endgame of Globalization* (New York: Routledge, 2005).
13. See, for example, William Greider, *One World, Ready or Not: The Manic Logic of Global Capitalism* (New York: Simon & Schuster, 1997).
14. David Rothkopf, "In Praise of Cultural Imperialism?" *Foreign Policy, 107* (Summer 1997), pp. 38–54.
15. See, for example, Joel Krieger, *Globalization and State Power: Who Wins When America Rules?* (New York: Pearson, Longman, 2005).
16. For a good selection of articles on the empire thesis, see Andrew J. Bacevich, ed., *The Imperial Tense: Prospects and Problems of American Empire* (New York: Ivan R. Dee, 2003).
17. Robert Hunter Wade, "The Rising Inequality of World Income Distribution," *Finance & Development, 38* (December 2001), pp. 37–40.
18. This is one of the main arguments of Jeffrey Sachs, *The End of Poverty: Economic Possibilities for Our Time* (New York: Penguin, 2005).
19. For an example of the World Bank's shifting emphasis on development that incorporates equity, see *The World Bank Development Report 2005: Equity and Development* (Washington, DC: The World Bank, 2005).
20. Jagdish Bhagwati, *In Defense of Globalization* (Oxford: Oxford University Press, 2004).
21. See Smith, *The Endgame of Globalization*, p. 14.
22. Ibid.
23. Morris Berman, *Dark Ages America: The Final Phase of Empire,* (New York: W. W. Norton, 2006), p. 15.
24. John Maynard Keynes, "Economic Possibilities for Our Grandchildren," in *Essays in Persuasion* (New York: W. W. Norton, 1963), p. 373.

# Glossary

**Absorption**   A term used in balance-of-payments analysis. Absorption is the total value of the resources used by consumers, businesses, and governments. Absorption is the national "consumption" of currently produced goods and services. See *Output*.

**Adaptancy platform**   A perspective on tourism that favors small-scale, responsible, and sustainable alternatives to mass tourism.

**Adventurism**   Efforts by Middle Eastern leaders or states to invade or take over the territory of other states, initiate punitive strikes, threaten to intervene or to use covert operations, or to otherwise destabilize other states, such as Saddam Hussein's (Iraq) attack on Kuwait in 1990.

**Advocacy platform**   A popular perspective on tourism, especially in the 1950s and 1960s but still common today among businesses and tourists, that advocates the development of mass tourism according to free-market principles.

*Amakudari*   A Japanese term meaning "descend from heaven." It refers to a Japanese bureaucrat gaining a job at a business over which he formerly had regulatory authority. There is concern that, in expectation of future private-sector jobs, bureaucrats have an incentive to treat some businesses they oversee preferentially. See *Iron triangle*.

**Appreciate**   A term used in foreign exchange markets when one currency rises in value relative to another currency. See *Depreciate*.

**Appropriability theory**   A theory of transnational corporations that hypothesizes that they engage in foreign direct investment in order to keep firm-specific advantages from being appropriated by competitors.

**Arbitrage**   Buying a product in a lower price market in order to sell it in a higher price market. Price differences between markets are often the result of differing laws, taxes, and regulations. When legislative action increases the price of a good that is available in neighboring jurisdictions at a cheaper price, smuggling is encouraged, which fuels a black market for the good.

**Asia-Pacific Economic Cooperation (APEC)**   A forum for discussion and negotiation of trade and other issues among Asia-Pacific nations, including the United States, Japan, China, and many other countries in this region. At the 1994 APEC meetings in Bogor, Indonesia, the group pledged to create a regional free-trade zone.

**Assimilation**   Process by which one adopts the customs and values of another culture. Relative to migration, assimilation implies that a person's original culture is replaced by the prevailing culture in the destination country.

**Asylum**   Refuge for a displaced person who cannot return to his or her country of origin because of fear of persecution on account of race, religion, nationality, membership in a particular social group, or political opinion. An asylum seeker solicits permanent residence in another country through application to that country's courts, often from within that state's territory.

**Asymmetric information**   A problem that exists especially in rural credit markets, in that the lender does not know what borrowers all know, which is who is trustworthy and who is not. This lack of information forces lenders to charge high interest rates, which discourages borrowing in general.

**Austerity policies**   Government policies designed to increase output and/or reduce absorption in order to produce favorable current account conditions. See *Structural adjustment programs*.

**Autonomous state**   A state that is independent and not controlled by outside forces. Autonomous states have *sovereignty* or final authority of matters inside of the state.

**Bail-in plan**   In a financial crisis, a plan under which lenders agree to keep their loans and extend additional credit in order to prevent a crisis. The opposite of a bail-out: In a bail-out, lenders pull out, making the crisis worse.

**Balance of payments (BoP)**    A tabulation of all international transactions involving a nation in a given year, the BoP is the best indicator of a nation's international economic status. The most important parts of the BoP are the *current account* and the *capital account.*

**Balance-of-payments deficit**    This term usually refers to a *current account deficit.* See *Current account.*

**Balance of power**    A concept that describes how states deal with the problems of national security in a context of shifting alliances and alignments. The balance system is produced by the clustering of individual national interests in opposition to those of other states. Peace among nations is usually associated with an approximate equilibrium in the distribution of power between nations in this system. Others argue that peace is enforced by a hegemon, not an equilibrium. See *Hegemony.*

**Benign mercantilism**    A defensive strategy that seeks to protect the domestic economy against damaging political and economic forces. In contrast to malevolent mercantilism, it seeks to expand a nation's political and economic influence intentionally at the expense of other nations, beyond what is needed for protection. But what one nation intends as benign can be interpreted by another as malevolent, as in the case of Unocal's attempted acquisition by China's state-owned oil company.

**Bicycle theory**    A theory relating to the European Union that holds that regional groups must constantly move forward (in terms of regional integration) in order to maintain political unity. A bicycle must keep moving to maintain its balance; if it stops, it falls over. The term is also applied to trade policies in the context of continuing to bring down tariff barriers for fear of protectionism setting back in (the bicycle falling over).

**Bipolar balance of power**    An international security structure with one or more centers of power that manage the security structure. Each "pole" or "sphere of influence" competes with others to keep the distribution of power relatively equal between them. The Cold War was mainly a bipolar security structure, with hegemonic military power distributed between the United States and the Soviet Union.

**Bloc**    A group of nation-states united or associated for some purpose. Examples of blocs are defense blocs, such as *NATO* and the *Warsaw Pact,* and trade blocs such as the *European Union* and *NAFTA.*

**Bonyads**    Quasi-independent conglomerates and charitable organizations dominated by clerics and private business allies in Iran that siphon off public resources and dominate some sectors of the economy.

**Bourgeoisie**    In Marxian analysis, the bourgeoisie is the capitalist class, made up of those who own the means of production. In everyday language, this term often refers to the middle class. See *Proletariat.*

**Brain drain**    The exodus of highly educated, professional migrants out of their country of origin toward economic or social opportunities in another country. This phenomenon is especially significant for Third World countries, whose most skilled residents often move to the First World.

**Bretton Woods system and conference**    Bretton Woods is a place, a meeting, and a set of institutions and practices. Bretton Woods, New Hampshire, was the site of a series of meetings that took place in July 1944 among representatives of the Allied Powers of World War II (including the United States, Britain, France, Canada, and the Soviet Union, and also involving many smaller states). The Bretton Woods agreements created the International Monetary Fund, the World Bank, and the system of fixed exchange rates that prevailed in international finance until 1973.

**Bubble**    A financial market condition in which expectations of higher prices drive prices higher, often unsustainably so. Bubbles usually burst when investors stop financing certain projects or industries and can result in economic recessions and unemployment. See *Lender of last resort.*

**Capital**    "Stuff that is used to make stuff." Broadly speaking, capital is any long-lasting productive resource. Types of capital include physical capital, such as machines and factories; human capital, such as knowledge and learned skills; and financial capital, which is another term for money available for investment. The term *capital* is used in Marxist analysis to identify the owners of physical capital (capital versus labor).

**Capital and financial account**    The part of the *balance of payments* that records international borrowing, lending, and investment. If a nation has a capital account surplus, it means that it is a net debtor during a particular period.

**Capital controls**    Government rules and regulations that seek to limit or control inflows and outflows of international investment funds. The goal of capital controls is to maintain orderly international capital movements and prevent financial and foreign exchange instability.

**Capital flight**    The process whereby investors transfer their money out of investments and bank accounts in a country that is suffering from an imbalance of payments. Often associated with downturns in an economy.

**Capital mobility**    The ability of investment funds to move from one nation to another. The degree of capital mobility depends on the domestic financial regulations of the nations involved, which can either encourage, permit, or restrict international investment flows, and on market forces seeking to profit from differences in returns between countries.

**Capitalism**    Originally, the term described a political ideology that was identified with the capitalists, the owners of capital. Today, however, it usually refers to a market-dominated system of economic organization based on private property and free markets.

**Capitulations**    Special economic privileges and legal rights granted to Europeans by the Ottoman Empire, which prevented the Ottomans from imposing tariffs to protect their infant industries. The enforcement of capitulations is offered as one explanation for the failure of the Ottoman Empire to catch up with Europe's growing power during the nineteenth century.

**Cartel**    A group of firms or nations that form a *bloc* to restrict the supply of and increase profits from a particular product. OPEC is an example of an oil cartel.

**Casino capitalism**    A term first used by John Maynard Keynes that refers to the volatile and unpredictable nature of capitalism, which is tantamount to legalized gambling. Even if there is a rational basis for making an economic decision, it is impossible to know reliably what the market outcome will be.

**Cautionary platform**   A critical perspective on tourism that highlights the negative economic, political, social, cultural, and environmental consequences of tourism on host societies.

**Central bank**   The chief monetary institution of a nation. Central banks regulate domestic financial institutions and influence domestic interest rates and foreign exchange rates. The central bank of the United States is the Federal Reserve System, which issues U.S. currency.

**Centrally planned economy**   Fundamental economic decisions flow not from the market, but from plans issued by the state. This system has a very difficult time accurately anticipating demand, and misjudgments in planning frequently lead to many shortages in some areas and overproduction in others—an especially acute problem because some products serve as inputs to other production processes. The gross inefficiency of central planning was a significant factor in the collapse of the Soviet Union.

**Chain migration**   Migrants move to "link up" with previous family members or social networks on the ground in a given destination.

**Circular migration**   Back-and-forth movement between two or more locations; part of an ongoing pattern of temporary migration and return.

**Class**   A collection of individuals who share certain socioeconomic attributes. Marx defined classes based on their relation to the means of production. See *Bourgeoisie* and *Proletariat*.

**Classical imperialism**   State-based imperialism as practiced, for example, through colonial systems.

**Classical mercantilism**   Policies focused on gaining wealth and power through unequal foreign trade; economic nationalism focused on the internal development of the national economy.

**Classical socialism**   The economic system usually associated with communism. Classical socialism is a highly centralized system of production and distribution. The Soviet Union typified the classical socialist system prior to 1989.

**CNN effect**   The pressure put on nation-states or the United Nations to "do something" where the news media generates a good deal of interest in situations such as massive starvation in Somalia (1992) or fleeing refugees in Rwanda (1994).

**Cold War**   A phrase first used by Bernard Baruch in 1948 to describe the bipolar security structure that lasted until 1989. The Cold War refers to the military and political confrontation between the United States and the Soviet Union and their respective allies.

**Collective good**   A tangible or intangible good that, once created, is available to all members of a group. The issue of collective goods raises questions about who should pay for these goods when they are to be provided to the entire group. No single person or entity has an incentive to pay for something from which everyone derives a benefit—for example, reducing air pollution.

**Colonialism**   The state of being a colony or extension of another government.

**Commercialization of sovereignty**   The process of one state renting out commercial privileges and protections to citizens and companies from another state. Examples of this trend include offering flags of convenience and serving as tax havens. In this way, one state's sovereign privilege is used to undermine the sovereign power of another state to regulate their citizens' and companies' behaviors.

**Commodification**   The process whereby an item is transformed into a commodity to be bought and sold. In the context of tourism, commodification refers to the transformation of cultural objects and values into commodities in response to tourist preferences and demands.

**Common Agricultural Policy (CAP)**   The system of agricultural subsidies employed by the *European Union* that protects farmers by a variety of means including export subsidies, tariffs, and income-support measures.

**The common heritage of mankind**   A term created by the UN Ambassador of Malta in 1964 that refers to those resources that are humanity's collective goods—those things that are shared by everybody but owned by nobody. The term is often applied to the *Law of the Sea Treaty*, to characterize the sea as a common good owned by no one state. See *Tragedy of the commons*.

**Communism**   The system of political economy in which control over state and market is centralized in a single, authoritarian party.

**Comparative advantage**   A nation has a comparative advantage in production of a good or service if it can produce it at a lower cost, or *opportunity cost*, than other nations. The theory of comparative advantage holds that nations should produce and export those goods and services for which they hold a comparative advantage and import those items that other nations can produce at lower cost.

**Competitive devaluation**   The 1930s problem in which nations competed to devalue their currencies the most, to gain advantages over foreign competitors.

**Conditionality**   A policy of the International Monetary Fund that ties short-term loans to certain conditions designed to improve *current account* balances. In general, the making of loans subject to domestic economic and political reforms that promotes economic liberal policies and values. See *World Bank* and *International Monetary Fund*.

**Conspiracism**   A political culture widespread in Iran and Arab countries that blames covert Western and Israeli manipulation for any and all regional or national problems. Some scholars worry that this mindset encourages extremism by engendering a mindset of permanent suspicion toward the West and Israel.

**Constructivism**   A critique of international political economy (IPE), which argues that the structures and institutions analyzed by IPE have no intrinsic causal power distinct from the values, beliefs, and interests that underlie them. States are not only political actors, but also social actors insofar as they adhere to rules, norms, and institutional constructs that reflect society's values and beliefs. These values are not static but are the result of ongoing social construction.

**Consumer economics**   An economic system organized primarily to satisfy consumer demands. See *Producer economics*.

**Contagion crisis**   A domestic financial crisis that spreads to other national economies through international linkages such as capital, currency, money, and commodity markets, trade interdependence effects, and shifting market psychology. This phenomenon was observed during the East Asian financial crisis of 1997–2000, which despite starting in Thailand quickly spread to Malay, Indonesia, South Korea, the Philippines, and other Asian economies, and later to Russia, Brazil, and Argentina.

**Coordination mechanisms**   Private and public institutions that organize the production and distribution of goods and services.

**Core**   A term used in modern world system analysis (core versus periphery) in reference to the more developed capitalist part of the economic system, which interacts with the *periphery*, or less developed part of the system. These terms can refer to international geographic regions (e.g., *North–South*) or to sectors within a particular economy. See *Modern world system*.

**Corn Laws**   Trade barriers that restricted agricultural imports into Great Britain from 1815 to 1846.

**Corporatism**   A system of political economy built on collective organizations within society such as labor and business organizations (rather than focusing on individuals or classes, for example).

**Counter trade**   A form of barter in international trade in which goods are paid for with other goods instead of money. Counter trade is most common in trade with *soft currency* nations, which often experience a shortage of *hard currency* funds with which to pay for imports.

**Countermovement**   A conceptual tool devised by Karl Polanyi to describe the rejection of the market by groups of working people, in response to its negative social effects. See *The Great Transformation*.

**Countervailing trade practices**   Defensive measures taken on the part of the state to counter the advantage gained by another state when it adopts protectionist measures. Such practices include antidumping measures and the imposition of countervailing tariffs or quotas.

**Crony capitalism**   A term applied to close business–government links in Asian countries, especially when links foster corruption.

***Cui bono?* (kwē bōnō) Who benefits?**   This term suggests that benefits drive actions, so we should "follow the money" to see in whose interest are the actions and institutions we perceive.

**Cultural citizenship**   An understanding of citizenship that refers not simply to legal rights but also to a sense of belonging and entitlement that is achieved through cultural difference rather than assimilation.

**Cultural Revolution**   The name for the political turmoil in China from 1966 until Mao Zedong's death in 1976. Mao encouraged China's people to attack the *party-state,* which he considered too resistant to the continuous revolution he advocated in China. The struggle seriously weakened the capacity of the party-state to centrally plan China's vast and complex economy and helped pave the way for the economic transition that began shortly after Mao's death.

**Currency board**   A government institution that regulates a nation's domestic money supply and its foreign exchange rate. The goal of a currency board is to use the commitment to a fixed foreign exchange rate as a tool to stabilize the domestic economy.

**Currency crisis**   A condition that occurs when a nation's currency suffers a substantial short-term drop in its foreign exchange value as a result of a financial bubble, a speculative attack, or another international financial situation.

**Currency devaluation (or depreciation)**   By devaluing their currency, countries cause exports to other countries to become cheaper, while imports from abroad become more expensive. Currency depreciation thus tends to achieve the effects, temporarily at least, of both a tariff (raising import prices) and an export subsidy (lowering the costs of exports). Currency changes affect the prices of all traded goods, however, whereas tariffs and subsidies generally apply to one good at a time.

**Current account**   A part of a nation's balance of payments that records financial flows due to international trade in goods and services and unilateral transfers (aid or gifts) between nations. A *current account deficit* means that a nation is paying out more for goods and services than it receives for the goods and services it sells on international markets; this leads to rising international indebtedness.

**Customs union**   A group of nations that agrees to eliminate trade barriers among themselves and adopt a unified system of external trade barriers. The *Treaty of Rome* created a customs union in the form of the *European Economic Community*.

**Defensive modernization**   Efforts to catch up with other states by reorganizing the government, military, economy, legal system, or other institutions. During the nineteenth century, the Ottoman Empire pursued defensive modernization in order to rival Europe's growing imperial power but met with limited success. The inability of the Middle East to modernize is variously blamed on a lack of separation of church and state, cultural immobilism, and lack of political freedom.

**Deficit**   Money outflows from some account exceed money inflows.

**Deflation**   When the general level of prices falls over a period of time. Deflation (falling prices) is commonly associated with falling incomes, as during a *depression*.

**Deforestation**   The destruction of forests, usually through excessive tree cutting by humans.

**Demographic transition**   The point at which population growth decreases as per-capita income levels rise. The argument often made by those who reject the idea that limiting population growth alone will lead to economic development.

**Dependency theory**   A theory of the relationship between industrialized (*core*) nations and less developed (*periphery*) nations that stresses the many linkages that exist to make less developed countries dependent on richer nations. These linkages include trade, finance, and technology.

**Depreciate**   A term used in foreign exchange markets when one currency falls in value relative to another currency. See *Appreciate*.

**Depression**   A period of very significant decreases in incomes and employment in a nation, as indicated by substantial decreases in Gross National Product and a high level of unemployment. A depression is more severe than a *recession*.

**Devaluation**   Also termed *currency depreciation*. A situation in which the value of the domestic currency is reduced relative to foreign currencies. Devaluation increases the prices of imported goods, while making exports relatively less costly to foreign buyers.

**Developmental capitalism**   A term used to describe the system of political economy of postwar Japan, where state policies are used to encourage industrial growth.

**Developmental state capitalism**   A term used to describe the system of political economy of postwar Japan, where state policies are used to encourage industrial growth, especially through expanded exports. Japan's policies became a model for other developing nations, especially in Southeast Asia.

**Diaspora**   Transnational communities that identify with a common homeland, history, and ethnic identity despite their citizenship in other countries. Diasporas may be tied to a particular nation-state or simply reflect a particular national identity.

**Differential taxation**   A major incentive for smuggling. When taxes on the same product differ significantly between countries, a black market opportunity is created to buy the product in the low-tax jurisdiction and resell it in the high-tax jurisdiction for a substantial markup.

**Direct foreign investment (DFI)**   Investments made by a company (often a *transnational corporation*) in production, distribution, or sales facilities in another country. The term *direct* implies a measure of control exercised by the parent company (U.S.–based IBM, for example) on resources in the host nation (such as Mexico).

**Displacement**   The first stage of a financial crisis, in which an external shock or some news fundamentally alters the economic outlook in a market, shifting expectations concerning future profits in some significant way, which attracts speculators and investors. See *Expansion*.

**Dispute Settlement Panel**   A part of the World Trade Organization (WTO), composed of impartial panels of trade experts that rule on trade disputes. The panel can impose trade sanctions on member states that violate trade agreements. By creating an enforcement mechanism for trade agreements, the WTO is a significant evolution from the preceding General Agreement on Tariffs and Trade (GATT) regime.

**Distress**   The fourth stage of a financial crisis, following euphoria, in which expectations about an investment begin to downturn out of fear that past investments have pushed the price above its real value, which is unsustainable. See *Euphoria* and *Revulsion*.

**Dumping**   The practice of selling an item for less abroad than at home. Dumping is an unfair trade practice when it is used to drive out competitors from an export market with the goal of creating monopoly power.

**Dynamic efficiency**   An economic structure that produces high rates of economic growth.

**Eastern Question Game**   Countries outside of the Middle East jockey to penetrate or otherwise control Middle Eastern states in the zero-sum style of power politics. Middle Eastern leaders responded to the opportunity for "quick grabs" at the expense of long-term development. See Chapter 9 and 14.

**Economic development**   Increase in the level of economic activity in a nation, often measured by growth in gross domestic product (GDP) or per-capita GDP. Generally, economic development involves structural changes, with populations moving from agricultural (primary sector) to manufacturing (secondary sector) to services (tertiary sector). The concept of economic development is rooted in the experiences of Western nations, especially Britain, the United States, and Germany.

**Economic globalization**   The expansion of market activity, including especially finance and production, from a national to a truly global scale.

**Economic integration**   The process by which a group of nation-states agrees to ignore their national boundaries for at least some economic purposes, creating a larger and more tightly connected system of markets.

**Economic liberalism**   The ideology of the free market. Economic liberalism holds that nations are best off when the role of the state is minimized. See *Laissez-faire*. Economic liberalism derives in part from fear of state abuse of power and in part from the philosophy of individualism and liberty of the eighteenth-century Enlightenment.

**Economic nationalism**   The ideology of *mercantilism*. Economic nationalism holds that nations are best off when state and market are joined in a partnership. The state protects domestic business firms, which become richer and more powerful, which in turn increases the power of the state. Alexander Hamilton and Friedrich List are two famous proponents of economic nationalism.

**Economic sanctions**   Trade and other barriers imposed against a country as part of a nation's foreign policy.

**Economic statecraft**   The use of economic policies as tools of international relations.

**Economic structuralism**   The idea that the economic structures of society, in particular, condition the outcomes for actors in society. See *Structuralism*.

**Economic union**   A degree of economic integration that goes beyond that found in a customs union. An economic union eliminates both tariff and nontariff barriers to trade and finance among a group of countries.

**Ecosystem**   An ecological community and its environment considered as a single unit.

**Ecotourism**   Responsible travel to natural areas that conserves the environment and improves the well-being of local people.

**Efficiency**   The economic goal of making the best use of scarce resources, that is, the allocation and distribution of goods and services that provides maximum benefit to society. See *Dynamic efficiency* and *Static efficiency*.

**Elastic demand**   The demand for a product is said to be elastic if a given change in price produces a relatively larger proportionate change in the quantity that is demanded. If a 10 percent price cut results in an increase in the quantity demanded of more than 10 percent (say, 15 percent), then the demand is elastic. See *Inelastic demand*.

**Embargo**   A government prohibition of a certain activity. A trade embargo is a prohibition of trade with a nation.

**Embedded liberalism**   A system of strong states and strong markets. Under the Bretton Woods economic system, states were responsible for management of the domestic economy but within a liberal international system featuring increasingly free trade. Embedded liberalism is different from mercantilism in that the focus of economic policy is on Keynesian domestic policies to reduce unemployment and encourage economic growth rather than the beggar-thy-neighbor mercantilist policies of the 1930s, which destroyed the open trading system among nations.

**Emerging market economies**   Nations making a transition from heavily state-controlled systems of political economy to more market-oriented policies. In 1999 the Institute of International Finance included the following countries in the list of "emerging market economies": China, India, Indonesia, Malaysia, the Philippines, South Korea, Thailand; Argentina, Brazil, Chile, Colombia, Ecuador, Mexico, Peru, Uruguay, Venezuela; Bulgaria, the Czech Republic, Hungary, Poland, Romania, the Russian Federation, Slovakia, Turkey, Algeria, Egypt, Morocco, South Africa, and Tunisia.

**Emission credits**   An implementation mechanism for the Kyoto Protocol, which allows countries to buy and sell carbon dioxide production quotas from one another. See *Kyoto Protocol*.

**Emulator**   The characteristic of Japan that it selectively adapts foreign political, economic, and cultural factors.

*Endaka*   A Japanese term for the problems associated with an overvalued yen.

**Epistemic communities**   A network of experts on a particular international problem, who try to frame the issue for policymakers and the public, and offer solutions. For example, an epistemic community has mobilized around the issue of global climate change, with many scientists, nongovernmental organizations, and the media bringing attention to the threat and advocating solutions.

**Equilibrium**   A balance of opposing forces, as with an equilibrium in an account, in which money inflows and outflows are equal.

**Ethnic cleansing**   The harassment, removal, or murder of citizens based solely on their ethnic or racial attributes. A term that emerged in the conflict following the breakup of the former Yugoslavia.

**Euphoria**   The third stage of a financial crisis, following expansion, in which expectations about an investment have become self-reinforcing, pushing the price up higher and higher as more investors race to it. See *Expansion* and *Distress*.

**Euro-Mediterranean Partnership**   A free-trade and cooperation agreement between the EU and a number of MENA (Middle Eastern and North African) states in effect since 1995. In exchange for lowering trade barriers and initiating economic reform, the Arab Mediterranean countries can expect greater market access into Europe, as well as more European aid, loans, and investment.

**European Coal and Steel Community (ECSC)**   An organization established in 1952 to integrate the coal and steel resources of six European nations. Eventually evolved into the European Economic Community.

**European Community (EC)**   A creation of the *Treaty of Rome*, the EC was a group that eventually numbered twelve nations engaged in economic (and to a lesser extent, political) integration. Taken together, the EC member states formed the largest single market in the world. EC members were France, Germany, Italy, Belgium, the Netherlands, and Luxembourg (the charter members), plus Great Britain, Ireland, Denmark, Greece, Spain, and Portugal. See *European Union*.

**European Economic Community (EEC)**   The original European "Common Market" of seven countries created in 1957 by the Treaty of Rome.

**European Economic Space (EES)**   A group of nations that are not members of the *European Union* but have negotiated free-trade or preferential trade agreements with the EU.

**European Free Trade Area (EFTA)**   Promoted by Great Britain in 1960, it was comprised of states that did not belong to the European Economic Community. Its members removed trade barriers among themselves, but maintained the right to levy tariffs on third countries.

**European Monetary Union (EMU)**   The agreement of several European countries to adopt a common currency—the euro, which was introduced in 2002. At the time of this printing, there are twelve members of the Euro-zone.

**European Union (EU)**   Successor organization to the *European Community* as defined by the *Maastricht Treaty*.

**Exchange rate**   The ratio of exchange between the currencies of different countries (for example, between the dollar and the yen). Changes in the exchange rate affect the prices of goods in international trade and therefore have important internal effects in nations. (See *Devaluation*.) The international system of exchange rates can be based on fixed (pegged) exchange rates, as during the Bretton Woods period (1946–1973) and the period of the gold standard in the late nineteenth century; or on flexible (floating) exchange rates, as during the period since 1973. Fixed exchange rates are determined by international agreements among states; flexible exchange rates are determined by market forces.

**Expansion**   The second stage of a financial crisis, following displacement, in which an expectations boom intensifies, perhaps transforming into a *bubble* as more and more money is poured into the investment opportunity. During this stage, a nation's financial resources are stretched to acquire the funds needed to invest further. See *Displacement* and *Euphoria*.

**Exploitation**   An economic relationship in which one side of a transaction selfishly attempts to achieve the maximum possible gain, generally at the expense of the well-being of others.

**Export**   A good or service that is sold to the citizens of another nation.

**Export quotas**   International agreements that limit the quantity of an item that a nation can export. The effect is to limit the number of goods imported into a country. Examples include Orderly Marketing Arrangements (OMAs), Voluntary Export Restraints (VERs), and Voluntary Restraint Agreements (VRAs). The Multifibre Agreement establishes a system of export quotas for less developed countries, for example.

**Export subsidies**   Any measure that effectively reduces the price of an exported product, making it more attractive to potential foreign buyers.

**Export-oriented growth**   A strategy for economic growth that focuses on exports and integration into global markets. Contrast this strategy with *Import-substituting industrialization*.

**External cost**   A cost that is not factored into market decisions. An external cost is created when an individual makes decisions that impose costs on others, such as when a factory pollutes.

**Fair trade**   Often presented as an alternative to free trade, fair trade mixes protectionism and free trade to "level the playing field" for domestic producers. The fair trade movement is also an initiative spearheaded by international nongovernmental organizations to provide higher prices for certified goods such as coffee, timber, and a host of other products of workers in developing countries.

**Feminism**   An alternative analytical perspective that applies the lens of gender to problems in the international political economy. Feminists theorize that gender accounts for societal norms and expectations related to what is appropriate for males and females. Feminism seeks to describe and explain many of the hidden assumptions about gender in mercantilism and realism, liberalism, and structuralist studies.

**Feudal system**   The medieval system of political economy, organized around land holdings or fiefs.

**Finance structure**   The system of institutions, practices, and arrangements that condition the use and exchange of financial resources. The international monetary system and the institutions that condition the distribution and payment of international debts are parts of the finance structure.

**Flags of convenience**   Legal businesses and criminals are permitted to register their airplanes and ships in a country even though they will conduct most of their business (licit or illicit) elsewhere. In exchange, host countries typically receive lucrative registration fees, payoffs, or "protection money."

**Food First**   A thesis introduced in the 1970s to counter the view that overpopulation is the underlying cause of world hunger. It argues that hunger is actually caused by deficiencies in income and land distribution, rather than of food production and distribution. According to the proponents of this theory, hunger is *not endemic* to less developed countries, but is a *byproduct* of their political and economic relationship to the industrialized nations.

**Food security**   An element of national security; concerns about the security of a nation's food supply.

**Foreign direct investment (FDI)**   Purchase of business assets such as factories, stores, warehouses, and the like, by a foreign firm. Investment that gives a foreign firm a tangible business presence in a country.

**Foreign exchange (FX)**   Foreign currencies and foreign currency markets.

**Free ride**   To utilize a service or contribute to a collective problem without paying the associated costs. A good example of a free rider is a high-polluting industry that is not required to pay for the cost of the environmental damage it causes. In this case, the industry gets a free ride because it is able to externalize the cost of pollution onto society at large, but unilaterally realizes the benefits that come with selling the good produced. See *Tragedy of the commons*.

**Free-rider problem**   Difficulty associated with *public goods*, in that an individual is able to enjoy the benefits of a good or service without paying for it.

**Free trade**   One of the popular policies advocated by economic liberals. In keeping with the laissez-faire notion that government intervention in the economy undermines efficiency and overall wealth, a regime of free trade would remove protectionist measures (tariffs, quotas, etc.) that are designed to insulate domestic producers from international competition. See *Comparative advantage*.

**Free-trade area (FTA)**   A group of nations that agrees to eliminate tariff barriers for trade among themselves, but that retains the right of individual nations to set their own tariffs for trade with nonmember nations.

**Friedman, Milton**   A prominent economist who advocated market liberalization as a means of expanding social and political freedom. His philosophy was highly influential in the mainstream adoption of neoliberal economic practices. See *neoliberalism*.

**General Agreement on Tariffs and Trade (GATT)**   An international organization, based in Geneva, that negotiated reductions in trade barriers among its many member nations. GATT negotiations took place over a period of years and were termed "rounds," as in the Kennedy round and the Tokyo round, which reduced trade barriers for manufactured goods, and the *Uruguay round*, which aimed to create freer trade in services and in agricultural goods. Replaced by the *World Trade Organization*.

**Generalized System of Preferences Act (GSP)**   Regulations regarding tariffs set as part of the General Agreement on Tariffs and Trade (GATT).

**Genetically Modified Organisms (GMOs)**   A living organism that has had its genetic code altered for commercial or scientific gain. For example, a crop might be genetically modified to enhance desirable nutritional qualities. Critics of GMOs worry about the loss of native biodiversity, the accompanying shift to monoculture farming techniques, a greater reliance on herbicides, and an incommensurability with the agricultural systems in many less developed countries.

**Genomics**   The study and manipulation of organisms' genetic codes for commercial and scientific gain. Examples include the development of food commodities that are genetically modified to enhance desirable nutritional qualities, and considerable research in the field of biotechnology with the aim of curing human genetic diseases.

**Geopolitics**   The combination of political and geographic factors that influence a nation within an IPE structure, especially the *security structure*.

*Glasnost*   Russian term for the policy initiated by Soviet Premier Mikhail Gorbachev in the late 1980s that involved opening up the Soviet state to political reform. It was meant to complement economic reform, or *Perestroika*.

**Global commodity chains**   Networks of firms created for the production, distribution, and marketing of various products.

**Global warming**   The increase in the temperature of the earth's atmosphere that results from the *greenhouse effect*. A hotly debated topic as to how much global warming is caused by man-made and natural forces.

**Globalism**   The ideology underlying economic *globalization*. Based on economic liberal principles and ideas globalism holds that the internationalization and integration of markets will provide a vehicle for enhancing global economic well-being. A popular ideology among supporters of globalization.

**Globalization**   The process by which all of the structures of IPE have become less strictly associated with the boundaries of the nation-state. Globalization also connotes increasing economic interdependence as well as the spread of Western (U.S.) cultural influence all over the world.

**Grameen Bank**   An important microcredit bank founded in Bangladesh by Mohammad Yunus in 1976. An increasingly popular method of helping usually poor women in poor countries create small business enterprises.

**Gramsci, Antonio**   Italian socialist thinker who theorized that hegemonic ideas were important in influencing state and human behavior. People followed a dominant figure or state because they agreed with its views.

**Great Depression**   The period starting in 1929 and lasting through most of the 1930s during which high unemployment and declining national income plagued the United States, much of Europe, and many developing regions of the world.

**Great Leap Forward**   A 1958 economic and social development program in China that organized a half-billion peasants into 24,000 "people's communes."

*The Great Transformation*   The title of the seminal work of Karl Polanyi that investigates the birth and development of the market economy and industrial society in England along with the concurrent maturation of economic liberal ideology. Polanyi challenged the notion that the market is a self-regulating entity, instead arguing that it is the product of human action in response to economic and social changes.

**Green**   The adjective *green* often indicates an emphasis on environmental and ecological issues. The Green Party in Germany, for example, is a political party devoted to furthering environmental and related positions.

**Green revolution**   Various scientific, technological, and economic programs that attempt to increase food production through introduction of advanced plant strains and farming techniques.

**Greenhouse effect**   The gradual increase in gaseous components such as carbon dioxide, methane, nitrous oxide, and chlorofluorocarbons in the earth's atmosphere that contribute to the earth's warming. While the surface of the earth has been warming, not all scientists agree as to the cause of this trend or its significance.

**Gross domestic product (GDP)**   Like Gross National Product (GNP), gross domestic product is a measure of a nation's economic production in a year. Unlike GNP, however, GDP measures only production that takes place within a nation. GDP is the accepted international measure of national economic performance. "Real" GDP adjusts GDP for changes in inflation. "Per-capita" GDP is a measure of average income per person in a country.

**Gross National Product (GNP)**   The total value of all goods and services produced in a country in a year. GNP is a measure of a nation's overall economic activity. "Real" GNP, which adjusts GNP for the effects of inflation, is a more reliable indicator of changes in a nation's production. GNP was the main measure of economic performance in the United States until 1991. Now the United States and most other nations rely on *gross domestic product* measurements.

**Group of Seven (G-7)**   The seven largest industrial democracies: the United States, Japan, Germany, France, Canada, Italy, and Great Britain. The leaders of the G-7 nations meet regularly to discuss common economic and political problems and to attempt to coordinate policies in some areas.

**Growth pole**   A strategically selected location meant to serve as the center of economic growth for surrounding areas. Through investments in infrastructure, and incentives meant to attract capital and labor, governments stimulate economic development by concentrating resources on the growth pole.

**Guest worker**   A nonresident foreign worker. Guest workers engage in temporary employment within a foreign state, but both the length of their residence and the conditions of labor are stipulated by that state, which also prohibits the possibility of their permanent residence or citizenship.

**Gulf Cooperation Council (GCC)**   A grouping composed of Saudi Arabia, the United Arab Emirates, Kuwait, Oman, Bahrain, and Qatar. These six countries share a heavy reliance on foreign workers, which make up a significant proportion of their combined workforce.

*Habeas corpus*   The right to a speedy trial. Some fear that U.S. policies post–9/11 have restricted this and other valuable rights.

**Hard currency**   A currency of known value that can readily be exchanged on foreign exchange markets and is therefore generally accepted in international transactions. Examples of hard currencies today include the U.S. dollar, the Japanese yen, the euro, and the Swiss franc. See *Soft currency.*

**Hard power**   Military and in some cases economic power. Hard power refers to state tools to influence, persuade, or coerce through the direct application of power and wealth. See *Soft power.*

*Hawala*   An informal network of money dealers who facilitate international money transfers.

**Hayek, Friedrich**   An influential twentieth-century economist, who advocated an aggressive *laissez-faire* model, in opposition to both Soviet collectivism and Keynesian economics. Hayek's philosophy influenced the economic policies of the United States under Ronald Reagan and the United Kingdom under Margaret Thatcher.

**Hedge funds**   Investment funds that seek to profit from small differences in asset prices that are likely to converge. In general, hedge funds "bet" that asset prices will move in certain predictable ways. Hedge funds play an important role in *Speculative attacks*.

**Hegemonic stability**   The theory that the international system is more stable in the presence of a *hegemon* or dominant power.

**Hegemony**   Dominance or leadership, especially by one nation over other nations. The theory of hegemonic stability holds that the international system achieves growth and stability only when one state acts as the hegemon, dominating the others but also paying the costs associated with counteracting problems in the international system.

**Hierarchy**   A social or organizational system using a clear ordering of rank, authority, and priorities.

**Highly indebted poor countries (HIPCs)**   A designation for forty-one of the world's poorest countries, mostly in Africa. These countries suffer from high poverty and high incidences of HIV/AIDS.

**HIPC Initiative**   An effort in the late 1990s to cancel the debt of the highly indebted poor countries. This effort largely failed, as only four countries received debt relief as part of the initiative.

**Historical materialism**   The idea, central to Marx, that social and political institutions are built on a foundation of the economy. The idea that natural laws are based on physical things, not ideas alone.

**Hot money**   Highly interest-sensitive short-term international capital movements.

**Hydra effect**   Efforts to reduce the supply of an illegal commodity (for example, drugs) are often counterproductive because a crackdown in one area triggers movement of illicit goods to a different area. U.S. antidrug efforts in Latin America have spawned new organizations in Mexico and Puerto Rico.

**Immigration**   Movement into another country with the intention of becoming a permanent resident in the destination country.

**Imperialism**   Idea associated with the works of J. A. Hobson, V. I. Lenin, and R. Luxemburg. A superior–inferior relationship in which an area and its people have been subordinated to the will or interests of a foreign state. Imperialism is often associated with historical periods that correspond to conquest and colonization of developing territories by developed "modern" industrialized nations. Economic imperialism may result from a conscious policy or from the capital flows of private foreign investment. See *Direct foreign investment*.

**Import**   A good or service purchased from citizens of a foreign country.

**Import quotas**   A limit on the quantity of an item that can be imported into a nation. By limiting the quantity of imports, the quota tends to drive up the price of a good while at the same time restricting competition.

**Import-substituting industrialization (ISI)**   An economic development strategy that attempts to encourage industrial development, often by restricting imports of industrial productions or encouraging exports of these items. Contrast this strategy with *Export-oriented growth*.

**Industrial policy**   Economic policies designed to guide or direct business investment and development. Such policies often include support for businesses and trade protection.

**Industrial Revolution**   The period, from approximately 1780 to 1840, when an industrial sector developed in Europe, especially in Great Britain. This period is sometimes called the "first industrial revolution" to distinguish it from the "second industrial revolution" (approximately 1880 to 1910). The first revolution relied on mechanical innovations, whereas the second revolution was based on chemical and electrical innovations.

**Inelastic demand**   The demand for a product is said to be inelastic if a given change in price produces a relatively smaller proportionate change in the quantity that is demanded. If a 10 percent price cut results in an increase in the quantity demanded of less than 10 percent (say, 5 percent), then the demand is inelastic. See *Elastic demand*.

**Inflation**   A rise in the general level of prices in a country (as opposed to a rise in the price of a particular good). Hyperinflation is a condition in which very high rates of inflation (1000 percent per year price increases and more) are experienced.

**Informal economy**   The part of an economy that is unregulated and usually does not pay taxes. In a less developed country, most street vendors, for example, would be classified as "informal."

**Integration**   In IPE, integration occurs when nation-states agree to unify or coordinate some political and economic activities.

**Intellectual hegemony**   Antonio *Gramsci*'s theory that the dominant class maintains its position through the creation of an ideology or worldview that is accepted by society and thereby controls its actions. Social control, in Gramsci's view, is achieved by both coercion (police and military action) and consent (achieved through intellectual hegemony).

**Intellectual property rights (IPRs)**   Patents, copyrights, trademarks, and other rights to ownership or control of ideas, innovation, and creations.

**Interdependence**   Usually thought of as interconnectedness between nations and other actors in the international political economy conditioned by trade, aid, finance, and investment. Reactions to interdependence include the need to cooperate but also negative reactions related to the vulnerability and sensitivity it engenders.

**Internal migration**   Migration of an individual or group within a single nation-state, often from one region to another or from the rural to urban locations.

**International division of labor**   The organization of global economic activity, often with special emphasis on the activities of the *core* and *periphery*.

**International Monetary Fund (IMF)**   Created as part of the *Bretton Woods* system, the IMF is an organization of over 150 member states charged with stabilizing the international monetary system. The IMF makes loans to member states when they experience severe *current account deficits*. These loans are made subject to enactment of economic reforms, a practice called *conditionality*.

**International organizations (IOs)**    Voluntary associations such as the United Nations that draw their members from the ranks of nation-states. See *Nongovernmental organizations.*

**International political economy (IPE)**    The interdisciplinary social science that studies questions raised by the political and economic interactions of nations. IPE studies complex interdependent webs created by international trade, migration, finance, and technology flows and the international security arrangements that condition them.

**International Trade Organization (ITO)**    An original element of the *Bretton Woods* system that was not successfully implemented. A weaker institution, the GATT, was eventually created to take the place of the ITO alongside the World Bank and the International Monetary Fund. See *General Agreement on Tariffs and Trade* and *World Trade Organization.*

**Intervene (in foreign exchange markets)**    Action by a government agency or central bank to alter the foreign exchange value of a currency, especially by buying or selling that currency.

**Intifada**    Literally means the "uprising" of the Palestinians against Israeli occupation of the West Bank and the Gaza Strip. There have been two intifadas—in 1987 and 2000.

**Intraregional trade bloc**    A trade agreement where nation-states in a particular region remove barriers to trade with the other members of the region. The Asian Pacific Economic Cooperation Forum (APEC) is an example of an intraregional trade bloc that aims to integrate eighteen Asian and Pacific nations into a nonbinding arrangement that would gradually remove trade barriers among members by 2020.

**The invisible hand**    A term first used by Adam *Smith* to describe the free market's ability to allocate scarce resources through the interplay of supply and demand. On the basis of this quality of the free market, states should play a limited role in the economy. See *Laissez-faire.*

**Iron triangle**    The relationship between politicians, bureaucrats, and business leaders in Japan's political economy.

**Irregular migrants**    Migrants who reside and work in a foreign country without the appropriate legal documents. These workers may have entered the country without permission or entered with a visa but then stayed on past the limits of that permission.

**Isolationism**    The policy of withdrawing from world affairs, especially to prevent disruption or exploitation from external sources.

**Keiretsu**    Japanese "business families"; groups of businesses in different economic sectors that engage in cooperative strategic behavior—buying and selling goods within the group whenever possible, for example.

**Keynesian compromise**    The Keynesian compromise is one aspect of the *Bretton Woods* system. Nations retain the ability to intervene in their domestic economies but are limited in this by their agreement to limit interference in international economic markets.

**Keynesian theory**    To be Keynesian is to be in agreement with the general thrust of the political economy of John Maynard *Keynes* (pronounced "Canes") (1883–1946). Because Keynes's views were complex, original, and constantly changing, there is no precise definition of what it means to be Keynesian. A general definition is to believe that there is a positive role for the state to play in domestic affairs (fighting unemployment and poverty, for example) and in international affairs (the kind of role conceived for the *International Monetary Fund* and the *World Bank*). Keynes's views were influenced by the catastrophe of World War I and the Great Depression of the interwar period. His ideas are also reflected in the *Bretton Woods* institutions and policies.

**Knowledge structure**    The set of institutions and practices that condition the production, exchange, and distribution of intellectual and technological goods and services, property rights, and their associated benefits.

**Knowledge and technology structure**    The set of institutions and practices that condition the production, exchange, and distribution of information and intellectual and technological goods and services, property rights, and their associated benefits.

**Kyoto Protocol**    Environmental rules that derive from the 1997 Kyoto, Japan, summit on global warming.

**Laissez-faire**    A French term ("let be" or "leave alone") commonly associated with Adam *Smith*, the eighteenth-century Scottish economist who advocated free-market solutions to economic and social problems. Today, it refers to a view that individuals are best left to solve problems themselves, through the "invisible hand" of market interactions, rather than through government policies.

**Law of the Sea Treaty**    Based on the principle that the seas are a collective good owned by no one nation state but shared by all states and people, this series of conventions was negotiated in the United Nations since the 1960s. The agreements attempt to regulate international fishing, mining of the ocean floor and seabeds, control of coastal waters and the continental shelf, and passage through narrow straits. See *Tragedy of the commons* and Collective good.

**Lender of last resort**    An institution that pledges to provide liquidity to financial markets during a panic in order to prevent the collapse of a financial *bubble*.

**Less developed country (LDC)**    A nation with relatively low levels of income and industrialization.

**Levels of analysis**    The three levels of analysis are the individual, the state, and the international system. The levels-of-analysis approach was originally developed by political scientist Kenneth Waltz to help in understanding differences of opinion regarding the fundamental sources of international conflict and war.

**Liberal imperialism**    The idea that liberal nations intervene in the internal affairs of premodern states with the intent to establish liberal values and institutions.

**Liberalism**    The IPE perspective that focuses on the individual and the primacy of freedom or liberty. There are many varieties of liberalism today, which reflect different points of view regarding the proper role of the state in private activities.

**Liquidity**    Money or assets that can readily be converted to money without substantial loss.

**List, Friedrich**   One of the principal organizers of the German nationalist movement in the nineteenth century, who proposed nationalism and protective tariffs as a means of unifying the German principalities into a single nation-state and countering British economic imperialism. List visited the United States from 1825 to 1830 and promoted many national economic projects such as rail transport. He is viewed by many as one of the modern founders of economic nationalist ideas.

**Maastricht Treaty**   This treaty creating the *European Union* was ratified by members of the *European Community* in 1993.

**Malevolent mercantilism**   Mercantilist policies that aim to defeat an enemy or potential enemy. Associated with Germany and Japan before World War II.

**Managed exchange rates**   An *exchange rate* system whereby day-to-day foreign exchange changes are determined by market forces, but long-run changes are conditioned by state actions. Sometimes termed a "dirty float."

**Managed trade system**   A mixture of liberal and mercantilist trade policies. Strong political and social interests often call for trade protection that often creates a political climate incompatible with completely free trade. A managed trade system often reflects a political compromise most states and even the World Trade Organization can adhere to.

*Maquiladora*   Assembly plants in Mexico that use foreign parts and semifinished products to produce final goods for export.

**Market**   A form of social organization based on individual action and self-interest. Individuals exchange goods and services through market institutions. Markets are sometimes distinct physical places (such as the New York Stock Exchange or Pike Place Market in Seattle), but the term *market* generally refers to the broader market forces of profit and self-interest.

**Market fundamentalism**   The notion that the creation of wealth is the most important priority and that this can best be accomplished by removing government obstacles. See *Neoliberalism*.

**Market Leninism**   See *Market socialism*.

**Market socialism**   A system of political economy that combines state ownership and control of some sectors of the economy with private ownership and market allocations in other sectors. See *Classical socialism*.

**Marketization**   Part of the process of economic transition from classical socialism to capitalism. When a particular commodity has been marketized, its exchange becomes governed by supply and demand rather than according to central planning.

**Market system**   The basic political, social, and economic elements that comprise the exchange of goods and services either locally or the world over. In an age of increasing globalization, the exchange of goods and services for most specific items cannot be thought of as discreet and independent. Rather, local markets have become part of a wider market network that links people and economies around the world. See *Globalization*.

**Marshall Plan**   Named for U.S. Secretary of State George C. Marshall, who proposed the program in 1947. A 1948–1951 U.S. postwar assistance program that provided $12 billion in aid to European countries. Also called the European Recovery Program.

**Marxism**   An ideology that originated in the works of the German sociologist Karl Marx (1818–1883). Many strains of Marxism have evolved from Marx's works. Generally, Marxism is a critique of *capitalism* (as distinct from *economic liberalism*). Marxism holds that capitalism is subject to several distinctive flaws. Marxism tends to view economic relations from a power perspective (capital versus labor) as opposed to the cooperative relationship implicit in economic liberalism. See *Structuralism*.

**Mashriq**   The region of Arab-speaking countries to the east of Egypt, including Syria, Lebanon, Jordan, Iraq, and the Palestinian Territories.

**Mercantilism**   A seventeenth-century idea that won't go away, mercantilism was an ideology that put accumulation of national treasure as the main goal of society. Today, it is an economic philosophy and practice of government regulation of a nation's economic life to increase state power and security. Policies of import restriction and export promotion (to accumulate treasure at the expense of other countries) follow from this goal. See *Economic nationalism*.

**Microcredit**   The practice of providing very small loans to groups of people (usually women) in less developed countries who share the risk of repaying the loans. Muhammad Yunus is credited as the founder of the movement and the Grameen Bank in Bangladesh, which dispurses microcredit loans. Microcredit has been heralded for its promise to directly overcome poverty by putting money into the hands of those who actually need it, thus encouraging sustainable private-sector development. It has also served as a model in some industrialized countries.

**Migration**   Movement of an individual or group from one place to another, often in pursuit of political or religious freedom, economic opportunity, reunification with family, or access to specific resources.

**Mill, John Stuart**   A nineteenth-century English philosopher and political economist who questioned the wisdom of an absolute *laissez-faire* attitude. Reacting to the often-wretched working conditions in England during the industrial revolution, Mill advocated limited state intervention, for example, by providing free education to children and assistance to the poor.

**Millennium Development Goals (MDG)**   United Nations–sponsored initiatives to work on a local level to achieve the eradication of extreme hunger and poverty, universal primary education, gender equality and the empowerment of women, reduction in child mortality, improvement of maternal health, as well as efforts to combat HIV/AIDs, malaria, and other diseases, ensure environmental sustainability, and develop a global partnership for development.

**Ministry of Economy, Trade, and Industry (METI)**   Along with the Ministry of Finance, one of the two most important economic agencies in the Japanese government. Formerly known as the Ministry of International Trade and Industry (MITI).

**Ministry of Finance (MoF)**   A Japanese government ministry that is very influential in setting economic policy for the nation.

**Ministry of International Trade and Industry (MITI)**   A Japanese government ministry that is credited by some for Japan's rapid industrialization in the 1960s and 1970s. Now known as the Ministry of Economy, Trade, and Industry (METI).

**Mixed economy**   An economy that combines important elements of *state* and *market* (although the relative importance of these two elements may vary). Britain and France are both mixed economies, for example, although the state is relatively larger in France and the market relatively more important in Britain.

**Modern world system (MWS)**   A theory of economic development based on Marxist-Leninist ideologies. The MWS views economic development as conditioned by the relationship between the capitalist *core* and the less developed *periphery* nations. The historic mission of the core is to develop the periphery (often through the *semiperiphery*), but this development is exploitive in nature. The MWS therefore presents a theory that runs counter to liberal theories such as "hegemonic stability."

**Monetarism**   A school of thought that focuses on the money supply as a key determinant of the level of economic activity in a nation. Monetarists tend to view state economic actions as likely to disrupt domestic and international affairs. Monetarists tend, therefore, to be closely associated with *economic liberals* in their dislike of state influences.

**Monetary autonomy**   The ability of a nation, through its central bank, to determine domestic monetary policy without regard for international agreements or restraints.

**Monetary union**   A group of nations that actively coordinates their monetary policies. Members of a monetary union might adopt a common currency, for example.

**Moral hazard**   The property that risky behavior increases when people are insulated in some way from the consequences of the risks they take.

**Most Favored Nation (MFN)**   Trade status under the World Trade Organization, whereby imports from a nation are granted the same degree of preference as those from the most preferred nations.

**Mujahideen**   A term meaning Islamic freedom fighters. It often refers to the warlord leaders of local tribes, who in the 1980s became famous for their resistance to the Soviet Union in Afghanistan, with the help of American weapons and training. This support has been blamed as a source of blowback, whereby America's former surrogates have formed terrorist organizations targeting the United States.

**Multinational corporation (MNC)**   A business firm that engages in production, distribution, and marketing activities that cross national boundaries (see *Foreign direct investment*). The critical factor is that the firm has a tangible productive presence in several countries. This factor distinguishes an MNC from an international firm, which produces in one country and exports to other countries. See *Transnational corporation*.

**Multipolar system**   A security structure with more than two centers of power.

**Mundel trilemma**   Named for Nobel laureate Robert Mundel. A property of international monetary systems. It is impossible for such systems to provide foreign exchange stability, capital mobility, and national economic independence. One of these goals must be sacrificed to achieve the other two.

**Mutual assured destruction (MAD)**   The Cold War strategy of the United States and the Soviet Union under which each had sufficient military power to destroy the other even if destroyed itself, thus ensuring that neither nation could realistically "win" a nuclear war.

**Name-and-shame campaigns**   A way of pressuring companies and countries to change practices that are illegal or perceived to be unethical by bringing international attention to them.

**Nation**   A social group that shares a common identity, history, language, set of values and beliefs, institutions, and sense of territory. Nations do not have to have a homogeneous ethnic culture but usually exhibit a sense of homogeneity. Nations may extend beyond states, be circumscribed by states, or be coterminous with states. Since the seventeenth century, the nation-state has been the major political (sovereign) unit of the international system.

**Nation-state**   Synonymous with the term "country," since the seventeenth century the nation-state has been the major political (sovereign) unit of the international system. The nation-state joins the nation—a group of people with a shared sense of cultural identity and territoriality—with the state—a legal concept describing a social group that occupies a territory and is organized under common political institutions and an effective government. As sovereign entities, nation-states have the right to determine their own national objectives and to decide how they will achieve them.

**Neoconservatism**   A term used in the United States to describe a movement that is liberal in fundamental nature and that arose in reaction to the growth of the state in the 1960s.

**Neoimperialism**   An element of the structuralist interpretation of capitalism. *Core* nations exploit the periphery and create dependency through financial and production structures in neoimperialism. See *Classical imperialism*.

**Neoliberal policies**   Economic policies that stress reductions in the size and influence of the state combined with free-market reforms. See *Structural adjustment policies*.

**Neoliberalism**   A viewpoint that favors a return to the economic policies advocated by classical liberals such as Adam Smith and David Ricardo. Neoliberalism emphasizes market deregulation, privatization of government enterprises, minimal government intervention, and open international markets. Unlike classical liberalism, neoliberalism is primarily an agenda of economic policies rather than a political economy perspective. See *Market fundamentalism* and *Neoconservatism*.

**Neomercantilism**   A version of mercantilism that evolved in the post–World War II period. Neomercantilism is basically mercantilist policy enacted with a liberal system of international trade.

**Network**   A set of connected actors and the nature of their linkages. Examples include terrorist networks, some diasporas, and *hawala* informal finance networks.

**New International Economic Order (NIEO)**   A set of proposals made by less developed nations to reform international trade and financial structures.

**Newly industrialized countries (NICs)**   Nations that have achieved a large measure of industrialization in the second half of the twentieth century. Most lists of the NICs include South Korea, Taiwan, and Brazil, and sometimes Singapore and Hong Kong.

**1940 System**   Characteristics of the Japanese political economy originally adopted as government policy in preparation for World War II.

*Nomenklatura*   In Russian this term means "list of names" and refers to individuals in privileged positions within the structure of classical socialism, who frequently benefited in material ways from their political status.

**Nondiscrimination**   A principal of the World Trade Organization system whereby products of different nations are treated equally (and equally with domestic products once imported). The products of a specific nation cannot be discriminated against under this rule. See *Most Favored Nation*.

**Nongovernmental organizations (NGOs)**   National and international voluntary organizations that exist at a level between the individual and the state. Examples of NGOs include Greenpeace and the Red Cross. See *International organizations*.

**Nontariff barriers (NTBs)**   Alternative ways of limiting imports, including government health and safety standards, domestic content legislation, licensing requirements, and labeling requirements. Such measures make it difficult for imported goods to be marketed or significantly raise the price of imported goods.

**North American Free Trade Agreement (NAFTA)**   A free-trade area among the United States, Canada, and Mexico, fully implemented in 2005. The NAFTA treaty was signed in 1992 and took effect in 1994.

**North Atlantic Treaty Organization (NATO)**   An international security organization founded in 1949. NATO served as the main Western alliance during the Cold War. See *Warsaw Pact*.

**North–South**   The relationship between developed, industrialized countries (the North) and less developed countries (the South). This concept is often associated with *core–periphery* analysis but can also be simply a descriptive device.

**North–South dilemma**   The continuing problem of the uneven distribution of income and wealth between the richer and poorer nations of the world.

**Odius debt**   Foreign liabilities incurred by a former corrupt regime that leaves the new government owing tremendous sums of money. The burden of servicing this debt often stifles development efforts.

**Official capital flows**   The issuance of cross-border loans by states, the International Monetary Fund, and a number of specific regional banks. See *Private capital flows*.

**Oil-for-Food program**   A UN program applied to Iraq after the Persian Gulf War (1990–1991) that allowed Iraq to sell some of its oil in international markets in exchange for income to buy food and emergency aid supplies. It was a controversial program to the extent that many Iraqi and some UN officials were accused of corruption related to implementing the program.

**Open society**   A term popularized by philosopher Karl Popper and adopted by George Soros, a billionaire businessman, to describe the type of global society he seeks to create through a network of foundations. In general terms, an open society is one that values the rule of law, democratic government, active civil society, individual rights, and active civic dialogue.

**Opportunity cost**   The value of the best foregone opportunity when a choice is made. See *Comparative advantage*.

**Organic intellectuals**   In Antonio *Gramsci*'s theory of *intellectual hegemony*, these are intellectuals who are raised within the prevailing system and whose ideas therefore reinforce that system.

**Organization of Economic Cooperation and Development (OECD)**   An international organization created by European countries in 1948 to coordinate aid from the United States to Europe under the *Marshall Plan*. When the United States and Canada joined in 1960, its focus shifted to coordinating economic policy among the Western industrialized developed nations. Mexico, the Czech Republic, Hungary, Poland, the Slovak Republic, and South Korea have been admitted to the OECD in recent years.

**Organization of Petroleum Exporting Countries (OPEC)**   An organization of nations formed in 1960 to advance the interests of Third World oil exporters. OPEC members include Saudi Arabia, Iran, Iraq, Kuwait, Qatar, Abu Dhabi, Algeria, Gabon, Libya, Nigeria, Indonesia, Ecuador, and Venezuela.

**Output**   In balance-of-payments analysis, output is the total value of current production by a nation (roughly the same as its gross domestic product). See *Absorption*.

**Outsourcing**   When a firm transfers part (or all) of the production process for a good or service to another country. Many economic liberals consider outsourcing to be part of the process of the globalization of international production and trade. This is a controversial idea due to the number of people who are displaced when jobs move overseas.

**Overvalued currency**   When a currency's purchasing power abroad (converted at the going exchange rate) is greater than its purchasing power in the home country. The exchange rate thus biases economic activity in favor of foreign goods over domestically produced items. See *Undervalued currency*.

**Paradox of globalization**   Opening up domestic markets to international competition stimulates demands to protect and insulate national economies from that competition, jeopardizing the supposed benefits of globalization.

**Paradox of thrift**   If one individual saves much more income, that individual may be more secure economically. If everyone does this, however, the combined actions can cause a recession and everyone is less secure economically. The paradox of thrift then is an example of the potential problems of an unregulated economy. Keynes supported an active role for the state in the economy to help overcome this problem.

**Party-state**   A term used to describe the symbiosis between the Communist Party and sate goverment in classic socialist systems. Rather than being autonomous, the state is dominated by the party, which direct its resources toward the party's political ends.

**Pax Americana**   The period of U.S. hegemony following World War II. "Pax" means "peace." Some critics use the phrase to equate U.S. power with imperialism, similar to the Pax Britannica of Great Britain during the eighteenth and nineteenth centuries.

**Pax Britannica**   The period of British hegemony following the Napoleonic wars. The idea of peace can in this case be either an imposed peace by the *hegemon* or the peace that results when other states buy into the order that the hegemon generates.

**Pax consortis**   A period of "universal peace" provided by a collective hegemon in a multipolar system.

**Peace dividend**   Resources that become available for other uses during peacetime due to decreased expenditures on national defense.

**Perestroika**   Russian term for restructuring or economic reform, especially economic programs implemented in the Soviet Union in the mid-1980s. See *Glasnost*.

**Periphery**   Nonindustrialized sector of the modern world system that produces agricultural goods and natural resources. See *Core* and *Modern world system*. The theory hypothesizes that peripheral states (e.g., developing countries) are usually made worse off as a result of interacion with core states.

**Perspectives**   In IPE this term refers to theoretical or philosophical frameworks, usually mercantilism or realism, liberalism, and Marxism or structuralism.

**Petrodollar recycling**   Since 1973, the system whereby payments for imported oil are recycled through the global financial structure to provide loans to oil purchasers. Oil exporters then financed purchases of their products with these monies paid to them for their oil.

**Plan Colombia**   A recent program of U.S. aid to Colombia to reduce coca production (and as a result, cocaine imports to the United States) by, among other things, dispersing defoliating chemicals from the air. Despite the $4.7 billion price tag between 2000 and 2006, coca cultivation has not dropped. This illustrates the difficulty of supply-side policies in the global fight against drugs.

**Plaza Accord**   An agreement in 1985 between the G5 states (Great Britain, West Germany, France, Japan, and the United States) reached in New York City to intervene in currency markets to cause the depreciation of the U.S. dollar.

**Pleasure periphery**   Regions in the periphery of the world system that serve as recipients of pleasure-seeking tourists from core nations in the industrialized world.

**Pluralism**   Existence of many different ethnic, social, and political groups within society.

**Political economy**   The social science that examines the dynamic interaction between the forces of market and state, and how the tension and conflict between these aspects of society affect the world. The term "political economy," in certain contexts, has different meanings. In economics, for example, political economy is the name sometimes applied to Marxist analysis and sometimes to economic tools used to analyze political behavior.

**Portfolio investment**   Pattern of international investment by which firms seek to acquire ownership in many industries or world regions in order to hedge investment risk.

**Positive-sum game**   Any interaction between actors that makes all participants simultaneously better off. See *Zero-sum game*.

**Postal Savings Bank**   A Japanese financial institution that channels private savings to uses determined by the government.

**Postmodernism**   A school of thought that reacts against "modern" institutions and ideas, such as the primacy of the nation-state.

**Primitive accumulation**   A Marxist concept that is hypothesized to be at the root of capitalism's initial development. The process is one of coercive or violent seizure of assets (particularly land).

**Prisoner's Dilemma**   A term coined by Princeton mathematics professor A. W. Tucker to describe a situation in which the best interests of persons in society taken individually are opposite from those of the same individuals taken as a group. A group may benefit the most if everyone cooperates on an issue, for example, but each individual member may face an incentive to "defect" and eschew cooperation.

**Private capital flows**   The cross-border movement of money by nonofficial sources. Private capital flows can occur as direct investments by transnational corporations, portfolio investments (such as purchases of foreign stocks by an international mutual fund), commercial bank lending, and nonbank lending. See *Official capital flows*.

**Privatization**   Part of the process of economic transition from classical socialism to capitalism, in which state-held property and assets are transferred into private hands.

**Process innovation**   Inventions and improvements for producing existing goods, services, and techniques that do not result in new items. See *Product innovation*.

**Producer economics**   An economic system organized primarily to generate sustained increases in production. See *Consumer economics*.

**Product cycle theory or Product life-cycle theory**   Terms coined by Harvard political economist Raymond Vernon to describe production and trade patterns stemming from product innovation and technological diffusion.

**Product innovation**   Pattern of inventions that focuses on creation of new goods and services, not refinements of existing items. See *Process innovation*.

**Production structure**   The institutions and practices that condition the production, exchange, and distribution of goods and services in the international political economy. International trade is a key component of the production structure. Essentially, the factors that determine what is produced, where, how, by whom, for whom, and on what terms. See *International division of labor*.

**Production and Trade Structure**   The institutions and practices that condition the production, exchange, and distribution of goods and services in the international political economy (IPE). International trade is a key component of the production structure. Essentially, the factors that determine what is produced, where, how, by whom, for whom, and on what terms. See *International division of labor*.

**Productive power**   A term used by Friedrich *List* to describe technology, education, and training, especially with respect to the industrial sector of the economy.

**Profit paradox**  When law enforcement tries to ban an item for which there is high demand (for example, drugs), the reduction in supply drives up prices in the short term, but this bolsters profits for those willing to illegally supply the item, thus encouraging others to enter the illegal business. Thus, the temporary reduction in supply is reversed as criminals find ways around the ban. Often criminals compete for dominance in the illegal market, which precipitates violence and associated crime.

**Proletariat**  In Marxian analysis, the class of workers who do not own capital.

**Property rights**  A bundle of rights associated with ownership of a resource. Property rights include the right to use a resource and exclude others from its use, to gain from or control its use by others, and to dispose of it. Property rights are defined by the state.

**Protectionism**  The theory of or belief in the advantages of restricting trade to encourage or benefit domestic producers.

**Public choice analysis**  An analytical perspective that focuses on official (public) decision makers and their individual interests that motivate them to make certain decisions. States do not make choices per se. Rather the "state's decision" is made by individuals, each of whom has distinct interests and motivations.

**Public goods**  Goods or services that, once provided, generate benefits that can be enjoyed by all simultaneously. A lighthouse is the classic example of a public good.

**Public Law 480**  A policy in the 1960s that made food aid available to nations whose governments were anticommunist and whose economies served as good markets for future sales of U.S. products. The program had limited effectiveness in stamping out hunger and malnutrition rampant in less developed countries.

**Purchasing power parity (PPP)**  An *exchange rate* such that a given amount of a currency will purchase the same amounts of goods and services at home as abroad.

**Qat**  A tree whose leaves contain a mild narcotic. A majority of Yemeni males habitually chew qat, lowering worker productivity and depleting family finances.

**Rational-choice theory**  A theory of *political economy* that focuses on the incentives facing individuals and states and how those incentives affect their behavior. The structure of incentives (costs and benefits) of the international system is seen as an important determinant of state behavior by rational-choice theorists.

**Realism**  A theory of state behavior that focuses on national interest as a determinant of state behavior. In the view of realists, states, like individuals, tend to act in their own self-interest.

**Recession**  A decline in the overall level of economic activity in a nation as indicated by a decrease in real *Gross National Product*.

**Reciprocity**  A principal of the World Trade Organization system whereby trading partners simultaneously reduce trade barriers, providing each greater access to foreign markets.

**Refugee**  A displaced person who cannot return to his country of origin because of fear of persecution or due to destruction caused by war or natural disaster. Refugees are often assisted and relocated by an international body such as the United Nations Office of the High Commissioner for Refugees.

**Regime**  The environment in which a particular type of IPE activity takes place, including the various rules, norms, and institutions that condition actor expectations regarding a specific problem. The oil regime, for example, includes the nation-states, international organizations, private-sector firms, markets, agreements, and so on, that condition expectations of oil production, exchange and distribution, and related activities.

**Regionalism**  A movement toward "clubs" or associations of nation-states in a geographic area that cooperate to achieve goals that may be very specific or very general.

**Regional trade agreements (RTAs)**  Agreements between different states in a geographic area to reduce trade barriers between them. RTAs are often easier to form than global trade agreements because there are fewer interests to reconcile. Some economic liberals oppose RTAs out of fear that they deter global free trade.

**Regional trade blocs**  A formal process of intergovernmental collaboration between two or more states in a geographical area that promotes a mix of economic liberal and mercantilist trade policies, bringing down barriers within the trade bloc while retaining trade barriers with nonmember nations. See *European Free Trade Area*.

**Relational power**  Power of one actor vis-à-vis another based on the *hard* and *soft power* that each possesses. See *Structural power*.

**Reluctant realism**  The trend in Japanese politics toward a more assertive foreign policy, including expanded collective security agreements, increased military spending, and heightened overseas involvement of Japan's Self-Defense Forces. This realism runs counter to Japan's post–World War II foreign policy stance and is the subject of considerable domestic debate.

**Remittances**  Payments made by a migrant to family or friends in the country of origin.

**Rentier state**  A country that earns a large proportion of its government revenue from taxes on oil and gas exports. In the cases of Iran, Iraq, Libya, Algeria, and other Gulf Cooperation Council states, the wealth generated from this income is usually concentrated in the hands of a few people.

**Rent-seeking behavior**  Efforts to achieve personal gain by creating an artificial scarcity rather than through efficient production. Many corrupt activities can be viewed as examples of rent-seeking behavior.

**Reserve currency**  A currency that is held by a nation's central bank in its foreign exchange reserves. The U.S. dollar is the world's most common reserve currency, and many international transactions and commodities are priced in U.S. dollars.

**Restriction-opportunity dilemma**  A situation in which efforts to ban a material in high demand (for example, drugs and guns) are often counterproductive because they make the black markets provision of the material more profitable.

**Revenue leakages**  In tourism, the loss of revenue resulting from imports of goods and services required by tourists and tourism businesses, including food, hotel fixtures, advertising costs, repatriated profits, and airport equipment.

**Revulsion**   The fifth stage of a financial crisis, following distress, in which new news about a market or investment cause investors to abandon their investments for fear of an imminent downturn in prices. This expectations shift precipitates a self-fulfilling prophesy, as prices collapse because of the rapid decline in demand. See *Distress* and *Torschlusspanik*.

**Ricardo, David**   A nineteenth-century English businessman, economic philosopher, and proponent of free trade. Ricardo argued that nations should specialize in producing the good for which they hold a comparative advantage—and if they have a comparative advantage in more than one good, to choose the good with the greatest comparative advantage—in order to maximize the gains from trade. See *Comparative advantage*.

**Rio Earth Summit**   International conference held in Rio de Janeiro, Brazil, in 1992 to discuss global environmental problems.

**Rogue regime**   A label applied to states seeking to acquire weapons of mass destruction or defying commonly accepted international norms. However, not all states that fit this description are declared "rogue" (for example, Israel), demonstrating the highly situational and politicized nature of this term.

**Rogue state**   A states that is regarded as hostile to or that refuses to cooperate with the Western industrialized nations: Iran, Iraq, Syria, and North Korea, among others. Often these states are cited as potential sources of arms sales and terrorism.

**Secrecy jurisdictions**   Countries with strong banking privacy laws, many in the Caribbean. Tax evaders and money launderers exploit these privacy guarantees to hide billions of dollars from their governments.

**Security structure**   The sets of institutions, practices, and beliefs that condition international behavior as it relates to national security issues.

**Self-Defense Forces (SDF)**   Japan's post–World War II constitution, written by the United States, prevents it from having a standing military. However, it is allowed to maintain a military for self-defense purposes. In recent years, Japanese politicians have sought to expand the SDF's mandate, and members of the SDF have been sent to Iraq on a noncombat mission and to Cambodia on a UN peacekeeping assignment.

**Semiperiphery**   An intermediate zone between the *core* and *periphery*. South Korea and Taiwan might be considered part of the semiperiphery today in the *modern world system* theory. See *Core*.

**Settler states**   Countries such as the United States and Australia, which allow immigrants the opportunity to become permanent residents and/or naturalized citizens.

**Smith, Adam**   Considered the intellectual founder of the laissez-faire philosophy of economics. Smith advocated the free market as a means of maximizing collective well-being. See *Laissez-faire*.

**Social Darwinism**   A structuralist characterization of the effect of globalization's competitive pressures, which simulates natural selection by killing off the firms that can't adapt to changing market conditions.

**Social safety net**   Social programs, such as old-age pensions and unemployment insurance, that provide for economically disadvantaged groups in society.

**Socialism**   A system of political economy that gives high priority to equity and economic equality. Socialist systems often feature communal or public ownership of some of the means of production.

**Socially responsible investing**   A trend whereby investors avoid certain types of companies and countries that they perceive to be socially or environmentally unethical, such as those involved in land expropriation, oil corruption, terrorist financing, human rights abuses, or unsustainable environmental practices. These investment strategies challenge economic liberal principles by subordinating market efficiency to concerns of justice.

**Soft currency**   Currencies of uncertain value (due, perhaps, to high inflation rates) that are not generally accepted in international transactions. Soft currency can usually be spent only within the nation that issues it, whereas a *hard currency* can be exchanged and spent in most nations. Some soft currencies, such as the ruble in the former Soviet Union, are called "inconvertible currencies" because it is illegal to convert them into hard currencies.

**Soft power**   The power to influence the environment of international affairs through such intangible factors as culture, values, and ideals. Soft power is less direct than *hard power* but sometimes more effective.

**Solidarity**   Polish labor union (and political party) founded in 1980 by Lech Walesa.

**Sovereignty**   Independence from foreign control. See *Autonomous state*.

**Special Economic Zones**   Regions of China where private ownership is permitted and market forces are used to encourage rapid economic growth. See *Market socialism*.

**Specialization**   Part of the economic liberal argument—an economic motive—for free trade. Adam Smith and others advocated that trading nations should concentrate their production on sectors where they possess a comparative advantage. When nations traded with one another they would see an increase in efficiency and, in turn, wealth. In an age of competitive globalization, different states and regions of the world are driven to specialize in particular parts of the production process. Quite often this specialization does not reflect a natural advantage but one that is fostered by different state policies, resulting in tensions over the motives behind different trade policies.

**Speculation**   To make an investment in a foreign currency based on the belief that the currency will increase in value, allowing the speculator to earn a return when the currency is converted back. See *Speculative attack*.

**Speculative attack**   A form of currency speculation whereby speculators sell large quantities of a currency in the hope that they will be able to buy it back later at a lower price.

**Sphere of influence**   The area or territory in which a *hegemon* or major state has interest and sustains either political, military, or economic influence. During the Vietnam War, it was common practice to refer to Southeast Asia as being in the United States's sphere of influence.

**State**   A legal concept describing a social group that occupies a defined territory and is organized under common political institutions and an effective government. A state has some degree of independence and autonomy. States are the primary units of the international political and legal community. As sovereign entities, states have the right to determine their own national objectives and the techniques (including the use of force) for their achievement.

**Static efficiency**   An efficient use of current resources, especially specialization according to the *comparative advantage*. See *Dynamic efficiency*.

**Strategic Arms Limitation Treaty (SALT)**   Arms control and reduction agreement between the United States and the Soviet Union, signed in 1972.

**Strategic resources**   Resources, such as oil and rubber, that have national security value to a nation.

**Strategic trade policies**   Efforts on the part of the *state* to create *comparative advantage* in trade by methods such as subsidizing research and development of a product, or providing subsidies to help an industry increase production to the point at which it can move down the "learning curve" to achieve greater production efficiency than foreign competitors. Strategic trade practices are often associated with state industrial policies—that is, intervention in the economy to promote specific patterns of industrial development.

**Structural Adjustment Programs (SAPs)**   Economic policies that seek to reduce state power and introduce free-market reforms to help less developed countries establish a foundation for economic growth. The International Monetary Fund often makes the adoption of structural adjustment policies a condition for financial assistance.

**Structural power**   The power that an actor possesses because of its position in the international system and its ability to shape the "rules of the game." See *Relational power*.

**Structural rigidities**   Inflexible elements of the structure of an organization that resist the forces of change.

**Structuralism**   A theory that accounts for the political–economic interconnectedness (structural relationship) between any number of entities: the *bourgeoisie* and *proletariat*, the *core* and *periphery*, the *North* and *South*. A number of ties bind these entities to one another, including trade, foreign aid, and direct investment. Much debate exists as to whether and how structural conditions can be changed or reformed. See *Marxism*.

**Subsidy**   Government payment to encourage some activity or benefit some group. See *Common Agricultural Policy*.

**Super 301**   Aggressive U.S. trade policy designed to open foreign markets to U.S. exports.

**Surplus**   In an economic account such as the current account, a situation whereby money inflows exceed money outflows.

**Sustainable development**   A pattern of economic development that is consistent with the goal of nondegradation of the environment.

**Symbolic analysts**   A term coined by U.S. political economist Robert Reich to describe a class of highly trained persons. To use the language of *modern world systems* analysis, symbolic analysts form the *core* of a knowledge-based global division of labor.

**Tariff**   A tax placed on imported goods to raise the price of those goods, making them less attractive to consumers. Though tariffs are used at times to raise government revenue (particularly in less developed countries), they are more commonly a means to protect domestic industry from foreign competition.

**Tax havens**   A name for mostly small countries and territories that have protective banking privacy laws. These sovereign jurisdictions attract tax evaders and money launderers who wish to hide their earnings from their home government so as to avoid paying taxes on the money or provoking inquiries into the (often illicit) source of the income.

**Terms of trade**   The value of a nation's exported goods relative to the value of the goods that are imported. A measure of the prices paid for imports relative to the prices received for exports.

**Third World**   A Cold War term that is still in use. During the Cold War, the term applied to less developed countries (LDCs) that were not part of either the First World (the United States and its allies) or the Second World (the Soviet Union and its allies). In the post–Cold War era, this term refers to LDCs generally.

**Top currency**   A currency in great demand because of its central role in international trade and financial transactions. The U.S. dollar has played the role of top currency since World War II.

**Torschlusspanik**   A German term to describe how during a financial crisis, falling prices feed on themselves, creating self-fulfilling prophecies. A good example of this phenomenon is the East Asian financial crisis of 1997–2000, when the fear of an imminent decline in real estate prices and currency values caused a mass exodus of foreign investment from these economies, precipitating the very collapse that had been the source of investors' anxiety in the first place. See *Revulsion* and *Capital flight*.

**Trade bloc**   A group of nation-states united by trade agreements (such as the European Union and the North American Free Trade Area).

**Trade diversion**   An effect of a trade bloc. Although trade is created among members of the trade bloc because of lower internal barriers, this comes partly at the expense of trade diverted from more efficient non–bloc countries that are still subject to trade barriers.

**Trade-related intellectual property rights (TRIPs)**   International agreements regarding the protection of copyright, digital software, production technologies, and drug patents.

**Tragedy of the commons**   Term coined by Garrett Hardin to describe situations in which human nature drives individuals to overuse communal resources.

**Transdniestra**   A part of Moldova that declared independence in 1992, though this claim has not been recognized by any other country. Ambiguity about its status and a lack of strong government has transformed the region into a hub of illegal activity, especially for trafficking in weapons, stolen cars, and other contraband. The case of Transdniestra illustrates one dark side to the end of the Cold War: the retreat of the Soviet Union often left power vacuums that could not be filled by the weak postcommunist governments, and therefore, illegal activity proliferated.

**Transit states**   States that serve as halfway points for transnational migrants en route to another destination country.

**Transnational advocacy networks (TANs)**   International networks of activists who attempt to influence states regarding various political and social issues, including migration and refugee policy, for example.

**Transnational corporation (TNC)**   The accepted term to describe businesses that compete in regional or global markets and whose business environment therefore extends beyond any given nation-state. The key characteristic of a TNC is a high level of *foreign direct investment*.

**Transnational migration**   Migration of an individual or group across national borders.

**Transparency**   The public's ability to see how decisions are made. In the case of global financial institutions such as the International Monetary Fund, some argue that greater transparency would improve investors' decision making and prevent financial crises from developing.

**Treaty of Rome**   A 1957 treaty among France, Great Britain, West Germany, Belgium, Italy, Luxembourg, and the Netherlands that established the European Economic Community.

**Triage**   The medical practice of dividing patients according to the severity of their afflictions when resources are limited.

**Undervalued currency**   A condition in which a currency's purchasing power within its home country is greater than its purchasing power abroad when converted at the going exchange rate. The exchange rate thus biases economic activity in favor of domestic goods over foreign goods. See *Overvalued currency*.

**United Nations Conference on Trade and Development (UNCTAD)**   A permanent conference of the United Nations General Assembly that focuses on the effects of international trade on nations at differing stages of development and with differing social and economic systems. UNCTAD is an important forum for multilateral discussions and negotiations regarding less developed countries and transnational corporation issues.

**(United States) Special Trade Representative (USTR)**   Created in 1962 as an office with the rank of ambassador, and appointed by the President with the consent of the Senate. The USTR advocates for the United States in World Trade Organization meetings and other forums where trade issues and policies are discussed and decided.

**Uruguay round**   Set of negotiations among the members of the *General Agreement on Tariffs and Trade* (1986–1994) that focused on reducing trade barriers, especially regarding services and agricultural goods.

**Vietnam syndrome**   A lesson the United States supposedly learned from having lost the Vietnam War: Essentially, don't intervene in Third World nations unless U.S. vital interests are at stake, the United States is assured of a quick and relatively inexpensive victory, and the U.S. public will support the operation.

**Voluntary export restraint (VER)** or **Voluntary export agreement (VEA)**   Agreements that limit the quantity of an item a nation can export. Importers ask exporters to "voluntarily" set limits on the numbers of exports, backed by an implied threat of economic sanctions or some form of retaliation if the exporter does not comply with the importer's request.

**Voucher privatization**   A method of privatization used by some transitional economies in which citizens are given vouchers that can be used to bid for shares in state-owned firms. In contrast to privatization through direct sale to an outside investor, voucher privatization is less able to bring new capital and expertise into the economy.

**Warsaw Pact**   The Warsaw Treaty Organization (1955–1991) military and defense alliance among Albania, Bulgaria, Czechoslovakia, East Germany, Hungary, Poland, Romania, and the Soviet Union. See *North Atlantic Treaty Organization*.

**Washington consensus**   The viewpoint, often evidenced in the policy proposals of the U.S. Treasury Department, the World Bank, and the International Monetary Fund, that less developed countries should adopt policies to reduce inflation and fiscal deficits, privatize, deregulate, and create open markets.

**Weapons of Mass Destruction (WMD)**   Technologically sophisticated weapons that have the potential to kill large numbers of people, such as nuclear, chemical, and biological weapons.

**Westoxication**   The idea prevalent in the Middle East of seduction to imported Western cultural ideas and institutions. Anti-Western leaders and some terrorists often cite it as a motive for their opposition to the United States and other industrialized states' values and institutions.

**World Bank**   Officially called the International Bank for Reconstruction and Development (IBRD), the World Bank is an international agency with over 150 members. Created by the Bretton Woods agreements in 1944, the World Bank originally worked on the reconstruction of Europe after World War II. Today, the World Bank makes low-interest loans and grants to *less developed countries* to stimulate economic development.

**World Intellectual Property Organization (WIPO)**   A United Nations agency created in 1967 to monitor adherence to the Berne and Paris conventions that established rules for copyright, patent, trademark, and industrial design protection.

**World Trade Organization (WTO)**   Successor organization to the *General Agreement on Tariffs and Trade (GATT)*.

**Yom Kippur War**   The 1973 war between Israel and several Arab nations in the Middle East.

***Zaibatsu***   Large and powerful family-controlled financial and industrial organizations of pre–World War II Japan. See *Keiretsu*.

**Zero-sum game**   An activity whereby gains by one party create equal losses for others. See *Positive-sum game*.

# Glossary of Acronyms

| | |
|---|---|
| **APEC** | Asia-Pacific Economic Cooperation |
| **BoP** | Balance of payments |
| **CAP** | Common Agricultural Policy |
| **DFI** | Direct foreign investment |
| **EEC** | European Economic Community |
| **EFTA** | European Free Trade Area |
| **EMU** | European Monetary Union |
| **EU** | European Union |
| **FDI** | Foreign direct investment |
| **FX** | Foreign exchange |
| **GATT** | General Agreement on Tariffs and Trade |
| **GDP** | Gross domestic product |
| **GNP** | Gross National Product |
| **GSP** | Generalized System of Preferences |
| **HPICs** | Highly indebted poor countries |
| **IBRD** | International Bank for Reconstruction and Development (also World Bank) |
| **IMF** | International Monetary Fund |
| **IOs** | International organizations |
| **IPE** | International political economy |
| **IPRs** | Intellectual property rights |
| **ITO** | International Trade Organization |
| **LDC** | Less developed country |
| **MAD** | Mutual assured destruction |
| **MDG** | Millennium Development Goals |
| **MENA** | Middle East and North Africa |
| **METI** | Ministry of Economy, Trade and Industry |
| **MFN** | Most Favored Nation |
| **MNC** | Multinational corporation |
| **NAFTA** | North American Free Trade Agreement |
| **NATO** | North Atlantic Treaty Organization |

| | |
|---|---|
| **NGOs** | Nongovernmental organizations |
| **NIC** | Newly industrialized country |
| **NIEO** | New International Economic Order |
| **NTB** | Nontariff barrier |
| **OECD** | Organization for Economic Cooperation and Development |
| **OPEC** | Organization of Petroleum Exporting Countries |
| **PPP** | Purchasing power parity |
| **SALT** | Strategic Arms Limitation Treaty |
| **SAP** | Structural Adjustment Program |
| **TNC** | Transnational corporation |
| **TRIPs** | Trade-related intellectual property rights |
| **UNCTAD** | United Nations Conference on Trade and Development |
| **USTR** | U.S. Trade Representative |
| **WIPO** | World Intellectual Property Rights Organization |
| **WTO** | World Trade Organization |

# *Index*